COMMERCIAL AND CONSUMER ARBITRATION STATUTES AND RULES

To
Eleonora, Freyja, Katerina,
Lisa and Marghanita

COMMERCIAL AND CONSUMER ARBITRATION STATUTES AND RULES

Edited by

Eur. Biol. M. J. Chapman, FCIArb

BLACKSTONE
PRESS LIMITED

First published in Great Britain 1997 by Blackstone Press Limited,
9–15 Aldine Street, London W12 8AW.
Telephone 0181-740 2277 (00 + 44-181-740 2277)

© M.J. Chapman, 1997

ISBN: 1 85431 587 0

British Library Cataloguing in Publication Data
A CIP catalogue record for this book is available from the British Library

Typeset by Style Photosetting Ltd, Mayfield, East Sussex
Printed by Bell and Bain Limited, Glasgow

FOREWORD

by Maître S Lazareff, Chairman of the French National Committee
of the ICC, and Avocat, J C Goldsmith et Associés, Paris

International arbitration, it is said, has its roots in history. Modern commercial arbitration is a true product of the City, even though there were precedents in the late XVIIIth century.

It is well-known that the first contracts to be submitted to arbitration dealt with commodities. As the disputes involved, in most cases, perishable goods, they had to be settled rapidly and confidentially. London became, in the XIXth century, the centre for martime and financial matters, insurance, commodities and then metals. This is still the case today.

International commercial arbitration, as we know it, started between the two World Wars. Eisemann, Secretary General of the ICC Court of Arbitration, used to say that the first ICC arbitration he conducted, was spontaneous, without Rules and, horrendously, without a fee! International commercial arbitration was then a procedure whereby gentlemen would settle in a gentlemanly way disputes between gentlemen. The penalty for noncompliance was blackballing — nothing more. How far away that seems today!

In the 1970s and even more so in the 1980s, arbitration gradually became the standard procedure for settling major commercial disputes. But, mainly due to the invasion of the arbitration world by professional litigators, arbitration is more and more becoming a specific form of litigation unfortunately getting closer and closer to an adversarial process before the Courts. Blood and money! The user is therefore, unless he is advised by someone quite familiar with the subject, at a loss when an arbitration provision or agreement is submitted to him.

Hence the importance of this very welcome book which brings to the users the major statutes and rules on commercial and consumer arbitration. As Michael Chapman wrote in the preface, these rules and statutes were so far only embodied in booklets of every imaginable size and shape, if even available. This book will also be of considerable use to practitioners. At last, they will be able to compare and, hopefully, to make the choice best adapted to their specific requirements, in particular, to assess the degree of autonomy granted to them in each of the key stages of an arbitration, such as the appointment of arbitrators (including nationality), the choice of law, of the situs and of the procedure, including the language, the duration of a case, etc.

At this point, it might be useful to give a word of advice to users: if you have decided to take the road of institutional arbitration, as opposed to *ad hoc* arbitration, inquire about the reliability, the seriousness and the solidity of the arbitration institution. Some contracts have survived the institution which was supposed to settle the disputes arising from them. This is certainly not the case here, as no user could have the slightest worry with the reputable international institutions included in this book.

Serge Lazareff
Paris, August 1996.

CONTENTS

EDITOR'S NOTE

NOTE: This book is published as the *Arbitration Act 1996* enters into the law of England. The Act though does not come into force until an order is made under s. 109. Thus notes are shown in other statutes that *will* be amended (or repealed) once the Act comes into force. Such amendments will, anyway, not apply to references commenced before the Act comes into force (s. 84).

It is appreciated that many rules and statutes share a common origin. Space could have been saved by merely reproducing the parts of statutes or rules that differed from the 'principal' version. However this is not a text that discusses comparative law. Its purpose as a sourcebook for examination students would be lost with such an approach. It is also appreciated that all statutes and rules are susceptible to amendment, and that full text reproduction does allow users to paste in amendments over the specific text to which they relate.

EDITOR'S PREFACE

I have sat through many, and even chaired the occasional, learned meeting where some discussion has emerged as to how a particular point is dealt with in differing arbitration rules. The tables are rapidly covered with booklets of every imaginable size and shape, as members of the group compare different rules. The need for a uniform compilation of such rules and of statutes is obvious for the scholar.

Comparison of rules has a more practical value. In an arbitral hearing if a point arises that is not covered by the particular rules (if any) applicable to that reference then the parties' advocates and members of the tribunal can find it useful to note how other bodies have approached the same problem. Such comparisons are obviously only 'persuasive' but can nevertheless assist, and even 'de-fuse' discussions.

For practical reasons it was decided to confine this book to the English language. Most international rules and other international documents (treaties, UNICITRAL texts, etc.) are available in English. Statutes are reproduced from what were known as the British Isles. These islands off the North-West coast of Europe contain a suprising number of jurisdictions, the majority not within the European Union. Eight are referred to in this text, and relevant statutes reproduced.

Some texts applicable to state entities are also included. The Permanent Court rules apply to private parties in dispute with a state (the state: state rules are not reproduced here), whilst the utility of the ICSID procedure in private disputes (even though designed for disputes involving a state) has been commented on by Brian Drewitt (62JCIArb1, 41). There is nothing to stop parties using these procedures, incorporating them into arbitration clauses, terms of reference or whatever.

The new (1996) English Arbitration Act was a motivating factor in deciding the 'time had come' to offer such a compilation. Originally I thought this volume would be an interesting valediction to old statute. The new Act was set to be consolidating. It however would not apply to arbitrations commenced before it came into operation. Thus the 1950, 1975 and 1979 acts could just be justified for inclusion. However, as it turns out a large section of the 1950 Act (by number of pages some 45%) remains in force throughout the United Kingdom. Even more curiously whilst the short Consumer Arbitration Agreements Act (of 1988) is repealed (and replaced by ss. 89–91 of the new Act), the 1975 Act is only repealed for England and Northern Ireland (being replaced by Part III of the new Act), it remains in force for Scotland (!).

The promise to my publishers of a 'neater' manuscript for a second edition looks to have been based on an illusion.

Collecting the material for this work has been more stimulating than I first imagined. It seems inconceivable that some error will not have crept in. All texts I consulted bar one, omit an amendment to one statute which is of some decades standing. I hope none are of the magnitude of that in Barker and Lucas's 1632 edition of The Bible. It is however our hope that this book will be produced regularly, so notes of errors would be gratefully received.

Suggestions for new material that might be included would also be most welcome.

There is no 'right time' to produce a work such as this. The 1996 Act will undoubtedly cause many, probably all, English domestic arbitration rules to be changed. Jersey is on the verge of publishing a (its first) arbitration law. Ireland is debating adopting the Model Law. German adoption of the Model Law would undoubtedly have repercussion of the DIS Rules. And, so on. Contact details are provided for all bodies referred to. It is hoped that these will allow for a quick check to be made that the edition included here is indeed the current (or applicable) text.

Michael Chapman,
Bianne,
November 1996.

ACKNOWLEDGEMENTS

Working on this book has been a pleasure. Compared with normal office life, let alone other more academic pursuits, then breaking off from these regular activities to prepare this manuscript has been a positive feature of the last few months.

Primarily this has been due to the courtesy and encouragement that I have met from colleagues throughout the World. Whilst there may be some 'enlightened self-interest' in seeing one's institute's arbitration rules more widely disseminated, the helpfulness and advice of colleagues has gone far beyond what was necessary to achieve such a selfish objective. The world arbitral community is truly a community.

For permission to reproduce material here I would like to thank Her Majesty's Greffier, K.H. Tough Esq of Guernsey. Also for granting their permission or obtaining their body's permission: Ted Pons (Senior Editor, American Arbitration Association), Marcel Veroone (President, CAREN), Kerry Harding (Secretary General, CIArb), Anne Bunni (Chairman, CIArb Irish Branch), Jens Bredow (Secretary General, DIS), Mauro Rubino-Sammartano (Co-chairman MMEIA), Stuart Logan (Chief Executive and Secretary, FOSFA), Pamela Kirby Johnson (Director General, GAFTA), Janine Uzan-Spira (General Counsel, CCIG), Ruth Eldon (Editorial Director, IBA), Eric Schwartz (Secretary General, ICC Court of Arbitration), Pascale Reins (Director, ICC Publishing), Alejandro Escobar, Margrete Stevens (Counsel, ICSID), Graham James (Thomas Telford Services), Hiroshi Hattori (JCAA), Madeleine May (Executive Director, LCIA), George Hardee (Honorary Secretary, LMAA), B.S. Dorkings, Esq. (Director of Operations, LME), Stefano Azzali (Vice-Secretary General, Milan Chamber), Bette Shifman (Deputy Secretary-General, Permanent Court of Arbitration), Liza Kershaw (RIBA Publications), D.G. Moon, Esq. (Secretary, RSA), Ulf Franke (Stockholm Chamber), Matthieu Reeb (Counsel, TAS), Gerold Herrmann (Secretary, UNCITRAL), Werner Melis (Chairman, Vienna Chamber), Francis Gurry (Director, WIPO Arbitration Center), and Lukas Briner (Zurich Chamber).

I would also like to thank those who have provided suggestions, texts or other materials, and arranged access to library facilities. In particular I would thank: The Tynwald Librarian (Douglas), Jean-Francois Bourque (Paris),

Burt Campbell (France), Mme Dumont (Strasbourg), Anne Kenny (London), Bill McLaughlin (Kent), Pat O'Loughlin (Basel), and Bob Waite (Guernsey).

A particular word of thanks to Serge Lazareff for his kind words of introduction to this book and for his encouragement.

My apologies to anyone omitted in what has been a project that 'just grew'.

Much of the texts in this book are the copyright of particular bodies, it is believed that permission has been obtained for each and every reproduction. Any errors are regretted and should be communicated to the publishers.

Many have assisted, all errors are mine alone.

MJC

PART I
STATUTES

I.1　ALDERNEY

Note:　The Arbitration (International Investment Disputes) (Guernsey) Order 1968 also applies to Alderney. This is reproduced in section I.2 'Guernsey'.

THE ARBITRATION (ALDERNEY) LAW 1983

THE STATES, in pursuance of their resolution of the eighteenth day of December, nineteen hundred and eighty-one, have approved the following provisions which, subject to the Sanction of Her Most Excellent Majesty in Council, shall have force of law in the Island of Alderney.

PART I

GENERAL PROVISIONS AS TO ARBITRATION

Effect of Arbitration Agreements, etc.

1.　Authority of arbitrators and umpires to be irrevocable.

The Authority of an arbitrator or umpire appointed by, or virtue of, an arbitration agreement shall, unless a contrary intention is expressed in the agreement, be irrevocable except by leave of the Court.

2.　Death of party.

(1)　An arbitration agreement shall not be discharged by the death of any party thereto, either as respects the deceased or any other party, but shall in such event be enforceable by or against the personal representative of the deceased.

(2)　The authority of an arbitrator shall not be revoked by the death of any party by whom he was appointed.

(3)　Nothing in this section shall be taken to affect the operation of any enactment or rule of law by virtue of which any right of action is extinguished by the death of a person.

3.　Insolvency.

Where it is provided by a term in a contract to which a person who is insolvent is a party that any differences arising thereout or in connection therewith shall be referred to arbitration, the said term shall, if the trustee or other person acting on behalf of his creditors adopts the contract, be enforceable by or against him so far as relates to any such differences.

4.　Staying Court proceedings where there is submission to arbitration.

Subject to the next succeedimg section, if any party to an arbitration agreement, or any person claiming through or under him, commences any legal proceedings in the Court against any other party to the agreement, or any person claiming through or under him, in respect of any matter agreed to be referred, any party to those legal proceedings may at any time after appearance or after the inscription of the cause on the Pleading List but before delivering any pleadings or taking any other steps in the proceedings, apply to the Court, if satisfied that there is no sufficient reason why the matter should not be referred in accordance with the agreement, and that the applicant was, at the time when the proceedings were commenced, and still remains ready and willing to do all things necessary to the proper conduct of the arbitration, may make an order staying the proceedings.

5. Staying Court proceedings where party proves arbitration agreement.

(1) If any party to an arbitration agreement to which this section applies, or any person claiming through or under him, commences any legal proceedings in the Court against any other party to the agreement, or any person claiming through him or under him, in respect of any matter agreed to be referred, any party to the proceedings may at any time after appearance or after the inscription of the cause on the Pleading List but before delivering any pleadings or taking any other steps in the proceedings, apply to the Court to stay the proceedings; and the Court, unless satisfied that the arbitration agreement is null and void, inoperative or incapable of being performed or that there is not in fact any dispute between the parties with regard to the matter agreed to be referred, shall make an order staying the proceedings.

(2) This section applies to any arbitration agreement which is not a domestic arbitration agreement; and the last preceding section shall not apply to an arbitration agreement to which this section applies.

(3) In this section, the expression 'domestic arbitration agreement' means an arbitration agreement which does not provide, expressly or by implication, for arbitration in a State other than the Island and to which neither—

    (a) an individual who is not—
        (i) a citizen of the United Kingdom and Colonies; or
        (ii) a British subject without citizenship; or
        (iii) a British protected person; or
        (iv) a Stateless person;
or who is habitually resident in any State other than the Island; nor

    (b) a body corporate which is incorporated in, or whose central management and control is exercised in, any State other than the Island;
is party at the time the proceedings are commenced.

Arbitrators and Umpires

6. When reference is to a single arbitrator.

Unless a contrary intention is expressed therein, every arbitration agreement shall, if no other mode of reference is provided, be deemed to include a provision that the reference shall be to a single arbitrator.

7. Power of parties in certain cases to supply vacancy.

(1) Subject to the next succeeding subsection, where an arbitration agreement provides that the reference shall be to two arbitrators, one to be

appointed by each party, then, unless a contrary intention is expressed therein—

(a) if either of the appointed arbitrators refuses to act, or is incapable of acting, or dies, the party who appointed him may appoint a new arbitrator in his place;

(b) if, on such a reference, one party fails to appoint an arbitrator, either originally or by way of substitution as aforesaid, for seven clear days after the other party, having appointed his arbitrator, has served the party making default with notice to make the appointment, the party who has appointed an arbitrator may appoint that arbitrator to act as sole arbitrator in the reference, and his award shall be binding on both parties as if he had been appointed by consent.

(2) The Court may set aside any appointment made in pursuance of this section.

8. Umpires.

(1) Unless a contrary intention is expressed therein, every arbitration agreement shall, where the reference is to two arbitrators, be deemed to include a provision that the two arbitrators may appoint an umpire at any time after they are themselves appointed and shall do so forthwith if they cannot agree.

(2) Unless a contrary intention is expressed therein, every arbitation agreement shall, where such a provision is applicable to the reference, be deemed to include a provision that, if the arbitrators have delivered to any party to the arbitration agreement, or to the umpire, a notice in writing stating that they cannot agree, the umpire may forthwith enter on the reference in lieu of the arbitrators.

(3) At any time after the appointment of an umpire, however appointed, the Court may, on the application of any party to the reference and not withstanding anything to the contrary in the arbitration agreement, order that the umpire shall enter upon the reference in lieu of the arbitrators and as if he were a sole arbitrator.

9. Majority award of three arbitrators.

Unless the contrary intention is expressed in the arbitration agreement, in any case where there is a reference to three arbitrators, the award of any two of the arbitrators shall be binding.

10. Power of Court in certain cases to appoint an arbitrator or umpire.

(1) In any of the following cases—

(a) where an arbitration agreement provides that the reference shall be to a single arbitrator, and all parties do not, after differences have arisen, concur in the appointment of an arbitrator;

(b) if an appointed arbitrator refuses to act, or is incapable of acting, or dies, and the arbitration agreement does not show that it was intended that the vacancy should not be supplied and the parties do not supply the vacancy;

(c)   where the parties or two arbitrators are required or are at liberty to appoint an umpire or third arbitrator and do not appoint him;

(d)   where an appointed umpire or third arbitrator refuses to act, or is incapable of acting, or dies, and the arbitration agreement does not show that it was intended that the vacancy should not be supplied, and the parties or arbitrators do not supply the vacancy;

any party may serve the other parties or the arbitrators, as the case may be, with a written notice to appoint or, as the case may be, concur in appointing, an arbitrator, umpire or third arbitrator; and, if the appointment is not made within seven days after the service of the notice, the Court may, on application by the party who gave the notice, appoint an arbitrator, umpire or third arbitrator who shall have the like powers to act in the reference and make an award as if he had been appointed by consent of all parties.

(2)   In any case where—

(a)   an arbitration agreement provides for the appointment of an arbitrator or umpire by a person who is neither one of the parties nor an existing arbitrator (whether the provision applies directly or in default of agreement by the parties or otherwise); and

(b)   that person refuses to make the appointment or does not make it within the time specified in the agreement or, if no time is so specified, within a reasonable time;

any party to the agreement may serve the person in question with a written notice to appoint an arbitrator or umpire and, if the appointment is not made within seven clear days after the service of the notice, the Court may, on the application of the party who gave the notice, appoint an arbitrator or umpire who shall have the like powers to act in the reference and make an award as if he had been appointed in accordance with the terms of the agreement.

Conduct of Proceedings, Witnesses, etc.

11.   Conduct of proceedings, witnesses, etc.

(1)   Unless a contrary intention is expressed therein, every arbitration agreement shall, where such a provision is applicable to the reference, be deemed to contain a provision that the parties to the reference, and all persons claiming through them respectively, shall, subject to any legal objection, submit to be examined by the arbitrator or umpire, on oath or affirmation, in relation to the matters in dispute, and shall, subject as aforesaid, produce before the arbitrator or umpire all documents within their possession or power respectively which may be required or called for, and do all other things which during the proceedings on the reference the arbitrator or umpire may require.

(2)   Unless a contrary intention is expressed therein, every arbitration agreement shall, where such a provision is applicable to the reference, be deemed to contain a provision that the witnesses on the reference shall, if the arbitrator or umpire thinks fit, be examined on oath or affirmation.

(3)   An arbitrator or umpire shall, unless a contrary intention is expressed in the arbitration agreement, have power to administer oaths to, or take the affirmations of, the parties to and witnesses on a reference under the agreement.

(4)   Any party to a reference under an arbitration agreement may apply to the Court for permission to summon a witness to give evidence or to produce documentary evidence and a party who is so authorised by the Court may cause a summons to be served on any person, in the same manner as a summons may be served upon any person in respect of a civil action before the Court, summoning that person to attend before the arbitrator or umpire for the purpose of giving evidence or producing any document likely to assist the arbitrator or umpire in determining the question in dispute; and a person so summoned shall be under a like obligation as to giving of any evidence and the production of any document as if he were so summoned in respect of such an action.

(5)   The Court shall have, for the purpose of and in relation to a reference under an arbitration agreement, the same power of making orders in respect of matters of procedure and other matters incidental to the reference as it has for the purpose of and in relation to a civil action before the Court.

Provisions as to Awards

12.   Time for making award.

(1)   Subject to the provisions of subsection (2) of section nineteen and subsection (2) of section twenty-two of this Law, and anything to the contrary in the arbitration agreement, an arbitrator or umpire shall have power to make an award at any time.

(2)   The time, if any, limited for making an award, whether under this Law or otherwise, may from time to time be enlarged by order of the Court, whether that time has expired or not.

(3)   The Court may, on the application of any party to a reference, remove an arbitrator or umpire who fails to use all reasonable despatch in entering on and proceeding with the reference and making an award, and an arbitrator or umpire who is removed by the Court under this subsection shall not be entitled to receive any remuneration in respect of his services.

(4)   For the purposes of the last preceding subsection the expression 'proceeding with a reference' includes, in a case where two arbitrators are unable to agree, giving notice of that fact to the parties and to the umpire.

13.   Interim awards.

Unless a contrary intention is expressed therein, every arbitration agreement shall, where such a provision is applicable to the reference, be deemed to contain a provision that the arbitrator or umpire may, if he thinks fit, make an interim award, and any reference in this Part of this Law to an award includes a reference to an interim award.

14.   Awards to be final.

Subject to the provisions of section nineteen of this Law and unless a contrary intention is expressed therein, every arbitration agreement shall, where such a provision is applicable to the reference, be deemed to contain a provision that the award to be made by the arbitrator or umpire shall be final and binding on the parties and the persons claiming under them respectively.

15. Power to correct slips.

Unless a contrary intention is expressed in the arbitration agreement, the arbitrator or umpire shall have power to correct in an award any clerical mistake or error arising from any accidental slip or omission.

Costs, Fees and Interest

16. Costs.

(1) Unless a contrary intention is expressed therein, every arbitration agreement shall be deemed to include a provision that the costs of the reference and award shall be in the discretion of the arbitrator or umpire, who may direct to and by whom and in what manner those costs or any part thereof shall be paid, and shall tax the amount of costs to be so paid.

(2) Subject to the provisions of the last preceding subsection in the event of any difference or dispute between any parties to any reference as to the fees, disbursements and allowances recoverable in pursuance of an award directing the payment of costs, the difference or dispute shall be referred to the Clerk of the Court whose decision shall be final.

(3) Subject to the next succeeding subsection, any provision in an arbitration agreement to the effect that the parties or any party thereto shall in any event pay their or his own costs of the reference or award or any part thereof shall be void, and this Part of this Law shall, in the case of an arbitration agreement containing any such provision, have effect as if that provision were not contained therein.

(4) Nothing in the last preceding subsection shall invalidate such a provision when it is a part of an agreement to submit to arbitration a dispute which has arisen before the making of that agreement.

(5) If no provision is made by an award with respect to the costs of the reference, any party to the reference may, within fourteen days of the publication of the award or such further time as the Court may direct, apply to the arbitrator for an order directing by and to whom those costs shall be paid, and thereupon the arbitrator shall, after hearing any party who may desire to be heard, amend his award by adding thereto such directions as he may think proper with respect of the payment of the costs of the reference and shall tax the amount of costs to be so paid.

17. Taxation of arbitrator's or umpires's fees.

(1) If, in any case, an arbitrator or umpire refuses to deliver his award except on payment of the fees demanded by him, the Court may, on application for the purpose, order that the arbitrator or umpire shall deliver the award to the applicant on payment into the Court by the applicant of the fees demanded, and further that the fees demanded shall be taxed bv the Clerk of the Court and that, out of the money paid into Court, there shall be paid out to the arbitrator or umpire, by way of fees, such sums as may be found reasonable on taxation, and that the balance of the money, if any, shall be paid out to the applicant.

(2) An application for the purposes of this section may be made by any party to the reference unless the fees demanded have been fixed by a written agreement between him and the arbitrator or umpire.

(3)   A taxation of fees by the Clerk of the Court under this section shall be final.

(4)   Any money required to be paid into Court under subsection (1) of this section shall be paid to the Clerk of the Court.

(5)   The arbitrator or umpire shall be entitled to appear and be heard on any taxation under this section.

18.   Interest on awards.

A sum directed to be paid by an award shall, unless the award otherwise directs, carry interest as from the date of the award and at the same rate as a judgment debt.

Judicial Review, Remission and Setting aside of
Awards, etc.

19.   Judicial review of arbitration awards.

(1)   Without prejudice to the right of appeal conferred by the next succeeding subsection, the Court shall not have jurisdiction to set aside or remit an award on an arbitration agreement on the ground of errors of fact or law on the face of the award.

(2)   Subject to the next succeeding subsection, an appeal shall lie to the Court on any question of law arising out of award made on an arbitration agreement; and on the determination of such an appeal the Court may by order—

(a)   confirm, vary or set aside the award; or

(b)   remit the award to the reconsideration of the arbitrator or umpire together with the Court's opinion on the question of law which was the subject of the appeal;

and where the award is remitted under paragraph (b) of this subsection the arbitrator or umpire shall, unless the order otherwise directs, make his award within three months after the date of the order.

(3)   An appeal under this section may be brought by any of the parties to the reference—

(a)   with the consent of all the other parties to the reference; or

(b)   subject to section 20A of this Law, with the leave of the Court.

[*Amended by The Arbitration (Amendment) (Alderney) Law, 1986.*]

(4)   The Court shall not grant leave under paragraph (b) of the last preceding subsection unless it considers that, having regard to all the circumstances, the determination of the question of law concerned could substantially affect the rights of one or more of the parties to the arbitration agreement; and the Court may make any leave which it gives conditional upon the applicant complying with such conditions as it considers appropriate.

(5)   Subject to the next succeeding subsection, if an award is made and, on an application made by any of the parties to the reference—

(a)   with the consent of all the other parties to the reference; or

(b)   subject to section 20A of this Law, with the leave of the Court;

[*Amended by The Arbitration (Amendment) (Alderney) Law, 1986.*]

it appears to the Court that the award does not or does not sufficiently set out the reasons for the award, the Court may order the arbitrator or umpire concerned to state the reasons for his award in sufficient detail to enable the Court, should an appeal be brought under this section, to consider any question of law arising out of the award.

(6) In any case where an award is made without any reason being given, the Court shall not make an order under the last preceding subsection unless it is satisfied—

    (a) that before the award was made one of the parties to the reference gave notice to the arbitrator or umpire concerned that a reasoned award would be required; or

    (b) that there is some special reason why such a notice was not given.

(7) No appeal shall lie to the Royal Court under section two of the Law of 1969 from a decision of the Court on an appeal under this section unless—

    (a) the court or the Royal Court gives leave; and

    (b) it is certified by the Court that the question of law to which its decision relates either is one of general public importance or is one which for some other special reason should be considered by the Royal Court.

(8) Where the award of an arbitrator or umpire is varied on appeal, the award as varied shall have effect (except for the purpose of this section) as if it were the award of the arbitrator or umpire.

(9) An appeal under the provisions of subsection (2) of this section shall be made to the Court within twenty-one days from the date of the publication of the award:

Provided that the Court may extend the period prescribed under this subsection for making an appeal upon application being made to the Court before the expiration of that period.

20. Determination of preliminary point of law by Court.

(1) Subject to section 20A of this Law and the next succeeding subsection, on an application to the Court made by any of the parties to a reference—

    (a) with the consent of an arbitrator who has entered on the reference or, if an umpire has entered on the reference, with his consent; or

    (b) with the consent of all the other parties; the Court shall have jurisdiction to determine any question of law arising in the course of the reference.

[*Section 20(1) amended by The Arbitration (Amendment) (Alderney) Law, 1986.*]

(2) The Court shall not entertain an application under paragraph (a) of the last preceding subsection with respect to any question of law unless it is satisfied that—

    (a) the determination of the application might produce substantial savings in costs to the parties; and

    (b) the question of law is one in respect of which leave to appeal would be likely to be given under paragraph (b) of subsection (3) of the last preceding section.

(3) A decision of the Court under this section shall be deemed to be a judgment of the Court for the purposes of appellate jurisdiction of the Royal

Court in civil matters under section two of the Lav of 1969, but no appeal shall lie from such a decision unless—

(a)   the Court or the Royal Court gives leave; and

(b)   it is certified by the Court that the question of law to which its decision relates either is one of general public importance or is one which for some other special reason should be considered by the Royal Court.

20A.   Exclusion agreements affecting rights under sections 19 and 20.

(1)   Subject to the following provisions of this section—

(a)   the Court shall not, under section 19(3)(b) of this Law, grant leave to appeal with respect to a question of law arising out of an award; and

(b)   the Court shall not, under section 19(5)(b) of this Law, grant leave to make an aplication with respect to an award; and

(c)   no application may be made under section 20(1)(a) of this Law with respect to a question of law;

if the parties to the reference in question have entered into an agreement in writing (in this section referred to as an 'exclusion agreement') which excludes the right of appeal under section 19 of this Law in relation to that award or, in a case falling within paragraph (c) of this subsection in relation to an award to which the determination of the question of law is material.

(2)   If the parties to an exclusion agreement subsequently enter into an agreement in writing to revoke the exclusion agreement the provisions of subsection (1) of this section shall cease to apply to the reference or references in question until such time as a further exclusion agreement is entered into by the parties.

(3)   An exclusion agreement may be expressed so as to relate to a particular award, to awards under a particular reference or to any other description of awards, whether arising out of the same reference or not; and an agreement may be an exclusion agreement for the purposes of this section whether it is entered into before or after the coming into force of the Arbitration (Amendment) (Alderney) Law, 1985, and whether or not it forms part of an arbitration agreement.

(4)   In any case where—

(a)   an arbitration agreement, other than a domestic arbitration agreement, provides for disputes between the parties to be referred to arbitration; and

(b)   a dispute to which the agreement relates involves the question whether a party has been guilty of fraud; and

(c)   the parties have entered into an exclusion agreement which is applicable to any award made on the reference of that dispute;

then, except in so far as the exclusion agreement otherwise provides, the Court shall not exercise its powers under section 24(2) of this Law (to take steps necessary to enable the question to be determined by the Court) in relation to that dispute.

(5)   Except as provided by subsection (1) of this section, sections 19 and 20 of this Law shall have effect notwithstanding anything in any agreement purporting—

(a)   to prohibit or restrict access to the Court; or

(b)   to restrict the jurisdiction of the Court; or

(c) to prohibit or restrict the making of a reasoned award.

(6) An exclusion agreement shall be of no effect in relation to an award made on, or a question of law arising in the course of a reference under, a statutory arbitration, that is to say, such an arbitration as is referred to in subsection (1) of section 30 of this Law.

(7) An exclusion agreement shall be of no effect in relation to an award made on, or a question of law arising in the course of a reference under, an arbitration agreement which is a domestic arbitration agreement unless the exclusion agreement is entered into after the commencement of the arbitration in which the award is made or, as the case may be, in which the question of law arises.

(8) In this section, the expression 'domestic arbitration agreement' has the same meaning as in subsection (3) of section 5 of this Law, save that the said subsection (3) shall have effect as if for the words therein 'is a party at the time the proceedings are commenced' there were substituted the words 'is a party at the time the arbitration agreement is entered into'.

[*Section 20A inserted by The Arbitration (Amendment) (Alderney) Law, 1986.*]

21. Interlocutory orders.

(1) If any party to a reference under an arbitration agreement fails within the time specified in the order or, if no time is so specified, within a reasonable time to comply with the order made by the arbitrator or umpire in the course of the reference, then on the application of the arbitrator or umpire or of any party to the reference, the Court may make an order extending the powers of the arbitrator or umpire as mentioned in the next succeeding subsection.

(2) If an order is made by the Court under this section, the arbitrator or umpire shall have power, to the extent and subject to any conditions specified in that order, to continue with the reference in default of appearance or of any other act by one of the parties in like manner as the Court might continue with proceedings in the Court where a party fails to comply with an order of the Court or a requirement of Rules of Court.

(3) The preceding provisions of this section shall have effect notwithstanding anything in any agreement but shall not derogate from any powers conferred on an arbitrator or umpire, whether by an arbitration agreement or otherwise.

22. Power to remit award.

(1) In all cases of reference to arbitration, the Court may from time to time remit the matters referred, or any of them, to the reconsideration of the arbitrator or umpire.

(2) Where an award is remitted, the arbitrator or umpire shall, unless the order otherwise directs, make his award within three months after the date of the order.

(3) An application to the Court to remit an award under subsection (1) of this section may be made at any time within six weeks after the award has been made and published to the parties.

23. Removal of arbitrator and setting aside of award.

(1)   Where an arbitrator or umpire has misconducted himself or the proceedings, the Court may remove him.

(2)   Where an arbitrator or umpire has misconducted himself or the proceedings, or an arbitration or award has been improperly procured, the Court may set the award aside.

(3)   Where an application is made to set aside an award, the Court may order that any money made payable by the award shall be brought into Court or otherwise secured pending the determination of the application.

(4)   Any money ordered to be brought into Court under the last preceding subsection shall be paid to the Clerk of the Court.

(5)   An application to the Court to set aside an award under subsection (2) of this section may be made at any time within six weeks after the award has been made and published to the parties.

24. Power of Court to give relief where arbitrator is not impartial or the dispute involves question of fraud.

(1)   Where an agreement between any parties provides that disputes which may arise in the future between them shall be referred to an arbitrator named or designated in the agreement, and after a dispute has arisen any party applies, on the ground that the arbitrator so named or designated is not or may not be impartial, for leave to revoke the authority of the arbitrator or for an order to restrain any other party or the arbitrator from proceeding with the arbitration, it shall not be a ground for refusing the application that the said party at the time when he made the agreement knew, or ought to have known, that the arbitrator, by reason of his relation towards any other party to the agreement or of his connection with the subject referred, might not be capable of impartiality.

(2)   Where an agreement between any parties provides that disputes which may arise in the future between them shall be referred to arbitration, and a dispute which so arises involves the question whether any such party has been guilty of fraud, the Court shall, so far as may be necessary to enable that question to be determined by the Court, have power to order that the agreement shall cease to have effect and power to give leave to revoke the authority of any arbitrator or umpire appointed by or by virtue of the agreement.

(3)   In any case where, by virtue of this section, the Court has power to order that an arbitration agreement shall cease to have effect or to give leave to revoke the authority of an arbitrator or umpire, the Court may refuse to stay any action brought in breach of the agreement.

25. Power of Court where arbitrator is removed or authority of arbitrator is revoked.

(1)   Where an arbitrator (not being a sole arbitrator) or two or more arbitrators (not being all the arbitrators) or an umpire who has not entered on the reference is or are removed by the Court, the Court may, on the application of any party to the arbitration agreement, appoint a person or

persons to act as arbitrator or arbitrators or umpire in place of the person or persons so removed.

(2) Where the authority of an arbitrator or arbitrators or umpire is revoked by leave of the Court, or a sole arbitrator or all the arbitrators or an umpire who has entered on the reference is or are removed by the Court, the Court may, on the application of any party to the arbitration agreement, either—

(a) appoint a person to act as sole arbitrator in place of the person or persons removed; or

(b) order that the arbitration agreement shall cease to have effect with respect to the dispute referred.

(3) A person appointed under this section by the Court as an arbitrator or umpire shall have the like power to act in the reference, and to make an award, as if he had been appointed in accordance with the terms of the arbitration agreement.

(4) Where it is provided (whether by means of a provision in the arbitration agreement or otherwise) that an award under an arbitration agreement shall be a condition precedent to the bringing of an action with respect to any matter to which the agreement applies, the Court, if it orders (whether under this section or under any other enactment) that the agreement shall cease to have effect as regards any particular dispute, may further order that the provision making an award a condition precedent to the bringing of an action shall also cease to have effect as regards that dispute.

Enforcement of Award

26. Enforcement of award.

An award on an arbitration agreement may, by leave of the Court, be enforced in the same manner as a judgment or order to the same effect; and, where leave is so given, the Act of Court shall specify the manner of enforcement.

Miscellaneous

27. Power of Court to extend time for commencing arbitration proceedings.

Where the terms of an agreement to refer disputes to arbitration provide that any claims to which the agreement applies shall be barred unless notice to appoint an arbitrator is given or an arbitrator is appointed or some other step to commence arbitration proceedings is taken within a time fixed by the agreement, and a dispute arises to which the agreement applies, the Court, if it is of the opinion that, in the circumstances of the case, undue hardship would otherwise be caused, and notwithstanding that the time so fixed has expired, may, on such terms, if any, as the justice of the case may require, but without prejudice to the provisions of any enactment limiting the time for the commencement of arbitration proceedings, extend the time for such period as it thinks proper.

28. Terms as to costs, etc.

Any order made under this Part of this Law may be made on such terms as to costs or otherwise as the authority making the order thinks just.

29. Limitation of action.

(1)   Subject to the provisions of this section the provisions of any enactment relating to the limitation of actions shall apply to arbitrations as they apply to civil actions before the Court.

(2)   No action to enforce an award on an arbitration agreement shall be brought before the Court after the expiration of six years from the date on which the cause of action arose.

(3)   Notwithstanding any term in an arbitration agreement to the effect that no cause of action shall accrue in respect of any matter required by the agreement to be referred until an award is made under the agreement, the cause of action shall, for the purpose of this section and of any such enactment as aforesaid (whether in application to arbitrations or to other proceedings), be deemed to have accrued in respect of any such matter at the time when it would have accrued but for that term in the agreement.

(4)   For the purpose of this section and of any such enactment as aforesaid, an arbitration shall be deemed to be commenced when one party to the arbitration serves on the other party or parties a notice requiring him or them to appoint an arbitrator or to agree to the appointment of an arbitrator, or, where the arbitration agreement provides that the reference shall be to a person named or designated in the agreement, requiring him or them to submit the dispute to the person so named or designated.

(5)   Where the Court orders that an award be set aside or orders, after the commencement of an arbitration, that the arbitration shall cease to have effect with respect to the dispute referred, the Court may further order that the period between the commencement of the arbitration and the date of the order of the Court shall be excluded in computing the time prescribed by this section or any such enactment as aforesaid for the commencement of proceedings (including arbitration) with respect to the dispute referred.

30. Application of Part I to statutory arbitrations.

(1)   This Part of this Law, except the provisions thereof specified in the next succeeding subsection shall apply to every arbitration under any other enactment (whether passed before or after the coming into force of this Law) as if the arbitration were pursuant to an arbitration agreement and as if that other enactment were an arbitration agreement, except in so far as this Law is inconsistent with that other enactment or with any rules or procedure authorised or recognised thereby:

Provided that in any arbitration under the provisions of any other enactment any reference to the award made by an arbitrator or umpire being final and binding on the parties and the persons claiming under them respectively shall be deemed to include a reference to such provisions being subject to the provisions of section nineteen of this Law.

(2)   The provisions referred to in the last preceeding subsection are subsection (1) of section two, section three, section five, subsection (2) of section sixteen, section twenty-four, section twenty-five and section twenty-seven of this Law.

PART II

ENFORCEMENT OF CERTAIN FOREIGN AWARDS

31.   Awards to which Part II applies.

(1)   Subject to section thirty-six of this Law, this Part of this Law applies to any award made after the twenty-eighth day of July, nineteen hundred and twenty-four—

(a)   in pursuance of an agreement for arbitration to which the Protocol applies; and

(b)   between persons of whom one is subject to the jurisdiction of some one of such Powers as Her Majesty may, by Order in Council, have declared to be parties to the Geneva Convention and of whom the other is subject to the jurisdiction of some other of the Powers aforesaid; and

(c)   in one of such territories as Her Majesty may, by Order in Council, have declared to be territories to which the Geneva Convention applies;

and an award to which this Part of this Law applies is, in this Part of this Law, referred to as 'a foreign award'.

(2)   In this section the expression 'Order in Council' means an Order in Council which is in force and which—

(a)   has been made under paragraph (b) of sub-section (1) of section thirty-five of the Arbitration Act 1950; or

(b)   has effect, by virtue of subsection (3) of that section, as if it had been so made.

32.   Effect of foreign awards.

(1)   A foreign award shall, subject to the provisions of this part of this Law, be enforceable in the Island either by action or in the same manner as the award of an arbitrator is enforceable by virtue of section twenty-six of this Law.

(2)   Any foreign award which would be enforceable under this Part of this Law shall be treated as binding for all purposes on the persons as between whom it was made, and may, accordingly, be relied on by any of those persons by way of defence, set off or otherwise in any legal proceedings in the Island, and any references in this Part of this Law to enforcing a foreign award shall be construed as including references to relying on an award.

33.   Conditions for enforcement of foreign awards.

(1)   In order that a foreign award may be enforceable under this Part of this Law, it must have—

(a)   been made in pursuance of an agreement for arbitration which was valid under the law by which it was governed;

(b)   been made by the tribunal provided for in the agreement or constituted in the mannner agreed upon by the parties;

(c)   been made in conformity with the law governing the arbitration procedure;

(d)   become final in the country in which it was made;

(e)   been in respect of a matter which may lawfully be referred to arbitration under the law of the Island;

and the enforcement thereof must not be contrary to the public policy or the law of the Island.

(2)   Subject to the provisions of this subsection, a foreign award shall not be enforceable under this Part of this Law if the Court is satisfied that—

(a)   the award has been annulled in the country in which it was made; or

(b)   the party against whom it is sought to enforce the award was not given notice of the arbitration proceedings in sufficient time to enable him to present his case, or was under some legal incapacity and was not properly represented; or

(c)   the award does not deal with all the questions referred or contains decisions on matters beyond the scope of the agreement for arbitration;

but, if the award does not deal with all the questions referred, the Court may, if it thinks fit either postpone the enforcement of the award or order its enforcement subject to the giving of such security by the person seeking to enforce it as the Court may think fit.

(3)   If a party seeking to resist the enforcement of a foreign award proves that there is any ground other than the non-existence of the conditions specified in paragraphs (a), (b) and (c) of subsection (1) of this section, or the existence of the conditions specified in paragraphs (b) and (c) of the last preceding subsection, entitling him to contest the validity of the award, the Court may, if it thinks fit, either refuse to enforce the award or adjourn the hearing until after the expiration of such period as appears to the Court to be reasonably sufficient to enable that party to take the necessary steps to have the award annulled by the competent tribunal.

34.   Evidence.

(1)   The party seeking to enforce a foreign award must produce—

(a)   the original award or a copy thereof duly authenticated in the manner required by the law of the country in which it was made;

(b)   evidence proving that the award has become final; and

(c)   such evidence as may be necessary to prove that the award is a foreign award and that the conditions mentioned in paragraphs (a), (b) and (c) of subsection (1) of the last preceding section are satisfied.

(2)   In any case where any document required to be produced under the last preceding subsection is in a foreign language, it shall be the duty of the party seeking to enforce the award to produce a translation thereof in the English language certified as correct by an official or sworn translator or by a diplomatic or consular agent of the country to which that party belongs, or certified as correct in such other manner as may be sufficient according to the law of the Island.

35.   Meaning of 'final award'.

For the purposes of this Part of this Law, an award shall not be deemed final if any proceedings for the purpose of contesting the validity of the award are pending in the country in which it was made.

PART III

ENFORCEMENT OF CONVENTION AWARDS

36.   Replacement of Part II in certain cases.

Sections thirty-seven, thirty-eight and thirty-nine of, and paragraph 3 of the First Schedule to, this Law shall have effect with respect of the enforcement of Convention awards; and, where a Convention award would, but for this section, be also a foreign award within the meaning of Part II of this Law, that Part shall not apply to it.

37.   Effect of Convention awards.

(1)   A Convention award shall, subject to the following provisions of this Part of this Law, be enforceable in the Island either by action or in the same manner as the award of an arbitrator is enforceable by virtue of section twenty-six of this Law.

(2)   Any Convention award which would be enforceable under this Part of this Law shall be treated as binding for all purposes on the persons as between whom it was made, and may, accordingly be relied on by any of those persons by way of defence, set off or otherwise in any legal proceedings in the Island; and any reference in this Part of this Law to enforcing a Convention award shall be construed as including references to relying on such an award.

38.   Evidence.

The party seeking to enforce a Convention award must produce—
  (a)   the original award or a copy thereof duly authenticated in the manner required by the law of the country in which it was made;
  (b)   the original arbitration agreement or a copy thereof duly authenticated in the manner required by the law of the country in which it was made; and
  (c)   where the award or agreement is in a foreign language, a translation thereof in the English language certified as correct by an official or sworn translator or by a diplomatic or consular agent of the country to which that party belongs, or certified as correct in such other manner as may be sufficient according to the law of the Island.

39.   Refusal of enforcement.

(1)   Enforcement of a Convention award shall not be refused except in the cases mentioned in this section.

(2)   Enforcement of a Convention award may be refused if the person against whom it is invoked proves—

(a)   that a party to the arbitration was under the law applicable to him, under some incapacity; or

(b)   that the arbitration agreement was not valid under the law to which the parties subjected it or, failing any indication thereon, under the law of the country where the award was made; or

(c)   that he was not given proper notice of the appointment of the arbitrator or of the arbitration proceedings or was otherwise unable to present his case; or

(d)   subject to subsection (4) of this section, that the award deals with a difference not contemplated by, or not falling within the terms of, the submission to arbitration or contains decisions on matters beyond the scope of the submission to arbitration; or

(e)   that the composition of the arbitral authority or the arbitral procedure was not in accordance with the ageement of the parties or, failing such agreement with the law of the country where the arbitration took place; or

(f)   that the award has not yet become binding on the parties, or has been set aside or suspended by a competent authority of the country in which, or under the law of which, it was made.

(3)   Enforcement of a Convention award may also be refused if the award is in respect of a matter which is not capable of settlement by arbitration, or if it would be contrary to public policy to enforce the award.

(4)   A convention award which contains decisions on matters not submitted to arbitration may be enforced to the extent that it contains decisions on matters submitted to arbitration which can be separated from those on matters not so submitted.

(5)   Where an application for the setting aside or suspension of a Convention award has been made to such a competent authority as is mentioned in paragraph (f) of subsection (2) of this section, the Court may, if it thinks fit, adjourn the proceedings and may, on the application of the party seeking to enforce the award, order the other party to give security.

PART IV

SUPPLEMENTARY

40.   Rules of Court.

The Royal Court may, from time to time, make rules dealing generally with all matters of procedure and incidental matters arising under this Law and for carrying out this Law into effect.

41.   Service of notices.

A notice which may be served for the purpose of this Law shall be validly served—

(a)   on any person, if delivered to him, left, or sent by registered post or by recorded delivery service to him, at his usual or last known place of abode;

(b)   on any firm, if delivered to any partner of the firm or left at, or sent by registered post or by recorded delivery service to, the principal or last known principal place of business of the firm;

(c)   on any body corporate, if left at, or sent by registered post or by recorded delivery service to, its registered office if situate in the Island or, if its registered office is not so situate, its principal or last known principal place of business in the Island;

and a notice shall, as well, be validly served if served on any person, firm or body corporate in any other manner provided in the arbitration agreement.

42.   Interpretation.

(1)   In this Law, except where the context otherwise requires, the following expressions have the meanings hereby respectively assigned to them, that is to say:—

'arbitration agreement' means—

(a)   in section five of this Law and in the definition below of 'Convention award', an agreement in writing (including an agreement contained in an exchange of letters or telegrams) to submit to arbitration present or future differences capable of settlement by arbitration; and

(b)   elsewhere, a written agreement to submit present or future differences to arbitration, whether an arbitrator is mentioned therein or not;

'Convention award' means an award made in pursuance of an arbitration agreement in the territory of a State, other than the United Kingdom, which is a party to the New York Convention;

'the Court' means the Court of Alderney;

'The Geneva Convention' means the Convention on the Execution of Foreign Arbitral Awards signed at Geneva on behalf of His late Majesty, King George V, on the 26th September, 1927;

'the Island' means the Island of Alderney;

'the Law of 1969' means the Court of Alderney (Appeals) Law, 1969;

'the New York Convention' means the Convention on the Recogition and Enforcement of Foreign Arbitral Awards adopted by the United Nations Conference on International Commercial Arbitration on the 10th June, 1958;

'the Protocol' means the Protocol on Arbitration Clauses signed on behalf of His late Majesty, King George V, at a Meeting of the Assembly of the League of Nations held on the 24th September, 1923;

'the Royal Court' means—

(a)   in sections nineteen and twenty of this Law, the Royal Court of Guernsey sitting as an Appellate Court for the Court of Alderney; and

(b)   in section forty of this Law, the Royal Court of Guernsey sitting as a Full Court.

(2)   If Her Majesty by Order in Council declares that any State specified in the Order is a party to the New York Convention, the Order shall, while in force, be conclusive evidence that that State is a party to that Convention.

(3)   Any reference in this Law to any other enactment shall, except where the context otherwise requires, be construed as including a reference to that enactment as amended, repealed or replaced, extended or applied by or under any other enactment including this Law.

(4)   The Interpretation (Guernsey) Law, 1948, shall apply to the interpretation of this Law as it applies to the interpretation of a Guernsey enactment.

43. Transitional provisions and savings.

The transitional provisions and savings in the First Schedule to this Law shall have effect.

44. Repeals.

The Laws set out in the Second Schedule to this Law are hereby repealed.

45. Citation.

This Law may be cited as the Arbitration (Alderney) Law, 1983.

46. Commencement.

This Law shall come into force on such day as the States may by Ordinance appoint, and different days may be so appointed for different provisions of this Law, or for different purposes.

['The Arbitration (Alderney) Law, 1983, shall come into force on the sixteenth day of January, nineteen hundred and eighty-four.' *The Arbitration (Alderney) Law, 1983 (Commencement) Ordinance, 1983.*]

FIRST SCHEDULE

Sections thirty-six and forty-three

TRANSITIONAL PROVISIONS AND SAVINGS

1. Any proceedings under the Law entitled 'Loi donnant effet à une Convention sur l'Exécution des Jugements Arbitraux et portant amendement à la Loi donnant effet à une Protocole sur l'Arbitrage enregistré le 28 juin 1926' registered on the twentieth day of December, nineteen hundred and thirty (hereinafter referred to as 'the Law of 1930') which are uncompleted on the coming into force of this Law may be carried on and completed under Part II of this Law as if they bad been instituted thereunder.

2. Nothing in Part II of this Law shall prejudice any rights which any person would have had of enforcing in the Island any award, or of availing himself in the Island of any award, if neither that Part nor the Law of 1930 had been enacted.

3. Nothing in Part III of this Law shall prejudice any right to enforce or rely on an award otherwise than under that Part or under Part II of this Law.

SECOND SCHEDULE

Section forty-four

LAWS REPEALED

The Law entitled 'Loi donnant effet à une Protocole sur l'Arbitrage, Aurigny' registered on the nineteenth day of June, nineteen hundred and twenty-six.

The Law entitled 'Loi donnant effet à une Convention sur l'Exécution des Jugements Arbitraux et portant amendment à la Loi donnant effet à un Protocole sur l'Arbitrage enregistré le 28 juin 1926' registered on the twentieth day of December, nineteen hundred and thirty.

D. J. ROBILLIARD,
Her Majesty's Deputy Greffier.

THE ROYAL COURT (ARBITRATION) (ALDERNEY) RULES 1984

THE ROYAL COURT, in exercise of the powers conferred upon it by section forty of the Arbitration (Alderney) Law, 1983, and of all other powers enabling it in that behalf, hereby makes the following Rules:—

Order in Council No. XIII of 1983.

1. Applications under the Law.

(1) Subject to the provisions of paragraphs (3) and (4) of these Rules, every application to the Court under the Law shall be made by filing a notice of application with the Clerk of the Court and serving a copy of the notice within the seven days next following the filing thereof on every party affected by the application.

(2) When a date has been fixed for the hearing by the Court of an application to which the last preceding paragraph applies, the Clerk of the Court shall inform the applicant of the date so fixed and notice thereof shall, as soon as may be, be served by the applicant on every other party affected by the application and shall in any case be so served not less than four clear days before the date so fixed.

(3) Every application to the Court under section nineteen, section twenty, section twenty-one, subsection (1) of section twenty-two, subsections (1) and (2) of section twenty-three and twenty-six (including applications under the said section twenty-six as extended by sections thirty-two and thirty-seven) of the Law shall be made by way of summons which shall be served on every party affected by the application.

(4) An application to the Court under subsection (4) of section eleven of the Law may be made ex parte.

(5) Every application to the Court shall state in general terms the grounds of the application.

2. Interpretation.

(1) In these Rules the expression 'the Law' means the Arbitration (Alderney) Law, 1983, and any other expressions have the same meanings as in the Law.

(2) The Interpretation (Guernsey) Law, 1948, shall apply to the interpretation of these Rules as it applies to the interpretation of a Guernsey enactment.

(3) Any reference in these Rules to any other enactment shall, except where the context otherwise requires, be construed as including a reference

to that enactment as amended, repealed or replaced, extended or applied by or under any other enactment including these Rules.

3. Citation.

These Rules may be cited as the Royal Court (Arbitration) (Alderney) Rules, 1984.

4. Commencement.

These Rules shall come into force on the sixteenth day of January, nineteen hundred and eighty-four.

K. H. TOUGH,
Her Majesty's Greffier.

I.2   GUERNSEY

THE ARBITRATION (INTERNATIONAL INVESTMENT DISPUTES) (GUERNSEY) ORDER 1968
(SI 1968, No. 1199)

Her Majesty, in exercise of the powers conferred upon Her by section 6 of the Arbitration (International Investment Disputes) Act 1966, is pleased, by and with the advice of Her Privy Council, to order, and it is hereby ordered, as follows:—

1.   The provisions of the Arbitration (International Investments Disputes) Act 1966 shall extend to the Bailiwick of Guernsey subject to the exceptions, adaptations and modifications specified in the Schedule to this Order.

2.   The Interpretation Act 1889 shall apply for the purpose of the interpretation of this Order as it applies for the purpose of the interpretation of an Act of Parliament.

3.   This Order may be cited as the Arbitration (International Investment Disputes) (Guernsey) Order 1968 and shall come into operation on 1st September 1968.

SCHEDULE

EXCEPTIONS, ADAPTATIONS AND MODIFICATIONS

1.   Any reference to the Arbitration (International Investment Disputes) Act 1966 shall be construed as a reference to that Act as extended to the Bailiwick of Guernsey by this Order.

2.—(1)   In section 1(2) for the words 'the High Court' there shall be substituted the words 'the appropriate Bailiwick court'.

(2)   For section 1(6) there shall be substituted the following subsection—

'''(6)   The Royal Court sitting as a Full Court may from time to time make rules of court—

(a)   prescribing the procedure for applying for registration under this section, and requiring an applicant to give prior notice of his intentions to other parties;

(b)   prescribing the matters to be proved on the application and the manner of proof and in particular requiring the applicant to furnish a copy of the award certified pursuant to the Convention;

(c)   prescribing the manner in which awards shall be registered;

(d)   providing for the service of notice of registration of the award by the applicant on other parties;

and in this and the next following section 'prescribed' means prescribed by such rules of court.'''.

(3)   In section 1(7) immediately before paragraph (a) thereof, there shall be inserted the following paragraph:—

'''(a)   'the appropriate Bailiwick court' means—

(i)   as respects the Islands of Guernsey, Herm and Jethou, the Royal Court sitting as an Ordinary Court,

(ii)   as respects the Island of Alderney, the Court of Alderney.

(iii)   as respects the Island of Sark, the Court of the Seneschal of Sark,''',

and the existing paragraphs (a) and (b) shall accordingly be respectively redesignated as paragraphs (b) and (c).

3.—(1)   In section 2(1) for the words 'the High Court', wherever they occur, there shall be substituted the words 'the appropriate Bailiwick court'.

(2)   In section 2(2) for the words 'Rules of court under section 99 of the Supreme Court of Judicature (Consolidation) Act 1925' there shall be substituted the words 'Rules of court under subsection (6) of the last preceding section'.

4.   For section 3 there shall be substituted the following section:—

'3.   Proceedings in the Bailiwick of Guernsey.

(1)   The Bailiff may, by rules made under this subsection—

(a)   make provision, in relation to such proceedings pursuant to the Convention as are specified in those rules, being proceedings taking place in the Bailiwick of Guernsey, for the attendance of witnesses, the taking of evidence and the production of documents;

(b)   direct that any of the provisions of the Foreign Tribunals Evidence Act 1856 (which relates to the taking of evidence for the purpose of proceedings before a foreign tribunal) shall apply to such proceedings pursuant to the Convention as are specified in those rules, with or without any modifications or exceptions specified in those rules.

(2)   Any rules made under subsection (1) of this section may be varied or revoked by subsequent rules so made.'

5.   Sections 5, 6(1)(a) and (c), 7, 8 and 9(2) shall be omitted.

EXPLANATORY NOTE

(This Note is not part of the Order.)

This Order extends to the Bailiwick of Guernsey, with exceptions, adaptations and modifications, the provisions of the Arbitration (International Investment Disputes) Act 1966 (which implements the Convention on the settlement of investment disputes between States and nationals of other States which was opened for signature in Washington on 18th March 1965).

THE ARBITRATION (GUERNSEY) LAW 1982

THE STATES, in pursuance of their Resolutions of the twelfth day of December, nineteen hundred and seventy-three and the twenty-eighth day of October, nineteen hundred and eighty-one, have approved the following provisions which, subject to the Sanction of Her Most Excellent Majesty in Council, shall have force of law in the Islands of Guernsey, Herm and Jethou.

PART I

GENERAL PROVISIONS AS TO ARBITRATION

Effect of Arbitration Agreements, etc.

1. Authority of arbitrators and umpires to be irrevocable.

The authority of an arbitrator or umpire appointed by, or by virtue of, an arbitration agreement shall, unless a contrary intention is expressed in the agreement, be irrevocable except by leave of the Court.

2. Death of party.

(1) An arbitration agreement shall not be discharged by the death of any party thereto, either as respects the deceased or any other party, but shall in such event be enforceable by or against the personal representative of the deceased.

(2) The authority of an arbitrator shall not be revoked by the death of any party by whom he was appointed.

(3) Nothing in this section shall be taken to affect the operation of any enactment or rule of law by virtue of which any right of action is extinguished by the death of a person.

3. Insolvency.

Where it is provided by a term in a contract to which a person who is insolvent is a party that any differences arising thereout or in connection therewith shall be referred to arbitration, the said term shall, if the trustee or other person acting on behalf of his creditors adopts the contract, be enforceable by or against him so far as relates to any such differences.

4. Staying Court proceedings where there is submission to arbitration.

Subject to the next succeeding section, if any party to an arbitration agreement, or any person claiming through or under him, commences any legal proceedings in the Court against any other party to the agreement, or any person claiming through or under him, in respect of any matter agreed to be referred, any party to those legal proceedings may at any time after appearance or after the inscription of the cause on the Pleading List but before delivering any pleadings or taking any other steps in the proceedings, apply to the Court to stay the proceedings; and the Court, if satisfied that there is no sufficient reason why the matter should not be referred in accordance with the agreement, and that the applicant was, at the time when the proceedings were commenced, and still remains, ready and willing to do all things necessary to the proper conduct of the arbitration, may make an order staying the proceedings.

5. Staying Court proceedings where party proves arbitration agreement.

(1) If any party to an arbitration agreement to which this section applies, or any person claiming through or under him, commences any legal proceedings in the Court against any other party to the agreement, or any person claiming through him or under him, in respect of any matter agreed to be referred, any party to the proceedings may at any time after appearance or after the inscription of the cause on the Pleading List but before delivering any pleadings or taking any other steps in the proceedings; apply to the Court to stay the proceedings; and the Court, unless satisfied that the arbitration agreement is null and void, inoperative or incapable of being performed or that there is not in fact any dispute between the parties with regard to the matter agreed to be referred, shall make an order staying the proceedings.

(2) This section applies to any arbitration agreement which is not a domestic arbitration agreement; and the last preceding section shall not apply to an arbitration agreement to which this section applies.

(3) In this section, the expression 'domestic arbitration agreement' means an arbitration agreement which does not provide, expressly or by implication, for arbitration in a State other than the Island and to which neither—
    (a) an individual who is not—
        (i) a citizen of the United Kingdom and Colonies; or
        (ii) a British subject without citizenship; or
        (iii) a British protected person; or
        (iv) a Stateless person;
        or who is habitually resident in any State other than the Island; nor
    (b) a body corporate which is incorporated in, or whose central management and control is exercised in, any State other than the Island;
is a party at the time the proceedings are commenced.

Arbitrators and Umpires

6. When reference is to a single arbitrator.

Unless a contrary intention is expressed therein, every arbitration agreement shall, if no other mode of reference is provided, be deemed to include a provision that the reference shall be to a single arbitrator.

7.   Power of parties in certain cases to supply vacancy.

(1)   Subject to the next succeeding subsection, where an arbitration agreement provides that the reference shall be to two arbitrators, one to be appointed by each party, then, unless a contrary intention is expressed therein—

(a)   if either of the appointed arbitrators refuses to act, or is incapable of acting, or dies, the party who appointed him may appoint a new arbitrator in his place;

(b)   if, on such a reference, one party fails to appoint an arbitrator, either originally or by way of substitution as aforesaid, for seven clear days after the other party, having appointed his arbitrator, has served the party making default with notice to make the appointment, the party who has appointed an arbitrator may appoint that arbitrator to act as sole arbitrator in the reference, and his award shall be binding on both parties as if he had been appointed by consent.

(2)   The Court may set aside any appointment made in pursuance of this section.

8.   Umpires.

(1)   Unless a contrary intention is expressed therein, every arbitration agreement shall, where the reference is to two arbitrators, be deemed to include a provision that the two arbitrators may appoint an umpire at any time after they are themselves appointed and shall do so forthwith if they cannot agree.

(2)   Unless a contrary intention is expressed therein, every arbitration agreement shall, where such a provision is applicable to the reference, be deemed to include a provision that, if the arbitrators have delivered to any party to the arbitration agreement, or to the umpire, a notice in writing stating that they cannot agree, the umpire may forthwith enter on the reference in lieu of the arbitrators.

(3)   At any time after the appointment of an umpire, however appointed, the Court may, on the application of any party to the reference and notwithstanding anything to the contrary in the arbitration agreement, order that the umpire shall enter upon the reference in lieu of the arbitrators and as if he were a sole arbitrator.

9.   Majority award of three arbitrators.

Unless the contrary intention is expressed in the arbitration agreement, in any case where there is a reference to three arbitrators, the award of any two of the arbitrators shall be binding.

10.   Power of Court in certain cases to appoint an arbitrator or umpire.

(1)   In any of the following cases—

(a)   where an arbitration agreement provides that the reference shall be to a single arbitrator, and all the parties do not, after differences have arisen, concur in the appointment of an arbitrator;

(b)   if an appointed arbitrator refuses to act, or is incapable of acting, or dies, and the arbitration agreement does not show that it was intended that the vacancy should not be supplied and the parties do not supply the vacancy;

(c)   where the parties or two arbitrators are required or are at liberty to appoint an umpire or third arbitrator and do not appoint him;

(d)   where an appointed umpire or third arbitrator refuses to act, or is incapable of acting, or dies, and the arbitration agreement does not show that it was intended that the vacancy should not be supplied, and the parties or arbitrators do not supply the vacancy;

any party may serve the other parties or the arbitrators, as the case may be, with a written notice to appoint or, as the case may be, concur in appointing, an arbitrator, umpire or third arbitrator; and, if the appointment is not made within seven days after the service of the notice, the Court may, on application by the party who gave the notice, appoint an arbitrator, umpire or third arbitrator who shall have the like powers to act in the reference and make an award as if he had been appointed by consent of all parties.

(2)   In any case where—

(a)   an arbitration agreement provides for the appointment of an arbitrator or umpire by a person who is neither one of the parties nor an existing arbitrator (whether the provision applies directly or in default of agreement by the parties or otherwise); and

(b)   that person refuses to make the appointment or does not make it within the time specified in the agreement or, if no time is so specified, within a reasonable time;

any party to the agreement may serve the person in question with a written notice to appoint an arbitrator or umpire and, if the appointment is not made within seven clear days after the service of the notice, the Court may, on the application of the party who gave the notice, appoint an arbitrator or umpire who shall have the like powers to act in the reference and make an award as if he had been appointed in accordance with the terms of the agreement.

Conduct of Proceedings, Witnesses, etc.

11.   Conduct of proceedings, witnesses, etc.

(1)   Unless a contrary intention is expressed therein, every, arbitration agreement shall, where such a provision is applicable to the reference, be deemed to contain a provision that the parties to the reference, and all persons claiming through them respectively, shall, subject to any legal objection, submit to be examined by tbe arbitrator or umpire, on oath or affirmation, in relation to the matters in dispute, and shall, subject as aforesaid, produce before the arbitrator or umpire all documents within their possession or power respectively which may be required or called for, and do all other things which during the proceedings on the reference the arbitrator or umpire may require.

(2)   Unless a contrary intention is expressed therein, every, arbitration agreement shall, where such a provision is applicable to the reference, be deemed to contain a provision that the witnesses on the reference shall, if the arbitrator or umpire thinks fit, be examined on oath or affirmation.

(3)   An arbitrator or umpire shall, unless a contrary intention is expressed in the arbitration agreement, have power to administer oaths to, or take the

affirmations of, the parties to and witnesses on a reference under the agreement.

(4)   Any party to a reference under an arbitration agreement may apply to the Court for permission to summon a witness to give evidence or to produce documentary evidence and a party who is so authorised by the Court may cause a summons to be served on any person, in the same manner as a summons may be served upon any person in respect of a civil action before the Court, summoning that person to attend before the arbitrator or umpire for the purpose of giving evidence or producing any document likely to assist the arbitrator or umpire in determining the question in dispute; and a person so summoned shall be under a like obligation as to the giving of any evidence and the production of any document as if he were so summoned in respect of such an action.

(5)   The Court shall have, for the purpose of and in relation to a reference under an arbitration agreement, the same power of making orders in respect of matters of procedure and other matters incidental to the reference as it has for the purpose of and in relation to a civil action before the Court.

Provisions as to Awards

12.   Time for making award.

(1)   Subject to the provisions of subsection (2) of section nineteen and subsection (2) of section twenty-two of this Law, and anything to the contrary in the arbitration agreement, an arbitrator or umpire shall have power to make an award at any time.

(2)   The time, if any, limited for making an award, whether under this Law or otherwise, may from time to time be enlarged by order of the Court, whether that time has expired or not.

(3)   The Court may, on the application of any party to a reference, remove an arbitrator or umpire who fails to use all reasonable dispatch in entering on and proceeding with the reference and making an award, and an arbitrator or umpire who is removed by the Court under this subsection shall not be entitled to receive any remuneration in respect of his services.

(4)   For the purposes of the last preceding subsection the expression 'proceeding with a reference' includes, in a case where two arbitrators are unable to agree, giving notice of that fact to the parties and to the umpire.

13.   Interim awards.

Unless a contrary intention is expressed therein, every arbitration agreement shall, where such a provision is applicable to the reference, be deemed to contain a provision that the arbitrator or umpire may, if he thinks fit, make an interim award, and any reference in this Part of this Law to an award includes a reference to an interim award.

14.   Awards to be final.

Subject to the provisions of section nineteen of this Law and unless a contrary intention is expressed therein, every arbitration agreement shall, where such a provision is applicable to the reference, be deemed to contain a provision that the award to be made by the arbitrator or umpire shall be final and binding on the parties and the persons claiming under them respectively.

15. Power to correct slips.

Unless a contrary intention is expressed in the arbitration agreement, the arbitrator or umpire shall have power to correct in an award any clerical mistake or error arising from any accidental slip or omission.

Costs, Fees and Interest

16. Costs.

(1) Unless a contrary intention is expressed therein, every arbitration agreement shall be deemed to include a provision that the costs of the reference and award shall be in the discretion of the arbitrator or umpire, who may direct to and by whom and in what manner those costs or any part thereof shall be paid, and shall tax the amount of costs to be so paid.

(2) Subject to the provisions of the last preceding subsection in the event of any difference or dispute between any parties to any reference as to the fees, disbursements and allowances recoverable in pursuance of an award directing the payment of costs, the difference or dispute shall be referred to Her Majesty's Procureur, whose decision shall be final.

(3) Subject to the next succeeding subsection, any provision in an arbitration agreement to the effect that the parties or any party thereto shall in any event pay their or his own costs of the reference or award or any part thereof shall be void, and this Part of this Law shall, in the case of an arbitration agreement containing any such provision, have effect as if that provision were not contained therein.

(4) Nothing in the last preceding subsection shall invalidate such a provision when it is a part of an agreement to submit to arbitration a dispute which has arisen before the making of that agreement.

(5) If no provision is made by an award with respect to the costs of the reference, any party to the reference may, within fourteen days of the publication of the award or such further time as the Court may direct, apply to the arbitrator for an order directing by and to whom those costs shall be paid, and thereupon the arbitrator shall, after hearing any party who may desire to be heard, amend his award by adding thereto such directions as he may think proper with respect of the payment of the costs of the reference and shall tax the amount of costs to be so paid.

17. Taxation of arbitrator's or umpire's fees.

(1) If, in any case, an arbitrator or umpire refuses to deliver his award except on payment of the fees demanded by him, the Court may, on application for the purpose, order that the arbitrator or umpire shall deliver the award to the applicant on payment into Court by the applicant of the fees demanded, and further that the fees demanded shall be taxed by Her Majesty's Procureur, and that, out of the money paid into Court, there shall

be paid out to the arbitrator or umpire, by way of fees, such sums as may be found reasonable on taxation, and that the balance of the money, if any, shall be paid out to the applicant.

(2)   An application for the purposes of this section may be made by any party to the reference unless the fees demanded have been fixed by a written agreement between him and the arbitrator or umpire.

(3)   A taxation of fees by Her Majesty's Procureur under this section shall be final.

(4)   Any money required to be paid into Court under subsection (1) of this section shall be paid to Her Majesty's Greffier.

(5)   The arbitrator or umpire shall be entitled to appear and be heard on any taxation under this section.

18.   Interest on awards.

A sum directed to be paid by an award shall, unless the award otherwise directs, carry interest as from the date of the award and at the same rate as a judgment debt.

Judicial Review, Remission and Setting aside of Awards, etc.

19.   Judicial review of arbitration awards.

(1)   Without prejudice to the right of appeal conferred by the next succeeding subsection, the Court shall not have jurisdiction to set aside or remit an award on an arbitration agreement on the ground of errors of fact or law on the face of the award.

(2)   Subject to the next succeeding subsection, an appeal shall lie to the Court on any question of law arising out of an award made on an arbitration agreement; and on the determination of such an appeal the Court may by order—

(a)   confirm, vary or set aside the award; or

(b)   remit the award to the reconsideration of the arbitrator or umpire together with the Court's opinion on the question of law which was the subject of the appeal;

and where the award is remitted under paragraph (b) of this subsection the arbitrator or umpire shall, unless the order otherwise directs, make his award within three months after the date of the order.

(3)   An appeal under this section may be brought by any of the parties to the reference—

(a)   with the consent of all the other parties to the reference; or

(b)   subject to section 20A of this Law,

[*Amended by The Arbitration (Amendment) (Guernsey) Law, 1986*] with leave of the Court.

(4)   The Court shall not grant leave under paragraph (b) of the last preceding subsection unless it considers that, having regard to all the circumstances, the determination of the question of law concerned could substantially affect the rights of one or more of the parties to the arbitration agreement; and the Court may make any leave which it gives conditional upon the appliant complying with such conditions as it considers appropriate.

(5)   Subject to the next succeeding subsection, if an award is made and, on an application made by any of the parties to the reference—

(a)   with the consent of all the other parties to the reference; or

(b)   subject to section 20A of this Law, with the leave of the Court;

it appears to the Court that the award does not or does not sufficiently set out the reasons for the award, the Court may order the arbitrator or umpire concerned to state the reasons for his award in sufficient detail to enable the Court, should an appeal be brought under this section, to consider any question of law arising out of the award.

[*Amended by The Arbitration (Amendment) (Guernsey) Law, 1986.*]

(6)   In any case where an award is made without any reason being given, the Court shall not make an order under the last preceding subsection unless it is satisfied—

(a)   that before the award was made one of the parties to the reference gave notice to the arbitrator or umpire concerned that a reasoned award would be required; or

(b)   that there is some special reason why such a notice was not given.

(7)   No appeal shall lie to the Court of Appeal under section thirteen of the Law of 1961 from a decision of the Court on an appeal under this section unless—

(a)   the Court or the Court of Appeal gives leave; and

(b)   it is certified by the Court that the question of law to which its decision relates either is one of general public importance or is one which for some other special reason should be considered by the Court of Appeal.

(8)   Where the award of an arbitrator or umpire is varied on appeal, the award as varied shall have effect (except for the purposes of this section) as if it were the award of the arbitrator or umpire.

(9)   An appeal under the provisions of subsection (2) of this section shall be made to the Court within twenty-one days from the date of the publication of the award:

Provided that the Court may extend the period prescribed under this subsection for making an appeal upon application being made to the Court before the expiration of that period.

20.   Determination of preliminary point of law by Court.

(1)   Subject to section 20A of this Law and to the next succeeding subsection, on an application to the Court made by any of the parties to a reference—

(a)   with the consent of an arbitrator who has entered on the reference or, if an umpire has entered on the reference, with his consent; or

(b)   with the consent of all the other parties;

the Court shall have jurisdiction to determine any question of law arising in the course of the reference.

[*Section 20(1) amended by The Arbitration (Amendment) (Guernsey) Law, 1986.*]

(2)   The Court shall not entertain an application under paragraph (a) of the last preceding subsection with respect to any question of law unless it is satisfied that—

(a)   the determination of the application might produce substantial savings in costs to the parties; and

(b)   the question of law is one in respect of which leave to appeal would be likely to be given under paragraph (b) of subsection (3) of the last preceding section.

(3)   A decision of the Court under this section shall be deemed to be a judgment of the Court for the purposes of appellate jurisdiction of the Court of Appeal in civil matters under section thirteen of the Law of 1961, but no appeal shall lie from such a decision unless—

(a)   the Court or the Court of Appeal gives leave; and

(b)   it is certified by the Court that the question of law to which its decision relates either is one of general public importance or is one which for some other special reason should be considered by the Court of Appeal.

20A.   Exclusion agreements affecting rights under sections 19 and 20.

(1)   Subject to the following provisions of this section—

(a)   the Court shall not, under section 19(3)(b) of this Law, grant leave to appeal with respect to a question of law arising out of an award; and

(b)   the Court shall not, under section 19(5)(b) of this Law, grant leave to make an application with respect to an award; and

(c)   no application may be made under section 20(1)(a) of this Law with respect to a question of law;

if the parties to the reference in question have entered into an agreement in writing (in this section referred to as an 'exclusion agreement') which excludes the right of appeal under section 19 of this Law in relation to that award or, in a case falling within paragraph (c) of this subsection in relation to an award to which the determination of the question of law is material.

(2)   If the parties to an exclusion agreement subsequently enter into an agreement in writing to revoke the exclusion agreement the provisions of subsection (1) of this section shall cease to apply to the reference or references in question until such time as a further exclusion agreement is entered into by the parties.

(3)   An exclusion agreement may be expressed so as to relate to a particular award, to awards under a particular reference or to any other description of awards, whether arising out of the same reference or not; and an agreement may be an exclusion agreement for the purposes of this section whether it is entered into before or after the coming into force of the Arbitration (Amendment) (Guernsey) Law, 1986, and whether or not it forms part of an arbitration agreement.

(4)   In any case where—

(a)   an arbitration agreement, other than a domestic arbitration agreement, provides for disputes between the parties to be referred to arbitration; and

(b)   a dispute to which the agreement relates involves the question whether a party has been guilty of fraud; and

(c)   the parties have entered into an exclusion agreement which is applicable to any award made on the reference of that dispute;

then, except in so far as the exclusion agreement otherwise provides, the Court shall not exercise its powers under section 24(2) of this Law (to take steps necessary to enable the question to be determined by the Court) in relation to that dispute.

(5)   Except as provided by subsection (1) of this section, sections 19 and 20 of this Law shall have effect notwithstanding anything in any agreement purporting—
    (a)   to prohibit or restrict access to the Court; or
    (b)   to restrict the jurisdiction of the Court; or
    (c)   to prohibit or restrict the making of a reasoned award.
(6)   An exclusion agreement shall be of no effect in relation to an award made on, or a question of law arising in the course of a reference under, a statutory arbitration, that is to say, such an arbitration as is referred to in subsection (1) of section 30 of this Law.
(7)   An exclusion agreement shall be of no effect in relation to an award made on, or a question of law arising in the course of a reference under, an arbitration agreement which is a domestic arbitration agreement unless the exclusion agreement is entered into after the commencement of the arbitration in which the award is made or, as the case may be, in which the question of law arises.
(8)   In this section, the expression 'domestic arbitration agreement' has the same meaning as in subsection (3) of section 5 of this Law, save that the said subsection (3) shall have effect as if for the words therein 'is a party at the time the proceedings are commenced' there were substituted the words 'is a party at the time the arbitration agreement is entered into'.
[*Section 20A inserted by The Arbitration (Amendment) (Guernsey) Law, 1986.*]

21.   Interlocutory orders.

(1)   If any party to a reference under an arbitration agreement fails within the time specified in the order or, if no time is so specified, within a reasonable time to comply with an order made by the arbitrator or umpire in the course of the reference, then, on the application of the arbitrator or umpire or of any party to the reference, the Court may make an order extending the powers of the arbitrator or umpire as mentioned in the next succeeding subsection.
(2)   If an order is made by the Court under this section, the arbitrator or umpire shall have power, to the extent and subject to any conditions specified in that order, to continue with the reference in default of appearance or of any other act by one of the parties in like manner as the Court might continue with proceedings in the Court where a party fails to comply with an order of the Court or a requirement of Rules of Court.
(3)   The preceding provisions of this section shall have effect notwithstanding anything in any agreement but shall not derogate from any powers conferred on an arbitrator or umpire, whether by an arbitration agreement or otherwise.

22.   Power to remit award.

(1)   In all cases of reference to arbitration, the Court may from time to time remit the matters referred, or any of them, to the reconsideration of the arbitrator or umpire.
(2)   Where an award is remitted, the arbitrator or umpire shall, unless the order otherwise directs, make his award within three months after the date of the order.

(3)   An application to the Court to remit an award under subsection (1) of this section may be made at any time within six weeks after the award has been made and published to the parties.

23.   Removal of arbitrator and setting aside of award.

(1)   Where an arbitrator or umpire has misconducted himself or the proceedings, the Court may remove him.

(2)   Where an arbitrator or umpire has misconducted himself or the proceedings, or an arbitration or award has been improperly procured, the Court may set the award aside.

(3)   Where an application is made to set aside an award, the Court may order that any money made payable by the award shall be brought into Court or otherwise secured pending the determination of the application.

(4)   Any money ordered to be brought into Court under the last preceding subsection shall be paid to Her Majesty's Greffier.

(5)   An application to the Court to set aside an award under subsection (2) of this section may be made at any time within six weeks after the award has been made and published to the parties.

24.   Power of Court to give relief where arbitrator is not impartial or the dispute involves question of fraud.

(1)   Where an agreement between any parties provides that disputes which may arise in the future between them shall be referred to an arbitrator named or designated in the agreement, and after a dispute has arisen any party applies, on the ground that the arbitrator so named or designated is not or may not be impartial, for leave to revoke the authority of the arbitrator or for an order to restrain any other party or the arbitrator from proceeding with the arbitration, it shall not be a ground for refusing the application that the said party at the time when he made the agreement knew, or ought to have known, that the arbitrator, by reason of his relation towards any other party to the agreement or of his connection with the subject referred, might not be capable of impartiality.

(2)   Where an agreement between any parties provides that disputes which may arise in the future between them shall be referred to arbitration, and a dispute which so arises involves the question whether any such party has been guilty of fraud, the Court shall, so far as may be necessary to enable that question to be determined by the Court, have power to order that the agreement shall cease to have effect and power to give leave to revoke the authority of any arbitrator or umpire appointed by or by virtue of the agreement.

(3)   In any case where, by virtue of this section, the Court has power to order that an arbitration agreement shall cease to have effect or to give leave to revoke the authority of an arbitrator or umpire, the Court may refuse to stay any action brought in breach of the agreement.

25.   Power of Court where arbitrator is removed or authority of arbitrator is revoked.

(1)   Where an arbitrator (not being a sole arbitrator) or two or more arbitrators (not being all the arbitrators) or an umpire who has not entered

on the reference is or are removed by the Court, the Court may, on the application of any party to the arbitration agreement, appoint a person or persons to act as arbitrator or arbitrators or umpire in place of the person or persons so removed.

(2)   Where the authority of an arbitrator or arbitrators or umpire is revoked by leave of the Court, or a sole arbitrator or all the arbitrators or an umpire who has entered on the reference is or are removed by the Court, the Court may, on the application of any party to the arbitration agreement, either—

(a)   appoint a person to act as sole arbitrator in place of the person or persons removed; or

(b)   order that the arbitration agreement shall cease to have effect with respect to the dispute referred.

(3)   A person appointed under this section by the Court as an arbitrator or umpire shall have the like power to act in the reference, and to make an award, as if he had been appointed in accordance with the terms of the arbitration agreement.

(4)   Where it is provided (whether by means of a provision in the arbitration agreement or otherwise) that an award under an arbitration agreement shall be a condition precedent to the bringing of an action with respect to any matter to which the agreement applies, the Court, if it orders (whether under this section or under any other enactment) that the agreement shall cease to have effect as regards any particular dispute, may further order that the provision making an award a condition precedent to the bringing of an action shall also cease to have effect as regards that dispute.

Enforcement of Award

26.   Enforcement of award.

An award on an arbitration agreement may, by leave of the Court, be enforced in the same manner as a judgment or order to the same effect; and, where leave is so given, the Act of Court shall specify the manner of enforcement.

Miscellaneous

27.   Power of Court to extend time for commencing arbitration proceedings.

Where the terms of an agreement to refer disputes to arbitration provide that any claims to which the agreement applies shall be barred unless notice to appoint an arbitrator is given or an arbitrator is appointed or some other step to commence arbitration proceedings is taken, within a time fixed by the agreement, and a dispute arises to which the agreement applies, the Court, if it is of the opinion that, in the circumstances of the case, undue hardship would otherwise be caused, and notwithstanding that the time so fixed has expired, may, on such terms, if any, as the justice of the case may require, but without prejudice to the provisions of any enactment limiting the time for the commencement of arbitration proceedings, extend the time for such period as it thinks proper.

28. Terms as to costs, etc.

Any order made under this Part of this Law may be made on such terms as to costs or otherwise as the authority making the order thinks just.

29. Limitation of action.

(1)   Subject to the provisions of this section the provisions of any enactment relating to the limitation of actions shall apply to arbitrations as they apply to civil actions before the Court.

(2)   No action to enforce an award on an arbitration agreement shall be brought before the Court after the expiration of six years from the date on which the cause of action arose.

(3)   Notwithstanding any term in an arbitration agreement to the effect that no cause of action shall accrue in respect of any matter required by the agreement to be referred until an award is made under the agreement, the cause of action shall, for the purpose of this section and of any such enactment as aforesaid (whether in their application to arbitrations or to other proceedings), be deemed to have accrued in respect of any such matter at the time when it would have accrued but for that term in the agreement.

(4)   For the purpose of this section and of any such enactment as aforesaid, an arbitration shall be deemed to be commenced when one party to the arbitration serves on the other party or parties a notice requiring him or them to appoint an arbitrator or to agree to the appointment of an arbitrator, or, where the arbitration agreement provides that the reference shall be to a person named or designated in the agreement, requiring him or them to submit the dispute to the person so named or designated.

(5)   Where the Court orders that an award be set aside or orders, after the commencement of an arbitration, that the arbitration shall cease to have effect with respect to the dispute referred, the Court may further order that the period between the commencement of the arbitration and the date of the order of the Court shall be excluded in computing the time prescribed by this section or any such enactment as aforesaid for the commencement of proceedings (including arbitration) with respect to the dispute referred.

30. Application of Part I to statutory arbitrations.

(1)   This Part of this Law, except the provisions thereof specified in the next succeeding subsection shall apply to every arbitration under any other enactment (whether passed before or after the coming into force of this Law) as if the arbitration were pursuant to an arbitration agreement and as if that other enactment were an arbitration agreement, except in so far as this Law is inconsistent with that other enactment or with any rules or procedure authorised or recognised thereby:

Provided that in any arbitration under the provisions of any other enactment any reference to the award made by an arbitrator or umpire being final and binding on the parties and the persons claiming under them respectively shall be deemed to include a reference to such provisions being subject to the provisions of section nineteen of this Law.

(2)   The provisions referred to in the last preceding subsection are subsection (1) of section two, section three, section five, subsection (2) of

section sixteen, section twenty-four, section twenty-five and section twenty-seven of this Law.

PART II

ENFORCEMENT OF CERTAIN FOREIGN AWARDS

31. Awards to which Part II applies.

(1) Subject to section thirty-six of this Law, this Part of this Law applies to any award made after the twenty-eighth day of July, nineteen hundred and twenty-four—

(a) in pursuance of an agreement for arbitration to which the Protocol applies; and

(b) between persons of whom one is subject to the jurisdiction of some one of such Powers as Her Majesty may, by Order in Council, have declared to be parties to the Geneva Convention and of whom the other is subject to the jurisdiction of some other of the Powers aforesaid; and

(c) in one of such territories as Her Majesty may, by Order in Council, have declared to be territories to which the Geneva Convention applies;

and an award to which this Part of this Law applies is, in this Part of this Law, referred to as 'a foreign award'.

(2) In this section the expression 'Order in Council' means an Order in Council which is in force and which—

(a) has been made under paragraph (b) of sub-section (1) of section thirty-five of the Arbitration Act 1950; or

(b) has effect, by virtue of subsection (3) of that section, as if it had been so made.

32. Effect of foreign awards.

(1) A foreign award shall, subject to the provisions of this Part of this Law, be enforceable in the Island either by action or in the same manner as the award of an arbitrator is enforceable by virtue of section twenty-six of this Law.

(2) Any foreign award which would be enforceable under this Part of this Law shall be treated as binding for all purposes on the persons as between whom it was made, and may, accordingly, be relied on by any of those persons by way of defence, set off or otherwise in any legal proceedings in the Island, and any references in this Part of this Law to enforcing a foreign award shall be construed as including references to relying on an award.

33. Conditions for enforcement of foreign awards.

(1) In order that a foreign award may be enforceable under this Part of this Law, it must have—

(a) been made in pursuance of an agreement for arbitration which was valid under the law by which it was governed;

(b) been made by the tribunal provided for in the agreement or constituted in the manner agreed upon by the parties;

(c)   been made in conformity with the law governing the arbitration procedure;

(d)   become final in the country in which it was made;

(e)   been in respect of a matter which may lawfully be referred to arbitration under the law of the Island;

and the enforcement thereof must not be contrary to the public policy or the law of the Island.

(2)   Subject to the provisions of this subsection, a foreign award shall not be enforceable under this Part of this Law if the Court is satisfied that—

(a)   the award has been annulled in the country in which it was made; or

(b)   the party against whom it is sought to enforce the award was not given notice of the arbitration proceedings in sufficient time to enable him to present his case, or was under some legal incapacity and was not properly represented; or

(c)   the award does not deal with all the questions referred or contains decisions on matters beyond the scope of the agreement for arbitration;

but, if the award does not deal with all the questions referred, the Court may, if it thinks fit, either postpone the enforcement of the award or order its enforcement subject to the giving of such security by the person seeking to enforce it as the Court may think fit.

(3)   If a party seeking to resist the enforcement of a foreign award proves that there is any ground other than the non-existence of the conditions specified in paragraphs (a), (b) and (c) of subsection (1) of this section, or the existence of the conditions specified in paragraphs (b) and (c) of the last preceding subsection, entitling him to contest the validity of the award, the Court may, if it thinks fit, either refuse to enforce the award or adjourn the hearing until after the expiration of such period as appears to the Court to be reasonably sufficient to enable that party to take the necessary steps to have the award annulled by the competent tribunal.

34.   Evidence.

(1)   The party seeking to enforce a foreign award must produce—

(a)   the original award or a copy thereof duly authenticated in the manner required by the law of the country in which it was made;

(b)   evidence proving that the award has become final; and

(c)   such evidence as may be necessary to prove that the award is a foreign award and that the conditions mentioned in paragraphs (a), (b) and (c) of subsection (1) of the last preceding section are satisfied.

(2)   In any case where any document required to be produced under the last preceding subsection is in a foreign language, it shall be the duty of the party seeking to enforce the award to produce a translation thereof in the English language certified as correct by an official or sworn translator or by a diplomatic or consular agent of the country to which that party belongs, or certified as correct in such other manner as may be sufficient according to the law of the Island.

35.   Meaning of 'final award'.

For the purposes of this Part of this Law, an award shall not be deemed final if any proceedings for the purpose of contesting the validity of the award are pending in the country in which it was made.

PART III

ENFORCEMENT OF CONVENTION AWARDS

36. Replacement of Part II in certain cases.

Sections thirty-seven, thirty-eight and thirty-nine of, and paragraph 3 of the First Schedule to, this Law shall have effect with respect of the enforcement of Convention awards; and, where a Convention award would, but for this section, be also a foreign award within the meaning of Part II of this Law, that Part shall not apply to it.

37. Effect of Convention awards.

(1) A Convention award shall, subject to the following provisions of this Part of this Law, be enforceable in the Island either by action or in the same manner as the award of an arbitrator is enforceable by virtue of section twenty-six of this Law.

(2) Any Convention award which would be enforceable under this Part of this Law shall be treated as binding for all purposes on the persons as between whom it was made, and may, accordingly, be relied on by any of those persons by way of defence, set off or otherwise in any legal proceedings in the Island; and any reference in this Part of this Law to enforcing a Convention award shall be construed as including references to relying on such an award.

38. Evidence.

The party seeking to enforce a Convention award must produce—

(a) the original award or a copy thereof duly authenticated in the manner required by the law of the country in which it was made;

(b) the original arbitration agreement or a copy thereof duly authenticated in the manner required by the law of the country in which it was made; and

(c) where the award or agreement is in a foreign language, a translation thereof in the English language certified as correct by an official or sworn translator or by a diplomatic or consular agent of the country to which that party belongs, or certified correct in such other manner as may be sufficient according to the law of the Island.

39. Refusal of enforcement.

(1) Enforcement of a Convention award shall not be refused except in the cases mentioned in this section.

(2) Enforcement of a Convention award may be refused if the person against whom it is invoked proves—

(a) that a party to the arbitration was under the law applicable to him, under some incapacity; or

(b) that the arbitration agreement was not valid under the law to which the parties subjected it or, failing any indication thereon, under the law of the country where the award was made; or

(c)   that he was not given proper notice of the appointment of the arbitrator or of the arbitration proceedings or was otherwise unable to present his case; or

(d)   subject to subsection (4) of this section, that the award deals with a difference not contemplated by, or not falling within the terms of, the submission to arbitration or contains decisions on matters beyond the scope of the submission to arbitration; or

(e)   that the composition of the arbitral authority or the arbitral procedure was not in accordance with the agreement of the parties or, failing such agreement with the law of the country where the arbitration took place; or

(f)   that the award has not yet become binding on the parties, or has been set aside or suspended by a competent authority of the country in which, or under the law of which, it was made.

(3)   Enforcement of a Convention award may also be refused if the award is in respect of a matter which is not capable of settlement by arbitration, or if it would be contrary to public policy to enforce the award.

(4)   A Convention award which contains decisions on matters not submitted to arbitration may be enforced to the extent that it contains decisions on matters submitted to arbitration which can be separated from those on matters not so submitted.

(5)   Where an application for the setting aside or suspension of a Convention award has been made to such a competent authority as is mentioned in paragraph (f) of subsection (2) of this section, the Court may, if it thinks fit, adjourn the proceedings and may, on the application of the party seeking to enforce the award, order the other party to give security.

PART IV

SUPPLEMENTARY

40.   Rules of Court.

The Royal Court may, from time to time, make rules dealing generally with all matters of procedure and incidental matters arising under this Law and for carrying out this Law into effect.

41.   Service of notices.

A notice which may be served for the purpose of this Law shall be validly served—

(a)   on any person, if delivered to him, left, or sent by registered post or by recorded delivery service to him, at his usual or last known place of abode;

(b)   on any firm, if delivered to any partner of the firm or left at, or sent by registered post or by recorded delivery service to, the principal or last known principal place of business of the firm;

(c)   on any body corporate, if left at, or sent by registered post or by recorded delivery service to, its registered office if situate in the Island or, if its registered office is not so situate, its principal or last known principal place of business in the Island;

and a notice shall, as well, be validly served if served on any person, firm or body corporate in any other manner provided in the arbitration agreement.

42. Interpretation.

(1)   In this Law, except where the context otherwise requires, the following expressions have the meanings hereby respectively assigned to them, that is to say:—

'arbitration agreement' means—

(a) in section five of this Law and in the definition below of 'Convention award', an agreement in writing (including an agreement contained in an exchange of letters or telegrams) to submit to arbitration present or future differences capable of settlement by arbitration; and

(b) elsewhere, a written agreement to submit present or future differences to arbitration, whether an arbitrator is mentioned therein or not;

'Convention award' means an award made in pursuance of an arbitration agreement in the territory of a State, other than the United Kingdom, which is a party to the New York Convention;

'the Court' means the Royal Court sitting as Ordinary Court;

'the Court of Appeal' means the Court of Appeal constituted under the Law of 1961;

'The Geneva Convention' means the Convention on the Execution of Foreign Arbitral Awards signed at Geneva on behalf of His late Majesty, King George V, on the 26th September, 1927;

'Her Majesty's Greffier' includes any Deputy Greffier;

'Her Majesty's Procureur' includes Her Majesty's Comptroller;

'the Island' means the Island of Guernsey and includes the Islands of Herm and Jethou;

'the Law of 1961' means the Court of Appeal (Guernsey) Law, 1961;

'the New York Convention' means the Convention on the Recognition and Enforcement of Foreign Arbitral Awards adopted by the United Nations Conference on International Commercial Arbitration on the 10th June, 1958;

'the Protocol' means the Protocol on Arbitration Clauses signed on behalf of His late Majesty, King George V, at a Meeting of the Assembly of the League of Nations held on the 24th September, 1923.

(2)   If Her Majesty by Order in Council declares that any State specified in the Order is a party to the New York Convention, the Order shall, while in force, be conclusive evidence that that State is a party to that Convention.

(3)   Any reference in this Law to any other enactment shall, except where the context otherwise requires, be construed as including a reference to that enactment as amended, repealed or replaced, extended or applied by or under any other enactment including this Law.

43. Transitional provisions and savings.

The transitional provisions and savings in the First Schedule to this Law shall have effect.

44. Repeals.

The Laws set out in the Second Schedule to this Law are hereby repealed.

45. Citation.

This Law may be cited as the Arbitration (Guernsey) Law, 1982.

46. Commencement.

This Law shall come into force on such day as the States may by Ordinance appoint, and different days may be so appointed for different provisions of this Law, or for different purposes.

['The Arbitration (Guernsey) Law, 1982, shall come into force on the eleventh day of April, nineteen hundred and eighty-three', *The Arbitration (Guernsey) Law, 1982 (Commencement) Ordinance, 1983.*]

FIRST SCHEDULE

Sections thirty-six and forty-three

TRANSITIONAL PROVISIONS AND SAVINGS

1. Any proceedings under the Law entitled 'Loi donnant effet à une Convention sur l'Exécution des Jugements Arbitraux et portant amendement à la Loi donnant effet à un Protocole sur l'Arbitrage du 20 juillet 1925' registered on the twentieth day of December, nineteen hundred and thirty (hereinafter referred to as 'the Law of 1930') which are uncompleted on the coming into force of this Law may be carried on and completed under Part II of this Law as if they had been instituted thereunder.

2. Nothing in Part II of this Law shall prejudice any rights which any person would have had of enforcing in the Island any award, or of availing himself in the Island of any award, if neither that Part nor the Law of 1930 had been enacted.

3. Nothing in Part III of this Law shall prejudice any right to enforce or rely on an award otherwise than under that Part or under Part II of this Law.

SECOND SCHEDULE

Section forty-four

LAWS REPEALED

The Law entitled 'Loi donnant effet à un Protocole sur l'Arbitrage' registered on the twentieth day of July, nineteen hundred and twenty-five.

The Law entitled 'Loi donnant effet à une Convention sur l'Exécution des Jugements Arbitraux et portant amendement à la Loi donnant effet à un Protocole sur l'Arbitrage du 20 juillet 1925' registered on the twentieth day of December, nineteen hundred and thirty.

K. H. TOUGH,
Her Majesty's Greffier.

THE INDUSTRIAL DISPUTES AND CONDITIONS OF EMPLOYMENT (AMENDMENT) (GUERNSEY) LAW 1986

THE STATES, in pursuance of their Resolution of the 28th day of November, 1985, have approved the following provisions which, subject to the Sanction of Her

Most Excellent Majesty in Council, shall have force of law in the Islands of Guernsey and Herm.

1.   Amendment to Law of 1947.

Immediately after Article 21 of the Industrial Disputes and Conditions of Employment Law, (1947), as amended, there is hereby inserted the following addition Article numbered '21A'—

'21A.   Exclusion of Arbitration Law of 1982 to voluntary arbitrations.

The provisions of Part I of the of Arbitration (Guernsey) Law, 1982, shall not apply to arbitration voluntarily submitted to by the parties to an industrial dispute under Article 3(c)(i) of this Law.'

2.   Citation.

This Law may be cited as the Industrial Disputes and Conditions of Employment (Amendment) (Guernsey) Law, 1986.

3.   Collective title.

This Law and the Industrial Disputes and Conditions of Employment Laws, 1947 to 1971, may be cited together as the Industrial Disputes and Conditions of Employment Laws, 1947 to 1986.

K. H. TOUGH,
Her Majesty's Greffier.

THE ROYAL COURT (ARBITRATION) (GUERNSEY) RULES 1983

THE ROYAL COURT, in exercise of the powers conferred upon it by section forty of the Arbitration (Guernsey) Law, 1982, and of all other powers enabling it in that behalf, hereby makes the following Rules:—

1.   Applications under the Law.

(1)   Subject to the provisions of paragraphs (3) and (4) of these Rules, every application to the Court under the Law shall be made by filing a notice of application with Her Majesty's Greffier and serving a copy of the notice within the seven days next following the filing thereof on every party affected by the application.

(2)   When a date has been fixed for the hearing by the Court of an application to which the last preceding paragraph applies, Her Majesty's Greffier shall inform the applicant of the date so fixed and notice thereof shall, as soon as may be, be served by the applicant on every other party affected by the application and shall in any case be so served not less than four clear days before the date so fixed.

(3)   Every application to the Court under section nineteen, section twenty, section twenty-one, subsection (1) of section twenty-two, subsections

(1) and (2) of section twenty-three and twenty-six (including applications under the said section twenty-six as extended by sections thirty-two and thirty-seven) of the Law shall be made by way of summons which shall be served on every party affected by the application.

(4) An application to the Court under subsection (4) of section eleven of the Law may be made ex parte.

(5) Every application to the Court shall state in general terms the grounds of the application.

2. Interpretation.

(1) In these Rules the expression 'the Law' means the Arbitration (Guernsey) Law, 1982, and any other expressions have the same meanings as in the Law.

(2) The Interpretation (Guernsey) Law, 1948, shall apply to the interpretation of these Rules as it applies to the interpretation of an enactment.

(3) Any reference in these Rules to any other enactment shall, except where the context otherwise requires, be construed as including a reference to that enactment as amended, repealed or replaced, extended or applied by or under any other enactment including these Rules.

3. Citation.

These Rules may be cited as the Royal Court (Arbitration) (Guernsey) Rules, 1983.

4. Commencement.

These Rules shall come into force on the eleventh day of April, nineteen hundred and eighty-three.

A. G. LE CHEMINANT,
Deputy Greffier.

I.3 IRELAND

ARBITRATION ACT 1954
(1954, C. 26)

An Act to make further and better provision in respect of arbitrations.

[9th December 1954]

BE IT ENACTED BY THE OIREACHTAS AS FOLLOWS:—

PART I

PRELIMINARY AND GENERAL.

1.—(1) This Act may be cited as the Arbitration Act, 1954.

(2) This Act (except subsection (2) of section 12 and Part V) shall come into operation on the 1st day of January, 1955.

(3)   Subsection (2) of section 12 and Part V of this Act shall come into operation on such day as may be fixed for that purpose by order of the Government.

2.—(1)   In this Act—
'arbitration agreement' means a written agreement to refer present or future differences to arbitration, whether an arbitrator is named therein or not:
'the Convention of 1927' means the Convention on the Execution of Foreign Arbitral Awards done at Geneva on the 26th day of September, 1927, set out in the Second Schedule to this Act;
'the Court' means the High Court;
'the operative date' means the 1st day of January, 1955;
'the Protocol of 1923' means the Protocol on Arbitration Clauses opened at Geneva on the 24th day of September, 1923, set out in the First Schedule to this Act:
'State authority' means any authority being—
(a)   a Minister of State.
(b)   the Commissioners of Public Works in Ireland.
(c)   the Irish Land Commission, or
(d)   the Revenue Commissioners;
'the statutes of limitation' includes any enactment limiting the time within which any particular proceedings may be commenced.
(2)   References in this Act to an award include reference to an interim award.

3.   Commencement of arbitration.

(1)   For the purposes of this Act and for the purpose of the statutes of limitation as applying to arbitrations and of section 496 of the Merchant Shipping Act 1894, as amended by section 46 of this Act, an arbitration shall be deemed to be commenced when one party to the arbitration agreement serves on the other party or parties a written notice requiring him or them to appoint or concur in appointing an arbitrator or, where the arbitration agreement provides that the reference shall be to a person named or designated in the agreement, requiring him or them to submit the dispute to the person so named or designated.
(2)   (a)   A notice under subsection (1) of this section may be served—
(i)   by delivering it to the person to whom it is to be served,
(ii)   by leaving it at the place in the State at which that person ordinarily resides or carries on business.
(iii)   by sending it by registered post in an envelope addressed to that person at the place in the State at which he ordinarily resides or carries on business.
(iv)   in any other manner provided in the arbitration agreement.
(b)   For the purposes of this subsection, a company registered under the Companies Acts, 1908 to 1924, shall be deemed to carry on business at its registered office in the State and every other body corporate and every unincorporated body shall be deemed to carry on business at its principal office or place of business in the State.

4. State authorities to be bound.

This Part, Part II (except subsection (2) of section 12) and Part III of this Act shall apply to an arbitration under an arbitration agreement to which a State authority is a party.

5. Exclusion of certain arbitrations.

Notwithstanding anything contained in this Act, this Act does not apply to—

(a)   an arbitration under an agreement providing for the reference to, or the settlement by, arbitration of any question relating to the terms or conditions of employment or the remuneration of any employees, including persons employed by or under the State or local authorities, or

(b)   an arbitration under section 70 of the Industrial Relations Act, 1946 (No. 26 of 1946).

6. Operation of Parts II and III.

(1)   Part II of this Act shall not affect any arbitration under an arbitration agreement which has commenced before the operative date, but shall apply to any arbitration commenced on or after the operative date under an arbitration agreement made before the operative date.

(2)   Part III of this Act shall not affect any arbitration under any other Act which has commenced before the operative date, but shall apply to any arbitration commenced on or after the operative date under any other Act passed before, on, or after the operative date.

7. Penalty for giving false evidence.

Any person who, upon any examination upon oath or affirmation before an arbitrator or umpire or in any affidavit in proceedings before an arbitrator or umpire, wilfully and corruptly gives false evidence or wilfully and corruptly swears or affirms anything which is false, being convicted thereof, shall be liable to the penalties for wilful and corrupt perjury.

8. Repeals.

(1)   The enactments mentioned in column (2) of the Third Schedule to this Act are (except in relation to arbitrations under arbitration agreements commenced before the operative date) hereby repealed to the extent mentioned in column (3) of that Schedule.

(2)   Any enactment or instrument referring to any enactment repealed by this Act shall be construed as referring to this Act.

PART II

ARBITRATION UNDER ARBITRATION AGREEMENTS

9. Authority of arbitrators and umpires to be irrevocable.

The authority of the arbitrator or umpire appointed by or by virtue of an arbitration agreement shall, unless a contrary intention is expressed in the agreement, be irrevocable except by leave of the Court.

10. Death of party.

(1) An arbitration agreement shall not be discharged by the death of any party thereto, either as respects the deceased or any other party, but shall in such an event be enforceable by or against the personal representatives of the deceased.

(2) The authority of an arbitrator shall not be revoked by the death of any party by whom he was appointed.

(3) Nothing in this section shall be taken to affect the operation of any enactment or rule of law by virtue of which any right of action is extinguished by the death of a person.

11. Provisions in case of bankruptcy.

(1) In this section the word 'assignee' means the Official Assignee in Bankruptcy and includes the assignee (if any) chosen by the creditors to act with the Official Assignee in Bankruptcy.

(2) Where an arbitration agreement forms part of a contract to which a bankrupt is a party, the agreement shall, if the assignee or trustee in bankruptcy does not disclaim the contract, be enforceable by or against him so far as it relates to any difference arising out of, or in connection with, such contract.

(3) Where—

(a) a person who has been adjudged bankrupt had, before the commencement of the bankruptcy, become a party to an arbitration agreement, and

(b) any matter to which the agreement applies requires to be determined in connection with or for the purposes of the bankruptcy proceedings, and

(c) the case is one to which subsection (2) of this section does not apply, then, any other party to the agreement or the asignee or, with the consent of the committee of inspection, the trustee in bankruptcy may apply to the court having jurisdiction in the bankruptcy proceedings for an order directing that the matter in question shall be referred to arbitration in accordance with the agreement and that court may, if it is of opinion that having regard to all the circumstances of the case, the matter ought to be determined by arbitration, make an order accordingly.

12. . . . [*This section has been repealed by Section 4 of the Arbitration Act 1980. It has been replaced by Section 5 the 1980 Act, q.v.*]

13.—Where relief by way of interpleader is granted and it appears to the Court that the claims in question are matters to which an arbitration agreement, to which the claimants are parties, applies, the Court may direct the issue between the claimants to be determined in accordance with the agreement.

Arbitrators and Umpires

14.—Unless a contrary intention is expressed therein, every arbitration agreement shall, if no other mode of reference is provided, be deemed to include a provision that the reference shall be to a single arbitrator.

15. Power of parties in certain cases to supply vacancy.

(1) Where—

  (a)   an arbitration agreement provides that the reference shall be to two arbitrators, one to be appointed by each party, and

  (b)   either of the appointed arbitrators refuses to act, or is incapable of acting, or dies,

then, unless the agreement expresses a contrary intention, the party, who appointed the arbitrator so refusing to act, becoming incapable of acting or dying, may appoint a new arbitrator in his place.

(2) (a) Where—

  (i)   an arbitration agreement provides that the reference shall be to two arbitrators, one to be appointed by each party, and

  (ii)   on such a reference one party fails to appoint an arbitrator, either originally or by way of substitution under subsection (1) of this section, for seven clear days after the other party, having appointed his arbitrator, has served the party making default with notice to make the appointment,

then unless a contrary intention is expressed in the agreement, the party who has appointed an arbitrator may appoint that arbitrator to act as sole arbitrator in the reference, and his award shall be binding on both parties as if he has been appointed by consent.

  (b)   The Court may set aside any appointment made under paragraph (a) of this subsection.

16. Umpires.

(1) Unless a contrary intention is expressed therein, every arbitration agreement shall, where the reference is to two arbitrators, be deemed to include a provision that the two arbitrators shall appoint an umpire immediately after they are themselves appointed.

(2) Unless a contrary intention is expressed therein, every arbitration agreement shall, where such a provision is applicable to the reference, be deemed to include a provision that if the arbitrators have delivered to any party to the arbitration agreement, or to the umpire, a notice in writing stating that they cannot agree, the umpire may forthwith enter upon the reference in lieu of the arbitrators, but nothing in this subsection shall be construed as preventing the umpire from sitting with the arbitrators and hearing the evidence.

(3) At any time after the appointment of an umpire, however appointed, the Court may, on the application of any party to the reference and notwithstanding anything to the contrary in the arbitration agreement, order that the umpire shall enter upon the reference in lieu of the arbitrators and as if he were a sole arbitrator.

17. Agreements for reference to three arbitrators.

(1) Where an arbitration agreement provides that the reference shall be to three arbitrators, one to be appointed by each party and the third to be appointed by the two appointed by the parties, the agreement shall have effect as if it provided for the appointment of an umpire, and not for the

appointment of a third arbitrator, by the two arbitrators appointed by the parties.

(2)   Where an arbitration agreement provides that the reference shall be to three arbitrators to be appointed otherwise than as is mentioned in subsection (1) of this section, the award of any two of the arbitrators shall be binding.

18.   Power of Court in certain cases to appoint an arbitrator or umpire.

In any of the following cases—
    (a)   where—
        (i)   an arbitration agreement provides that the reference shall be to a single arbitrator, and
        (ii)   all the parties do not, after differences have arisen, concur in the appointment of an arbitrator;
    (b)   if—
        (i)   an appointed arbitrator refuses to act, or is incapable of acting or dies, and
        (ii)   the arbitration agreement does not show that it was intended that the vacancy should not be supplied, and
        (iii)   the parties do not supply the vacancy;
    (c)   where the parties or two arbitrators are at liberty to appoint an umpire or third arbitrator and do not appoint him;
    (d)   where two arbitrators are required to appoint an umpire and do not appoint him;
    (e)   where—
        (i)   an appointed umpire or third arbitrator refuses to act, or is incapable of acting, or dies, and
        (ii)   the arbitration agreement does not show that it was intended that the vacancy should not be supplied, and
        (iii)   the parties or arbitrators do not supply the vacancy,
the following provisions shall have effect—
(1)   any party may serve the other parties or the arbitrators, as the case may be, with a written notice to appoint or, as the case may be, concur in appointing an arbitrator, umpire or third arbitrator,
(2)   if the appointment is not made within seven clear days after the service of the notice, the Court may, on the application of the party who gave the notice, appoint an arbitrator, umpire or third arbitrator, who shall have the like powers to act in the reference and make an award as if he had been appointed by consent of all parties.

Witnesses, Security for Costs, Discovery of Documents, etc.

19.   Powers of arbitrators and umpires as to witnesses.

(1)   Unless a contrary intention is expressed therein every arbitration agreement shall, where such a provision is applicable to the reference, be deemed to contain a provision that the parties to the reference, and all persons claiming through them respectively, shall, subject to any legal

objection, submit to be examined by the arbitrator or umpire, on oath or affirmation, in relation to the matters in dispute and shall subject to any legal objection, produce before the arbitrator or umpire all documents (other than documents the production of which could not be compelled on the trial of an action) within their possession or power respectively which may be required or called for, and do all such other things which during the proceedings on the reference the arbitrator or umpire may require.

(2)   Unless a contrary intention is expressed therein, every arbitration agreement shall, where such a provision is applicable to the reference, be deemed to contain a provision that the witnesses on the reference shall, if the arbitrator or umpire thinks fit, be examined on oath or affirmation.

(3)   An arbitrator or umpire shall, unless a contrary intention is expressed in an arbitration agreement, have power to administer oaths to, or take the affirmations of, the parties and and witnesses on a reference under the agreement.

20.   Powers of parties to a reference to compel attendance of witnesses.

Any party to a reference under an arbitration agreement may sue out an order in the nature of a writ of subpoena ad testificandum or of a writ of subpoena duces tecum, but no person shall be compelled under any such order to produce any document which he could not be compelled to produce on the trial of an action.

21.   Power of Court to compel attendance of prisoner as a witness.

The Court may order that an order in the nature of a writ of habeas corpus ad testificandum shall issue to bring up a prisoner for examination before an arbitrator or umpire.

22.   Orders by Court in relation to security for costs, discovery of documents etc.

(1)   The Court shall have, for the purpose of and in relation to a reference, the same power of making orders in respect of—
   (a)   security for costs;
   (b)   discovery and inspection of documents and interrogatories;
   (c)   the giving of evidence by affidavit;
   (d)   examination on oath of any witness before an officer of the Court or any other person, and the issue of a commission or request for the examination of a witness out of the jurisdiction;
   (e)   the preservation, interim custody or sale of any goods which are the subject matter of the reference;
   (f)   securing the amount in dispute in the reference;
   (g)   the detention, preservation or inspection of any property or thing which is the subject of the reference or as to which any question may arise therein, and authorising for any of the purposes aforesaid any persons to enter upon or into any land or building in the possession of any party to the reference, or authorising any samples to be taken or any observation to be

made or experiment to be tried which may be necessary or expedient for the
purpose of obtaining full information or evidence; and

    (h)   interim injunctions or the appointment of a receiver,

as it has for the purpose of and in relation to an action or matter in the Court.

    (2)   Nothing in subsection (1) of this section shall be taken to prejudice
any power which may be vested in an arbitrator or umpire of making orders
with respect to any of the matters mentioned in the said subsection.

Provisions as to Awards

23.   Time for making an award.

    (1)   Subject to subsection (2) of section 36 of this Act and anything to the
contrary in the arbitration agreement, an arbitrator or umpire shall have
power to make an award at any time.

    (2)   The time, if any, limited for making an award, whether under this Act
or otherwise, may from time to time be enlarged by order of the Court or by
agreement in writing of the parties, whether that time has expired or not.

24.   Removal of arbitrator or umpire on failure to use due dispatch.

    (1)   The Court may, on the application of any party to a reference, remove
an arbitrator or umpire who fails to use all reasonable dispatch in entering on
and proceeding with the reference and making an award.

    (2)   An arbitrator or umpire who is removed by the Court under subsec-
tion (1) of this section shall not be entitled to receive any remuneration in
respect of his services.

    (3)   For the purposes of this section the expression 'proceeding with a
reference' includes, in a case where two arbitrators are unable to agree, giving
notice of that fact to the parties and to the umpire.

25.   Interim awards.

Unless a contrary intention is expressed therein, every arbitration agreement
shall, where such a provision is applicable to the reference, be deemed to
contain a provision that the arbitrator or umpire may, if he thinks fit, make
an interim award.

26.   Specific performance.

Unless a contrary intention is expressed therein, every arbitration agreement
shall, where such a provision is applicable to the reference, be deemed to
contain a provision that the arbitrator or umpire shall have the same power
as the Court to order specific performance of any contract other than a
contract relating to land or any interest in land.

27.   Awards to be final.

Unless a contrary intention is expressed therein, every arbitration agreement
shall, where such a provision is applicable to the reference, be deemed to

contain a provision that the award to be made by the arbitrator or umpire shall be final and binding on the parties and the persons claiming under them respectively.

28. Power to correct slips.

Unless a contrary intention is expressed in the arbitration agreement, the arbitrator or umpire shall have power to correct in an award any clerical mistake or error arising from any accidental slip or omission.

Costs, Fees and Interest

29. Costs of reference and award to be in the discretion of the arbitrator or umpire.

(1) Unless a contrary intention is expressed therein, every arbitration agreement shall be deemed to include a provision that the costs of the reference and award shall be in the discretion of the arbitrator or umpire who may direct to and by whom and in what manner those costs or any part thereof shall be paid, and may, with the consent of the parties, tax or settle the amount of costs to be so paid or any part thereof, and may award costs to be paid as between solicitor and client.

(2) Where an award directs any costs to be paid, then, unless the arbitrator or umpire, with the consent of the parties, taxes or settles the amount thereof—

(a) the costs shall be taxed and ascertained by a Taxing Master,

(b) the procedure to obtain taxation and the rules, regulations and scales of costs of the Court relative to taxation and to the review thereof shall apply to the costs to be so taxed and ascertained as if the award were a judgment or order of the court.

30. Avoidance of certain provisions as to costs in arbitration agreements.

(1) Any provision in an arbitration agreement to the effect that the parties or any party thereto shall in any event pay their or his own costs of the reference or award or any part thereof shall be void, and this Part shall, in the case of an arbitration agreement containing any such provision, have effect as if that provision were not contained therein.

(2) Nothing in subsection (1) of this section shall invalidate any such provision as is mentioned in that subsection when it is part of an agreement to submit to arbitration a dispute which has arisen before the making of that agreement.

31. Application to arbitrator or umpire to give directions as to costs where award contains no provision.

If no provision is made by an award with respect to the costs of the reference, any party to the reference may, within fourteen days of the publication of the award or such further time as the Court may direct, apply to the arbitrator or umpire for an order directing by and to whom those costs shall be paid, and thereupon the arbitrator or umpire shall, after hearing any party who may desire to be heard, amend his award by adding thereto such directions as he may think proper with respect to the payment of the costs of the reference.

32.   Application of section 3 of Legal Practitioners (Ireland) Act, 1876, to solicitors' costs in arbitrations.

Section 3 of the Legal Practitioners (Ireland) Act, 1876, (which empowers a court before which any proceeding has been heard or is pending to charge property recovered or preserved in the proceeding with the payment of solicitors' costs) shall apply as if an arbitration were a proceeding in the Court, and the Court may make declarations and orders accordingly.

33.   Taxation of arbitrator's or umpire's fee.

(1)   If in any case an arbitrator or umpire refuses to deliver his award except on payment of the fees demanded by him, the Court may, on an application for the purpose, order that the arbitrator or umpire shall deliver the award to the applicant on payment into Court by the applicant of the fees demanded, and further that the fees demanded shall be taxed by a Taxing Master and that out of the money paid into Court there shall be paid out to the arbitrator or umpire by way of fees such sum as may be found reasonable on taxation and that the balance of the money, if any, shall be paid out to the applicant.

(2)   An application for the purpose of this section may be made by any party to the reference unless the fees demanded have been fixed by a written agreement between him and the arbitrator or umpire.

(3)   A taxation of fees under this section may be reviewed in the same manner as a taxation of costs.

(4)   The arbitrator or umpire shall be entitled to appear and be heard on any taxation or review of taxation under this section.

34.   Interest on awards.

A sum directed to be paid by an award shall, unless the award otherwise directs, carry interest as from the date of the award and at the same rate as a judgment debt.

Special Cases, Remission and Setting aside of Awards, Removal of Arbitrator or Umpire, and Relief where Arbitrator not impartial or Questions of Fraud involved

35.   Statement of case by arbitrator or umpire.

(1)   An arbitrator or umpire may, and shall if so directed by the Court, state—
    (a)   any question of law arising in the course of the reference, or
    (b)   any award or any part of an award,
in the form of a special case for the decision of the Court.

(2)   A special case with respect to an interim award or with respect to a question of law arising in the course of a reference may be stated, or may be ordered by the Court to be stated, notwithstanding that proceedings under the reference are still pending.

36.   Power of Court to remit award.

(1)   In all cases of reference to arbitration, the Court may from time to time remit the matters referred or any of them to the reconsideration of the arbitrator or umpire.

(2)   Where an award is remitted, the arbitrator or umpire shall, unless the order otherwise directs, make his award within three months after the date of the order.

37.   Power of Court to remove arbitrator or umpire on ground of misconduct.

Where an arbitrator or umpire has misconducted himself or the proceedings, the Court may remove him.

38.   Power of Court to set aside award on ground of misconduct.

(1)   Where—

(a)   an arbitrator or umpire has misconducted himself or the proceedings, or

(b)   an arbitration or award has been improperly procured,

the Court may set the award aside.

(2)   Where an application is made to set aside an award, the Court may order that any money made payable by the award shall be brought into Court or otherwise secured pending the determination of the application.

39.   Power of Court to give relief where arbitrator is not impartial or dispute referred involves question of fraud.

(1)   Where—

(a)   an agreement between any parties provides that disputes which may arise in the future between them shall be referred to an arbitrator named or designated in the agreement, and

(b)   after a dispute has arisen any party, on the ground that the arbitrator so named or designated is not or may not be impartial, applies to the Court for leave to revoke the authority of the arbitrator or for an injunction to restrain any other party or the arbitrator from proceeding with the arbitration,

it shall not be a ground for refusing the application that the said party at the time when he made the agreement knew, or ought to have known, that the arbitrator, by reason of his relation towards any other party to the agreement or of his connection with the subject referred, might not be impartial.

(2)   Where—

(a)   an agreement between any parties provides that disputes which may arise in the future between them shall be referred to arbitration, and

(b)   a dispute which so arises involves the question whether any party has been guilty of fraud,

the Court shall, so far as may be necessary to enable the question to be determined by the Court, have power to order that the agreement shall cease to have effect and power to give leave to revoke the authority of any arbitrator or umpire appointed by or by virtue of the agreement.

(3)   In any case where by virtue of this section the Court has power to order that any arbitration agreement shall cease to have effect or to give leave to revoke the authority of any arbitrator or umpire, the Court may refuse to stay any action brought in breach of the agreement.

40.   Power of Court where arbitrator is removed or authority of arbitrator is revoked.

(1)   Where an arbitrator (not being a sole arbitrator) or two or more arbitrators (not being all the arbitrators) or an umpire who has not entered on the reference is or are removed by the Court, the Court may, on the application of any party to the arbitration agreement, appoint a person or persons to act as arbitrator or arbitrators or umpire in place of the person or persons so removed.

(2)   Where—

(a)   the authority of the arbitrator or arbitrators or umpire is revoked by leave of the Court, or

(b)   a sole arbitrator or all the arbitrators or an umpire who has entered on the reference is or are removed by the Court,

the Court may, on the application of any party to the arbitration agreement, either—

(i)   appoint a person to act as sole arbitrator in place of the person or persons removed, or

(ii)   order that the arbitration agreement shall cease to have effect with respect to the dispute referred.

(3)   A person appointed under this section by the Court as an arbitrator or umpire shall have the like power to act in the reference and to make an award as if he had been appointed in accordance with the terms of the arbitration agreement.

(4)   Where it is provided (whether by means of a provision in an arbitration agreement or otherwise) that an award under an arbitration agreement shall be a condition precedent to the bringing of an action with respect to any matter to which the agreement applies, the Court, if it orders (whether under this section or any other enactment) that the agreement shall cease to have effect as regards any particular dispute, may order that the provision making an award a condition precedent to the bringing of an action shall also cease to have effect as regards that dispute.

Enforcement of Award

41.   Enforcement of award.

An award on an arbitration agreement may, by leave of the Court, be enforced in the same manner as a judgment or order to the same effect and, where leave is so given judgment may be entered in terms of the award.

Limitation of Time for Commencing Arbitration Proceedings

42.   Application of statutes of limitation to arbitration under arbitration agreements.

The statutes of limitation shall apply to an arbitration under an arbitration agreement as they apply to actions in the Court.

43.   Accrual for purposes of statutes of limitation of right of action in respect of matters required by arbitration agreement to be referred to arbitration, where agreement provides that arbitration shall be a condition precedent to commencement of action.

Notwithstanding any term in an arbitration agreement to the effect that no cause of action shall accrue in respect of any matter required by the agreement to be referred until an award is made under the agreement, a cause of action shall, for the purposes of the statutes of limitation (whether in their application to arbitrations or to other proceedings), be deemed to have accrued in respect of any such matter at the time when it would have accrued but for that term in the agreement.

44.   Power of Court to extend period of limitation where it sets aside award or orders arbitration to cease to have effect.

Where the Court orders that an award be set aside or orders, after the commencement of an arbitration, that the arbitration should cease to have effect with respect to the dispute referred, the Court may further order that the period between the commencement of the arbitration and the date of the order of the Court shall be excluded in computing the time prescribed by the statutes of limitation for the commencement of the proceedings (including arbitration) with respect to the dispute referred.

45.   Power of Court to extend time for commencing arbitration proceedings, where agreement provides that claims are to be barred unless proceedings are commenced within a specified time.

Where—
    (a)   the terms of an agreement to refer future disputes to arbitration provide that any claims to which the agreement applies shall be barred unless notice to appoint an arbitrator is given or an arbitrator is appointed or some other step to commence arbitration proceedings is taken within a time fixed by the agreement, and
    (b)   a dispute arises to which the agreement applies,
the Court, if it is of opinion that in the circumstances of the case undue hardship would otherwise be caused, and notwithstanding that the time so fixed has expired, may on such terms, if any, as the justice of the case may require, but without prejudice to section 42 of this Act, extend the time for such period as it thinks proper.

46.   Extension of section 496 of the Merchant Shipping Act, 1894.

In subsection (3) of section 496 of the Merchant Shipping Act, 1894 (which requires a sum deposited with a wharfinger by an owner of goods to be repaid unless legal proceedings are instituted by the shipowner) the references to legal proceedings shall be construed as including references to arbitration.

Terms of Orders

47.   Terms of orders.

(1)   Any order made under this Part by a court may be made on such terms as to costs or otherwise as that court thinks just.

(2)   Subsection (1) of this section shall not apply to an order made under subsection (2) of section 12 of this Act.

PART III

ARBITRATION UNDER OTHER ACTS

48.   Application of Parts I and II to arbitrations under other Acts.

(1)   In this section, the expression 'the excluded provisions' means the following provisions of this Act, subsection (1) of section 10, section 11, subsection (2) of section 12, and sections 13, 30, 39, 40, 45 and 46.

(2)   Parts I and II of this Act (except the excluded provisions) shall apply to every arbitration under any other Act as if the arbitration were pursuant to an arbitration agreement and as if that other Act were an arbitration agreement, except in so far as Part II of this Act is inconsistent with that other Act or with any rules or procedure authorised or recognised thereby.

PART IV

REFERENCES UNDER ORDER OF THE COURT

49.   Power of Court and Circuit Court to refer in certain cases.

(1)   If, in any cause or matter (including any cause or matter to which a State authority is a party, but excluding a criminal proceeding at the suit of the Attorney General), the question in dispute consists wholly or in part of matter of account, the Court or the Circuit Court may at any time order the whole cause or matter or any question or issue of fact arising therein to be tried before an arbitrator agreed on by the parties or before an officer of the Court or the Circuit Court (as the case may be), upon such terms as to costs or otherwise as the Court of Circuit Court (as the case may be) thinks just.

(2)   The references in sections 50 and 52 of this Act and the first and second references in section 51 of this Act to the Court shall be construed as including references to the Circuit Court.

50. Powers of arbitrators in references under section 49.

(1)   In all cases of references to an arbitrator under an order of the Court under section 49 of this Act, the arbitrator shall be deemed to be an officer of the Court, and, subject to rules of court, shall have such authority and conduct the reference in such manner as the Court may direct.

(2)   The award of an arbitrator on any reference under section 49 of this Act shall, unless set aside by the Court, be equivalent to the verdict of a jury.

(3)   The remuneration to be paid to an arbitrator to whom any matter is referred under section 49 of this Act shall be determined by the Court.

51. Court to have Powers as in references under arbitration agreements.

The Court shall, in relation to references under an order of the Court made under section 49 of this Act, have all the powers which are by Part II of this Act conferred on the Court in relation to references under arbitration agreements.

52. Statement of case pending arbitration.

An arbitrator on any reference under section 49 of this Act may at any stage of the proceedings under the reference, and shall, if so directed by the Court, state in the form of a special case for the opinion of the Court any question of law arising in the course of the reference.

53. Powers of Supreme Court.

The Supreme Court shall have all such powers as are conferred by this Part on the Court.

PART V

ENFORCEMENT OF CERTAIN FOREIGN AWARDS

54. 'Foreign award'.

(1)   (a)   The Government, if satisfied that any State which has ratified the Convention of 1927 has made such reciprocal provisions as will enable the Convention of 1927 to be operative in any territory to which the Convention of 1927 is applicable, may by order declare—

(i)   that State to be a party to the Convention of 1927,

(ii)   that territory to be a territory to which the Convention of 1927 applies.

(b)   The Government may by order vary or revoke any order made under this subsection.

(2)   In this Part, 'foreign award' means any award made after the commencement of this Part—

(a)   in pursuance of an agreement for arbitration to which the Protocol of 1923 applies, and

(b)   between persons—
(i)   of whom one is subject to the jurisdiction of a State which is declared by an order under subsection (1) of this section to be a party to the Convention of 1927, and
(ii)   of whom the other is subject to the jurisdiction of another such State, and
(c)   in a territory which is declared by an order under subsection (1) of this section to be a territory to which the Convention of 1927 applies.

55.   Effect of foreign awards.

(1)   A foreign award shall, subject to the provisions of this Part, be enforceable in the State either by action or in the same manner as an award of an arbitrator is enforceable by virtue of section 41 of this Act.

(2)   Any foreign award which would be enforceable under this Part shall be treated as binding for all purposes on the persons as between whom it was made, and may accordingly be relied on by any of those persons by way of defence, set-off or otherwise in any legal proceedings in the State, and any references in this Part to enforcing a foreign award shall be construed as including references to relying on an award.

56.   Conditions for enforcement of foreign awards.

(1)   In order that a foreign award may be enforceable under this Part it must have—
(a)   been made in pursuance of an agreement for arbitration which was valid under the law by which it was governed,
(b)   been made by the tribunal provided for in the agreement or constituted in manner agreed upon by the parties,
(c)   been made in conformity with the law governing the arbitration procedure,
(d)   become final in the country in which it was made.
(e)   been in respect of a matter which may lawfully be referred to arbitration under the law of the State,
and the enforcement thereof must not be contrary to the public policy or the law of the State.

(2)   Subject to subsection (3) of this section, a foreign award shall not be enforceable under this Part if the Court is satisfied that—
(a)   the award has been annulled in the country in which it was made, or
(b)   the party against whom it is sought to enforce the award was not given notice of the arbitration proceedings in sufficient time to enable him to present his case or was under some legal incapacity and was not properly represented, or
(c)   the award does not deal with all the questions referred or contains decisions beyond the scope of the agreement for arbitration.

(3)   Where a foreign award does not deal with all the questions referred, the Court may, if it thinks fit, either postpone the enforcement of the award or order its enforcement subject to the giving of such security by the person seeking to enforce it as the Court may think fit.

(4)   If the party seeking to resist the enforcement of a foreign award proves that there is any ground, other than the non-existence of the conditions specified in paragraphs (a) (b) and (c) of subsection (1) of this section or the existence of the conditions specified in paragraphs (b) and (c) of subsection (2) of this section, entitling him to contest the validity of the award, the Court may, if it thinks fit, either refuse to enforce the award, the Court may, if it thinks fit, either refuse to enforce the award or adjourn the hearing until after the expiration of such period as appears to the Court to be reasonably sufficient to enable that party to take the necessary steps to have the award annulled by the competent tribunal.

57.   Evidence.

(1)   The party seeking to enforce a foreign award must produce—
(a)   the original award or a copy thereof duly authenticated in manner required by the law of the country in which it was made, and
(b)   evidence proving that the award has become final, and
(c)   such evidence as may be necessary to prove that the award is a foreign award and that the conditions specified in paragraphs (a), (b) and (c) of subsection (1) of section 56 of this Act are satisfied.
(2)   In any case where any document required to be produced under subsection (1) of this section is in a language, other than one of the official languages, it shall be the duty of the party seeking to enforce the award to produce a translation certified as correct by a diplomatic or consular agent of the country to which that party belongs, or certified as correct in such other manner as may be sufficient according to the law of the State.
(3)   Subject to the provisions of this section, rules of court may be made under section 36 of the Courts of Justice Act, 1924 (No. 10 of 1924), as amended by section 68 of the Courts of Justice Act, 1936 (No. 48 of 1936), with respect to the evidence which must be furnished by a party seeking to enforce a foreign award under this Part.

58.   Meaning of 'final award'.

For the purposes of this Part, an award shall not be deemed final if any proceedings for the purposes of contesting the validity of the award are pending in the country in which it was made.

59.   Saving for other rights, etc.

Nothing in this Part shall—
(a)   prejudice any rights which any person would have had of enforcing in the State any award or of availing himself in the State of an award if this Part had not been enacted, or
(b)   apply to any award made on an arbitration agreement governed by the law of the State.
[The texts of the Geneva Protocol and the Geneva Convention — the First and Second Schedules, respectively, of this Act — are in Part V of this book. The Schedules are not reproduced here.]

ARBITRATION ACT 1980

An act to enable effect to be given to the Convention on the Recognition and Enforcement of Foreign Arbitral Awards done at New York on the 10th day of June, 1958, and to certain provisions of the Convention on the Settlement of Investment Disputes between States and Nationals of Other States opened for signature in Washington on the 18th day of March, 1965, and otherwise to amend the Arbitration Act, 1954.   [4th June 1980]

BE IT ENACTED BY THE OIREACHTAS AS FOLLOWS:

PART 1

PRELIMINARY AND GENERAL

1. Short title and collective citation.

(1)   This Act may be cited as the Arbitration Act, 1980.

(2)   The Arbitration Act, 1954, and this Act may be cited together as the Arbitration Acts, 1954 and 1980.

2. Definitions.

In this Act—
    'arbitration agreement' means an agreement in writing (including an agreement contained in an exchange of letters or telegrams) to submit to arbitration present or future differences capable of settlement by arbitration;
    'the Principal Act' means the Arbitration Act, 1954.

3. Commencement.

Parts III and IV of this Act shall come into operation on such day or days as the Minister for Justice may by order appoint.

4. Repeal.

Section 12 of the Principal Act is hereby repealed.

PART II

EFFECT OF ARBITRATION AGREEMENT ON COURT PROCEEDINGS

5. Staying court proceedings where party proves arbitration agreement.

(1)   If any party to an arbitration agreement, or any person claiming through or under him, commences any proceedings in any court against any other party to such agreement, or any person claiming through or under him, in respect of any matter agreed to be referred to arbitration, any party to the

proceedings may at any time after an appearance has been entered, and before delivery any pleadings or taking any other steps in the proceedings, apply to the court to stay the proceedings, and the court, unless it is satisfied that the arbitration agreement is null and void, inoperative or incapable of being performed or that there is not in fact any dispute between the parties with regard to the matter agreed to be referred, shall make an order staying the proceedings.

(2) Nothing in this section shall be construed as limiting or otherwise affecting the power conferred on the High Court pursuant to section 39(3) of the Principal Act to refuse to stay any action brought in breach of an arbitration agreement.

PART III

ENFORCEMENT OF NEW YORK CONVENTION AWARDS

6. Interpretation (Part III).

(1) In this Part of this Act—

'award' means an award (other than an award within the meaning of *Part IV* of this Act) made in pursuance of an arbitration agreement in the territory of a state, other than the State, which is a party to the New York Convention:

'the New York Convention' means the Convention on the Recognition and Enforcement of Foreign Arbitral Awards done at New York on the 10th day of June, 1958, which Convention is set out in the *First Schedule* to this Act.

(2) The Minister for Foreign Affairs may by order declare that any state specified in the order is a party to the New York Convention and, while such order is in force, the order shall be evidence that such state is a party to that Convention.

(3) The Minister for Foreign Affairs may by order revoke or amend an order under this section, including an order under this subsection.

7. Effect of awards.

(1) An award shall, subject to the subsequent provisions of this Part, be enforceable either by action or in the same manner as the award of an arbitrator is enforceable by virtue of section 41 of the Principal Act.

(2) An award that would be enforceable under this Part shall be treated as binding for all purposes on the persons between whom it was made, and may accordingly be relied on by any of those persons by way of defence, set off or otherwise in any legal proceedings in the State, and any reference in this Part to the enforcement of an award shall be construed as including a reference to the reliance on such an award.

8. Evidence.

Any person who seeks to enforce an award shall produce—

(a) the duly authenticated original award or a duly certified copy of that award, and

(b)   the original arbitration agreement or a duly certified copy of that agreement, and

(c)   in any case where the award or the arbitration agreement is in a language other than one of the official languages of the State, a translation of the award or the agreement, as the case may be, certified by an official or sworn translator or by a diplomatic or consular agent.

9.   Refusal of enforcement.

(1)   Enforcement of an award shall not be refused otherwise than pursuant to the subsequent provisions of this section.

(2)   Enforcement of an award may be refused if the person against whom it is invoked proves that—

(a)   a party to the arbitration agreement was (under the law applicable to him) under some incapacity, or

(b)   the arbitration agreement was not valid under the law of the country to which the parties subjected it or, failing any indication thereon, under the law of the country where the award was made, or

(c)   he was not given proper notice of the appointment of the arbitrator or of the arbitration proceedings or was otherwise unable to present his case, or

(d)   subject to *subsection (4)* of this section, the award deals with a difference not contemplated by or not falling within the terms of the submission to arbitration or contains decisions on matters beyond the scope of the submission to arbitration, or

(e)   the composition of the arbitral authority or the arbitral procedure was not in accordance with the agreement of the parties or, failing such agreement, with the law of the country where the arbitration took place, or

(f)   the award has not yet become binding on the parties or has been set aside or suspended by a competent authority of the country in which, or under the law of which, the award was made.

(3)   Enforcement of an award may also be refused if the award is in respect of a matter which is not capable of settlement by arbitration under the law of the State, or if it would be contrary to public policy to enforce the award.

(4)   An award which contains decisions on matters not submitted to arbitration which can be separated from any decisions on matters not so submitted.

(5)   In any case where an application for the setting aside or suspension of an award has been made to such a competent authority as is mentioned in *subsection (2) (f)* of this section, a court before which enforcement of the award is sought may, if it thinks fit, adjourn the proceedings and may, on the application of the party seeking to enforce the award, order the other party to give such security as the court may think fit.

10.   Non-application of Part V of Principal Act.

In any case where an award is also a foreign award within the meaning of Part V of the Principal Act, that Part shall not apply to such award.

11. Saving for other rights.

Nothing in this Part shall prejudice the right of any person to enforce or to rely on an award otherwise than under this Part or under Part V of the Principal Act.

PART IV

ENFORCEMENT OF WASHINGTON CONVENTION AWARDS

12. Interpretation (Part IV).

In this Part—
'award' means an award rendered pursuant to the Washinton Convention and includes any decision made—

(a) pursuant to Article 49(2) of that Convention in relation to any question which the Tribunal referred to in that Article had omitted to decide in the award, or in relation to the rectification of any clerical, arithmetical or similar error in the award.

(b) pursuant to Articles 50,51 and 52 of that Convention, interpreting, revising or annulling the award, and

(c) pursuant to Article 61(2) of that Convention in relation to costs;
'the Washington Convention' means the Convention on the Settlement of Investment Disputes between States and Nationals of Other States opened for signature in Washington on the 18th day of March, 1965, which Convention is set out in the *Second Schedule* to this Act.

13. Approval of acceptance

Acceptance by the State of the Washington Convention is hereby approved.

14. Government contribution under Washington Convention and expenses.

(1) The Minister for Finance may discharge any obligations of the Government arising under Article 17 of the Washington Convention (which obliges for Contracting States to meet any deficit of the International Centre for Settlement of Investment Disputes established under that Convention).

(2) Any sums required for the purposes of *subsection (1)* of this section and any administrative expenses incurred by the Minister for Finance as a result of acceptance by the State of the Washington Convention shall be paid out of moneys provided by the Oireachtas.

15. Application of Principal Act and other enactments.

(1) The Minister for Justice may by order direct that any of the provisions contained in—

(a) sections 19, 20, 21 and 22 of the Principal Act (which relate to attendance of witnesses, security for costs, discovery of documents, etc.), and

(b) the Foreign Evidence Act, 1856 (which relates to taking of evidence for the purpose of proceedings before a foreign tribunal),
shall apply to such proceedings pursuant to the Washington Conventions as are specified in the order, and the order may contain such modifications or

exceptions as may appear to the Minister for Justice to be expedient for the purposes of the order.

(2) Subject to *subsection (1)* of this section, the Principal Act shall not apply to proceedings pursuant to the Washington Convention.

(3) The Minister for Justice may by order revoke or amend an order under this section, including an order under this subsection.

16. Enforcement of pecuniary obligations imposed by award.

(1) The pecuniary obligations imposed by an award shall, by leave of the High Court, be enforceable in the same manner as a judgment or order of the High Court to the same effect and, where leave is so given, judgment may be entered for the amount due or, as the case may be, the balance outstanding under the award.

(2) Any person who applies to the High Court pursuant to *subsection (1)* of this section for leave to enforce the pecuniary obligations imposed by an award shall lodge with his application a copy of the award certified in accordance with Article 54(2) of the Washington Convention.

17. Power of High Court to stay enforcement.

Where an application is made to the High Court pursuant to *section 16* of this Act, the High Court shall, in any case where enforcement of an award has been stayed, whether provisionally or otherwise, in accordance with Article 50, Article 51 or Article 52 of the Washington Convention, stay enforcement of the pecuniary obligations imposed by the award and may, in any case where an application has been made in accordance with any of those Articles which, if granted, might result in a stay on the enforcement of the award, stay enforcement of the pecuniary obligations imposed by the award.

I.4   ISLE OF MAN

ARBITRATION ACT 1976

We, your Majesty's most dutiful and loyal subjects, the Lieutenant Governor, Council, and Keys, of the said Isle, do humbly beseech your Majesty that it may be enacted, and be it enacted, by the Queen's Most Excellent Majesty, by and with the advice and consent of the Lieutenant Governor, Council, and Keys, in Tynwald assembled, and by the authority of the same, as follows (that is to say):—

PART I

GENERAL PROVISIONS AS TO ARBITRATION

Effect of Arbitration Agreements, &c.

1.   Authority of arbitrators and umpires to be irrevocable.

The authority of an arbitrator or umpire appointed by, or by virtue of, an arbitration agreement shall, unless a a contrary intention is expressed in the agreement, be irrevocable except by leave of the Court.

2. Death of party.

(1)   An arbitration agreement shall not be discharged by the death of any party thereto, either as respects the deceased or any other party, but shall in such event be enforceable by or against the personal representative of the deceased.

(2)   The authority of an arbitrator shall not be revoked by the death of any party by whom he was appointed.

(3)   Nothing in this section shall be taken to affect the operation of any enactment or rule of law by virtue of which any right of action is extinguished by the death of a person.

3. Bankruptcy.

(1)   Where it is provided by a term in a contract to which a bankrupt is a party that any differences arising thereout or in connection therewith shall be referred to arbitration, the said term shall, if the trustee in bankruptcy adopts the contract, be enforceable by or against him so far as relates to any such differences.

(2)   Where a person who has been adjudged bankrupt had, before the commencement of the bankruptcy, become a party to an arbitration agreement, and any matter to which the agreement applies requires to be determined in connection with or for the purposes of the bankruptcy proceedings, then, if the case is one to which subsection (1) above does not apply, any other party to the agreement or the trustee in bankruptcy may apply to the Court for an order directing that the matter in question shall be referred to arbitration in accordance with the agreement, and the Court may, if it is of the opinion that, having regard to all the circumstances of the case, the matter ought to be determined by arbitration, make an order accordingly.

4. Staying court proceedings where there is submission to arbitration.

Subject to section 5 of this Act, if any party to an arbitration agreement, or any person claiming through or under him, commences any legal proceedings in the Court against any other party to the agreement, or any person claiming through or under him, in respect of any matter agreed to be referred, any party to those legal proceedings may at any time after appearance, and before delivering any pleadings or taking any other steps in the proceedings, apply to the Court to stay the proceedings; and the Court, if satisfied that there is no sufficient reason why the matter should not be referred in accordance with the agreement, and that the applicant was, at the time when the proceedings were commenced, and still remains, ready and willing to do all things necessary to the proper conduct of the arbitration, may make an order staying the proceedings.

5. Staying court proceedings where party proves arbitration agreement.

(1)   If any party to an arbitration agreement to which this section applies, or any person claiming through or under him, commences any legal

proceedings in the Court against any other party to the agreement, or any person claiming through him or under him, in respect of any matter agreed to be referred, any party to the proceedings may at any time after appearance, and before delivering any pleadings or taking any other steps in the proceedings, apply to the Court to stay the proceedings: and the Court, unless satisfied that the arbitration agreement is null and void, inoperative or incapable of being performed or that there is not in fact any dispute between the parties with regard to the matter agreed to be referred, shall make an order staying the proceedings.

(2)   This section applies to any arbitration agreement which is not a domestic arbitration agreement; and section 4 of this Act shall not apply to an arbitration agreement to which this section applies.

(3)   In this section 'domestic arbitration agreement' means an arbitration agreement which does not provide, expressly or by implication, for arbitration in a country other than the Island and to which neither—

(a)   an individual who is a national of any state other than the United Kingdom, or who is habitually resident in any country other than the Island; nor

(b)   a body corporate which is incorporated in, or whose central management and control is exercised in, any country other than the Island, is a party at the time the proceedings are commenced.

(4)   In subsection (3), 'the United Kingdom' means Great Britain, Northern Ireland, the Island and the Channel Islands, taken together.

[*Section 5(3)(a) substituted, and s. 5(4) inserted, by Statute Law Revision Act 1983, sch. 1, para. 25.*]

6.   Reference of interpleader issues to arbitration.

Where relief by way of interpleader is granted and it appears to the Court that the claims in question are matters to which an arbitration agreement, to which the claimants are parties, applies, the Court may direct the issue between the claimants to be determined in accordance with the agreement.

Arbitrators and Umpires

7.   When reference is to a single arbitrator.

Unless a contrary intention is expressed therein, every arbitration agreement shall, if no other mode of reference is provided, be deemed to include a provision that the reference shall be to a single arbitrator.

8.   Power of parties in certain cases to supply vacancy.

(1)   Subject to subsection (2) below, where an arbitration agreement provides that the reference shall be to two arbitrators, one to be appointed by each party, then, unless a contrary intention is expressed therein—

(a)   if either of the appointed arbitrators refuses to act, or is incapable of acting, or dies, the party who appointed him may appoint a new arbitrator in his place;

(b)   if, on such a reference, one party fails to appoint an arbitrator, either originally or by way of substitution as aforesaid, for seven clear days after the other party, having appointed his arbitrator, has served the party making default with notice to make the appointment, the party who has appointed an arbitrator may appoint that arbitrator to act as sole arbitrator in the reference, and his award shall be binding on both parties as if he had been appointed by consent.

(2)   The Court may set aside any appointment made in pursuance of this section.

9.   Umpires.

(1)   Unless a contrary intention is expressed therein, every arbitration agreement shall, where the reference is to two arbitrators, be deemed to include a provision that the two arbitrators shall appoint an umpire immediately after they are themselves appointed.

(2)   Unless a contrary intention is expressed therein, every arbitration agreement shall, where such a provision is applicable to the reference, be deemed to include a provision that, if the arbitrators have delivered to any party to the arbitration agreement, or to the umpire, a notice in writing stating that they cannot agree, the umpire may forthwith enter on the reference in lieu of the arbitrators.

(3)   At any time after the appointment of an umpire, however appointed, the Court may, on the application of any party to the reference and notwithstanding anything to the contrary in the arbitration agreement, order that the umpire shall enter upon the reference in lieu of the arbitrators and as if he were a sole arbitrator.

10.   Agreements for references to three arbitrators.

(1)   Where an arbitration agreement provides that the reference shall be to three arbitrators, one to be appointed by each party and the third to be appointed by the two appointed by the parties, the agreement shall have effect as if it provided for the appointment of an umpire, and not for the appointment of a third arbitrator, by the two arbitrators appointed by the parties.

(2)   Where an arbitration agreement provides that the reference shall be to three arbitrators to be appointed otherwise than as mentioned in subsection (1) above, the award of any two of the arbitrators shall be binding.

(3)   In any case where—

(a)   an arbitration agreement provides that the reference shall be to three arbitrators, one to be appointed by each party and the third to be appointed by the two appointed by the parties or in some other manner specified in the agreement; and

(b)   one of the parties ('the party in default') refuses to appoint an arbitrator or does not do so within the time specified in the agreement or, if no time is specified, within a reasonable time,

the other party to the agreement, having appointed his arbitrator, may serve the party in default with a written notice to appoint an arbitrator and, if the appointment is not made within seven clear days after the service of the notice, the High Court or a judge thereof may, on the application of the party who gave the notice, appoint an arbitrator on behalf of the party in default who shall have the like powers to act in the reference and make an award (and, if the case so requires, the like duty in relation to the appointment of a third arbitrator) as if he had been appointed in accordance with the terms of the agreement.

(4)   Except in a case where the arbitration agreement shows that it was intended that the vacancy should not be supplied, paragraph (b) of subsection (3) shall be construed as extending to any such refusal or failure by a person as is there mentioned arising in connection with the replacement of an arbitrator who was appointed by that person (or in default of being so appointed, was appointed under that subsection) but who refuses to act, or is incapable of acting or has died.

[*Section 10(3) to (4) inserted by the High Court Act 1991, sch. 3, para. 30(1). See also text of para. 30(4) given after s. 14A.*]

11.   Power of court in certain cases to appoint an arbitrator or umpire.

In any of the following cases—

(a)   where an arbitration agreement provides that the reference shall be to a single arbitrator, and all the parties do not, after differences have arisen, concur in the appointment of an arbitrator:

(b)   if an appointed arbitrator refuses to act, or is incapable of acting, or dies, and the arbitration agreement does not show that it was intended that the vacancy should not be supplied and the parties do not supply the vacancy;

(c)   where the parties or two arbitrators are at liberty to appoint an umpire or third arbitrator and do not appoint him, or where two arbitrators are required to appoint an umpire and do not appoint him:

(d)   where an appointed umpire or third arbitrator refuses to act, or is incapable of acting, or dies, and the arbitration agreement does not show that it was intended that the vacancy should not be supplied, and the parties or arbitrators do not supply the vacancy,

any party may serve the other parties or the arbitrators, as the case may be, with a written notice to appoint or, as the case may be, concur in appointing, an arbitrator, umpire or third arbitrator; and, if the appointment is not made within seven clear days after the service of the notice, the Court may, on application by the party who gave the notice, appoint an arbitrator, umpire or third arbitrator who shall have the like powers to act in the reference and make an award as if he had been appointed by consent of all parties.

12.   Reference to special referee.

(1)   The Deemsters may, subject to subsection (3) below, make rules prescribing the cases in which the jurisdiction or powers, or both, of the Court may be exercised by special referees and, without prejudice to the generality of the foregoing, such rules may—

(a)   authorise the whole of any cause or matter or any question or issue therein to be ordered to be tried before, or any question arising in any cause or matter to be ordered to be referred for inquiry and report to, any such referee; and

(b)   make any provision incidental to any of the matters in respect of which rules may be made under this subsection.

(2)   The decision of a special referee may be called in question in such manner, whether by—
    (a)   an appeal to the Staff of Government Division; or
    (b)   an appeal or application to the Court or to a Deemster in Chambers; or
    (c)   an adjournment to the Court or to a Deemster in Chambers,
as may, subject to subsection (3) below, be prescribed by rules made by the Deemsters.
    (3)   No rules under subsection (1) or (2) above shall have effect until they have been approved by Tynwald.

12A.   Specific powers of arbitrator exercisable by High Court.

In any cause or matter proceeding in the High Court in connection with any contract incorporating an arbitration clause which confers specific powers upon the arbitrator, the High Court may, if all parties to the proceedings agree, exercise any such powers.
[*Section 12A inserted by the High Court Act 1991, sch. 3, para. 30(2). See also text of para. 30(4) given after s. 14A.*]

Conduct of Proceedings, Witnesses &c.

13.   Conduct of proceedings, witnesses, &c.

(1)   Unless a contrary intention is expressed therein, every arbitration agreement shall, where such a provision is applicable to the reference, be deemed to contain a provision that the parties to the reference, and all persons claiming through them respectively, shall, subject to any legal objection, submit to be examined by the arbitrator or umpire, on oath or affirmation, in relation to the matters in dispute, and shall, subject as aforesaid, produce before the arbitrator or umpire all documents within their possession or power respectively which may be required or called for, and do all other things which during the proceedings on the reference the arbitrator or umpire may require.
    (2)   Unless a contrary intention is expressed therein, every arbitration agreement shall, where such a provision is applicable to the reference, be deemed to contain a provision that the witnesses on the reference shall, if the arbitrator or umpire thinks fit, be examined on oath or affirmation.
    (3)   An arbitrator or umpire shall, unless a contrary intention is expressed in the arbitration agreement, have power to administer oaths to, or take the affirmations of, the parties to and witnesses on a reference under the agreement.
    (4)   Any party to a reference under an arbitration agreement may apply to the Court for a warrant to summon a witness to give evidence or to produce documentary evidence, but no person shall be compelled, under any such warrant, to produce any document which he could not be compelled to produce on the trial of an action; and the Court may, on any such application, order that such a warrant shall issue to compel the attendance of a witness before an arbitrator or umpire, wherever the witness may be within the Island.

(5)   A detainee may be brought up for examination before any arbitrator or umpire, pursuant to a direction of the Department of Home Affairs given under section 20(2) of the Custody Act 1995.

[*Section 13(5) substituted by the Custody Act 1995, sch. 4, para. 3.*]

(6)   Subject to subsection (7) below, the Court shall have, for the purpose of and in relation to a reference, the same power of making orders in respect of—

(a)   security for costs;

(b)   discovery of documents and interrogatories;

(c)   the giving of evidence by affidavit;

(d)   examination on oath of any witness before an officer of the Court or any other person, and the issue of a commission or request for the examination of a witness out of the jurisdiction;

(e)   the preservation, interim custody or sale of any goods which are the subject matter of the reference;

(f)   securing the amount in dispute in the reference;

(g)   the detention, preservation or inspection of any property or thing which is the subject of the reference or as to which any question may arise therein, and authorising for any of the purposes aforesaid any persons to enter upon or into any land in the possession of any party to the reference, or authorising any samples to be taken or any observation to be made or experiment to be tried which may be necessary or expedient for the purpose of obtaining full information or evidence; and

(h)   interim injunctions or the appointment of a receiver,

as it has for the purpose of and in relation to an action or matter in the Court.

(7)   Nothing in subsection (6) above shall be taken to prejudice any power which may be vested in an arbitrator or umpire of making orders with respect to any of the matters mentioned in that subsection.

Provisions as to Awards

14.   Time for making award.

(1)   Subject to the provisions of section 23(2) of this Act, and anything to the contrary in the arbitration agreement, an arbitrator or umpire shall have power to make an award at any time.

(2)   The time, if any, limited for making an award, whether under this Act or otherwise, may from time to time be enlarged by order of the Court, whether that time has expired or not.

(3)   The Court may, on the application of any party to a reference, remove an arbitrator or umpire who fails to use all reasonable dispatch in entering on and proceeding with the reference and making an award, and an arbitrator or umpire who is removed by the Court under this subsection shall not be entitled to receive any remuneration in respect of his services.

(4)   For the purposes of subsection (3) above, 'proceeding with a reference' includes, in a case where two arbitrators are unable to agree, giving notice of that fact to the parties and to the umpire.

14A.   Want of prosecution.

(1)   Unless a contrary intention is expressed in the arbitration agreement, the arbitrator or umpire shall have power to make an award dismissing the

claim in a dispute referred to him if it appears to him that the conditions
mentioned in subsection (2) are satisfied.

(2)   The conditions are—

(a)   that there has been inordinate and inexcusable delay on the part of
the claimant in pursuing the claim; and

(b)   that the delay —

(i)   will give rise to a substantial risk that it is not possible to have a
fair resolution of the issues in that claim; or

(ii)   has caused, or is likely to cause or to have caused, serious
prejudice to the respondent.

[*Section 14A inserted by the High Court Act 1991, sch. 3, para, 30(3), para.
30(4) goes on to state:* 'This entry applies to an arbitration agreement whether
it was entered into before or after the commencement of this entry.']

15.   Interim awards.

Unless a contrary intention is expressed therein, every arbitration agreement
shall, where such a provision is applicable to the reference, be deemed to
contain a provision that the arbitrator or umpire may, if he thinks fit, make
an interim award, and any reference in this Part to an award includes a
reference to an interim award.

16.   Specific performance.

Unless a contrary intention is expressed therein, every arbitration agreement
shall, where such a provision is applicable to the reference, be deemed to
contain a provision that the arbitrator or umpire shall have the same power
as the Court to order specific performance of any contract other than a
contract relating to land.

17.   Awards to be final.

Unless a contrary intention is expressed therein, every arbitration agreement
shall, where such a provision is applicable to the reference, be deemed to
contain a provision that the award to be made by the arbitrator or umpire
shall be final and binding on the parties and the persons claiming under them
respectively.

18.   Power to correct slips.

Unless a contrary intention is expressed in the arbitration agreement, the
arbitrator or umpire shall have power to correct in an award any clerical
mistake or error arising from any accidental slip or omission.

Costs, Fees and Interest

19.   Costs.

(1)   Unless a contrary intention is expressed therein, every arbitration
agreement shall be deemed to include a provision that the costs of the

reference and award shall be in the discretion of the arbitrator or umpire, who may direct to and by whom and in what manner those costs or any part thereof shall be paid, and may tax or settle the amount of costs to be so paid or any part thereof, and may award costs to be paid as between attorney and client.

(2)　Any costs directed by an award to be paid shall, unless the award otherwise directs, be taxable by the Taxing Master.

(3)　Subject to subsection (4) below, any provision in an arbitration agreement to the effect that the parties or any party thereto shall in any event pay their or his own costs of the reference or award or any party thereof shall be void, and this Part shall, in the case of an arbitration agreement containing any such provision, have effect as if that provision were not contained therein.

(4)　Nothing in subsection (3) above shall invalidate such a provision when it is a part of an agreement to submit to arbitration a dispute which has arisen before the making of that agreement.

(5)　If no provision is made by an award with respect to the costs of the reference, any party to the reference may, within fourteen days of the publication of the award or such further time as the Court may direct, apply to the arbitrator for an order directing by and to whom those costs shall be paid, and thereupon the arbitrator shall, after hearing any party who may desire to be heard, amend his award by adding thereto such directions as he may think proper with respect to the payment of the costs of the reference.

(6)　Section 12 of the Advocates' Act 1874 (which empowers a court before which any proceeding is being heard or is pending to charge property recovered or preserved in the proceeding with the payment of advocates' costs) shall apply as if an arbitration were a proceeding in the Court, and the Court may make declarations and orders accordingly.

20.　Taxation of arbitrator's or umpire's fees.

(1)　If, in any case, an arbitrator or umpire refuses to deliver his award except on payment of the fees demanded by him, the Court may, on application for the purpose, order that the arbitrator or umpire shall deliver the award to the applicant on payment into court by the applicant of the fees demanded, and further that the fees demanded shall be taxed by the Taxing Master, and that, out of the money paid into Court, there shall be paid out to the arbitrator or umpire, by way of fees, such sum as may be found reasonable on taxation, and that the balance of the money, if any, shall be paid out to the applicant.

(2)　An application for the purposes of this section may be made by any party to the reference unless the fees demanded have been fixed by a written agreement between him and the arbitrator or umpire.

(3)　A taxation of fees under this section may be reviewed in the same manner as a taxation of costs.

(4)　The arbitrator or umpire shall be entitled to appear and be heard on any taxation or review of taxation under this section.

20A.　Power of arbitrator to award interest.

(1)　Unless a contrary intention is expressed therein, every arbitration agreement shall, where such provision is applicable to the reference, be deemed to contain a provision that the arbitrator or umpire may, if he thinks fit, award simple interest at such rate as he thinks fit —

(a)   on any sum which is the subject of the reference but which is paid before the award for such period ending not later than the date of the payment as he thinks fit; and

(b)   on any sum which he awards, for such period ending not later than the date of the award as he thinks fit.

(2)   The power to award interest conferred on an arbitrator or umpire by subsection (1) above is without prejudice to any other power of an arbitrator or umpire to award interest.

[*Section 20A inserted by the High Court Act 1991, sch. 3, para. 31.*]

21.   Interest on awards

A sum directed to be paid by an award shall, unless the award otherwise directs, carry interest as from the date of the award and at the same rate as a judgment debt.

Special Cases, Remission and
Setting aside of Awards, &c.

22.   Statement of case.

(1)   An arbitrator or umpire may, and shall if so directed by the Court, state—

(a)   any question of law arising in the course of the reference; or

(b)   an award or any part of an award in the form of a special case for the decision of the Court.

(2)   A special case with respect to an interim award or with respect to a question of law arising in the course of a reference may be stated, or may be directed by the Court to be stated, notwithstanding that proceedings under the reference are still pending.

(3)   An appeal shall lie to the Staff of Government Division from a decision of the Court under this section, but no appeal shall lie from the decision of the Court on any case stated under subsection (1)(a) without the leave of the Staff of Government Division.

[*Section 23(3) substituted by the High Court Act 1991, sch. 3, para. 32.*]

23.   Power to remit award.

(1)   In all cases of reference to arbitration, the Court may from time to time remit the matters referred, or any of them to the reconsideration of the arbitrator or umpire.

(2)   Where an award is remitted, the arbitrator or umpire shall, unless the order otherwise directs, make his award within three months after the date of the order.

24.   Removal of arbitrator and setting aside of award.

(1)   Where an arbitrator or umpire has misconducted himself or the proceedings, the Court may remove him.

(2)   Where an arbitrator or umpire has misconducted himself or the proceedings, or an arbitration or award has been improperly procured, the Court may set the award aside.

(3)   Where an application is made to set aside an award, the Court may order that any money made payable by the award shall be brought into court or otherwise secured pending the determination of the application.

25.   Power of court to give relief where arbitrator is not impartial or the dispute involves question of fraud.

(1)   Where an agreement between any parties provides that disputes which may arise in the future between them shall be referred to an arbitrator named or designated in the agreement, and after a dispute has arisen any party applies, on the ground that the arbitrator so named or designated is not or may not be impartial, for leave to revoke the authority of the arbitrator or for an injunction to restrain any other party or the arbitrator from proceeding with the arbitration, it shall not be a ground for refusing the application that the said party at the time when he made the agreement knew, or ought to have known, that the arbitrator, by reason of his relation towards any other party to the agreement or of his connection with the subject referred, might not be capable of impartiality.

(2)   Where an agreement between any parties provides that disputes which may arise in the future between them shall be referred to arbitration, and a dispute which so arises involves the question whether any such party has been guilty of fraud, the Court shall, so far as may be necessary to enable that question to be determined by the Court, have power to order that the agreement shall cease to have effect and power to give leave to revoke the authority of any arbitrator or umpire appointed by or by virtue of the agreement.

(3)   In any case where, by virtue of this section, the Court has power to order that an arbitration agreement shall cease to have effect or to give leave to revoke the authority of an arbitrator or umpire, the Court may refuse to stay any action brought in breach of the agreement.

26.   Power of court where arbitrator is removed or authority of arbitrator is revoked.

(1)   Where an arbitrator (not being a sole arbitrator) or two or more arbitrators (not being all the arbitrators) or an umpire who has not entered on the reference is or are removed by the Court, the Court may, on the application of any party to the arbitration agreement, appoint a person or persons to act as arbitrator or arbitrators or umpire in place of the person or persons so removed.

(2)   Where the authority of an arbitrator or arbitrators or umpire is revoked by leave of the Court, or a sole arbitrator or all the arbitrators or an umpire who has entered on the reference is or are removed by the Court, the Court may, on the application of any party to the arbitration agreement either—

(a)   appoint a person to act as sole arbitrator in place of the person or persons removed; or

(b)   order that the arbitration agreement shall cease to have effect with respect to the dispute referred.

(3)   A person appointed under this section by the Court as an arbitrator or umpire shall have the like power to act in the reference, and to make an award, as if he had been appointed in accordance with the terms of the arbitration agreement.

(4)   Where it is provided (whether by means of a provision in the arbitration agreement or otherwise) that an award under an arbitration agreement shall be a condition precedent to the bringing of an action with respect to any matter to which the agreement applies, the Court, if it orders (whether under this section or under any other enactment) that the agreement shall cease to have effect as regards any particular dispute, may further order that the provision making an award a condition precedent to the bringing of an action shall also cease to have effect as regards that dispute.

Enforcement of Award

27.   Enforcement of award.

An award on an arbitration agreement may, by leave of the Court, be enforced in the same manner as a judgment or order to the same effect: and, where leave is so given, judgment may be entered in terms of the award.

Miscellaneous

28.   Power of court to extend time for commencing arbitration proceedings.

Where the terms of an agreement to refer disputes to arbitration provide that any claims to which the agreement applies shall be barred unless notice to appoint an arbitrator is given or an arbitrator is appointed or some other step to commence arbitration proceedings is taken within a time fixed by the agreement, and a dispute arises to which the agreement applies, the Court, if it is of the opinion that, in the circumstances of the case, undue hardship would otherwise be caused, and notwithstanding that the time so fixed has expired, may, on such terms, if any, as the justice of the case may require, but without prejudice to the provisions of any enactment limiting the time for the commencement of arbitration proceedings, extend the time for such period as it thinks proper.

'28A.   Limitation of time for commencing arbitration proceedings.

(1)   The statutes of limitation shall apply to arbitrations as they apply to proceedings in the Court.

(2)   Notwithstanding any term in an arbitration agreement to the effect that no cause of action shall accrue in respect of any matter required by the agreement to be referred until an award is made under the agreement, a cause of action shall, for the purpose of the statutes of limitation (whether in their application to arbitrations or to other proceedings), be deemed to have accrued in respect of any such matter at the time when it would have accrued but for that term in the agreement.

(3)   For the purpose of this section and for the purpose of the statutes of limitation as applying to arbitrations, an arbitration shall be deemed to be commenced when one party to the arbitration agreement serves on the other party or parties a notice requiring him or them to appoint an arbitrator or to agree to the appointment of an arbitrator, or, where the arbitration agreement provides that the reference shall be to a person named or designated in the agreement, requiring him or them to submit the dispute to the person so named or designated.

(4)   Any such notice as is mentioned in subsection (3) may be served either—

(a)   by delivering it to the person on whom it is to be served; or

(b)   by leaving it at the usual or last known place of abode or business in the Island of that person; or

(c)   by sending it by post by the recorded delivery service addressed to that person at his usual or last known place of abode;

as well as in any other manner provided in the arbitration agreement; and where a notice is sent by post in accordance with paragraph (c), service shall, unless the contrary is proved, be deemed to have been effected at the time at which the letter would have been delivered in the ordinary course of post.

(5)   Where the Court orders that an award be set aside or orders, after the commencement of an arbitration, that the arbitration shall cease to have effect with respect to the dispute referred, the Court may further order that the period between the commencement of the arbitration and the date of the order of the Court shall be excluded in computing the time prescribed by the statutes of limitation for the commencement of proceedings (including arbitration) with respect to the dispute referred.

(6)   This section shall apply to an arbitration under any enactment as well as to an arbitration pursuant to an arbitration agreement, and subsections (3) and (4) shall have effect, in relation to an arbitration under an enactment, as if for the references to the arbitration agreement there were substituted references to such of the provisions of the enactment or of any public document made there under as relate to the arbitration.

(7)   In this section the words "the statutes of limitation" includes any enactment limiting the time within which any particular proceeding may be commenced.'

[*Section 28A added by the Limitation (Miscellaneous Provisions) Act 1981, s. 3.*]

29.   Terms as to costs, &c.

Any order made under this Part may be made on such terms as to costs or otherwise as the authority making the order thinks just.

30.   Government to be bound.

(1)   This Part shall apply to any arbitration to which the Government is a party.

(2)   In this section, 'the Government' includes a Board of Tynwald and a Statutory Board.

31. Application of Part I to statutory arbitrations.

(1) This Part, except the provisions thereof specified in subsection (2) below, shall apply to every arbitration under any other Act (whether passed before or after the appointed day) as if the arbitration were pursuant to an arbitration agreement and as if that other Act were an arbitration agreement, except in so far as this Act is inconsistent with that other Act or with any rules or procedure authorised or recognised thereby.

(2) The provisions referred to in subsection (1) above are sections 2(1), 3, 5, 6, 19(3), 25, 26 and 28.

PART II

ENFORCEMENT OF CERTAIN
FOREIGN AWARDS

32. Awards to which Part II applies.

(1) Subject to section 37 of this Act, this Part applies to any award made after the 28th July 1924—

(a) in pursuance of an agreement for arbitration to which the Protocol applies; and

(b) between persons of whom one is subject to the jurisdiction of some one of such Powers as Her Majesty may, by Order in Council, have declared to be parties to the Geneva Convention and of whom the other is subject to the jurisdiction of some other of the Powers aforesaid: and

(c) in one of such territories as Her Majesty may, by Order in Council, have declared to be territories to which the Geneva Convention applies, and an award to which this Part applies is, in this Part, referred to as 'a foreign award'.

(2) In this section, 'Order in Council' means an Order in Council which is in force and which—

(a) has been made under subsection (1)(b) or, as the case may be, subsection (1)(c) of section 35 of the Arbitration Act 1950 (an Act of Parliament); or

(b) has effect, by virtue of subsection (3) of that section, as if it had been so made.

33. Effect of foreign awards.

(1) A foreign award shall, subject to the provisions of this Part, be enforceable in the Island either by action or in the same manner as the award of an arbitrator is enforceable by virtue of section 27 of this Act.

(2) Any foreign award which would be enforceable under this Part shall be treated as binding for all purposes on the persons as between whom it was made, and may, accordingly, be relied on by any of those persons by way of defence, set off or otherwise in any legal proceedings in the Island, and any references in this Part to enforcing a foreign award shall be construed as including references to relying on an award.

34. Conditions for enforcement of foreign awards.

(1)   In order that a foreign award may be enforceable under this Part, it must have —

(a)   been made in pursuance of an agreement for arbitration which was valid under the law by which it was governed:

(b)   been made by the tribunal provided for in the agreement or constituted in the manner agreed upon by the parties:

(c)   been made in conformity with the law governing the arbitration procedure:

(d)   become final in the country in which it was made:

(e)   been in respect of a matter which may lawfully be referred to arbitration under the law of the Island,

and the enforcement thereof must not be contrary to the public policy or the law of the Island.

(2)   Subject to the provisions of this subsection, a foreign award shall not be enforceable under this Part if the Court is satisfied that —

(a)   the award has been annulled in the country in which it was made; or

(b)   the party against whom it is sought to enforce the award was not given notice of the arbitration proceedings in sufficient time to enable him to present his case, or was under some legal incapacity and was not properly represented; or

(c)   the award does not deal with all the questions referred or contains decisions on matters beyond the scope of the agreement for arbitration;

but, if the award does not deal with all the questions referred, the Court may, if it thinks fit, either postpone the enforcement of the award or order its enforcement subject to the giving of such security by the person seeking to enforce it as the court may think fit.

(3)   If a party seeking to resist the enforcement of a foreign award proves that there is any ground other than the non-existence of the conditions specified in subsection (1)(a), (b) and (c) above, or the existence of the conditions specified in subsection (2)(b) and (c) above, etitling him to contest the validity of the award, the Court may, if it thinks fit, either refuse to enforce the award or adjourn the hearing until after the expiration of such period as appears to the Court to be reasonably sufficient to enable that party to take the necessary steps to have the award annulled by the competent tribunal.

35. Evidence.

(1)   The party seeking to enforce a foreign award must produce —

(a)   the original award or a copy thereof duly authenticated in the manner required by the law of the country in which it was made;

(b)   evidence proving that the award has become final; and

(c)   such evidence as may be necessary to prove that the award is a foreign award and that the conditions mentioned in section 34(1)(a), (b) and (c) of this Act are satisfied.

(2)   In any case where any document required to be produced under subsection (1) above is in a foreign language, it shall be the duty of the party seeking to enforce the award to produce a translation certified as correct by

a diplomatic or consular agent of the country to which that party belongs, or certified as correct in such other manner as may be sufficient according to the law of the Island.

(3)   Subject to the provisions of this section, rules of court may be made with respect to the evidence which must be furnished by a party seeking to enforce an award under this Part.

36. Meaning of 'final award'.

For the purposes of this Part, an award shall not be deemed final if any proceedings for the purpose of contesting the validity of the award are pending in the country in which it was made.

PART III

ENFORCEMENT OF CONVENTION AWARDS

37. Replacement of Part II in certain cases.

Sections 38 to 40 of, and paragraph 5 of Schedule 1 to, this Act shall have effect with respect to the enforcement of Convention awards; and, where a Convention award would, but for this section, be also a foreign award within the meaning of Part II of this Act, that Part shall not apply to it.

38. Effect of Convention awards.

(1)   A Convention award shall, subject to the following provisions of this Part, be enforceable either by action or in the same manner as the award of an arbitrator is enforceable by virtue of section 27 of this Act.

(2)   Any Convention award which would be enforceable under this Part shall be treated as binding for all purposes on the persons as between whom it was made, and may, accordingly, be relied on by any of those persons by way of defence, set off or otherwise in any legal proceedings in the Island; and any reference in this Part to enforcing a Convention award shall be construed as including references to relying on such an award.

39. Evidence.

The party seeking to enforce a Convention award must produce —
    (a)   the duly authenticated original award or a duly certified copy of it;
    (b)   the original arbitration agreement or a duly certified copy of it; and
    (c)   where the award or agreement is in a foreign language, a translation of it certified by an official or sworn translator or by a diplomatic or consular agent.

40. Refusal of enforcement.

(1)   Enforcement of a Convention award shall not be refused except in the cases mentioned in this section.

(2)   Enforcement of a Convention award may be refused if the person against whom it is invoked proves—

(a)   that a party to the arbitration was (under the law applicable to him) under some incapacity; or

(b)   that the arbitration agreement was not valid under the law to which the parties subjected it or, failing any indication thereon, under the law of the country where the award was made; or

(c)   that he was not given proper notice of the appointment of the arbitrator or of the arbitration proceedings or was otherwise unable to present his case; or

(d)   subject to subsection (4) below, that the award deals with a difference not contemplated by, or not falling within the terms of, the submission to arbitration or contains decisions on matters beyond the scope of the submission to arbitration; or

(e)   that the composition of the arbitral authority or the arbitral procedure was not in accordance with the agreement of the parties or, failing such agreement, with the law of the country where the arbitration took place; or

(f)   that the award has not yet become binding on the parties, or has been set aside or suspended by a competent authority of the country in which, or under the law of which, it was made.

(3)   Enforcement of a Convention award may also be refused if the award is in respect of a matter which is not capable of settlement by arbitration, or if it would be contrary to public policy to enforce the award.

(4)   A Convention award which contains decisions on matters not submitted to arbitration may be enforced to the extent that it contains decisions on matters submitted to arbitration which can be separated from those on matters not so submitted.

(5)   Where an application for the setting aside or suspension of a Convention award has been made to such a competent authority as is mentioned in subsection (2)(f) above, the Court may, if it thinks fit, adjourn the proceedings and may, on the application of the party seeking to enforce the award, order the other party to give security.

PART IV

SUPPLEMENTARY

41.   Interpretation.

(1)   In this Act, unless the context otherwise requires—
'the appointed day' means the day on which this Act takes effect;
'arbitration agreement' means—

(a)   in section 5 and in the definition below of 'Convention award', an agreement in writing (including an agreement contained in an exchange of letters or telegrams) to submit to arbitration present or future differences capable of settlement by arbitration; and

(b)   elsewhere, a written agreement to submit present or future differences to arbitration, whether an arbitrator is mentioned therein or not;
'Convention award' means an award made in pursuance of an arbitration agreement in the territory of a State, other than the United Kingdom, which is a party to the New York Convention;

'the Court' means the High Court;

'the Geneva Convention' means the Convention on the Execution of Foreign Arbitral Awards signed at Geneva on behalf of His late Majesty, King George V, on the 26th September 1927;

'the New York Convention' means the Convention on the Recognition and Enforcement of Foreign Arbitral Awards adopted by the United Nations Conference on International Commercial Arbitration on the 10th June 1958;

'the Protocol' means the Protocol on Arbitration Clauses signed on behalf of His late Majesty, King George V, at a meeting of the Assembly of the League of Nations held on the 24th September 1923.

(2)   If Her Majesty by Order in Council declares that any State specified in the Order is a party to the New York Convention, the Order shall, while in force, be conclusive evidence that that State is a party to that Convention.

42.   Transitional provisions and savings.

The transitional provisions and savings in Schedule 1 to this Act shall have effect.

43.   Repeals.

The enactments mentioned in Schedule 2 to this Act are hereby repealed to the extent specified in the third column of that Schedule.

44.   Short title and commencement.

(1)   This Act may be cited as the Arbitration Act 1976.

(2)   This Act shall come into operation when the Royal Assent thereto has been by the Governor announced to Tynwald and a certificate thereof has been signed by the Governor and the Speaker of the House of Keys, but shall not take effect until such day as the governor may by order appoint.

Sections 37 and 42   SCHEDULE 1

TRANSITIONAL PROVISIONS AND SAVINGS

1.   Any proceedings under Part I of the Arbitration (Foreign Awards) Act 1931 which are uncompleted on the appointed day may be carried on and completed under Part II of this Act as if they had been instituted thereunder.

2.   Notwithstanding the repeal by this Act of the Arbitration Act 1910, the Arbitration Clauses (Protocol) Act 1925 and the Arbitration Act 1935, those Acts shall continue to have effect to arbitrations commenced before the appointed day.

3.   Any reference in any enactment or other document to any enactment repealed by this Act shall be construed as including a reference to the corresponding provision of this Act.

4.   Nothing in Part II of this Act shall —

(a)   prejudice any rights which any person would have had of enforcing in the Island any award, or of availing himself in the Island of any award, if neither that Part nor Part I of the said Act of 1931 had been enacted; or

(b)   apply to any award made on an arbitration agreement governed by the law of the Island.

5.   Nothing in Part III of this Act shall prejudice any right to enforce or rely on an award otherwise than under that Part or under Part II of this Act.

6.   Nothing in this Schedule shall prejudice the provisions of section 10 of the Interpretation Act 1970 (which relates to repeals).

Section 43   SCHEDULE 2
                              ENACTMENTS REPEALED

[Schedule 2 is not reproduced here.]

ARBITRATION (INTERNATIONAL INVESTMENT DISPUTES) ACT 1983

We, your Majesty's most dutiful and loyal subjects, the Lieutenant Governor, Council and Keys of the said Isle, do humbly beseech your Majesty that it may be enacted, and be it enacted, by the Queen's Most Excellent Majesty, by and with the advice and consent of the Lieutenant Governor, Council and Keys in Tynwald assembled, and by the authority of the same, as follows (that is to say):—

1.   Registration of Convention awards.

(1)   This section has effect as respects awards rendered pursuant to the Convention on the settlement of investment disputes between States and nationals of other States which was opened for signature in Washington on 18th March 1965 (in this Act called 'the Convention').

(2)   A person seeking recognition or enforcement of such an award shall be entitled to have the award registered in the High Court subject to proof of the prescribed matters and to the other provisions of this Act.

(3)   Where any pecuniary obligation imposed by the award is expressed in a currency other than the currency of the United Kingdom, the award shall be registered as if that obligation were expressed in the currency of the United Kingdom converted on the basis of the rate of exchange prevailing at the date when the award was rendered pursuant to the Convention.

(4)   In addition to the pecuniary obligations imposed by the award, the award shall be registered for the reasonable costs of and incidental to registration.

(5)   If at the date of the application for registration the pecuniary obligations imposed by the award have been partly satisfied, the award shall be registered only in respect of the balance, and accordingly if those obligations have been wholly satisfied, the award shall not be registered.

(6)   Rules of court may—

(a)   prescribe the procedure for applying for registration under this section, and require an applicant to give prior notice of his intention to other parties,

(b)   prescribe the matters to be proved on the application and the manner of proof, and in particular require the applicant to furnish a copy of the award certified pursuant to the Convention, and

(c)   provide for the service of notice of registration of the award by the applicant on other parties.

(7)   For the purposes of this section and section 2, an award shall be deemed to have been rendered pursuant to the Convention on the date on which certified copies of the award were pursuant to the Convention dispatched to the parties.

(8)   This section and section 2 shall bind the Crown (but not so as to make an award enforceable against the Crown in a manner in which a judgment would not be enforceable against the Crown).

2. Effect of registration.

(1)   Subject to the provisions of this Act, an award registered under section 1 shall, as respects the pecuniary obligations which it imposes, be of the same force and effect for the purposes of execution as if it had been a judgment of the High Court given when the award was rendered pursuant to the Convention and entered on the date of registration under this Act, and, so far as relates to such pecuniary obligations—
(a)   proceedings may be taken on the award,
(b)   the sum for which the award is registered shall carry interest, and
(c)   the High Court shall have the same control over the execution of the award,
as if the award had been such a judgment of the High Court.

(2)   Rules of court may contain provisions requiring the court on proof of the prescribed matters to stay execution of any award registered under this Act so as to take account of cases where enforcement of the award has been stayed (whether provisionally or otherwise) pursuant to the Convention, and may provide for the provisional stay of execution of the award where an application is made pursuant to the Convention which, if granted, might result in a stay of enforcement of the award.

Procedural provisions

3. Application of Arbitration Act 1976.

(1)   The Clerk of the Rolls may by order direct that any of the provisions contained in section 13 of the Arbitration Act 1976 (attendance of witnesses, production of documents, etc.) shall apply to such proceedings pursuant to the Convention as are specified in the order, with or without any modifications or exceptions specified in the order.

(2)   Subject to subsection (1), the Arbitration Act 1976 shall not apply to proceedings pursuant to the Convention, but this subsection shall not be taken as affecting section 4 of the said Act (stay of proceedings).

Immunities and privileges

4. Status, immunities and privileges conferred by the Convention.

(1)   Articles 18 to 20, 21(a) (with article 22 as it applies article 21(a)), 23(1) and 24 of the Convention (which confer status, immunities and privileges on the Centre and certain other persons, and are set out in the Schedule) shall have the force of law in the Island.

(2)   Nothing in article 24(1) of the Convention as given the force of law by this section shall be construed as—

(a)   entitling the Centre to import goods free of customs duty without any restriction on their subsequent sale in the country to which they were imported, or

(b)   conferring on the Centre any exemption from duties or taxes which form part of the price of goods sold, or

(c)   conferring on the Centre any exemption from duties or taxes which are no more than charges for services rendered.

(3)   For the purposes of articles 20 and 21(a) of the Convention as given the force of law by this section, a statement to the effect that the Centre has waived an immunity in the circumstances specified in the statement, being a statement certified by the Secretary-General of the Centre (or by the person acting as Secretary-General), shall be conclusive evidence.

Supplemental

5.   Interpretation.

In this Act—

'award' includes any decision interpreting, revising or annulling an award, being a decision pursuant to the Convention, and any decision as to the costs which under the Convention is to form part of the award;

'the Centre' means the International Centre for Settlement of Investment Disputes established by the Convention;

'the Convention' means the convention referred to in section 1(1);

'prescribed' means prescribed by rules of court.

6.   Short title and commencement.

(1)   This Act may be cited as the Arbitration (International Investment Disputes) Act 1983.

(2)   This Act shall come into force on such day as the Governor in Council may by order appoint.

Section 4   SCHEDULE

SECTION 6 OF THE CONVENTION AS GIVEN THE FORCE OF LAW

Status, Immunities and Privileges

Article 18

The Centre shall have full international legal personality. The legal capacity of the Centre shall include the capacity—

(a)   to contact;

(b)   to acquire and dispose of movable and immovable property;

(c)   to institute legal proceedings.

Article 19

To enable the Centre to fulfil its functions, it shall enjoy in the territories of each Contracting State the immunities and privileges set forth in this Section.

Article 20

The Centre, its property and assets shall enjoy immunity from all legal processes, except when the Centre waives this immunity.

Article 21

The Chairman, the members of the Administrative Council, persons acting as conciliators or arbitrators or members of a Committee appointed pursuant to paragraph (3) of Article 52, and the officers and employees of the Secretariat—

(a) shall enjoy immunity from legal process with respect to acts performed by them in the exercise of their functions, except when the Centre waives this immunity;

(b) . . .

Article 22

The provisions of Article 21 shall apply to persons appearing in proceedings under this Convention as parties, agents, counsel, advocates, witnesses or experts; . . .

Article 23

(1) The archives of the Centre shall be inviolable, wherever they may be.

(2) . . .

Article 24

(1) The Centre, its assets, property and income, and its operations and transactions authorised by this Convention shall be exempt from all taxation and customs duties. The Centre shall also be exempt from liability for the collection or payment of any taxes or customs duties.

(2) Except in the case of local nationals, no tax shall be levied on or in respect of expense allowances paid by the Centre to the Chairman or members of the Administrative Council, or on or in respect of salaries, expense allowances or other emoluments paid by the Centre to officials or employees of the Secretariat.

(3) No tax shall be levied on or in respect of fees or expense allowances received by persons acting as conciliators, or arbitrators, or members of the Committee appointed pursuant to paragraph (3) of Article 52, in proceedings under this Convention, if the sole jurisdictional basis for such tax is the location of the Centre or the place where such proceedings are conducted or the place where such fees or allowances are paid.

I.5 JERSEY

ARBITRATION (INTERNATIONAL INVESTMENT DISPUTES) (JERSEY) ORDER 1979
(SI 1979, No. 572)

Her Majesty, in exercise of the powers conferred upon Her by section 6 of the Arbitration (International Investment Disputes) Act 1966, is pleased, by and with the advice of Her Privy Council, to order, and it is hereby ordered as follows:—

1. This Order may be cited as the Arbitration (International Investment Disputes) (Jersey) Order 1979 and shall come into operation on 1st July 1979.

2. The provisions of the Arbitration (International Investment Disputes) Act 1966 shall extend to the Bailiwick of Jersey subject to the exceptions, adaptations and modifications specified in the Schedule to this Order.

SCHEDULE

EXCEPTIONS, ADAPTATIONS AND MODIFICATIONS IN THE EXTENTION OF THE ARBITRATION (INTERNATIONAL INVESTMENT DISPUTES) ACT 1966 TO THE BAILIWICK OF JERSEY

1.—(1) In section 1(2), for the reference to the High Court there shall be substituted a reference to the Royal Court.

(2) In section 1(6), for the words 'to make rules of court under section 99 of the Supreme Court of Judicature (Consolidation) Act 1925', there shall be substituted the words 'of the Royal Court to make rules of court under Article 11 of the Royal Court (Jersey) Law 1948'.

(3) Section 1(8) shall be omitted.

2.—(1) In section 2(1), for any reference to the High Court, there shall be substituted a reference to the Royal Court.

(2) In section 2(2), for the words 'Rules of court under section 99 of the Supreme Court of Judicature (Consolidation) Act 1925', there shall be substituted the words 'Rules of court made by the Royal Court under Article 11 of the Royal Court (Jersey) Law 1948'.

3. For section 3 there shall be substituted the following section:—

'Proceedings in the Bailiwick of Jersey

3.—(1) The power of the Royal Court to make rules of court under Article 11 of the Royal Court (Jersey) Law 1948, as extended by this Act, shall include power to make provision, in relation to such proceedings pursuant to the Convention as are specified in the rules of court, for the attendance of witnesses, the taking of evidence and the production of documents.

(2) Such rules of court may contain provisions directing that Part II of the Service of Process and Taking of Evidence (Jersey) Law 1960 (which relates to the taking of evidence in Jersey for the purpose of proceedings

before courts and tribunals outside Jersey) shall apply to such proceedings pursuant to the Convention as are specified in the rules of court, with or without any modifications or exceptions specified in the rules of court.'

4.   Section 5, 6, 7, 8 and 9(2) shall be omitted.

EXPLANATORY NOTE

(This Note is not part of the Order.)

This Order extends to the Bailiwick of Jersey, with exceptions, adaptations and modifications, the provisions of the Arbitration (International Investment Disputes) Act 1966. The Act implements the Convention on the settlement of investment disputes between States and nationals of other States which was opened for signature in Washington on 18th March 1965.

I.6   UNITED KINGDOM OF GREAT BRITAIN AND NORTHERN IRELAND

I.6.1   England

BOARD OF TRADE ARBITRATIONS, &c. ACT 1874
(1874, c. 40)

This Act is not necessarily in the form in which it has effect in Northern Ireland.

An Act to amend the powers of the Board of Trade with respect to inquiries, arbitrations, appointments, and other matters under special Acts, and to amend the Regulation of Railways Act 1873, so far as regards the reference of differences to the Railway Commissioners in lieu of Arbitrators.   [30th July 1874]

Preliminary

1.   Short title.

This Act may be cited as 'The Board of Trade Arbitrations, &c. Act 1874.'

PART I

Board of Trade Inquiries, &c.

2.   Power of Board of Trade as to inquiry.

Where, under the provisions of any special Act, passed either before or after the passing of this Act, the Board of Trade are required, or authorised to sanction, approve, confirm, or determine any appointment, matter, or thing, or to make any order or to do any other act or thing for the purposes of such a special Act, the Board of Trade may make such inquiry as they may think necessary for the purpose of enabling them to comply with such requisition or exercise such authority.

Where an inquiry is held by the Board of Trade for the purposes of this section, or in pursuance of any general or special Act passed either before or after the passing of this Act, directing or authorising them to hold any inquiry, the Board of Trade may hold such inquiry by any person or persons duly authorised in that behalf by an order of the Board of Trade, and such inquiry if so held shall be deemed to be duly held.

3. Expenses connected with arbitration, sanction, &c.

Where application is made in pursuance of any special Act passed either before or after the passing of this Act, to the Board of Trade to be arbitrators, or to appoint any arbitrator, referee, engineer, or other person, or to hold any inquiry, or to sanction, approve, confirm, or determine, any appointment, matter, or thing, or to make any order, or to do any other act or thing for the purposes of such special Act, all expenses incurred by the Board of Trade in relation to such application and the proceedings consequent thereon, shall, to such amount as the Board of Trade may certify by their order to be due, be defrayed by the parties to such application, and (subject to any provision contained in the said special Act) shall be defrayed by such of the parties as the Board of Trade may by order direct, or if so directed by an order of the Board of Trade shall be paid as costs of the arbitration or reference.

The Board of Trade may, if they think fit, on or at any time after the making the application, by order require the parties to the application, or any of them, to pay to the Board of Trade such sum as the Board of Trade think requisite for or on account of those expenses, or to give security to the satisfaction of the Board of Trade for the payment of those expenses on demand, and if such payment or security is not made or given may refuse to act in pursuance of the application.

All expenses directed by an order of the Board of Trade or an award in pursuance of this section to be paid may be recovered in any court of competent jurisdiction as a debt, and if payable to the Board of Trade, as a debt to the Crown; and an order of the Board of Trade shall be conclusive evidence of the amount of such expenses.

4. Meaning of 'special Act'.

In this part of this Act the term 'special Act' means a local or local and personal Act, or an Act of a local and personal nature, and includes a provisional order of the Board of Trade confirmed by Act of Parliament and a certificate granted by the Board of Trade under the Railways Construction Facilities Act 1864.

5–8. [*Sections repealed.*]

ARBITRATION ACT 1950
(1950, c. 27)

An Act to consolidate the Arbitration Acts, 1889 to 1934.   [28th July 1950]

PART I

GENERAL PROVISIONS AS TO ARBITRATION

[This Part is to be repealed by the Arbitration Act 1996, sch. 4.]

Effect of Arbitration Agreements, etc.

1. Authority of arbitrators and umpires to be irrevocable.

The authority of an arbitrator or umpire appointed by or by virtue of an arbitration agreement shall, unless a contrary intention is expressed in the agreement, be irrevocable except by leave of the High Court or a judge thereof.

2. Death of party.

(1) An arbitration agreement shall not be discharged by the death of any party thereto, either as respects the deceased or any other party, but shall in such an event be enforceable by or against the personal representative of the deceased.

(2) The authority of an arbitrator shall not be revoked by the death of any party by whom he was appointed.

(3) Nothing in this section shall be taken to affect the operation of any enactment or rule of law by virtue of which any right of action is extinguished by the death of a person.

3. Bankruptcy.

(1) Where it is provided by a term in a contract to which a bankrupt is a party that any differences arising thereout or in connection therewith shall be referred to arbitration, the said term shall, if the trustee in bankruptcy adopts the contract, be enforceable by or against him so far as relates to any such differences.

(2) Where a person who has been adjudged bankrupt had, before the commencement of the bankruptcy, become a party to an arbitration agreement, and any matter to which the agreement applies requires to be determined in connection with or for the purposes of the bankruptcy proceedings, then, if the case is one to which subsection (1) of this section does not apply, any other party to the agreement or, with the consent of the [creditors' committee established under section 301 of the Insolvency Act 1986], the trustee in bankruptcy, may apply to the court having jurisdiction in the bankruptcy proceedings for an order directing that the matter in question shall be referred to arbitration in accordance with the agreement, and that court may, if it is of opinion that, having regard to all the circumstances of the case, the matter ought to be determined by arbitration, make an order accordingly.

[Substituted by the Insolvency Acts 1985, 1986.]

4. Staying court proceedings where there is submission to arbitration.

(1) If any party to an arbitration agreement, or any person claiming through or under him, commences any legal proceedings in any court against any other party to the agreement, or any person claiming through or under him, in respect of any matter agreed to be referred, any party to those legal proceedings may at any time after appearance, and before delivering any pleadings or taking any other steps in the proceedings, apply to that court to stay the proceedings, and that court or a judge thereof, if satisfied that there is no sufficient reason, why the matter should not be referred in accordance with the agreement, and that the applicant was, at the time when the proceedings were commenced, and still remains, ready and willing to do all things necessary to the proper conduct of the arbitration, may make an order staying the proceedings.

(2) [*Repealed by the Arbitration Act 1975, s. 8(2)(a).*]

5. Reference of interpleader issues to arbitration.

Where relief by way of interpleader is granted and it appears to the High Court that the claims in question are matters to which an arbitration agreement, to which the claimants are parties, applies, the High Court may direct the issue between the claimants to be determined in accordance with the agreement.

Arbitrators and Umpires

6. When reference is to a single arbitrator.

Unless a contrary intention is expressed therein, every arbitration agreement shall, if no other mode of reference is provided, be deemed to include a provision that the reference shall be to a single arbitrator.

7. Power of parties in certain cases to supply vacancy.

Where an arbitration agreement provides that the reference shall be two arbitrators, one to be appointed by each party, then, unless a contrary intention is expressed therein—

(a) if either of the appointed arbitrators refuses to act, or is incapable of acting, or dies, the party who appointed him may appoint a new arbitrator in his place;

(b) if, on such a reference, one party fails to appoint an arbitrator, either originally, or by way of substitution as foresaid, for seven clear days after the other party, having appointed his arbitrator, has served the party making default with notice to make the appointment, the party who has appointed an arbitrator may appoint that arbitrator to act as sole arbitrator in the reference and his award shall be binding on both parties as if he had been appointed by consent:

Provided that the High Court or a judge thereof may set aside any appointment made in pursuance of this section.

8. Umpires.

(1)   Unless a contrary intention is expressed therein, every arbitration agreement shall, where the reference is to two, arbitrators, be deemed to include provision that the two arbitrators may appoint an umpire at any time after they are themselves appointed and shall do so forthwith if they cannot agree.
[*Amended by the Arbitration Act 1979 s. 6(1).*]

(2)   Unless a contrary intention is expressed therein, every arbitration agreement shall, where such a provision is applicable to the reference, be deemed to include a provision that if the arbitrators have delivered to any party to the arbitration agreement, or to the umpire, a notice in writing stating that they cannot agree, the umpire may forthwith enter on the reference in lieu of the arbitrators.

(3)   At any time after the appointment of an umpire, however appointed, the High Court may, on the application of any party to the reference and notwithstanding anything to the contrary in the arbitration agreement, order that the umpire shall enter upon the reference in lieu of the arbitrators and as if he were a sole arbitrator.

[9.   Majority award of three arbitrators.

Unless the contrary intention is expressed in the arbitration agreement, in any case where there is a reference to three arbitrators, the award of any two of the arbitrators shall be binding.]
[*Substituted by the Arbitration Act 1979, s. 6(2).*]

10.   Power of court in certain cases to appoint an arbitrator or umpire.

In any of the following cases—
    (a)   where an arbitration agreement provides that the reference shall be to a single arbitrator, and all the parties do not, after differences have arisen, concur in the appointment of an arbitrator;
    (b)   if an appointed arbitrator refuses to act, or is incapable of acting or dies, and the arbitration agreement does not show that it was intended that the vacancy should not be supplied and the parties do not supply the vacancy;
    (c)   where the parties or two arbitrators are required or are at liberty to appoint an umpire or third arbitrator and do not appoint him;
[*Section 10(c) amended by the Arbitration Act 1979, s. 6(3).*]
    (d)   where an appointed umpire or third arbitrator refuses to act, or is incapable of acting, or dies, and the arbitration agreement does not show that it was intended that the vacancy should not be supplied, and the parties or arbitrators do not supply the vacancy;
any party may serve the other parties or the arbitrators, as the case may be, with a written notice to appoint or, as the case may be, concur in appointing, an arbitrator, umpire or third arbitrator, and if the appointment is not made within seven clear days after the service of the notice, the High Court or a judge thereof may, on application by the party who gave the notice, appoint an arbitrator, umpire or third arbitrator who shall have the like powers to act

in the reference and make an award as if he had been appointed by consent of all parties.

[(2)   In any case where—

(a)   an arbitration agreement provides for the appointment of an arbitrator or umpire by a person who is neither one of the parties nor an existing arbitrator (whether the provision applies directly or in default of agreement by the parties or otherwise), and

(b)   that person refuses to make the appointment or does not make it within the time specified in the agreement or, if no time is so specified, within a reasonable time,

any party to the agreement may serve the person in question with a written notice to appoint an arbitrator or umpire and, if the appointment is not made within seven clear days after the service of the notice, the High Court or a judge thereof may, on the application of the party who gave the notice, appoint an arbitrator or umpire who shall have the like powers to act in the reference and make an award as if he had been appointed in accordance with the terms of the agreement.

[*Section 10(2) added by the Arbitration Act 1979 s. 6(4).*]

[(3)   In any case where—

(a)   an arbitration provides that the reference shall be to three arbitrators, one to be appointed by each party and the third to be appoted by the two appointed parties or in some other manner specified in the agreement; and

(b)   one of the parties ('the party in default') refuses to appoint an arbitrator or does not do so within the time specified in the agreement or, if no time is specified, within a reasonable time,

the other party to the agreement, having appointed his arbitrator, may serve the party in default with a written notice to appoint an arbitrator.

(3A)   A notice under subsection (3) must indicate whether it is served for the purposes of subsection (3B) or for the purposes of subsection (3C).

(3B)   Where a notice is served for the purposes of this subsection, then unless a contrary intention is expressed in the agreement, if the required appointment is not made within seven clear days after the service of the notice—

(a)   the party who gave the notice may appoint his arbitrator to act as sole arbitrator in the reference; and

(b)   his award shall be binding on both parties as if he had been appointed by consent.

(3C)   Where a notice is served for the purposes of this subsection, then, if the required appointment is not made within seven clear days after the service of the notice, the High Court or a judge thereof may, on the application of the party who gave the notice, appoint an arbitrator on behalf of the party in default who shall have the like powers to act in the reference and make an award (and, if the case so requires, the like duty in relation to the appointment of a third arbitrator) as if he had been appointed in accordance with the terms of the agreement.

(3D)   The High Court or a judge thereof may set aside any appoinment made by virtue of subsection (3B).]

[*Section 10(3) substituted by the Courts and Legal Services Act 1990, s. 101.*]

[11. Power of official referee to take arbitrations.

(1)   An official referee may, if in all the circumstances he thinks fit, accept appointment as sole arbitrator, or as umpire, by or by virtue of an arbitration agreement.

(2)   An official referee shall not accept appointment as arbitrator or umpire unless the Lord Chief Justice has informed him that, having regard to the state of official referees' business, he can be made available to do so.

(3)   The fees payable for the services of an official referee as arbitrator or umpire shall be taken in the High Court.

(4)   Schedule 3 to the Administration of Justice Act 1970 (which modifies this Act in relation to arbitration by judges, in particular by substituting the Court of Appeal for the High Court in provisions whereby arbitrators and umpires, their proceedings and awards are subject to control and review by the court) shall have effect in relation to official referees appointed as arbitrators or umpires as it has effect in relation to judge-arbitrators and judge-umpires (within the meaning of that Schedule).

(5)   Any jurisdiction which is exercisable by the High Court in relation to arbitrators and umpires otherwise than under this Act shall, in relation to an official referee appointed as arbitrator or umpire, be exercisable instead by the Court of Appeal.

(6)   In this section 'official referee' means any person nominated under section 68(1)(a) of the Supreme Court Act 1981 to deal with official referees' business.

(7)   Rules of the Supreme Court may make provision for—

(a)   cases in which it is necessary to allocate references made under or by virtue of arbitration agreements to official referees;

(b)   the transfer of references from one official referee to another.]

[*Section 11 substituted by the Courts and Legal Services Act 1990, s. 99.*]

Conduct of Proceedings, Witnesses, etc.

12. Conduct of proceedings, witnesses, etc.

(1)   Unless a contrary intention is expressed therein, every arbitration agreement shall, where such a provision is applicable to the reference, be deemed to contain a provision that the parties to the reference, and all persons claiming through them respectively, shall, subject to any legal objection, submit to be examined by the arbitrator or umpire, on oath or affirmation, in relation to the matters in dispute, and shall, subject as aforesaid, produce before the arbitrator or umpire all documents within their possession or power respectively which may be required or called for, and do all other things which during the proceedings on the reference the arbitrator or umpire may require.

(2)   Unless a contrary intention is expressed therein, every arbitration agreement shall, where such a provision is applicable to the reference, be deemed to contain a provision that the witnesses on the reference shall, if the arbitrator or umpire thinks fit, be examined on oath or affirmation.

(3)   An arbitrator or umpire shall, unless a contrary intention is expressed in the arbitration agreement, have power to administer oaths to, or take the

affirmations of, the parties to and witnesses on a reference under the agreement.

(4)   Any party to a reference under an arbitration agreement may sue out a writ of subpoena and testificandum or a writ of subpoena duces tecum, but no person shall be compelled under any such writ to produce any such document which he could not be compelled to produce on the trial of an action, and the High Court or a judge thereof may order that a writ of subpoena ad testificandum or of subpoena duces tecum shall issue to compel the attendance before an arbitrator or umpire of a witness wherever he may be within the United Kingdom.

(5)   The High Court or a judge thereof may also order that a writ of habeas corpus ad testificandum shall issue to bring up a prisoner for examination before an arbitrator or umpire.

(6)   The High Court shall have, for the purpose of and in relation to a reference, the same power of making orders in respect of—

(a)   security for costs;

(b)   [repealed by the Courts and Legal Services Act 1990, s. 103]

(c)   the giving of evidence by affidavit;

(d)   examination on oath of any witness before an officer of the High Court or any other person, and the issue of a commission or request for the examination of a witness out of the jurisdiction;

(e)   the preservation, interim custody or sale of any goods which are the subject matter of the reference;

(f)   securing the amount in dispute in the reference;

(g)   the detention, preservation or inspection of any property or thing which is the subject of the reference or as to which any question may arise therein, and authorising for any of the purposes aforesaid any persons to enter upon or into any land or building in the possession of any party to the reference, or authorising any samples to be taken or any observation to be made or experiment to be tried which may be necessary or expedient for the purpose of obtaining full information or evidence; and

(h)   interim injunctions or the appointment of a receiver;

as it has for the purpose of and in relation to an action or matter in the High Court;

Provided that nothing in this subsection shall be taken to prejudice any power which may be vested in an arbitrator or umpire of making orders with respect to any of the matters aforesaid.

Provisions as to Awards

13.   Time for making award.

(1)   Subject to the provisions of subsection (2) of section twenty-two of this Act, and anything to the contrary in the arbitration agreement, an arbitrator or umpire shall have power to make an award at any time.

(2)   The time, if any, limited for making an award, whether under this Act or otherwise, may from time to time be enlarged by order of the High Court or a judge thereof, whether that time has expired or not.

(3)   The High Court may, on the application of any party to a reference, remove an arbitrator or umpire who fails to use all reasonable dispatch in

entering on and proceeding with the reference and making an award, and an arbitrator or umpire who is removed by the High Court under this subsection shall not be entitled to receive any remuneration in respect of his services.

For the purposes of this subsection, the expression 'proceeding with a reference' includes, in a case where two arbitrators are unable to agree, giving notice of the fact to the parties and to the umpire.

[13A.   Want of prosecution.

(1)   Unless a contrary intention is expressed in the arbitration agreement, the arbitrator or umpire shall have power to make and award dismissing any claim in a dispute referred to him if it appears to him that the conditions mentioned in subsection (2) are satisfied.

(2)   The conditions are—

(a)   that there has been inordinate and inexcusable delay on the part of the claimant in pursuing the claim; and

(b)   that the delay—

(i)   will give rise to a substantial risk that it is not possible to have a fair resolution of the issues in that claim; or

(ii)   has caused, or is likely to cause or to have caused, serious prejudice to the respondent.

(3)   For the purpose of keeping the provision made by this section and the corresponding provision which applies in relation to proceedings in the High Court in step, the Secretary of State may by order made by statutory instrument amend subsection (2) above.

(4)   Before making any such order the Secretary of State shall consult the Lord Chancellor and such other persons as he considers appropriate.

(5)   No such order shall be made unless a draft of the order has been laid before, and approved by resolution of, each House of Parliament.]

[*Section 13A inserted by the Courts and Legal Services Act 1990, s. 102.*]

14.   Interim awards.

Unless a contrary intention is expressed therein, every arbitration agreement shall, where such a provision is applicable to the reference, be deemed to contain a provision that the arbitrator or umpire may, if he thinks fit, make an interim award, and any reference in this Part of the Act to an award includes a reference to an interim award.

15.   Specific performance.

Unless a contrary intention is expressed therein, every arbitration agreement shall, where such a provision is applicable to the reference, be deemed to contain a provision that the arbitrator or umpire shall have the same power as the High Court to order specific performance of any contract other than a contract relating to land or any interest in land.

16.   Awards to be final.

Unless a contrary intention is expressed therein, every arbitration agreement shall, where such a provision is applicable to the reference, be deemed to contain a provision that the award to be made by the arbitrator or umpire shall be final and binding on the parties and the persons claiming under them respectively.

17. Power to correct slips.

Unless a contrary intention is expressed in the arbitration agreement, the arbitrator or umpire shall have power to correct in an award any clerical mistake or error arising from any accidental slip or omission.

Costs, Fees and Interest

18. Costs.

(1) Unless a contrary intention is expressed therein, every arbitration agreement shall be deemed to include a provision that the costs of the reference and award shall be in the discretion of the arbitrator or umpire, who may direct to and by whom and in what manner those costs or any part thereof shall be paid, and may tax or settle the amount of costs to be so paid or any part thereof, and may award costs to be paid as between solicitor and client.

(2) Any costs directed by an award to be paid shall, unless the award otherwise directs, be taxable in the High Court.

(3) Any provision in an arbitration agreement to the effect that the parties or any party thereto shall in any event pay their or his own costs of the reference or award or any part thereof shall be void, and this Part of this Act, shall in the case of an arbitration agreement containing any such provision, have effect as if that provision were not contained therein:

Provided that nothing in this subsection shall invalidate such a provision when it is a part of an agreement to submit to arbitration a dispute which has arisen before the making of that agreement.

(4) If no provision is made by an award with respect to the costs of the reference, any party to the reference may, within fourteen days of the publication of the award or such further time as the High Court or a judge thereof may direct, apply to the arbitrator for an order directing by and to whom those costs shall be paid, and thereupon the arbitration shall, after hearing any party who may desire to be heard, amend his award by adding thereto such directions as he may think proper with respect to the payment of the costs of the reference.

(5) Section sixty-nine of the Solicitors Act 1932 (which empowers a court before which any proceeding is being heard or is pending to charge property recovered or preserved in the proceeding with the payment of solicitors' costs) shall apply as if an arbitration were a proceeding in the High Court and the High Court may make declarations and orders accordingly.

19. Taxation of arbitrator's or umpire's fees.

(1) If in any case an arbitrator or umpire refuses to deliver his award except on payment of the fees demanded by him, the High Court may, on application for the purpose, order that the arbitration or umpire shall deliver

the award to the applicant on payment into court by the applicant of the fees demanded, and further that the fees demanded shall be taxed by the taxing officer and that out of the money paid into court there shall be paid out to the arbitrator or umpire by way of fees such sums as may be found reasonable on taxation and that the balance of the money, if any, shall be paid out to the applicant.

(2)   An application for the purpose of this section may be made by any party to the reference unless the fees demanded have been fixed by a written agreement between him and the arbitrator or umpire.

(3)   A taxation of fees under this section may be reviewed in the same manner as a taxation of costs.

(4)   The arbitrator or umpire shall be entitled to appear and be heard on any taxation or review of taxation under this section.

[19A.   Power of arbitrator to award interest.

(1)   Unless a contrary intention is expressed therein, every arbitration agreement shall, where such a provision is applicable to the reference, be deemed to contain a provision that the arbitrator or umpire may, if he thinks fit, award simple interest at such rate as he thinks fit—

(a)   on any sum which is the subject of the reference but which is paid before the award, for such period ending not later than the date of the payment as he thinks fit; and

(b)   on any sum which he awards, for such period ending not later than the date of the award as he thinks fit.

(2)   The power to award interest conferred on an arbitrator or umpire by subsection (1) above is without prejudice to any other power of an arbitrator or umpire to award interest.]

[*Section 19A added by the Administration of Justice Act 1982.*]

20.   Interest on awards.

A sum directed to be paid by an award shall, unless the award otherwise directs, carry interest as from the date of that award and at the same rate as a judgment debt.

Special Cases, Remission and Setting aside of Awards, etc.

21.   Statement of case. [*Repealed by Arbitration Act 1979, s. 8(3)(b)*]

22.   Power to remit award.

(1)   In all cases of reference to arbitration the High Court or a judge thereof may from time to time remit the matters referred, or any of them, to the reconsideration of the arbitrator or umpire.

(2)   Where an award is remitted, the arbitrator or umpire shall, unless the order otherwise directs, make his award within three months after the date of the order.

23. Removal of arbitrator and setting aside of award.

(1)   Where an arbitrator or umpire has misconducted himself or the proceedings, the High Court may remove him.

(2)   Where an arbitrator or umpire has misconducted himself or the proceedings, or an arbitration or award has been improperly procured the High Court may set the award aside.

(3)   Where an application is made to set aside an award, the High Court may order that any money made payable by the award shall be brought into court or otherwise secured pending the determination of the application.

24. Power of court to give relief where arbitrator is not impartial or the dispute involves question of fraud.

(1)   Where an agreement between any parties provides that disputes which may arise in the future between them shall be referred to an arbitrator named or designated in the agreement, and after a dispute has arisen any party applies, on the ground that the arbitrator so named or designated is not or may not be impartial, for leave to revoke the authority of the arbitrator or for an injunction to restrain any other party or the arbitrator from proceeding with the arbitrator, it shall not be a ground for refusing the application that the said party at the time when he made the agreement knew, or ought to have known, that the arbitrator, by reason of his relation towards any other party to the agreement or of his connection with the subject referred, might not be capable of impartiality.

(2)   Where an agreement between any parties provided that disputes which may arise in the future between them shall be referred to arbitration, and a dispute which so arises involves the question whether any such party has been guilty of fraud, the High Court shall, so far as may be necessary to enable that question to be determined by the High Court, have power to order that the agreement shall cease to have effect and power to give leave to revoke the authority of any arbitrator or umpire appointed by or by virtue of the agreement.

(3)   In any case where by virtue of this section the High Court has power to order that an arbitration agreement shall cease to have effect or to give leave to revoke the authority of an arbitrator or umpire the High Court may refuse to stay any action brought in breach of the agreement.

25. Power of court where arbitrator is removed or authority of arbitrator is revoked.

(1)   Where an arbitrator (not being a sole arbitrator), or two or more arbitrators (not being all the arbitrators) or an umpire who has not entered on the reference is or are removed by the High Court or the Court of Appeal, the High Court or the Court of Appeal as the case may be, may, on the application of any party to the arbitration agreement, appoint a person or persons to act as arbitrator or arbitrators or umpire in place of the person or persons so removed.

(2)   Where the authority of an arbitrator or arbitrators or umpire is revoked by leave of the High Court or the Court of Appeal, or a sole arbitrator or all the arbitrators or an umpire who has entered on the reference

is or are removed by the High Court or the Court of Appeal, the High Court or the Court of Appeal as the case may be, may, on the application of any party to the arbitration agreement, either—

(a)   appoint a person to act as sole arbitrator in place of the person or persons removed; or

(b)   order that the arbitration agreement shall cease to have effect with respect to the dispute referred.

(3)   A person appointed under this section by the High Court or the Court of Appeal as an arbitrator or umpire shall have the like power to act in the reference and to make an award as if he had been appointed in accordance with the terms of the arbitration agreement.

(4)   Where it is provided (whether by means of a provision in the arbitration agreement or otherwise) that an award under an arbitration agreement shall be a condition precedent to the bringing of an action with respect to any matter to which the agreement applies, the High Court or the Court of Appeal, if it orders (whether under this section or under any other enactment) that the agreement shall cease to have effect as regards any particular dispute, may further order that the provision making an award a condition precedent to the bringing of an action shall also cease to have effect as regards that dispute.

Enforcement of Award

26.   Enforcement of award.

(1)   An award on an arbitration agreement may, by leave of the High Court or a judge thereof, be enforced in the same manner as a judgment or order to the same effect, and where leave is so given, judgment may be entered in terms of the award.

[(2)   If—

(a)   the amount sought to be recovered does not exceed the current limit on jurisdiction in section 40 of the Country Courts Act 1959, and

(b)   a county court so orders,

it shall be recoverable (by execution issued from the court or otherwise) as if payable under an order of that court and shall not be enforceable under subsection (1) above.

(3)   An application to the High Court under this section shall preclude an application to a county court and an application to a county court under this section shall preclude an application to the High Court.]

[*Section 26(2) and (3) added by the Administration of Justice Act 1977, s. 18(2).*]

Miscellaneous

27.   Power of court to extend time for commencing arbitration proceedings.

Where the terms of an agreement to refer future disputes to arbitration provide that any claims to which the agreement applies shall be barred unless notice to appoint an arbitrator is given or an arbitrator is appointed or some other step to commence arbitration proceedings is taken within a time fixed by the agreement, and a dispute arises to which the agreement applies, the High Court, if it is of opinion that in the circumstances of the case undue hardship would otherwise be caused, and notwithstanding that the time so fixed has expired, may, on such terms, if any, as the justice of the case may require, but without prejudice to the provisions of any enactment limiting the time for the commencement of arbitration proceedings, extend the time for such period as it thinks proper.

28. Terms as to costs, etc.

Any costs made under this Part of this Act may be made on such terms as to costs or otherwise as the authority making the order thinks just.

29. Extension of section 496 of the Merchant Shipping Act 1894.

(1) In subsection (3) of section four hundred and ninty-six of the Merchant Shipping Act 1894 (which requires a sum deposited with a wharfinger by an owner of goods to be repaid unless legal proceedings are instituted by the shipowner), the expression 'legal proceedings' shall be deemed to include arbitration.

(2) For the purposes of the said section four hundred and ninety-six, as amended by this section, an arbitration shall be deemed to be commenced when one party to the arbitration agreement serves on the other party or parties a notice requiring him or them to appoint or concur in appointing an arbitrator, or, where the arbitration agreement provides that the reference shall be to a person named or designated in the agreement, requiring him or them to submit the dispute to the person so named or designated.

(3) Any such notice as is mentioned in subsection (2) of this section may be served either—

(a) by delivering it to the person on whom it is to be served; or

(b) by leaving it at the usual or last known place of abode in England of that person; or

(c) by sending it by post in a registered letter addressed to that person at his usual or last known place of abode in England;

as well as in any other manner provided in the arbitration agreement; and where a notice is sent by post in manner prescribed by paragraph (c) of this subsection, service thereof shall, unless the contrary is proved, be deemed to have been effected at the time at which the latter would have been delivered in the ordinary course of post.

30. Crown to be bound.

This part of this Act [. . .] shall apply to any arbitration to which his Majesty, either in right of the Crown or of the Duchy of Lancaster or otherwise, or the Duke of Cornwall, is a party.

31. Application of Part I to statutory arbitrations.

(1) Subject to the provisions of section thirty-three of this Act, this Part of this Act, except the provisions thereof specified in subsection (2) of this section, shall apply to every arbitration under any other Act (whether passed before or after the commencement of this Act) as if the arbitration were pursuant to an arbitration agreement and as if that other Act were an

arbitration agreement, except in so far as this Act is inconsistent with that other Act or with any rules or procedure authorised or recognised thereby.

(2) The provisions referred to in subsection (1) of this section are subsection (1) of section two, section three [*words deleted by the Arbitration Act 1975, s. 8(2)(d)*], section five, subsection (3) of section eighteen and sections twenty-four, twenty-five, twenty-seven and twenty-nine.

32. Meaning of 'arbitration agreement'.

In this Part of this Act, unless the context otherwise requires, the expression 'arbitration agreement' means a written agreement to submit present or future differences to arbitration, whether an arbitrator is named therein or not.

33. Operation of Part I.

This Part of this Act shall not affect any arbitration commenced (within the meaning of subsection (2) of section twenty-nine of this Act) before the commencement of this Act, but shall apply to an arbitration so commenced after the commencement of this Act under an agreement made before the commencement of this Act.

34. Extent of Part I.
[. . .] Save as aforesaid, none of the provisions of this Part of the Act shall extend to Scotland or Northern Ireland.

PART II

ENFORCEMENT OF CERTAIN FOREIGN AWARDS

35. Awards to which Part II applies.

(1) This Part of this Act applies to any award made after the twenty-eighth day of July, nineteen hundred and twenty-four—

(a) in pursuance of an agreement for arbitration to which the protocol set out in the First Schedule to this Act applies; and

(b) between persons of whom one is subject to the jurisdiction of some one of such Powers as His Majesty, being satisfied that reciprocal provisions have been made, may by Order in Council declare to be parties to the convention set out in the Second Schedule to this Act, and of whom the other is subject to the jurisdiction of some other of the Powers aforesaid; and

(c) in one of such territories as His Majesty, being satisfied that reciprocal provisions have been made, may by Order in Council declare to be territories to which the said convention applies;
and an award to which this Part of this Act applies in this Part of this Act referred to as 'a foreign award.'

(2) His Majesty may by a subsequent Order in Council vary or revoke any Order previously made under this section.

(3) Any Order in Council under section one of the Arbitration (Foreign Awards) Act 1930, which is in force at the commencement of this Act shall have effects as if it had been made under this section.

36. Effect of foreign awards.

(1)   A foreign award shall, subject to the provisions of this Part of this Act, be enforceable in England either by action or in the same manner as the award of an arbitrator is enforceable by virtue of section twenty-six of this Act.

[*Section 36(1) is to be amended by the Arbitration Act 1996, sch. 3(10).*]

(2)   Any foreign award which would be enforceable under this Part of this Act shall be treated as binding for all purposes on the persons as between whom it was made, and may accordingly be relied on by any of those persons by way of defence, set off or otherwise in any legal proceedings in England, and any references in this Part of this Act to enforcing a foreign award shall be construed as including references to relying on an award.

37. Conditions for enforcement of foreign awards.

(1)   In order that a foreign award may be enforceable under this part of this Act it must have—

(a)   been made in pursuance of an agreement for arbitration which was valid under the law by which it was governed;

(b)   been made by the tribunal provided for in the agreement or constituted in manner agreed upon by the parties;

(c)   been made in conformity with the law governing the arbitration procedure;

(d)   become final in the country in which it was made;

(e)   been in respect of a matter which may lawfully be referred to arbitration under the law of England;

and the enforcement thereof must not be contrary to the public policy or the law of England.

(2)   Subject to the provisions of this subsection, a foreign award shall not be enforceable under this Part of this Act if the court dealing with the case is satisfied that—

(a)   the award has been annulled in the country in which it was made; or

(b)   the party against whom it is sought to enforce the award was not given notice of the arbitration proceedings in sufficient time to enable him to present his case, or was under some legal incapacity and was not properly represented; or

(c)   the award does not deal with all the questions referred to or contains decisions on matters beyond the scope of the agreement for arbitration:

Provided that, if the award does not deal with all the questions referred, the court may, if it thinks fit, either postpone the enforcement of the award or order its enforcement subject to the giving of such security by the person seeking to enforce it as the court may think fit.

(3)   If a party seeking to resist the enforcement of a foreign award proves that there is any ground other than the non-existence of the conditions specified in paragraphs (a), (b), (c) of subsection (1) of this section, or the existence of the conditions specified in paragraphs (b) and (c) of subsection (2) of this section, entitling him to contest the validity of the award, the court may, if it thinks fit, either refuse to enforce the award or adjourn the hearing until after the expiration of such period as appears to the court to be

reasonably sufficient that party to take the necessary steps to have the award annulled by the competent tribunal.

38. Evidence.

(1) The party seeking to enforce a foreign award must produce—

(a) the original award or a copy thereof duly authenticated in manner required by the law of the country in which it was made; and

(b) evidence proving that the award has become final; and

(c) such evidence as may be necessary to prove that the award is a foreign award and that the conditions mentioned in paragraphs (a), (b), and (c) of subsection (1) of the last foregoing section are satisfied.

(2) In any case where any document required to be produced under subsection (1) of this section is in a foreign language, it shall be the duty of the party seeking to enforce the award to produce a translation certified as correct by a diplomatic or consular agent of the country to which that party belongs, or certified as correct in such other manner as may be sufficient according to the law of England.

(3) Subject to the provisions of this section, rules of court may be made under section [84 of the Supreme Court Act 1981] with respect to the evidence which must be furnished by a party seeking to enforce an award under this Part of this Act.

[*For Northern Ireland s. 38(3) reads:*

'(3) Subject to the provisions of this section, rules of the court may be made under section 55 of the Judicature (Northern Ireland) Act 1978 with respect to the evidence which must be furnished by a party seeking to enforce an award under this Part of this Act.'

substituted by the Judicature (Northern Ireland) Act 1978, s. 122(1), sch. 5, Pt. II.]

39. Meaning of 'final award'.

For the purposes of this Part of this Act, an award shall not be deemed final if any proceedings for the purpose of contesting the validity of the award are pending in the country in which it was made.

40. Saving for rights, etc.

Nothing in this Part of this Act shall—

(a) prejudice any rights which any person would have had of enforcing in England any award or of availing himself in England of any award if neither this Part of this Act nor Part I of the Arbitration (Foreign Awards) Act 1930 had been enacted; or

(b) apply to any award made on an arbitration agreement governed by the law of England.

41. Application of Part II to Scotland.

(1) The following provisions of this section shall have effect for the purpose of the application of this Part of this Act to Scotland.

(2)   For the references to England there shall be substituted references to Scotland.

(3)   For subsection (1) of section thirty-six there shall be substituted the following subsection:

'(1)   A foreign award shall, subject to the provisions of this Part of this Act, be enforceable by action, or, if the agreement for arbitration contains consent to the registration of the award in the Books of Council and Session for execution and the award is so registered, it shall, subject as aforesaid, be enforceable by summary diligence.'

(4)   For subsections (3) of section thirty-eight there shall be substituted the following subsection:

'(3)   The Court of Session shall, subject to the provisions of this section, have power to make provision by Act of Sederunt with respect to the evidence which must be furnished by a party seeking to enforce in Scotland an award under this Part of this Act.'

42.   Application of Part II to Northern Ireland.

(1)   The following provisions of this section shall have effect for the purpose of the application of this Part of this Act to Northern Ireland.

(2)   For the references to England there shall be substituted references to Northern Ireland.

(3)   For subsection (1) of section thirty-six there shall be substituted the following subsection:—

'(1)   A foreign award shall, subject to the provisions of this Part of this Act, be enforceable either by action or in thee same manner as the award of an arbitrator under the provisions of the Common Law Procedure Amendment Act (Ireland) 1856 was enforceable at the date of the passing of the Arbitration (Foreign Awards) Act 1930.'

[Section 42(3) to be repealed by the Arbitration Act 1996, sch. 4.]
    (4)   [Repealed by the Judicature (Northern Ireland) Act 1978, sch. 7.]

43.   Saving for pending proceedings.

[Repealed by the Statute Law (Repeals) Act 1978, sch. 1.]

PART III

GENERAL

44.   Short title, commencement and repeal.

(1)   This Act may be cited as the Arbitration Act 1950.

(2)   This Act shall come into operation on the first day of September, nineteen hundred and fifty.

(3)   The Arbitration Act 1889, the Arbitration Clauses (Protocol) Act 1924 and the Arbitration Act 1934 are hereby repealed except in relation to

arbitrations commenced (within the meaning of subsection (2) of section twenty-nine of this Act) before the commencement of this Act, and the Arbitration (Foreign Awards) Act 1930 is hereby repealed; and any reference in Act or other document to any enactment hereby repealed shall be construed as including a reference to the corresponding provision of this Act.

SCHEDULES

Sections 4, 35   FIRST SCHEDULE

PROTOCOL ON ARBITRATION CLAUSES SIGNED ON BEHALF OF HIS MAJESTY AT A MEETING OF THE LEAGUE OF NATIONS HELD ON THE TWENTY-FOURTH DAY OF SEPTEMBER, NINETEEN HUNDRED AND TWENTY-THREE

[Reproduced in Part V *International Documents* as *Geneva Protocol 1923.*]

Section 35   SECOND SCHEDULE

CONVENTION ON THE EXECUTION OF FOREIGN ARBITRAL AWARDS SIGNED AT GENEVA ON BEHALF OF HIS MAJESTY ON THE TWENTY-SIXTH DAY OF SEPTEMBER, NINETEEN HUNDRED AND TWENTY-SEVEN

[*Reproduced in Part V, International Documents as Geneva Convention 1927.*]

CARRIAGE BY AIR ACT 1961
(1961, c. 27)

An Act to give effect to the Convention concerning international carriage by air known as 'the Warsaw Convention as amended at The Hague, 1955', to enable the rules contained in that Convention to be applied, with or without modification, in other cases and, in particular, to non-international carriage by air; and for connected purposes.   [22nd June 1961]

SCHEDULES

FIRST SCHEDULE

THE WARSAW CONVENTION WITH THE AMENDMENTS MADE IN IT BY THE HAGUE PROTOCOL

PART I

THE ENGLISH TEXT

CONVENTION
FOR THE UNIFICATION OF CERTAIN RULES RELATING TO INTERNATIONAL CARRIAGE BY AIR

Article 28

(1)   An action for damages must be brought, at the option of the plaintiff, in the territory of one of the High Contracting Parties, either before the court

having jurisdiction where the carrier is ordinarily resident, or has his principal place of business, or has an establishment by which the contract has been made or before the court having jurisdiction at the place of destination.

(2) Questions of procedure shall be governed by the law of the court seised of the case.

Article 32

Any clause contained in the contract and all special agreements entered into before the damage occurred by which the parties purport to infringe the rules laid down by this Convention, whether by deciding the law to be applied, or by altering the rules to jurisdiction, shall be null and void. Nevertheless for the carriage of cargo arbitration clauses are allowed, subject to this Convention, if the arbitration is to take place within one of the jurisdictions referred to in the first paragraph of Article 28.

ARBITRATION (INTERNATIONAL INVESTMENT DISPUTES) ACT 1966
(1966, c. 41)

An Act to implement an international Convention on the settlement of investment disputes between States and nationals of other States.   [13th December 1966]

Enforcement of Convention Awards

1. Registration of Convention awards.

(1) This section has effect as respects awards rendered pursuant to the Convention on the settlement of investment disputes between States and nationals of other States which was opened for signature in Washington on 18th March 1965.

That Convention is in this Act called 'the Convention', and its text is set out in the Schedule to this Act.

(2) A person seeking recognition or enforcement of such an award shall be entitled to have the award registered in the High Court subject to proof of the prescribed matters and to the other provisions of this Act.

(3) [*Repealed by the Administration of Justice Act 1977.*]

(4) In addition to the pecuniary obligations imposed by the award, the award shall be registered for the reasonable costs of and incidental to registration.

(5) If at the date of the application for registration the pecuniary obligations imposed by the award have been partly satisfied, the award shall be registered only in respect of the balance, and accordingly if those obligations have then been wholly satisfied, the award shall not be registered.

(6) The power to make rules of court under section [84 of the Supreme Court Act 1981] shall include power —

(a) to prescribe the procedure for applying for registration under this section, and to require an applicant to give prior notice of his intention to other parties,

(b)   to prescribe the matters to be proved on the application and the manner of proof, and in particular to require the applicant to furnish a copy of the award certified pursuant to the Convention,

(c)   to provide for the service of notice of registration of the award by the applicant on other parties,

and in this and the next following section 'prescribed' means prescribed by rules of court.

(7)   For the purposes of this and the next following section—

(a)   'award' shall include any decision interpreting, revising or annulling an award, being a decision pursuant to the Convention, and any decision as to costs which under the Convention is to form part of the award,

(b)   an award shall be deemed to have been rendered pursuant to the Convention on the date on which certified copies of the award were pursuant to the Convention dispatched to the parties.

(8)   This and the next following section shall bind the Crown (but not so as to make an award enforceable against the Crown in a manner in which a judgment would not be enforceable against the Crown).

2.   Effect of registration.

(1)   Subject to the provisions of this Act, an award registered under section 1 above shall, as respects the pecuniary obligations which it imposes, be of the same force and effect for the purposes of execution as if it had been a judgment of the High Court given when the award was rendered pursuant to the Convention and entered on the date of registration under this Act, and, so far as relates to such pecuniary obligations —

(a)   proceedings may be taken on the award,

(b)   the sum for which the award is registered shall carry interest,

(c)   the High Court shall have the same control over the execution of the award,

as if the award had been such a judgment of the High Court.

(2)   Rules of court under section [84 of the Supreme Court Act 1981] may contain provisions requiring the court on proof of the prescribed matters to stay execution of any award registered under this Act so as to take account of cases where enforcement of the award has been stayed (whether provisionally or otherwise) pursuant to the Convention, and may provide for the provisional stay of execution of the award where an application is made pursuant to the Convention which, if granted, might result in a stay of enforcement of the award. [*Words in brackets substituted by the Supreme Court Act 1981, s. 152(1), sch. 5.*]

Procedural Provisions

3.   Application of Arbitration Act 1950 and other enactments.

[*Section 3 is to be amended by the Arbitration Act 1996, sch. 3(24).*]

(1)   The Lord Chancellor may by order direct that any of the provision contained in—

(a)   section 12 of the Arbitration Act 1950 (attendance of witnesses, production of documents, etc) or any corresponding enactments forming part of the law of Northern Ireland, [*Repealed by the Evidence (Proceedings in Other Jurisdictions) Act 1975.*]

(b) [*Repealed by the Evidence (Proceedings in Other Jurisdictions) Act 1975.*] shall apply to such proceedings pursuant to the Convention as are specified in the order, with or without any modifications or exceptions specified in the order.

(2)   Subject to subsection (1) above, neither the Arbitration Act 1950 nor the Arbitration Act (Northern Ireland) 1937 shall apply to proceedings pursuant to the Convention, but this subsection shall not be taken as affecting section 4(1) of the Arbitration Act 1950 (stay of court proceedings where there is submission to arbitration) or section 4 of the said Act of Northern Ireland.

(3)   An order made under this section—
(a)   may be varied or revoked by a subsequent order so made, and
(b)   shall be contained in a statutory instrument.

Immunities and Privileges

4.   Status, immunities and privileges conferred by the Convention.

(1)   In Section 6 of Chapter I of the Convention (which governs the status, immunities and privileges of the International Centre for Settlements of Investment Disputes established by the Convention, of members of its Council and Secretariat and of persons concerned with conciliation or arbitration under the Convention) Articles 18 to 20, Article 21(a) (with Article 22 as it applies Article 21(a)), Article 23(1) and Article 24 shall have the force of law.

(2)   Nothing in Article 24(1) of the Convention as given the force of law by this section shall be construed as—
(a)   entitling the said Centre to import goods free of customs duty without any restriction on their subsequent sale in the country to which they were imported, or
(b)   conferring on that Centre any exemption from duties or taxes which form part of the price of goods sold, or
(c)   conferring on that Centre any exemption from duties or taxes which are no more than charges for services rendered.

(3)   For the purposes of Article 20 and Article 21(a) of the Convention as given the force of law by this section, a statement to the effect that the said Centre has waived an immunity in the circumstances specified in the statement, being a statement certified by the Secretary-General of the said Centre (or by the person acting as Secretary-General), shall be conclusive evidence.

Supplemental

5.   Government contribution to expenses under the Convention.

The Treasury may discharge any obligations of Her Majesty's Government in the United Kingdom arising under Article 17 of the Convention (which obliges the Contracting States to meet any deficit of the International Centre for Settlement of Investment Disputes established under the Convention), and any sums required for that purpose shall be met out of money provided by Parliament.

6.   Application to British possessions, etc.

(1)   Her Majesty may by Order in Council direct that the provisions of this Act shall extend, with such exceptions, adaptations and modifications as may be specified in the Order, to—

(a)   the Isle of Man,

(b)   any of the Channel Islands,

(c)   any colony, or any country or place outside Her Majesty's dominions in which for the time being Her Majesty has jurisdiction, or any territory consisting partly of one or more colonies and partly of one or more such countries or places.

(2)   An Order in Council under this section—

(a)   may contain such transitional and other supplemental provisions as appear to Her Majesty to be expedient;

(b)   may be varied or revoked by a subsequent Order in Council under this section.

7.   Application to Scotland.

In the application of this Act to Scotland—

(a)   for any reference to the High Court there shall be substituted a reference to the Court of Session;

(b)   the Court of Session shall have power by Act of Sederunt to make rules for the purposes specified in section 1(6) and section 2(2) of this Act;

(c)   registration under section 1 of this Act shall be effected by registering in the Books of Council and Session, or in such manner as the Court of Session may by Act of Sederunt prescribe;

(d)   for any reference to the entering of a judgment there shall be substituted a reference to the signing of the interlocutor embodying the judgment;

(e)   for section 3 of this Act there shall be substituted the following section:

'3.   Proceedings in Scotland.

(1)   The Secretary of State may by order make provision, in relation to such proceedings pursuant to the Convention as are specified in the order, being proceedings taking place in Scotland, for the attendance of witnesses, the taking of evidence and the production of documents.

(2)   The Secretary of State may by order direct that the Foreign Tribunals Evidence Act 1856 (which relates to the taking of evidence in the United Kingdom for the purpose of proceedings before a foreign tribunal) shall apply to such proceedings pursuant to the Convention as are specified in the order, with or without any modifications or exceptions specified in the order.

(3)   An order made under this section —

(a)   may be varied or revoked by a subsequent order so made, and

(b)   shall be contained in a statutory instrument.';

and in any reference in this Act, or in the Convention as given the force of law in Scotland by this Act, to the staying of execution or enforcement of an award registered under this Act the expression 'stay' shall be construed as meaning sist.

8. Application to Northern Ireland.

In the application of this Act to Northern Ireland—
    (a) references to the High Court shall, unless the context otherwise requires, be construed as references to the High Court in Northern Ireland,
    (b) for the references to section 99 of the Supreme Court of Judicature (Consolidation) Act 1925 there shall be substituted references to [section 55 of the Judicature (Northern Ireland) Act 1978].
[*Words in brackets substituted by the Judicature (Northern Ireland) Act 1978, s. 122(1), sch. 5, Pt. II.*]

9. Short title and commencement.

(1) This Act may be cited as the Arbitration (International Investment Disputes) Act 1966.
(2) This Act shall come into force on such day as Her Majesty may by Order in Council certify to be the day on which the Convention comes into force as regards the United Kingdom.

Note: The Arbitration (International Investment Disputes) Act 1966 (Commencement) Order 1966, SI 1966, No. 1597 certified that the Convention came into force as regards the United Kingdom on 18 January 1967.

Section 1   SCHEDULE

TEXT OF CONVENTION

CONVENTION ON THE SETTLEMENT OF INVESTMENT DISPUTES BETWEEN STATES AND NATIONALS OF OTHER STATES

[*The Schedule is reproduced in Part V, International Documents as the Washington Convention 1965.*]

Note: The Arbitration (International Investment Disputes) Act (Application to Colonies etc) Order 1967 (SI 1967, No. 159) as amended (by SI 1967, No's 249 and 585) extends this Act to a large number of other territories.
    Of relevance to the jurisdictions considered here, the following Orders extend this Act as indicated:

— Arbitration (International Investment Disputes) (Guernsey) Order 1968 (SI 1968, No. 1199)
— Arbitration (International Investment Disputes) (Jersey) Order 1979 (SI 1979, No. 572).

(The Isle of Man has its own Act — of 1983.)

ARBITRATION ACT 1975
(1975, c. 3)

Note: This Act is to be repealed for England and for Northern Ireland. See Arbitration Act, 1996 s. 108(4).

An Act to give effect to the New York Convention on the Recognition and Enforcement of Foreign Arbitral Awards.   [25th February 1975]

Effect of arbitration agreement on court proceedings

1. Staying court proceedings where party proves arbitration agreement.

(1)   If any party to an arbitration agreement to which this section applies, or any person claiming through or under him, commences any legal proceedings in any court against any other party to the agreement, or any person claiming through or under him, in respect of any matter agreed to be referred, any party to the proceedings may at any time after appearance, and before delivering any pleadings or taking any other steps in the proceedings, apply to the court to stay the proceedings; and the court, unless satisfied that the arbitration agreement is null and void, inoperative or incapable of being performed or that there is not in fact any dispute between the parties with regard to the matter agreed to be referred, shall make an order staying the proceedings.

(2)   This section applies to any arbitration agreement which is not a domestic arbitration agreement; and neither section 4(1) of the Arbitration Act 1950 nor section 4 of the Arbitration Act (Northern Ireland) 1937 shall apply to an arbitration agreement to which this section applies.

(3)   In the application of this section to Scotland, for the references to staying proceedings there shall be substituted references to sisting proceedings.

(4)   In this section 'domestic arbitration agreement' means an arbitration agreement which does not provide, expressly or by implication, for arbitration in a State other than the United Kingdom and to which neither—

(a)   an individual who is a national of, or habitually resident in, any State other than the United Kingdom; nor

(b)   a body corporate which is incorporated in, or whose central management and control is exercised in, any State other than the United Kingdom;

is a party at the time the proceedings are commenced.

Enforcement of Convention awards

2. Replacement of former provisions.

Sections 3 to 6 of this Act shall have effect with respect to the enforcement of Convention awards; and where a Convention award would, but for this section, be also a foreign award within the meaning of Part II of the Arbitration Act 1950, that Part shall not apply to it.

3. Effect of Convention awards.

(1)   A Convention award shall, subject to the following provisions of this Act, be enforceable—

(a)   in England and Wales, either by action or in the same manner as the award of an arbitrator is enforceable by virtue of section 26 of the Arbitration Act 1950;

(b)   in Scotland, either by action or, in a case where the arbitration agreement contains consent to the registration of the award in the Books of Council and Session for execution and the award is so registered, by summary diligence;

(c)   in Northern Ireland, either by action or in the same manner as the award of an arbitrator is enforceable by virtue of section 16 of the Arbitration Act (Northern Ireland) 1937.

(2)   Any Convention award which would be enforceable under this Act shall be treated as binding for all purposes on the persons as between whom it was made, and may accordingly be relied on by any of those persons by way of defence, set off or otherwise in any legal proceedings in the United Kingdom; and any reference in this Act to enforcing a Convention award shall be construed as including references to relying on such an award.

4. Evidence.

The party seeking to enforce a Convention award must produce—

(a)   the duly authenticated original award or a duly certified copy of it; and

(b)   the original arbitration agreement or a duly certified copy of it; and

(c)   where the award or agreement is in a foreign language, a translation of it certified by an official or sworn translator or by a diplomatic or consular agent.

5. Refusal of enforcement.

(1)   Enforcement of a Convention award shall not be refused except in the cases mentioned in this section.

(2)   Enforcement of a Convention award may be refused if the person against whom it is invoked proves—

(a)   that a party to the arbitration agreement was (under the law applicable to him) under some incapacity; or

(b)   that the arbitration agreement was not valid under the law to which the parties subjected it or, failing any indication thereon, under the law of the country where the award was made; or

(c)   that he was not given proper notice of the appointment of the arbitrator or of the arbitration proceedings or was otherwise unable to present his case; or

(d)   (subject to subsection (4) of this section) that the award deals with a difference not contemplated by or not failing within the terms of the submission to arbitration or contains decisions on matters beyond the scope of the submission to arbitration; or

(e)   that the composition of the arbitral authority or the arbitral procedure was not in accordance with the agreement of the parties or, failing such agreement, with the law of the country where the arbitration took place; or

(f)   that the award has not yet become binding on the parties, or has been set aside or suspended by a competent authority of the country in which, or under the law of which, it was made.

(3)   Enforcement of a Convention award may also be refused if the award is in respect of a matter which is not capable of settlement by arbitration, or if it would be contrary to public policy to enforce the award.

(4)   A Convention award which contains decisions on matters not submitted to arbitration may be enforced to the extent that it contains decisions on matters submitted to arbitration which can be separated from those on matters not so submitted.

(5)   Where an application for the setting aside or suspension of a Convention award has been made to such a competent authority as is mentioned in subsection (2)(f) of this section, the court before which enforcement of the award is sought may, if it thinks fit, adjourn the proceedings and may, on the application of the party seeking to enforce the award, order the other party to give security.

6. Saving.

Nothing in this Act shall prejudice any right to enforce or rely on an award otherwise than under this Act or Part II of the Arbitration Act 1950.

General

7. Interpretation.

(1)   In this Act—
'arbitration agreement' means an agreement in writing (including an agreement contained in an exchange of letters or telegrams) to submit to arbitration present or future differences capable of settlement by arbitration;
'Convention award' means an award made in pursuance of an arbitration agreement in the territory of a State, other than the United Kingdom, which is a party to the New York Convention; and
'the New York Convention' means the Convention on the Recognition and Enforcement of Foreign Arbitral Awards adopted by the United Nations Conference on International Commercial Arbitration on 10th June 1958.

(2)   If Her Majesty by Order in Council declares that any State specified in the Order is a party to the New York Convention the Order shall, while in force, be conclusive evidence that that State is a party to that Convention.

(3)   An Order in Council under this section may be varied or revoked by a subsequent Order in Council.

8. Short title, repeals, commencement and extent.

(1)   This Act may be cited as the Arbitration Act 1975.
(2)   . . .
(3)   This Act shall come into operation on such date as the Secretary of State may by order made by statutory instrument appoint.
(4)   This Act extends to Northern Ireland.

ARBITRATION ACT 1979
(1979, c. 42)

Note: This Act is to be repealed by the Arbitration Act 1996, sch. 4.

An Act to amend the law relating to arbitrations and for purposes connected therewith.   [4th April 1979]

1. Judicial review of arbitration awards.

(1)   In the Arbitration Act 1950 (in this Act referred to as 'the principal Act') section 21 (statement of case for a decision of the High Court) shall cease to have effect and, without prejudice to the right of appeal conferred by subsection (2) below, the High Court shall not have jurisdiction to set aside or remit an award on an arbitration agreement on the ground of errors of fact or law on the face of the award.

(2)   Subject to subsection (3) below, an appeal shall lie to the High Court on any question of law arising out of an award made on an arbitration agreement; and on the determination of such an appeal the High Court may by order—

(a)   confirm, vary or set aside the award; or

(b)   remit the award to the reconsideration of the arbitrator or umpire together with the court's opinion on the question of law which was the subject of the appeal;

and where the award is remitted under paragraph (b) above the arbitrator or umpire shall, unless the order otherwise directs, make his award within three months after the date of the order.

(3)   An appeal under this section may be brought by any of the parties to the reference—

(a)   with the consent of all the other parties to the reference; or

(b)   subject to section 3 below, with the leave of the court.

(4)   The High Court shall not grant leave under subsection (3)(b) above unless it considers that, having regard to all the circumstances, the determination of the question of law concerned could substantially affect the rights of one or more of the parties to the arbitration agreement; and the court may make any leave which it gives conditional upon the applicant complying with such conditions as it considers appropriate.

(5)   Subject to subsection (6) below, if an award is made and, on an application made by any of the parties to the reference,—

(a)   with the consent of all the other parties to the reference, or

(b)   subject to section 3 below, with the leave of the court,

it appears to the High Court that the award does not or does not sufficiently set out the reasons for the award, the court may order the arbitrator or umpire concerned to state the reasons for his award in sufficient detail to enable the court, should an appeal be brought under this section, to consider any question of law arising out of the award.

(6)   In any case where an award is made without any reason being given, the High Court shall not make an order under subsection (5) above unless it is satisfied—

(a)   that before the award was made one of the parties to the reference gave notice to the arbitrator or umpire concerned that a reasoned award would be required; or

(b)   that there is some special reason why such a notice was not given.

[(6A) Unless the High Court gives leave, no appeal shall lie to the Court of Appeal from a decision of the High Court—

(a)   to grant or refuse leave under subsection (3)(b) or (5)(b) above; or

(b)   to make or not to make an order under subsection (5) above.]

[*Subsection (6A) added by the Supreme Court Act 1981, s. 148(1).*]

(7)   No appeal shall lie to the Court of Appeal from a decision of the High Court on an appeal under this section unless—

(a)   the High Court or the Court of Appeal gives leave; and

(b)   it is certified by the High Court that the question of law to which its decision relates either is one of general public importance or is one which for some other special reason should be considered by the Court of Appeal.

(8)   Where the award of an arbiter or umpire is varied on appeal, the award as varied shall have effect (except for the purposes of this section) as if it were the award of the arbitrator or umpire.

2.   Determination of preliminary point of law by court.

(1)   Subject to subsection (2) and section (3) below, on an application to the High Court made by any of the parties to a reference—

(a)   with the consent of an arbitrator who has entered on the reference or, if an umpire has entered on the reference, with his consent, or

(b)   with the consent of all the other parties,

the High Court shall have jurisdiction to determine any question of law arising in the course of the reference.

(2)   The High Court shall not entertain an application under subsection (1)(a) above with respect to any question of law unless it is satisfied that—

(a)   the determination of the application might produce substantial savings in costs to the parties; and

(b)   the question of law is one in respect of which leave to appeal would be likely to be given under section 1(3)(b) above.

[(2A)   Unless the High Court gives leave, no appeal shall lie to the Court of Appeal from a decision of the High Court to entertain or not to entertain an application under subsection (1)(a) above.]

[*Subsection (2A) added by the Supreme Court Act 1981, s. 148(1).*]

(3)   A decision of the High Court under [subsection (1) above] shall be deemed to be a judgment of the court within the meaning of section [16 of the Supreme Court Act 1981] (appeals to the Court of Appeal), but no appeal shall lie from such a decision unless—

(a)   the High Court or the Court of Appeal gives leave; and

(b)   it is certified by the High Court that the question of law to which its decision relates either is one of general public importance or is one which for some other special reason should be considered by the Court of Appeal.

3.   Exclusion agreements affecting rights under sections 1 and 2.

(1)   Subject to the following provisions of this section and section 4 below—

(a)   the High Court shall not, under section 1(3)(b) above, grant leave to appeal with respect to a question of law arising out of an award, and

    (b)   the High Court shall not, under section 1(5)(b) above, grant leave to make an application with respect to an award, and

    (c)   no application may be made under section 2(1)(a) above with respect to a question of law,

if the parties to the reference in question have entered into an agreement in writing (in this section referred to as an 'exclusion agreement') which excludes the right of appeal under section 1 above in relation to that award or, in a case falling within paragraph (c) above, in relation to an award to which the determination of the question of law is material.

    (2)   An exclusion agreement may be expressed so as to relate to a particular award, to awards under a particular reference or to any other description of awards, whether arising out of the same reference or not; and an agreement may be an exclusion agreement for the purposes of this section whether it is entered into before or after the passing of this Act and whether or not it forms part of an arbitration agreement.

    (3)   In any case where—

    (a)   an arbitration agreement, other than a domestic arbitration agreement, provides for disputes between the parties to be referred to arbitration, and

    (b)   a dispute to which the agreement relates involves the question whether a party has been guilty of fraud, and

    (c)   the parties have entered into an exclusion agreement which is applicable to any award made on the reference of that dispute,

then, except in so far as the exclusion agreement otherwise provides, the High Court shall not exercise its powers under section 24(2) of the principal Act (to take steps necessary to enable the question to be determined by the High Court) in relation to that dispute.

    (4)   Except as provided by subsection (1) above, sections 1 and 2 above shall have effect notwithstanding anything in any agreement purporting—

    (a)   to prohibit or restrict access to the High Court; or

    (b)   to restrict the jurisdiction of that court; or

    (c)   to prohibit or restrict the making of a reasoned award.

    (5)   An exclusion agreement shall be of no effect in relation to an award made on, or a question of law arising in the course of a reference under, a statutory arbitration, that is to say, such an arbitration as is referred to in subsection (1) of section 31 of the principal Act.

    (6)   An exclusion agreement shall be of no effect in relation to an award made on, or a question of law arising in the course of a reference under, an arbitration agreement which is a domestic arbitration agreement unless the exclusion agreement is entered into after the commencement of the arbitration in which the award is made or, as the case may be, in which the question of law arises.

    (7)   In this section 'domestic arbitration agreement' means an arbitration agreement which does not provide, expressly or by implication, for arbitration in a State other than the United Kingdom and to which neither—

    (a)   an individual who is a national of, or habitually resident in, any State other than the United Kingdom, nor

    (b)   a body corporate which is incorporated in, or whose central management and control is exercised in, any State other than the United Kingdom,

is a party at the time the arbitration agreement is entered into.

4. Exclusion agreements not to apply in certain cases.

(1)   Subject to subsection (3) below, if an arbitration award or a question of law arising in the course of a reference relates, in whole or in part to—

(a)   a question or claim falling within the Admiralty jurisdiction of the High Court, or

(b)   a dispute arising out of a contract of insurance, or

(c)   a dispute arising out of a commodity contract,

an exclusion agreement shall have no effect in relation to the award or question unless either—

(i)   the exclusion agreement is entered into after the commencement of the arbitration in which the award is made or, as the case may be, in which the question of law arises, or

(ii)   the award or question relates to a contract which is expressed to be governed by a law other than the law of England and Wales.

(2)   In subsection (1)(c) above 'commodity contract' means a contract—

(a)   for the sale of goods regularly dealt with on a commodity market or exchange in England or Wales which is specified for the purposes of this section by an order made by the Secretary of State; and

(b)   of a description so specified.

(3)   The Secretary of State may by order provide that subsection (1) above—

(a)   shall cease to have effect; or

(b)   subject to such conditions as may be specified in the order, shall not apply to any exclusion agreement made in relation to an arbitration award of a description so specified;

and an order under this subsection may contain such supplementary, incidental and transitional provisions as appear to the Secretary of State to be necessary or expedient.

[See SI 1979, No. 54.]

(4)   The power to make an order under subsection (2) or subsection (3) above shall be exercisable by statutory instrument which shall be subject to annulment in pursuance of a resolution of either House of Parliament.

(5)   In this section 'exclusion agreement' has the same meaning as in section 3 above.

5. Interlocutory orders.

(1)   If any party to a reference under an arbitration agreement falls within the time specified in the order or, if no time is so specified, within a reasonable time to comply with an order made by the arbitrator or umpire in the course of the reference, then, on the application of the arbitrator or umpire or of any party to the reference, the High Court may make an order extending the powers of the arbitrator or umpire as mentioned in subsection (2) below.

(2)   In an order made by the High Court under this section, the arbitrator or umpire shall have power, to the extent and subject to any conditions specified in that order, to continue with the reference in default of appearance or of any other act by one of the parties in like manner as a judge of the High Court might continue with proceedings in that court where a party fails to comply with an order of that court or a requirement of rules of court.

(3)   Section 4(5) of the Administration of Justice Act 1970 (jurisdiction of the High Court to be exercisable by the Court of Appeal in relation to judge-arbitrators and judge-umpires) shall not apply in relation to the power of the High Court to make an order under this section, but in the case of a reference to a judge-arbitrator or judge-umpire that power shall be exercisable as in the case of any other reference to arbitration and also by the judge-arbitrator or judge-umpire himself.

(4)   Anything done by a judge-arbitrator or judge-umpire in the exercise of the power conferred by subsection (3) above shall be done by him in his capacity as judge of the High Court and have effect as if done by that court.

6.   Minor amendments relating to awards and appointment of arbitrators and umpires.

(1)   In subsection (1) of section 8 of the principal Act (agreements where reference is to two arbitrators deemed to include provision that the arbitrators shall appoint an umpire immediately after their own appointment)—
      (a)   for the words 'shall appoint an umpire immediately' there shall be substituted the words 'may appoint an umpire at any time'; and
      (b)   at the end there shall be added the words 'and shall do so forthwith if they cannot agree.'

(2)   For section 9 of the principal Act (agreements for reference to three arbitrators) there shall be substituted the following section:—

'9.   Majority award of three arbitrators.

Unless the contrary intention is expressed in the arbitration agreement, in any case where there is a reference to three arbitrators, the award of any two of the arbitrators shall be binding.'

(3)   In section 10 of the principal Act (power of court in certain cases to appoint an arbitrator or umpire) in paragraph (c) after the word 'are,' in the first place where it occurs, there shall be inserted the words 'required or are' and the words from 'or where' to the end of the paragraph shall be omitted.

(4)   At the end of section 10 of the principal Act there shall be added the following subsection:—

'(2) In any case where—
      (a)   an arbitration agreement provided for the appointment of an arbitrator or umpire by a person who is neither one of the parties nor an existing arbitrator (whether the provision applies directly or in default of agreement by the parties or otherwise), and
      (b)   that person refuses to make the appointment or does not make it within the time specified in the agreement or, if no time is so specified, within a reasonable time,
any party to the agreement may serve the person in question with a written notice to appoint an arbitrator or umpire and, if the appointment is not made within seven clear days after the service of the notice, the High Court or a judge thereof may, on the application of the party who gave the notice, appoint an arbitrator or umpire who shall have the like powers to act in the reference and make an award as if he had been appointed in accordance with the terms of the agreement.'

7.   Application and interpretation of certain provisions of Part I of principal Act.

(1)   References in the following provisions of Part I of the principal Act to that Part of that Act shall have effect as if the preceding provisions of this Act were included in that Part, namely,—

(a)   section 14 (interim awards);
(b)   section 28 (terms as to costs of orders);
(c)   section 30 (Crown to be bound);
(d)   section 31 (application to statutory arbitrations); and
(e)   section 32 (meaning of 'arbitration agreement').

(2)   Subsections (2) and (3) of section 29 of the principal Act shall apply to determine when an arbitration is deemed to be commenced for the purpose of this Act.

(3)   For the avoidance of doubt, it is hereby declared that the reference in subsection (1) of section 31 of the principal Act (statutory arbitrations) to arbitration under any other Act does not extend to arbitration under [section 64 of the County Courts Act 1984] (cases in which proceedings are to be or may be referred to arbitration) and accordingly nothing in this Act or in Part I of the principal Act applies to arbitration under the said section 92.

8.   Short title, commencement, repeals and extent.

(1)   This Act may be cited as the Arbitration Act 1979.

(2)   This Act shall come into operation on such day as the Secretary of State may appoint by order made by statutory instrument; and such an order—

(a)   may appoint different days for different provisions of this Act and for the purposes of the operation of the same provision in relation to different descriptions of arbitration agreement; and

(b)   may contain such supplementary, incidental and transitional provisions as appear to the Secretary of State to be necessary or expedient.

(3)   In consequence of the preceding provisions of this Act, the following provisions are hereby repealed, namely—

(a)   in paragraph (c) of section 10 of the principal Act the words from 'or where' to the end of the paragraph;

(b)   section 21 of the principal Act;

(c)   in paragraph 9 of Schedule 3 to the Administration of Justice Act 1970, in sub-paragraph (1) the words '2(1) and (2)' and sub-paragraph (2).

(4)   This Act forms part of the law of England and Wales only.

LIMITATION ACT 1980
(1980, c. 58)

34.   Application of Act and other limitation enactments to arbitrations.

(1)   This Act and any other limitation enactment shall apply to arbitrations as they apply to actions in the High Court.

(2)   Notwithstanding any term in an arbitration agreement to the effect that no cause of action shall accrue in respect of any matter required by the agreement to be referred until an award is made under the agreement, the

cause of action shall, for the purposes of this Act and any other limitation enactment (whether in their application to arbitrations or to other proceedings), be deemed to have accrued in respect of any such matter at the time when it would have accrued but for that term in the agreement.

(3)   For the purposes of this Act and of any other limitation enactment an arbitration shall be treated as being commenced—

(a)   when one party to the arbitration serves on the other party or parties a notice requiring him or them to appoint an arbitrator or to agree to the appointment of an arbitrator; or

(b)   where the arbitration agreement provides that the reference shall be to a person named or designated in the agreement, when one party to the arbitration serves on the other party or parties a notice requiring him or them to submit the dispute to the person so named or designated.

(4)   Any such notice may be served either—

(a)   by delivering it to the person on whom it is to be served; or

(b)   by leaving it at the usual or last-known place of abode in England and Wales of that person; or

(c)   by sending it by post in a registered letter addressed to that person at his usual or last-known place of abode in England and Wales:
as well as in any other manner provided in the arbitration agreement.

(5)   Where the High Court—

(a)   orders that an award be set aside; or

(b)   orders, after the commencement of an arbitration, that the arbitration agreement shall cease to have effect with respect to the dispute referred; the court may further order that the period between the commencement of the arbitration and the date of the order of the court shall be excluded in computing the time prescribed by this Act or by any other limitation enactment for the commencement of proceedings (including arbitration) with respect to the dispute referred.

(6)   This section shall apply to an arbitration under an Act of Parliament as well as to an arbitration pursuant to an arbitration agreement.

Subsections (3) and (4) above shall have effect, in relation to an arbitration under an Act, as if for the references to the arbitration agreement there were substituted references to such of the provisions of the Act or of any order scheme, rules, regulations or byelaws made under the Act as relate to the arbitration.

(7)   In this section—

(a)   'arbitration', 'arbitration agreement' and 'award' have the same meanings as in Part I of the Arbitration Act 1950; and

(b)   references to any other limitation enactment are references to any other enactment relating to the limitation of actions, whether passed before or after the passing of this Act.

[*Section 34 is to be repealed by the Arbitration Act 1996, sch. 4.*]

SUPREME COURT ACT 1981
(1981, c. 54)

[43A.   Specific powers of arbitrator exercisable by High Court.

In any cause or matter proceeding in the High Court in connection with any contract incorporating an arbitration agreement which confers specific

powers upon the arbitrator, the High Court may, if all parties to the agreement agree, exercise any such powers.]
[*Section 43A inserted by the Courts and Legal Services Act 1990, s. 100.*]

TELECOMMUNICATIONS ACT 1984
(1984, c. 12)

Section 10   SCHEDULE 2

THE TELECOMMUNICATIONS CODE

Linear obstacles

12.—(1)   Subject to the following provisions of this code, the operator shall, for the statutory purposes, have the right in order to cross any relevant land with a line, to install and keep the line and other telecommunication apparatus on, under or over that land and—

(a)   to execute any works on that land for or in connection with the installation, maintenance, adjustment, repair or alteration of that line or the other telecommunication apparatus; and

(b)   to enter on that land to inspect the line or the other apparatus.

(2)   A line installed in pursuance of any right conferred by this paragraph need not cross the relevant land in question by a direct route or by the shortest route from the point at which the line enters that land, but it shall not cross that land by any route which, in the horizontal plane, exceeds the said shortest route by more than 400 metres.

(3)   Telecommunication apparatus shall not be installed in pursuance of any right conferred by this paragraph in any position on the relevant land in which it interferes with traffic on the railway, canal or tramway on that land.

(4)   The operator shall not execute any works on any land in pursuance of any right conferred by this paragraph unless—

(a)   he has given the person with control of the land 28 days' notice of his intention to do so; or

(b)   the works are emergency works.

(5)   A notice under sub-paragraph (4) above shall contain a plan and section of the proposed works or (in lieu of a plan and section) any description of the proposed works (whether or not in the form of a diagram) which the person with control of the land has agreed to accept for the purposes of this sub-paragraph.

(6)   If, at any time before a notice under sub-paragraph (4) above expires, the person with control of the land gives the operator notice of objection to the works, the operator shall be entitled to execute the works only—

(a)   if, within the period of 28 days beginning with the giving of the notice of objection, neither the operator nor that person has given notice to the other requiring him to agree to an arbitrator to whom the objection may be referred under paragraph 13 below; or

(b)   in accordance with an award made on such a reference; or

(c)   to the extent that the works have at any time become emergency works.

(7)   If the operator exercises any power conferred by this paragraph to execute emergency works on any land, he shall, as soon as reasonably

practicable after commencing those works, give the person with control of the land a notice identifying the works and containing—

(a) a statement of the reason why the works are emergency works; and

(b) either the matters which would be required to be contained in a notice under sub-paragraph (4) above with respect to those works or, as the case may require, a reference to an earlier notice under that sub-paragraph with respect to those works.

(8) If within the period of 28 days beginning with the giving of a notice under sub-paragraph (7) above the person to whom that notice was given gives a notice to the operator requiring him to pay compensation, the operator shall be liable to pay that person compensation in respect of loss or damage sustained in consequence of the carrying out of the emergency works in question; and any question as to the amount of that compensation shall, in default of agreement, be referred to arbitration under paragraph 13 below.

(9) If the operator commences the execution of any works in contravention of any provision of this paragraph, he shall be guilty of an offence and liable on summary conviction to a fine not exceeding level 3 on the standard scale.

(10) In this paragraph 'relevant land' means land which is used wholly or mainly either as a railway, canal or tramway or in connection with a railway, canal or tramway on that land, and a reference to the person with control of any such land is a reference to the person carrying on the railway, canal or tramway undertaking in question.

Arbitration in relation to linear obstacles

13.—(1) Any objection or question which, in accordance with paragraph 12 above, is referred to arbitration under this paragraph shall be referred to the arbitration of a single arbitrator appointed by agreement between the parties concerned or, in default of agreement, by the President of the Institution of Civil Engineers.

(2) Where an objection under paragraph 12 above is referred to arbitration under this paragraph the arbitrator shall have the power—

(a) to require the operator to submit to the arbitrator a plan and section in such form as the arbitrator may think requisite for the purposes of the arbitration;

(b) to require the observations on any such plan or section of the person who objects to the works to be submitted to the arbitrator in such form as the arbitrator may think requisite for those purposes;

(c) to direct the operator or that person to furnish him with such information and to comply with such other requirements as the arbitrator may think requisite for those purposes;

(d) to make an award requiring modifications to the proposed works and specifying the terms on which and the conditions subject to which the works may be executed; and

(e) to award such sum as the arbitrator may determine in respect of one or both of the following matters, that is to say—

(i) compensation to the person who objects to the works in respect of loss or damage sustained by that person in consequence of the carrying out of the works, and

(ii)   consideration payable to that person for the right to carry out the works.

(3)   Where a question as to compensation in respect of emergency works is referred to arbitration under this paragraph, the arbitrator—

(a)   shall have the power to direct the operator or the person who requires the payment of compensation to furnish him with such information and to comply with such other requirements as the arbitrator may think requisite for the purposes of the arbitration; and

(b)   shall award to the person requiring the payment of compensation such sum (if any) as the arbitrator may determine in respect of the loss or damage sustained by that person in consequence of the carrying out of the emergency works in question.

(4)   The arbitrator may treat compliance with any requirement made in pursuance of sub-paragraph (2)(a) to (c) or (3)(a) above as a condition of his making an award.

(5)   In determining what award to make on a reference under this paragraph, the arbitrator shall have regard to all the circumstances and to the principle that no person should unreasonably be denied access to a telecommunication system.

(6)   For the purposes of the making of an award under this paragraph—

(a)   the references in sub-paragraphs (2)(e) and (3)(b) above to loss shall, in relation to a person carrying on a railway, canal or tramway undertaking, include references to any increase in the expenses of carrying on that undertaking; and

(b)   the consideration mentioned in sub-paragraph (2)(e) above shall be determined on the basis of what would have been fair and reasonable if the person who objects to the works had given his authority willingly for the works to be executed on the same terms and subject to the same conditions (if any) as are contained in the award.

(7)   In the application of this paragraph to Scotland, the reference to an arbitrator shall have effect as a reference to an arbiter and the arbiter may and, if so directed by the Court of Session, shall state a case for the decision of that Court on any question of law arising in the arbitration.

(8)   In the application of this paragraph to Northern Ireland, the Arbitration Act (Northern Ireland) 1937 shall apply in relation to an arbitration under this paragraph as if this code related exclusively to matters in respect of which the Parliament of Northern Ireland had power to make laws.

[*Para. 13(8) is to be repealed by the Arbitration Act 1996, sch. 4.*]

AGRICULTURAL HOLDINGS ACT 1986
(1986, c. 5)

12.   Arbitration of rent.

(1)   Subject to the provisions of Schedule 2 of this Act, the landlord or tenant of an agricultural holding may by notice in writing served on the other demand that the rent to be payable in respect of the holding as from the next termination date shall be referred to arbitration under this Act.

(2)   On a reference under this section the arbitrator shall determine what rent should be properly payable in respect of the holding at the date of reference and accordingly shall, with effect from the next terminations date following the date of demand for arbitration, increase or reduce the rent previously payable or direct that it shall continue unchanged.

(3)   A demand for arbitration under this section shall cease to be effective for the purposes of this section on the next termination date following the date of the demand unless before the said termination date—

(a)   an arbitrator has been appointed by agreement between the parties, or

(b)   an application has been made to the President of the Royal Institution of Chartered Surveyors for the appointment of an arbitrator by him.

(4)   Reference in this section (and in Schedule 2 of this Act) in relation to a demand for arbitration with respect to the rent of any holding, to the next termination date following the date of the demand are references to the next day following the date of the demand on which the tenancy of the holding could have been determined by notice to quit given at the date of the demand.

(5)   Schedule 2 of this Act shall have effect for supplementing this section.

84.   Arbitrations.

(1)   Any matter which by or by virtue of this Act or regulations made under this Act is required to be determined by arbitration under this Act shall, notwithstanding any agreement (under a contract of tenancy or otherwise) providing for a different method of arbitration, be determined by the arbitration of a single arbitrator in accordance with the provisions of any order under this section, together with the provisions of Schedule 11 of this Act (as for the time being in force); and the Arbitration Act 1950 shall not apply to any such arbitration.

(2)   The Lord Chancellor may by order make provisions as to the procedure to be followed in, or in connection with, proceedings on arbitrations under this Act.

(3)   An order under this section may in particular—

(a)   provide for the provisions of Schedule 11 to this Act, exclusive of those mentioned in subsection (4) below, to have effect subject to such modification as may be specified in the order;

(b)   prescribe forms for proceedings on arbitrations under this Act which, if used, shall be sufficient;

(c)   prescribe the form in which awards in such proceedings are to be made.

(4)   An order under this section shall not make provision inconsistent with the following provisions of Schedule 11 to this Act, namely paragraphs 1 to 6, 11 to 13, 14(2), 17, 19, 21, 22, 26 to 29 and 32.

(5)   In this section 'modifications' includes additions, omissions and amendments.

[*Section 84(1) is to be amended by the Arbitration Act 1996, sch. 3(4).*]

SCHEDULE 11

ARBITRATIONS

Appointment and remuneration of arbitrator

1.—(1)   The arbitrator shall be a person appointed by agreement between the parties or, in default of agreement, a person appointed on the application of either of the parties by the President of the Royal Institution of Chartered Surveyors (referred to in this Schedule as 'the President') from among the members of the panel constituted for the purposes of this paragraph.

(2)   No application may be made to the President for an arbitrator to be appointed by him under this paragraph unless the application is accompanied by such fee as may be prescribed as the fee for such an application; but once the fee has been paid in connection with any such application no further fee shall be payable in connection with any subsequent application for the President to exercise any function exercisable by him in relation to the arbitration by virtue of this Schedule (including an application for the appointment by him in an appropriate case of a new arbitrator).

(3)   Any such appointment by the President shall be made by him as soon as possible after receiving the application; but where the application is referable to a demand for arbitration made under section 12 of this Act any such appointment shall in any event not be made by him earlier than four months before the next termination date following the date of the demand (as defined by subsection (4) of that section).

(4)   A person appointed by the President as arbitrator shall, where the arbitration relates to an agricultural holding in Wales, be a person who possesses a knowledge of Welsh agricultural conditions, and, if either party to the arbitration so requires, a knowledge also of the Welsh language.

(5)   For the purposes of this Schedule there shall be constituted a panel consisting of such number of persons as the Lord Chancellor may determine, to be appointed by him.

2.   If the arbitrator dies, or is incapable of acting, or for seven days after notice from either party requiring him to act fails to act, a new arbitrator may be appointed as if no arbitrator had been appointed.

3.   In relation to an arbitrator who is appointed in place of another arbitrator (whether under paragraph 2 above or otherwise) the reference in section 12(2) of this Act to the date of the reference shall be construed as a reference to the date when the original arbitrator was appointed.

4.   Neither party shall have power to revoke the appointment of the arbitrator without the consent of the other party; and his appointment shall not be revoked by the death of either party.

5.   Every appointment, application, notice, revocation and consent under the foregoing paragraphs must be in writing.

6.   The remuneration of the arbitrator shall be—

(a)   where he is appointed by agreement between the parties, such amount as may be agreed upon by him and the parties or, in default of agreement, fixed by the registrar of the county court (subject to an appeal to the judge of the court) on an application made by the arbitrator or either of the parties,

(b)   where he is appointed by the President, such amount as may be agreed upon by the arbitrator and the parties or, in default of agreement, fixed by the President,
and shall be recoverable by the arbitrator as a debt due from either of the parties to the arbitration.

Conduct of proceedings and witnesses

7.   The parties to the arbitration shall, within thirty-five days from the appointment of the arbitrator, deliver to him a statement of their respective cases with all necessary particulars and—
(a)   no amendment or addition to the statement or particulars delivered shall be allowed after the expiry of the said thirty-five days except with the consent of the arbitrator,
(b)   a party to the arbitration shall be confined at the hearing to the matters alleged in the statement and particulars delivered by him and any amendment or addition duly made.

8.   The parties to the arbitration and all persons claiming through them respectively shall, subject to any legal objection, submit to be examined by the arbitrator, on oath or affirmation, in relation to the matters in dispute and shall, subject to any such objection, produce before the arbitrator all samples and documents within their possession or power respectively which may be required or called for, and do all other things which during the proceedings the arbitrator may require.

9.   Witnesses appearing at the arbitration shall, if the arbitrator thinks fit, be examined on oath or affirmation, and the arbitrator shall have power to administer oaths to, or to take the affirmation of, the parties and witnesses appearing.

10.   The provisions of county court rules as to the issuing of witness summonses shall, subject to such modifications as may be prescribed by such rules, apply for the purposes of the arbitration as if it were an action or matter in the county court.

11.—(1)   Subject to sub-paragraphs (2) and (3) below, any person who—
(a)   having been summoned in pursuance of county court rules as a witness in the arbitration refuses or neglects, without sufficient cause, to appear or to produce any documents required by the summons to be produced, or
(b)   having been so summoned or being present at the arbitration and being required to give evidence, refuses to be sworn or give evidence,
shall forfeit such fine as the judge of the county court may direct.

(2)   A judge shall not have power under sub-paragraph (1) above to direct that a person shall forfeit a fine of an amount exceeding £10.

(3)   No person summoned in pursuance of county court rules as a witness in the arbitration shall forfeit a fine under this paragraph unless there has been paid or tendered to him at the time of the service of the summons such sum in respect of his expenses (including, in such cases as may be prescribed by county court rules, compensation for loss of time) as may be so prescribed for the purposes of section 55 of the County Court Act 1984.

(4)   The judge of the county court may at his discretion direct that the whole or any part of any such fine, after deducting costs, shall be applicable towards indemnifying the party injured by the refusal or neglect.

12.—(1) Subject to sub-paragraph (2) below, the judge of the county court may, if he thinks fit, upon application on affidavit by either party to the arbitration, issue an order under his hand for bringing up before the arbitrator any person (in this paragraph referred to as a 'prisoner') confined in any place under any sentence or under committal for trial or otherwise, to be examined as a witness in the arbitration.

(2) No such order shall be made with respect to a person confined under process in any civil action or matter.

(3) Subject to sub-paragraph (4) below, the prisoner mentioned in any such order shall be brought before the arbitrator under the same custody, and shall be dealt with in the same manner in all respects, as a prisoner required by a writ of habeas corpus to be brought before the High Court and examined there as a witness.

(4) The person having the custody of the prisoner shall not be bound to obey the order unless there is tendered to him a reasonable sum for the conveyance and maintenance of a proper officer or officers and of the prisoner in going to, remaining at, and returning from, the place where the arbitration is held.

13. The High Court may order that a writ of habeas corpus ad testificandum shall issue to bring up a prisoner for examination before the arbitrator, if the prisoner is confined in any prison under process in any civil action or matter.

Award

14.—(1) Subject to sub-paragraph (2) below, the arbitrator shall make and sign his award within fifty-six days of his appointment.

(2) The President may from time to time enlarge the time limited for making the award, whether that time has expired or not.

15. The arbitrator may if he thinks fit make an interim award for the payment of any sum on account of the sum to be finally awarded.

16. The arbitrator shall—

(a) state separately in the award the amounts awarded in respect of the several claims referred to him, and

(b) on the application of either party, specify the amount awarded in respect of any particular improvement or any particular matter the subject of the award.

17. Where by virtue of this Act compensation under an agreement is to be substituted for compensation under this Act for improvements or for any such matters as are specified in Part II of Schedule 8 to this Act, the arbitrator shall award compensation in accordance with the agreement instead of in accordance with this Act.

18. The award shall fix a day not later than one month after the delivery of the award for the payment of the money as compensation, costs or otherwise.

19. The award shall be final and binding on the parties and the persons claiming under them respectively.

20. The arbitrator shall have power to correct in the award any clerical mistake or error arising from any accidental slip or omission.

Reasons for award

21.   Section 12 of the Tribunals and Inquiries Act 1971 (reasons to be given for decisions of tribunals etc) shall apply in relation to the award of an arbitrator appointed under this Schedule by agreement between the parties as it applies in relations to the award of an arbitrator appointed under this Schedule otherwise than by such agreement.

Interest on awards

22.   Any sum directed to be paid by the award shall, unless the award otherwise directs, carry interest as from the date of the award and at the same rate as a judgment debt.

Costs

23.   The costs of, and incidental to, the arbitration and award shall be in the discretion of the arbitrator who may direct to and by whom and in what manner the costs, or any part of the costs, are to be paid.

24.   On the application of either party, any such costs shall be taxable in the county court according to such of the scales prescribed by county court rules for proceedings in the county court as may be directed by the arbitrator under paragraph 23 above, or, in the absence of any such direction, by the county court.

25.—(1)   The arbitrator shall, in awarding costs, take into consideration—

(a)   the reasonableness or unreasonableness of the claim of either party, whether in respect of amount or otherwise,

(b)   any unreasonable demand for particulars or refusal to supply particulars, and

(c)   generally all the circumstances of the case.

(2)   The arbitrator may disallow the costs of any witness whom he considers to have been called unnecessarily and any other costs which he considers to have been unnecessarily incurred.

Special case, setting aside award and remission

26.   The arbitrator may, at any stage of the proceedings, and shall, upon a direction in that behalf given by the judge of the county court upon an application made by either party, state in the form of a special case for the opinion of the county court any question of law arising in the course of the arbitration and any question as to the jurisdiction of the arbitrator.

27.—(1)   Where the arbitrator has misconducted himself, the county court may remove him.

(2)   Where the arbitrator has misconducted himself, or an arbitration or award had been improperly procured, or there is an error of law on the face of the award, the county court may set the award aside.

28.—(1)   The county court may from time to time remit the award, or any part of the award, to the reconsideration of the arbitrator.

(2)   In any case where it appears to the county court that there is an error of law on the face of the award, the court may, instead of exercising its power of remission under sub-paragraph (1) above, vary the award by substituting

for so much of it as is affected by the error such award as the court considers that it would have been proper for the arbitrator to make in the circumstances; and the award shall thereupon have effect as so varied.

(3)   Where remission is ordered under that sub-paragraph, the arbitrator shall, unless the order otherwise directs, make and sign his award within thirty days after the date of the order.

(4)   If the county court is satisfied that the time limited for making the said award is for any good reason insufficient, the court may extend or further extend that time for such period as it thinks proper.

Miscellaneous

29.   Any amount paid, in respect of the remuneration of the arbitrator by either party to the arbitration, in excess of the amount, if any, directed by the award to be paid by him in respect of the costs of the award shall be recoverable from the other party.

30.   The provisions of this Schedule relating to the fixing and recovery of the remuneration of an arbitrator and the making and enforcement of an award as to costs, together with any other provision in Schedule applicable for the purposes of or in connection with those provisions, shall apply where the arbitrator has no jurisdiction to decide the question referred to him as they apply where the arbitrator has jurisdiction to decide that question.

31.   For the purposes of this Schedule, an arbitrator appointed by the President shall be taken to have been so appointed at the time when the President executed the instrument of appointment; and in the case of any such arbitrator the periods mentioned in paragraphs 7 and 14 above shall accordingly run from that time.

32.   Any instrument of appointment or other document purporting to be made in the exercise of any function exercisable by the President under paragraph 1, 6 or 14 above and to be signed by or on behalf of the President shall be taken to be such an instrument or document unless the contrary is shown.

CONSUMER ARBITRATION AGREEMENTS ACT 1988
(1988, c. 21)

[This Act is to be repealed by the Arbitration Act 1996, sch. 4.]

An Act to extend to consumers certain rights as regards agreements to refer future differences to arbitration and for purposes connected therewith. [28th June 1988]

Be it enacted by the Queen's most Excellent Majesty, by and with the advice and consent of the Lords Spiritual and Temporal, and Commons, in this present Parliament assembled, and by the authority of the same, as follows:—

England, Wales and Northern Ireland

1.   Arbitration agreements.

(1)   Where a person (referred to in section 4 below as 'the consumer') enters into a contract as a consumer, an agreement that future differences

arising between parties to the contract are to be referred to arbitration cannot be enforced against him in respect of any cause of action so arising to which this section applies except—

(a) with his written consent signified after the differences in question have arisen; or

(b) where he has submitted to arbitration in pursuance of the agreement, whether in respect of those or any other differences; or

(c) where the court makes an order under section 4 below in respect of that cause of action.

(2) This section applies to a cause of action—

(a) if proceedings in respect of it would be within the jurisdiction of a county court; or

(b) if it satisfies such other conditions as may be prescribed for the purposes of this paragraph in an order under section 5 below.

(3) Neither section 4(1) of the Arbitration Act 1950 nor section 4 of the Arbitration Act (Northern Ireland) 1937 (which provide for the staying of court proceedings where an arbitration agreement is in force) shall apply to an arbitration agreement to the extent that it cannot be enforced by virtue of this section.

2. Exclusions.

Section 1 above does not affect—

(a) the enforcement of an arbitration agreement to which section 1 of the Arbitration Act 1975 applies, that is, an arbitration agreement other than a domestic arbitration agreement within the meaning of that section;

(b) the resolution of differences arising under any contract so far as it is, by virtue of section 1(2) of, and Schedule 1 to, the Unfair Contract Terms Act 1977 ('the Act of 1977'), excluded from the operation of section 2, 3, 4 or 7 of that Act.

3. Contracting 'as a consumer'.

(1) For the purposes of section 1 above a person enters into a contract 'as a consumer' if—

(a) he neither makes the contract in the course of a business nor holds himself out as doing so; and

(b) the other party makes the contract in the course of a business; and

(c) in the case of a contract governed by the law of sale of goods or hire-purchase, or by section 7 of the Act of 1977, the goods passing under or in pursuance of the contract are of a type ordinarily supplied for private use or consumption;

but on a sale by auction or by competitive tender the buyer is not in any circumstances to be regarded as entering into the contract as a consumer.

(2) In subsection (1) above—

'business' includes a profession and the activities of any government department, Northern Ireland department or local or public authority; and

'goods' has the same meaning as in the Sale of Goods Act 1979.

(3)   It is for those claiming that a person entered into a contract otherwise than as a consumer to show that he did so.

4. Power of court to disapply section 1 where no detriment to consumer.

(1)   The High Court or a county court may, on an application made after the differences in question have arisen, order that a cause of action to which this section applies shall be treated as one to which section 1 above does not apply.

(2)   Before making an order under this section the court must be satisfied that it is not detrimental to the interests of the consumer for the differences in question to be referred to arbitration in pursuance of the arbitration agreement instead of being determined by proceedings before a court.

(3)   In determining for the purposes of subsection (2) above whether a reference to arbitration is or is not detrimental to the interests of the consumer, the court shall have regard to all factors appearing to be relevant, including, in particular, the availability of legal aid and the relative amount of any expense which may result to him—

(a)   if the differences in question are referred to arbitration in pursuance of the arbitration agreement; and

(b)   if they are determined by proceedings before a court.

(4)   This section applies to a cause of action—

(a)   if proceedings in respect of it would be within the jurisdiction of a county court and would not fall within the small claims limit; or

(b)   if it satisfies the conditions referred to in section 1(2)(b) above and the order under section 5 below prescribing the conditions in question provides for this section to apply to causes of action which satisfy them.

(5)   For the purposes of subsection (4)(a) above proceedings 'fall within the small claims limit'—

(a)   in England and Wales, if in a county court they would stand referred to arbitration (without any order of the court) under rules made by virtue of section 64(1)(a) of the County Courts Act 1984;

(b)   in Northern Ireland, if in a county court the action would be dealt with by way of arbitration by a circuit registrar by virtue of Article 30(3) of the County Courts (Northern Ireland) Order 1980.

(6)   Where the consumer submits to arbitration in consequence of an order under this section, he shall not be regarded for the purposes of section 1(1)(b) above as submitting to arbitration in pursuance of the agreement there mentioned.

5. Orders adding to the causes of action to which section 1 applies.

(1)   Orders under this section may prescribe the conditions referred to in section 1(2)(b) above; and any such order may provide that section 4 above shall apply to a cause of action which satisfies the conditions so prescribed.

(2)   Orders under this section may make different provision for different cases and for different purposes.

(3)   The power to make orders under this section for England and Wales shall be exercisable by statutory instrument made by the Secretary of State

with the concurrence of the Lord Chancellor: but no such order shall be made unless a draft of it has been laid before, and approved by resolution of, each House of Parliament.

(4) The power to make orders under this section for Northern Ireland shall be exercisable by the Department of Economic Development for Northern Ireland with the concurrence of the Lord Chancellor; and any such order—

(a) shall be a statutory rule for the purposes of the Statutory Rules (Northern Ireland) Order 1979; and

(b) shall be subject to affirmative resolution, within the meaning of section 41(4) of the Interpretation Act (Northern Ireland) 1954.

Scotland

6. Arbitration agreements: Scotland.

(1) In the case of a consumer contract to which, by virtue of subsections (2) to (4) of section 15 of the Act of 1977 (scope of Part II of that Act), sections 16 to 18 of that Act apply, an agreement to refer future differences arising out of the contract to arbitration cannot, if it is a domestic arbitration agreement, be enforced against the consumer in respect of a relevant difference so arising except—

(a) with his written consent given after that difference has arisen; or

(b) where, subject to subsection (2) below, he has submitted to arbitration in pursuance of the agreement (whether or not the arbitration was in respect of that difference); or

(c) by virtue of an order under section 7 below in respect of that difference.

(2) In determining for the purposes of subsection (1)(b) above whether the consumer has submitted to arbitration, any arbitration which takes place in consequence of an order of the court under section 7 below shall be disregarded.

7. Power of court to disapply section 6 where no detriment to consumer.

(1) Subject to subsection (4) below, the Court of Session or the sheriff ('the court') may, on an application made after a relevant difference has arisen, order that section 6 above shall not apply as respects that difference.

(2) No such order shall be made unless the court is satisfied that it would not be detrimental to the interests of the consumer were the difference to be referred to arbitration in pursuance of the arbitration agreement.

(3) In determining for the purposes of subsection (2) above whether there would be any detriment to the consumer's interests, the court shall have regard to all factors appearing to be relevant, including, in particular, the availability of legal aid and the relative amounts of any expenses which he might incur—

(a) if the difference is referred to arbitration; and

(b) if it is determined by proceedings before a court.

(4) No order shall be made under subsection (1) above where, if (disregarding the arbitration agreement) the difference were to be resolved by civil

proceedings in the sheriff court, the form of summary cause process to be used for the purposes of those proceedings would be that of a small claim.

8. Construction of sections 6 and 7.

(1) In sections 6 and 7 above 'consumer' and 'consumer contract' have the meanings assigned to those expressions by section 25(1) of the Act of 1977 and 'domestic arbitration agreement' has the same meaning as in section 1 of the Arbitration Act 1975.

(2) For the purposes of sections 6 and 7 above a difference is 'relevant' where, if (disregarding the arbitration agreement) it were to be resolved by civil proceedings in the sheriff court—

(a) the form of process to be used for the purposes of those proceedings would be that of a summary cause; or

(b) the proceedings would come within such description of proceedings as may, by order, be specified by the Secretary of State for the purposes of this paragraph.

(3) The power to make an order under paragraph (b) of subsection (2) above shall be exercisable by statutory instrument made with the concurrence of the Lord Advocate; but no order shall be so made unless a draft has been laid before, and approved by resolution of, each House of Parliament.

Supplementary

9. Short title, commencement, interpretation and extent.

(1) This Act may be cited as the Consumer Arbitration Agreements Act 1988.

(2) This Act shall have effect in relation to contracts made on or after such day as the Secretary of State may by order made by statutory instrument appoint; and different days may be so appointed for different provisions and different purposes.

(3) In this Act 'the Act of 1977' means the Unfair Contract Terms Act 1977.

(4) Sections 1 to 5 above do not extend to Scotland, sections 6 to 8 extend to Scotland only, and this Act, apart from sections 6 to 8, extends to Northern Ireland.

AGRICULTURAL TENANCIES ACT 1995
(1995, c. 8)

An Act to make further provision with respect to tenancies which include agricultural land. [9th May 1995]

12. Appointment of arbitrator.

Where a statutory review notice has been given in relation to a farm business tenancy, but—

(a) no arbitrator has been appointed under an agreement made since the notice was given, and

(b)   no person has been appointed under such an agreement to determine the question of the rent (otherwise than as arbitrator) on a basis agreed
by the parties,
either party may, at any time during the period of six months ending with the
review date, apply to the President of the Royal Institution of Chartered
Surveyors (in this Act referred to as 'the RICS') for the appointment of an
arbitrator by him.

13.   Amount of rent.

(1)   On any reference made in pursuance of a statutory review notice, the
arbitrator shall determine the rent properly payable in respect of the holding
at the review date and accordingly shall, with effect from that date, increase
or reduce the rent previously payable or direct that it shall continue unchanged.

(2)   For the purposes of subsection (1) above, the rent properly payable
in respect of a holding is the rent at which the holding might reasonably I be
expected to be let on the open market by a willing landlord to a willing tenant,
taking into account (subject to subsections (3) and (4) below) all relevant
factors, including (in every case) the terms of the tenancy (including those
which are relevant for the purposes of section 10(4) to (6) of this Act, but
not those relating to the criteria by reference to which any new rent is to be
determined).

(3)   The arbitrator shall disregard any increase in the rental value of the
holding which is due to tenant's improvements other than—

(a)   any tenant's improvement provided under an obligation which was
imposed on the tenant by the terms of his tenancy or any previous tenancy
and which arose on or before the beginning of the tenancy in question,

(b)   any tenant's improvement to the extent that any allowance or
benefit has been made or given by the landlord in consideration of its
provision, and

(c)   any tenant's improvement to the extent that the tenant has received
any compensation from the landlord in respect of it.

(4)   The arbitrator—

(a)   shall disregard any effect on the rent of the fact that the tenant who
is a party to the arbitration is in occupation of the holding, and

(b)   shall not fix the rent at a lower amount by reason of any dilapida-
tion or deterioration of, or damage to, buildings or land caused or permitted
by the tenant.

. . .

PART IV

MISCELLANEOUS AND SUPPLEMENTAL

Resolution of disputes

28.   Resolution of disputes.

(1)   Subject to subsections (4) and (5) below and to section 29 of this Act,
any dispute between the landlord and the tenant under a farm business

tenancy, being a dispute concerning their rights and obligations under this Act, under the terms of the tenancy or under any custom, shall be determined by arbitration.

(2)   Where such a dispute has arisen, the landlord or the tenant may give notice in writing to the other specifying the dispute and stating that, unless before the end of the period of two months beginning with the day on which the notice is given the parties have appointed an arbitrator by agreement, he proposes to apply to the President of the RICS for the appointment of an arbitrator by him.

(3)   Where a notice has been given under subsection (2) above, but no arbitrator has been appointed by agreement, either party may, after the end of the period of two months referred to in that subsection, apply to the President of the RICS for the appointment of an arbitrator by him.

(4)   Subsection (1) above does not affect the jurisdiction of the courts, except to the extent provided by section 4(1) of the Arbitration Act 1950 (staying of court proceedings where there is submission to arbitration), as applied to statutory arbitrations by section 31 of that Act.

[*Section 28(4) is to be repealed by the Arbitration Act 1996, sch. 4.*]

(5)   Subsections (1) to (3) above do not apply in relation to—

(a)   the determination of rent in pursuance of a statutory review notice (as defined in section 10(1) of this Act),

(b)   any case falling within section 19(1) of this Act, or

(c)   any claim for compensation under Part III of this Act.

29.   Cases where right to refer claim to arbitration under section 28 does not apply.

(1)   Section 28 of this Act does not apply in relation to any dispute if—

(a)   the tenancy is created by an instrument which includes provision for disputes to be resolved by any person other than—

(i)   the landlord or the tenant, or

(ii)   a third party appointed by either of them without the consent or concurrence of the other, and

(b)   either of the following has occurred—

(i)   the landlord and the tenant have jointly referred the dispute to the third party under the provision, or

(ii)   the landlord or the tenant has referred the dispute to the third party under the provision and notified the other in writing of the making of the reference, the period of four weeks beginning with the date on which the other was so notified has expired and the other has not given a notice under section 28(2) of this Act in relation to the dispute before the end of that period.

(2)   For the purposes of subsection (1) above, a term of the tenancy does not provide for disputes to be 'resolved' by any person unless that person (whether or not acting as arbitrator) is enabled under the terms of the tenancy to give a decision which is binding in law on both parties.

30.   General provisions applying to arbitration under Act.

(1)   Any matter which is required to be determined by arbitration under this Act shall be determined by the arbitration of a sole arbitrator.

(2)   Any application under this Act to the President of the RICS for the appointment of an arbitrator by him must be made in writing and must be accompanied by such reasonable fee as the President may determine in respect of the costs of making the appointment.

(3)   Where an arbitrator appointed for the purposes of this Act dies or is incapable of acting and no new arbitrator has been appointed by agreement, either party may apply to the President of the RICS for the appointment of a new arbitrator by him.

41.   Short title, commencement and extent.

(1)   This Act may be cited as the Agricultural Tenancies Act 1995.

(2)   This Act shall come into force on 1st September 1995.

(3)   Subject to subsection (4) below, this Act extends to England and Wales only.

(4)   The amendment by a provision of the Schedule to this Act of an enactment which extends to Scotland or Northern Ireland also extends there, except that paragraph 9 of the Schedule does not extend to Northern Ireland.

ARBITRATION ACT 1996
(1996, c. 23)

ARRANGEMENT

PART I

ARBITRATION PURSUANT TO AN ARBITRATION AGREEMENT

PART II

OTHER PROVISIONS RELATING TO ARBITRATION

Domestic arbitration agreements (ss. 85–88)

Consumer arbitration agreements (ss. 89–91)

Small claims arbitration in the county court (s. 92)

Appointment of judges as arbitrators (s. 93)

Statutory arbitrations (ss. 94–98)

PART III

RECOGNITION AND ENFORCEMENT OF CERTAIN FOREIGN AWARDS

Enforcement of Geneva Convention awards (s. 99)

Recognition and enforcement of New York Convention awards (ss. 100–104)

PART IV

GENERAL PROVISIONS (ss. 105–110)

SCHEDULES:

Schedule 1—Mandatory provisions of Part I.
Schedule 2—Modifications of Part I in relation to judge-arbitrators.
Schedule 3—Consequential amendments.
Schedule 4—Repeals.

ARBITRATION ACT 1996

An Act to restate and improve the law relating to arbitration pursuant to an arbitration agreement; to make other provision relating to arbitration and arbitration awards; and for connected purposes. [17th June 1996]

PART I

ARBITRATION PURSUANT TO AN ARBITRATION AGREEMENT

Introductory

1. General principles.

The provisions of this Part are founded on the following principles, and shall be construed accordingly—

    (a) the object of arbitration is to obtain the fair resolution of disputes by an impartial tribunal without unnecessary delay or expense;

(b)   the parties should be free to agree how their disputes are resolved, subject only to such safeguards as are necessary in the public interest;

(c)   in matters governed by this Part the court should not intervene except as provided by this Part.

2.   Scope of application of provisions.

(1)   The provisions of this Part apply where the seat of the arbitration is in England and Wales or Northern Ireland.

(2)   The following sections apply even if the seat of the arbitration is outside England and Wales or Northern Ireland or no seat has been designated or determined—

(a)   sections 9 to 11 (stay of legal proceedings, &c.), and

(b)   section 66 (enforcement of arbitral awards).

(3)   The powers conferred by the following sections apply even if the seat of the arbitration is outside England and Wales or Northern Ireland or no seat has been designated or determined—

(a)   section 43 (securing the attendance of witnesses), and

(b)   section 44 (court powers exercisable in support of arbitral proceedings);

but the court may refuse to exercise any such power if, in the opinion of the court, the fact that the seat of the arbitration is outside England and Wales or Northern Ireland, or that when designated or determined the seat is likely to be outside England and Wales or Northern Ireland, makes it inappropriate to do so.

(4)   The court may exercise a power conferred by any provision of this Part not mentioned in subsection (2) or (3) for the purpose of supporting the arbitral process where—

(a)   no seat of the arbitration has been designated or determined, and

(b)   by reason of a connection with England and Wales or Northern Ireland the court is satisfied that it is appropriate to do so.

(5)   Section 7 (separability of arbitration agreement) and section 8 (death of a party) apply where the law applicable to the arbitration agreement is the law of England and Wales or Northern Ireland even if the seat of the arbitration is outside England and Wales or Northern Ireland or has not been designated or determined.

3.   The seat of the arbitration.

In this Part 'the seat of the arbitration' means the juridical seat of the arbitration designated—

(a)   by the parties to the arbitration agreement, or

(b)   by any arbitral or other institution or person vested by the parties with powers in that regard, or

(c)   by the arbitral tribunal if so authorised by the parties,

or determined, in the absence of any such designation, having regard to the parties' agreement and all the relevant circumstances.

4.   Mandatory and non-mandatory provisions.

(1)   The mandatory provisions of this Part are listed in Schedule 1 and have effect notwithstanding any agreement to the contrary.

(2)   The other provisions of this Part (the 'non-mandatory provisions') allow the parties to make their own arrangements by agreement but provide rules which apply in the absence of such agreement.

(3)   The parties may make such arrangements by agreeing to the application of institutional rules or providing any other means by which a matter may be decided.

(4)   It is immaterial whether or not the law applicable to the parties' agreement is the law of England and Wales or, as the case may be, Northern Ireland.

(5)   The choice of a law other than the law of England and Wales or Northern Ireland as the applicable law in respect of a matter provided for by a non-mandatory provision of this Part is equivalent to an agreement making provision about that matter.

For this purpose an applicable law determined in accordance with the parties' agreement, or which is objectively determined in the absence of any express or implied choice, shall be treated as chosen by the parties.

5.   Agreements to be in writing.

(1)   The provisions of this Part apply only where the arbitration agreement is in writing, and any other agreement between the parties as to any matter is effective for the purposes of this Part only if in writing.

The expressions 'agreement', 'agree' and 'agreed' shall be construed accordingly.

(2)   There is an agreement in writing—

(a)   if the agreement is made in writing (whether or not it is signed by the parties),

(b)   if the agreement is made by exchange of communications in writing, or

(c)   if the agreement is evidenced in writing.

(3)   Where parties agree otherwise than in writing by reference to terms which are in writing, they make an agreement in writing.

(4)   An agreement is evidenced in writing if an agreement made otherwise than in writing is recorded by one of the parties, or by a third party, with the authority of the parties to the agreement.

(5)   An exchange of written submissions in arbitral or legal proceedings in which the existence of an agreement otherwise than in writing is alleged by one party against another party and not denied by the other party in his response constitutes as between those parties an agreement in writing to the effect alleged.

(6)   References in this Part to anything being written or in writing include its being recorded by any means.

The arbitration agreement

6.   Definition of arbitration agreement.

(1)   In this Part an 'arbitration agreement' means an agreement to submit to arbitration present or future disputes (whether they are contractual or not).

(2)   The reference in an agreement to a written form of arbitration clause or to a document containing an arbitration clause constitutes an arbitration

agreement if the reference is such as to make that clause part of the agreement.

7.   Separability of arbitration agreement.

Unless otherwise agreed by the parties, an arbitration agreement which forms or was intended to form part of another agreement (whether or not in writing) shall not be regarded as invalid, non-existent or ineffective because that other agreement is invalid, or did not come into existence or has become ineffective, and it shall for that purpose be treated as a distinct agreement.

8.   Whether agreement discharged by death of a party.

(1)   Unless otherwise agreed by the parties, an arbitration agreement is not discharged by the death of a party and may be enforced by or against the personal representatives of that party.

(2)   Subsection (1) does not affect the operation of any enactment or rule of law by virtue of which a substantive right or obligation is extinguished by death.

Stay of legal proceedings

9.   Stay of legal proceedings.

(1)   A party to an arbitration agreement against whom legal proceedings are brought (whether by way of claim or counterclaim) in respect of a matter which under the agreement is to be referred to arbitration may (upon notice to the other parties to the proceedings) apply to the court in which the proceedings have been brought to stay the proceedings so far as they concern that matter.

(2)   An application may be made notwithstanding that the matter is to be referred to arbitration only after the exhaustion of other dispute resolution procedures.

(3)   An application may not be made by a person before taking the appropriate procedural step (if any) to acknowledge the legal proceedings against him or after he has taken any step in those proceedings to answer the substantive claim.

(4)   On an application under this section the court shall grant a stay unless satisfied that the arbitration agreement is null and void, inoperative, or incapable of being performed.

(5)   If the court refuses to stay the legal proceedings, any provision that an award is a condition precedent to the bringing of legal proceedings in respect of any matter is of no effect in relation to those proceedings.

10.   Reference of interpleader issue to arbitration.

(1)   Where in legal proceedings relief by way of interpleader is granted and any issue between the claimants is one in respect of which there is an arbitration agreement between them, the court granting the relief shall direct that the issue be determined in accordance with the agreement unless the

circumstances are such that proceedings brought by a claimant in respect of the matter would not be stayed.

(2)   Where subsection (1) applies but the court does not direct that the issue be determined in accordance with the arbitration agreement, any provision that an award is a condition precedent to the bringing of legal proceedings in respect of any matter shall not affect the determination of that issue by the court.

11.   Retention of security where Admiralty proceedings stayed.

(1)   Where Admiralty proceedings are stayed on the ground that the dispute in question should be submitted to arbitration, the court granting the stay may, if in those proceedings property has been arrested or bail or other security has been given to prevent or obtain release from arrest—

(a)   order that the property arrested be retained as security for the satisfaction of any award given in the arbitration in respect of that dispute, or

(b)   order that the stay of those proceedings be conditional on the provision of equivalent security for the satisfaction of any such award.

(2)   Subject to any provision made by rules of court and to any necessary modifications, the same law and practice shall apply in relation to property retained in pursuance of an order as would apply if it were held for the purposes of proceedings in the court making the order.

Commencement of arbitral proceedings

12.   Power of court to extend time for beginning arbitral proceedings, &c.

(1)   Where an arbitration agreement to refer future disputes to arbitration provides that a claim shall be barred, or the claimant's right extinguished, unless the claimant takes within a time fixed by the agreement some step–

(a)   to begin arbitral proceedings, or

(b)   to begin other dispute resolution procedures which must be exhausted before arbitral proceedings can be begun,
the court may by order extend the time for taking that step.

(2)   Any party to the arbitration agreement may apply for such an order (upon notice to the other parties), but only after a claim has arisen and after exhausting any available arbitral process for obtaining an extension of time.

(3)   The court shall make an order only if satisfied—

(a)   that the circumstances are such as were outside the reasonable contemplation of the parties when they agreed the provision in question, and that it would be just to extend the time, or

(b)   that the conduct of one party makes it unjust to hold the other party to the strict terms of the provision in question.

(4)   The court may extend the time for such period and on such terms as it thinks fit, and may do so whether or not the time previously fixed (by agreement or by a previous order) has expired.

(5)   An order under this section does not affect the operation of the Limitation Acts (see section 13).

(6)   The leave of the court is required for any appeal from a decision of the court under this section.

13. Application of Limitation Acts.

(1) The Limitation Acts apply to arbitral proceedings as they apply to legal proceedings.

(2) The court may order that in computing the time prescribed by the Limitation Acts for the commencement of proceedings (including arbitral proceedings) in respect of a dispute which was the subject matter—

(a) of an award which the court orders to be set aside or declares to be of no effect, or

(b) of the affected part of an award which the court orders to be set aside in part, or declares to be in part of no effect,

the period between the commencement of the arbitration and the date of the order referred to in paragraph (a) or (b) shall be excluded.

(3) In determining for the purposes of the Limitation Acts when a cause of action accrued, any provision that an award is a condition precedent to the bringing of legal proceedings in respect of a matter to which an arbitration agreement applies shall be disregarded.

(4) In this Part 'the Limitation Acts' means—

(a) in England and Wales, the Limitation Act 1980, the Foreign Limitation Periods Act 1984 and any other enactment (whenever passed) relating to the limitation of actions;

(b) in Northern Ireland, the Limitation (Northern Ireland) Order 1989, the Foreign Limitation Periods (Northern Ireland) Order 1985 and any other enactment (whenever passed) relating to the limitation of actions.

14. Commencement of arbitral proceedings.

(1) The parties are free to agree when arbitral proceedings are to be regarded as commenced for the purposes of this Part and for the purposes of the Limitation Acts.

(2) If there is no such agreement the following provisions apply.

(3) Where the arbitrator is named or designated in the arbitration agreement, arbitral proceedings are commenced in respect of a matter when one party serves on the other party or parties a notice in writing requiring him or them to submit that matter to the person so named or designated.

(4) Where the arbitrator or arbitrators are to be appointed by the parties, arbitral proceedings are commenced in respect of a matter when one party serves on the other party or parties notice in writing requiring him or them to appoint an arbitrator or to agree to the appointment of an arbitrator in respect of that matter.

(5) Where the arbitrator or arbitrators are to be appointed by a person other than a party to the proceedings, arbitral proceedings are commenced in respect of a matter when one party gives notice in writing to that person requesting him to make the appointment in respect of that matter.

The arbitral tribunal

15. The arbitral tribunal.

(1) The parties are free to agree on the number of arbitrators to form the tribunal and whether there is to be a chairman or umpire.

(2)   Unless otherwise agreed by the parties, an agreement that the number of arbitrators shall be two or any other even number shall be understood as requiring the appointment of an additional arbitrator as chairman of the tribunal.

(3)   If there is no agreement as to the number of arbitrators, the tribunal shall consist of a sole arbitrator.

16. Procedure for appointment of arbitrators.

(1)   The parties are free to agree on the procedure for appointing the arbitrator or arbitrators, including the procedure for appointing any chairman or umpire.

(2)   If or to the extent that there is no such agreement, the following provisions apply.

(3)   If the tribunal is to consist of a sole arbitrator, the parties shall jointly appoint the arbitrator not later than 28 days after service of a request in writing by either party to do so.

(4)   If the tribunal is to consist of two arbitrators, each party shall appoint one arbitrator not later than 14 days after service of a request in writing by either party to do so.

(5)   If the tribunal is to consist of three arbitrators—

(a)   each party shall appoint one arbitrator not later than 14 days after service of a request in writing by either party to do so, and

(b)   the two so appointed shall forthwith appoint a third arbitrator as the chairman of the tribunal.

(6)   If the tribunal is to consist of two arbitrators and an umpire—

(a)   each party shall appoint one arbitrator not later than 14 days after service of a request in writing by either party to do so, and

(b)   the two so appointed may appoint an umpire at any time after they themselves are appointed and shall do so before any substantive hearing or forthwith if they cannot agree on a matter relating to the arbitration.

(7)   In any other case (in particular, if there are more than two parties) section 18 applies as in the case of a failure of the agreed appointment procedure.

17. Power in case of default to appoint sole arbitrator.

(1)   Unless the parties otherwise agree, where each of two parties to an arbitration agreement is to appoint an arbitrator and one party ('the party in default') refuses to do so, or fails to do so within the time specified, the other party, having duly appointed his arbitrator, may give notice in writing to the party in default that he proposes to appoint his arbitrator to act as sole arbitrator.

(2)   If the party in default does not within 7 clear days of that notice being given—

(a)   make the required appointment, and

(b)   notify the other party that he has done so,

the other party may appoint his arbitrator as sole arbitrator whose award shall be binding on both parties as if he had been so appointed by agreement.

(3)   Where a sole arbitrator has been appointed under subsection (2), the party in default may (upon notice to the appointing party) apply to the court which may set aside the appointment.

(4)   The leave of the court is required for any appeal from a decision of the court under this section.

18.   Failure of appointment procedure.

(1)   The parties are free to agree what is to happen in the event of a failure of the procedure for the appointment of the arbitral tribunal.

There is no failure if an appointment is duly made under section 17 (power in case of default to appoint sole arbitrator), unless that appointment is set aside.

(2)   If or to the extent that there is no such agreement any party to the arbitration agreement may (upon notice to the other parties) apply to the court to exercise its powers under this section.

(3)   Those powers are—

    (a)   to give directions as to the making of any necessary appointments;

    (b)   to direct that the tribunal shall be constituted by such appointments (or any one or more of them) as have been made;

    (c)   to revoke any appointments already made;

    (d)   to make any necessary appointments itself.

(4)   An appointment made by the court under this section has effect as if made with the agreement of the parties.

(5)   The leave of the court is required for any appeal from a decision of the court under this section.

19.   Court to have regard to agreed qualifications.

In deciding whether to exercise, and in considering how to exercise, any of its powers under section 16 (procedure for appointment of arbitrators) or section 18 (failure of appointment procedure), the court shall have due regard to any agreement of the parties as to the qualifications required of the arbitrators.

20.   Chairman.

(1)   Where the parties have agreed that there is to be a chairman, they are free to agree what the functions of the chairman are to be in relation to the making of decisions, orders and awards.

(2)   If or to the extent that there is no such agreement, the following provisions apply.

(3)   Decisions, orders and awards shall be made by all or a majority of the arbitrators (including the chairman).

(4)   The view of the chairman shall prevail in relation to a decision, order or award in respect of which there is neither unanimity nor a majority under subsection (3).

21.   Umpire.

(1)   Where the parties have agreed that there is to be an umpire, they are free to agree what the functions of the umpire are to be, and in particular—

    (a)   whether he is to attend the proceedings, and

(b)   when he is to replace the other arbitrators as the tribunal with power to make decisions, orders and awards.

(2)   If or to the extent that there is no such agreement, the following provisions apply.

(3)   The umpire shall attend the proceedings and be supplied with the same documents and other materials as are supplied to the other arbitrators.

(4)   Decisions, orders and awards shall be made by the other arbitrators unless and until they cannot agree on a matter relating to the arbitration.

In that event they shall forthwith give notice in writing to the parties and the umpire, whereupon the umpire shall replace them as the tribunal with power to make decisions, orders and awards as if he were sole arbitrator.

(5)   If the arbitrators cannot agree but fail to give notice of that fact, or if any of them fails to join in the giving of notice, any party to the arbitral proceedings may (upon notice to the other parties and to the tribunal) apply to the court which may order that the umpire shall replace the other arbitrators as the tribunal with power to make decisions, orders and awards as if he were sole arbitrator.

(6)   The leave of the court is required for any appeal from a decision of the court under this section.

22.   Decision-making where no chairman or umpire.

(1)   Where the parties agree that there shall be two or more arbitrators with no chairman or umpire, the parties are free to agree how the tribunal is to make decisions, orders and awards.

(2)   If there is no such agreement, decisions, orders and awards shall be made by all or a majority of the arbitrators.

23.   Revocation of arbitrator's authority.

(1)   The parties are free to agree in what circumstances the authority of an arbitrator may be revoked.

(2)   If or to the extent that there is no such agreement the following provisions apply.

(3)   The authority of an arbitrator may not be revoked except—
   (a)   by the parties acting jointly, or
   (b)   by an arbitral or other institution or person vested by the parties with powers in that regard.

(4)   Revocation of the authority of an arbitrator by the parties acting jointly must be agreed in writing unless the parties also agree (whether or not in writing) to terminate the arbitration agreement.

(5)   Nothing in this section affects the power of the court—
   (a)   to revoke an appointment under section 18 (powers exercisable in case of failure of appointment procedure), or
   (b)   to remove an arbitrator on the grounds specified in section 24.

24.   Power of court to remove arbitrator.

(1)   A party to arbitral proceedings may (upon notice to the other parties, to the arbitrator concerned and to any other arbitrator) apply to the court to remove an arbitrator on any of the following grounds—

(a)   that circumstances exist that give rise to justifiable doubts as to his impartiality;

(b)   that he does not possess the qualifications required by the arbitration agreement;

(c)   that he is physically or mentally incapable of conducting the proceedings or there are justifiable doubts as to his capacity to do so;

(d)   that he has refused or failed—

(i)   properly to conduct the proceedings, or

(ii)   to use all reasonable despatch in conducting the proceedings or making an award,

and that substantial injustice has been or will be caused to the applicant.

(2)   If there is an arbitral or other institution or person vested by the parties with power to remove an arbitrator, the court shall not exercise its power of removal unless satisfied that the applicant has first exhausted any available recourse to that institution or person.

(3)   The arbitral tribunal may continue the arbitral proceedings and make an award while an application to the court under this section is pending.

(4)   Where the court removes an arbitrator, it may make such order as it thinks fit with respect to his entitlement (if any) to fees or expenses, or the repayment of any fees or expenses already paid.

(5)   The arbitrator concerned is entitled to appear and be heard by the court before it makes any order under this section.

(6)   The leave of the court is required for any appeal from a decision of the court under this section.

25.   Resignation of arbitrator.

(1)   The parties are free to agree with an arbitrator as to the consequences of his resignation as regards—

(a)   his entitlement (if any) to fees or expenses, and

(b)   any liability thereby incurred by him.

(2)   If or to the extent that there is no such agreement the following provisions apply.

(3)   An arbitrator who resigns his appointment may (upon notice to the parties) apply to the court—

(a)   to grant him relief from any liability thereby incurred by him, and

(b)   to make such order as it thinks fit with respect to his entitlement (if any) to fees or expenses or the repayment of any fees or expenses already paid.

(4)   If the court is satisfied that in all the circumstances it was reasonable for the arbitrator to resign, it may grant such relief as is mentioned in subsection (3)(a) on such terms as it thinks fit.

(5)   The leave of the court is required for any appeal from a decision of the court under this section.

26.   Death of arbitrator or person appointing him.

(1)   The authority of an arbitrator is personal and ceases on his death.

(2)   Unless otherwise agreed by the parties, the death of the person by whom an arbitrator was appointed does not revoke the arbitrator's authority.

27. Filling of vacancy, &c.

(1) Where an arbitrator ceases to hold office, the parties are free to agree—
(a) whether and if so how the vacancy is to be filled,
(b) whether and if so to what extent the previous proceedings should stand, and
(c) what effect (if any) his ceasing to hold office has on any appointment made by him (alone or jointly).

(2) If or to the extent that there is no such agreement, the following provisions apply.

(3) The provisions of sections 16 (procedure for appointment of arbitrators) and 18 (failure of appointment procedure) apply in relation to the filling of the vacancy as in relation to an original appointment.

(4) The tribunal (when reconstituted) shall determine whether and if so to what extent the previous proceedings should stand.

This does not affect any right of a party to challenge those proceedings on any ground which had arisen before the arbitrator ceased to hold office.

(5) His ceasing to hold office does not affect any appointment by him (alone or jointly) of another arbitrator, in particular any appointment of a chairman or umpire.

28. Joint and several liability of parties to arbitrators for fees and expenses.

(1) The parties are jointly and severally liable to pay to the arbitrators such reasonable fees and expenses (if any) as are appropriate in the circumstances.

(2) Any party may apply to the court (upon notice to the other parties and to the arbitrators) which may order that the amount of the arbitrators' fees and expenses shall be considered and adjusted by such means and upon such terms as it may direct.

(3) If the application is made after any amount has been paid to the arbitrators by way of fees or expenses, the court may order the repayment of such amount (if any) as is shown to be excessive, but shall not do so unless it is shown that it is reasonable in the circumstances to order repayment.

(4) The above provisions have effect subject to any order of the court under section 24(4) or 25(3)(b) (order as to entitlement to fees or expenses in case of removal or resignation of arbitrator).

(5) Nothing in this section affects any liability of a party to any other party to pay all or any of the costs of the arbitration (see sections 59 to 65) or any contractual right of an arbitrator to payment of his fees and expenses.

(6) In this section references to arbitrators include an arbitrator who has ceased to act and an umpire who has not replaced the other arbitrators.

29. Immunity of arbitrator.

(1) An arbitrator is not liable for anything done or omitted in the discharge or purported discharge of his functions as arbitrator unless the act or omission is shown to have been in bad faith.

(2)   Subsection (1) applies to an employee or agent of an arbitrator as it applies to the arbitrator himself.

(3)   This section does not affect any liability incurred by an arbitrator by reason of his resigning (but see section 25).

Jurisdiction of the arbitral tribunal

30.   Competence of tribunal to rule on its own jurisdiction.

(1)   Unless otherwise agreed by the parties, the arbitral tribunal may rule on its own substantive jurisdiction, that is, as to—
  (a)   whether there is a valid arbitration agreement,
  (b)   whether the tribunal is properly constituted, and
  (c)   what matters have been submitted to arbitration in accordance with the arbitration agreement.

(2)   Any such ruling may be challenged by any available arbitral process of appeal or review or in accordance with the provisions of this Part.

31.   Objection to substantive jurisdiction of tribunal.

(1)   An objection that the arbitral tribunal lacks substantive jurisdiction at the outset of the proceedings must be raised by a party not later than the time he takes the first step in the proceedings to contest the merits of any matter in relation to which he challenges the tribunal's jurisdiction.

A party is not precluded from raising such an objection by the fact that he has appointed or participated in the appointment of an arbitrator.

(2)   Any objection during the course of the arbitral proceedings that the arbitral tribunal is exceeding its substantive jurisdiction must be made as soon as possible after the matter alleged to be beyond its jurisdiction is raised.

(3)   The arbitral tribunal may admit an objection later than the time specified in subsection (1) or (2) if it considers the delay justified.

(4)   Where an objection is duly taken to the tribunal's substantive jurisdiction and the tribunal has power to rule on its own jurisdiction, it may—
  (a)   rule on the matter in an award as to jurisdiction, or
  (b)   deal with the objection in its award on the merits.

If the parties agree which of these courses the tribunal should take, the tribunal shall proceed accordingly.

(5)   The tribunal may in any case, and shall if the parties so agree, stay proceedings whilst an application is made to the court under section 32 (determination of preliminary point of jurisdiction).

32.   Determination of preliminary point of jurisdiction.

(1)   The court may, on the application of a party to arbitral proceedings (upon notice to the other parties), determine any question as to the substantive jurisdiction of the tribunal.

A party may lose the right to object (see section 73).

(2)   An application under this section shall not be considered unless—
  (a)   it is made with the agreement in writing of all the other parties to the proceedings, or

(b) it is made with the permission of the tribunal and the court is satisfied—

    (i) that the determination of the question is likely to produce substantial savings in costs,

    (ii) that the application was made without delay, and

    (iii) that there is good reason why the matter should be decided by the court.

(3) An application under this section, unless made with the agreement of all the other parties to the proceedings, shall state the grounds on which it is said that the matter should be decided by the court.

(4) Unless otherwise agreed by the parties, the arbitral tribunal may continue the arbitral proceedings and make an award while an application to the court under this section is pending.

(5) Unless the court gives leave, no appeal lies from a decision of the court whether the conditions specified in subsection (2) are met.

(6) The decision of the court on the question of jurisdiction shall be treated as a judgment of the court for the purposes of an appeal.

But no appeal lies without the leave of the court which shall not be given unless the court considers that the question involves a point of law which is one of general importance or is one which for some other special reason should be considered by the Court of Appeal. .

The arbitral proceedings

33. General duty of the tribunal.

(1) The tribunal shall—

    (a) act fairly and impartially as between the parties, giving each party a reasonable opportunity of putting his case and dealing with that of his opponent, and

    (b) adopt procedures suitable to the circumstances of the particular case, avoiding unnecessary delay or expense, so as to provide a fair means for the resolution of the matters falling to be determined.

(2) The tribunal shall comply with that general duty in conducting the arbitral proceedings, in its decisions on matters of procedure and evidence and in the exercise of all other powers conferred on it.

34. Procedural and evidential matters.

(1) It shall be for the tribunal to decide all procedural and evidential matters, subject to the right of the parties to agree any matter.

(2) Procedural and evidential matters include—

    (a) when and where any part of the proceedings is to be held;

    (b) the language or languages to be used in the proceedings and whether translations of any relevant documents are to be supplied;

    (c) whether any and if so what form of written statements of claim and defence are to be used, when these should be supplied and the extent to which such statements can be later amended;

    (d) whether any and if so which documents or classes of documents should be disclosed between and produced by the parties and at what stage;

(e)   whether any and if so what questions should be put to and answered by the respective parties and when and in what form this should be done;

(f)   whether to apply strict rules of evidence (or any other rules) as to the admissibility, relevance or weight of any material (oral, written or other) sought to be tendered on any matters of fact or opinion, and the time, manner and form in which such material should be exchanged and presented;

(g)   whether and to what extent the tribunal should itself take the initiative in ascertaining the facts and the law;

(h)   whether and to what extent there should be oral or written evidence or submissions.

(3)   The tribunal may fix the time within which any directions given by it are to be complied with, and may if it thinks fit extend the time so fixed (whether or not it has expired).

35.   Consolidation of proceedings and concurrent hearings.

(1)   The parties are free to agree—

(a)   that the arbitral proceedings shall be consolidated with other arbitral proceedings, or

(b)   that concurrent hearings shall be held,

on such terms as may be agreed.

(2)   Unless the parties agree to confer such power on the tribunal, the tribunal has no power to order consolidation of proceedings or concurrent hearings.

36.   Legal or other representation.

Unless otherwise agreed by the parties, a party to arbitral proceedings may be represented in the proceedings by a lawyer or other person chosen by him.

37.   Power to appoint experts, legal advisers or assessors.

(1)   Unless otherwise agreed by the parties—

(a)   the tribunal may—

(i)   appoint experts or legal advisers to report to it and the parties, or

(ii)   appoint assessors to assist it on technical matters,

and may allow any such expert, legal adviser or assessor to attend the proceedings; and

(b)   the parties shall be given a reasonable opportunity to comment on any information, opinion or advice offered by any such person.

(2)   The fees and expenses of an expert, legal adviser or assessor appointed by the tribunal for which the arbitrators are liable are expenses of the arbitrators for the purposes of this Part.

38.   General powers exercisable by the tribunal.

(1)   The parties are free to agree on the powers exercisable by the arbitral tribunal for the purposes of and in relation to the proceedings.

(2)   Unless otherwise agreed by the parties the tribunal has the following powers.

(3)   The tribunal may order a claimant to provide security for the costs of the arbitration.

This power shall not be exercised on the ground that the claimant is—

(a)   an individual ordinarily resident outside the United Kingdom, or

(b)   a corporation or association incorporated or formed under the law of a country outside the United Kingdom, or whose central management and control is exercised outside the United Kingdom.

(4)   The tribunal may give directions in relation to any property which is the subject of the proceedings or as to which any question arises in the proceedings, and which is owned by or is in the possession of a party to the proceedings—

(a)   for the inspection, photographing, preservation, custody or detention of the property by the tribunal, an expert or a party, or

(b)   ordering that samples be taken from, or any observation be made of or experiment conducted upon, the property.

(5)   The tribunal may direct that a party or witness shall be examined on oath or affirmation, and may for that purpose administer any necessary oath or take any necessary affirmation.

(6)   The tribunal may give directions to a party for the preservation for the purposes of the proceedings of any evidence in his custody or control.

39.   Power to make provisional awards.

(1)   The parties are free to agree that the tribunal shall have power to order on a provisional basis any relief which it would have power to grant in a final award.

(2)   This includes, for instance, making—

(a)   a provisional order for the payment of money or the disposition of property as between the parties, or

(b)   an order to make an interim payment on account of the costs of the arbitration.

(3)   Any such order shall be subject to the tribunal's final adjudication; and the tribunal's final award, on the merits or as to costs, shall take account of any such order.

(4)   Unless the parties agree to confer such power on the tribunal, the tribunal has no such power.

This does not affect its powers under section 47 (awards on different issues, &c.).

40.   General duty of parties.

(1)   The parties shall do all things necessary for the proper and expeditious conduct of the arbitral proceedings.

(2)   This includes—

(a)   complying without delay with any determination of the tribunal as to procedural or evidential matters, or with any order or directions of the tribunal, and

(b)   where appropriate, taking without delay any necessary steps to obtain a decision of the court on a preliminary question of jurisdiction or law (see sections 32 and 45).

41. Powers of tribunal in case of party's default.

(1) The parties are free to agree on the powers of the tribunal in case of a party's failure to do something necessary for the proper and expeditious conduct of the arbitration.

(2) Unless otherwise agreed by the parties, the following provisions apply.

(3) If the tribunal is satisfied that there has been inordinate and inexcusable delay on the part of the claimant in pursuing his claim and that the delay—

(a) gives rise, or is likely to give rise, to a substantial risk that it is not possible to have a fair resolution of the issues in that claim, or

(b) has caused, or is likely to cause, serious prejudice to the respondent,

the tribunal may make an award dismissing the claim.

(4) If without showing sufficient cause a party—

(a) fails to attend or be represented at an oral hearing of which due notice was given, or

(b) where matters are to be dealt with in writing, fails after due notice to submit written evidence or make written submissions,

the tribunal may continue the proceedings in the absence of that party or, as the case may be, without any written evidence or submissions on his behalf, and may make an award on the basis of the evidence before it.

(5) If without showing sufficient cause a party fails to comply with any order or directions of the tribunal, the tribunal may make a peremptory order to the same effect, prescribing such time for compliance with it as the tribunal considers appropriate.

(6) If a claimant fails to comply with a peremptory order of the tribunal to provide security for costs, the tribunal may make an award dismissing his claim.

(7) If a party fails to comply with any other kind of peremptory order, then, without prejudice to section 42 (enforcement by court of tribunal's peremptory orders), the tribunal may do any of the following—

(a) direct that the party in default shall not be entitled to rely upon any allegation or material which was the subject matter of the order;

(b) draw such adverse inferences from the act of non-compliance as the circumstances justify;

(c) proceed to an award on the basis of such materials as have been properly provided to it;

(d) make such order as it thinks fit as to the payment of costs of the arbitration incurred in consequence of the non-compliance.

Powers of court in relation to arbitral proceedings

42. Enforcement of peremptory orders of tribunal.

(1) Unless otherwise agreed by the parties, the court may make an order requiring a party to comply with a peremptory order made by the tribunal.

(2) An application for an order under this section may be made—

(a) by the tribunal (upon notice to the parties),

(b)   by a party to the arbitral proceedings with the permission of the tribunal (and upon notice to the other parties), or

(c)   where the parties have agreed that the powers of the court under this section shall be available.

(3)   The court shall not act unless it is satisfied that the applicant has exhausted any available arbitral process in respect of failure to comply with the tribunal's order.

(4)   No order shall be made under this section unless the court is satisfied that the person to whom the tribunal's order was directed has failed to comply with it within the time prescribed in the order or, if no time was prescribed, within a reasonable time.

(5)   The leave of the court is required for any appeal from a decision of the court under this section.

43.   Securing the attendance of witnesses.

(1)   A party to arbitral proceedings may use the same court procedures as are available in relation to legal proceedings to secure the attendance before the tribunal of a witness in order to give oral testimony or to produce documents or other material evidence.

(2)   This may only be done with the permission of the tribunal or the agreement of the other parties.

(3)   The court procedures may only be used if—

(a)   the witness is in the United Kingdom, and

(b)   the arbitral proceedings are being conducted in England and Wales or, as the case may be, Northern Ireland.

(4)   A person shall not be compelled by virtue of this section to produce any document or other material evidence which he could not be compelled to produce in legal proceedings.

44.   Court powers exercisable in support of arbitral proceedings.

(1)   Unless otherwise agreed by the parties, the court has for the purposes of and in relation to arbitral proceedings the same power of making orders about the matters listed below as it has for the purposes of and in relation to legal proceedings.

(2)   Those matters are—

(a)   the taking of the evidence of witnesses;

(b)   the preservation of evidence;

(c)   making orders relating to property which is the subject of the proceedings or as to which any question arises in the proceedings—

(i)   for the inspection, photographing, preservation, custody or detention of the property, or

(ii)   ordering that samples be taken from, or any observation be made of or experiment conducted upon, the property;

(iii)   and for that purpose authorising any person to enter any premises in the possession or control of a party to the arbitration;

(d)   the sale of any goods the subject of the proceedings;

(e)   the granting of an interim injunction or the appointment of a receiver.

(3)   If the case is one of urgency, the court may, on the application of a party or proposed party to the arbitral proceedings, make such orders as it thinks necessary for the purpose of preserving evidence or assets.

(4)   If the case is not one of urgency, the court shall act only on the application of a party to the arbitral proceedings (upon notice to the other parties and to the tribunal) made with the permission of the tribunal or the agreement in writing of the other parties.

(5)   In any case the court shall act only if or to the extent that the arbitral tribunal, and any arbitral or other institution or person vested by the parties with power in that regard, has no power or is unable for the time being to act effectively.

(6)   If the court so orders, an order made by it under this section shall cease to have effect in whole or in part on the order of the tribunal or of any such arbitral or other institution or person having power to act in relation to the subject-matter of the order.

(7)   The leave of the court is required for any appeal from a decision of the court under this section.

45.   Determination of preliminary point of law.

(1)   Unless otherwise agreed by the parties, the court may on the application of a party to arbitral proceedings (upon notice to the other parties) determine any question of law arising in the course of the proceedings which the court is satisfied substantially affects the rights of one or more of the parties.

An agreement to dispense with reasons for the tribunal's award shall be considered an agreement to exclude the court's jurisdiction under this section.

(2)   An application under this section shall not be considered unless—

(a)   it is made with the agreement of all the other parties to the proceedings, or

(b)   it is made with the permission of the tribunal and the court is satisfied—

(i)   that the determination of the question is likely to produce substantial savings in costs, and

(ii)   that the application was made without delay.

(3)   The application shall identify the question of law to be determined and, unless made with the agreement of all the other parties to the proceedings, shall state the grounds on which it is said that the question should be decided by the court.

(4)   Unless otherwise agreed by the parties, the arbitral tribunal may continue the arbitral proceedings and make an award while an application to the court under this section is pending.

(5)   Unless the court gives leave, no appeal lies from a decision of the court whether the conditions specified in subsection (2) are met.

(6)   The decision of the court on the question of law shall be treated as a judgment of the court for the purposes of an appeal.

But no appeal lies without the leave of the court which shall not be given unless the court considers that the question is one of general importance, or is one which for some other special reason should be considered by the Court of Appeal.

The award

46. Rules applicable to substance of dispute.

(1)   The arbitral tribunal shall decide the dispute—

(a)   in accordance with the law chosen by the parties as applicable to the substance of the dispute, or

(b)   if the parties so agree, in accordance with such other considerations as are agreed by them or determined by the tribunal.

(2)   For this purpose the choice of the laws of a country shall be understood to refer to the substantive laws of that country and not its conflict of laws rules.

(3)   If or to the extent that there is no such choice or agreement, the tribunal shall apply the law determined by the conflict of laws rules which it considers applicable.

47. Awards on different issues, &c.

(1)   Unless otherwise agreed by the parties, the tribunal may make more than one award at different times on different aspects of the matters to be determined.

(2)   The tribunal may, in particular, make an award relating—

(a)   to an issue affecting the whole claim, or

(b)   to a part only of the claims or cross-claims submitted to it for decision.

(3)   If the tribunal does so, it shall specify in its award the issue, or the claim or part of a claim, which is the subject matter of the award.

48. Remedies.

(1)   The parties are free to agree on the powers exercisable by the arbitral tribunal as regards remedies.

(2)   Unless otherwise agreed by the parties, the tribunal has the following powers.

(3)   The tribunal may make a declaration as to any matter to be determined in the proceedings.

(4)   The tribunal may order the payment of a sum of money, in any currency.

(5)   The tribunal has the same powers as the court—

(a)   to order a party to do or refrain from doing anything;

(b)   to order specific performance of a contract (other than a contract relating to land);

(c)   to order the rectification, setting aside or cancellation of a deed or other document.

49. Interest.

(1)   The parties are free to agree on the powers of the tribunal as regards the award of interest.

(2)   Unless otherwise agreed by the parties the following provisions apply.

(3)   The tribunal may award simple or compound interest from such dates, at such rates and with such rests as it considers meets the justice of the case—

(a)   on the whole or part of any amount awarded by the tribunal, in respect of any period up to the date of the award;

(b)   on the whole or part of any amount claimed in the arbitration and outstanding at the commencement of the arbitral proceedings but paid before the award was made, in respect of any period up to the date of payment.

(4)   The tribunal may award simple or compound interest from the date of the award (or any later date) until payment, at such rates and with such rests as it considers meets the justice of the case, on the outstanding amount of any award (including any award of interest under subsection (3) and any award as to costs).

(5)   References in this section to an amount awarded by the tribunal include an amount payable in consequence of a declaratory award by the tribunal.

(6)   The above provisions do not affect any other power of the tribunal to award interest.

50.   Extension of time for making award.

(1)   Where the time for making an award is limited by or in pursuance of the arbitration agreement, then, unless otherwise agreed by the parties, the court may in accordance with the following provisions by order extend that time.

(2)   An application for an order under this section may be made—

(a)   by the tribunal (upon notice to the parties), or

(b)   by any party to the proceedings (upon notice to the tribunal and the other parties),

but only after exhausting any available arbitral process for obtaining an extension of time.

(3)   The court shall only make an order if satisfied that a substantial injustice would otherwise be done.

(4)   The court may extend the time for such period and on such terms as it thinks fit, and may do so whether or not the time previously fixed (by or under the agreement or by a previous order) has expired.

(5)   The leave of the court is required for any appeal from a decision of the court under this section.

51.   Settlement.

(1)   If during arbitral proceedings the parties settle the dispute, the following provisions apply unless otherwise agreed by the parties.

(2)   The tribunal shall terminate the substantive proceedings and, if so requested by the parties and not objected to by the tribunal, shall record the settlement in the form of an agreed award.

(3)   An agreed award shall state that it is an award of the tribunal and shall have the same status and effect as any other award on the merits of the case.

(4)   The following provisions of this Part relating to awards (sections 52 to 58) apply to an agreed award.

(5)   Unless the parties have also settled the matter of the payment of the costs of the arbitration, the provisions of this Part relating to costs (sections 59 to 65) continue to apply.

52.   Form of award.

(1)   The parties are free to agree on the form of an award.

(2)   If or to the extent that there is no such agreement, the following provisions apply.

(3)   The award shall be in writing signed by all the arbitrators or all those assenting to the award.

(4)   The award shall contain the reasons for the award unless it is an agreed award or the parties have agreed to dispense with reasons.

(5)   The award shall state the seat of the arbitration and the date when the award is made.

53.   Place where award treated as made.

Unless otherwise agreed by the parties, where the seat of the arbitration is in England and Wales or Northern Ireland, any award in the proceedings shall be treated as made there, regardless of where it was signed, despatched or delivered to any of the parties.

54.   Date of award.

(1)   Unless otherwise agreed by the parties, the tribunal may decide what is to be taken to be the date on which the award was made.

(2)   In the absence of any such decision, the date of the award shall be taken to be the date on which it is signed by the arbitrator or, where more than one arbitrator signs the award, by the last of them.

55.   Notification of award.

(1)   The parties are free to agree on the requirements as to notification of the award to the parties.

(2)   If there is no such agreement, the award shall be notified to the parties by service on them of copies of the award, which shall be done without delay after the award is made.

(3)   Nothing in this section affects section 56 (power to withhold award in case of non-payment).

56.   Power to withhold award in case of non-payment.

(1)   The tribunal may refuse to deliver an award to the parties except upon full payment of the fees and expenses of the arbitrators.

(2)   If the tribunal refuses on that ground to deliver an award, a party to the arbitral proceedings may (upon notice to the other parties and the tribunal) apply to the court, which may order that—

(a)   the tribunal shall deliver the award on the payment into court by the applicant of the fees and expenses demanded, or such lesser amount as the court may specify,

(b) the amount of the fees and expenses properly payable shall be determined by such means and upon such terms as the court may direct, and

(c) that out of the money paid into court there shall be paid out such fees and expenses as may be found to be properly payable and the balance of the money (if any) shall be paid out to the applicant.

(3) For this purpose the amount of fees and expenses properly payable is the amount the applicant is liable to pay under section 28 or any agreement relating to the payment of the arbitrators.

(4) No application to the court may be made where there is any available arbitral process for appeal or review of the amount of the fees or expenses demanded.

(5) References in this section to arbitrators include an arbitrator who has ceased to act and an umpire who has not replaced the other arbitrators.

(6) The above provisions of this section also apply in relation to any arbitral or other institution or person vested by the parties with powers in relation to the delivery of the tribunal's award.

As they so apply, the references to the fees and expenses of the arbitrators shall be construed as including the fees and expenses of that institution or person.

(7) The leave of the court is required for any appeal from a decision of the court under this section.

(8) Nothing in this section shall be construed as excluding an application under section 28 where payment has been made to the arbitrators in order to obtain the award.

57. Correction of award or additional award.

(1) The parties are free to agree on the powers of the tribunal to correct an award or make an additional award.

(2) If or to the extent there is no such agreement, the following provisions apply.

(3) The tribunal may on its own initiative or on the application of a party—

(a) correct an award so as to remove any clerical mistake or error arising from an accidental slip or omission or clarify or remove any ambiguity in the award, or

(b) make an additional award in respect of any claim (including a claim for interest or costs) which was presented to the tribunal but was not dealt with in the award.

These powers shall not be exercised without first affording the other parties a reasonable opportunity to make representations to the tribunal.

(4) Any application for the exercise of those powers must be made within 28 days of the date of the award or such longer period as the parties may agree.

(5) Any correction of an award shall be made within 28 days of the date the application was received by the tribunal or, where the correction is made by the tribunal on its own initiative, within 28 days of the date of the award or, in either case, such longer period as the parties may agree.

(6) Any additional award shall be made within 56 days of the date of the original award or such longer period as the parties may agree.

(7) Any correction of an award shall form part of the award.

58. Effect of award.

(1)   Unless otherwise agreed by the parties, an award made by the tribunal pursuant to an arbitration agreement is final and binding both on the parties and on any persons claiming through or under them.

(2)   This does not affect the right of a person to challenge the award by any available arbitral process of appeal or review or in accordance with the provisions of this Part.

Costs of the arbitration

59. Costs of the arbitration.

(1)   References in this Part to the costs of the arbitration are to—
   (a)   the arbitrators' fees and expenses,
   (b)   the fees and expenses of any arbitral institution concerned, and
   (c)   the legal or other costs of the parties.

(2)   Any such reference includes the costs of or incidental to any proceedings to determine the amount of the recoverable costs of the arbitration (see section 63).

60. Agreement to pay costs in any event.

An agreement which has the effect that a party is to pay the whole or part of the costs of the arbitration in any event is only valid if made after the dispute in question has arisen.

61. Award of costs.

(1)   The tribunal may make an award allocating the costs of the arbitration as between the parties, subject to any agreement of the parties.

(2)   Unless the parties otherwise agree, the tribunal shall award costs on the general principle that costs should follow the event except where it appears to the tribunal that in the circumstances this is not appropriate in relation to the whole or part of the costs.

62. Effect of agreement or award about costs.

Unless the parties otherwise agree, any obligation under an agreement between them as to how the costs of the arbitration are to be borne, or under an award allocating the costs of the arbitration, extends only to such costs as are recoverable.

63. The recoverable costs of the arbitration.

(1)   The parties are free to agree what costs of the arbitration are recoverable.

(2)   If or to the extent there is no such agreement, the following provisions apply.

(3)   The tribunal may determine by award the recoverable costs of the arbitration on such basis as it thinks fit.

If it does so, it shall specify—
    (a)   the basis on which it has acted, and
    (b)   the items of recoverable costs and the amount referable to each.
    (4)   If the tribunal does not determine the recoverable costs of the arbitration, any party to the arbitral proceedings may apply to the court (upon notice to the other parties) which may—
    (a)   determine the recoverable costs of the arbitration on such basis as it thinks fit, or
    (b)   order that they shall be determined by such means and upon such terms as it may specify.
    (5)   Unless the tribunal or the court determines otherwise—
    (a)   the recoverable costs of the arbitration shall be determined on the basis that there shall be allowed a reasonable amount in respect of all costs reasonably incurred, and
    (b)   any doubt as to whether costs were reasonably incurred or were reasonable in amount shall be resolved in favour of the paying party.
    (6)   The above provisions have effect subject to section 64 (recoverable fees and expenses of arbitrators).
    (7)   Nothing in this section affects any right of the arbitrators, any expert, legal adviser or assessor appointed by the tribunal, or any arbitral institution, to payment of their fees and expenses.

64.   Recoverable fees and expenses of arbitrators.

    (1)   Unless otherwise agreed by the parties, the recoverable costs of the arbitration shall include in respect of the fees and expenses of the arbitrators only such reasonable fees and expenses as are appropriate in the circumstances.
    (2)   If there is any question as to what reasonable fees and expenses are appropriate in the circumstances, and the matter is not already before the court on an application under section 63(4), the court may on the application of any party (upon notice to the other parties)—
    (a)   determine the matter, or
    (b)   order that it be determined by such means and upon such terms as the court may specify.
    (3)   Subsection (1) has effect subject to any order of the court under section 24(4) or 25(3)(b) (order as to entitlement to fees or expenses in case of removal or resignation of arbitrator).
    (4)   Nothing in this section affects any right of the arbitrator to payment of his fees and expenses.

65.   Power to limit recoverable costs.

    (1)   Unless otherwise agreed by the parties, the tribunal may direct that the recoverable costs of the arbitration, or of any part of the arbitral proceedings, shall be limited to a specified amount.
    (2)   Any direction may be made or varied at any stage, but this must be done sufficiently in advance of the incurring of costs to which it relates, or the taking of any steps in the proceedings which may be affected by it, for the limit to be taken into account.

Powers of the court in relation to award

66. Enforcement of the award.

(1)   An award made by the tribunal pursuant to an arbitration agreement may, by leave of the court, be enforced in the same manner as a judgment or order of the court to the same effect.

(2)   Where leave is so given, judgment may be entered in terms of the award.

(3)   Leave to enforce an award shall not be given where, or to the extent that, the person against whom it is sought to be enforced shows that the tribunal lacked substantive jurisdiction to make the award.

The right to raise such an objection may have been lost (see section 73).

(4)   Nothing in this section affects the recognition or enforcement of an award under any other enactment or rule of law, in particular under Part II of the Arbitration Act 1950 (enforcement of awards under Geneva Convention) or the provisions of Part III of this Act relating to the recognition and enforcement of awards under the New York Convention or by an action on the award.

67. Challenging the award: substantive jurisdiction.

(1)   A party to arbitral proceedings may (upon notice to the other parties and to the tribunal) apply to the court—

  (a)   challenging any award of the arbitral tribunal as to its substantive jurisdiction; or

  (b)   for an order declaring an award made by the tribunal on the merits to be of no effect, in whole or in part, because the tribunal did not have substantive jurisdiction.

A party may lose the right to object (see section 73) and the right to apply is subject to the restrictions in section 70(2) and (3).

(2)   The arbitral tribunal may continue the arbitral proceedings and make a further award while an application to the court under this section is pending in relation to an award as to jurisdiction.

(3)   On an application under this section challenging an award of the arbitral tribunal as to its substantive jurisdiction, the court may by order—

  (a)   confirm the award,

  (b)   vary the award, or

  (c)   set aside the award in whole or in part.

(4)   The leave of the court is required for any appeal from a decision of the court under this section.

68. Challenging the award: serious irregularity.

(1)   A party to arbitral proceedings may (upon notice to the other parties and to the tribunal) apply to the court challenging an award in the proceedings on the ground of serious irregularity affecting the tribunal, the proceedings or the award.

A party may lose the right to object (see section 73) and the right to apply is subject to the restrictions in section 70(2) and (3).

(2) Serious irregularity means an irregularity of one or more of the following kinds which the court considers has caused or will cause substantial injustice to the applicant—

(a) failure by the tribunal to comply with section 33 (general duty of tribunal);

(b) the tribunal exceeding its powers (otherwise than by exceeding its substantive jurisdiction: see section 67);

(c) failure by the tribunal to conduct the proceedings in accordance with the procedure agreed by the parties;

(d) failure by the tribunal to deal with all the issues that were put to it;

(e) any arbitral or other institution or person vested by the parties with powers in relation to the proceedings or the award exceeding its powers;

(f) uncertainty or ambiguity as to the effect of the award;

(g) the award being obtained by fraud or the award or the way in which it was procured being contrary to public policy;

(h) failure to comply with the requirements as to the form of the award; or

(i) any irregularity in the conduct of the proceedings or in the award which is admitted by the tribunal or by any arbitral or other institution or person vested by the parties with powers in relation to the proceedings or the award.

(3) If there is shown to be serious irregularity affecting the tribunal, the proceedings or the award, the court may—

(a) remit the award to the tribunal, in whole or in part, for reconsideration,

(b) set the award aside in whole or in part, or

(c) declare the award to be of no effect, in whole or in part.

The court shall not exercise its power to set aside or to declare an award to be of no effect, in whole or in part, unless it is satisfied that it would be inappropriate to remit the matters in question to the tribunal for reconsideration.

(4) The leave of the court is required for any appeal from a decision of the court under this section.

69. Appeal on point of law.

(1) Unless otherwise agreed by the parties, a party to arbitral proceedings may (upon notice to the other parties and to the tribunal) appeal to the court on a question of law arising out of an award made in the proceedings.

An agreement to dispense with reasons for the tribunal's award shall be considered an agreement to exclude the court's jurisdiction under this section.

(2) An appeal shall not be brought under this section except—

(a) with the agreement of all the other parties to the proceedings, or

(b) with the leave of the court.

The right to appeal is also subject to the restrictions in section 70(2) and (3).

(3) Leave to appeal shall be given only if the court is satisfied—

(a) that the determination of the question will substantially affect the rights of one or more of the parties,

    (b)   that the question is one which the tribunal was asked to determine,

    (c)   that, on the basis of the findings of fact in the award—

        (i)   the decision of the tribunal on the question is obviously wrong, or

        (ii)   the question is one of general public importance and the decision of the tribunal is at least open to serious doubt, and

    (d)   that, despite the agreement of the parties to resolve the matter by arbitration, it is just and proper in all the circumstances for the court to determine the question.

(4)   An application for leave to appeal under this section shall identify the question of law to be determined and state the grounds on which it is alleged that leave to appeal should be granted.

(5)   The court shall determine an application for leave to appeal under this section without a hearing unless it appears to the court that a hearing is required.

(6)   The leave of the court is required for any appeal from a decision of the court under this section to grant or refuse leave to appeal.

(7)   On an appeal under this section the court may by order—

    (a)   confirm the award,

    (b)   vary the award,

    (c)   remit the award to the tribunal, in whole or in part, for reconsideration in the light of the court's determination, or

    (d)   set aside the award in whole or in part.

The court shall not exercise its power to set aside an award, in whole or in part, unless it is satisfied that it would be inappropriate to remit the matters in question to the tribunal for reconsideration.

(8)   The decision of the court on an appeal under this section shall be treated as a judgment of the court for the purposes of a further appeal.

But no such appeal lies without the leave of the court which shall not be given unless the court considers that the question is one of general importance or is one which for some other special reason should be considered by the Court of Appeal.

70.   Challenge or appeal: supplementary provisions.

(1)   The following provisions apply to an application or appeal under section 67, 68 or 69.

(2)   An application or appeal may not be brought if the applicant or appellant has not first exhausted—

    (a)   any available arbitral process of appeal or review, and

    (b)   any available recourse under section 57 (correction of award or additional award).

(3)   Any application or appeal must be brought within 28 days of the date of the award or, if there has been any arbitral process of appeal or review, of the date when the applicant or appellant was notified of the result of that process.

(4)   If on an application or appeal it appears to the court that the award—

    (a)   does not contain the tribunal's reasons, or

    (b)   does not set out the tribunal's reasons in sufficient detail to enable the court properly to consider the application or appeal,

the court may order the tribunal to state the reasons for its award in sufficient detail for that purpose.

(5)   Where the court makes an order under subsection (4), it may make such further order as it thinks fit with respect to any additional costs of the arbitration resulting from its order.

(6)   The court may order the applicant or appellant to provide security for the costs of the application or appeal, and may direct that the application or appeal be dismissed if the order is not complied with.

The power to order security for costs shall not be exercised on the ground that the applicant or appellant is—

(a)   an individual ordinarily resident outside the United Kingdom, or

(b)   a corporation or association incorporated or formed under the law of a country outside the United Kingdom, or whose central management and control is exercised outside the United Kingdom.

(7)   The court may order that any money payable under the award shall be brought into court or otherwise secured pending the determination of the application or appeal, and may direct that the application or appeal be dismissed if the order is not complied with.

(8)   The court may grant leave to appeal subject to conditions to the same or similar effect as an order under subsection (6) or (7).

This does not affect the general discretion of the court to grant leave subject to conditions.

71.   Challenge or appeal: effect of order of court.

(1)   The following provisions have effect where the court makes an order under section 67, 68 or 69 with respect to an award.

(2)   Where the award is varied, the variation has effect as part of the tribunal's award.

(3)   Where the award is remitted to the tribunal, in whole or in part, for reconsideration, the tribunal shall make a fresh award in respect of the matters remitted within three months of the date of the order for remission or such longer or shorter period as the court may direct.

(4)   Where the award is set aside or declared to be of no effect, in whole or in part, the court may also order that any provision that an award is a condition precedent to the bringing of legal proceedings in respect of a matter to which the arbitration agreement applies, is of no effect as regards the subject matter of the award or, as the case may be, the relevant part of the award.

Miscellaneous

72.   Saving for rights of person who takes no part in proceedings.

(1)   A person alleged to be a party to arbitral proceedings but who takes no part in the proceedings may question—

(a)   whether there is a valid arbitration agreement,

(b)   whether the tribunal is properly constituted, or

(c)   what matters have been submitted to arbitration in accordance with the arbitration agreement,

by proceedings in the court for a declaration or injunction or other appropriate relief.

(2)   He also has the same right as a party to the arbitral proceedings to challenge an award—

(a) by an application under section 67 on the ground of lack of substantive jurisdiction in relation to him, or

(b) by an application under section 68 on the ground of serious irregularity (within the meaning of that section) affecting him;
and section 70(2) (duty to exhaust arbitral procedures) does not apply in his case.

73. Loss of right to object.

(1) If a party to arbitral proceedings takes part, or continues to take part, in the proceedings without making, either forthwith or within such time as is allowed by the arbitration agreement or the tribunal or by any provision of this Part, any objection—

(a) that the tribunal lacks substantive jurisdiction,

(b) that the proceedings have been improperly conducted,

(c) that there has been a failure to comply with the arbitration agreement or with any provision of this Part, or

(d) that there has been any other irregularity affecting the tribunal or the proceedings,
he may not raise that objection later, before the tribunal or the court, unless he shows that, at the time he took part or continued to take part in the proceedings, he did not know and could not with reasonable diligence have discovered the grounds for the objection.

(2) Where the arbitral tribunal rules that it has substantive jurisdiction and a party to arbitral proceedings who could have questioned that ruling—

(a) by any available arbitral process of appeal or review, or

(b) by challenging the award,
does not do so, or does not do so within the time allowed by the arbitration agreement or any provision of this Part, he may not object later to the tribunal's substantive jurisdiction on any ground which was the subject of that ruling.

74. Immunity of arbitral institutions, &c.

(1) An arbitral or other institution or person designated or requested by the parties to appoint or nominate an arbitrator is not liable for anything done or omitted in the discharge or purported discharge of that function unless the act or omission is shown to have been in bad faith.

(2) An arbitral or other institution or person by whom an arbitrator is appointed or nominated is not liable, by reason of having appointed or nominated him, for anything done or omitted by the arbitrator (or his employees or agents) in the discharge or purported discharge of his functions as arbitrator.

(3) The above provisions apply to an employee or agent of an arbitral or other institution or person as they apply to the institution or the person himself.

75. Charge to secure payment of solicitors' costs.

The powers of the court to make declarations and orders under section 73 of the Solicitors Act 1974 or Article 71H of the Solicitors (Northern Ireland)

Order 1976 (power to charge property recovered in the proceedings with the payment of solicitors' costs) may be exercised in relation to arbitral proceedings as if those proceedings were proceedings in the court.

Supplementary

76.   Service of notices, &c.

(1)   The parties are free to agree on the manner of service of any notice or other document required or authorised to be given or served in pursuance of the arbitration agreement or for the purposes of the arbitral proceedings.

(2)   If or to the extent that there is no such agreement the following provisions apply.

(3)   A notice or other document may be served on a person by any effective means.

(4)   If a notice or other document is addressed, pre-paid and delivered by post—

(a)   to the addressee's last known principal residence or, if he is or has been carrying on a trade, profession or business, his last known principal business address, or

(b)   where the addressee is a body corporate, to the body's registered or principal office,

it shall be treated as effectively served.

(5)   This section does not apply to the service of documents for the purposes of legal proceedings, for which provision is made by rules of court.

(6)   References in this Part to a notice or other document include any form of communication in writing and references to giving or serving a notice or other document shall be construed accordingly.

77.   Powers of court in relation to service of documents.

(1)   This section applies where service of a document on a person in the manner agreed by the parties, or in accordance with provisions of section 76 having effect in default of agreement, is not reasonably practicable.

(2)   Unless otherwise agreed by the parties, the court may make such order as it thinks fit—

(a)   for service in such manner as the court may direct, or

(b)   dispensing with service of the document.

(3)   Any party to the arbitration agreement may apply for an order, but only after exhausting any available arbitral process for resolving the matter.

(4)   The leave of the court is required for any appeal from a decision of the court under this section.

78.   Reckoning periods of time.

(1)   The parties are free to agree on the method of reckoning periods of time for the purposes of any provision agreed by them or any provision of this Part having effect in default of such agreement.

(2)   If or to the extent there is no such agreement, periods of time shall be reckoned in accordance with the following provisions.

(3)   Where the act is required to be done within a specified period after or from a specified date, the period begins immediately after that date.

(4)   Where the act is required to be done a specified number of clear days after a specified date, at least that number of days must intervene between the day on which the act is done and that date.

(5)   Where the period is a period of seven days or less which would include a Saturday, Sunday or a public holiday in the place where anything which has to be done within the period falls to be done, that day shall be excluded.

In relation to England and Wales or Northern Ireland, a 'public holiday' means Christmas Day, Good Friday or a day which under the Banking and Financial Dealings Act 1971 is a bank holiday.

79.   Power of court to extend time limits relating to arbitral proceedings.

(1)   Unless the parties otherwise agree, the court may by order extend any time limit agreed by them in relation to any matter relating to the arbitral proceedings or specified in any provision of this Part having effect in default of such agreement.

This section does not apply to a time limit to which section 12 applies (power of court to extend time for beginning arbitral proceedings, &c.).

(2)   An application for an order may be made—

    (a)   by any party to the arbitral proceedings (upon notice to the other parties and to the tribunal), or

    (b)   by the arbitral tribunal (upon notice to the parties).

(3)   The court shall not exercise its power to extend a time limit unless it is satisfied—

    (a)   that any available recourse to the tribunal, or to any arbitral or other institution or person vested by the parties with power in that regard, has first been exhausted, and

    (b)   that a substantial injustice would otherwise be done.

(4)   The court's power under this section may be exercised whether or not the time has already expired.

(5)   An order under this section may be made on such terms as the court thinks fit.

(6)   The leave of the court is required for any appeal from a decision of the court under this section.

80.   Notice and other requirements in connection with legal proceedings.

(1)   References in this Part to an application, appeal or other step in relation to legal proceedings being taken 'upon notice' to the other parties to the arbitral proceedings, or to the tribunal, are to such notice of the originating process as is required by rules of court and do not impose any separate requirement.

(2)   Rules of court shall be made—

    (a)   requiring such notice to be given as indicated by any provision of this Part, and

(b)   as to the manner, form and content of any such notice.

(3)   Subject to any provision made by rules of court, a requirement to give notice to the tribunal of legal proceedings shall be construed—

(a)   if there is more than one arbitrator, as a requirement to give notice to each of them; and

(b)   if the tribunal is not fully constituted, as a requirement to give notice to any arbitrator who has been appointed.

(4)   References in this Part to making an application or appeal to the court within a specified period are to the issue within that period of the appropriate originating process in accordance with rules of court.

(5)   Where any provision of this Part requires an application or appeal to be made to the court within a specified time, the rules of court relating to the reckoning of periods, the extending or abridging of periods, and the consequences of not taking a step within the period prescribed by the rules, apply in relation to that requirement.

(6)   Provision may be made by rules of court amending the provisions of this Part—

(a)   with respect to the time within which any application or appeal to the court must be made,

(b)   so as to keep any provision made by this Part in relation to arbitral proceedings in step with the corresponding provision of rules of court applying in relation to proceedings in the court, or

(c)   so as to keep any provision made by this Part in relation to legal proceedings in step with the corresponding provision of rules of court applying generally in relation to proceedings in the court.

(7)   Nothing in this section affects the generality of the power to make rules of court.

81.   Saving for certain matters governed by common law.

(1)   Nothing in this Part shall be construed as excluding the operation of any rule of law consistent with the provisions of this Part, in particular, any rule of law as to—

(a)   matters which are not capable of settlement by arbitration;

(b)   the effect of an oral arbitration agreement; or

(c)   the refusal of recognition or enforcement of an arbitral award on grounds of public policy.

(2)   Nothing in this Act shall be construed as reviving any jurisdiction of the court to set aside or remit an award on the ground of errors of fact or law on the face of the award.

82.   Minor definitions.

(1)   In this Part—

'arbitrator', unless the context otherwise requires, includes an umpire;

'available arbitral process', in relation to any matter, includes any process of appeal to or review by an arbitral or other institution or person vested by the parties with powers in relation to that matter;

'claimant', unless the context otherwise requires, includes a counterclaimant, and related expressions shall be construed accordingly;

'dispute' includes any difference;

'enactment' includes an enactment contained in Northern Ireland legislation;

'legal proceedings' means civil proceedings in the High Court or a county court;

'peremptory order' means an order made under section 41(5) or made in exercise of any corresponding power conferred by the parties;

'premises' includes land, buildings, moveable structures, vehicles, vessels, aircraft and hovercraft;

'question of law' means—

    (a) for a court in England and Wales, a question of the law of England and Wales, and

    (b) for a court in Northern Ireland, a question of the law of Northern Ireland;

'substantive jurisdiction', in relation to an arbitral tribunal, refers to the matters specified in section 30(1)(a) to (c), and references to the tribunal exceeding its substantive jurisdiction shall be construed accordingly.

(2) References in this Part to a party to an arbitration agreement include any person claiming under or through a party to the agreement.

83. Index of defined expressions: Part I.

In this Part the expressions listed below are defined or otherwise explained by the provisions indicated—

agreement, agree and agreed	section 5(1)
agreement in writing	section 5(2) to (5)
arbitration agreement	sections 6 and 5(1)
arbitrator	section 82(1)
available arbitral process	section 82(1)
claimant	section 82(1)
commencement (in relation to arbitral proceedings)	section 14
costs of the arbitration	section 59
the court	section 105
dispute	section 82(1)
enactment	section 82(1)
legal proceedings	section 82(1)
Limitation Acts	section 13(4)
notice (or other document)	section 76(6)
party—	
—in relation to an arbitration agreement	section 82(2)
—where section 106(2) or (3) applies	section 106(4)
peremptory order	section 82(1) (and see section 41(5))
premises	section 82(1)
question of law	section 82(1)
recoverable costs	sections 63 and 64
seat of the arbitration	section 3
serve and service (of notice or other document)	section 76(6)

substantive jurisdiction (in relation to an arbitral tribunal)	section 82(1) (and see section 30(1)(a) to (c))
upon notice (to the parties or the tribunal)	section 80
written and in writing	section 5(6)

84. Transitional provisions.

(1)   The provisions of this Part do not apply to arbitral proceedings commenced before the date on which this Part comes into force.

(2)   They apply to arbitral proceedings commenced on or after that date under an arbitration agreement whenever made.

(3)   The above provisions have effect subject to any transitional provision made by an order under section 109(2) (power to include transitional provisions in commencement order).

PART II

OTHER PROVISIONS RELATING TO ARBITRATION

Domestic arbitration agreements

85. Modification of Part I in relation to domestic arbitration agreement.

(1)   In the case of a domestic arbitration agreement the provisions of Part I are modified in accordance with the following sections.

(2)   For this purpose a 'domestic arbitration agreement' means an arbitration agreement to which none of the parties is—

(a)   an individual who is a national of, or habitually resident in, a state other than the United Kingdom, or

(b)   a body corporate which is incorporated in, or whose central control and management is exercised in, a state other than the United Kingdom, and under which the seat of the arbitration (if the seat has been designated or determined) is in the United Kingdom.

(3)   In subsection (2) 'arbitration agreement' and 'seat of the arbitration' have the same meaning as in Part I (see sections 3, 5(1) and 6).

86. Staying of legal proceedings.

(1)   In section 9 (stay of legal proceedings), subsection (4) (stay unless the arbitration agreement is null and void, inoperative, or incapable of being performed) does not apply to a domestic arbitration agreement.

(2)   On an application under that section in relation to a domestic arbitration agreement the court shall grant a stay unless satisfied—

(a)   that the arbitration agreement is null and void, inoperative, or incapable of being performed, or

(b)   that there are other sufficient grounds for not requiring the parties to abide by the arbitration agreement.

(3)   The court may treat as a sufficient ground under subsection (2)(b) the fact that the applicant is or was at any material time not ready and willing to

do all things necessary for the proper conduct of the arbitration or of any other dispute resolution procedures required to be exhausted before resorting to arbitration.

(4) For the purposes of this section the question whether an arbitration agreement is a domestic arbitration agreement shall be determined by reference to the facts at the time the legal proceedings are commenced.

87. Effectiveness of agreement to exclude court's jurisdiction.

(1) In the case of a domestic arbitration agreement any agreement to exclude the jurisdiction of the court under—
    (a) section 45 (determination of preliminary point of law), or
    (b) section 69 (challenging the award: appeal on point of law),
is not effective unless entered into after the commencement of the arbitral proceedings in which the question arises or the award is made.

(2) For this purpose the commencement of the arbitral proceedings has the same meaning as in Part I (see section 14).

(3) For the purposes of this section the question whether an arbitration agreement is a domestic arbitration agreement shall be determined by reference to the facts at the time the agreement is entered into.

88. Power to repeal or amend sections 85 to 87.

(1) The Secretary of State may by order repeal or amend the provisions of sections 85 to 87.

(2) An order under this section may contain such supplementary, incidental and transitional provisions as appear to the Secretary of State to be appropriate.

(3) An order under this section shall be made by statutory instrument and no such order shall be made unless a draft of it has been laid before and approved by a resolution of each House of Parliament.

Consumer arbitration agreements

89. Application of unfair terms regulations to consumer arbitration agreements.

(1) The following sections extend the application of the Unfair Terms in Consumer Contracts Regulations 1994 in relation to a term which constitutes an arbitration agreement.

For this purpose 'arbitration agreement' means an agreement to submit to arbitration present or future disputes or differences (whether or not contractual).

(2) In those sections 'the Regulations' means those regulations and includes any regulations amending or replacing those regulations.

(3) Those sections apply whatever the law applicable to the arbitration agreement.

90. Regulations apply where consumer is a legal person.

The Regulations apply where the consumer is a legal person as they apply where the consumer is a natural person.

91.   Arbitration agreement unfair where modest amount sought.

(1)   A term which constitutes an arbitration agreement is unfair for the purposes of the Regulations so far as it relates to a claim for a pecuniary remedy which does not exceed the amount specified by order for the purposes of this section.

(2)   Orders under this section may make different provision for different cases and for different purposes.

(3)   The power to make orders under this section is exercisable—

(a)   for England and Wales, by the Secretary of State with the concurrence of the Lord Chancellor,

(b)   for Scotland, by the Secretary of State with the concurrence of the Lord Advocate, and

(c)   for Northern Ireland, by the Department of Economic Development for Northern Ireland with the concurrence of the Lord Chancellor.

(4)   Any such order for England and Wales or Scotland shall be made by statutory instrument which shall be subject to annulment in pursuance of a resolution of either House of Parliament.

(5)   Any such order for Northern Ireland shall be a statutory rule for the purposes of the Statutory Rules (Northern Ireland) Order 1979 and shall be subject to negative resolution, within the meaning of section 41(6) of the Interpretation Act (Northern Ireland) 1954.

Small claims arbitration in the county court

92.   Exclusion of Part I in relation to small claims arbitration in the county court.

Nothing in Part I of this Act applies to arbitration under section 64 of the County Courts Act 1984.

Appointment of judges as arbitrators

93.   Appointment of judges as arbitrators.

(1)   A judge of the Commercial Court or an official referee may, if in all the circumstances he thinks fit, accept appointment as a sole arbitrator or as umpire by or by virtue of an arbitration agreement.

(2)   A judge of the Commercial Court shall not do so unless the Lord Chief Justice has informed him that, having regard to the state of business in the High Court and the Crown Court, he can be made available.

(3)   An official referee shall not do so unless the Lord Chief Justice has informed him that, having regard to the state of official referees' business, he can be made available.

(4)   The fees payable for the services of a judge of the Commercial Court or official referee as arbitrator or umpire shall be taken in the High Court.

(5)   In this section—

'arbitration agreement' has the same meaning as in Part I; and

'official referee' means a person nominated under section 68(1)(a) of the Supreme Court Act 1981 to deal with official referees' business.

(6)   The provisions of Part I of this Act apply to arbitration before a person appointed under this section with the modifications specified in Schedule 2.

Statutory arbitrations

94.   Application of Part I to statutory arbitrations.

(1)   The provisions of Part I apply to every arbitration under an enactment (a 'statutory arbitration'), whether the enactment was passed or made before or after the commencement of this Act, subject to the adaptations and exclusions specified in sections 95 to 98.

(2)   The provisions of Part I do not apply to a statutory arbitration if or to the extent that their application—

(a)   is inconsistent with the provisions of the enactment concerned, with any rules or procedure authorised or recognised by it, or

(b)   is excluded by any other enactment.

(3)   In this section and the following provisions of this Part 'enactment'—

(a)   in England and Wales, includes an enactment contained in subordinate legislation within the meaning of the Interpretation Act 1978;

(b)   in Northern Ireland, means a statutory provision within the meaning of section 1(f) of the Interpretation Act (Northern Ireland) 1954.

95.   General adaptation of provisions in relation to statutory arbitrations.

(1)   The provisions of Part I apply to a statutory arbitration—

(a)   as if the arbitration were pursuant to an arbitration agreement and as if the enactment were that agreement, and

(b)   as if the persons by and against whom a claim subject to arbitration in pursuance of the enactment may be or has been made were parties to that agreement.

(2)   Every statutory arbitration shall be taken to have its seat in England and Wales, or, as the case may be, in Northern Ireland.

96.   Specific adaptations of provisions in relation to statutory arbitrations.

(1)   The following provisions of Part I apply to a statutory arbitration with the following adaptations.

(2)   In section 30(1) (competence of tribunal to rule on its own jurisdiction), the reference in paragraph (a) to whether there is a valid arbitration agreement shall be construed as a reference to whether the enactment applies to the dispute or difference in question.

(3)   Section 35 (consolidation of proceedings and concurrent hearings) applies only so as to authorise the consolidation of proceedings, or concurrent hearings in proceedings, under the same enactment.

(4)   Section 46 (rules applicable to substance of dispute) applies with the omission of subsection (1)(b) (determination in accordance with considerations agreed by parties).

97. Provisions excluded from applying to statutory arbitrations.

The following provisions of Part I do not apply in relation to a statutory arbitration—
    (a)   section 8 (whether agreement discharged by death of a party);
    (b)   section 12 (power of court to extend agreed time limits);
    (c)   sections 9(5), 10(2) and 71(4) (restrictions on effect of provision that award condition precedent to right to bring legal proceedings).

98. Power to make further provision by regulations.

    (1)   The Secretary of State may make provision by regulations for adapting or excluding any provision of Part I in relation to statutory arbitrations in general or statutory arbitrations of any particular description.
    (2)   The power is exercisable whether the enactment concerned is passed or made before or after the commencement of this Act.
    (3)   Regulations under this section shall be made by statutory instrument which shall be subject to annulment in pursuance of a resolution of either House of Parliament.

PART III

RECOGNITION AND ENFORCEMENT OF CERTAIN FOREIGN AWARDS

Enforcement of Geneva Convention awards

99. Continuation of Part II of the Arbitration Act 1950.

Part II of the Arbitration Act 1950 (enforcement of certain foreign awards) continues to apply in relation to foreign awards within the meaning of that Part which are not also New York Convention awards.

Recognition and enforcement of New York Convention awards

100. New York Convention awards.

    (1)   In this Part a 'New York Convention award' means an award made, in pursuance of an arbitration agreement, in the territory of a state (other than the United Kingdom) which is a party to the New York Convention.
    (2)   For the purposes of subsection (1) and of the provisions of this Part relating to such awards—
    (a)   'arbitration agreement' means an arbitration agreement in writing, and
    (b)   an award shall be treated as made at the seat of the arbitration, regardless of where it was signed, despatched or delivered to any of the parties.
    In this subsection 'agreement in writing' and 'seat of the arbitration' have the same meaning as in Part I.
    (3)   If Her Majesty by Order in Council declares that a state specified in the Order is a party to the New York Convention, or is a party in respect of

any territory so specified, the Order shall, while in force, be conclusive evidence of that fact.

(4)   In this section 'the New York Convention' means the Convention on the Recognition and Enforcement of Foreign Arbitral Awards adopted by the United Nations Conference on International Commercial Arbitration on 10th June 1958.

101.   Recognition and enforcement of awards.

(1)   A New York Convention award shall be recognised as binding on the persons as between whom it was made, and may accordingly be relied on by those persons by way of defence, set-off or otherwise in any legal proceedings in England and Wales or Northern Ireland.

(2)   A New York Convention award may, by leave of the court, be enforced in the same manner as a judgment or order of the court to the same effect.

As to the meaning of 'the court' see section 105.

(3)   Where leave is so given, judgment may be entered in terms of the award.

102.   Evidence to be produced by party seeking recognition or enforcement.

(1)   A party seeking the recognition or enforcement of a New York Convention award must produce—
    (a)   the duly authenticated original award or a duly certified copy of it, and
    (b)   the original arbitration agreement or a duly certified copy of it.

(2)   If the award or agreement is in a foreign language, the party must also produce a translation of it certified by an official or sworn translator or by a diplomatic or consular agent.

103.   Refusal of recognition or enforcement.

(1)   Recognition or enforcement of a New York Convention award shall not be refused except in the following cases.

(2)   Recognition or enforcement of the award may be refused if the person against whom it is invoked proves—
    (a)   that a party to the arbitration agreement was (under the law applicable to him) under some incapacity;
    (b)   that the arbitration agreement was not valid under the law to which the parties subjected it or, failing any indication thereon, under the law of the country where the award was made;
    (c)   that he was not given proper notice of the appointment of the arbitrator or of the arbitration proceedings or was otherwise unable to present his case;
    (d)   that the award deals with a difference not contemplated by or not falling within the terms of the submission to arbitration or contains decisions on matters beyond the scope of the submission to arbitration (but see subsection (4));

(e)   that the composition of the arbitral tribunal or the arbitral procedure was not in accordance with the agreement of the parties or, failing such agreement, with the law of the country in which the arbitration took place;

(f)   that the award has not yet become binding on the parties, or has been set aside or suspended by a competent authority of the country in which, or under the law of which, it was made.

(3)   Recognition or enforcement of the award may also be refused if the award is in respect of a matter which is not capable of settlement by arbitration, or if it would be contrary to public policy to recognise or enforce the award.

(4)   An award which contains decisions on matters not submitted to arbitration may be recognised or enforced to the extent that it contains decisions on matters submitted to arbitration which can be separated from those on matters not so submitted.

(5)   Where an application for the setting aside or suspension of the award has been made to such a competent authority as is mentioned in subsection (2)(f), the court before which the award is sought to be relied upon may, if it considers it proper, adjourn the decision on the recognition or enforcement of the award.

It may also on the application of the party claiming recognition or enforcement of the award order the other party to give suitable security.

104.   Saving for other bases of recognition or enforcement.

Nothing in the preceding provisions of this Part affects any right to rely upon or enforce a New York Convention award at common law or under section 66.

PART IV

GENERAL PROVISIONS

105.   Meaning of 'the court': jurisdiction of High Court and county court.

(1)   In this Act 'the court' means the High Court or a county court, subject to the following provisions.

(2)   The Lord Chancellor may by order make provision—

(a)   allocating proceedings under this Act to the High Court or to county courts; or

(b)   specifying proceedings under this Act which may be commenced or taken only in the High Court or in a county court.

(3)   The Lord Chancellor may by order make provision requiring proceedings of any specified description under this Act in relation to which a county court has jurisdiction to be commenced or taken in one or more specified county courts.

Any jurisdiction so exercisable by a specified county court is exercisable throughout England and Wales or, as the case may be, Northern Ireland.

(4)   An order under this section—

(a)   may differentiate between categories of proceedings by reference to such criteria as the Lord Chancellor sees fit to specify, and

(b)   may make such incidental or transitional provision as the Lord Chancellor considers necessary or expedient.

(5)   An order under this section for England and Wales shall be made by statutory instrument which shall be subject to annulment in pursuance of a resolution of either House of Parliament.

(6)   An order under this section for Northern Ireland shall be a statutory rule for the purposes of the Statutory Rules (Northern Ireland) Order 1979 which shall be subject to annulment in pursuance of a resolution of either House of Parliament in like manner as a statutory instrument and section 5 of the Statutory Instruments Act 1946 shall apply accordingly.

106.   Crown application.

(1)   Part I of this Act applies to any arbitration agreement to which Her Majesty, either in right of the Crown or of the Duchy of Lancaster or otherwise, or the Duke of Cornwall, is a party.

(2)   Where Her Majesty is party to an arbitration agreement otherwise than in right of the Crown, Her Majesty shall be represented for the purposes of any arbitral proceedings—

(a)   where the agreement was entered into by Her Majesty in right of the Duchy of Lancaster, by the Chancellor of the Duchy or such person as he may appoint, and

(b)   in any other case, by such person as Her Majesty may appoint in writing under the Royal Sign Manual.

(3)   Where the Duke of Cornwall is party to an arbitration agreement, he shall be represented for the purposes of any arbitral proceedings by such person as he may appoint.

(4)   References in Part I to a party or the parties to the arbitration agreement or to arbitral proceedings shall be construed, where subsection (2) or (3) applies, as references to the person representing Her Majesty or the Duke of Cornwall.

108.   Extent.

(1)   The provisions of this Act extend to England and Wales and, except as mentioned below, to Northern Ireland.

(2)   The following provisions of Part II do not extend to Northern Ireland—

section 92 (exclusion of Part I in relation to small claims arbitration in the county court), and

section 93 and Schedule 2 (appointment of judges as arbitrators).

(3)   Sections 89, 90 and 91 (consumer arbitration agreements) extend to Scotland and the provisions of Schedules 3 and 4 (consequential amendments and repeals) extend to Scotland so far as they relate to enactments which so extend, subject as follows.

(4)   The repeal of the Arbitration Act 1975 extends only to England and Wales and Northern Ireland.

109.   Commencement.

(1)   The provisions of this Act come into force on such day as the Secretary of State may appoint by order made by statutory instrument, and different days may be appointed for different purposes.

(2)   An order under subsection (1) may contain such transitional provisions as appear to the Secretary of State to be appropriate.

110.   Short title.

This Act may be cited as the Arbitration Act 1996.

SCHEDULES

Section 4(1)   SCHEDULE I

MANDATORY PROVISIONS OF PART I

sections 9 to 11	(stay of legal proceedings);
section 12	(power of court to extend agreed time limits);
section 13	(application of Limitation Acts);
section 24	(power of court to remove arbitrator);
section 26(1)	(effect of death of arbitrator);
section 28	(liability of parties for fees and expenses of arbitrators);
section 29	(immunity of arbitrator);
section 31	(objection to substantive jurisdiction of tribunal);
section 32	(determination of preliminary point of jurisdiction);
section 33	(general duty of tribunal);
section 37(2)	(items to be treated as expenses of arbitrators);
section 40	(general duty of parties);
section 43	(securing the attendance of witnesses);
section 56	(power to withhold award in case of non-payment);
section 60	(effectiveness of agreement for payment of costs in any event);
section 66	(enforcement of award);
sections 67 and 68	(challenging the award: substantive jurisdiction and serious irregularity), and sections 70 and 71 (supplementary provisions; effect of order of court) so far as relating to those sections;
section 72	(saving for rights of person who takes no part in proceedings);
section 73	(loss of right to object);
section 74	(immunity of arbitral institutions, &c.);
section 75	(charge to secure payment of solicitors' costs).

Section 93(6)   SCHEDULE 2

MODIFICATIONS OF PART I IN RELATION
TO JUDGE-ARBITRATORS

Introductory

1.   In this Schedule 'judge-arbitrator' means a judge of the Commercial Court or official referee appointed as arbitrator or umpire under section 93.

General

2.—(1)   Subject to the following provisions of this Schedule, references in Part I to the court shall be construed in relation to a judge-arbitrator, or in relation to the appointment of a judge-arbitrator, as references to the Court of Appeal.

(2)   The references in sections 32(6), 45(6) and 69(8) to the Court of Appeal shall in such a case be construed as references to the House of Lords.

Arbitrator's fees

3.—(1)   The power of the court in section 28(2) to order consideration and adjustment of the liability of a party for the fees of an arbitrator may be exercised by a judge-arbitrator.

(2)   Any such exercise of the power is subject to the powers of the Court of Appeal under sections 24(4) and 25(3)(b) (directions as to entitlement to fees or expenses in case of removal or resignation).

Exercise of court powers in support of arbitration

4.—(1)   Where the arbitral tribunal consists of or includes a judge-arbitrator the powers of the court under sections 42 to 44 (enforcement of peremptory orders, summoning witnesses, and other court powers) are exercisable by the High Court and also by the judge-arbitrator himself.

(2)   Anything done by a judge-arbitrator in the exercise of those powers shall be regarded as done by him in his capacity as judge of the High Court and have effect as if done by that court.

Nothing in this sub-paragraph prejudices any power vested in him as arbitrator or umpire.

Extension of time for making award

5.—(1)   The power conferred by section 50 (extension of time for making award) is exercisable by the judge-arbitrator himself.

(2)   Any appeal from a decision of a judge-arbitrator under that section lies to the Court of Appeal with the leave of that court.

Withholding award in case of non-payment

6.—(1)   The provisions of paragraph 7 apply in place of the provisions of section 56 (power to withhold award in the case of non-payment) in relation to the withholding of an award for non-payment of the fees and expenses of a judge-arbitrator.

(2)   This does not affect the application of section 56 in relation to the delivery of such an award by an arbitral or other institution or person vested by the parties with powers in relation to the delivery of the award.

7.—(1)   A judge-arbitrator may refuse to deliver an award except upon payment of the fees and expenses mentioned in section 56(1).

(2)   The judge-arbitrator may, on an application by a party to the arbitral proceedings, order that if he pays into the High Court the fees and expenses demanded, or such lesser amount as the judge-arbitrator may specify—

(a)   the award shall be delivered,

(b)   the amount of the fees and expenses properly payable shall be determined by such means and upon such terms as he may direct, and

(c)   out of the money paid into court there shall be paid out such fees and expenses as may be found to be properly payable and the balance of the money (if any) shall be paid out to the applicant.

(3)   For this purpose the amount of fees and expenses properly payable is the amount the applicant is liable to pay under section 28 or any agreement relating to the payment of the arbitrator.

(4)   No application to the judge-arbitrator under this paragraph may be made where there is any available arbitral process for appeal or review of the amount of the fees or expenses demanded.

(5)   Any appeal from a decision of a judge-arbitrator under this paragraph lies to the Court of Appeal with the leave of that court.

(6)   Where a party to arbitral proceedings appeals under sub-paragraph (5), an arbitrator is entitled to appear and be heard.

Correction of award or additional award

8.   Subsections (4) to (6) of section 57 (correction of award or additional award: time limit for application or exercise of power) do not apply to a judge-arbitrator.

Costs

9.   Where the arbitral tribunal consists of or includes a judge-arbitrator the powers of the court under section 63(4) (determination of recoverable costs) shall be exercised by the High Court.

10.—(1)   The power of the court under section 64 to determine an arbitrator's reasonable fees and expenses may be exercised by a judge-arbitrator.

(2)   Any such exercise of the power is subject to the powers of the Court of Appeal under sections 24(4) and 25(3)(b) (directions as to entitlement to fees or expenses in case of removal or resignation).

Enforcement of award

11.   The leave of the court required by section 66 (enforcement of award) may in the case of an award of a judge-arbitrator be given by the judge-arbitrator himself.

Solicitors' costs

12.   The powers of the court to make declarations and orders under the provisions applied by section 75 (power to charge property recovered in arbitral proceedings with the payment of solicitors' costs) may be exercised by the judge-arbitrator.

Powers of court in relation to service of documents

13.—(1)   The power of the court under section 77(2) (powers of court in relation to service of documents) is exercisable by the judge-arbitrator.

(2)   Any appeal from a decision of a judge-arbitrator under that section lies to the Court of Appeal with the leave of that court.

Powers of court to extend time limits relating to arbitral proceedings

14.—(1)   The power conferred by section 79 (power of court to extend time limits relating to arbitral proceedings) is exercisable by the judge-arbitrator himself.

(2)   Any appeal from a decision of a judge-arbitrator under that section lies to the Court of Appeal with the leave of that court.

Section 107(1)   SCHEDULE 3

CONSEQUENTIAL AMENDMENTS

Merchant Shipping Act 1894 (c.60)

1.   In section 496 of the Merchant Shipping Act 1894 (provisions as to deposits by owners of goods), after subsection (4) insert—

'(5) In subsection (3) the expression 'legal proceedings' includes arbitral proceedings and as respects England and Wales and Northern Ireland the provisions of section 14 of the Arbitration Act 1996 apply to determine when such proceedings are commenced.'.

Stannaries Court (Abolition) Act 1896 (c.45)

2.   In section 4(1) of the Stannaries Court (Abolition) Act 1896 (references of certain disputes to arbitration), for the words from 'tried before' to 'any such reference' substitute 'referred to arbitration before himself or before an arbitrator agreed on by the parties or an officer of the court'.

Tithe Act 1936 (c.43)

3.   In section 39(1) of the Tithe Act 1936 (proceedings of Tithe Redemption Commission)—
   (a)   for 'the Arbitration Acts 1889 to 1934' substitute 'Part I of the Arbitration Act 1996';
   (b)   for paragraph (e) substitute—

   '(e)   the making of an application to the court to determine a preliminary point of law and the bringing of an appeal to the court on a point of law;';

   (c)   for 'the said Acts' substitute 'Part I of the Arbitration Act 1996'.

Education Act 1944 (c.31)

4.   In section 75(2) of the Education Act 1944 (proceedings of Independent School Tribunals) for 'the Arbitration Acts 1889 to 1934' substitute 'Part I of the Arbitration Act 1996'.

Commonwealth Telegraphs Act 1949 (c.39)

5.   In section 8(2) of the Commonwealth Telegraphs Act 1949 (proceedings of referees under the Act) for 'the Arbitration Acts 1889 to 1934, or the Arbitration Act (Northern Ireland) 1937,' substitute 'Part I of the Arbitration Act 1996'.

Lands Tribunal Act 1949 (c.42)

6.   In section 3 of the Lands Tribunal Act 1949 (proceedings before the Lands Tribunal)—
    (a)   in subsection (6)(c) (procedural rules: power to apply Arbitration Acts), and
    (b)   in subsection (8) (exclusion of Arbitration Acts except as applied by rules),
for 'the Arbitration Acts 1889 to 1934' substitute 'Part I of the Arbitration Act 1996'.

Wireless Telegraphy Act 1949 (c.54)

7.   In the Wireless Telegraphy Act 1949, Schedule 2 (procedure of appeals tribunal), in paragraph 3(1)—
    (a)   for the words 'the Arbitration Acts 1889 to 1934' substitute 'Part I of the Arbitration Act 1996';
    (b)   after the word 'Wales' insert 'or Northern Ireland'; and
    (c)   for 'the said Acts' substitute 'Part I of that Act'.

Patents Act 1949 (c.87)

8.   In section 67 of the Patents Act 1949 (proceedings as to infringement of pre-1978 patents referred to comptroller), for 'The Arbitration Acts 1889 to 1934' substitute 'Part I of the Arbitration Act 1996'.

National Health Service (Amendment) Act 1949 (c.93)

9.   In section 7(8) of the National Health Service (Amendment) Act 1949 (arbitration in relation to hardship arising from the National Health Service Act 1946 or the Act), for 'the Arbitration Acts 1889 to 1934' substitute 'Part I of the Arbitration Act 1996' and for 'the said Acts' substitute 'Part I of that Act'.

Arbitration Act 1950 (c.27)

10.   In section 36(1) of the Arbitration Act 1950 (effect of foreign awards enforceable under Part II of that Act) for 'section 26 of this Act' substitute 'section 66 of the Arbitration Act 1996'.

Interpretation Act (Northern Ireland) 1954 (c.33 (N.I.))

11.   In section 46(2) of the Interpretation Act (Northern Ireland) 1954 (miscellaneous definitions), for the definition of 'arbitrator' substitute—

'"arbitrator" has the same meaning as in Part I of the Arbitration Act 1996;'.

Agricultural Marketing Act 1958 (c.47)

12. In section 12(1) of the Agricultural Marketing Act 1958 (application of provisions of Arbitration Act 1950)—
(a) for the words from the beginning to 'shall apply' substitute 'Sections 45 and 69 of the Arbitration Act 1996 (which relate to the determination by the court of questions of law) and section 66 of that Act (enforcement of awards) apply'; and
(b) for 'an arbitration' substitute 'arbitral proceedings'.

Carriage by Air Act 1961 (c.27)

13.—(1) The Carriage by Air Act 1961 is amended as follows.
(2) In section 5(3) (time for bringing proceedings)—
(a) for 'an arbitration' in the first place where it occurs substitute 'arbitral proceedings'; and
(b) for the words from 'and subsections (3) and (4)' to the end substitute 'and the provisions of section 14 of the Arbitration Act 1996 apply to determine when such proceedings are commenced.'.
(3) In section 11(c) (application of section 5 to Scotland)—
(a) for 'subsections (3) and (4)' substitute 'the provisions of section 14 of the Arbitration Act 1996'; and
(b) for 'an arbitration' substitute 'arbitral proceedings'.

Factories Act 1961 (c.34)

14. In the Factories Act 1961, for section 171 (application of Arbitration Act 1950), substitute—

'*Application of the Arbitration Act 1996*
171. Part I of the Arbitration Act 1996 does not apply to proceedings under this Act except in so far as it may be applied by regulations made under this Act.'.

Clergy Pensions Measure 1961 (No. 3)

15. In the Clergy Pensions Measure 1961, section 38(4) (determination of questions), for the words 'The Arbitration Act 1950' substitute 'Part I of the Arbitration Act 1996'.

Transport Act 1962 (c. 46)

16.—(1) The Transport Act 1962 is amended as follows.
(2) In section 74(6)(f) (proceedings before referees in pension disputes), for the words 'the Arbitration Act 1950' substitute 'Part I of the Arbitration Act 1996'.

(3)   In section 81(7) (proceedings before referees in compensation disputes), for the words 'the Arbitration Act 1950' substitute 'Part I of the Arbitration Act 1996'.

(4)   In Schedule 7, Part IV (pensions), in paragraph 17(5) for the words 'the Arbitration Act 1950' substitute 'Part I of the Arbitration Act 1996'.

Corn Rents Act 1963 (c.14)

17.   In the Corn Rents Act 1963, section 1(5) (schemes for apportioning corn rents, &c.), for the words 'the Arbitration Act 1950' substitute 'Part I of the Arbitration Act 1996'.

Plant Varieties and Seeds Act 1964 (c.14)

18.   In section 10(6) of the Plant Varieties and Seeds Act 1964 (meaning of 'arbitration agreement'), for 'the meaning given by section 32 of the Arbitration Act 1950' substitute 'the same meaning as in Part I of the Arbitration Act 1996'.

Lands Tribunal and Compensation Act (Northern Ireland) 1964 (c.29 (N.I.))

19.   In section 9 of the Lands Tribunal and Compensation Act (Northern Ireland) 1964 (proceedings of Lands Tribunal), in subsection (3) (where Tribunal acts as arbitrator) for 'the Arbitration Act (Northern Ireland) 1937' substitute 'Part I of the Arbitration Act 1996'.

Industrial and Provident Societies Act 1965 (c.12)

20.—(1)   Section 60 of the Industrial and Provident Societies Act 1965 is amended as follows.

(2)   In subsection (8) (procedure for hearing disputes between society and member, &c.)—

(a)   in paragraph (a) for 'the Arbitration Act 1950' substitute 'Part I of the Arbitration Act 1996'; and

(b)   in paragraph (b) omit 'by virtue of section 12 of the said Act of 1950'.

(3)   For subsection (9) substitute—

'(9)   The court or registrar to whom any dispute is referred under subsections (2) to (7) may at the request of either party state a case on any question of law arising in the dispute for the opinion of the High Court or, as the case may be, the Court of Session.'.

Carriage of Goods by Road Act 1965 (c.37)

21.   In section 7(2) of the Carriage of Goods by Road Act 1965 (arbitrations: time at which deemed to commence), for paragraphs (a) and (b) substitute—

'(a)   as respects England and Wales and Northern Ireland, the provisions of section 14(3) to (5) of the Arbitration Act 1996 (which determine the time at which an arbitration is commenced) apply;'.

Factories Act (Northern Ireland) 1965 (c.20 (N.I.))

22. In section 171 of the Factories Act (Northern Ireland) 1965 (application of Arbitration Act), for 'The Arbitration Act (Northern Ireland) 1937' substitute 'Part I of the Arbitration Act 1996'.

Commonwealth Secretariat Act 1966 (c.10)

23. In section 1(3) of the Commonwealth Secretariat Act 1966 (contracts with Commonwealth Secretariat to be deemed to contain provision for arbitration), for 'the Arbitration Act 1950 and the Arbitration Act (Northern Ireland) 1937' substitute 'Part I of the Arbitration Act 1996'.

Arbitration (International Investment Disputes) Act 1966 (c.41)

24. In the Arbitration (International Investment Disputes) Act 1966, for section 3 (application of Arbitration Act 1950 and other enactments) substitute—

'Application of provisions of Arbitration Act 1996
3.—(1) The Lord Chancellor may by order direct that any of the provisions contained in sections 36 and 38 to 44 of the Arbitration Act 1996 (provisions concerning the conduct of arbitral proceedings, &c.) shall apply to such proceedings pursuant to the Convention as are specified in the order with or without any modifications or exceptions specified in the order.

(2) Subject to subsection (1), the Arbitration Act 1996 shall not apply to proceedings pursuant to the Convention, but this subsection shall not be taken as affecting section 9 of that Act (stay of legal proceedings in respect of matter subject to arbitration).

(3) An order made under this section—
   (a) may be varied or revoked by a subsequent order so made, and
   (b) shall be contained in a statutory instrument.'.

Poultry Improvement Act (Northern Ireland) (c.12) (N.I.))

25. In paragraph 10(4) of the Schedule to the Poultry Improvement Act (Northern Ireland) 1968 (reference of disputes), for 'The Arbitration Act (Northern Ireland) 1937' substitute 'Part I of the Arbitration Act 1996'.

Industrial and Provident Societies Act (Northern Ireland) 1969 (c.24 (N.I.))

26.—(1) Section 69 of the Industrial and Provident Societies Act (Northern Ireland) 1969 (decision of disputes) is amended as follows.

(2) In subsection (7) (decision of disputes)—
   (a) in the opening words, omit the words from 'and without prejudice' to '1937';
   (b) at the beginning of paragraph (a) insert 'without prejudice to any powers exercisable by virtue of Part I of the Arbitration Act 1996,'; and

(c)   in paragraph (b) omit 'the registrar or' and 'registrar or' and for the words from 'as might have been granted by the High Court' to the end substitute 'as might be granted by the registrar'.

(3)   For subsection (8) substitute—

'(8)   The court or registrar to whom any dispute is referred under subsections (2) to (6) may at the request of either party state a case on any question of law arising in the dispute for the opinion of the High Court.'.

Health and Personal Social Services (Northern Ireland) Order 1972 (N.I. 14)

27.   In Article 105(6) of the Health and Personal Social Services (Northern Ireland) Order 1972 (arbitrations under the Order), for 'the Arbitration Act (Northern Ireland) 1937' substitute 'Part I of the Arbitration Act 1996'.

Consumer Credit Act 1974 (c.39)

28.—(1)   Section 146 of the Consumer Credit Act 1974 is amended as follows.

(2)   In subsection (2) (solicitor engaged in contentious business), for 'section 86(1) of the Solicitors Act 1957' substitute 'section 87(1) of the Solicitors Act 1974'.

(3)   In subsection (4) (solicitor in Northern Ireland engaged in contentious business), for the words from 'business done' to 'Administration of Estates (Northern Ireland) Order 1979' substitute 'contentious business (as defined in Article 3(2) of the Solicitors (Northern Ireland) Order 1976.'.

Friendly Societies Act 1974 (c.46)

29.—(1)   The Friendly Societies Act 1974 is amended as follows.

(2)   For section 78(1) (statement of case) substitute—

'(1)   Any arbitrator, arbiter or umpire to whom a dispute falling within section 76 above is referred under the rules of a registered society or branch may at the request of either party state a case on any question of law arising in the dispute for the opinion of the High Court or, as the case may be, the Court of Session.'.

(3)   In section 83(3) (procedure on objections to amalgamations &c. of friendly societies), for 'the Arbitration Act 1950 or, in Northern Ireland, the Arbitration Act (Northern Ireland) 1937' substitute 'Part I of the Arbitration Act 1996'.

Industry Act 1975 (c.68)

30.   In Schedule 3 to the Industry Act (arbitration of disputes relating to vesting and compensation orders), in paragraph 14 (application of certain provisions of Arbitration Acts)—

(a)   for 'the Arbitration Act 1950 or, in Northern Ireland, the Arbitration Act (Northern Ireland) 1937' substitute 'Part I of the Arbitration Act 1996', and

(b)   for 'that Act' substitute 'that Part'.

Industrial Relations (Northern Ireland) Order 1976 (N.I. 16)

31.   In Article 59(9) of the Industrial Relations (Northern Ireland) Order 1976 (proceedings of industrial tribunal), for 'The Arbitration Act (Northern Ireland) 1937' substitute 'Part I of the Arbitration Act 1996'.

Aircraft and Shipbuilding Industries Act 1977 (c. 3)

32.   In Schedule 7 to the Aircraft and Shipbuilding Industries Act 1977 (procedure of Arbitration Tribunal), in paragraph 2—

(a)   for 'the Arbitration Act 1950 or, in Northern Ireland, the Arbitration Act (Northern Ireland) 1937' substitute 'Part I of the Arbitration Act 1996', and

(b)   for 'that Act' substitute 'that Part'.

Patents Act 1977 (c. 37)

33.   In section 130 of the Patents Act 1977 (interpretation), in subsection (8) (exclusion of Arbitration Act) for 'The Arbitration Act 1950' substitute 'Part I of the Arbitration Act 1996'.

Judicature (Northern Ireland) Act 1978 (c. 23)

34.—(1)   The Judicature (Northern Ireland) Act 1978 is amended as follows.

(2)   In section 35(2) (restrictions on appeals to the Court of Appeal), after paragraph (f) insert—

'(fa)   except as provided by Part I of the Arbitration Act 1996, from any decision of the High Court under that Part;'.

(3)   In section 55(2) (rules of court) after paragraph (c) insert—

'(cc)   providing for any prescribed part of the jurisdiction of the High Court in relation to the trial of any action involving matters of account to be exercised in the prescribed manner by a person agreed by the parties and for the remuneration of any such person;'.

Health and Safety at Work (Northern Ireland) Order 1978 (N.I. 9)

35.   In Schedule 4 to the Health and Safety at Work (Northern Ireland) Order 1978 (licensing provisions), in paragraph 3, for 'The Arbitration Act (Northern Ireland) 1937' substitute 'Part I of the Arbitration Act 1996'.

County Courts (Northern Ireland) Order 1980 (N.I.3)

36.—(1)   The County Courts (Northern Ireland) Order 1980 is amended as follows.
   (2)   In Article 30 (civil jurisdiction exercisable by district judge)—
      (a)   for paragraph (2) substitute—

'(2)   Any order, decision or determination made by a district judge under this Article (other than one made in dealing with a claim by way of arbitration under paragraph (3)) shall be embodied in a decree which for all purposes (including the right of appeal under Part VI) shall have the like effect as a decree pronounced by a county court judge.';

      (b)   for paragraphs (4) and (5) substitute—

'(4)   Where in any action to which paragraph (1) applies the claim is dealt with by way of arbitration under paragraph (3)—
      (a)   any award made by the district judge in dealing with the claim shall be embodied in a decree which for all purposes (except the right of appeal under Part VI) shall have the like effect as a decree pronounced by a county court judge;
      (b)   the district judge may, and shall if so required by the High Court, state for the determination of the High Court any question of law arising out of an award so made;
      (c)   except as provided by sub-paragraph (b), any award so made shall be final; and
      (d)   except as otherwise provided by county court rules, no costs shall be awarded in connection with the action.
   (5)   Subject to paragraph (4), county court rules may—
      (a)   apply any of the provisions of Part I of the Arbitration Act 1996 to arbitrations under paragraph (3) with such modifications as may be prescribed;
      (b)   prescribe the rules of evidence to be followed on any arbitration under paragraph (3) and, in particular, make provision with respect to the manner of taking and questioning evidence.
   (5A)   Except as provided by virtue of paragraph (5)(a), Part I of the Arbitration Act 1996 shall not apply to an arbitration under paragraph (3).'.

   (3)   After Article 61 insert—
'61A.   Appeals from decisions under Part I of the Arbitration Act 1996

   (1)   Article 61 does not apply to a decision of a county court judge made in the exercise of the jurisdiction conferred by Part I of the Arbitration Act 1996.
   (2)   Any party dissatisfied with a decision of the county court made in the exercise of the jurisdiction conferred by any of the following provisions of Part I of the Arbitration Act 1996, namely—

    (a)   section 32 (question as to substantive jurisdiction of arbitral tribunal);

    (b)   section 45 (question of law arising in course of arbitral proceedings);

    (c)   section 67 (challenging award of arbitral tribunal: substantive jurisdiction);

    (d)   section 68 (challenging award of arbitral tribunal: serious irregularity);

    (e)   section 69 (appeal on point of law),

may, subject to the provisions of that Part, appeal from that decision to the Court of Appeal.

    (3)   Any party dissatisfied with any decision of a county court made in the exercise of the jurisdiction conferred by any other provision of Part I of the Arbitration Act 1996 may, subject to the provisions of that Part, appeal from that decision to the High Court.

    (4)   The decision of the Court of Appeal on an appeal under paragraph (2) shall be final.'.

Supreme Court Act 1981 (c.54)

37.—(1)   The Supreme Court Act 1981 is amended as follows.

(2)   In section 18(1) (restrictions on appeals to the Court of Appeal), for paragraph (g) substitute—

'(g)   except as provided by Part I of the Arbitration Act 1996, from any decision of the High Court under that Part;'.

(3)   In section 151 (interpretation, &c.), in the definition of 'arbitration agreement', for 'the Arbitration Act 1950 by virtue of section 32 of that Act;' substitute 'Part I of the Arbitration Act 1996;'.

Merchant Shipping (Liner Conferences) Act 1982 (c.37)

38.   In section 7(5) of the Merchant Shipping (Liner Conferences) Act 1982 (stay of legal proceedings), for the words from 'section 4(1)' to the end substitute 'section 9 of the Arbitration Act 1996 (which also provides for the staying of legal proceedings).'.

Agricultural Marketing (Northern Ireland) Order 1982 (N.I.12)

39.   In Article 14 of the Agricultural Marketing (Northern Ireland) Order 1982 (application of provisions of Arbitration Act (Northern Ireland) 1937)—

    (a)   for the words from the beginning to 'shall apply' substitute 'Section 45 and 69 of the Arbitration Act 1996 (which relate to the determination by the court of questions of law) and section 66 of that Act (enforcement of awards)' apply; and

    (b)   for 'an arbitration' substitute 'arbitral proceedings'.

Mental Health Act 1983 (c. 20)

40. In section 78 of the Mental Health Act 1983 (procedure of Mental Health Review Tribunals), in subsection (9) for 'The Arbitration Act 1950' substitute 'Part I of the Arbitration Act 1996'.

Registered Homes Act 1984 (c. 23)

41. In section 43 of the Registered Homes Act 1984 (procedure of Registered Homes Tribunals), in subsection (3) for 'The Arbitration Act 1950' substitute 'Part I of the Arbitration Act 1996'.

Housing Act 1985 (c. 68)

42. In section 47(3) of the Housing Act 1985 (agreement as to determination of matters relating to service charges) for 'section 32 of the Arbitration Act 1950' substitute 'Part I of the Arbitration Act 1996'.

Landlord and Tenant Act 1985 (c. 70)

43. In section 19(3) of the Landlord and Tenant Act 1985 (agreement as to determination of matters relating to service charges), for 'section 32 of the Arbitration Act 1950' substitute 'Part I of the Arbitration Act 1996'.

Credit Unions (Northern Ireland) Order 1985 (N.I. 12)

44.—(1) Article 72 of the Credit Unions (Northern Ireland) Order 1985 (decision of disputes) is amended as follows.

(2) In paragraph (7)—

(a) in the opening words, omit the words from 'and without prejudice' to '1937';

(b) at the beginning of sub-paragraph (a) insert 'without prejudice to any powers exercisable by virtue of Part I of the Arbitration Act 1996,'; and

(c) in sub-paragraph (b) omit 'the registrar or' and 'registrar or' and for the words from 'as might have been granted by the High Court' to the end substitute 'as might be granted by the registrar'.

(3) For paragraph (8) substitute—

'(8) The court or registrar to whom any dispute is referred under paragraphs (2) to (6) may at the request of either party state a case on any question of law arising in the dispute for the opinion of the High Court.'.

Agricultural Holdings Act 1986 (c. 5)

45. In section 84(1) of the Agricultural Holdings Act 1986 (provisions relating to arbitration), for 'the Arbitration Act 1950' substitute 'Part I of the Arbitration Act 1996'.

Insolvency Act 1986 (c.45)

46.   In the Insolvency Act 1986, after section 349 insert—

'349A.   Arbitration agreements to which bankrupt is party
(1)   This section applies where a bankrupt had become party to a contract containing an arbitration agreement before the commencement of his bankruptcy.
(2)   If the trustee in bankruptcy adopts the contract, the arbitration agreement is enforceable by or against the trustee in relation to matters arising from or connected with the contract.
(3)   If the trustee in bankruptcy does not adopt the contract and a matter to which the arbitration agreement applies requires to be determined in connection with or for the purposes of the bankruptcy proceedings—
(a)   the trustee with the consent of the creditors' committee, or
(b)   any other party to the agreement,
may apply to the court which may, if it thinks fit in all the circumstances of the case, order that the matter be referred to arbitration in accordance with the arbitration agreement.
(4)   In this section—
"arbitration agreement" has the same meaning as in Part I of the Arbitration Act 1996; and
"the court" means the court which has jurisdiction in the bankruptcy proceedings.'.

Building Societies Act 1986 (c.53)

47.   In Part II of Schedule 14 to the Building Societies Act 1986 (settlement of disputes: arbitration), in paragraph 5(6) for 'the Arbitration Act 1950 and the Arbitration Act 1979 or, in Northern Ireland, the Arbitration Act (Northern Ireland) 1937' substitute 'Part I of the Arbitration Act 1996'.

Mental Health (Northern Ireland) Order 1986 (N.I.4)

48.   In Article 83 of the Mental Health (Northern Ireland) Order 1986 (procedure of Mental Health Review Tribunal), in paragraph (8) for 'The Arbitration Act (Northern Ireland) 1937' substitute 'Part I of the Arbitration Act 1996'.

Multilateral Investment Guarantee Agency Act 1988 (c.8)

49.   For section 6 of the Multilateral Investment Guarantee Agency Act 1988 (application of Arbitration Act) substitute—

'6.   Application of Arbitration Act
(1)   The Lord Chancellor may by order made by statutory instrument direct that any of the provisions of sections 36 and 38 to 44 of the Arbitration Act 1996 (provisions in relation to the conduct of the arbitral

proceedings, &c.) apply, with such modifications or exceptions as are specified in the order, to such arbitration proceedings pursuant to Annex II to the Convention as are specified in the order.

(2)   Except as provided by an order under subsection (1) above, no provision of Part I of the Arbitration Act 1996 other than section 9 (stay of legal proceedings) applies to any such proceedings.'.

Copyright, Designs and Patents Act 1988 (c.48)

50.   In section 150 of the Copyright, Designs and Patents Act 1988 (Lord Chancellor's power to make rules for Copyright Tribunal), for subsection (2) substitute—

'(2)   The rules may apply in relation to the Tribunal, as respects proceedings in England and Wales or Northern Ireland, any of the provisions of Part I of the Arbitration Act 1996.'.

Fair Employment (Northern Ireland) Act 1989 (c.32)

51.   In the Fair Employment (Northern Ireland) Act 1989, section 5(7) (procedure of Fair Employment Tribunal), for 'The Arbitration Act (Northern Ireland) 1937' substitute 'Part I of the Arbitration Act 1996'.

Limitation (Northern Ireland) Order 1989 (N.I.11)

52.   In Article 2(2) of the Limitation (Northern Ireland) Order 1989 (interpretation), in the definition of 'arbitration agreement', for 'the Arbitration Act (Northern Ireland) 1937' substitute 'Part I of the Arbitration Act 1996'.

Insolvency (Northern Ireland) Order 1989 (N.I.19)

53.   In the Insolvency (Northern Ireland) Order 1989, after Article 320 insert—

'320A.   Arbitration agreements to which bankrupt is party

(1)   This Article applies where a bankrupt had become party to a contract containing an arbitration agreement before the commencement of his bankruptcy.

(2)   If the trustee in bankruptcy adopts the contract, the arbitration agreement is enforceable by or against the trustee in relation to matters arising from or connected with the contract.

(3)   If the trustee in bankruptcy does not adopt the contract and a matter to which the arbitration agreement applies requires to be determined in connection with or for the purposes of the bankruptcy proceedings—

    (a)   the trustee with the consent of the creditors' committee, or

    (b)   any other party to the agreement,

may apply to the court which may, if it thinks fit in all the circumstances of the case, order that the matter be referred to arbitration in accordance with the arbitration agreement.

(4)   In this Article—

"arbitration agreement" has the same meaning as in Part I of the Arbitration Act 1996; and

"the court" means the court which has jurisdiction in the bankruptcy proceedings.'.

Social Security Administration Act 1992 (c.5)

54.   In section 59 of the Social Security Administration Act 1992 (procedure for inquiries, &c.), in subsection (7), for 'The Arbitration Act 1950' substitute 'Part I of the Arbitration Act 1996'.

Social Security Administration (Northern Ireland) Act 1992 (c.8)

55.   In section 57 of the Social Security Administration (Northern Ireland) Act 1992 (procedure for inquiries, &c.), in subsection (6) for 'the Arbitration Act (Northern Ireland) 1937' substitute 'Part I of the Arbitration Act 1996'.

Trade Union and Labour Relations (Consolidation) Act 1992 (c.52)

56.   In sections 212(5) and 263(6) of the Trade Union and Labour Relations (Consolidation) Act 1992 (application of Arbitration Act) for 'the Arbitration Act 1950' substitute 'Part I of the Arbitration Act 1996'.

Industrial Relations (Northern Ireland) Order 1992 (N.I.5)

57.   In Articles 84(9) and 92(5) of the Industrial Relations (Northern Ireland) Order 1992 (application of Arbitration Act) for 'The Arbitration Act (Northern Ireland) 1937' substitute 'Part I of the Arbitration Act 1996'.

Registered Homes (Northern Ireland) Order 1992 (N.I.20)

58.   In Article 33(3) of the Registered Homes (Northern Ireland) Order 1992 (procedure of Registered Homes Tribunal) for 'The Arbitration Act (Northern Ireland) 1937' substitute 'Part I of the Arbitration Act 1996'.

Education Act 1993 (c.35)

59.   In section 180(4) of the Education Act 1993 (procedure of Special Educational Needs Tribunal), for 'The Arbitration Act 1950' substitute 'Part I of the Arbitration Act 1996'.

Roads (Northern Ireland) Order 1993 (N.I.15)

60.—(1)   The Roads (Northern Ireland) Order 1993 is amended as follows.

(2)   In Article 131 (application of Arbitration Act) for 'the Arbitration Act (Northern Ireland) 1937' substitute 'Part I of the Arbitration Act 1996'.

(3)   In Schedule 4 (disputes), in paragraph 3(2) for 'the Arbitration Act (Northern Ireland) 1937' substitute 'Part I of the Arbitration Act 1996'.

Merchant Shipping Act 1995 (c.21)

61.   In Part II of Schedule 6 to the Merchant Shipping Act 1995 (provisions having effect in connection with Convention Relating to the Carriage of Passengers and Their Luggage by Sea), for paragraph 7 substitute—

'7.   Article 16 shall apply to arbitral proceedings as it applies to an action; and, as respects England and Wales and Northern Ireland, the provisions of section 14 of the Arbitration Act 1996 apply to determine for the purposes of that Article when an arbitration is commenced.'.

Industrial Tribunals Act 1996 (c.17)

62.   In section 6(2) of the Industrial Tribunals Act 1996 (procedure of industrial tribunals), for 'The Arbitration Act 1950' substitute 'Part I of the Arbitration Act 1996.'

Section 107(2)   SCHEDULE 4
                                      REPEALS

Chapter	Short title	Extent of repeal
1892 c. 43.	Military Land Act 1892.	In section 21(b), the words 'under the Arbitration Act 1889'.
1922 c. 51.	Allotments Act 1922.	In section 21(3), the words 'under the Arbitration Act 1889'.
1937 c. 8 (N.I.).	Arbitration Act (Northern Ireland) 1937.	The whole Act.
1949 c. 54	Wireless Telegraphy Act 1949.	In Schedule 2, paragraph 3(3).
1949 c. 97	National Parks and Access to the Countryside Act 1949.	In section 18(4), the words from 'Without prejudice' to 'England or Wales'.
1950 c. 27.	Arbitration Act 1950.	Part I. Section 42(3).
1958 c. 47.	Agricultural Marketing Act 1958.	Section 53(8).
1962 c. 46.	Transport Act 1962.	In Schedule 11, Part II, paragraph 7.
1964 c. 14.	Plant Varieties and Seeds Act 1964.	In section 10(4) the words from 'or in section 9' to 'three arbitrators)'. Section 39(3)(b)(i).
1964 c. 29 (N.I.)	Land Tribunal and Compensation Act (Northern Ireland) 1964.	In section 9(3) the words from 'so, however, that' to the end.

Chapter	Short title	Extent of repeal
1965 c. 12.	Industrial and Provident Societies Act 1965.	In section 60(8)(b), the words 'by virtue of section 12 of the said Act of 1950'.
1965 c. 37	Carriage of Goods by Road Act 1965.	Section 7(2)(b).
1965 c. 13 (N.I.).	New Towns Act (Northern Ireland) 1965	In section 27(2), the words from 'under and in accordance with' to the end.
1969 c. 24 (N.I).	Industrial and Provident Societies Act (Northern Ireland) 1969.	In section 69(7)— (a) in the opening words, the words from 'and without prejudice' to '1937'; (b) in paragraph (b), the words, 'the registrar or' and 'registrar or'.
1970 c. 31.	Administration of Justice Act 1970.	Section 4. Schedule 3.
1973 c. 41.	Fair Trading Act 1973.	Section 33(2)(d).
1973 N.I. 1.	Drainage (Northern Ireland) Order 1973.	In Article 15(4), the words from 'under and in accordance' to the end. Article 40(4). In Schedule 7, in paragraph 9(2), the words from 'under and in accordance' to the end.
1974 c. 47.	Solicitors Act 1974.	In section 87(1), in the definition of 'contentious business', the words 'appointed under the Arbitration Act 1950'.
1975 c. 3	Arbitration Act 1975.	The whole Act.
1975 c. 74.	Petroleum and Submarine Pipe-Lines Act 1975.	In Part II of Schedule 2— (a) in model clause 40(2), the words 'in accordance with the Arbitration Act 1950'; (b) in model clause 40(2B), the words 'in accordance with the Arbitration Act (Northern Ireland) 1937'. In Part II of Schedule 3, in model clause 38(2), the words 'in accordance with the Arbitration Act 1950'.

Chapter	Short title	Extent of repeal
1976 N.I. 12.	Solicitors (Northern Ireland) Order 1976.	In Article 3(2), in the entry 'contentious business' the words 'appointed under the Arbitration Act (Northern Ireland) 1937'. Article 71H(3).
1977 c. 37.	Patents Act 1977.	In section 52(4) the words 'section 21 of the Arbitration Act 1950 or, as the case may be, section 22 of the Arbitration Act (Northern Ireland) 1937 (statement of cases by arbitrators); but'. Section 131(e).
1977 c. 38.	Administration of Justice Act 1977.	Section 17(2).
1978 c. 23.	Judicature (Northern Ireland) Act 1978.	In section 35(2), paragraph (g)(v). In Schedule 5, the amendment to the Arbitration Act 1950.
1979 c. 42.	Arbitration Act 1979.	The whole Act.
1980 c. 58.	Limitation Act 1980.	Section 34.
1980 N.I. 3.	County Courts (Northern Ireland) Order 1980.	Article 31(3).
1981 c. 54.	Supreme Court Act 1981.	Section 148.
1982 c. 27.	Civil Jurisdiction and Judgments Act 1982.	Section 25(3)(c) and (5). In section 26— (a) in subsection (1), the words 'to arbitrator or'; (b) in subsection (1)(a)(i), the words 'arbitration or'; (c) in subsection (2), the words 'arbitration or'.
1982 c. 53.	Administration of Justice Act 1982.	Section 15(6). In Schedule 1, Part IV.
1984 c. 5.	Merchant Shipping Act 1984.	Section 4(8).
1984 c. 12.	Telecommunications Act 1984.	Schedule 2, paragraph 13(8).
1984 c. 16.	Foreign Limitation Periods Act 1984.	Section 5.
1984 c. 28.	County Courts Act 1984.	In Schedule 2, paragraph 70.

Chapter	Short title	Extent of repeal
1985 c. 61	Administration of Justice Act 1985.	Section 58. In Schedule 9, paragraph 15.
1985 c. 68.	Housing Act 1985.	In Schedule 18, in paragraph 6(2) the words from 'and the Arbitration Act 1950' to the end.
1985 N.I. 12.	Credit Unions (Northern Ireland) Order 1985.	In Article 72(7)— (a) in the opening words, the words from 'and without prejudice' to '1937'; (b) in sub-paragraph (b), the words 'the registrar or' and 'registrar or'.
1986 c. 45.	Insolvency Act 1986.	In Schedule 14, the entry relating to the Arbitration Act 1950.
1988 c. 8.	Multilateral Investment Guarantee Agency Act 1988.	Section 8(3).
1988 c. 21.	Consumer Arbitration Agreements Act 1988.	The whole Act.
1989 N.I. 11.	Limitation (Northern Ireland) Order 1989.	Article 72. In Schedule 3, paragraph 1.
1989 N.I. 19.	Insolvency (Northern Ireland) Order 1989.	In Part II of Schedule 9, paragraph 66.
1990 c. 41.	Courts and Legal Services Act 1990.	Sections 99 and 101 to 103.
1991 N.I. 7.	Food Safety (Northern Ireland) Order 1991.	In Articles 8(8) and 11(10), the words from 'and the provisions' to the end.
1992 c. 40.	Friendly Societies Act 1992.	In Schedule 16, paragraph 30(1).
1995 c. 8.	Agricultural Tenancies Act 1995.	Section 28(4).
1995 c. 21.	Merchant Shipping Act 1995.	Section 96(10). Section 264(9).
1995 c. 42.	Private International Law (Miscellaneous Provisions) Act 1995.	Section 3.

I.6.2 Scotland

Note: Statutory material that applies to both England and Scotland is not duplicated in this section. (For example, the Arbitration Act 1975 and part II of the Arbitration Act 1950 also apply in Scotland. The Arbitration Act 1996 does not repeal the 1975 Act for Scotland. It will, however, repeal the Consumer Arbitration Agreements Act 1988.)

THE 25TH ACT OF THE ARTICLES OF REGULATION 1695

That, for the cutting off of groundless and expensive pleas and processes in time coming, the Lords of Session sustain no reduction of any decreet-arbitral that shall be pronounced hereafter upon a Subscribed Submission, at the instance of either of the parties-submitters, upon any cause or reason whatsoever, unless that of corruption, bribery, or falsehood, to be alleged against the judges arbitrators who pronounced the same.

ARBITRATION (SCOTLAND) ACT 1894
(1894, c. 13)

An Act to amend the Law of Arbitration in Scotland.   [3rd July 1894]

1.   Reference to arbiter not named, &c. not to be invalid.

. . . , an agreement to refer to arbitration shall not be invalid or ineffectual by reason of the reference being to a person not named, or to a person to be named by another person, or to a person merely described as the holder for the time being of any office or appointment.
[*Opening words repealed by Statute Law Revision Act 1908.*]

2.   On failure to concur in nomination of single arbiter, court may appoint.

Should one of the parties to an agreement to refer to a single arbiter refuse to concur in the nomination of such arbiter, and should no provision have been made for carrying out the reference in that event, or should such provision have failed, an arbiter may be appointed by the court, on the application of any party to the agreement, and the arbiter so appointed shall have the same powers as if he had been duly nominated by all the parties.

3.   On failure of one party to nominate arbiter, court may appoint.

Should one of the parties to an agreement to refer to two arbiters refuse to name an arbiter, in terms of the agreement, and should no provision have been made for carrying out the reference in that event, or should such provision have failed, an arbiter may be appointed by the court, on the application of the other party, and the arbiter so appointed shall have the same powers as if he had been duly nominated by the party so refusing.

4.   Arbiters may devolve on oversmen unless otherwise agreed.

Unless the agreement to refer shall otherwise provide, arbiters shall have power to name an oversman on whom the reference shall be devolved in the event of their differing in opinion. Should the arbiters fail to agree in the nomination of an oversman, the court may on the application of any party to the agreement, appoint an oversman. The decision of such oversman, whether he has been named by the arbiters or appointed by the court, shall be final.

5.   Act not to apply to certain agreements.

This Act shall not apply to any agreement, made before its passing, to refer to an arbiter not named or to be named by another person or merely described as the holder for the time being of an office or appointment, if any party to such agreement shall, before the passing of this Act, or within six months thereafter, have intimated to the other party by writing that he declines to be bound by such agreement.

6.   Interpretation.

For the purposes of this Act the expression 'the court' shall mean any sheriff having jurisdiction or any Lord Ordinary of the Court of Session;
except that where—
(a)   any arbiter appointed is; or
(b)   in terms of the agreement to refer to arbitration an arbiter or oversman to be appointed must be,
a Senator of the College of Justice, 'the Court' shall mean the Inner House of the Court of Session.
[*As amended by the Law Reform (Miscellaneous Provisions) (Scotland) Act 1980, s. 17(4).*]

7.   Extent of Act and Short Title.

This Act shall apply to Scotland only, and may be cited as the Arbitration (Scotland) Act, 1894.

ADMINISTRATION OF JUSTICE (SCOTLAND) ACT 1972
(1972, c. 59)

An Act to confer extended powers on the courts in Scotland to order the inspection of documents and other property, and related matters; to enable an appeal to be taken to the House of Lords from an interlocutor of the Court of Session on a motion for a new trial; to enable a case to be stated on a question of law to the Court of Session in an arbitration; and to enable alterations to be made by act of sederunt in the rate of interest to be included in sheriff court decrees or extracts.
[9th August 1972]

1.   . . .

2.   . . .

3.   Power of arbiter to state case to Court of Session.

(1)   Subject to express provision to the contrary in an agreement to refer to arbitration, the arbiter or oversman may, on the application of a party to the arbitration, and shall, if the Court of Session on such an application so directs, at any stage in the arbitration state a case for the opinion of that Court on any question of law arising in the arbitration.

(2)   This section shall not apply to an arbitration under any enactment which confers a power to appeal to or state a case for the opinion of a court or tribunal in relation to that arbitration.

(3)   This section shall not apply to any form of arbitration relating to a trade dispute within the meaning of the [Employment Protection Act 1975] to any other arbitration arising from a collective agreement within the meaning of the [Trade Union and Labour Relations Act, 1974]; or to proceedings before the Industrial Arbitration Board . . .

(4)   This section shall not apply in relation to an agreement to refer to arbitration made before the commencement of this Act.

4.   . . .

5.   Short title, interpretation, commencement and extent.

(1)   This Act may be cited as the Administration of Justice (Scotland) Act 1972.

(2)   In this Act any reference to an enactment shall be construed as a reference to that enactment as amended by or under any other enactment.

(3)   Sections 1 and 3 of this Act shall come into operation on such day as the Secretary of State may by order made by statutory instrument appoint, and different days may be appointed for different purposes.
[*2/4/1973 appointed for s. 1 and s. 3.*]

(4)   This Act shall extend to Scotland only.

LAW REFORM (MISCELLANEOUS PROVISIONS) (SCOTLAND) ACT 1990
(1990, c. 40)

An Act, as respects Scotland, . . .   [1st November 1990]

Arbitration

66.   UNCITRAL Model Law on International Commercial Arbitration.

(1)   In this section, 'the Model Law' means the UNCITRAL Model Law on International Commercial Arbitration as adopted by the United Nations Commission on International Trade Law on 21st June 1985.

(2)   The Model Law shall have the force of law in Scotland in the form set out in Schedule 7 to this Act (which contains the Model Law with certain modifications to adapt it for application in Scotland).

(3)   The documents of the United Nations Commission on International Trade Law and its working group relating to the preparation of the Model Law may be considered in ascertaining the meaning or effect of any provision of the Model Law as set out in Schedule 7 to this Act.

(4)   The parties to an arbitration agreement may, notwithstanding that the arbitration would not be an international commercial arbitration within the meaning of article 1 of the Model Law as set out in Schedule 7 to this Act,

agree that the Model Law as set out in that Schedule shall apply, and in such a case the Model Law as so set out shall apply to that arbitration.

(5) Subsection (4) above is without prejudice to any other enactment or rule of law relating to arbitration.

(6) Subject to subsections (7) and (8) below, this section shall apply in relation to an arbitration agreement whether entered into before or after the date when this section comes into force.

(7) Notwithstanding subsection (6) above, this section shall not apply with respect to any arbitration which has commenced but has not been concluded on the date when this section comes into force.

(8) The parties to an arbitration agreement entered into before the date when this section comes into force may agree that the foregoing provisions of this section shall not apply to that arbitration agreement.

Section 66   SCHEDULE 7

UNCITRAL

MODEL LAW ON INTERNATIONAL COMMERCIAL ARBITRATION

CHAPTER I

GENERAL PROVISIONS

Article 1   Scope of application.

(1) This Law applies to international commercial arbitration, subject to any agreement in force between the United Kingdom and any other State or States which applies in Scotland.

(2) The provisions of this Law, except articles 8, 9, 35 and 36, apply only if the place of arbitration is in Scotland.

(3) An arbitration is international if:

(a) the parties to an arbitration agreement have, at the time of the conclusion of that agreement, their places of business in different States; or

(b) one of the following places is situated outside the State in which the parties have their places of business:

(i) the place of arbitration if determined in, or pursuant to, the arbitration agreement;

(ii) any place where a substantial part of the obligations of the commercial relationship is to be performed or the place with which the subject-matter of the dispute is most closely connected.

(4) For the purposes of paragraph (3) of this article:

(a) if a party has more than one place of business, the place of business is that which has the closest relationship to the arbitration agreement;

(b) if a party does not have a place of business, reference is to be made to his habitual residence.

(5) This Law shall not affect any other enactment or rule of law in force in Scotland by virtue of which certain disputes may not be submitted to arbitration or may be submitted to arbitration only according to provisions other than those of this Law.

Article 2   Definitions and rules of interpretation.

For the purposes of this Law:

(a)   'arbitration' means any arbitration whether or not administered by a permanent arbitral institution;

(b)   'arbitral tribunal' means an arbitrator or a panel of arbitrators;

(c)   'arbitrator' includes an arbiter:

(d)   'commercial', in relation to an arbitration, includes matters arising from all relationships of a commercial nature, whether contractual or not;

(e)   'country' includes Scotland;

(f)   'court' means a body or organ of the judicial system of a State;

(g)   'relationships of a commercial nature' include, but are not limited to, the following transactions, namely any trade transaction for the supply or exchange of goods or services; distribution agreement; commercial representation or agency; factoring; leasing; construction of works; consulting; engineering; licensing; investment; financing; banking; insurance; exploitation agreement or concession; joint venture and other forms of industrial or business co-operation; carriage of goods or passengers by air, sea, rail or road;

(h)   'State', except in article 1(1), includes Scotland;

(i)   where a provision of this Law, except article 28, leaves the parties free to determine a certain issue, such freedom includes the right of the parties to authorise a third party, including an institution, to make that determination;

(j)   where a provision of this Law refers to the fact that the parties have agreed or that they may agree or in any other way refers to an agreement of the paities, such agreement includes any arbitration rules referred to in that agreement;

(k)   where a provision of this Law, other than in articles 25(a) and 32(2)(a), refers to a claim, it also applies to a counter-claim, and where it refers to a defence, it also applies to a defence to such counter-claim;

(l)   article headings are for reference purposes only and are not to be used for purposes of interpretation.

Article 3   Receipt of written communications.

(1)   Unless otherwise agreed by the parties:

(a)   any written communication is deemed to have been received if it is delivered to the addressee personally or if it is delivered at his place of business, habitual residence or mailing address; if none of these can be found after making a reasonable inquiry, a written communication is deemed to have been received if it is sent to the addressee's last-known place of business, habitual residence or mailing address by registered letter or any other means which provides a record of the attempts to deliver it;

(b)   the communication is deemed to have been received on the day it is so delivered.

(2)   The provisions of this article do not apply to communications in court proceedings.

Article 4   Waiver of right to object.

A party who knows that any provision of this Law from which the parties may derogate or any requirement under the arbitration agreement has not been complied with and yet proceeds with the arbitration without stating his objections to such non-compliance without undue delay or, if a time-limit is provided therefor, within such period of time, shall be deemed to have waived his right to object.

Article 5   Extent of court intervention.

In matters governed by this Law, no court shall intervene except where so provided in this Law.

Article 6   Court for certain functions of arbitration assistance, supervision and enforcement.

The functions referred to in articles 11(3), 11(4), 13(3), 14, 16(3), 34(2), 35 and 36 shall be performed by:
  (a)   the Court of Session; or
  (b)   where it has jurisdiction, the sheriff court.

CHAPTER II

ARBITRATION AGREEMENT

Article 7   Definition and form of arbitration agreement.

(1)   'Arbitration agreement' is an agreement by the parties to submit to arbitration all or certain disputes which have arisen or which may arise between them in respect of a defined legal relationship, whether contractual or not. An arbitration agreement may be in the form of an arbitration clause in a contract or in the form of a separate agreement.

(2)   The arbitration agreement shall be in writing. An agreement is in writing if it is contained in a document signed by the parties or in an exchange of letters, telex, telegrams or other means of telecommunication which provide a record of the agreement, or in an exchange of statements of claim and defence in which the existence of an agreement is alleged by one party and not denied by another. The reference in a contract to a document containing an arbitration clause constitutes an arbitration agreement provided that the contract is in writing and the reference is such as to make that clause part of the contract.

Article 8   Arbitration agreement and substantive claim before court.

(1)   A court before which an action is brought in a matter which is the subject of an arbitration agreement shall, if a party so requests at any time before the pleadings in the action are finalised, refer the parties to arbitration unless it finds that the agreement is null and void, inoperative or incapable of being performed.

(2)   Where an action referred to in paragraph (1) of this article has been brought, arbitral proceedings may nevertheless be commenced or continued, and an award may be made, while the issue is pending before the court.

Article 9   Arbitration agreement and interim measures by court.

(1)   It is not incompatible with an arbitration agreement for a party to request, before or during arbitral proceedings, from a court an interim measure of protection and for a court to grant such measure.

(2)   In paragraph (1) of this article 'interim measure of protection' includes, but is not limited to, the following:

(a)   arrestment or inhibition to ensure that any award which may be made in the arbitral proceedings is not rendered ineffectual by the dissipation of assets by another party;

(b)   interim interdict or other interim order.

(3)   Where:

(a)   a party applies to a court for an interim interdict or other interim order; and

(b)   an arbitral tribunal has already ruled on the matter,

the court shall treat the ruling or any finding of fact made in the course of the ruling as conclusive for the purposes of the application.

CHAPTER III

COMPOSITION OF ARBITRATION TRIBUNAL

Article 10   Number of arbitrators.

(1)   The parties are free to determine the number of arbitrators.

(2)   Failing such determination, there shall be a single arbitrator.

Article 11   Appointment of arbitrators.

(1)   No person shall be precluded by reason of his nationality from acting as an arbitrator, unless otherwise agreed by the parties.

(2)   The parties are free to agree on a procedure of appointing the arbitrator or arbitrators, subject to the provisions of paragraphs (4) and (5) of this article.

(3)   Failing such agreement,

(a)   in an arbitration with three arbitrators, each party shall appoint one arbitrator, and the two arbitrators thus appointed shall appoint the third arbitrator; if a party fails to appoint the arbitrator within thirty days of receipt of a request to do so from the other party, or if the two arbitrators fail to agree on the third arbitrator within thirty days of their appointment, the appointment shall be made, upon request of a party, by the court specified in article 6;

(b)   in an arbitration with a single arbitrator, if the parties are unable to agree on the arbitrator, he shall be appointed, upon request of a party, by the court specified in article 6.

(4)   Where, under an appointment procedure agreed upon by the parties:

(a)   a party fails to act as required under such procedure, or

(b)   the parties, or two arbitrators, are unable to reach an agreement expected of them under such procedure, or

(c)   a third party, including an institution, fails to perform any function entrusted to it under such procedure, any party may request the court specified in article 6 to take the necessary measure, unless the agreement on the appointment procedure provides other means for securing the appointment.

(5)   A decision on a matter entrusted by paragraph (3) or (4) of this article to the court specified in article 6 shall be subject to no appeal. The court, in appointing an arbitrator, shall have due regard to any qualifications required of the arbitrator by the agreement of the parties and to such considerations as are likely to secure the appointment of an independent and impartial arbitrator and, in the case of a sole or third arbitrator, shall take into account as well the advisability of appointing an arbitrator of a nationality other than those of the parties.

Article 12   Grounds for challenge.

(1)   When a person is approached in connection with his possible appointment as an arbitrator, he shall disclose any circumstances likely to give rise to justifiable doubts as to his impartiality or independence. An arbitrator, from the time of his appointment and throughout the arbitral proceedings, shall without delay disclose any such circumstances to the parties unless they have already been informed of them by him.

(2)   An arbitrator may be challenged only if circumstances exist that give rise to justifiable doubts as to his impartiality or independence, or if he does not possess qualifications agreed to by the parties. A party may challenge an arbitrator appointed by him, or in whose appointment he has participated, only for reasons of which he becomes aware after the appointment has been made.

Article 13   Challenge procedure.

(1)   The parties are free to agree on a procedure for challenging an arbitrator, subject to the provisions of paragraph (3) of this article.

(2)   Failing such agreement, a party who intends to challenge an arbitrator shall, within fifteen days after becoming aware of the constitution of the arbitral tribunal or after becoming aware of any circumstances referred to in article 12(2), send a written statement of the reasons for the challenge to the arbitral tribunal. Unless the challenged arbitrator withdraws from his office or the other party agrees to the challenge, the arbitral tribunal shall decide on the challenge.

(3)   If a challenge under any procedure agreed upon by the parties or under the procedure of paragraph (2) of this article is not successful, the challenging party may, within thirty days after having received notice of the decision rejecting the challenge, request the court specified in article 6 to decide on the challenge, which decision shall be subject to no appeal. While such a request is pending, the arbitral tribunal, including the challenged arbitrator, may continue the arbitral proceedings and make an award.

Article 14   Failure or impossibility to act.

(1)   If an arbitrator becomes de jure or de facto unable to perform his functions or for other reasons fails to act without undue delay, his mandate

terminates if he withdraws from his office or if the parties agree on the termination. Otherwise, if a controversy remains concerning any of these grounds, any party may request the court specified in article 6 to decide on the termination of the mandate, which decision shall be subject to no appeal.

(2)　If, under this article or article 13(2), an arbitrator withdraws from his office or a party agrees to the termination of the mandate of an arbitrator, this does not imply acceptance of the validity of any ground referred to in this article or article 12(2).

Article 15　Appointment of substitute arbitrator.

Where the mandate of an arbitrator terminates under article 13 or 14 or because of his withdrawal from office for any other reason or because of the revocation of his mandate by agreement of the parties or in any other case of termination of his mandate, a substitute arbitrator shall be appointed according to the rules that were applicable to the appointment of the arbitrator being replaced.

CHAPTER IV

JURISDICTION OF ARBITRAL TRIBUNAL

Article 16　Competence of arbitral tribunal to rule on its jurisdiction.

(1)　The arbitral tribunal may rule on its own jurisdiction, including any objections with respect to the existence or validity of the arbitration agreement. For that purpose, an arbitration clause which forms part of a contract shall be treated as an agreement independent of the other terms of the contract. A decision by the arbitral tribunal that the contract is null and void shall not entail ipso jure the invalidity of the arbitration clause.

(2)　A plea that the arbitral tribunal does not have jurisdiction shall be raised not later than the submission of the statement of defence. A party is not precluded from raising such a plea by the fact that he has appointed, or participated in the appointment of, an arbitrator. A plea that the arbitral tribunal is exceeding the scope of its authority shall be raised as soon as the matter alleged to be beyond the scope of its authority is raised during the arbitral proceedings. The arbitral tribunal may, in either case, admit a later plea if it considers the delay justified.

(3)　The arbitral tribunal may rule on a plea referred to in paragraph (2) of this article either as a preliminary question or in an award on the merits. If the arbitral tribunal rules on such a plea as a preliminary question, any party may, within thirty days after having received notice of that ruling, request the court specified in article 6 to decide the matter, which decision shall be subject to no appeal. While such a request is pending, the arbitral tribunal may continue the arbitral proceedings and make an award.

Article 17　Power of arbitral tribunal to order interim measures.

(1)　Unless otherwise agreed by the parties, the arbitral tribunal may, at the request of a party, order any party to take such interim measures of protection as the arbitral tribunal may consider necessary in respect of the subject-matter of the dispute. The arbitral tribunal may require any party to provide appropriate security in connection with such measure.

(2) An order under paragraph (1) of this article shall take the form of an award and articles 31, 35 and 36 shall apply accordingly.

CHAPTER V

CONDUCT OF ARBITRAL PROCEEDINGS

Article 18 Equal treatment of parties.

The parties shall be treated with equality and each party shall be given a full opportunity of presenting his case.

Article 19 Determination of rules of procedure.

(1) Subject to the provisions of this Law, the parties are free to agree on the procedure to be followed by the arbitral tribunal in conducting the proceedings.

(2) Failing such agreement, the arbitral tribunal may, subject to the provisions of this Law, conduct the arbitration in such manner as it considers appropriate. The power conferred upon the arbitral tribunal includes the power to determine the admissibility, relevance, materiality and weight of any evidence.

Article 20 Place of arbitration.

(1) The parties are free to agree on the place of arbitration. Failing such agreement, the place of arbitration shall be determined by the arbitral tribunal having regard to the circumstances of the case, including the convenience of the parties.

(2) Notwithstanding the provisions of paragraph (1) of this article, the arbitral tribunal may, unless otherwise agreed by the parties, meet at any place it considers appropriate for consultation among its members, for hearing witnesses, experts or the parties, or for inspection of goods, other property or documents.

Article 21 Commencement of arbitral proceedings.

Unless otherwise agreed by the parties, the arbitral proceedings in respect of a particular dispute commence on the date on which a request for that dispute to be referred to arbitration is received by the respondent.

Article 22 Language.

(1) The parties are free to agree on the language or languages to be used in the arbitral proceedings. Failing such agreement, the arbitral tribunal shall determine the language or languages to be used in the proceedings. This agreement or determination, unless otherwise specified therein, shall apply to

any written statement by a party, any hearing and any award, decision or other communication by the arbitral tribunal.

(2) The arbitral tribunal may order that any documentary evidence shall be accompanied by a translation into the language or languages agreed upon by the parties or determined by the arbitral tribunal.

Article 23   Statements of claim and defence.

(1) Within the period of time agreed by the parties or determined by the arbitral tribunal, the claimant shall state the facts supporting his claim, the points at issue and the relief or remedy sought, and the respondent shall state his defence in respect of these particulars, unless the parties have otherwise agreed as to the required elements of such statements. The parties may submit with their statements all documents they consider to be relevant or may add a reference to the documents or other evidence they will submit.

(2) Unless otherwise agreed by the parties, either party may amend or supplement his claim or defence during the course of the arbitral proceedings, unless the arbitral tribunal considers it inappropriate to allow such amendment having regard to the delay in making it.

Article 24   Hearings and written proceedings.

(1) Subject to any contrary agreement by the parties, the arbitral tribunal shall decide whether to hold oral hearings for the presentation of evidence or for oral argument, or whether the proceedings shall be conducted on the basis of documents and other materials. However, unless the parties have agreed that no hearings shall be held, the arbitral tribunal shall hold such hearings at an appropriate stage of the proceedings, if so requested by a party.

(2) The parties shall be given sufficient advance notice of any hearing and of any meeting of the arbitral tribunal for the purposes of inspection of goods, other property or documents.

(3) All statements, documents or other information supplied to the arbitral tribunal by one party shall be communicated to the other party. Also any expert report or evidentiary document on which the arbitral tribunal may rely in making its decision shall be communicated to the parties.

Article 25   Default of a party.

Unless otherwise agreed by the parties, if, without showing sufficient cause,

(a) the claimant fails to communicate his statement of claim in accordance with article 23(1), the arbitral tribunal shall terminate the proceedings;

(b) the respondent fails to communicate his statement of defence in accordance with article 23(1), the arbitral tribunal shall continue the proceedings without treating such failure in itself as an admission of the claimant's allegations;

(c) any party fails to appear at a hearing or to produce documentary evidence, the arbitral tribunal may continue the proceedings and make the award on the evidence before it.

Article 26   Expert appointed by arbitral tribunal.

(1)   Unless otherwise agreed by the parties, the arbitral tribunal:
    (a)   may appoint one or more experts to report to it on specific issues to be determined by the arbitral tribunal;
    (b)   may require a party to give the expert any relevant information or to provide access to any relevant documents, goods or other property for his inspection.

(2)   Unless otherwise agreed by the parties, if a party so requests or if the arbitral tribunal considers it necessary, the expert shall, after delivery of his written or oral report, participate in a hearing where the parties have the opportunity to put questions to him and to present expert witnesses in order to testify on the points at issue.

Article 27   Court assistance in taking evidence.

The arbitral tribunal or a party with the approval of the arbitral tribunal may request from the Court of Session or the sheriff court assistance in taking evidence and recovering documents. The court may execute the request within its competence and according to its rules on taking evidence and recovery of documents.

CHAPTER VI

MAKING OF AWARD AND TERMINATION OF PROCEEDINGS

Article 28   Rules applicable to substance of dispute.

(1)   The arbitral tribunal shall decide the dispute in accordance with such rules of law as are chosen by the parties as applicable to the substance of the dispute. Any designation of the law or legal system of a given State shall be construed, unless otherwise expressed, as directly referring to the substantive law of that State and not to its conflict of laws rules.

(2)   Failing any designation by the parties, the arbitral tribunal shall apply the law determined by the conflict of laws rules which it considers applicable.

(3)   The arbitral tribunal shall decide ex aequo et bono or as amiable compositeur only if the parties have expressly authorised it to do so.

(4)   In all cases, the arbitral tribunal shall decide in accordance with the terms of the contract and shall take into account the usages of the trade applicable to the transaction.

Article 29   Decision making by panel of arbitrators.

In arbitral proceedings with more than one arbitrator, any decision of the arbitral tribunal shall be made, unless otherwise agreed by the parties, by a majority of all its members. However, questions of procedure may be decided by a presiding arbitrator, if so authorised by the parties or all members of the arbitral tribunal.

Article 30   Settlement.

(1)   If, during arbitral proceedings, the parties settle the dispute, the arbitral tribunal shall terminate the proceedings and, if so requested by the parties and not objected to by the arbitral tribunal, record the settlement in the form of an arbitral award on agreed terms.

(2)   An award on agreed terms shall be made in accordance with the provisions of article 31 and shall state that it is an award. Such an award has the same status and effect as any other award on the merits of the case.

Article 31   Form and contents of award.

(1)   The award shall be made in writing and shall be signed by the arbitrator or arbitrators. In arbitral proceedings with more than one arbitrator, the signatures of the majority of all members of the arbitral tribunal shall suffice, provided that the reason for any omitted signature is stated.

(2)   The award shall state the reasons upon which it is based, unless the parties have agreed that no reasons are to be given or the award is on agreed terms under article 30.

(3)   The award shall state its date and the place of arbitration as determined in accordance with article 20(1). The award shall be deemed to have been made at that place.

(4)   After the award is made, a copy signed by the arbitrators in accordance with paragraph (1) of this article shall be delivered to each party.

Article 32   Termination of proceedings.

(1)   The arbitral proceedings are terminated by the final award or by an order of the arbitral tribunal in accordance with paragraph (2) of this article.

(2)   The arbitral tribunal shall issue an order for the termination of the arbitral proceedings when:

(a)   the claimant withdraws his claim, unless the respondent objects thereto and the arbitral tribunal recognises a legitimate interest on his part in obtaining a final settlement of the dispute;

(b)   the parties agree on the termination of the proceedings;

(c)   the arbitral tribunal finds that the continuation of the proceedings has for any other reason become unnecessary or impossible.

(3)   The mandate of the arbitral tribunal terminates with the termination of the arbitral proceedings, subject to the provisions of articles 33 and 34(4).

Article 33   Correction and interpretation of award and making of additional award.

(1)   Within thirty days of receipt of the award, unless another period of time has been agreed upon by the parties:

(a)   a party, with notice to the other party, may request the arbitral tribunal to correct in the award any errors in computation, any clerical or typographical errors or any errors of similar nature;

(b)   if so agreed by the parties, a party, with notice to the other party, may request the arbitral tribunal to give an interpretation of a specific point or part of the award.

If the arbitral tribunal considers the request to be justified, it shall make the correction or give the interpretation within thirty days of receipt of the request. The interpretation shall form part of the award.

(2)   The arbitral tribunal may correct any error of the type referred to in paragraph (1)(a) of this article on its own initiative within thirty days of the date of the award.

(3)   Unless otherwise agreed by the parties, a party, with notice to the other party, may, within thirty days of receipt of the award request the arbitral tribunal to make an additional award as to claims presented in the arbitral proceedings but omitted from the award. If the arbitral tribunal considers the request to be justified, it shall make the additional award.

(4)   The arbitral tribunal may extend, if necessary, the period of time within which it shall make a correction or interpretation under paragraph (1) of this article.

(5)   The provisions of article 31 shall apply to a correction or interpretation of the award or to an additional award.

CHAPTER VII

RECOURSE AGAINST AWARD

Article 34   Application for setting aside as exclusive recourse against arbitral award.

(1)   Recourse to a court against an arbitral award may be made only by an application for setting aside in accordance with paragraphs (2) and (3) of this article.

(2)   An arbitral award may be set aside by the court specified in article 6 only if:

    (a)   the party making the application furnishes proof that:

        (i)   a party to the arbitration agreement referred to in article 7 was under some incapacity, or the said agreement is not valid under the law to which the parties have subjected it or, failing any indication thereon, under the law of Scotland; or

        (ii)   the party making the application was not given proper notice of the appointment of an arbitrator or of the arbitral proceedings or was otherwise unable to present his case; or

        (iii)   the award deals with a dispute not contemplated by or not falling within the terms of the submission to arbitration, or contains decisions on matters beyond the scope of the submission to arbitration, provided that, if the decisions on matters submitted to arbitration can be separated from those not so submitted, only that part of the award which contains decisions on matters not submitted to arbitration may be set aside; or

        (iv)   the composition of the arbitral tribunal or the arbitral procedure was not in accordance with the agreement of the parties, unless such agreement was in conflict with a provision of this Law from which the parties cannot derogate, or, failing such agreement, was not in accordance with this Law; or

        (v)   the award was procured by fraud, bribery or corruption; or

    (b)   the court finds that:

(i)   the subject-matter of the dispute is not capable of settlement by arbitration under the law of Scotland; or

(ii)   the award is in conflict with public policy.

(3)   An application for setting aside may not be made after three months have elapsed from the date on which the party making that application had received the award or, if a request had been made under article 33, from the date on which that request had been disposed of by the arbitral tribunal. This paragraph does not apply to an application for setting aside on the ground mentioned in paragraph (2)(a)(v) of this article.

(4)   The court, when asked to set aside an award, may, where appropriate and so requested by a party, suspend the setting aside proceedings for a period of time determined by it in order to give the arbitral tribunal an opportunity to resume the arbitral proceedings or to take such other action as in the arbitral tribunal's opinion will eliminate the grounds for setting aside.

CHAPTER VIII

RECOGNITION AND ENFORCEMENT OF AWARDS

Article 35   Recognition and enforcement.

(1)   An arbitral award, irrespective of the country in which it was made, shall be recognised as binding and, upon application in writing to the competent court, shall be enforced subject to the provisions of this article and of article 36.

(2)   The party relying on an award or applying for its enforcement shall supply the duly authenticated original award or a duly certified copy thereof, and the original arbitration agreement referred to in article 7 or a duly certified copy thereof. If the award or agreement is not made in English, the party shall supply a duly certified translation thereof into English.

Article 36   Grounds for refusing recognition or enforcement.

(1)   Recognition or enforcement of an arbitral award, irrespective of the country in which it was made, may be refused only:

(a)   at the request of the party against whom it is invoked, if that party furnishes to the competent court where recognition or enforcement is sought proof that:

(i)   a party to the arbitration agreement referred to in article 7 was under some incapacity; or the said agreement is not valid under the law to which the parties have subjected it or, failing any indication thereon, under the law of the country where the award was made; or

(ii)   the party against whom the award is invoked was not given proper notice of the appointment of an arbitrator or of the arbitral proceedings or was otherwise unable to present his case; or

(iii)   the award deals with a dispute not contemplated by or not falling within the terms of the submission to arbitration, or it contains decisions on matters beyond the scope of the submission to arbitration, provided that, if the decision on matters submitted to arbitration can be separated from those not so submitted, that part of the award which contains decisions on matters submitted to arbitration may be recognized and enforced; or

(iv)   the composition of the arbitral tribunal or the arbitral procedure was not in accordance with the agreement of the parties or, failing such agreement, was not in accordance with the law of the country where the arbitration took place; or

(v)   the award has not yet become binding on the parties or has been set aside or suspended by a court of the country in which, or under the law of which, that award was made, or

(b)   if the court finds that:

(i)   the subject-matter of the dispute is not capable of settlement by arbitration under the law of Scotland; or

(ii)   the recognition or enforcement of the award would be contrary to public policy.

(2)   If an application for setting aside or suspension of an award has been made to a court referred to in paragraph (1)(a)(v) of this article, the court where recognition or enforcement is sought may, if it considers it proper, adjourn its decision and also, on the application of the party claiming recognition or enforcement of the award, order the other party to provide appropriate security.

I.6.3   Northern Ireland

Note: Statutory material that applies to both England and Northern Ireland is not duplicated in this section. (For example, the Arbitration Act 1975 and part II of the Arbitration Act 1950 also apply in Northern Ireland.)

The Arbitration Act 1996 will repeal the 1937 Act, and the 1975 Act for Northern Ireland. It also repeals the Consumer Arbitration Agreements Act, 1988.

ARBITRATION ACT (NORTHERN IRELAND) 1937
(1 Edw. 8 & 1 Geo. 6. Ch. 8.)

An Act to amend the law relating to arbitrations, and to make provision for other matters connected therewith.   [7th July 1937]

[This Act is to be repealed by the Arbitration Act 1996, sch. 4.]

References under arbitration agreements

1.   Provisions as to arbitration agreements and references thereunder.

(1)   A reference under an arbitration agreement shall, unless a contrary intention is expressed therein, be irrevocable, except by leave of the court, and shall have the same effect in all respects as if it had been made an order of court.

(2)   An arbitration agreement shall, unless a contrary intention is expressed therein, be deemed to include the provisions set forth in the First Schedule to this Act, so far as they are applicable to the reference under the agreement.

2. Arbitration agreement not to be discharged by death of party thereto.

(1) An arbitration agreement shall not be discharged by the death of any party thereto, either as respects the deceased or any other party, but shall in such an event be enforceable by or against the personal representative of the deceased.

(2) The authority of an arbitrator shall not be revoked by the death of any party by whom he was appointed.

3. Provisions in case of bankruptcy.

(1) Where an arbitration agreement forms part of a contract to which a bankrupt is a party, the said agreement shall, if the assignee or the trustee in bankruptcy does not disclaim the contract, be enforceable by or against him so far as it relates to any difference arising out of, or in connection with, such contract.

(2) Where a person who has been adjudged bankrupt had before the commencement of the bankruptcy become a party to an arbitration agreement and any matter to which the agreement applies requires to be determined in connection with or for the purposes of the bankruptcy proceedings, then, if the case is one to which sub-section (1) of this section does not apply, any other party to the agreement or the assignee, or, with the consent of the committee of inspection, the trustee in bankruptcy, may apply to the court having jurisdiction in the bankruptcy proceedings for an order directing that the matter in question shall be referred to arbitration in accordance with the agreement, and that court may, if it is of opinion that, having regard to all the circumstances of the case, the matter ought to be determined by arbitration, make an order accordingly.

4. Power to stay proceedings.

If any party to an arbitration agreement, or any person claiming through or under him, commences any proceedings in any court against any other party to the agreement, or any person claiming through or under him, in respect of any matter to be referred, any party to such proceedings may at any time after appearance, and before delivering any pleadings or taking any other steps in the proceedings, apply to that court to stay the proceedings, and that court, if satisfied that there is no sufficient reason why the matter should not be referred in accordance with the agreement, and that the applicant was, at the time when the proceedings were commenced, and still remains, ready and willing to do all things necessary to the proper conduct of the arbitration, may make an order staying the proceedings.

Provisions as to arbitrators and umpires under arbitration agreements

5. Power for the court in certain cases to appoint an arbitrator, umpire or third arbitrator.

In any of the following cases, namely—

(a)   where an arbitration agreement provides that the reference shall be to a single arbitrator, and all the parties do not after differences have arisen concur in the appointment of an arbitrator.

(b)   if an appointed arbitrator refuses to act, or is incapable of acting, or dies, and the arbitration agreement or the references under the agreement does not show that it was intended that the vacancy should not be supplied, and the parties do not supply the vacancy;

(c)   where the parties or two arbitrators are at liberty to appoint an umpire or third arbitrator, or where two arbitrators are required to appoint an umpire, and do not appoint him;

(d)   where an appointed umpire or third arbitrator refuses to act, or is incapable of acting, or dies, and the arbitration agreement or the reference under the agreement does not show that it was intended that the vacancy should not be supplied, and the parties or arbitrators do not supply the vacancy;

any party may serve the other parties or the arbitrators, as the case may be, with a written notice that in default of concurrence in appointing an arbitrator, umpire or third arbitrator, as the case may be, an application will be made to the court under this section.

If the appointment is not made within seven days after the day of service of the notice, the court may, on application by the party who gave the notice, appoint an arbitrator, umpire, or third arbitrator, who shall have the like powers to act in the reference and make an award as if he had been appointed by consent of all parties.

6.   Power of parties in certain cases to supply vacancy.

Where an arbitration agreement provides that the reference shall be to two arbitrators, one to be appointed by each party, then, unless the agreement expresses a contrary intention—

(a)   if either of the appointed arbitrators refuses to act, or is incapable of acting, or dies, the party who appointed him may appoint a new arbitrator in his place;

(b)   if, on such a reference, one party fails to appoint an arbitrator, either originally or by way of subscription as aforesaid, for seven clear days after the other party, having appointed his arbitrator, has served the party making default with notice to make the appointment, the party who has appointed an arbitrator may appoint that arbitrator in the reference, and his award shall be binding on both parties as if he had been appointed by consent:

Provided that the court may set aside any appointment made in pursuance of paragraph (b) of this section.

7.   Power of court to remove arbitration or umpire and to set aside award.

(1)   Where an arbitrator or umpire has misconducted himself or the proceedings, the court may remove him.

(2)   Where an arbitrator or umpire has misconducted himself or the proceedings, or an arbitration or award has been improperly procured, the court may set aside the award.

8. Removal of arbitrator or umpire on failure to use due dispatch.

(1)   The court may, on the application of any party to a reference under an arbitration agreement, remove an arbitrator or umpire who fails to use all reasonable dispatch in entering on and proceeding with the reference and making an award.

(2)   An arbitrator or umpire who is removed by the court under this section shall not be entitled to receive any remuneration in respect of his services.

(3)   For the purposes of this section the expression 'proceeding with a reference' includes, in a case where two arbitrators are unable to agree, giving notice of that fact to the parties and to the umpire.

9. Provisions as to time for making an award.

(1)   Subject to the provisions of section fifteen of this Act and anything to the contrary in the arbitration agreement, an arbitrator or umpire shall have power to make an award at any time.

(2)   Where an arbitration agreement provides that the award shall be delivered within a certain time, or where an award has been remitted under the provisions of section fifteen of this Act, the time for making the award may from time to time be enlarged by order of the court whether the time for making the award has expired or not.

10. Power of court to give relief where arbitrator is not impartial or dispute referred involves question of fraud.

(1)   Where an agreement between any parties provides that disputes which may arise in the future between them shall be referred to an arbitrator named or designated in the agreement, and after a dispute has arisen any party applies, on the ground that the arbitrator so named or designated is not or may not be impartial, for leave to revoke the reference under the agreement or for an injunction to restrain any other party or the arbitrator from proceeding with the arbitration, it shall not be a ground for refusing the application that the said party at the time when he made the agreement knew, or ought to have known, that the arbitrator by reason of his relation towards any other party to the agreement or of his connection with the subject referred might not be capable of impartiality.

(2)   Where an agreement between any parties provides that disputes which may arise in the future between them shall be referred, and a dispute which so arises involves the question whether any party has been guilty of fraud, the court shall, so far as may be necessary to enable that question to be determined by the court, have power to order that the agreement shall cease to have effect and power to give leave to revoke any reference made thereunder.

(3)   In any case where by virtue of this section the court has power to order that an arbitration agreement shall cease to have effect or to give leave to revoke a reference under an arbitration agreement, the court may refuse to stay any action brought in breach of the agreement.

11. Power of court where arbitrator is removed or appointment of arbitrator is revoked.

(1)   Where an arbitrator (not being a sole arbitrator), or two or more arbitrators (not being all the arbitrators), or an umpire who has not entered on the reference, is or are removed by the court, the court may, on the application of any party to the arbitration agreement, appoint a person or persons to act as arbitrator or arbitrators or umpire in place of the person or persons so removed.

(2)   Where the appointment of an arbitrator or arbitrators or umpire is revoked by leave of the court, or a sole arbitrator or all the arbitrators or an umpire who has entered on the reference is or are removed by the court, the court may, on the application of any party to the arbitration agreement, either—

(a)   appoint a person to act as sole arbitrator in place of the person or persons removed: or

(b)   order that the arbitration agreement shall cease to have effect with respect to the dispute referred.

(3)   A person appointed under this section by the court as an arbitrator or umpire shall have the like power to act in the reference and to make an award as if he had been appointed in accordance with the terms of the arbitration agreement.

(4)   Where it is provided (whether by means of a provision in the arbitration agreement or otherwise) that an award under an arbitration agreement shall be a condition precedent to the bringing of an action with respect to any matter to which the agreement applies, the court, if it orders (whether under this section or any other enactment) that the agreement shall cease to have effect as regards any particular dispute, may further order that the provision making an award a condition precedent to the bringing of an action shall also cease to have effect as regards that dispute.

12. Provisions applicable where three arbitrators appointed and as to umpires.

(1)   Where an arbitration agreement provides that the reference shall be to three arbitrators, one to be appointed by each party and the third to be appointed by the two appointed by the parties, the agreement shall have effect as if it provided for the appointment of an umpire, and not for the appointment of a third arbitrator by the two arbitrators appointed by the parties.

(2)   Where an arbitration agreement provides that the reference shall be to three arbitrators to be appointed otherwise than as mentioned in the foregoing subsection, the award of any two of the arbitrators shall be binding.

(3)   At any time after the appointment of an umpire, however appointed, the court may, on the application of any party to the reference, and notwithstanding anything to the contrary in the arbitration agreement, order that the umpire shall enter on the reference in lieu of the arbitrators and as if he were a sole arbitrator.

13. Power of arbitrators.

The arbitrators or umpire acting under a reference in an arbitration agreement shall, unless the arbitration agreement or the reference thereunder expresses a contrary intention, have power to administer oaths to or take the affirmations of the parties and witnesses appearing, and to correct in an award any clerical mistake or error arising from any accidental slip or omission.

14. Attendance of witnesses.

Any party to a reference under an arbitration agreement may sue out a writ of subpoena ad testificandum, or a writ of subpoena duces tecum, but no person shall be compelled under any such writ to produce any document which he could not be compelled to produce on the trial of an action:

Provided that no writ shall issue under this section unless the arbitrator has entered on the reference or has been called on to act by notice in writing from a party to the reference and has agreed to do so.

Provisions as to awards under arbitration agreements

15. Power to remit award.

(1) In all cases of reference to arbitration the court may from time to time remit the matters referred, or any of them, to the reconsideration of the arbitrators or umpire.

(2) Subject to the provisions of section nine of this Act, where an award is remitted the arbitrators or umpire shall, unless the order otherwise directs, make their award within three months after the date of the order.

16. Entry of judgment in terms of award.

An award on a reference under an arbitration agreement may, by leave of the court, be entered as a judgment in terms of the award, and shall thereupon have the same force and effect as a judgment or order of the court.

17. Interests on awards.

A sum directed to be paid by an award shall, unless the award otherwise directs, carry interest as from the date of the award and at the same rate as a judgment debt.

18. Taxation of arbitrator's or umpire's fees.

(1) If in any case an arbitrator or umpire refuses to deliver his award except on payment of the fees demanded by him, the court may, on an application for the purpose, order that the arbitrator or umpire shall deliver the award to the applicant on payment into court by the applicant of the fees demanded, and further that the fees demanded shall be taxed by the taxing master, and that out of the money paid into court there shall be paid out to the arbitrator or umpire by way of fees such sum as may be found reasonable on taxation, and that the balance of the money, if any, shall be paid out to the applicant.

(2) An application for the purposes of this section may be made by any party to the reference unless the fees demanded have been fixed by a written agreement between him and the arbitrator or umpire.

(3)   A taxation of fees under this section may be reviewed in the same manner as a taxation of costs.

(4)   The arbitrator or umpire shall be entitled to appear and be heard on any taxation or review of taxation under this section.

Limitation of time for proceedings under arbitration agreements

19.   Limitation of time for commencing arbitration proceedings.

(1)   The statutes of limitation shall apply to an arbitration under an arbitration agreement as they apply to proceedings in the court.

(2)   Notwithstanding any term in an arbitration agreement to the effect that no cause of action shall accrue in respect of any matter required by the agreement to be referred until an award is made under the agreement, a cause of action shall, for the purpose of the statutes of limitation both as originally enacted and as applying to arbitrations, be deemed to have accrued in respect of any such matter at the time when it would have accrued but that term in the agreement.

(3)   For the purpose of this section and for the purpose of the statutes of limitation as applying to arbitrations, an arbitration shall be deemed to be commenced when one party to the arbitration agreement serves on the other party or parties a notice requiring him or them to appoint an arbitrator, or, where the arbitration agreement provides that the reference shall be to a person named or designated in the agreement, serves on the other party or parties a notice requiring him or them to submit the dispute to the person so named or designated.

(4)   Any such notice as is mentioned in the preceding sub-section may be served—

(a)   by delivering it to the person on whom it is to be served; or

(b)   by leaving it at the usual or last known place of abode in Northern Ireland of that person; or

(c)   by sending it by post in a registered letter addressed to that person at his usual or last known place of abode in Northern Ireland;

as well as in any other manner provided in the arbitration agreement; and where a notice is sent by post in manner prescribed by paragraph (c) of this sub-section service thereof shall, unless the contrary is provided, be deemed to have been effected at the time at which the letter would have been delivered in the ordinary course of post.

(5)   Where the terms of an agreement to refer future disputes to arbitration provide that any claims to which the agreement applies shall be barred unless notice to appoint an arbitrator is given, or an arbitrator is appointed, or some other step to commence arbitration proceedings is taken within a time fixed by the agreement, and a dispute arises to which the agreement applies, the court, if it is of opinion that in the circumstances of the case undue hardship would otherwise be caused, and notwithstanding that the time so fixed has expired, may, on such terms, if any, as the justice of the case may require, but without prejudice to the foregoing provisions of this section, extend the time for such period as it thinks proper.

(6)   Where the court orders that an award be set aside or orders, after the commencement of an arbitration, that the arbitration agreement shall cease

to have effect with respect to the dispute referred, the court may further order that the period between the commencement of the arbitration and the date of the order of the order of the court shall be excluded in computing the time prescribed by the statutes of limitation for the commencement of proceedings (including arbitration) with respect to the dispute referred.

(7) For the purposes of this section the expression 'the statutes of limitation' includes any enactment limiting the time within any particular proceeding may be commenced.

References under order of court

20. Power to make rules as to reference under order of court.

(1) Rules of court may be made providing that—

(a) in any cause or matter (other than a criminal proceeding by the Crown) if the question in dispute consists wholly or in part of matters of account, the court may at any time order the whole cause or matter, or any question or issue of fact arising therein to be tried before a referee or arbitrator respectively agreed on by the paries, or before an officer of the court;

(b) in all cases of reference to a referee or arbitrator under an order of the court in any cause or matter, the referee or arbitrator shall be deemed to be an officer of the court and shall have such authority, and shall conduct the reference in such manner, as may be prescribed by the said rules, and, subject thereto, as the court may direct;

(c) the report or award of any referee or arbitrator on any such reference shall, unless set aside by the court, be equivalent to the verdict of a jury;

(d) the remuneration to be paid to any referee or arbitrator to whom any matter is referred under order of the court shall be determined by the court.

Upon the making of such rules of court the following provisions of this section shall come into operation, and the rules may provide for any matters for which provision may be necessary in order to give full effect to this section, and may prescribe anything which is to be prescribed thereunder.

(2) The court shall as to references under an order of a court, have all the powers which are by this Act conferred on the court as to references under arbitration agreements.

(3) The provisions of sections six to twenty of the Common Law Procedure Amendment Act (Ireland), 1856, relating to the reference of matters of account under order of court to an arbitrator, master of the court, or assistant barrister, and sections sixty-three and sixty-four of the Debtors (Ireland) Act, 1840, so far as they relate to references by order of court, shall cease to have effect.

General

21. Additional powers of court.

(1) the court shall have, for the purpose of and in relation to a reference, the same power of making orders in respect of any of the matters set out in

the Second Schedule to this Act as it has for the purpose of and in relation to an action or matter in the court:

Provided that nothing in the foregoing provision shall be taken to prejudice any power which may be vested in an arbitrator or umpire of making orders with respect to any of the matters aforesaid.

(2) Where relief by way of interpleader is granted and it appears to the court that the claims in question are matters to which an arbitration agreement, to which the claimants are parties, applies, the court may direct the issue between the claimants to be determined in accordance with the agreement.

(3) Where an application is made to set aside an award the court may order that any money made payable by the award shall be brought into court or otherwise secured pending the determination of the application.

22. Statement of case by arbitrator or umpire.

(1) An arbitrator or umpire may, and shall if so ordered by the court, state—
    (a) any question of law arising in the course of the reference; or
    (b) an award or any part of an award;
in the form of a special case for the determination of the court.

(2) A special case with respect to an interim award or with respect to a question of law arising in the course of a reference may be ordered by the court to be stated, notwithstanding that proceedings under the reference are still pending.

23. Provisions as to costs.

(1) Any order made under this Act by the court may be made on such terms as to costs or otherwise as the court thinks just.

(2) Any provision in an arbitration agreement to the effect that the parties or any party thereto shall in any event pay their or own costs of the reference or award or any part thereof shall be void:

Provided that nothing herein shall invalidate such a provision when it is part of an agreement to submit to arbitration a dispute which has arisen before the making of such agreement.

(3) If no provision is made by an award with respect to the costs of the reference, any party to the reference may, within fourteen days of the publication of the award or such further time as a court may direct, apply to the arbitrator for an order directing by and to whom such costs shall be paid, and thereupon the arbitrator shall, after hearing any party who may desire to be heard, amend his award by adding thereto such directions as he may think proper with respect to the payment of the costs of the reference.

(4) Section three of the Legal Practitioners (Ireland) Act, 1876, which empowers a court before which any proceeding has been heard or is depending to charge property recovered or preserved in the proceeding with the payment of solicitors' costs, shall apply as if an arbitrator were a proceeding in the court, and the court may make declarations and orders accordingly.

24. Additional powers to compel attendance of witnesses.

(1) The court may order that a writ of subpoena ad testificandum or of subpoena duces tecum shall issue to compel the attendance of a witness before any referee, arbitrator or umpire.

(2) The court may also order that a writ of habeas corpus ad testificandum shall issue to bring up a prisoner for examination before any referee, arbitrator or umpire.

25. Exercise of jurisdiction conferred on the court.

The jurisdiction conferred on the court by this Act shall be exercisable in such manner as may be provided by the rules of court, and such rules may, in particular, confer all or any of the said jurisdiction upon a judge sitting in court or, if so provided, upon a judge in chambers.

26. Penalty for perjury.

Any person who wilfully and corruptly gives false evidence before any referee, arbitrator or umpire shall be liable to the penalties for wilful and corrupt perjury.

Statute law applicable to Northern Ireland

27. Saving for pending arbitrations.

Subject as hereinafter provided, the provisions of this Act shall not affect any arbitration which has been commenced within the meaning of section nineteen of this Act before the date on which this Act comes into operation, but shall apply to any arbitration so commenced after the said date under an arbitrator agreement made before the said date.

28. Application of Act to statutory arbitrations.

This Act, except the provisions thereof set out in the Third Schedule to this Act, shall apply in relation to every arbitration under any other Act passed before or after the commencement of this Act, as if the arbitration were pursuant to an arbitration agreement and as if that other Act were an arbitration agreement, except in so far as this Act is inconsistent with that other Act or with any rules or procedure authorised or recognised thereby.

Supplemental

29. Repeals.

(1) The enactments set out in the Fourth Schedule to this Act are hereby repealed to the extent specified in the third column of that Schedule.

(2) Any enactment or instument referring to any enactment repealed by this Act shall be construed as referring to this Act.

30. Interpretation.

(1) In this Act, unless the context otherwise requires, the following expressions have the meanings hereby assigned to them, that is to say:—

'Act' and 'enactment' include an Act or enactment passed by the Parliament of the United Kingdom in so far as it relates to a a matter in respect of which the Parliament of Northern Ireland has power to make laws:

'Arbitration agreement' means a written agreement to refer present or future difference to arbitration, whether an arbitrator is named therein or not:

'Assignee' means the official assignee appointed in Northern Ireland under section fifty-nine of the Irish Bankrupt and Insolvent Act,1857, as amended by section four of the Supreme Court of Judicature (Ireland) (No. 2) Act, 1897, and includes the assignee (if any) chosen by the creditors to act with the official assignee:

'Court' means the High Court:

'Judge' means a judge of the High Court:

'Rules of court' means rules of the Supreme Court made under section sixty-one of the Supreme Court of Judicature Act (Ireland), 1877, as amended by the Supreme Court of Judicature (Ireland) (No. 2) Act, 1897.

(2) References in this Act to an award include references to an interim award.

(3) References in this Act to those enactments of the Parliament of the United Kingdom shall be construed as references to those enactments as they apply in Northern Ireland.

31. Short title and commencement.

(1) This act may be cited as the Arbitration Act (Northern Ireland), 1937.

(2) This act shall come into operation on the first day of January, nineteen hundred and thirty-eight.

FIRST SCHEDULE

Provisions to be implied in arbitration agreements

1. If no other mode of reference is provided the reference shall be to a single arbitrator.

2. If the reference is to two arbitrators the two arbitrators shall appoint an umpire immediately after they are themselves appointed.

3. If the arbitrators have delivered to any party to the arbitration agreement, or to the umpire a notice in writing stating that they cannot agree, the umpire may forthwith enter on the reference in lieu of the arbitrators.

4. The parties to the reference and all persons claiming through them respectively shall, subject to any legal objection, submit to be examined by the arbitrators or umpire on oath or affirmation in relation to the matters in dispute and shall, subject as aforesaid, produce before the arbitrators or umpire all books, deeds, papers, accounts, writings and documents within their possesion or power respectively which may be required or called for, and do all other things which during the proceedings on the reference the arbitrators or umpire may require.

5. The witnesses on the reference shall, if the arbitrators or umpire think fit, be examined on oath or affirmation.

6. The arbitrators or umpire shall have the same power as the Court to order specific performance of any contract, other than a contract relating to land or any interest in land.

7. The award to be made by the arbitrators or umpire shall be final and binding on the parties and the persons claiming under them respectively.

8. The arbitrators or umpire may, if they think fit, make an interim award.

9. The costs of the reference and award shall be in the discretion of the arbitrators or umpire who may direct to, and whom, and in what manner, those costs, or any part thereof, shall be paid and may tax or settle the amount of costs to be so paid, or any part thereof, and may award costs to be paid as between solicitor and client.

SECOND SCHEDULE

Matters in respect of which the Court may make Orders

1. Security for costs.
2. Discovery of documents and interrogatories.
3. The giving of evidence by affidavit.
4. Examination on oath of any witness before an officer of the court or any other person, and the issue of a commision or request for the examination of a witness out of the jurisdiction.
5. The preservation, interim custody, or sale, of any goods which are the subject matter of the reference.
6. Securing the amount in dispute in the reference.
7. The detention, preservation or inspection of any property or thing which is the subject of the reference or as to which any question may arise therein, and authorising for any of the purposes aforesaid any persons to enter upon or into any land or building in the possession of any party to the reference, or authorising any samples to be taken or any observation to be made or experiment to be tried which may be necessary or expedient for the purpose of obtaining full information or evidence.
8. Interim injunctions or the appointment of a receiver.

THIRD SCHEDULE

Provisions of Act which do no apply to statutory arbitrations

Sub-section (1) of section two.
Section three.
Section ten.
Section eleven.
Section nineteen.
Sub-section (2) of section twenty-one.
Sub-section (2) of section twenty-three.

FOURTH SCHEDULE

Enactments repealed

[*Not reproduced here.*]

PART II
STATUTORY INSTRUMENTS
(United Kingdom)

Note: For the Arbitration (International Investment Disputes) (Guernsey) Order 1968 No. 1199, see under Guernsey in Part I.

For the Arbitration (International Investment Disputes) (Jersey) Order 1968 No. 572, see under Jersey in Part I.

ARBITRATION (COMMODITY CONTRACTS) ORDER 1979
(SI 1979 No. 754)

1.—(1)   This Order may be cited as the Arbitration (Commodity Contracts) Order 1979 and shall come into operation on 1st August 1979.

(2)   In this Order—

'the Act' means the Arbitration Act 1979;

'market' means a commodity market or exchange.

2.   The following markets are hereby specified for the purpose of section 4 of the Act—

(a)   the markets set out in Part I of the Schedule hereto;

(b)   any market in which contracts for sale are subject to the rules or regulations of one or other of the associations set out in Part II of the Schedule, whether or not the market is a market on which commodities are bought and sold at a particular place.

3.   The following descriptions of contract are hereby specified for the purpose of section 4 of the Act—

(a)   contracts for the sale of goods or any market specified in Article 2 of this Order;

(b)   contracts for the sale of goods which are subject to arbitration rules of the London Metal Exchange or of an association set out in Part II of the Schedule hereto.

SCHEDULE

PART I

Markets

The London Cocoa Terminal Market
The London Coffee Terminal Market
The London Grain Futures Market
The London Metal Exchange
The London Rubber Terminal Market
The Gafta Soya Bean Meal Futures Market
The London Sugar Terminal Market
The London Vegetable Oil Terminal Market
The London Wool Terminal Market

PART II

Markets in which contracts are subject to rules or regulations of the following Associations—

The Cocoa Association of London Limited
The Coffee Trade Federation
The Combined Edible Nut Trade Association
Federation of Oils, Seeds and Fats Associations Limited
The General Produce Brokers' Association of London
The Grain and Feed Trade Association Limited
The Hull Seed, Oil and Cake Association
The Liverpool Cotton Association Limited
London Jute Association
London Rice Brokers' Association
The National Federation of Fruit and Potato Trades Limited
The Rubber Trade Association of London
Skin, Hide and Leather Traders' Association Limited
The Sugar Association of London
The Refined Sugar Association
The Tea Brokers' Association of London
The British Wool Confederation.

ARBITRATION (FOREIGN AWARDS) ORDER 1984
(SI 1984 No. 1168)

Whereas a Convention on the Execution of Foreign Arbitral Awards (herein-after called 'the Geneva Convention') was, on 26th September 1927, signed at Geneva on behalf of His Late Majesty King George the Fifth:

And whereas it is provided by section 35(1) of the Arbitration Act 1950 that Part II of that Act (which provides for the enforcement of certain foreign awards under the Geneva Convention) applies to any award made after 28th July 1928—

(a)   in pursuance of an agreement for arbitration to which the Protocol set out in the First Schedule to that Act applies; and

(b)   between persons of whom one is subject to the jurisdiction of some one of such Powers as Her Majesty, being satisfied that reciprocal provisions have been made, may by Order in Council declare to be parties to the Geneva Convention, and of whom the other is subject to the jurisdiction of some other of the Powers aforesaid; and

(c)   in one of such territories as Her Majesty, being satisfied that reciprocal provisions have been made, may by Order in Council declare to be territories to which the Geneva Convention applies:

And whereas Her Majesty is satisfied that reciprocal provisions have been made:

And whereas a Convention on the Recognition and Enforcement of Foreign Arbitral Awards (hereinafter called 'the New York Convention') adopted on 10th June 1958 entered into force for the United Kingdom of Great Britain and Northern Ireland on 23rd December 1975:

And whereas it is provided by section 7(2) of the Arbitration Act 1975 (which Act provides for the enforcement of foreign awards under the New York Convention) that if Her Majesty by Order in Council declares that any State specified in the Order is a party to the New York Convention the Order shall, while in force, be conclusive evidence that that State is a party to that Convention:

Now, therefore, Her Majesty, by and with the advice of Her Privy Council, in pursuance of the powers conferred upon Her by section 35(1) and (2) of the Arbitration Act 1950 and section 7(2) and (3) of the Arbitration Act 1975, and of all other powers enabling Her in that behalf, is pleased to declare, and it is hereby declared, as follows:

1. Citation and commencement.

This Order may be cited as the Arbitration (Foreign Awards) Order 1984 and shall come into operation on 1st August 1984.

2. Geneva Convention States.

(1) The Powers listed in Column 1 of Schedule 1 to this Order are parties to the Geneva Convention.
(2) The territories specified in Column 2 of the said Schedule are territories to which the Geneva Convention applies.

3. New York Convention States.

The States listed in Schedule 2 to this Order are parties to the New York Convention.

4. Revocation.

The Arbitration (Foreign Awards) Order 1978 [SI 1978/86] and the Arbitration (Foreign Awards) Order 1979 [SI 1979/304] are hereby revoked.

SCHEDULE 1

GENEVA CONVENTION STATES

Column 1	Column 2
Powers party to the Geneva Convention	Territories to which the Geneva Convention applies
The United Kingdom of Great Britain and Northern Ireland	The United Kingdom of Great Britain and Northern Ireland
	Anguilla
	British Virgin Islands
	Cayman Islands
	Falkland Islands
	Falkland Islands Dependencies
	Gibraltar
	Hong Kong
	Montserrat
	Turks and Caicos Islands
Antigua and Barbuda	Antigua and Barbuda
Austria	Austria
Bahamas	Bahamas
Bangladesh	Bangladesh

Column 1	Column 2
Powers party to the Geneva Convention	Territories to which the Geneva Convention applies
Belgium	Belgium
Belize	Belize
Czechoslovakia	Czechoslovakia
Denmark	Denmark
Dominica	Dominica
Finland	Finland
France	France
Federal Republic of Germany	Federal Republic of Germany
German Democratic Republic	German Democratic Republic
Greece	Greece
Grenada	Grenada
Guyana	Guyana
India	India
Republic of Ireland	Republic of Ireland
Israel	Israel
Italy	Italy
Japan	Japan
Kenya	Kenya
Luxembourg	Luxembourg
Malta	Malta
Mauritius	Mauritius
Netherlands	Netherlands (including Curacao)
New Zealand	New Zealand
Pakistan	Pakistan
Portugal	Portugal
Romania	Romania
Saint Christopher and Nevis	Saint Christopher and Nevis
St. Lucia	St. Lucia
Spain	Spain
Sweden	Sweden
Switzerland	Switzerland
Tanzania	Tanzania
Thailand	Thailand
Western Samoa	Western Samoa
Yugoslavia	Yugoslavia
Zambia	Zambia

SCHEDULE 2

NEW YORK CONVENTION STATES

Australia (including all the external territories for the international relations of which Australia is responsible)	Bulgaria
	Byelorussian Soviet Socialist Republic
	Cambodia
	Central African Republic
Austria	Chile
Belgium	Colombia
Belize	Cuba
Benin	Cyprus
Botswana	Czechoslovakia

Denmark (including Greenland and the Faroe Islands)
Djibouti
Ecuador
Egypt
Finland
France (including all the territories of the French Republic)
Federal Republic of Germany
German Democratic Republic
Ghana
Greece
Guatemala
Haiti
Holy See
Hungary
India
Indonesia
Republic of Ireland
Israel
Italy
Japan
Jordan
Korea
Kuwait
Luxembourg
Madagascar
Mexico
Monaco

Morocco
Netherlands (including the Netherlands Antilles)
New Zealand
Niger
Nigeria
Norway
Philippines
Poland
Romania
San Marino
South Africa
Spain
Sri Lanka
Sweden
Switzerland
Syria
Tanzania
Thailand
Trinidad and Tobago
Tunisa
Ukrainian Soviet Socialist Republic
Union of Soviet Socialist Republics
United States of America (including all the territories for the international relations of which the United States of America is responsible)
Uruguay
Yugoslavia

EXPLANATORY NOTE

(This note is not part of the Order)

This Order specifies (in Schedule 1) States which are parties to the 1927 Geneva Convention on the Execution of Foreign Arbitral Awards ('the Geneva Convention'), and which have satisfied Her Majesty that they have made reciprocal provisions. Arbitral awards made in such States are enforceable in the United Kingdom under Part II of the Arbitration Act 1950, except, where the State in question is also a New York Convention State, in so far as the award is enforceable under the Arbitration Act 1975.

The Order also specifies (in Schedule 2) States which are parties to the 1958 New York Convention on the Recognition and Enforcement of Foreign Arbitral Awards ('the New York Convention'). Arbitral awards made in such States are enforceable in the United Kingdom under the Arbitration Act 1975.

The Order replaces the Arbitration (Foreign Awards) Order 1978 and the Arbitration (Foreign Awards) Order 1979, which are revoked. The two Schedules have been revised to take account of the accession of certain States to the two Conventions and to take account of the independence of certain States which were formerly territories for whose international relations another State was responsible.

The States now added as being parties to the Geneva Convention are: Antigua and Barbuda; Bahamas; Bangladesh; Belize; Dominica; Guyana; Malta; Saint Christopher and Nevis; St. Lucia; Western Samoa and Zambia. In respect of the New York Convention the additional States are: Belize; Byelorussian Soviet Socialist Republic; Colombia; Djibouti; Guatemala; Haiti; Jordan; Luxembourg; New Zealand; San Marino; Ukrainian Soviet Socialist Republic; Uruguay; and Yugoslavia.

ARBITRATION (FOREIGN AWARDS) ORDER 1987
(SI 1987 No. 1029)

Whereas a Convention on the Recognition and Enforcement of Foreign Arbitral Awards (hereinafter called the 'New York Convention') (adopted on 10th June 1958 entered into force for the United Kingdom of Great Britain and Northern Ireland on 23rd December 1975:

And whereas it is provided by section 7(2) of the Arbitration Act 1975 (which Act provides for the enforcement of foreign awards under the New York Convention) that if Her Majesty by Order in Council declares that any State specified in the Order is a party to the New York Convention the Order shall, while in force, be conclusive evidence that that State is a party to that Convention:

Now, therefore, Her Majesty, by and with the advice of Her Privy Council, in pursuance of the powers conferred on Her by section 7(2) of the Arbitration Act 1975 and of all other powers enabling Her in that behalf, is pleased to declare, and it is hereby declared, as follows:

1.   This Order may be cited as the Arbitration (Foreign Awards) Order 1987 and shall come into force on 1st July 1987.

2.   The People's Republic of China and the Republic of Singapore are parties to the New York Convention.

EXPLANATORY NOTE

(This Note is not part of the Order)

This Order specifies that the People's Republic of China and the Republic of Singapore are parties to the 1958 New York Convention on the Recognition and Enforcement of Foreign Arbitral Awards. Arbitral awards made in States which are parties to the Convention are enforceable in the United Kingdom under the Arbitration Act 1975.

ARBITRATION (FOREIGN AWARDS) ORDER 1989
(SI 1989 No. 1348)

Her Majesty, in pursuance of the powers conferred on Her by section 7(2) and (3) of the Arbitration Act 1975 and of all other powers enabling Her in that behalf, is pleased, by and with the advice of Her Privy Council, to declare, and it is hereby declared, as follows:

1.   This Order may be cited as the Arbitration (Foreign Awards) Order 1993 and shall come into force on 1st September 1989.

2.   The States listed in the Schedule to this Order are parties to the New York Convention on the Recognition and Enforcement of Foreign Arbitral Awards which was adopted on 10th June 1958 and came into force in the United Kingdom of Great Britain and Northern Ireland on 23rd December 1975.

3.   The Arbitration (Foreign Awards) (Amendment) Order 1985 [SI 1985/ 455] and the Arbitration (Foreign Awards) Order 1986 [SI 1986/949] are hereby revoked.

THE SCHEDULE

NEW YORK CONVENTION STATES

Algeria

Antigua and Barbados

Argentina

Bahrain

Burkina Faso

Cameroon

Canada

China

Costa Rica

Dominica

Kenya

Malaysia

Panama

Peru

Singapore

EXPLANATORY NOTE

(This Note is not part of the Order)

This Order declares Algeria, Antigua and Barbados, Argentina, Bahrain, Burkina Faso, Cameroon, Canada, China, Costa Rica, Dominica, Kenya, Peru and Singapore as parties to the 1958 New York Convention on the Recognition and Enforcement of Foreign Arbitral Awards. Arbitral awards made in these States are enforceable in the United Kingdom under the Arbitration Act 1975. Two previous Orders (the Arbitration (Foreign Awards) (Amendment) Order 1985 (SI 1985/455) and the Arbitration (Foreign Awards) Order 1986) (SI 1986/949) have been revoked and the States concerned (Panama and Malaysia) included in the Schedule to this Order. Schedule 2 of the Arbitration (Foreign Awards) Order 1984 (S.I. 1984/1168) and the Schedule to this Order now contain a comprehensive list of the States declared to be parties to the New York Convention.

ARBITRATION (FOREIGN AWARDS) ORDER 1993
(SI 1993 No. 1256)

Her Majesty, in pursuance of the powers conferred on Her by section 7(2) and (3) of the Arbitration Act 1975 and of all other powers enabling Her in that behalf, is pleased, by and with the advice of Her Privy Council, to declare, and it is hereby declared, as follows:

1. This Order may be cited as the Arbitration (Foreign Awards) Order 1993 and shall come into force on 3rd June 1993.

2. Antigua and Barbuda is a party to the New York Convention on the Recognition and Enforcement of Foreign Arbitral Awards which was adopted on 10th June 1958 and came into force in the United Kingdom of Great Britain and Northern Ireland on 23rd December 1975.

3. The Arbitration (Foreign Awards) Order 1989 [SI 1989/1348] shall be amended by the deletion from the Schedule thereto of the words 'Antigua and Barbados'.

EXPLANATORY NTOE

(This Note is not part of the Order)

This Order declares Antigua and Barbuda as a party to the New York Convention on the Recognition and Enforcement of Foreign Arbitral Awards. It had been intended to declare that country in the Arbitration (Foreign Awards) Order 1989 but that Order misdescribed it as 'Antigua and Barbados' and Barbados itself is not a party to the Convention. Accordingly, the 1989 Order is amended by deleting the reference in the Schedule to Antigua and Barbados.

COAL MINING SUBSIDENCE (ARBITRATION SCHEMES) REGULATIONS 1994
(SI 1994 No. 2566)

The Secretary of State, in exercise of the powers conferred on him by section 47(2), (7), (8) and (10) of the Coal Industry Act 1994 and section 50 of the Coal Mining Subsidence Act 1991, and of all other powers enabling him in that behalf, hereby makes the following Regulations—

1. Citation, commencement and interpretation.

(1) These Regulations may be cited as the Coal Mining Subsidence (Arbitration Schemes) Regulations 1994 and shall come into force on 31st October 1994.

(2) In these Regulations and the Schedules to them, unless the context otherwise requires—

'the 1991 Act' means the Coal Mining Subsidence Act 1991;

'the 1994 Act' means the Coal Industry Act 1994;

'the Arbitration Body' means the person or body of persons for the time being appointed in accordance with regulation 7;

'arbitrator' means, in relation to an arbitration, the person for the time being appointed to act as the arbitrator therein;

'claimant' means a person who has made an application in accordance with paragraph 1 of Schedule 1 to these Regulations or paragraph 1 of Schedule 2;

'dispute' means any question to which these Regulations apply by virtue of Regulation 2;

'document' includes any map, plan, drawing, photograph, computer record and other record kept otherwise than in documentary form;

'financial year' means the period of 12 months commencing on 1st April;

'the General Arbitration Scheme' means the provisions of Schedule 2 to these Regulations;

'the Householders' Arbitration Scheme' means the provisions of Schedule 1 to these Regulations;

'householder' means a person who occupies a dwelling-house and who either is the owner of it or is liable to make good any damage to it in whole or in part;

'notify' means notify in writing;

'respondent' means, in relation to a dispute, the responsible person involved in it;

'responsible person' means a person with responsibility for subsidence affecting land;

'subsidence requirement' means a requirement referred to in section 47(9) of the 1994 Act.

(3) In the application of these Regulations to arbitration proceedings which are subject to the law of Scotland—

(a) references to an arbitrator shall be construed as references to an arbiter; and

(b) in any reference to the costs of an arbitration or to the costs of a party, the word 'costs' shall be construed as 'expenses'.

(4) Unless the context otherwise requires, other expressions appearing in these Regulations shall have the same meaning, if any, as they have in the 1991 Act or the 1994 Act.

(5) References in a Schedule to these Regulations to a numbered paragraph are references to the relevant paragraph of that Schedule.

(6) The amounts payable as registration fees in accordance with Schedules 1 and 2 to these Regulations shall be exclusive of any value added tax that may be chargeable on such fees.

2. Questions to which Regulations apply.

(1) Subject to paragraph (2) below, these Regulations shall apply to any question arising under the 1991 Act and, without prejudice to the generality of the foregoing—

(a) any question as to who is the person with responsibility for subsidence affecting particular land;

(b) the question of whether there has been a contravention of any subsidence requirement;

(c) the question of how any such contravention is to be remedied.

(2) These Regulations do not apply to any question arising under section 32 of the 1991 Act (*compensation for death or disablement*) or section 36 of that Act (*land drainage systems*).

3. Resolution of questions by arbitration.

(1) The provisions of Schedule 1 to these Regulations ('the Householders' Arbitration Scheme') shall apply to any question to which these Regulations apply arising between a responsible person and a householder.

(2) The provisions of Schedule 2 to these Regulations ('the General Arbitration Scheme') shall apply to any question to which these Regulations apply which is not for the time being the subject of the procedures specified in Schedule 1.

4. Arbitrators.

(1) Disputes referred to arbitration in accordance with these Regulations shall be determined by a single arbitrator appointed by the Arbitration Body.

(2) The Arbitration Body may, where it considers that special circumstances apply, appoint one or more persons to assist the arbitrator on matters of a technical nature.

(3) The Arbitration Body may appoint a substitute for the arbitrator, or any person appointed under paragraph (2) above, in the event of him misconducting himself or dying, becoming incapacitated or for any other reason being unable to attend expeditiously to his duties.

(4) The Arbitration Body shall notify all the parties to a dispute of the appointments made by it under this regulation in connection with the dispute.

5. Costs of arbitration proceedings.

(1) Subject to paragraph (2) below and to the provisions of Schedule 1 concerning the payment of registration fees—

(a) each party to an arbitration under the Householders' Arbitration Scheme shall pay his own costs and the respondent pay all the fees and expenses by the arbitrator and any person appointed to assist him under regulation 4(2); and

(b) the costs of an arbitration under the General Arbitration Scheme shall be paid by the parties to the dispute in accordance with the provisions of Schedule 2.

(2) Paragraph (1) above shall not apply—

(a) where any arbitration proceedings under these Regulations are subject to the law of England and Wales, to the costs of any appeal or application to the High Court in respect of the proceedings; or

(b) where any arbitration proceedings under these Regulations are subject to the law of Scotland, to the expenses of any proceedings brought in the Court of Session for the opinion of that Court on any question of law arising in the proceedings, or for the challenge or correction of an award made by the arbiter.

6. Applicable law.

(1) A dispute refenced to arbitration in accordance with these Regulations shall be determined, in relation to any question concerning the arbitration procedure, according to the law of the place where the arbitration is held.

(2) Subject to paragraph (1) above, the dispute shall be determined according to the law for the time being in force in England Wales or to the law for the time being in force in Scotland as the parties to the dispute may agree or, in default of agreement, as determined by the arbitrator.

7. Appointment of Arbitration Body.

The Secretary of State shall appoint a person or body of persons ('the Arbitration Body') to administer the reference of disputes to arbitration in accordance with these Regulations.

8. Costs of Arbitration Body.

(1) Subject to paragraph (2) below, the Secretary of State shall, in consultation with the Arbitration Body, as soon as reasonably practicable after the beginning of the financial year commencing on 1st April 1995 and every financial year thereafter make a determination for the purposes of this regulation by—

(a) estimating the likely costs and expenses of the Arbitration Body during the financial year in question in connection with the carrying out of its functions under these Regulations; and

(b) adding to or subtracting from that estimate, as appropriate, the amount, if any, by which the estimate made by him in accordance with this regulation for the preceding financial year, fell short of, or exceeded, the costs and expenses actually so incurred during that financial year.

(2) In the case of the determination made by the Secretary of State in accordance with paragraph (1) above for the financial year commencing on 1st April 1995, the Secretary of State shall add to the amount estimated in accordance with paragraph (1)(a) above the costs and expenses of the Arbitration Body for the period from the making of these Regulations to 31st March 1995 in connection with the carrying out of its functions under these Regulations.

(3) The Secretary of State shall notify the Coal Authority of the amount determined by him in accordance with paragraphs (1) and (2) above and request the Authority to apportion that amount between itself and every other responsible person on the basis of the number of applications for arbitration received by the Arbitration Body during the financial year immediately preceding that to which the determination applies which relate to the area for which they are the responsible person.

(4) The Coal Authority shall notify every responsible person of—

(a) the total amount notified to it by the Secretary of State in accordance with paragraph (3) above; and

(b) the amount apportioned by it to that responsible person and the calculation of that amount.

(5) Every responsible person to whom a notification has been given in accordance with paragraph (4) above may, within 21 days of the giving of that notification, make representations to the Coal Authority concerning it.

(6) The Coal Authority, having considered any such representations, shall notify the responsible person of its final determination with respect to the amount to be apportioned to that person.

(7) A responsible person shall forthwith pay to the Coal Authority the amount notified to it in accordance with paragraph (6) above; and, in default of payment, the sum due shall be recoverable by the Coal Authority from that person as a civil debt.

(8) The Coal Authority shall, when so requested by him, pay to the Secretary of State in respect of each financial year the amount determined by

the Secretary of State for that year in accordance with paragraphs (1) and (2) above.

(9) It shall be the duty of the Arbitration Body to provide the Coal Authority with such information as it may reasonably request for the purpose of discharging its obligations under this regulation.

SCHEDULE 1

THE HOUSEHOLDERS' ARBITRATION SCHEME

Institution of arbitration proceedings

1.—(1) Subject to sub-paragraph (2) below, a claimant may make an application for the arbitration of a dispute in accordance with the provisions of this Schedule by sending to the Arbitration Body an application in that behalf and a registration fee of £50.

(2) No application for arbitration may be made by a person in respect of a dispute, concerning the same, or substantially the same, matter as that in respect of which a notification has been given under paragraph 11 or 12(1).

2.—(1) On receipt of an application in accordance with paragraph 1, the Arbitration Body shall—

(a) decide whether, in its opinion, the dispute appears to be suitable for resolution in accordance with the provisions of this Schedule; and

(b) notify both the claimant and the respondent of its decision and, if it decides that the dispute is not suitable for such resolution, its reasons for so deciding.

3. If the Arbitration Body notifies the respondent that the dispute is, in its opinion, suitable for resolution in accordance with the provisions of this Schedule—

(a) the respondent shall forthwith send to the Arbitration Body a registration fee of £50; and

(b) the Arbitration Body shall within 21 days commencing with the date of the giving of that notification—

(i) appoint an arbitrator to determine the dispute;

(ii) notify the parties of the identity of the person so appointed; and

(iii) send to the claimant a claim form.

Arbitration procedure

4. The claimant shall within—

(a) the period of 28 days commencing with the date of receiving the claim form forwarded in accordance with paragraph 3; or

(b) such further period as the arbitrator may at any time specify by notice given to each party

complete and return the claim form to the arbitrator and send a copy of the completed form to the respondent.

5.—(1) Subject to sub-paragraph (2) below, the respondent shall, within 28 days of receiving his copy of the completed claim form, send to both the arbitrator and the claimant—

(a) a statement of his response to the claim; and

(b) a copy of every document upon which he wishes to rely.

(2)   The arbitrator may on the application of the respondent extend the period of 28 days referred to in sub-paragraph (1) above by a period not exceeding 14 days, by notifying each party of the extension.

6.   The claimant shall be entitled to submit to the arbitrator and to the respondent written comments on the matters specified in paragraph 5(1) within the period of 14 days commencing with the date of his receiving those matters.

7.   The arbitrator may request any party to the dispute to submit to him, within such period as the arbitrator may specify, such further documents, information or other evidence as the arbitrator considers desirable and the arbitrator shall provide the other party to the dispute with an opportunity to comment on any matters so submitted within such period as the arbitrator may specify.

8.—(1)   Within 28 days beginning with the date of whichever is the later of—

(a)   the expiry of the period of 14 days referred to in paragraph 6;

(b)   if any further evidence has been requested in accordance with paragraph 7, the expiry of the second period referred to in that paragraph; or

(c)   if an inspection has taken place following a notification under paragraph 9, the completion of that inspection

the arbitrator shall send to each party a statement in writing of his award with respect to the matters in dispute and of his reasons for making it.

(2)   The arbitrator may as part of his decision direct that one party reimburse the registration fee paid by the other party.

Site inspections

9.—(1)   The arbitrator shall give to the parties to the dispute reasonable notice of any inspection he proposes to make of the dwelling-house by virtue of which the claimant is a qualifying householder.

(2)   The claimant shall permit the arbitrator to carry out such inspection of the dwelling-house as he may reasonably require and shall permit the respondent or his authorised representative to be present at any such inspection.

Effect of failure to submit evidence

10.—(1)   If the claimant fails to submit a completed claim form in accordance with paragraph 4—

(a)   the claimant shall be deemed to have abandoned his claim; and

(b)   the Arbitration Body shall so notify the claimant and return the registration fee paid by the respondent in accordance with paragraph 3.

(2)   If—

(a)   the respondent fails to comply with the requirements of paragraph 5; or

(b)   any party fails to comply with the requirements of paragraph 7

the arbitrator shall, subject to any directions he may give, decide the dispute by reference to the documents submitted to him.

Withdrawal of claims

11.   The claimant may at any time by notifying the arbitrator and the respondent withdraw the dispute from the arbitration and

(a)   the dispute shall forthwith cease to be the subject of arbitration in accordance with the provisions of this Schedule;

(b)   the Arbitration Body shall be entitled to retain the registration fees paid by the claimant and the respondent; and

(c)   the arbitrator may direct that one party reimburse the registration fee paid by the other party.

Termination of arbitration

12.—(1)   If at any time before the making of his award in accordance with paragraph 8 the arbitrator determines that in his opinion the claim is not capable of proper resolution under the provisions of this Schedule he shall notify the parties to the dispute—

(a)   of his determination; and

(b)   of whether, in his opinion, the dispute is capable of resolution in accordance with the General Arbitration Scheme.

(2)   If notification is given in accordance with sub-paragraph (1) above the claim shall cease to be subject to arbitration in accordance with the provisions of this Schedule and, unless the claimant gives notice in accordance with sub-paragraph (3) below, the Arbitration Body shall repay the registration fees paid by the claimant and the respondent,

(3)   In the event of the arbitrator notifying the parties in accordance with sub-paragraph (1)(b) above that, in his opinion, the dispute is capable of resolution in accordance with the General Arbitration Scheme, the claimant may within 14 days of his receiving that notification notify the arbitrator and the respondent that he wishes the arbitration to proceed in accordance with that Scheme, and accordingly—

(a)   the notification by the claimant shall, if accompanied by a registration fee of £25, constitute the making of an application for the purposes of paragraph 1 of Schedule 2;

(b)   the Arbitration Body shall be deemed for the purposes of paragraph 2(a) of Schedule 2 to have decided that the dispute is suitable for resolution in accordance with the provisions of that Schedule, and to have notified the parties accordingly;

(c)   the sum due from the respondent in accordance with paragraph 3(a) of Schedule 2 shall be reduced by the amount of the registration fee paid by him in accordance with paragraph 3(a) of this Schedule; and

(d)   the arbitrator shall conduct the arbitration in accordance with Schedule 2 as if he had been appointed by the Arbitration Body under paragraph 3(b)(i) of that Schedule.

SCHEDULE 2

THE GENERAL ARBITRATION SCHEME

Institution of arbitration proceedings

1.   A claimant may make an application for the arbitration of a dispute in accordance with the provisions of this Schedule by sending to the Arbitration Body an application in that behalf and a registration fee of £75.

2.   On receipt of an application in accordance with paragraph 1, the Arbitration Body shall—

(a)   decide whether, in its opinion, the dispute appears to be suitable for resolution in accordance with the provisions of this Schedule; and

(b)   notify both the claimant and the respondent of its decision and, if it decides that the dispute is not suitable for such resolution, its reasons for so deciding.

3.   If the Arbitration Body notifies the parties that the dispute is, in its opinion, suitable for resolution in accordance with the provisions of this Schedule—

(a)   the respondent shall forthwith send to the Arbitration Body a registration fee of £75; and

(b)   the Arbitration Body shall within 21 days commencing with the date of the giving of that notification—

(i)   appoint an arbitrator to determine the dispute; and

(ii)   notify the parties of the person so appointed.

Arbitration procedure

4.   The claimant shall, within the period of 28 days commencing with the date of his receiving notification from the Arbitration Body as mentioned in paragraph 3, send by registered post to the arbitrator and to the respondent a claim file containing—

(a)   a brief statement of the claimant's principal arguments of fact and law and of the remedies sought by him; and

(b)   a copy of every document upon which he intends to rely.

5.   Within 28 days commencing with the date of his receiving his copy of the claim file the respondent shall send by registered post to the arbitrator and to the claimant a respondent's file containing—

(a)   a brief statement of the respondent's principal arguments of fact and law; and

(b)   a copy of every document upon which he wishes to rely.

6.   Within the period of 14 days commencing with the date of his receiving the respondent's file, the claimant may send by registered post to the arbitrator and to the respondent—

(a)   comments on the matters contained in that file

(b)   a copy of any further documents relating to those matters upon which he wishes to rely.

7.   The arbitrator may, at his discretion and upon notifying the other party—

(a)   permit either party to send to him and to the other party further comments on the other party's case; and

(b)   extend any of the time limits in paragraphs 4 to 6.

Directions as to further conduct of arbitration

8.—(1)   Within 28 days commencing with the completion of the procedure described in paragraphs 4 to 7 the arbitrator shall invite the parties to make representations to him concerning the conduct of the arbitration either in writing or at a meeting convened by the arbitrator at a place which is reasonably convenient for each party.

(2)   Within 14 days of making of representations in accordance with sub-paragraph (1) above the arbitrator shall give directions to the parties as to the further conduct of the arbitration.

(3)   Without prejudice to the generality of sub-paragraph (2) above, the directions which may be made under that sub-paragraph may include a direction—

(a)   that an inspection of any premises the subject of the dispute take place;

(b)   convening an oral hearing of the parties;

(c)   that, in the interests of the expeditious determination of the claim—

(i)   a particular issue be determined by the arbitrator before other issues; or

(ii)   that particular steps be taken by one or both parties;

(d)   that a party to the arbitration provide such further documents, information or other evidence as may be specified;

(e)   that a party to the arbitration provide security for costs.

(4)   If any direction by the arbitrator under this paragraph is not complied with he may proceed with the arbitration on the assumption that compliance with the direction would not have favoured the party in default.

Oral hearings

9.—(1)   Any direction under paragraph 8 as to the convening of an oral hearing of the parties shall—

(a)   specify a date for the commencement of the hearing which shall be as soon as reasonably practicable after the giving of the direction; and

(b)   specify a place for the hearing which shall be reasonably convenient for each of the parties.

(2)   The procedure to be followed at the hearing shall be determined by the arbitrator.

Arbitrator's awards

10.—(1)   In respect of every award made by him the arbitrator shall send to each party a written statement of the terms of the award and of his reasons for making it.

(2)   The arbitrator may make an award in respect of liability for the costs of the arbitration and of every award made in the course of it, including the fees of all persons who have acted as an arbitrator or have been appointed to assist the arbitrator under regulation 4(2).

(3)   In respect of arbitration proceedings which are subject to the law of Scotland, the costs referred to in sub-paragraph (2) above shall be subject to taxation by the auditor of the sheriff court on the application of either party, but that taxation shall be subject to review by the sheriff.

(4)   The arbitrator shall make his final award in respect of the substantive issues in dispute before the expiry of 28 days commencing with the first day on which all fees properly payable to him and to any other person who has acted in the arbitration as an arbitrator or as a person appointed to assist the arbitrator under regulation 4(2) have been paid.

Fees

11.—(1)   Subject to sub-paragraph (2) below, the parties to the arbitration shall be jointly and severally liable for the fees of the arbitrator and of any other person as mentioned in paragraph 10(4).

(2)   Sub-paragraph (1) above shall be without prejudice to the right of a party to the arbitration to recover from the other party in accordance with an award of the arbitrator any fees paid by him under that sub-paragraph.

UNFAIR TERMS IN CONSUMER CONTRACTS REGULATIONS
(SI 1994 No. 3159)

Whereas the Secretary of State is a Minister designated for the purposes of section 2(2) of the European Communities Act 1972 in relation to measures relating to consumer protection;

Now, the Secretary of State, in exercise of the powers conferred upon him by section 2(2) of that Act and of all other powers enabling him in that behalf hereby makes the following Regulations:—

1.   Citation and commencement

These Regulations may be cited as the Unfair Terms in Consumer Contracts Regulations 1994 and shall come into force on 1st July 1995.

2.   Interpretation

(1)   In these Regulations—

'business' includes a trade or profession and the activities of any government department or local or public authority;

'the Community' means the European Economic Community and the other States in the European Economic Area;

'consumer' means a natural person who, in making a contract to which these Regulations apply, is acting for purposes which are outside his business;

'court' in relation to England and Wales and Northern Ireland means the High Court, and in relation to Scotland, the Court of Session;

'Director' means the Director General of Fair Trading;

'EEA Agreement' means the Agreement on the European Economic Area signed at Oporto on 2 May 1992 as adjusted by the protocol signed at Brussels on 17 March 1993;

'member State' shall mean a State which is a contracting party to the EEA Agreement but until the EEA Agreement comes into force in relation to Liechtenstein does not include the State of Liechtenstein;

'seller' means a person who supplies goods or services and who, in making a contract to which these Regulations apply, is acting for purposes relating to his business.

'supplier' means a person who supplies goods or services and who, in making a contract to which these Regulations apply, is acting for purposes relating to his business.

(2)   In the application of these Regulations to Scotland for references to an 'injunction' or an 'interlocutory injunction' there shall be substituted references to an 'interdict' or 'interim interdict' respectively.

3. Terms to which these Regulations apply

(1)   Subject to the provisions of Schedule 1, these Regulations apply to any term in a contract concluded between a seller, or supplier and a consumer where the said term has not been individually negotiated.

(2)   In so far as it is in plain, intelligible language, no assessment shall be made of the fairness of any term which—

(a)   defines the main subject matter of the contract, or

(b)   concerns the adequacy of the price or remuneration, as against the goods or services sold or supplied.

(3)   For the purposes of these Regulations, a term shall always be regarded as not having been individually negotiated where it has been drafted in advance and the consumer has not been able to influence the substance of the term.

(4)   Notwithstanding that a specific term or certain aspects of it in a contract has been individually negotiated, these Regulations shall apply to the rest of a contract if an overall assessment of the contract indicates that it is a pre-formulated standard contract.

(5)   It shall be for any seller or supplier who claims that a term was individually negotiated to show that it was.

4. Unfair terms

(1)   In these Regulations, subject to paragraphs (2) and (3) below, 'unfair term' means any term which contrary to the requirement of good faith causes a significant imbalance in the parties' rights and obligations under the contract to the detriment of the consumer.

(2)   An assessment of the unfair nature of a term shall be made taking into account the nature of the goods or services for which the contract was concluded and referring, as at the time of the conclusion of the contract, to all circumstances attending the conclusion of the contract and to all the other terms of the contract or of another contract on which it is dependent.

(3)   In determining whether a term satisfies the requirement of good faith, regard shall be had in particular to the matters specified in Schedule 2 to these regulations.

(4)   Schedule 3 to these Regulations contains an indicative and non-exhaustive list of the terms which may be regarded as unfair.

5. Consequence of inclusion of unfair terms in contracts

(1)   An unfair term in a contract concluded with a consumer by a seller of supplier shall not be binding on the consumer.

(2)   The contract shall continue to bind the parties if it is capable of continuing in existence without the unfair term.

6. Construction of written contracts

A seller or supplier shall ensure that any written term of a contract is expressed in plain, intelligible language, and if there is doubt about the meaning of a written term, the interpretation most favourable to the consumer shall prevail.

7. Choice of law clauses

These Regulations shall apply notwithstanding any contract term which applies or purports to apply the law of a non member State, if the contract has a close connection with the territory of the member States.

8. Prevention of continued use of unfair terms

(1)   It shall be the duty of the Director to consider any complaint made to him that any contract term drawn up for general use is unfair, unless the complaint appears to the Director to be frivolous or vexatious.

(2)   If having considered a complaint about any contract term pursuant to paragraph (1) above the Director considers that the contract term is unfair he may, if he considers it appropriate to do so, bring proceedings for an injunction (in which proceedings he may also apply for an interlocutory injunction) against any person appearing to him to be using or recommending use of such a term in contracts concluded with consumers.

(3)   The Director may, if he considers it appropriate to do so, have regard to any undertakings given to him by or on behalf of any person as to the continued use of such a term in contracts concluded with consumers.

(4)   The Director shall give reasons for his decision to apply or not to apply, as the case may be, for an injunction in relation to any complaint which these Regulations require him to consider.

(5)   The court on an application by the Director may grant an injunction on such terms as it thinks fit.

(6)   An injunction may relate not only to use of a particular contract term drawn up for general use but to any similar term, or a term having like effect, used or recommended for use by any party to the proceedings.

(7)   The Director may arrange for the dissemination in such form and manner as he considers appropriate of such information and advice concerning the operation of these Regulations as may appear to him to be expedient to give to the public and to all persons likely to be affected by these Regulations.

[. . .]

SCHEDULE 3

INDICATIVE AND ILLUSTRATIVE LIST OF TERMS WHICH MAY BE REGARDED AS UNFAIR

1.   Terms which have the object or effect of—

[. . .]

(q)   excluding or hindering the consumer's right to take legal action or exercise any other legal remedy, particularly by requiring the consumer to take disputes exclusively to arbitration not covered by legal provisions, unduly restricting the evidence available to him or imposing on him a burden of proof which, according to the applicable law, should lie with another party to the contract.

[. . .]

PART III
RULES OF THE SUPREME COURT
(England)

RULES OF THE SUPREME COURT

ORDER 73

ARBITRATION PROCEEDINGS

1. Arbitration proceedings not to be assigned to Chancery Division (Ord. 73, r. 1)
[*Revoked.*]

2. Matters for a judge in court (Ord. 73, r. 2)

Every application to the Court—
    (a) to remit an award under section 22 of the Arbitration Act 1950, or
    (b) to remove an arbitrator or umpire under section 23(1) of that Act,
or
    (c) to set aside an award under section 23(2) thereof, or
    (d) [*Revoked by R.S.C. (Amendment No. 2) 1983 (S.I. 1983 No. 1181).*]
    (e) to determine, under section 2(1) of that Act, any question of law
arising in the course of a reference,
must be made by originating motion to a single judge in court.
    (2) Any appeal to the High Court under section 1(2) of the Arbitration
Act 1979 shall be made by originating motion to a single judge in court and
notice thereof may be included in the notice of application for leave to appeal,
where leave is required.
    (3) An application for a declaration that an award made by an arbitrator
or umpire is not binding on a party to the award on the ground that it was
made without jurisdiction may be made by originating motion to a single
judge in court, but the foregoing provision shall not be taken as affecting the
judge's power to refuse to make such a declaration in proceedings begun by
motion.
[*Amended by R.S.C. (Amendment No. 3) 1979 and R.S.C. (Amendment
No. 3).*]

3. Matters for judge in chambers or master (Ord. 73, r. 3)

    (1) Subject to the foregoing provision of this Order and the provisions of
this rule, the jurisdiction of the High Court or a judge thereof under the
Arbitration Act 1950 and the jurisdiction of the High Court under the
Arbitration Act 1975 and the Arbitration Act 1979 may be exercised by a
judge in chambers, a master or the Admiralty Registrar.
    (2) Any application
    (a) for leave to appeal under s. 1(2) of the Arbitration Act 1979, or
    (b) under s. 1(5) of that Act (including any application for leave), or
    (c) under s. 5 of that Act.
shall be made to a judge in chambers.
    (3) Any application to which this rule applies shall, where an action is
pending, be made by summons in the action, and in any other case by an
originating summons which shall be in Form No. 10 in Appendix A.

(4)   Where an application is made under section 1(5) of the Arbitration Act 1979 (including any application for leave) the summons must be served on the arbitrator or umpire and on any other party to the reference.
[*Amended by R.S.C. (Amendment No. 3) 1979; R.S.C. (Writ and Appearance) 1979 and R.S.C. (Amendment No. 2) 1983.*]

4.   Applications in district registries (Ord. 73, r. 4)

An application under section 12(4) of the Arbitration Act 1950 for an order that a writ of subpoena ad testificandum or of subpoena duces tecum shall issue to compel the attendance before an arbitrator or umpire of a witness may, if the attendance of the witness is required within the district of any district registry, be made at that registry, instead of at the Admiralty and Commercial Registry, at the option of the applicant.
[*This Rule was taken from R.S.C. (Rev.) 1962, Ord. 88, r. 4, which had been taken from the former Ord. 37, r. 27B. The reference to the Registry was inserted by S.I. 1987 No. 1423.*]

5.   Time-limits and other special provisions as to appeals and applications under the Arbitration Acts (Ord. 73, r. 5)

(1)   An application to the Court—
   (a)   to remit an award under section 22 of the Arbitration Act 1950, or
   (b)   to set aside an award under section 23(2) of that Act or otherwise,
or
   (c)   to direct an arbitrator or umpire to state the reasons for an award under section 1(5) of the Arbitration Act 1979,
must be made, and the summons or notice must be served, within 21 days after the award has been made and published to the parties.
(2)   In the case of an appeal to the Court under section 1(2) of the Arbitration Act 1979, the summons for leave to appeal, where leave is required, and the notice of originating motion must be served and the appeal entered within 21 days after the award has been made and published to the parties:
Provided that, where reasons material to the appeal are given on a date subsequent to the publication of the award, the period of 21 days shall run from the date on which the reasons are given.
(3)   An application, under section 2(1) of the Arbitration Act 1979, to determine any question of law arising in the course of a reference, must be made, and notice thereof served, within 14 days after the arbitrator or umpire has consented to the application being made, or the other parties have so consented.
(4)   For the purpose of paragraph (2) the consent must be given in writing.
(5)   In the case of every appeal or application to which this rule applies, the notice of originating motion or, as the case may be, the originating summons, must state the grounds of the appeal of application and, where the appeal or application is founded on evidence by affidavit, or is made with the consent of the arbitrator or umpire or of the other parties, a copy of every affidavit intended to be used, or, as the case may be, of every consent given in writing, must be served with that notice.

(6)   Without prejudice to paragraph (5), in an appeal under section 1(2) of the Arbitration Act 1979 the statement of the grounds of the appeal shall specify the relevant parts of the award and reasons, and a copy of the award and reasons, or the relevant parts thereof, shall be lodged with the court and served with the notice of originating motion.

(7)   Without prejudice to paragraph (5), in an application for leave to appeal under section 1(2) of the Arbitration Act 1979, any affidavit verifying the facts in support of a convention that the question of law concerns a term of a contract or an event which is not a one-off term or event must be lodged with the court and served with the notice of originating motion.

(8)   Any affidavit in reply to an affidavit under paragraph (7) shall be lodged with the court and served on the applicant not less than two clear days before the hearing of the application.

(9)   A respondent to an application for leave to appeal under section 1(2) of the Arbitration Act 1979 who desires to contend that the award should be upheld on grounds not expressed or not fully expressed in the award and reasons shall not less than two clear days before the hearing of the application lodge with the court and serve on the applicant a notice specifying the grounds of his contention.

[*Substituted by R.S.C. (Amendment No. 3) 1979 (S.I. 1979 No. 522). Amended by R.S.C. (Amendment) 1986. Paragraphs (6)-(9) added by R.S.C. (Amendment No. 3) 1986.*]

6.   Applications and appeals to be heard by Commercial Judges

(1)   Any matter which is required, by rule 2 or 3, to be heard by a judge, shall be heard by a Commercial Judge, unless any such judge otherwise directs.

(2)   Nothing in the foregoing paragraph shall be construed as preventing the powers of a Commercial Judge from being exercised by any judge of the High Court.

[*Substituted by R.S.C. (Amendment No. 3) 1979 (S.I. 1979 No. 522).*]

7.   Service out of the jurisdiction of summons, notice, etc. (Ord. 73, r. 7)

(1)   Subject to paragraph (1A), service out of the jurisdiction of—

(a)   any originating summons or notice of originating motion under the Arbitration Act 1950 or the Arbitration Act 1979, or

(b)   any order made on such a summons or motion as aforesaid,

is permissible with the leave of the Court provided that the arbitration to which the summons, motion or order relates is governed by English law or has been, is being, or is to be held, within the jusdiction.

(1A)   Service out of the jurisdiction of an originating summons for leave to enforce an award is permissible with the leave of the Court whether or not the arbitration is governed by English law.

(2)   An application for the grant of leave under this rule must be supported by an affidavit stating the grounds on which the application is made and showing in what place or country the person to be served is, or probably may be found, and so such leave shall be granted unless it shall be made sufficiently to appear to the Court that the case is a proper one for service out of the jurisdiction under his rule.

(3)   Order 11, rules 5, 6 and 8, shall apply in relation to any such summons, notice or order as is referred to in paragraph (1) as they apply in relation to a writ.

[Amendment by R.S.C. (Amendment No. 4) 1979 (S.I. 1979 No. 1542); R.S.C. (Amendment No. 4) 1980 (S.I. 1980 No. 2000) and (with effect from the date s.2 of the Civil Jurisdiction and Judgments Act 1982 comes into force) by R.S.C. (Amendment No. 2) 1983 (S.I. 1983 No. 1181). Further amended by R.S.C. (Amendment) 1987.]

8.   Registration in High Court of foreign awards (Ord. 73, r. 8)

Where an award is made in proceedings on an arbitration in any part of Her Majesty's dominions or other territory to which Part I of the Foreign Judgments (Reciprocal Enforcement) Act 1933 extends, being a part to which Part II of the Administration of Justice Act 1920 extended immediately before the said Part I was extended thereto, then, if the award has, in pursuance of the law in force in the place where it was made, become enforceable in the same manner as a judgment given by a court in that place, Order 71 shall apply in relation to the award as it applies in relation to a judgment given by that court, subject, however, to the following modifications:—

(a)   for references to the country of the original court there shall be substituted references, to the place where the award was made; and

(b)   the affidavit required by rule 3 of the said Order must state (in addition to the other matters required by that rule) that to the best of the information or belief of the deponent the award has, in pursuance of the law in force in the place where it was made, become enforceable in the same manner as a judgment given by a court in that place.

[Taken from R.S.C. (Rev.) 1962, Ord. 88, r. 7, which replaced the former Ord. 41B, r. 15.]

9.   Registration of awards under Arbitration (International Investment Disputes) Act 1966 (Ord. 73, r. 9)

[(1)   In this rule and in any provision of these rules as applied by this rule—]
'The Act of 1966' means the Arbitration (International Investment Disputes) Act 1966;

'award' means an award rendered pursuant to the Convention;

'the Convention' means the Convention referred to in section 1(1) of the Act of 1966;

'judgment creditor' and 'judgment debtor' means respectively the person seeking recognition of enforcement of an award and the other party to the award.

(2)   Subject to the provisions of his rule, the following provisions of Order 7, namely, rules 1, 3(1) (except sub-paragraphs (c)(iv) and (d) thereof) 7 (except (3)(c) and (d) thereof) and 10(3) shall apply with the necessary modifications in relation to an award as they apply in relation to a judgment to which Part II of the Foreign Judgments (Reciprocal Enforcement) Act 1933 applies.

(3)   An application to have an award registered in the High Court under section 1 of the Act of 1966 shall be made by originating summons which shall be in Form No. 10 in Appendix A.

(4)   The affidavit required by Order 71, rule 3, in support of an application for registration shall—

(a)   in lieu of exhibiting the judgment or a copy thereof, exhibit a copy of an award certified pursuant to the Convention, and

(b)   in addition to stating the matters mentioned in paragraph 3(1)(c)(i) and (ii) of the said rule 3, state whether at the date of application the enforcement of the award has been stayed (provisionally or otherwise) pursuant to the Convention and whether any, and if so what, application has been made pursuant to the Convention which, if granted, might result in a stay of the enforcement of the award.

(5)   There shall be kept in the Admiralty and Commercial Registry under the direction of the Senior Master a register of the awards ordered to be registered under the Act of 1966 and particulars shall be entered in the register of any execution issued on such an award.

(6)   Where it appears to the court on granting leave to register an award or on an application made by the judgment debtor after an award has been registered—

(a)   that the enforcement of the award has been stayed (whether provisionally or otherwise) pursuant to the Convention, or

(b)   that an application has been made pursuant to the Convention which, if granted, might result in a stay of the enforcement of the award, the court shall, or, in the case referred to in sub-paragraph (b) may, stay execution of the award for such time as it considers appropriate in the circumstances.

(7)   An application by the judgment debtor under paragraph (6) shall be made by summons and supported by affidavit.

[Added by R.S.C. (Amendment No. 1) 1968 (S.I. 1968 No. 1244) and amended by R.S.C. (Amendment No. 3) 1977 (S.I. 1977 No. 1955); R.S.C. (Writ and Appearance) 1979 (S.I. 1979 No. 1716) and R.S.C. (Amendment No. 2) 1982 (S.I. 1982 No. 1111) and R.S.C. (Amendment) 1987.

9A.   Registration of awards under Multilateral Investment Guarantee Agency Act 1988 (Ord. 73, r. 9A)

Rule 9 shall apply, with necessary modifications, in relation to an award rendered pursuant to the convention referred to in section 1(1) of the Multilateral Guarantee Agency Act 1988 as it applies in relation to an award rendered pursuant to the convention referred to in section 1(1) of the Arbitration (International Investment Disputes) Act 1966.

[Added bv R.S.C. (Amendment No. 2) 1988 (S.I. 1988 No. 1340).]

10.   Enforcement of arbitration awards (Ord. 73, r. 10)

(1)   An application for leave under section 26 of the Arbitration Act 1950 or under section 3(1)(a) of the Arbitration Act 1975 to enforce an award on an arbitration agreement in the same manner as a judgment or order may be made ex parte but the Court hearing the application may direct a summons to be issued.

(2)   If the Court directs a summons to be issued, the summons shall be an originating summons which shall be in Form No, 10 in Appendix A.

(3)   An application for leave must be supported by affidavit—

    (a)   exhibiting

        (i)   where the application is under section 26 of the Arbitration Act 1950, the arbitration agreement and the original award or, in either case, a copy thereof;

        (ii)   where the application is under section 3(1)(a) of the Arbitration Act 1975, the documents required to be produced by section 4 of that Act,

    (b)   stating the name and the usual or last known place of abode or business of the applicant (hereinafter referred to as 'the creditor') and the person against whom it is sought to enforce the award (hereinafter referred to as 'the debtor') respectively,

    (c)   as the case may require, either that the award has not been complied with or the extend to which it has been complied with at the date of the application.

(4)   An order giving leave must be drawn up by or on behalf of the creditor and must be served on the debtor by delivering a copy to him personally or by sending a copy to him at his usual or last known place of above or business or in such other manner as the Court may direct

(5)   Service of the order out of the jurisdiction is permissible without leave, and Order 11, rules 5, 6 and 8, shall apply in relation to such an order as they apply in relation to a writ.

(6)   Within 14 days after the service of the order or, if the order is to be served out of the jurisdiction, within such other period as the Court may fix, the debtor may apply to set aside the order and the award shall not be enforced until after the expiration of that period or, if the debtor applies within that period to set aside the order, until the application is finally disposed of.

(7)   The copy of that order served on the debtor shall state the effect of paragraph (6).

(8)   In relation to a body corporate this rules shall have effect as if for any reference to the place of abode or business of the creditor or the debtor were were substituted a reference to the registered or principal address of the body corporate; so, however, that nothing in this rule shall affect any enactment which provides for the manner in which a document may be served on a body corporate.

[Added by R.S.C. (Amendment No. 4) 1978 (S.I. 1978 No. 1066) and amended by R.S.C. (Amendment) 1979 (S.I. No. 35); R.S.C. (Writ and Appearance) 1979 (S.I. 1979 No. 1716) and R.S.C. (Amendment No. 4) 1980 (S.I. No. 2000).]

PART IV
EUROPEAN UNION DOCUMENTS

COUNCIL DIRECTIVE
of 5 April 1993
on unfair terms in consumer contracts
(93/13/EEC:L 95/29)

THE COUNCIL OF THE EUROPEAN COMMUNITIES,

Having regard to [. . .]

HAS ADOPTED THIS DIRECTIVE:

Article 1.

1.   The purpose of this Directive is to approximate the laws, regulations and administrative provisions of the Member States relating to unfair terms in contracts concluded between a seller or supplier and a consumer.

2.   The contractual terms which reflect mandatory statutory or regulatory provisions and the provisions or principles of international conventions to which the Member States or the Community are party, particularly in the transport area, shall not be subject to the provisions of this Directive.

Article 2.

For the purposes of this Directive:

(a)   'unfair terms' means the contractual terms defined in Article 3;

(b)   'consumer' means any natural person who, in contracts covered by this Directive, is acting for purposes which are outside his trade, business or profession;

(c)   'seller or supplier' means any natural or legal person who, in contracts covered by this Directive, is acting for purposes relating to his trade, business or profession, whether publicly owned or privately owned.

Article 3.

1.   A contractual term which has not been individually negotiated shall be regarded as unfair if, contrary to the requirement of good faith, it causes a significant imbalance in the parties' rights and obligations arising under the contract, to the detriment of the consumer.

2.   A term shall always be regarded as not individually negotiated where it has been drafted in advance and the consumer has therefore not been able to influence the substance of the term, particularly in the context of a pre-formulated standard contract.

The fact that certain aspects of a term or one specific term have been individually negotiated shall not exclude the application of this Article to the rest of a contract if an overall assessment of the contract indicates that it is nevertheless a pre-formulated standard contract.

Where any seller or supplier claims that a standard term has been individually negotiated, the burden of proof in this respect shall be incumbent on him.

3.   The Annex shall contain an indicative and non-exhaustive list of the terms which may be regarded as unfair.

[. . .]

ANNEX

TERMS REFERRED TO IN ARTICLE 3(3)

1.   Terms which have the object or effect of:

[. . .]

(q)   excluding or hindering the consumer's right to take legal action or exercise any other legal remedy, particularly by requiring the consumer to take disputes exclusively to arbitration not covered by legal provisions, unduly restricting the evidence available to him or imposing on him a burden of proof which, according to the applicable law, should lie with another party to the contract.

[. . .]

PART V
INTERNATIONAL DOCUMENTS

GENEVA PROTOCOL 1923

[The text reproduced here is that of Schedule 1 of the United Kingdom's Arbitration Act 1950 — hence the preamble.]

PROTOCOL ON ARBITRATION CLAUSES SIGNED ON BEHALF OF HIS MAJESTY AT A MEETING OF THE ASSEMBLY OF THE LEAGUE OF NATIONS HELD ON THE TWENTY-FOURTH DAY OF SEPTEMBER, NINETEEN HUNDRED AND TWENTY-THREE

The undersigned, being duly authorised, declare that they accept, on behalf of the countries which they represent, the following provisions:—

1. Each of the Contracting States recognises the validity of an agreement whether relating to existing or future differences between parties, subject respectively to the jurisdiction of different Contracting States by which the parties to a contract agree to submit to arbitration all or any differences that may arise in connection with such contract relating to commercial matters or to any other matter capable of settlement by arbitration, whether or not the arbitration is to take place in a country to whose jurisdiction none of the parties is subject.

Each Contracting State reserves the right to limit the obligation mentioned above to contracts which are considered as commercial under its national law, Any Contracting State which avails itself of this right will notify the Secretary-General of the League of Nations, in order that the other Contracting States may be so informed.

2. The arbitral procedure, including the constitution of the arbitral tribunal, shall be governed by the will of the parties and by the law of the country in whose territory the arbitration takes place.

The Contracting States agree to facilitate all steps in the procedure which require to be taken in their own territories, in accordance with the provisions of their law governing arbitral procedure applicable to existing differences.

3. Each Contracting State undertakes to ensure the execution by its authorities and in accordance with the provisions of its national laws of arbitral awards made in its own territory under the preceding articles.

4. The tribunals of the Contracting Parties, on being seized of a dispute regarding a contract made between persons to whom Article 1 applies and including an arbitration agreement whether referring to present or future differences which is valid in virtue of the said article and capable of being carried into effect, shall refer the parties on the application of either of them to the decision of the arbitrators.

Such reference shall not prejudice the competence of the judicial tribunals in case the agreement or the arbitration cannot proceed or become inoperative.

5. The present Protocol, which shall remain open for signature by all States, shall be ratified. The ratifications shall be deposited as soon as

possible with the Secretary-General of the League of Nations, who shall notify such deposit to all the signatory States.

6.   The present Protocol shall come into force as soon as two ratifications have been deposited. Thereafter it will take effect, in the case of each Contracting State, one month after the notification by the Secretary-General of the deposit of its ratification.

7.   The present Protocol may be denounced by any Contracting State on giving one year's notice. Denunciation shall be effected by a notification addressed to the Secretary-General of the League, who will immediately transmit copies of such notification to, all the other signatory States and inform them of the date of which it was received. The denunciation shall take effect one year after the date on which it was notified to the Secretary-General, and shall operate only in respect of the notifying State.

8.   The Contracting States may declare that their acceptance of the present Protocol does not include any or all of the under-mentioned territories: that is to say, their colonies, overseas possessions or territories, protectorates or the territories over which they exercise a mandate.

The said States may subsequently adhere separately on behalf of any territory thus excluded. The Secretary-General of the League of Nations shall be informed as soon as possible of such adhesions. He shall notify such adhesions to all signatory States. They will take effect one month after the notification by the Secretary-General to all signatory States.

The Contracting States may also denounce the Protocol separately on behalf of any of the territories referred to above. Article 7 applies to such denunciation.

GENEVA CONVENTION 1927

[*The text reproduced here is that of Schedule 2 of the United Kingdom's Arbitration Act 1950 — hence the preamble.*]

CONVENTION ON THE EXECUTION OF FOREIGN ARBITRAL AWARDS SIGNED AT GENEVA ON BEHALF OF HIS MAJESTY ON THE TWENTY-SIXTH DAY OF SEPTEMBER, NINETEEN HUNDRED AND TWENTY-SEVEN

Article 1

In the territories of any High Contracting Party to which the present Convention applies, an arbitral award made in pursuance of an agreement, whether relating to existing or future differences (hereinafter called 'a submission to arbitration') covered by the Protocol on Arbitration Clauses, opened at Geneva on September 24, 1923, shall be recognised as binding and shall be enforced. in accordance with the rules of the procedure of the territory where the award is relied upon, provided that the said award has been made in a territory of one of the High Contracting Parties to which the present Convention applies and between: persons who are subject to the jurisdiction of one of the High Contracting Parties.

To obtain such recognition or enforcement, it shall, further, be necessary:—

(a)   That the award has been made in pursuance of a submission to arbitration which is valid under the law applicable thereto;

(b)   That the subject-matter of the award is capable of settlement by arbitration under the law of the country in which the award is sought to be relied upon;

(c)   That the award has been made by the Arbitral Tribunal provided for in the submission to arbitration or constituted in the manner agreed upon by the parties and in conformity with the law governing the arbitration procedure;

(d)   That the award has become final in the country in which it has been made, in the sense that it will not be considered as such if it is open to *opposition, appel* or *pourvoi en cassation* (in the countries where such forms of procedure exist) or if it is proved that any proceedings for the purpose of contesting the validity of the award are pending;

(e)   That the recognition or enforcement of the award is not contrary to the public policy or to the principles of the law of the country in which it is sought to be relied upon.

Article 2

Even if the conditions laid down in Article 1 hereof are fulfilled, recognition and enforcement of the award shall be refused if the Court is satisfied:—

(a)   That the award has been annulled in the country in which it was made;

(b)   That the party against whom it is sought to use the award was not given notice of the arbitration proceedings in sufficient time to enable him to present his case; or that, being under a legal incapacity, he was not properly represented;

(c)   That the award does not deal with the differences contemplated by or falling within the terms of the submission to arbitration or that it contains decisions on matters beyond the scope of the submission to arbitration.

If the award has not covered all the questions submitted to the arbitral tribunal, the competent authority of the country where recognition or enforcement of the award is sought can, if it think fit, postpone such recognition or enforcement or grant it subject to such guarantee as that authority may decide.

Article 3

If the party against whom the award has been made proves that, under the law governing the arbitration procedure, there is a ground, other than the grounds referred to in Article 1(a) and (c), and Article 2(b) and (c), entitling him to contest the validity of the award in a Court of Law, the Court may, if it thinks fit, either refuse recognition or enforcement of the award or adjourn the consideration thereof, giving such party a reasonable time within which to have the award annulled by the competent tribunal.

Article 4

The party relying upon an award or claiming its enforcement must supply, in particular:—

(1)   The original award or a copy thereof duly authenticated, according to the requirements of the law of the country in which it was made;

(2)   Documentary or other evidence to prove that the award has become final, in the sense defined in Article 1(d), in the country in which it was made;

(3)   When necessary, documentary or other evidence to prove that the conditions laid down in Article 1, paragraph 1 and paragraph 2(a) and (c), have been fulfilled.

A translation of the award and of the other documents mentioned in this Article into the official language of the country where the award is sought to be relied upon may be demanded. Such translation must be certified correct by a diplomatic or consular agent of the country to which the party who seeks to rely upon the award belongs or by a sworn translator of the country where the award is sought to be relied upon.

Article 5

The provisions of the above Articles shall not deprive any interested party of the right of availing himself of an arbitral award in the manner and to the extent allowed by the law or the treaties of the country where such award is sought to be relied upon.

Article 6

The present Convention applies only to arbitral awards made after the coming into force of the Protocol on Arbitration Clauses, opened at Geneva on September 24th, 1923.

Article 7

The present Convention, which will remain open to the signature of all the signatories of the Protocol of 1923 on Arbitration Clauses, shall be ratified.

It may be ratified only on behalf of those Members of the League of Nations and non-Member States on whose behalf the Protocol of 1923 shall have been ratified.

Ratifications shall be deposited as soon as possible with the Secretary-General of the League of Nations, who will notify such deposit to all the signatories.

Article 8

The present Convention shall come into force three months after it shall have been ratified on behalf of two High Contracting Parties. Thereafter, it shall take effect, in the case of each High Contracting Party, three months after the deposit of the ratifications on its behalf with the Secretary-General of the League of Nations.

Article 9

The present Convention may be denounced on behalf of any Member of the League or non-Member State. Denunciation shall be notified in writing to the Secretary-General of the League of Nations, who will immediately send a copy thereof, certified to be in conformity with the notification, to all the other Contracting Parties, at the same time informing them of the date on which he received it.

The denunciation shall come into force only in respect of the High Contracting Party which shall have notified it and one year after such notification shall have reached the Secretary-General of the League of Nations.

The denunciation of the Protocol on Arbitration Clauses shall entail, ipso facto, the denunciation of the present Convention.

Article 10

The present Convention does not apply to the Colonies, Protectorates or territories under suzerainty or mandate of any High Contracting Party unless they are specially mentioned.

The application of this Convention to one or more of such Colonies, Protectorates or territories to which the Protocol on Arbitration Clauses, opened at Geneva on September 24th, 1923, applies, can be effected at any time by means of a declaration addressed to the Secretary-General of the League of Nations by one of the High Contracting Parties.

Such declaration shall take effect three months after the deposit thereof.

The High Contracting Parties can at any time denounce the Convention for all or any of the Colonies, Protectorates or territories referred to above. Article 9 hereof applies to such denunciation.

Article 11

A certified copy of the present Convention shall be transmitted by the Secretary-General of the League of Nations to every Member of the League of Nations and to every non-Member State which signs the same.

NEW YORK CONVENTION 1958

CONVENTION ON THE RECOGNITION AND ENFORCEMENT OF FOREIGN ARBITRAL AWARDS. DONE AT NEW YORK, ON 10 JUNE 1958

Article I

1. This Convention shall apply to the recognition and enforcement of arbitral awards made in the territory of a State other than the State where the recognition and enforcement of such awards are sought, and arising out of differences between persons, whether physical or legal. It shall also apply to arbitral awards not considered as domestic awards in the State where their recognition and enforcement are sought.

2.   The term 'arbitral awards' shall include not only awards made by arbitrators appointed for each case but also those made by permanent arbitral bodies to which the parties have submitted.

3.   When signing, ratifying or acceding to this Convention, or notifying extension under article X hereof, any State may on the basis of reciprocity declare that it will apply the Convention to the recognition and enforcement of awards made only in the territory of another Contracting State. It may also declare that it will apply the Convention only to differences arising out of legal relationships, whether contractual or not, which are considered as commercial under the national law of the State making such declaration.

Article II

1.   Each Contracting State shall recognize an agreement in writing under which the parties undertake to submit to arbitration all or any differences which have arisen or which may arise between them in respect of a defined legal relationship, whether contractual or not, concerning a subject matter capable of settlement by arbitration.

2.   The term 'agreement in writing' shall include an arbitral clause in a contract or an arbitration agreement, signed by the parties or contained in an exchange of letters or telegrams.

3.   The court of a Contracting State, when seized of an action in a matter in respect of which the parties have made an agreement within the meaning of this article, at the request of one of the parties, refer the parties to arbitration, unless it finds that the said agreement is null and void, inoperative or incapable of being performed.

Article III

Each Contracting State shall recognize arbitral awards as binding and enforce them in accordance with the rules of procedure of the territory where the award is relied upon, under the conditions laid down in the following articles. There shall not be imposed substantially more onerous conditions or higher fees or charges on the recognition or enforcement of arbitral awards to which this Convention applies than are imposed on the recognition or enforcement of domestic arbitral awards.

Article IV

1.   To obtain the recognition and enforcement mentioned in the preceding article, the party applying for recognition and enforcement shall, at the time of the application, supply:

(a)   The duly authenticated original award or a duly certified copy thereof;

(b)   The original agreement referred to in article II or a duly certified copy thereof.

2.   If the said award or agreement is not made in an official language of the country in which the award is relied upon, the party applying for recognition and enforcement of the award shall produce a translation of these documents into such language. The translation shall be certified by an official or sworn translator or by a diplomatic or consular agent.

Article V

1. Recognition and enforcement of the award may be refused, at the request of the party against whom it is invoked, only if that party furnishes to the competent authority where the recognition and enforcement is sought, proof that:

(a) The parties to the agreement referred to in article II were, under the law applicable to them, under some incapacity, or the said agreement is not valid under the law to which the parties have subjected it or, failing any indication thereon, under the law of the country where the award was made; or

(b) The party against whom the award is invoked was not given proper notice of the appointment of the arbitrator or of the arbitration proceedings or was otherwise unable to present his case; or

(c) The award deals with a difference not contemplated by or not falling within the terms of the submission to arbitration, or it contains decisions on matters beyond the scope of the submission to arbitration, provided that, if the decisions on matters submitted to arbitration can be separated from those not so submitted, that part of the award which contains decisions on matters submitted to arbitration may be recognized and enforced; or

(d) The composition of the arbitral authority or the arbitral procedure was not in accordance with the agreement of the parties, or, failing such agreement, was not in accordance with the law of the country where the arbitration took place; or

(e) The award has not yet become binding on the parties, or has been set aside or suspended by a competent authority of the country in which, or under the law of which, that award was made.

2. Recognition and enforcement of an arbitral award may also be refused if the competent authority in the country where recognition and enforcement is sought finds that:

(a) The subject matter of the difference is not capable of settlement by arbitration under the law of that country; or

(b) The recognition or enforcement of the award would be contrary to the public policy of that country.

Article VI

If an application for the setting aside or suspension of the award has been made to a competent authority referred to in article, V(1)(e), the authority before which the award is sought to be relied upon may, if it considers it proper, adjourn the decision on the enforcement of the award and may also, on the application of the party claiming enforcement of the award, order the other party to give suitable security.

Article VII

1. The provisions of the present Convention shall not affect the validity of multilateral or bilateral agreements concerning the recognition and enforcement of arbitral awards entered into by the Contracting States nor

deprive any interested party of any right he may have to avail himself of an arbitral award in the manner and to the extent allowed by the law or the treaties of the country where such award is sought to be relied upon.

2.   The Geneva Protocol on Arbitration Clauses of 1923 and the Geneva Convention on the Execution of Foreign Arbitral Awards 1927 shall cease to have effect between Contracting States on their becoming bound and to the extent that they become bound, by this Convention.

Article VIII

1.   This Convention shall be open until 31 December 1958 for signature on behalf of any Member of the United Nations and also on behalf of any other State which is or hereafter becomes a member of any specialized agency of the United Nations, or which is or hereafter becomes a party to the Statute of the International Court of Justice, or any other State to which an invitation has been addressed by the General Assembly of the United Nations.

2.   This Convention shall be ratified and the instrument of ratification shall be deposited with the Secretary-General of the United Nations.

Article IX

1.   This Convention shall be open for accession to all States referred to in article VIII.

2.   Accession shall be effected by the deposit of an instrument of accession with the Secretary-General of the United Nations.

Article X

1.   Any State may, at the time of signature, ratification or accession, declare that this Convention shall extend to all or any of the territories for the international relations of which it is responsible. Such a declaration shall take effect when the Convention enters into force for the State concerned.

2.   At any time thereafter any such extension shall be made by notification addressed to the Secretary-General of the United Nations and shall take effect as from the ninetieth day after the day of receipt by the Secretary-General of the United Nations of this notification, or as from the date of entry into force of the Convention for the State concerned, whichever is the later.

3.   With respect to those territories to which this Convention is not extended at the time of signature, ratification or accession, each State concerned shall consider the possibility of taking the necessary steps in order to extend the application of this Convention to such territories, subject, where necessary for constitutional reasons, to the consent of the Govern-ments of such territories.

Article XI

In the case of a federal or non-unitary State, the following provisions shall apply:

(a)   With respect to those articles of this Convention that come within the legislative jurisdiction of the federal authority, the obligations of the federal Government shall to this extent be the same as those of Contracting States which are not federal States;

(b)   With respect to those articles of this Convention that come within the legislative jurisdiction of constituent states or provinces which are not, under the constitutional system of the federation, bound to take legislative action, the federal Government shall bring such articles with a favourable recommendation to the notice of the appropriate authorities of constituent states or provinces at the earliest possible moment;

(c)   A federal State Party to this Convention shall, at the request of any other Contracting State transmitted through the Secretary-General of the United Nations, supply a statement of the law and practice of the federation and its constituent units in regard to any particular provision of this Convention, showing the extent to which effect has been given to that provision by legislative or other action.

Article XII

1.   This Convention shall come into force on the ninetieth day following the date of deposit of the third instrument of ratification or accession.

2.   For each State ratifying or acceeding to this Convention after the deposit of the third instrument of ratification or accession, this Convention shall enter into force on the ninetieth day after deposit by such State of its instrument of ratification or accession.

Article XIII

1.   Any Contracting State may denounce this Convention by a written notification to the Secretary-General of the United Nations. Denunciation shall take effect one year after the date of receipt of the notification by the Secretary-General.

2.   Any State which has made a declaration or notification under article X may, at any time thereafter, by notification to the Seretary-General of the United Nations, declare that this Convention shall cease to extend to the territory concerned one year after the date .of the receipt of the notification by the Secretary-General.

3.   This Convention shall continue to be applicable to arbitral awards in respect of which recognition or enforcement proceedings have been instituted before the denunciation takes effect.

Article XIV

A Contracting State shall not be entitled to avail itself of the present Convention against other Contracting States except to the extent that it is itself bound to apply the Convention.

Article XV

The Secretary-General of the United Nations shall notify the States contemplated in article VIII of the following:

(a)   Signatures and ratifications in accordance with article VIII;

(b)   Accessions in accordance with article IX
(c)   Declarations and notifications under articles I, X and XI;
(d)   The date upon which this Convention enters into force in accordance with article XII;
(e)   Denunciations and notifications in accordance with article XIII.

Article XVI

1.   This Convention, of which the Chinese, English, French, Russian and Spanish texts shall be equally authentic, shall be deposited in the archives of the United Nations.
2.   The Secretary-General of the United Nations shall transmit a certified copy of this Convention to the States contemplated in article VIII.

GENEVA CONVENTION 1961

EUROPEAN CONVENTION ON INTERNATIONAL COMMERCIAL ARBITRATION. DONE AT GENEVA, ON 21 APRIL 1961

The undersigned, duly authorized,
Convened under the auspices of the Economic Commission for Europe of the United Nations,
Having noted that on 10th June 1958 at the United Nations Conference on International Commercial Arbitration has been signed in New York a Convention on the recognition and Enforcement of Foreign Arbitral awards,
Desirous of promoting the development of European trade by, as far as possible, removing certain difficulties that may impede the organization and operation of international commercial arbitration in relation between physical or legal persons of different European countries,
Have agreed on the following provisions:

Article I   Scope of the convention

1.   This Convention shall apply:
    (a)   to arbitration agreements concluded for the purpose of settling disputes arising from international trade between physical or legal persons having, when concluding the agreement, their habitual place of residence or their seat in different Contracting States;
    (b)   to arbitral procedures and awards based on agreements referred to in paragraph 1(a) above.
2.   For the purpose of this Convention,
    (a)   the term 'arbitration agreement' shall mean either an arbitral clause in a contract or an arbitration agreement, the contract or arbitration agreement being signed by the parties, or contained in an exchange of letters, telegrams, or in a communication by teleprinter and, in relations between States whose laws do not require that an arbitration agreement be made in writing, any arbitration agreement concluded in the form authorized by these laws;
    (b)   the term 'arbitration' shall mean not only settlement by arbitrators appointed for each case (*ad hoc* arbitration) but also by permanent arbitral institutions;

(c)   the term 'seat' shall mean the place of the situation of the establishment that has made the arbitration agreement.

Article II   Right of legal persons of public law to resort to arbitration

1.   In the cases refered to in Article I, paragraph 1, of this Convention,
legal persons considered by the law which is applicable to them as 'legal
persons of public law' have the right to conclude valid arbitration agreements.
2.   On signing, ratifying or acceding to this convention any State shall be
entitled to declare that it limits the above faculty to such conditions as may
be stated in its declaration.

Article III   Right of foreign nationals to be designated as arbitrators

In arbitration covered by this Convention, foreign nationals may be
designated as arbitrators.

Article IV   Organization of the arbitration

1.   The parties to an arbitration agreement shall be free to submit their
disputes:
(a)   to a permanent arbitral institution; in this case, the arbitration
proeedings shall be held in conformity with the rules of the said institution;
(b)   to an *ad hoc* arbitral procedure; in this case, they shall be free *inter
alia*
(i)   to appoint arbitrators or to establish means for their appointment in the event of an actual dispute;
(ii)   to determine the place of arbitration; and
(iii)   to lay down the procedure to be followed by the arbitrators.
2.   Where the parties have agreed to submit any disputes to an *ad hoc*
arbitration, and where within thirty days of the notification of the request for
arbitration to the respondent one of the parties fails to appoint his arbitrator,
the latter shall, unless otherwise provided, be appointed at the request of the
other party by the President of the competent Chamber of Commerce of the
country of the defaulting party's habitual place of residence or seat at the time
of the introduction of the request for arbitration. This paragraph shall also
apply to the replacement of the arbitrator(s) appointed by one of the parties
or by the President of the Chamber of Commerce above referred to.
3.   Where the parties have agreed to submit any disputes to an *ad hoc*
arbitration by one or more arbitrators and the arbitration agreement contains
no indication regarding the organization of the arbitration, as mentioned in
paragraph 1 of this article, the necessary steps shall be taken by the
arbitrator(s) already appointed, unless the parties are able to agree thereon
and without prejudice to the case referred to in paragraph 2 above. Where
the parties cannot agree on the appointment of the sole arbitrator or where
the arbitrators appointed cannot agree on the measures to be taken, the
claimant shall apply for the necessary action, where the place of arbitration
has been agreed upon by the parties, at his option to the President of the
Chamber of Commerce of the place of arbitration agreed upon or to the

President of the competent Chamber of Commerce of the respondent's habitual place of residence or seat at the time of the introduction of the request for arbitration. Where such a place has not been agreed upon, the claimant shall be entitled at his option to apply for the necessary action either to the President of the competent Chamber of Commerce of the respondent's habitual place of residence or seat at the time of the introduction of the request for arbitration, or to the Special Committee whose composition and procedure are specified in the Annex to this Convention. Where the claimant fails to exercise the rights given to him under this paragraph the respondent or the arbitrator(s) shall be entitled to do so.

4.   When seized of a request the President or the Special Committee shall be entitled as need be:

   (a)   to appoint the sole arbitrator, presiding arbitrator, umpire, or referee;

   (b)   to replace the arbitrator(s) appointed under any procedure other than that referred to in paragraph 2 above;

   (c)   to determine the place of arbitration, provided that the arbitrator(s) may fix another place of arbitration;

   (d)   to establish directly or by reference to the rules and statutes of a permanent abitral institution the rules of procedure to be followed by the arbitrator(s), provided that the arbitrators have not established these rules themselves in the absence of any agreement thereon between the parties.

5.   Where the parties have agreed to submit their disputes to a permanent arbitral institution without determining the institution in question and cannot agree thereon, the claimant may request the determination of such institution in conformity with the procedure referred to in paragraph 3 above.

6.   Where the arbitration agreement does not specify the mode of arbitration (arbitration by a permanent arbitral institution or an *ad hoc* arbitration) to which the parties have agreed to submit their dispute, and where the parties cannot agree thereon, the claimant shall be entitled to have recourse in this case to the procedure refered to in paragraph 3 above to determine the question. The President of the competent Chambers of Commerce or the Special Committee, shall be entitled either to refer the parties to a permanent arbitral institution or to request the parties to appoint their arbitrators within such time-limits as the President of the competent Chamber of Commerce or the Special Committee may have fixed and to agree within such time-limits on the necessary measures for the functioning of the arbitration. In the latter case, the provisions of paragraph 2, 3 and 4 of this Article shall apply.

7.   Where within a period of sixty days from the moment he was requested to fulfil one of the functions set out in paragraphs 2, 3, 4, 5 and 6 of this Article the President of the Chamber of Commerce designated by virtue of these paragraphs has not fulfilled one of these functions, the party requesting shall be entitled to ask the Special Committee to do so.

Article V   Plea as to arbitral jurisdiction

1.   The party which intends to raise a plea as to the arbitrator's jurisdiction based on the fact that the arbitration agreement was either non-existent or null and void or had lapsed shall do so during the arbitration proceedings, not later than the delivery of its statement of claim or defence relating to the

substance of the dispute; those based on the fact that an arbitrator has exceeded his terms of reference shall be raised during the arbitration proceedings as soon as the question on which the arbitrator is alleged to have no jurisdiction is raised during the arbitral procedure. Where the delay in raising the plea is due to a cause which the arbitrator deems justified, the arbitrator shall declare the plea admissible.

2.   Pleas to the jurisdiction referred to in paragraph 1 above that have not been raised during the time-limits there referred to, may not be entered either during a subsequent stage of the arbitral proceedings where they are pleas left to the sole discretion of the parties under the law applicable by the arbitrator, or during subsequent court proceedings concerning the substance or the enforcement of the award where such pleas are left to the discretion of the parties under the rule of conflict of the court seized of the substance of the dispute or the enforcement of the award. The arbitrator's decision on the delay in raising the plea, will, however, be subject to judicial control.

3.   Subject to any subsequent judicial control provided for under the *lex fori*, the arbitrator whose jurisdiction is called in question shall be entitled to proceed with the arbitration, to rule on his own jurisdiction and to decide upon the existence or the validity of the arbitration agreement or of the contract of which the agreement forms part.

Article VI   Jurisdiction of courts of law

1.   A plea as to the jurisdiction of the court made before the court seized by either party to the arbitration agreement, on the basis of the fact than an arbitration agreement exists shall, under penalty of estoppel, be presented by the respondent before or at the same time as the presentation of his substantial defence, depending upon whether the law of the court seized regards this plea as one of procedure or of substance.

2.   In taking a decision concerning the existence or the validity of an arbitration agreement, courts of Contracting States shall examine the validity of such agreement with reference to the capacity of the parties, under the law applicable to them, and with reference to other questions.

(a)   under the law to which the parties have subjected their arbitration agreement;

(b)   failing any indication thereon, under the law of the country in which the award is to be made;

(c)   failing any indication as to the law to which the parties have subjected the agreement, and where at the time when the question is raised in court the country in which the award is to be made cannot be determined, under the competent law by virtue of the rules of conflict of the court seized of the dispute.

The courts may also refuse recognition of the arbitration agreement if under the law of their country the dispute is not capable of settlement by arbitration.

3.   Where either party to an arbitration agreement has initiated arbitration proceedings before any resort is had to a court, courts of Contracting States subsequently asked to deal with the same subject-matter between the same parties or with the question whether the arbitration agreement was non-existent or null and void or had lapsed, shall stay their ruling on the

arbitrator's jurisdiction until the arbitral award is made, unless they have good and substantial reasons to the contrary.

4.   A request for interim measures or measures of conservation addressed to a judicial authority shall not be deemed incompatible with the arbitration agreement, or regarded as a submission of the substance of the case to the court.

Article VII   Applicable law

1.   The parties shall be free to determine, by agreement, the law to be applied by the arbitrators to the substance of the dispute. Failing any indication by the parties as to the applicable law, the arbitrators shall apply the proper law under the rule of conflict that the arbitrators deem applicable. In both cases the arbitrators shall take account of the terms of the contract and trade usages.

2.   The arbitrators shall act as *amiables compositeurs* if the parties so decide and if they may do so under the law applicable to the arbitration.

Article VIII   Reasons for the award

The parties shall be presumed to have agreed that reasons shall be given for the award unless they
(a)   either expressly declare that reasons shall not be given; or
(b)   have assented to an arbitral procedure under which it is not customary to give reasons for awards, provided that in this case neither party requests before the end of the hearing, or if there has not been a hearing then before the making of the award, that reasons be given.

Article IX   Setting aside of the arbitral award

1.   The setting aside in a Contracting State of an arbitral award covered by this Convention shall only constitute a ground for the refusal of recognition or enforcement in another Contracting State where such setting aside took place in a State in which, or under the law of which, the award has been made and for one of the following reasons:
(a)   the parties to the arbitration agreement were under the law applicable to them, under some incapacity or the said agreement is not valid under the law to which the parties have subjected it or, failing any indication thereon, under the law of the country where the award was made, or
(b)   the party requesting the setting aside of the award was not given proper notice of the appointment of the arbitrator or of the arbitration proceedings or was otherwise unable to present his case; or
(c)   the award deals with a difference not contemplated by or not falling within the terms of the submission to arbitration, or it contains decisions on matters beyond the scope of the submission to arbitration, provided that, if the decisions on matters submitted to arbitration can be separated from those not so submitted, that part of the award which contains decisions on matters submitted to arbitration need not be set aside;
(d)   the composition of the arbitral authority or the arbitral procedure was not in accordance with the agreement of the parties, or failing such agreement, with the provisions of Article IV of this Convention.

2.   In relations between Contracting States that are also parties to the New York Convention on the Recognition and Enforcement of Foreign Arbitral Awards of 10th June 1958, paragraph 1 of this Article limits the application of Article V(1)(e) of the New York Convention solely to the cases of setting aside set out under paragraph 1 above.

Article X   Final clauses

1.   This Convention is open for signature or accession by countries members of the Economic Commission for Europe and countries admitted to the Commission in a consultative capacity under paragraph 8 of the Commission's terms of reference.

2.   Such countries as may participate in certain activities of the Economic Commission for Europe in accordance with paragraph 11 of the Commission's terms of reference may become Contracting Parties to this Convention by acceding thereto after its entry into force.

3.   The Convention shall be open for signature until 31 December 1961 inclusive. Thereafter, it shall be open for accession.

4.   This Convention shall be ratified.

5.   Ratification or accession shall be effected by the deposit of an instrument with the Secretary-General of the United Nations.

6.   When signing, ratifying or acceding to this Convention, the Contracting Parties shall communicate to the Secretary-General of the United Nations a list of the Chambers of Commerce or other institutions in their country who will exercise the functions conferred by virtue of Article IV of this Convention on Presidents of the competent Chambers of Commerce.

7.   The provisions of the present Convention shall not affect the validity of multilateral or bilateral agreements concerning arbitration entered into by Contracting States.

8.   This Convention shall come into force on the ninetieth day after five of the countries referred to in paragraph 1 above have deposited their instruments of ratification or accession. For any country ratifying or acceding to it later this Convention shall enter into force on the ninetieth day after the said country has deposited its instrument of ratification or accession.

9.   Any Contracting Party may denounce this Convention by so notifying the Secretary-General of the United Nations. Denunciation shall take effect twelve months after the date of receipt by the Secretary-General of the notification of denunciation.

10.   If, after the entry into force of this Convention, the number of Contracting Parties is reduced, as a result of denunciations, to less than five, the Convention shall cease to be in force from the date on which the last of such denunciations takes effect.

11.   The Secretary-General of the United Nations shall notify the countries referred to in paragraph 1, and the countries which have become Contracting Parties under paragraph 2 above, of

(a)   declarations made under Article II, paragraph 2;

(b)   ratifications and accessions under paragraphs 1 and 2 above;

(c)   communications received in pursuance of paragraph 6 above;

(d)   the dates of entry into force of this Convention in accordance with paragraph 8 above;

(e)   denunciations under paragraph 9 above;
(f)   the termination of this Convention in accordance with paragraph 10 above.

12.   After 31 December 1961, the original of this Convention shall be deposited with the Secretary-General of the United Nations, who shall transmit certified true copies to each of the countries mentioned in paragraphs 1 and 2 above.

IN WITNESS WHEREOF the undersigned, being duly authorized thereto, have signed this Convention.

DONE at Geneva, this twenty-first day of April, one thousand nine hundred and sixty-one, in a single copy in the English, French and Russian languages, each text being equally authentic.

ANNEX

COMPOSITION AND PROCEDURE OF THE SPECIAL COMMITTEE REFERRED TO IN ARTICLE IV OF THE CONVENTION

1.   The Special Committee referred to in Article IV of the Convention shall consist of two regular members and a Chairman. One of the regular members shall be elected by the Chambers of Commerce or other institutions designated, under Article X, paragraph 6, of the Convention, by States in which at the time when the Convention is open to signature National Committees of the International Chamber of Commerce exist, and which at the time of the election are parties to the Convention. The other member shall be elected by the Chambers of Commerce or other institutions designated, under Article X, paragraph 6, of the Convention, by States in which at the time when the Convention is open to signature no National Committees of the International Chamber of Commerce exist and which at the time of the election are parties to the Convention.

2.   The persons who are to act as Chairman of the Special Committee pursuant to paragraph 7 of this Annex shall also be elected in like manner by the Chambers of Commerce or other institutions referred to in paragraph 1 of this Annex.

3.   The Chambers of Commerce or other institutions referred to in paragraph 1 of this Annex shall elect alternates at the same time and in the same manner as they elect the Chairman and other regular members, in case of the temporary inability of the Chairman or regular members to act. In the event of the permanent inability to act or of the resignation of a Chairman or of a regular member, then the alternate elected to replace him shall become, as the case may be, the Chairman or regular member, and the group of Chambers of Commerce or other institutions which had elected the alternate who has become Chairman or regular member shall elect another alternate.

4.   The first elections to the Committee shall be held within ninety days from the date of the deposit of the fifth instrument of ratification or accession. Chambers of Commerce and other institutions designated by Signatory States who are not yet parties to the Convention shall also be entitled to take part in these elections. If however it should not be possible to hold elections within the prescribed period, the entry into force of paragraphs 3 to 7 of

Article IV of the Convention shall be postponed until elections are held as provided for above.

5.   Subject to the provisions of paragraph 7 below, the members of the Special Committee shall be elected for a term of four years. New elections shall be held within the first six months of the fourth year following the previous elections. Nevertheless, if a new procedure for the election of the members of the Special Committee has not produced results, the members previously elected shall continue to exercise their functions until the election of new members.

6.   The results of the elections of the members of the Special Committee shall be communicated to the Secretary-General of the United Nations who shall notify the States referred to in Article X, paragraph 1, of this Convention and the States which have become Contracting Parties under Article X, paragraph 2. The Secretary-General shall likewise notify the said States of any postponement and of the entry into force of paragraphs 3 to 7 of Article IV of the Convention in pursuance of paragraph 4 of this Annex.

7.   The persons elected to the office of Chairman shall exercise their functions in rotation, each during a period of two years. The question which of these two persons shall act as Chairman during the first two-year period after the entry into force of the Convention shall be decided by the drawing of lots. The office of Chairman shall thereafter be vested, for each successive two-year period, in the person elected Chairman by the group of countries other than that by which the Chairman exercising his functions during the immediately preceding two-year period was elected.

8.   The reference to the Special Committee of one of the requests referred to in paragraphs 3 to 7 of the aforesaid Article IV shall be addressed to the Executive Secretary of the Economic Commission for Europe. The Executive Secretary shall in the first instance lay the request before the member of the Special Committee elected by the group of countries other than that by which the Chairman holding office at the time of the introduction of the request was elected. The proposal of the member applied to in the first instance shall be communicated by the Executive Secretary to the other member of the Committee and, if that other member agrees to this proposal, it shall be deemed to be the Committee's ruling and shall be communicated as such by the Executive Secretary to the person who made the request.

9.   If the two members of the Special Committee applied to by the Executive Secretary are unable to agree on a ruling by correspondence, the Executive Secretary of the Economic Commission for Europe shall convene a meeting of the said Committee at Geneva in an attempt to secure a unanimous decision on the request. In the absence of unanimity, the Committee's decision shall be given by a majority vote and shall be communicated by the Executive Secretary to the person who made the request.

10.   The expenses connected with the Special Committee's action shall be advanced by the person requesting such action but shall be considered as costs in the cause.

LIST OF THE CHAMBERS OF COMMERCE OR OTHER INSTITUTIONS COMMUNICATED TO THE SECRETARY-GENERAL PURSUANT TO ARTICLE X, PARAGRAPH 6

[*Not reproduced here.*]

PARIS AGREEMENT 1962

AGREEMENT
RELATING TO APPLICATION
OF THE EUROPEAN CONVENTION
ON INTERNATIONAL COMMERCIAL ARBITRATION,

PARIS, 17. XII. 1962
COUNCIL OF EUROPE
EUROPEAN TREATY SERIES No. 42.

The signatory Governments of the member States of the Council of Europe,

Considering that a European Convention on International Commercial Arbitration was opened for signature at Geneva on 21st April 1961;

Considering, however, that certain measures relating to the organisation of the arbitration, provided for in Article IV of the Convention, are not to be recommended except in the case of disputes between physical or legal persons having, on the one hand, their habitual place of residence or seat in Contracting States where, according to the terms of the Annex to the Convention, there exist National Committees of the International Chamber of Commerce, and, on the other, in States where no such Committees exist;

Considering that under the terms of paragraph 7 of Article X of the said Convention the provisions of that Convention shall not affect the validity of multilateral or bilateral agreements concerning arbitration entered into by States which are Parties thereto;

Without prejudice to the intervention of a Convention relating to a uniform law on arbitration now being drawn up within the Council of Europe,

Have agreed as follows:

Article 1

In relations between physical or legal persons whose habitual residence or seat is in States Parties to the present Agreement, paragraphs 2 to 7 of Article IV of the European Convention on International Commercial Arbitration, opened for signature at Geneva on 21st April 1961, are replaced by the following provision:

'If the arbitral Agreement contains no indication regarding the measures referred to in paragraph 1 of Article IV of the European Convention on International Commercial Arbitration as a whole, or some of these measures, any difficulties arising with regard to the constitution or functioning of the arbitral tribunal shall be submitted to the decision of the competent authority at the request of the party instituting proceedings.'

Article 2

1.   This Agreement shall be open for signature by the member States of the Council of Europe. It shall be ratified or accepted. Instruments of

ratification or acceptance shall be deposited with the Secretary-General of the Council of Europe.

2. Subject to the provisions of Article 4, this Agreement shall come into force thirty days after the date of deposit of the second instrument of ratification or acceptance.

3. Subect to the provisions of Article 4, in respect of any signatory Government ratifying or accepting it subsequently, the Agreement shall come into force thirty days after the date of deposit of its instrument of ratification or acceptance.

Article 3

1. After the entry into force of this Agreement, the Committee of Ministers of the Council of Europe may invite any State which is not a member of the Council and in which there exists a National Committee of the International Chamber of Commerce to accede to this Agreement.

2. Accession shall be effected by the deposit with the Secretary-General of the Council of Europe of an instrument of accession, which shall take effect, subject to the provisions of Article 4, thirty days after the date of its deposit.

Article 4

The entry into force of this Agreement in respect of any State after ratification, acceptance or accession in accordance with the terms of Articles 2 and 3 shall be conditional upon the entry into force of the European Convention on International Commercial Arbitration in respect of that State.

Article 5

Any Contracting Party may, in so far as it is concerned, denounce this Agreement by giving notice to the Secretary-General of the Council of Europe. Denunciation shall take effect six months after the date of receipt by the Secretary-General of the Council of such notification.

Article 6

The Secretary-General of the Council of Europe shall notify member States of the Council and the Government of any State which has acceded to this Agreement of:

(a) any signature;

(b) the deposit of any instrument of ratification, acceptance or accession;

(c) any date of entry into force;

(d) any notification received in pursuance of the provisions of Article 5.

In witness whereof, the undersigned, being duly authorised thereto, have signed this Agreement

Done at Paris, this 17th day of December 1962 in English and in French, both texts being equally authoritative, in a single copy which shall remain deposited in the archives of the Council of Europe. The Secretary-General shall transmit copies to each of the signatory and acceding Governments.

WASHINGTON CONVENTION 1965

CONVENTION ON THE SETTLEMENT OF INVESTMENT DISPUTES BETWEEN STATES AND NATIONALS OF OTHER STATES

PREAMBLE

The Contracting States

Considering the need for international co-operation for economic development, and the role of private international investment therein;

Bearing in mind the possibility that from time to time disputes may arise in connection with such investment between Contracting States and nationals of other Contracting States;

Recognizing that while such disputes would usually be subject to national legal processes, international methods of settlement may be appropriate in certain cases;

Attaching particular importance to the availability of facilities for international conciliation or arbitration to which Contracting States and nationals of other Contracting States may submit such disputes if they so desire;

Desiring to establish such facilities under the auspices of the International Bank for Reconstruction and Development;

Recognizing that mutual consent by the parties to submit such disputes to conciliation or to arbitration through such facilities constitutes a binding agreement which requires in particular that due consideration be given to any recommendation of conciliators, and that any arbitral award be complied with; and

Declaring that no Contracting State shall by the mere fact of its ratification, acceptance or approval of this Convention and without its consent be deemed to be under any obligation to submit any particular dispute to conciliation or arbitration,

Have agreed as follows:

CHAPTER I

INTERNATIONAL CENTRE FOR SETTLEMENT OF INVESTMENT DISPUTES

SECTION 1

Establishment and Organization

Article 1

(1) There is hereby established the International Centre for Settlement of Investment Disputes (hereinafter called the Centre).

(2)   The purpose of the Centre shall be to provide facilities for conciliation and arbitration of investment disputes between Contracting States and nationals of other Contracting States in accordance with the provisions of this Convention.

Article 2

The seat of the Centre shall be at the principal office of the International Bank for Reconstruction and Development (hereinafter called the Bank). The seat may be moved to another place by decision of the Administrative Council adopted by a majority of two-thirds of its members.

Article 3

The Centre shall have an Administrative Council and a Secretariat and shall maintain a Panel of Conciliators and a Panel of Arbitrators.

SECTION 2

The Administrative Council

Article 4

(1)   The Administrative Council shall be composed of one representative of each Contracting State. An alternate may act as representative in case of his principal's absence from a meeting or inability to act.

(2)   In the absence of a contrary designation, each governor and alternate governor of the Bank appointed by a Contracting State shall be *ex officio* its representative and its alternate respectively.

Article 5

The President of the Bank shall be *ex officio* Chairman of the Administrative Council (hereinafter called the Chairman) but shall have no vote. During his absence or inability to act and during any vacancy in the office of President of the Bank, the person for the time being acting as President shall act as Chairman of the Administrative Council.

Article 6

(1)   Without prejudice to the powers and functions vested in it by other provisions of this Convention, the Administrative Council shall

(a)   adopt the administrative and financial regulations of the Centre;

(b)   adopt the rules of procedure for the institution of conciliation and arbitration proceedings;

(c)   adopt the rules of procedure for conciliation and arbitration proceedings (hereinafter called the Conciliation Rules and the Arbitration Rules);

(d)   approve arrangements with the Bank for the use of the Bank's administrative facilities and services;

(e)   determine the conditions of service of the Secretary-General and of any Deputy Secretary-General;

(f)   adopt the annual budget of revenues and expenditures of the Centre;

(g)   approve the annual report on the operation of the Centre.

The decisions referred to in sub-paragraphs (a), (b), (c) and (f) above shall be adopted by a majority of two-thirds of the members of the Administrative Council.

(2)   The Administrative Council may appoint such committees as it considers necessary.

(3)   The Administrative Council shall also exercise such other powers and perform such other functions as it shall determine to be necessary for the implementation of the provisions of this Convention.

Article 7

(1)   The Administrative Council shall hold an annual meeting and such other meetings as may be determined by the Council, or convened by the Chairman, or convened by the Secretary-General at the request of not less than five members of the Council.

(2)   Each member of the Administrative Council shall have one vote and, except as otherwise herein provided, all matters before the Council shall be decided by a majority of the votes cast.

(3)   A quorum for any meeting of the Administrative Council shall be a majority of its members.

(4)   The Administrative Council may establish, by a majority of two-thirds of its members, a procedure whereby the Chairman may seek a vote of the Council without convening a meeting of the Council. The vote shall be considered valid only if the majority of the members of the Council cast their votes within the time limit fixed by the said procedure.

Article 8

Members of the Administrative Council and the Chairman shall serve without remuneration from the Centre.

SECTION 3

The Secretariat

Article 9

The Secretariat shall consist of a Secretary-General, one or more Deputy Secretaries-General and staff.

Article 10

(1) The Secretary-General and any Deputy Secretary-General shall be elected by the Administrative Council by a majority of two-thirds of its

members upon the nomination of the Chairman for a term of service not exceeding six years and shall be eligible for re-election. After consulting the members of the Administrative Council, the Chairman shall propose one or more candidates for each such office.

(2)   The offices of Secretary-General and Deputy Secretary-General shall be incompatible with the exercise of any political function. Neither the Secretary-General nor any Deputy Secretary-General may hold any other employment or engage in any other occupation except with the approval of the Administrative Council.

(3)   During the Secretary-General's absence or inability to act, and during any vacancy of the office of Secretary-General, the Deputy Secretary-General shall act as Secretary-General. If there shall be more than one Deputy Secretary-General, the Administrative Council shall determine in advance the order in which they shall act as Secretary-General.

Article 11

The Secretary-General shall be the legal representative and the principal officer of the Centre and shall be responsible for its administration, including the appointment of staff, in accordance with the provisions of this Convention and the rules adopted by the Administrative Council. He shall perform the function of registrar and shall have the power to authenticate arbitral awards rendered pursuant to this Convention, and to certify copies thereof.

SECTION 4

The Panels

Article 12

The Panel of Conciliators and the Panel of Arbitrators shall each consist of qualified persons, designated as hereinafter provided, who are willing to serve thereon.

Article 13

(1)   Each Contracting State may designate to each Panel four persons who may but need not be its nationals.

(2)   The Chairman may designate ten persons to each Panel. The persons so designated to a Panel shall each have a different nationality.

Article 14

(1)   Persons designated to serve on the Panels shall be persons of high moral character and recognized competence in the fields of law, commerce, industry or finance, who may be relied upon to exercise independent judgment. Competence in the field of law shall be of particular importance in the case of persons on the Panel of Arbitrators.

(2)   The Chairman, in designating persons to serve on the Panels, shall in addition pay due regard to the importance of assuring representation on the Panels of the principal legal systems of the world and of the main forms of economic activity.

Article 15

(1)   Panel members shall serve for renewable periods of six years.

(2)   In case of death or resignation of a member of a Panel, the authority which designated the member shall have the right to designate another person to serve for the remainder of that member's term.

(3)   Panel members shall continue in office until their successors have been designated.

Article 16

(1)   A person may serve on both Panels.

(2)   If a person shall have been designated to serve on the same Panel by more than one Contracting State, or by one or more Contracting States and the Chairman, he shall be deemed to have been designated by the authority which first designated him or, if one such authority is the State of which he is a national, by that State.

(3)   All designations shall be notified to the Secretary-General and shall take effect from the date on which the notification is received.

SECTION 5

Financing the Centre

Article 17

If the expenditure of the Centre cannot be met out of charges for the use of its facilities, or out of other receipts, the excess shall be borne by Contracting States which are members of the Bank in proportion to their respective subscriptions to the capital stock of the Bank, and by Contracting States which are not members of the Bank in accordance with rules adopted by the Administrative Council.

SECTION 6

Status, Immunities and Privileges

Article 18

The Centre shall have full international legal personality. The legal capacity of the Centre shall include the capacity
    (a)   to contract;
    (b)   to acquire and dispose of movable and immovable property;
    (c)   to institute legal proceedings.

Article 19

To enable the Centre to fulfil its functions, it shall enjoy in the territories of each Contracting State the immunities and privileges set forth in this Section.

Article 20

The Centre, its property and assets shall enjoy immunity from all legal process, except when the Centre waives this immunity.

Article 21

The Chairman, the members of the Administrative Council, persons acting as conciliators or arbitrators or members of a Committee appointed pursuant to paragraph (3) of Article 52, and the officers and employees of the Secretariat

(a)   shall enjoy immunity from legal process with respect to acts performed by them in the exercise of their functions, except when the Centre waives this immunity;

(b)   not being local nationals, shall enjoy the same immunities from immigration restrictions, alien registration requirements and national service obligations, the same facilities as regards exchange restrictions and the same treatment in respect of travelling facilities as are accorded by Contracting States to the representatives, officials and employees of comparable rank of other Contracting States.

Article 22

The provisions of Article 21 shall apply to persons appearing in proceedings under this Convention as parties, agents, counsel, advocates, witnesses or experts; provided, however, that sub-paragraph (b) thereof shall apply only in connection with their travel to and from, and their stay at, the place where the proceedings are held.

Article 23

(1)   The archives of the Centre shall be inviolable, wherever they may be.

(2)   With regard to its official communications, the Centre shall be accorded by each Contracting State treatment not less favourable than that accorded to other international organizations.

Article 24

(1)   The Centre, its assets, property and income, and its operations and transactions authorized by this Convention shall be exempt from all taxation and customs duties. The Centre shall also be exempt from liability for the collection or payment of any taxes or customs duties.

(2)   Except in the case of local nationals, no tax shall be levied on or in respect of expense allowances paid by the Centre to the Chairman or

members of the Administrative Council, or on or in respect of salaries, expense allowances or other emoluments paid by the Centre to officials or employees of the Secretariat.

(3)   No tax shall be levied on or in respect of fees or expense allowances received by persons acting as conciliators, or arbitrators, or members of a Committee appointed pursuant to paragraph (3) of Article 52, in proceedings under this Convention, if the sole jurisdictional basis for such tax is the location of the Centre or the place where such proceedings are conducted or the place where such fees or allowances are paid.

CHAPTER II

JURISDICTION OF THE CENTRE

Article 25

(1)   The jurisdiction of the Centre shall extend to any legal dispute arising directly out of an investment, between a Contracting State (or any constituent subdivision or agency of a Contracting State designated to the Centre by that State) and a national of another Contracting State, which the parties to the dispute consent in writing to submit to the Centre. When the parties have given their consent, no party may withdraw its consent unilaterally.

(2)   'National of another Contracting State' means:

(a)   any natural person who had the nationality of a Contracting State other than the State party to the dispute on the date on which the parties consented to submit such dispute to conciliation or arbitration as well as on the date on which the request was registered pursuant to paragraph (3) of Article 28 or paragraph (3) of Article 36, but does not include any person who on either date also had the nationality of the Contracting State party to the dispute; and

(b)   any juridical person which had the nationality of a Contracting State other than the State party to the dispute on the date on which the parties consented to submit such dispute to conciliation or arbitration and any juridical person which had the nationality of the Contracting State party to the dispute on that date and which, because of foreign control, the parties have agreed should be treated as a national of another Contracting State for the purposes of this Convention.

(3)   Consent by a constituent subdivision or agency of a Contracting State shall require the approval of that State unless that State notifies the Centre that no such approval is required.

(4)   Any Contracting State may, at the time of ratification, acceptance or approval of this Convention or at any time thereafter, notify the Centre of the class or classes of disputes which it would or would not consider submitting to the jurisdiction of the Centre. The Secretary-General shall forthwith transmit such notification to all Contracting States. Such notification shall not constitute the consent required by paragraph (1).

Article 26

Consent of the parties to arbitration under this Convention shall, unless otherwise stated, be deemed consent to such arbitration to the exclusion of any other remedy. A Contracting State may require the exhaustion of local administrative or judicial remedies as a condition of its consent to arbitration under this Convention.

Article 27

(1) No Contracting State shall give diplomatic protection, or bring an international claim, in respect of a dispute which one of its nationals and another Contracting State shall have consented to submit or shall have submitted to arbitration under this Convention, unless such other Contracting State shall have failed to abide by and comply with the award rendered in such dispute.

(2) Diplomatic protection, for the purposes of paragraph (1), shall not include informal diplomatic exchanges for the sole purpose of facilitating a settlement of the dispute.

CHAPTER III

CONCILIATION

SECTION 1

Request for Conciliation

Article 28

(1) Any Contracting State or any national of a Contracting State wishing to institute conciliation proceedings shall address a request to that effect in writing to the Secretary-General who shall send a copy of the request to the other party.

(2) The request shall contain information concerning the issues in dispute, the identity of the parties and their consent to conciliation in accordance with the rules of procedure for the institution of conciliation and arbitration proceedings.

(3) The Secretary-General shall register the request unless he finds, on the basis of the information contained in the request, that the dispute is manifestly outside the jurisdiction of the Centre. He shall forthwith notify the parties of registration or refusal to register.

SECTION 2

Constitution of the Conciliation Commission

Article 29

(1) The Conciliation Commission (hereinafter called the Commission) shall be constituted as soon as possible after registration of a request pursuant to Article 28.

(2)(a) The Commission shall consist of a sole conciliator or any uneven number of conciliators appointed as the parties shall agree.

(b)   Where the parties do not agree upon the number of conciliators and the method of their appointment, the Commission shall consist of three conciliators, one conciliator appointed by each party and the third, who shall be the president of the Commission, appointed by agreement of the parties.

Article 30

If the Commission shall not have been constituted within 90 days after notice of registration of the request has been dispatched by the Secretary-General in accordance with paragraph (3) of Article 28, or such other period as the parties may agree, the Chairman shall, at the request of either party and after consulting both parties as far as possible, appoint the conciliator or conciliators not yet appointed.

Article 31

(1)   Conciliators may be appointed from outside the Panel of Conciliators, except in the case of appointments by the Chairman pursuant to Article 30.

(2)   Conciliators appointed from outside the Panel of Conciliators shall possess the qualities stated in paragraph (1) of Article 14.

SECTION 3

Conciliation Proceedings

Article 32

(1)   The Commission shall be the judge of its own competence.

(2)   Any objection by a party to the dispute that that dispute is not within the jurisdiction of the Centre, or for other reasons is not within the competence of the Commission, shall be considered by the Commission which shall determine whether to deal with it as a preliminary question or to join it to the merits of the dispute.

Article 33

Any conciliation proceeding shall be conducted in accordance with the provisions of this Section and, except as the parties otherwise agree, in accordance with the Conciliation Rules in effect on the date on which the parties consented to conciliation. If any question of procedure arises which is not covered by this Section or the Conciliation Rules or any rules agreed by the parties, the Commission shall decide the question.

Article 34

(1)   It shall be the duty of the Commission to clarify the issues in dispute between the parties and to endeavour to bring about agreement between them upon mutually acceptable terms. To that end, the Commission may at any stage of the proceedings and from time to time recommend terms of settlement to the parties. The parties shall cooperate in good faith with the

Commission in order to enable the Commission to carry out its functions, and shall give their most serious consideration to its recommendations.

(2)   If the parties reach agreement, the Commission shall draw up a report noting the issues in dispute and recording that the parties have reached agreement. If, at any stage of the proceedings, it appears to the Commission that there is no likelihood of agreement between the parties, it shall close the proceedings and shall draw up a report noting the submission of the dispute and recording the failure of the parties to reach agreement. If one party fails to appear or participate in the proceedings, the Commission shall close the proceedings and shall draw up a report noting that party's failure to appear or participate.

Article 35

Except as the parties to the dispute shall otherwise agree, neither party to a conciliation proceeding shall be entitled in any other proceeding, whether before arbitrators or in a court of law or otherwise, to invoke or rely on any views expressed or statements or admissions or offers of settlement made by the other party in the conciliation proceedings, or the report or any recommendations made by the Commission.

CHAPTER IV

ARBITRATION

SECTION 1

Request for Arbitration

Article 36

(1)   Any contracting State or any national of a Contracting State wishing to institute arbitration proceedings shall address a request to that effect in writing to the Secretary-General who shall send a copy of the request to the other party.

(2)   The request shall contain information concerning the issues in dispute, the identity of the parties and their consent to arbitration in accordance with the rules of procedure for the institution of conciliation and arbitration proceedings.

(3)   The Secretary-General shall register the request unless he finds, on the basis of the information contained in the request, that the dispute is manifestly outside the jurisdiction of the Centre. He shall forthwith notify the parties of registration or refusal to register.

SECTION 2

Constitution of the Tribunal

Article 37

(1)   The Arbitral Tribunal (hereinafter called the Tribunal) shall be constituted as soon as possible after registration of a request pursuant to Article 36.

(2)(a) The Tribunal shall consist of a sole arbitrator or any uneven number of arbitrators appointed as the parties shall agree.

(b) Where the parties do not agree upon the number of arbitrators and the method of their appointment, the Tribunal shall consist of three arbitrators, one arbitrator appointed by each party and the third, who shall be the president of the Tribunal, appointed by agreement of the parties.

Article 38

If the Tribunal shall not have been constituted within 90 days after notice of registration of the request has been dispatched by the Secretary-General in accordance with paragraph (3) of Article 36, or such other period as the parties may agree, the Chairman shall, at the request of either party and after consulting both parties as far as possible, appoint the arbitrator or arbitrators not yet appointed. Arbitrators appointed by the Chairman pursuant to this Article shall not be nationals of the Contracting State party to the dispute or of the Contracting State whose national is a party to the dispute.

Article 39

The majority of the arbitrators shall be nationals of States other than the Contracting State party to the dispute and the Contracting State whose national is a party to the dispute; provided, however, that the foregoing provisions of this Article shall not apply if the sole arbitrator or each individual member of the Tribunal has been appointed by agreement of the parties.

Article 40

(1) Arbitrators may be appointed from outside the Panel of Arbitrators, except in the case of appointments by the Chairman pursuant to Article 38.

(2) Arbitrators appointed from outside the Panel of Arbitrators shall possess the qualities stated in paragraph (1) of Article 14.

SECTION 3

Powers and Functions of the Tribunal

Article 41

(1) The Tribunal shall be the judge of its own competence.

(2) Any objection by a party to the dispute that that dispute is not within the jurisdiction of the Centre, or for other reasons is not within the competence of the Tribunal, shall be considered by the Tribunal which shall determine whether to deal with it as a preliminary question or to join it to the merits of the dispute.

Article 42

(1) The Tribunal shall decide a dispute in accordance with such rules of law as may be agreed by the parties. In the absence of such agreement, the

Tribunal shall apply the law of the Contracting State party to the dispute (including its rules on the conflict of laws) and such rules of international law as may be applicable.

(2) The Tribunal may not bring in a finding of *non liquet* on the ground of silence or obscurity of the law.

(3) The provisions of paragraphs (1) and (2) shall not prejudice the power of the Tribunal to decide a dispute *ex aequo et bono* if the parties so agree.

Article 43

Except as the parties otherwise agree, the Tribunal may, if it deems it necessary at any stage of the proceedings,
(a) call upon the parties to produce documents or other evidence, and
(b) visit the scene connected with the dispute, and conduct such enquiries there as it may deem appropriate.

Article 44

Any arbitration proceeding shall be conducted in accordance with the provisions of this Section and, except as the parties otherwise agree, in accordance with the Arbitration Rules in effect on the date on which the parties consented to arbitration. If any question of procedure arises which is not covered by this Section or the Arbitration Rules or any rules agreed by the parties, the Tribunal shall decide the question.

Article 45

(1) Failure of a party to appear or to present his case shall not be deemed an admission of the other party's assertions.

(2) If a party fails to appear or to present his case at any stage of the proceedings the other party may request the Tribunal to deal with the questions submitted to it and to render an award. Before rendering an award, the Tribunal shall notify, and grant a period of grace to, the party failing to appear or to present its case, unless it is satisfied that that party does not intend to do so.

Article 46

Except as the parties otherwise agree, the Tribunal shall, if requested by a party, determine any incidental or additional claims or counter-claims arising directly out of the subject-matter of the dispute provided that they are within the scope of the consent of the parties and are otherwise within the jurisdiction of the Centre.

Article 47

Except as the parties otherwise agree, the Tribunal may, if it considers that the circumstances so require, recommend any provisional measures which should be taken to preserve the respective rights of either party.

SECTION 4

The Award

Article 48

(1)   The Tribunal shall decide questions by a majority of the votes of all its members.

(2)   The award of the Tribunal shall be in writing and shall be signed by the members of the Tribunal who voted for it.

(3)   The award shall deal with every question submitted to the Tribunal, and shall state the reasons upon which it is based.

(4)   Any member of the Tribunal may attach his individual opinion to the award, whether he dissents from the majority or not, or a statement of his dissent.

(5)   The Centre shall not publish the award without the consent of the parties.

Article 49

(1)   The Secretary-General shall promptly dispatch certified copies of the award to the parties. The award shall be deemed to have been rendered on the date on which the certified copies were dispatched.

(2)   The Tribunal upon the request of a party made within 45 days after the date on which the award was rendered may after notice to the other party decide any question which it had omitted to decide in the award, and shall rectify any clerical, arithmetical or similar error in the award. Its decision shall become part of the award and shall be notified to the parties in the same manner as the award. The periods of time provided for under paragraph (2) of Article 51 and paragraph (2) of Article 52 shall run from the date on which the decision was rendered.

SECTION 5

Interpretation, Revision and Annulment of the Award

Article 50

(1)   If any dispute shall arise between the parties as to the meaning or scope of an award, either party may request interpretation of the award by an application in writing addressed to the Secretary-General.

(2)   The request shall, if possible, be submitted to the Tribunal which rendered the award. If this shall not be possible, a new Tribunal shall be constituted in accordance with Section 2 of this Chapter. The Tribunal may, if it considers that the circumstances so require, stay enforcement of the award pending its decision.

Article 51

(1)   Either party may request revision of the award by an application in writing addressed to the Secretary-General on the ground of discovery of

some fact of such a nature as decisively to affect the award, provided that when the award was rendered that fact was unknown to the Tribunal and to the applicant and that the applicant's ignorance of that fact was not due to negligence.

(2) The application shall be made within 90 days after the discovery of such fact and in any event within three years after the date on which the award was rendered.

(3) The request shall, if possible, be submitted to the Tribunal which rendered the award. If this shall not be possible, a new Tribunal shall be constituted in accordance with Section 2 of this Chapter.

(4) The Tribunal may, if it considers that the circumstances so require, stay enforcement of the award pending its decision. If the applicant requests stay of enforcement of the award in his application, enforcement shall be stayed provisionally until the Tribunal rules on such request.

Article 52

(1) Either party may request annulment of the award by an application in writing addressed to the Secretary-General on one or more of the following grounds:

   (a) that the Tribunal was not properly constituted;
   (b) that the Tribunal has manifestly exceeded its powers;
   (c) that there was corruption on the part of a member of the Tribunal;
   (d) that there has been a serious departure from a fundamental rule of procedure; or
   (e) that the award has failed to state the reasons on which it is based.

(2) The application shall be made within 120 days after the date on which the award was rendered except that when annulment is requested on the ground of corruption such application shall be made within 120 days after discovery of the corruption and in any event within three years after the date on which the award was rendered.

(3) On receipt of the request the Chairman shall forthwith appoint from the Panel of Arbitrators an *ad hoc* Committee of three persons. None of the members of the Committee shall have been a member of the Tribunal which rendered the award, shall be of the same nationality as any such member, shall be a national of the State party to the dispute or of the State whose national is a party to the dispute, shall have been designated to the Panel of Arbitrators by either of those States, or shall have acted as a conciliator in the same dispute. The Committee shall have the authority to annul the award or any part thereof on any of the grounds set forth in paragraph (1).

(4) The provisions of Articles 41–45, 48, 49, 53 and 54, and of Chapters VI and VII shall apply *mutatis mutandis* to proceedings before the Committee.

(5) The Committee may, if it considers that circumstances so require, stay enforcement of the award pending its decision. If the applicant requests a stay of enforcement of the award in his application, enforcement shall be stayed provisionally until the Committee rules on such request.

(6) If the award is annulled the dispute shall, at the request of either party, be submitted to a new Tribunal constituted in accordance with Section 2 of this Chapter.

SECTION 6

Recognition and Enforcement of the Award

Article 53

(1)   The award shall be binding on the parties and shall not be subject to any appeal or to any other remedy except those provided for in this Convention. Each party shall abide by and comply with the terms of the award except to the extent that enforcement shall have been stayed pursuant to the relevant provisions of this Convention.

(2)   For the purposes of this Section, 'award' shall include any decision interpreting, revising or annulling such award pursuant to Articles 50, 51 or 52.

Article 54

(1)   Each Contracting State shall recognize an award rendered pursuant to this Convention as binding and enforce the pecuniary obligations imposed by that award within its territories as if it were a final judgment of a court in that State. A Contracting State with a federal constitution may enforce such an award in or through its federal courts and may provide that such courts shall treat the award as if it were a final judgment of the courts of a constituent state.

(2)   A party seeking recognition or enforcement in the territories of a Contracting State shall furnish to a competent court or other authority which such State shall have designated for this purpose a copy of the award certified by the Secretary-General. Each Contracting State shall notify the Secretary-General of the designation of the competent court or other authority for this purpose and of any subsequent change in such designation.

(3)   Execution of the award shall be governed by the laws concerning the execution of judgments in force in the State in whose territories such execution is sought.

Article 55

Nothing in Article 54 shall be construed as derogating from the law in force in any Contracting State relating to immunity of that State or of any foreign State from execution.

CHAPTER V

REPLACEMENT AND DISQUALIFICATION OF
CONCILIATORS AND ARBITRATORS

Article 56

(1)   After a Commission or a Tribunal has been constituted and proceedings have begun, its composition shall remain unchanged; provided, however,

that if a conciliator or an arbitrator should die, become incapacitated, or resign, the resulting vacancy shall be filled in accordance with the provisions of Section 2 of Chapter III or Section 2 of Chapter IV.

(2)   A member of the Commission or Tribunal shall continue to serve in that capacity notwithstanding that he shall have ceased to be a member of the Panel.

(3)   If a conciliator or arbitrator appointed by a party shall have resigned without the consent of the Commission or Tribunal of which he was a member, the Chairman shall appoint a person from the appropriate Panel to fill the resulting vacancy.

Article 57

A party may propose to a Commission or Tribunal the disqualification of any of its members on account of any fact indicating a manifest lack of the qualities required by paragraph (1) of Article 14. A party to arbitration proceedings may, in addition, propose the disqualification of an arbitrator on the ground that he was ineligible for appointment to the Tribunal under Section 2 of Chapter IV.

Article 58

The decision on any proposal to disqualify a conciliator or arbitrator shall be taken by the other members of the Commission or Tribunal as the case may be, provided that where those members are equally divided, or in the case of a proposal to disqualify a sole conciliator or arbitrator, or a majority of the conciliators or arbitrators, the Chairman shall take that decision. If it is decided that the proposal is well-founded the conciliator or arbitrator to whom the decision relates shall be replaced in accordance with the provisions of Section 2 of Chapter III or Section 2 of Chapter IV.

CHAPTER VI

COST OF PROCEEDINGS

Article 59

The charges payable by the parties for the use of the facilities of the Centre shall be determined by the Secretary-General in accordance with the regulations adopted by the Administrative Council.

Article 60

(1)   Each Commission and each Tribunal shall determine the fees and expenses of its members within limits established from time to time by the Administrative Council and after consultation with the Secretary-General.

(2)   Nothing in paragraph (1) of this Article shall preclude the parties from agreeing in advance with the Commission or Tribunal concerned upon the fees and expenses of its members.

Article 61

(1) In the case of conciliation proceedings the fees and expenses of members of the Commission as well as the charges for the use of the facilities of the Centre, shall be borne equally by the parties. Each party shall bear any other expenses it incurs in connection with the proceedings.

(2) In the case of arbitration proceedings the Tribunal shall, except as the parties otherwise agree, assess the expenses incurred by the parties in connection with the proceedings, and shall decide how and by whom those expenses, the fees and expenses of the members of the Tribunal and the charges for the use of the facilities of the Centre shall be paid. Such decision shall form part of the award.

CHAPTER VII

PLACE OF PROCEEDINGS

Article 62

Conciliation and arbitration proceedings shall be held at the seat of the Centre except as hereinafter provided.

Article 63

Conciliation and arbitration proceedings may be held, if the parties so agree,
    (a)   at the seat of the Permanent Court of Arbitration or of any other appropriate institution, whether private or public, with which the Centre may make arrangements for that purpose; or
    (b)   at any other place approved by the Commission or Tribunal after consultation with the Secretary-General.

CHAPTER VIII

DISPUTES BETWEEN CONTRACTING STATES

Article 64

Any dispute arising between Contracting States concerning the interpretation or application of this Convention which is not settled by negotiation shall be referred to the International Court of Justice by the application of any party to such dispute, unless the States concerned agree to another method of settlement.

CHAPTER IX

AMENDMENT

Article 65

Any Contracting State may propose amendment of this Convention. The text of a proposed amendment shall be communicated to the Secretary-

General not less than 90 days prior to the meeting of the Administrative Council at which such amendment is to be considered and shall forthwith be transmitted by him to all the members of the Administrative Council.

Article 66

(1) If the Administrative Council shall so decide by a majority of two-thirds of its members, the proposed amendment shall be circulated to all Contracting States for ratification, acceptance or approval. Each amendment shall enter into force 30 days after dispatch by the depositary of this Convention of a notification to Contracting States that all Contracting States have ratified, accepted or approved the amendment.

(2) No amendment shall affect the rights and obligations under this Convention of any Contracting State or of any of its constituent subdivisions or agencies, or of any national of such State arising out of consent to the jurisdiction of the Centre given before the date of entry into force of the amendment.

CHAPTER X

FINAL PROVISIONS

Article 67

This Convention shall be open for signature on behalf of States members of the Bank. It shall also be open for signature on behalf of any other State which is a party to the Statute of the International Court of Justice and which the Administrative Council, by a vote of two-thirds of its members, shall have invited to sign the Convention.

Article 68

(1) This Convention shall be subject to ratification, acceptance or approval by the signatory States in accordance with their respective constitutional procedures.

(2) This Convention shall enter into force 30 days after the date of deposit of the twentieth instrument of ratification, acceptance or approval. It shall enter into force for each State which subsequently deposits its instrument of ratification, acceptance or approval 30 days after the date of such deposit.

Article 69

Each Contracting State shall take such legislative or other measures as may be necessary for making the provisions of this Convention effective in its territories.

Article 70

This Convention shall apply to all territories for whose international relations a Contracting State is responsible, except those which are excluded by such State by written notice to the depositary of this Convention either at the time of ratification, acceptance or approval or subsequently.

Article 71

Any Contracting State may denounce this Convention by written notice to the depositary of this Convention. The denunciation shall take effect six months after receipt of such notice.

Article 72

Notice by a Contracting State pursuant to Article 70 or 71 shall not affect the rights or obligations under this Convention of that State or of any of its constituent subdivisions or agencies or of any national of that State arising out of consent to the jurisdiction of the Centre given by one of them before such notice was received by the depositary.

Article 73

Instruments of ratification, acceptance or approval of this Convention and of amendments thereto shall be deposited with the Bank which shall act as the depositary of this Convention. The depositary shall transmit certified copies of this Convention to States members of the Bank and to any other State invited to sign the Convention.

Article 74

The depositary shall register this Convention with the Secretariat of the United Nations in accordance with Article 102 of the Charter of the United Nations and the Regulations thereunder adopted by the General Assembly.

Article 75

The depositary shall notify all signatory States of the following:
    (a)   signatures in accordance with Article 67;
    (b)   deposits of instruments of ratification, acceptance and approval in accordance with Article 73;
    (c)   the date on which this Convention enters into force in accordance with Article 68;
    (d)   exclusions from territorial application pursuant to Article 70;
    (e)   the date on which any amendment of this Convention enters into force in accordance with Article 66; and
    (f)   denunciations in accordance with Article 71.

DONE at Washington in the English, French and Spanish languages, all three texts being equally authentic, in a single copy which shall remain deposited in the archives of the International Bank for Reconstruction and Development, which has indicated by its signature below its agreement to fulfil the functions with which it is charged under this Convention.
    (Here follow the signatures)

UNCITRAL MODEL LAW ON INTERNATIONAL COMMERCIAL ARBITRATION

UNCITRAL Secretariat
United Nations Commission on International Trade Law
Vienna International Centre,
POB 500
A-1400 WIEN
tel: 00 + 43-1-21 345–4060
fax: 00 + 43-1-21 345–5813

(As adopted by the United Nations Commission on International Trade Law on 21 June 1985.)

CHAPTER I

GENERAL PROVISIONS

Article 1   Scope of application

(1)   This Law applies to international commercial arbitration, subject to any agreement in force between this State and any other State or States.

(2)   The provisions of this Law, except articles 8, 9, 35 and 36, apply only if the place of arbitration is in the territory of this State.

(3)   An arbitration is international if:

(a)   the parties to an arbitration agreement have, at the time of the conclusion of that agreement, their places of business in different States; or

(b)   one of the following places is situated outside the State in which the parties have their places of business:

(i)   the place of arbitration if determined in, or pursuant to, the arbitration agreement;

(ii)   any place where a substantial part of the obligations of the commercial relationship is to be performed or the place with which the subject-matter of the dispute is most closely connected; or

(c)   the parties have expressly agreed that the subject-matter of the arbitration agreement relates to more than one country.

(4)   For the purposes of paragraph (3) of this article:

(a)   if a party has more than one place of business, the place of business is that which has the closest relationship to the arbitration agreement;

(b)   if a party does not have a place of business, reference is to be made to his habitual residence.

(5)   This Law shall not affect any other law of this State by virtue of which certain disputes may not be submitted to arbitration or may be submitted to arbitration only according to provisions other than those of this Law.

Article 2   Definitions and rules of interpretation

For the purposes of this Law:

(a)   'arbitration' means any arbitration whether or not administered by a permanent arbitral institution;

(b) 'arbitral tribunal' means a sole arbitrator or a panel of arbitrators;

(c) 'court' means a body or organ of the judicial system of a State;

(d) where a provision of this Law, except article 28, leaves the parties free to determine a certain issue, such freedom includes the right of the parties to authorize a third party, including an institution, to make that determination;

(e) where a provision of this Law refers to the fact that the parties have agreed or that they may agree or in any other way refers to an agreement of the parties, such agreement includes any arbitration rules referred to in that agreement;

(f) where a provision of this Law, other than in articles 25(a) and 32(2)(a), refers to a claim, it also applies to a counter-claim, and where it refers to a defence, it also applies to a defence to such counter-claim.

Article 3   Receipt of written communications

(1) Unless otherwise agreed by the parties:

(a) any written communication is deemed to have been received if it is delivered to the addressee personally or if it is delivered at his place of business, habitual residence or mailing address; if none of these can be found after making a reasonable inquiry, a written communication is deemed to have been received if it is sent to the addressee's last-known place of business, habitual residence or mailing address by registered letter or any other means which provides a record of the attempt to deliver it;

(b) the communication is deemed to have been received on the day it is so delivered.

(2) The provisions of this article do not apply to communications in court proceedings.

Article 4   Waiver of right to object

A party who knows that any provision of this Law from which the parties may derogate or any requirement under the arbitration agreement has not been complied with and yet proceeds with the arbitration without stating his objection to such non-compliance without undue delay or, if a time-limit is provided therefor, within such period of time, shall be deemed to have waived his right to object.

Article 5   Extent of court intervention

In matters governed by this Law, no court shall intervene except where so provided in this Law.

Article 6   Court or other authority for certain functions of arbitration assistance and supervision

The functions referred to in articles 11(3), 11(4), 13(3), 14, 16(3,) and 34(2) shall be performed by . . . [Each State enacting this model law specifies the court, courts or, where referred to therein, other authority competent to perform these functions.]

CHAPTER II

ARBITRATION AGREEMENT

Article 7   Definition and form of arbitration agreement

(1) 'Arbitration agreement' is an agreement by the parties to submit to arbitration all or certain disputes which have arisen or which may arise between them in respect of a defined legal relationship, whether contractual or not. An arbitration agreement may be in the form of an arbitration clause in a contract or in the form of a separate agreement.

(2) The arbitration agreement shall be in writing. An agreement is in writing if it is contained in a document signed by the parties or in an exchange of letters, telex, telegrams or other means of telecommunication which provide a record of the agreement, or in an exchange of statements of claim and defence in which the existence of an agreement is alleged by one party and not denied by another. The reference in a contract to a document containing an arbitration clause constitutes an arbitration agreement provided that the contract is in writing and the reference is such as to make that clause part of the contract.

Article 8   Arbitration agreement and substantive claim before court

(1) A court before which an action is brought in a matter which is the subject of an arbitration agreement shall, if a party so requests not later than when submitting his first statement on the substance of the dispute, refer the parties to arbitration unless it finds that the agreement is null and void, inoperative or incapable of being performed.

(2) Where an action referred to in paragraph (1) of this article has been brought, arbitral proceedings may nevertheless be commenced or continued, and an award may be made, while the issue is pending before the court.

Article 9   Arbitration agreement and interim measures by court

It is not incompatible with an arbitration agreement for a party to request, before or during arbitral proceedings, from a court an interim measure of protection and for a court to grant such measure.

CHAPTER III

COMPOSITION OF ARBITRAL TRIBUNAL

Article 10   Number of arbitrators

(1) The parties are free to determine the number of arbitrators.
(2) Failing such determination, the number of arbitrators shall be three.

Article 11   Appointment of arbitrators

(1) No person shall be precluded by reason of his nationality from acting as an arbitrator, unless otherwise agreed by the parties.

(2) The parties are free to agree on a procedure of appointing the arbitrator or arbitrators, subject to the provisions of paragraphs (4) and (5) of this article.

(3) Failing such agreement,

(a) in an arbitration with three arbitrators, each party shall appoint one arbitrator, and the two arbitrators thus appointed shall appoint the third arbitrator; if a party fails to appoint the arbitrator within thirty davs of receipt of a request to do so from the other party, or if the two arbitrators fail to agree on the third arbitrator within thirty days of their appointment, the appointment shall be made, upon request of a party, by the court or other authority specified in article 6;

(b) in an arbitration with a sole arbitrator, if the parties are unable to agree on the arbitrator, he shall be appointed, upon request of a party, by the court or other authority specified in article 6.

(4) Where, under an appointment procedure agreed upon by the parties,

(a) a party fails to act as required under such procedure, or

(b) the parties, or two arbitrators, are unable to reach an agreement expected of them under such procedure, or

(c) a third party, including an institution, fails to perform any function entrusted to it under such procedure,

any party may request the court or other authority specified in article 6 to take the necessary measure, unless the agreement on the appointment procedure provides other means for securing the appointment.

(5) A decision on a matter entrusted by paragraph (3) or (4) of this article to the court or other authority specified in article 6 shall be subject to no appeal. The court or other authority, in appointing an arbitrator, shall have due regard to any qualifications required of the arbitrator by the agreement of the parties and to such considerations as are likely to secure the appointment of an independent and impartial arbitrator and, in the case of a sole or third arbitrator shall take into account as well the advisability of appointing an arbitrator of a nationality other than those of the parties.

Article 12   Grounds for challenge

(1) When a person is approached in connection with his possible appointment as an arbitrator, he shall disclose any circumstances likely to give rise to justifiable doubts as to his impartiality or independence. An arbitrator, from the time of his appointment and throughout the arbitral proceedings, shall without delay disclose any such circumstances to the parties unless they have already been informed of them by him.

(2) An arbitrator may be challenged only if circumstances exist that give rise to justifiable doubts as to his impartiality or independence, or if he does not possess qualifications agreed to by the parties. A party may challenge an arbitrator appointed by him, or in whose appointment he has participated, only for reasons of which he becomes aware after the appointment has been made.

Article 13   Challenge procedure

(1) The parties are free to agree on a procedure for challenging an arbitrator, subject to the provisions of paragraph (3) of this article.

(2)   Failing such agreement, a party who intends to challenge an arbitrator shall, within fifteen days after becoming aware of the constitution of the arbitral tribunal or after becoming aware of any circumstance referred to in article 12(2), send a written statement of the reasons for the challenge to the arbitral tribunal. Unless the challenged arbitrator withdraws from his office or the other party agrees to the challenge, the arbitral tribunal shall decide on the challenge.

(3)   If a challenge under any procedure agreed upon by the parties or under the procedure of paragraph (2) of this article is not successful, the challenging party may request, within thirty days after having received notice of the decision rejecting the challenge, the court or other authority specified in article 6 to decide on the challenge, which decision shall be subject to no appeal; while such a request is pending, the arbitral tribunal, including the challenged arbitrator, may continue the arbitral proceedings and make an award.

Article 14   Failure or impossibility to act

(1)   If an arbitrator becomes *de jure* or *de facto* unable to perform his functions or for other reasons fails to act without undue delay, his mandate terminates if he withdraws from his office or if the parties agree on the termination. Otherwise, if a controversy remains concerning any of these grounds, any party may request the court or other authority specified in article 6 to decide on the termination of the mandate, which decision shall be subject to no appeal.

(2)   If, under this article or article 13(2), an arbitrator withdraws from his office or a party agrees to the termination of the mandate of an arbitrator, this does not imply acceptance of the validity of any ground referred to in this article or article 12(2).

Article 15   Appointment of substitute arbitrator

Where the mandate of an arbitrator terminates under article 13 or 14 or because of his withdrawal from office for any other reason or because of the revocation of his mandate by agreement of the parties or in any other case of termination of his mandate, a substitute arbitrator shall be appointed according to the rules that were applicable to the appointment of the arbitrator being replaced.

CHAPTER IV

JURISDICTION OF ARBITRAL TRIBUNAL

Article 16   Competence of arbitral tribunal to rule on its jurisdiction

(1)   The arbitral tribunal may rule on its own jurisdiction, including any objections with respect to the existence or validity of the arbitration agreement. For that purpose, an arbitration clause which forms part of a contract shall be treated as an agreement independent of the other terms of the contract. A decision by the arbitral tribunal that the contract is null and void shall not entail *ipso jure* the invalidity of the arbitration clause.

(2)   A plea that the arbitral tribunal does not have jurisdiction shall be raised not later than the submission of the statement of defence. A party is not precluded from raising such a plea by the fact that he has appointed, or participated in the appointment of, an arbitrator. A plea that the arbitral tribunal is exceeding the scope of its authority shall be raised as soon as the matter alleged to be beyond the scope of its authority is raised during the arbitral proceedings. The arbitral tribunal may, in either case, admit a later plea if it considers the delay justified.

(3)   The arbitral tribunal may rule on a plea referred to in paragraph (2) of this article either as a preliminary question or in an award on the merits. If the arbitral tribunal rules as a preliminary question that it has jurisdiction, any party may request, within thirty days after having received notice of that ruling, the court specified in article 6 to decide the matter, which decision shall be subject to no appeal; while such a request is pending, the arbitral tribunal may continue the arbitral proceedings and make an award.

Article 17   Power of arbitral tribunal to order interim measures

Unless otherwise agreed by the parties, the arbitral tribunal may, at the request of a party, order any party to take such interim measure of protection as the arbitral tribunal may consider necessary in respect of the subject-matter of the dispute. The arbitral tribunal may require any party to provide appropriate security in connection with such measure.

CHAPTER V

CONDUCT OF ARBITRAL PROCEEDINGS

Article 18   Equal treatment of parties

The parties shall be treated with equality and each party shall be given a full opportunity of presenting his case.

Article 19   Determination of rules of procedure

(1)   Subject to the provisions of this Law, the parties are free to agree on the procedure to be followed by the arbitral tribunal in conducting the proceedings.

(2)   Failing such agreement, the arbitral tribunal may, subject to the provisions of this Law, conduct the arbitration in such manner as it considers appropriate. The power conferred upon the arbitral tribunal includes the power to determine the admissibility, relevance, materiality and weight of any evidence.

Article 20   Place of arbitration

(1)   The parties are free to agree on the place of arbitration. Failing such agreement, the place of arbitration shall be determined by the arbitral tribunal having regard to the circumstances of the case, including the convenience of the parties.

(2)   Notwithstanding the provisions of paragraph (1) of this article, the arbitral tribunal may, unless otherwise agreed by the parties, meet at any place it considers appropriate for consultation among its members, for hearing witnesses, experts or the parties, or for inspection of goods, other property or documents.

Article 21   Commencement of arbitral proceedings

Unless otherwise agreed by the parties, the arbitral proceedings in respect of a particular dispute commence on the date on which a request for that dispute to be referred to arbitration is received by the respondent.

Article 22   Language

(1)   The parties are free to agree on the language or languages to be used in the arbitral proceedings. Failing such agreement, the arbitral tribunal shall determine the language or languages to be used in the proceedings. This agreement or determination, unless otherwise specified therein, shall apply to any written statement by a party, any hearing and any award, decision or other communication by the arbitral tribunal.

(2)   The arbitral tribunal may order that any documentary evidence shall be accompanied by a translation into the language or languages agreed upon by the parties or determined by the arbitral tribunal.

Article 23   Statements of claim and defence

(1)   Within the period of time agreed by the parties or determined by the arbitral tribunal, the claimant shall state the facts supporting his claim, the points at issue and the relief of remedy sought, and the respondent shall state his defence in respect of these particulars, unless the parties have otherwise agreed as to the required elements of such statements. The parties may submit with their statements all documents they consider to be relevant or may add a reference to the documents or other evidence they will submit.

(2)   Unless otherwise agreed by the parties, either party may amend or supplement his claim or defence during the course of the arbitral proceedings, unless the arbitral tribunal considers it inappropriate to allow such amendment having regard to the delay in making it.

Article 24   Hearings and written proceedings

(1)   Subject to any contrary agreement by the parties, the arbitral tribunal shall decide whether to hold oral hearings for the presentation of evidence or for oral argument, or whether the proceedings shall be conducted on the basis of documents and other materials. However, unless the parties have agreed that no hearings shall be held, the arbitral tribunal shall hold such hearings at an appropriate stage of the proceedings, if so requested by a party.

(2)   The parties shall be given sufficient advance notice of any hearing and of any meeting of the arbitral tribunal for the purposes of inspection of goods, other property or documents.

(3)   All statements, documents or other information supplied to the arbitral tribunal by one party shall be communicated to the other party. Also

any expert report or evidentiary document on which the arbitral tribunal may rely in making its decision shall be communicated to the parties.

Article 25   Default of a party

Unless otherwise agreed by the parties, if, without showing sufficient cause,

(a)   the claimant fails to communicate his statement of claim in accordance with article 23(1), the arbitral tribunal shall terminate the proceedings;

(b)   the respondent fails to communicate his statement of defence in accordance with article 23(1), the arbitral tribunal shall continue the proceedings without treating such failure in itself as an admission of the claimant's allegations;

(c)   any party fails to appear at a hearing or to produce documentary evidence, the arbitral tribunal may continue the proceedings and make the award on the evidence before it.

Article 26   Expert appointed by arbitral tribunal

(1)   Unless otherwise agreed by the parties, the arbitral tribunal

(a)   may appoint one or more experts to report to it on specific issues to be determined by the arbitral tribunal;

(b)   may require a party to give the expert any relevant information or to produce, or to provide access to, any relevant documents, goods or other property for his inspection.

(2)   Unless otherwise agreed by the parties, if a party so requests or if the arbitral tribunal considers it necessary, the expert shall, after delivery of his written or oral report, participate in a hearing where the parties have the opportunity to put questions to him and to present expert witnesses in order to testify on the points at issue.

Article 27   Court assistance in taking evidence

The arbitral tribunal or a party with the approval of the arbitral tribunal may request from a competent court of this State assistance in taking evidence. The court may execute the request within its competence and according to its rules on taking evidence.

CHAPTER VI

MAKING OF AWARD AND TERMINATION OF PROCEEDINGS

Article 28   Rules applicable to substance of dispute

(1)   The arbitral tribunal shall decide the dispute in accordance with such rules of law as are chosen by the parties as applicable to the substance of the dispute. Any designation of the law or legal system of a given State shall be construed, unless otherwise expressed, as directly referring to the substantive law of that State and not to its conflict of laws rules.

(2)   Failing any designation by the parties, the arbitral tribunal shall apply the law determined by the conflict of laws rules which it considers applicable.

(3)   The arbitral tribunal shall decide *ex aequo et bono* or as *amiable compositeur* only if the parties have expressly authorized it to do so.

(4)   In all cases, the arbitral tribunal shall decide in accordance with the terms of the contract and shall take into account the usages of the trade applicable to the transaction.

Article 29   Decision making by panel of arbitrators

In arbitral proceedings with more than one arbitrator, any decision of the arbitral tribunal shall be made, unless otherwise agreed by the parties, by a majority of all its members. However, questions of procedure may be decided by a presiding arbitrator, if so authorized by the parties or all members of the arbitral tribunal.

Article 30   Settlement

(1)   If, during arbitral proceedings, the parties settle the dispute, the arbitral tribunal shall terminate the proceedings and, if requested by the parties and not objected to by the arbitral tribunal, record the settlement in the form of an arbitral award on agreed terms.

(2)   An award on agreed terms shall be made in accordance with the provisions of article 31 and shall state that it is an award. Such an award has the same status and effect as any other award on the merits of the case.

Article 31   Form and contents of award

(1)   The award shall be made in writing and shall be signed by the arbitrator or arbitrators. In arbitral proceedings with more than one arbitrator, the signatures of the majority of all members of the arbitral tribunal shall suffice, provided that the reason for any omitted signature is stated.

(2)   The award shall state the reasons upon which it is based, unless the parties have agreed that no reasons are to be given or the award is an award on agreed terms under article 30.

(3)   The award shall state its date and the place of arbitration as determined in accordance with article 20(1). The award shall be deemed to have been made at that place.

(4)   After the award is made, a copy signed by the arbitrators in accordance with paragraph (1) of this article shall be delivered to each party.

Article 32   Termination of proceedings

(1)   The arbitral proceedings are terminated by the final award or by an order of the arbitral tribunal in accordance with paragraph (2) of this article.

(2)   The arbitral tribunal shall issue an order for the termination of the arbitral proceedings when:

(a)   the claimant withdraws his claim, unless the respondent objects thereto and the arbitral tribunal recognizes a legitimate interest on his part in obtaining a final settlement of the dispute;

(b)   the parties agree on the termination of the proceedings;

(c)   the arbitral tribunal finds that the continuation of the proceedings has for any other reason become unnecessary or impossible.

(3)   The mandate of the arbitral tribunal terminates with the termination of the arbitral proceedings, subject to the provisions of articles 33 and 34(4).

Article 33   Correction and interpretation of award: additional award

(1)   Within thirty days of receipt of the award, unless another period of time has been agreed upon by the parties:

(a)   a party, with notice to the other party, may request the arbitral tribunal to correct in the award any errors in computation, any clerical or typographical errors or any errors of similar nature;

(b)   if so agreed by the parties, a party, with notice to the other party, may request the arbitral tribunal to give an interpretation of a specific point or part of the award.

If the arbitral tribunal considers the request to be justified, it shall make the correction or give the interpretation within thirty days of receipt of the request. The interpretation shall form part of the award.

(2)   The arbitral tribunal may correct any error of the type referred to in paragraph (1)(a) of this article on its own initiative within thirty days of the date of the award.

(3)   Unless otherwise agreed by the parties, a party, with notice to the other party, may request, within thirty days of receipt of the award, the arbitral tribunal to make an additional award as to claims presented in the arbitral proceedings but omitted from the award. If the arbitral tribunal considers the request to be justified, it shall make the additional award within sixty days.

(4)   The arbitral tribunal may extend, if necessary, the period of time within which it shall make a correction, interpretation or an additional award under paragraph (1) or (3) of this article.

(5)   The provisions of article 31 shall apply to a correction or interpretation of the award or to an additional award.

CHAPTER VII

RECOURSE AGAINST AWARD

Article 34   Application for setting aside as exclusive recourse against arbitral award

(1)   Recourse to a court against an arbitral award may be made only by an application for setting aside in accordance with paragraphs (2) and (3) of this article.

(2)   An arbitral award may be set aside by the court specified in article 6 only if:

(a)   the party making the application furnishes proof that:

(i)   a party to the arbitration agreement referred to in article 7 was under some incapacity; or the said agreement is not valid under the law to which the parties have subjected it or, failing any indication thereon, under the law of this State; or

(ii)   the party making the application was not given proper notice of the appointment of an arbitrator or of the arbitral proceedings or was otherwise unable to present his case; or

(iii)   the award deals with a dispute not contemplated by or not falling within the terms of the submission to arbitration, or contains decisions on matters beyond the scope of the submission to arbitration, provided that, if the decisions on matters submitted to arbitration can be separated from those not so submitted, only that part of the award which contains decisions on matters not submitted to arbitration may be set aside; or

(iv)   the composition of the arbitral tribunal or the arbitral procedure was not in accordance with the agreement of the parties, unless such agreement was in conflict with a provision of this Law from which the parties cannot derogate, or, failing such agreement, was not in accordance with this Law; or

(b)   the court finds that:

(i)   the subject-matter of the dispute is not capable of settlement by arbitration under the law of this State; or

(ii)   the award is in conflict with the public policy of this State.

(3)   An application for setting aside may not be made after three months have elapsed from the date on which the party making that application had received the award or, if a request had been made under article 33, from the date on which that request had been disposed of by the arbitral tribunal.

(4)   The court, when asked to set aside an award, may, where appropriate and so requested by a party, suspend the setting aside proceedings for a period of time determined by it in order to give the arbitral tribunal an opportunity to resume the arbitral proceedings or to take such other action as in the arbitral tribunal's opinion will eliminate the grounds for setting aside.

CHAPTER VIII

RECOGNITION AND ENFORCEMENT OF AWARDS

Article 35   Recognition and enforcement

(1)   An arbitral award, irrespective of the country in which it was made, shall be recognized as binding and, upon application in writing to the competent court, shall be enforced subject to the provisions of this article and of article 36.

(2)   The party relying on an award or applying for its enforcement shall supply the duly authenticated original award or a duly certified copy thereof, and the original arbitration agreement referred to in article 7 or a duly certified copy thereof. If the award or agreement is not made in an official language of this State, the party shall supply a duly certified translation thereof into such language.

Article 36   Grounds for refusing recognition or enforcement

(1)   Recognition or enforcement of an arbitral award, irrespective of the country in which it was made, may be refused only:

(a)   at the request of the part against whom it is invoked, if that party furnishes to the competent court where recognition or enforcement is sought proof that:

(i)   a party to the arbitration agreement referred to in article 7 was under some incapacity; or the said agreement is not valid under the law to which the parties have subjected it or, failing any indication thereon, under the law of the country where the award was made; or;

(ii)   the party against whom the award is invoked was not given proper notice of the appointment of an arbitrator or of the arbitral proceedings or was otherwise unable to present his case; or

(iii)   the award deals with a dispute not contemplated by or not falling within the terms of the submission to arbitration, or it contains decisions on matters beyond the scope of the submission to arbitration, provided that, if the decisions on matters submitted to arbitration can be separated from those not so submitted, that part of the award which contains decisions on matters submitted to arbitration may be recognized and enforced; or

(iv)   the composition of the arbitral tribunal or the arbitral procedure was not in accordance with the agreement of the parties or, failing such agreement, was not in accordance with the law of the country where the arbitration took place; or

(v)   the award has not yet become binding on the parties or has been set aside or suspended by a court of the country in which, or under the law of which, that award was made; or

(b)   if the court finds that:

(i)   the subject-matter of the dispute is not capable of settlement by arbitration under the law of this State; or

(ii)   the recognition or enforcement of the award would be contrary to the public policy of this State.

(2)   If an application for setting aside or suspension of an award has been made to a court referred to in paragraph (1)(a)(v) of this article, the court where recognition or enforcement is sought may, if it considers it proper, adjourn its decision and may also, on the application of the party claiming recognition or enforcement of the award, order the other party to provide appropriate security.

PART VI
RULES

AMERICAN ARBITRATION ASSOCIATION

140 West 51st Street, New York, NY 10020-1203
Tel: 001-212-484-4000
Fax: 001-212-765-4874

INTERNATIONAL ARBITRATION RULES

Article 1

1.   Where parties have agreed in writing to arbitrate disputes under these International Arbitration Rules, the arbitration shall take place in accordance with their provisions, as in effect at the date of commencement of the arbitration, subject to whatever modifications the parties may adopt in writing.
2.   These rules govern the arbitration, except that, where any such rule is in conflict with any provision of the law applicable to the arbitration from which the parties cannot derogate, that provision shall prevail.
3.   These rules specify the duties and responsibilities of the administrator, the American Arbitration Association. The administrator may provide services through its own facilities or through the facilities of arbitral institutions with whom it has agreements of cooperation.

I.   COMMENCING THE ARBITRATION

Notice of Arbitration and Statement of Claim

Article 2

1.   The party initiating arbitration ('claimant') shall give written notice of arbitration to the administrator and to the party or parties against whom a claim is being made ('respondent(s)').
2.   Arbitral proceedings shall be deemed to commence on the date on which the notice of arbitration is received by the administrator.
3.   The notice of arbitration shall include the following:
   (a)   a demand that the dispute be referred to arbitration;
   (b)   the names and addresses of the parties;
   (c)   a reference to the arbitration clause or agreement that is invoked;
   (d)   a reference to any contract out of or in relation to which the dispute arises;
   (e)   a description of the claim and an indication of the facts supporting it;
   (f)   the relief or remedy sought and the amount claimed; and
   (g)   may include proposals as to the number of arbitrators, the place of arbitration and the language(s) of the arbitration.
Upon receipt of such notice, the administrator will communicate with all parties with respect to the arbitration, including the matters set forth in (g) above, if the parties have not already agreed on these matters, and will acknowledge the commencement of the arbitration.

Statement of Defense and Counterclaim

Article 3

1.   Within forty-five days after the date of the commencement of the arbitration, a respondent shall file a statement of defense in writing with the claimant and any other parties, and with the administrator for transmittal to the tribunal when appointed.

2.   At the time a respondent submits its statement of defense, a respondent may make counterclaims or assert set-offs as to any claim covered by the agreement to arbitrate, as to which the claimant shall within forty-five days file a statement of defense.

3.   A respondent shall respond to the administrator, the claimant and other parties within forty-five days as to any proposals the claimant may have made as to the number of arbitrators, the place of the arbitration or the language(s) of the arbitration, except to the extent that the parties have previously agreed as to these matters.

Amendments to Claims

Article 4

During the arbitral proceedings, any party may amend or supplement its claim, counterclaim or defense unless the tribunal considers it inappropriate to allow such amendment because of the party's delay in making it or of prejudice to the other parties or any other circumstances. A claim or counterclaim may not be amended if the amendment would fall outside the scope of the agreement to arbitrate.

II.   THE TRIBUNAL

Number of Arbitrators

Article 5

If the parties have not agreed on the number of arbitrators, one arbitrator shall be appointed unless the administrator determines in its discretion that three arbitrators are appropriate because of the large size, complexity or other circumstances of the case.

Appointment of Arbitrators

Article 6

1.   The parties may mutually agree upon any procedure for appointing arbitrators and shall inform the administrator as to such procedure.

2.   The parties may mutually designate arbitrators, with or without the assistance of the administrator. When such designations are made, the parties shall notify the administrator so that notice of the appointment can be communicated to the arbitrators, together with a copy of these rules.

3.   If within sixty days after the commencement of the arbitration, all of the parties have not mutually agreed on a procedure for appointing the arbitrator(s) or have not mutually agreed on the designation of the arbitrator(s), the administrator shall, at the written request of any party, appoint the arbitrator(s) and designate the presiding arbitrator. If all of the parties have mutually agreed upon a procedure for appointing the arbitrator(s), but all appointments have not been made within the time limits provided in that procedure, the administrator shall, at the written request of any party, perform all functions provided for in that procedure.

4.   In making such appointments, the administrator, after inviting consultation with the parties, shall endeavor to select suitable arbitrators. At the request of any party or on its own initiative, the administrator may appoint nationals of a country other than that of any of the parties.

Challenge of Arbitrators

Article 7

Unless the parties agree otherwise, arbitrators acting under these rules shall be impartial and independent. Prior to accepting appointment, a prospective arbitrator shall disclose to the administrator any circumstance likely to give rise to justifiable doubts as to the arbitrator's impartiality or independence. Once appointed, an arbitrator shall disclose any additional such information to the parties and to the administrator. Upon receipt of such information from an arbitrator or a party, the administrator shall communicate it to the parties and to the arbitrator.

Article 8

1.   A party may challenge any arbitrator whenever circumstances exist that give rise to justifiable doubts as to the arbitrator's impartiality or independence. A party wishing to challenge an arbitrator shall send notice of the challenge to the administrator within fifteen days after being notified of the appointment of the arbitrator, or within fifteen days after the circumstances giving rise to the challenge became known to that party.

2.   The challenge shall state in writing the reasons for the challenge.

3.   Upon receipt of such a challenge, the administrator shall notify the other parties of the challenge. When an arbitrator has been challenged by one party, the other parties may agree to the acceptance of the challenge and, if there is agreement, the arbitrator shall withdraw. The challenged arbitrator may also withdraw from office in the absence of such agreement. In neither case does this imply acceptance of the validity of the grounds for the challenge.

Article 9

If the other party or parties do not agree to the challenge or the challenged arbitrator does not withdraw, the decision on the challenge shall be made by the administrator in its sole discretion.

Replacement of an Arbitrator

Article 10

If an arbitrator withdraws after a challenge, or the administrator sustains the challenge, or the administrator determines that there are sufficient reasons to accept the resignation of an arbitrator, or an arbitrator dies, a substitute arbitrator shall be appointed pursuant to the provisions of Article 6, unless the parties otherwise agree.

Article 11

1. If an arbitrator on a three-person tribunal fails to participate in the arbitration, the two other arbitrators shall have the power in their sole discretion to continue the arbitration and to make any decision, ruling or award, notwithstanding the failure of the third arbitrator to participate. In determining whether to continue the arbitration or to render any decision, ruling or award without the participation of an arbitrator, the two other arbitrators shall take into account the stage of the arbitration, the reason, if any, expressed by the third arbitrator for such nonparticipation, and such other matters as they consider appropriate in the circumstances of the case. In the event that the two other arbitrators determine not to continue the arbitration without the participation of the third arbitrator, the administrator on proof satisfactory to it shall declare the office vacant, and a substitute arbitrator shall be appointed pursuant to the provisions of Article 6, unless the parties otherwise agree.

2. If a substitute arbitrator is appointed, the tribunal shall determine at its sole discretion whether all or part of any prior hearings shall be repeated.

III. GENERAL CONDITIONS

Representation

Article 12

Any party may be represented in the arbitration. The names, addresses and telephone numbers of representatives shall be communicated in writing to the other parties and to the administrator. Once the tribunal has been established, the parties or their representatives may communicate in writing directly with the tribunal.

Place of Arbitration

Article 13

1. If the parties disagree as to the place of arbitration, the place of arbitration may initially be determined by the administrator, subject to the power of the tribunal to determine finally the place of arbitration within sixty days after its constitution. All such determinations shall be made having regard for the contentions of the parties and the circumstances of the arbitration.

2. The tribunal may hold conferences or hear witnesses or inspect property or documents at any place it deems appropriate. The parties shall be given sufficient written notice to enable them to be present at any such proceedings.

Language

Article 14

If the parties have not agreed otherwise, the language(s) of the arbitration shall be that of the documents containing the arbitration agreement, subject to the power of the tribunal to determine otherwise based upon the contentions of the parties and the circumstances of the arbitration. The tribunal may order that any documents delivered in another language shall be accompanied by a translation into such language or languages.

Pleas as to Jurisdiction

Article 15

1. The tribunal shall have the power to rule on its own jurisdiction, including any objections with respect to the existence or validity of the arbitration agreement.

2. The tribunal shall have the power to determine the existence or validity of a contract of which an arbitration clause forms a part. Such an arbitration clause shall be treated as an agreement independent of the other terms of the contract.

3. Objections to the arbitrability of a claim must be raised no later than forty-five days after the commencement of the arbitration and, in respect to a counterclaim, no later than forty-five days after filing the counterclaim.

Conduct of the Arbitration

Article 16

1. Subject to these rules, the tribunal may conduct the arbitration in whatever manner it considers appropriate, provided that the parties are treated with equality and that each party has the right to be heard and is given a fair opportunity to present its case.

2. Documents or information supplied to the tribunal by one party shall at the same time be communicated by that party to the other party or parties.

Further Written Statements

Article 17

The tribunal may decide whether any written statements, in addition to statements of claims and counterclaims and statements of defense, shall be required from the parties or may be presented by them, and shall fix the periods of time for submitting such statements.

Periods of Time

Article 18

The periods of time fixed by the tribunal for the communication of written statements should not exceed forty-five days. However, the tribunal may extend such time limits if it considers such an extension justified.

Notices

Article 19

1.   Unless otherwise agreed by the parties or ordered by the tribunal, all notices, statements and written communications may be served on a party by air mail or air courier addressed to the party or its representative at the last known address or by personal service. Facsimile transmission, telex, telegram, or other written forms of electronic communication may be used to give any such notices, statements or written communications.

2.   For the purpose of calculating a period of time under these rules, such period shall begin to run on the day following the day when a notice, statement or written communication is received. If the last day of such period is an official holiday at the place received, the period is extended until the first business day which follows. Official holidays occurring during the running of the period of time are included in calculating the period.

Evidence

Article 20

1.   Each party shall have the burden of proving the facts relied on to support its claim or defense.

2.   The tribunal may order a party to deliver to the tribunal and to the other parties a summary of the documents and other evidence which that party intends to present in support of its claim, counterclaim or defense.

3.   At any time during the proceedings, the tribunal may order parties to produce other documents, exhibits or other evidence it deems necessary or appropriate.

Hearings

Article 21

1.   The tribunal shall give the parties at least thirty days' advance notice of the date, time and place of the initial oral hearing. The tribunal shall give reasonable notice of subsequent hearings.

2.   At least fifteen days before the hearings, each party shall give the tribunal and the other parties the names and addresses of any witnesses it intends to present, the subject of their testimony and the languages in which such witnesses will give their testimony.

3.   At the request of the tribunal or pursuant to mutual agreement of the parties, the administrator shall make arrangements for the interpretation of oral testimony or for a record of the hearing.

4.   Hearings are private unless the parties agree otherwise or the law provides to the contrary. The tribunal may require any witness or witnesses to retire during the testimony of other witnesses. The tribunal may determine the manner in which witnesses are examined.

5.   Evidence of witnesses may also be presented in the form of written statements signed by them.

6.   The admissibility, relevance, materiality and weight of the evidence offered by any party shall be determined by the tribunal.

Interim Measures of Protection

Article 22

1.   At the request of any party, the tribunal may take whatever interim measures it deems necessary in respect of the subject-matter of the dispute, including measures for the conservation of the goods which are the subject-matter in dispute, such as ordering their deposit with a third person or the sale of perishable goods.

2.   Such interim measures may be taken in the form of an interim award and the tribunal may require security for the costs of such measures.

3.   A request for interim measures addressed by a party to a judicial authority shall not be deemed incompatible with the agreement to arbitrate or a waiver of the right to arbitrate.

Experts

Article 23

1.   The tribunal may appoint one or more independent experts to report to it, in writing, on specific issues designated by the tribunal and communicated to the parties.

2.   The parties shall provide such an expert with any relevant information or produce for inspection any relevant documents or goods that the expert may require. Any dispute between a party and the expert as to the relevance of the requested information or goods shall be referred to the tribunal for decision.

3.   Upon receipt of an expert's report, the tribunal shall send a copy of the report to all parties, who shall be given an opportunity to express, in writing their opinion on the report. A party may examine any document on which the expert has relied in such a report.

4.   At the request of any party, the parties shall be given an opportunity to question the expert at a hearing. At this hearing, parties may present expert witnesses to testify on the points at issue.

Default

Article 24

1.   If a party fails to file a statement of defense within the time established by the tribunal without showing sufficient cause for such failure, as determined by the tribunal, the tribunal may proceed with the arbitration.

2.   If a party, duly notified under these rules, fails to appear at a hearing without showing sufficient cause for such failure, as determined by the tribunal, the tribunal may proceed with the arbitration.

3.   If a party, duly invited to produce evidence, fails to do so within the time established by the tribunal without showing sufficient cause for such failure, as determined by the tribunal, the tribunal may make the award on the evidence before it.

Closure of Hearing

Article 25

1.   After asking the parties if they have any further testimony or evidentiary submissions and upon receiving negative replies or if satisfied that the record is complete, the tribunal may declare the hearings closed.

2.   If it considers it appropriate, on its own motion or upon application of a party, the tribunal may reopen the hearings at any time before the award is made.

Waiver of Rules

Article 26

A party who knows that any provision of the rules or requirement under the rules has not been complied with, but proceeds with the arbitration without promptly stating an objection in writing thereto, shall be deemed to have waived the right to object.

Awards, Decisions and Rulings

Article 27

1.   When there is more than one arbitrator, any award, decision or ruling of the arbitral tribunal shall be made by a majority of the arbitrators.

2.   When the parties or the tribunal so authorize, decisions or rulings on questions of procedure may be made by the presiding arbitrator, subject to revision by the tribunal.

Form and Effect of the Award

Article 28

1.   Awards shall be made in writing, promptly by the tribunal, and shall be final and binding on the parties. The parties undertake to carry out any such award without delay.

2.   The tribunal shall state the reasons upon which the award is based, unless the parties have agreed that no reasons need be given.

3.   An award signed by a majority of the arbitrators shall be sufficient. Where there are three arbitrators and one of them fails to sign, the award shall be accompanied by a statement of whether the third arbitrator was given the

opportunity to sign. The award shall contain the date and the place where the award was made, which shall be the place designated pursuant to Article 13.

4. An award may be made public only with the consent of all parties or as required by law.

5. Copies of the award shall be communicated to the parties by the administrator.

6. If the arbitration law of the country where the award is made requires the award to be filed or registered, the tribunal shall comply with such requirement.

7. In addition to making a final award, the tribunal may make interim, interlocutory, or partial orders and awards.

Applicable Laws

Article 29

1. The tribunal shall apply the substantive law or laws designated by the parties as applicable to the dispute. Failing such a designation by the parties, the tribunal shall apply such law or laws as it determines to be appropriate.

2. In arbitrations involving the application of contracts, the tribunal shall decide in accordance with the terms of the contract and shall take into account usages of the trade applicable to the contract.

3. The tribunal shall not decide as *amiable compositeur* or *ex aequo et bono* unless the parties have expressly authorized it to do so.

Settlement or Other Reasons for Termination

Article 30

1. If the parties settle the dispute before an award is made, the tribunal shall terminate the arbitration and, if requested by all parties, may record the settlement in the form of an award on agreed terms. The tribunal is not obliged to give reasons for such an award.

2. If the continuation of the proceedings becomes unnecessary or impossible for any other reason, the tribunal shall inform the parties of its intention to terminate the proceedings. The tribunal shall there after issue an order terminating the arbitration, unless a party raises justifiable grounds for objection.

Interpretation or Correction of the Award

Article 31

1. Within thirty days after the receipt of an award, any party, with notice to the other parties, may request the tribunal to interpret the award or correct any clerical, typographical or computation errors or make an additional award as to claims presented but omitted from the award.

2. If the tribunal considers such a request justified, after considering the contentions of the parties, it shall comply with such a request within thirty days after the request.

Costs

Article 32

The tribunal shall fix the costs of arbitration in its award. The tribunal may apportion such costs among the parties if it determines that such apportionment is reasonable, taking into account the circumstances of the case. Such costs may include:

    (a)   the fees and expenses of the arbitrators;

    (b)   the costs of assistance required by the tribunal, including its experts;

    (c)   the fees and expenses of the administrator;

    (d)   the reasonable costs for legal representation of a successful party.

Compensation of Arbitrators

Article 33

Arbitrators shall be compensated based upon their amount of service, taking into account the size and complexity of the case. An appropriate daily or hourly rate, based on such considerations, shall be arranged by the administrator with the parties and the arbitrators prior to the commencement of the arbitration. If the parties fail to agree on the terms of compensation, an appropriate rate shall be established by the administrator and communicated in writing to the parties.

Deposit of Costs

Article 34

1.   When claims are filed, the administrator may request the filing party to deposit appropriate amounts, as an advance for the costs referred to in Article 32, paragraphs (a), (b) and (c).

2.   During the course of the arbitral proceedings, the tribunal may request supplementary deposits from the parties.

3.   If the deposits requested are not paid in full within thirty days after the receipt of the request, the administrator shall so inform the parties, in order that one or the other of them may make the required payment. If such payments are not made, the tribunal may order the suspension or termination of the proceedings.

4.   After the award has been made, the administrator shall render an accounting to the parties of the deposits received and return any unexpended balance to the parties.

Confidentiality

Article 35

Confidential information disclosed during the proceedings by the parties or by witnesses shall not be divulged by an arbitrator or by the administrator. Unless otherwise agreed by the parties, or required by applicable law, the members of the tribunal and the administrator shall keep confidential all matters relating to the arbitration or the award.

Exclusion of Liability

Article 36

The members of the tribunal and the administrator shall not be liable to any party for any act or omission in connection with any arbitration conducted under these rules.

Interpretation of Rules

Article 37

The tribunal shall interpret and apply these rules insofar as they relate to its powers and duties. All other rules shall be interpreted and applied by the administrator.

CAREN
COUR D'ARBITRAGE

SECRETARIAT ADMINISTRATIF:
8, rue d'Angleterre
59800 LILLE (FRANCE]
Tel. 0033-3-20.31.91.42
Fax: 0033-3-20065161

Draft Arbitration Agreements

Draft A

Note: It should be noted that the following clause is only enforceable under *French law* if entered into between French parties who are 'commerçants', or shareholders in a limited company which carries on a business coming within the category of 'commerce', or under certain of the French Codes. On the other hand this clause is always enforceable in France when the contract involves a French party and one resident in another country.

English law does not restrict the groups of persons which can enter into such an agreement.

'The parties hereby agree that any dispute arising from or out of the present contract shall be settled by arbitration under the supervision of CAREN'.

or

'The parties hereby agree that all disputes relating to the interpretation or execution of all future contracts and business dealings between them shall be settled by arbitration under the supervision of CAREN'.

Draft B

Note: An agreement of this nature may be entered into where two or more persons involved in a dispute agree to have the matter resolved by arbitration.

Under *French law* any person may enter into an agreement of this nature so long as they are of age and of full mental capacity. The matter in dispute is not restricted save in certain prescribed areas of public interest and where the status of the individual is in issue.

Article 1450 of the French Civil Code provides that even though proceedings have been instituted in the courts an agreement can subsequently be entered into for the matter to be resolved by arbitration.

Under *English law* parties who have the ability to enter into contractual obligations can also agree that disputes arising therefrom be settled by arbitration.

Agreement to arbitrate

This agreement is made the   day of   19

between

                                          (The Claimant)

and

                                          (The Respondent)

WHEREAS:

A dispute has arisen between the parties hereto relative to the following points:
(Here summarise the matters in issue).

The parties have agreed to go to arbitration for the matter to be decided under the CAREN rules.

NOW THIS AGREEMENT WITNESSES

    1.   The Claimant appoints as arbitrator :

The Respondent appoints as Arbitrator :

CAREN shall nominate and appoint the third arbitrator to chair the tribunal.

(Alternatively)

The parties jointly appoint

as sole arbitrator subject to the approval of his appointment by CAREN.

    2.   The arbitrator(s) shall be required to answer the points of claim set out in the claim and reply.

3.   (Optional) The arbitrator (s) may act in the role of Amiable compositeur (ex aequo et bono).

4.   The awards shall be made within (   ) months of the date hereof.

5.   Either party may lodge this agreement with CAREN at any of the addresses shown hereafter whereupon CAREN shall be empowered to deal with the matter.

SIGNED by the Parties in (   ) copies (one for each party and one copy for CAREN).

CAREN
ARBITRATION RULES

PART I

INITIAL CONSIDERATIONS

Clause   1   These rules apply when CAREN has been appointed following an arbitration clause in a contract or an agreement to arbitrate.

CAREN is responsible for the organisation of those arbitrations both national and international that are entrusted to it.

A CAREN Arbitration Committee is responsible for the organisation and supervision of arbitrations carried out under CAREN's jurisdiction. A Secretariat exists which acts as clerk for the arbitration and also provides support for the Arbitration Committee.

Definitions

Clause   1.1   'Arbitration Committee' or 'Committee' means the Arbitration Committee referred to above.

'Arbitration Agreement' means the agreement whereby CAREN is given jurisdiction whether by way of an arbitration clause or by agreement to arbitrate.

'Tribunal' is the the Arbitrator(s) appointed under the CAREN rules.

Time limits

Clause   1.2   The time limits mentioned in these rules are in months. Time expires at midnight on the day of the final month being the same numbered day of the month as the event decision or service causing time to run. In the event that the final month lacks the same numbered day of the month time will run out on the last day of that month.

Time that would normally expire on a public holiday or a non-working day is extended until the first working day thereafter.

Time runs in the case of giving a notice from the date on which that notice was sent.

Domicile

From the time when the mission statement referred to in Clause 16 hereof has been registered with the secretariat the parties' domicile is as set out therein.

Manner of Service

Clause 1.4 All notices or correspondence that are required under these rules to be effected by the committee or the parties must be effected by registered post with receipt or by such procedure as may be the equivalent in the country to which the correspondence is being sent by post or by any means whereby there is written proof of a document having been sent and received. The parties must use the most rapid means of communication possible.

PART II

APPOINTMENT OF CAREN AS ARBITRATOR

Request for arbitration

Clause 2 The parties themselves are responsible for bringing a matter to arbitration. They are also at liberty to bring that appointment to an end before it naturally determines as a result of the Award being made.

Arbitration proceedings are initiated by a request to arbitrate sent to the secretariat who will date it and record that it has been registered.

The request must include:—

The family name, personal name, title and address of the party making the request and where appropriate all details necessary to identify a body corporate and the names, christian names and offices held by the officers acting in the company's name;

The agreement to arbitrate;

A summary of the dispute;

The claimants submission;

Any submission as to the number of arbitrators and the manner by which they are to be chosen.

Inadmissible request for arbitration

Clause 3 When the request for arbitration is defective, either because of the nature of the claim or as a result of the drafting, and as a result the request fails to establish the existence of an agreement to arbitrate between the parties or the jurisdiction of CAREN, the secretariat will ask the respondent for its observations.

If the respondent objects to CAREN's jurisdiction or does not reply within one month of receipt of the request for its observation, the secretariat will advise the claimant that, in the circumstances, arbitration cannot take place.

The Arbitration Committee will give a ruling on all such problems.

Service of notice upon the defendant

Clause 4 When the request for arbitration appears to be in order, the secretariat will send one copy of the request and the documents accompanying it to the defendant. Using the language of the arbitration clause or agreement the notice will also make reference in the clearest terms to the provisions of Clause 6 hereof.

Respondents reply

Clause 5 Within one month of receipt of this information the respondent shall notify the secretariat of its requirements regarding the number of arbitrators and the manner of their choice. Should it be the case that it accepts the proposal set out in the request, it may, if need be, appoint an arbitrator. The respondent shall briefly set out the grounds for opposing the claimants case. It may disclose its documents or raise a counterclaim. The secretariat will advise the Claimant of the Respondent's reply.

Failure of respondent to reply

Clause 6 Arbitration may proceed and an award may be made despite the objection or non-participation of the respondent.

Before the Arbitration Proceedings begin, the arbitrator will satisfy himself that service has been properly effected upon the respondent.

PART III

CONSTITUTION OF THE ARBITRATION TRIBUNAL

Number of arbitrators

Clause 7 Arbitration can be by one or three arbitrators.

In the following Clauses the expression nominated arbitrator or the nomination of an arbitrator applies both to an nomination of an arbitrator by one of the parties or by the Arbitration Committee.

Appointed arbitrator or the appointment of an arbitrator refers to an arbitrator who has accepted to act as such.

Enrolled Arbitrator means a person enrolled on the list of CAREN Arbitrators. The jurisdiction of CAREN is deemed to begin once the last of the arbitrators has been appointed and has accepted to act as such.

Appointment of arbitrators

Clause 8-1 When the parties have agreed that the matter shall be decided by a sole arbitrator they may by agreement appoint an arbitrator and ask the Committee to confirm such appointment. In the absence of agreement, the arbitrator will be appointed by the Arbitrations Committee after the expiry of one month from the date of notification of the request for arbitration to the respondent.

Clause 8-2 When three arbitrators are to be appointed, each party in the request for arbitration, or in the reply thereto, shall nominate an arbitrator for confirmation by the Committee.

Should one of the parties fail to do so, that appointment shall be made by the Committee.

Where there is more than one Respondent or Claimant, the individuals making up the party shall come to agreement for an nomination of their arbitrator.

In default of agreement, an abitrator will be appointed by the Committee.

The third arbitrator who shall be chairperson, is appointed by the Committee unless the parties agreed that the arbitrators they have nominated shall choose the third arbitrator within a fixed period of time. In this case, the Committee will approved the appointment of the third arbitrator.

The third arbitrator will be appointed by the Committee in the event that, at the expiry of the time limits fixed by the parties or imposed by the Court, the arbitrators nominated by the parties have not been able to agree on an appointment.

Clause 8-3 Where the arbitration agreement does not specify the number of arbitrators, the Tribunal shall consist of one arbitrator unless the matters in issue appear to the Arbitration Committee to justify the appointment of three arbitrators. The parties shall, within one month of the service of the request for arbitration, take steps to nominate the arbitrator(s). The Arbitration Committee shall appoint the arbitrators in default of agreement between parties.

Approval of arbitrators

Clause 9 When the nomination of an arbitrator is not effected by the Arbitration Committee, the arbitrator must be approved by the Arbitration Committee. In the event that the Committee do not approve, it must propose a new arbitrator and submit the arbitrator's name for approval by the party whose nominee was not approved.

In the event that the party concerned does not accept the new nominee within one month of nomination, the Committee will appoint an arbitrator from the CAREN list of arbitrators.

Acceptance of office of arbitrator

Clause 10 The arbitrator shall accept the appointment in writing the secretariat. By accepting, the arbitrator agrees to act throughout the matter in its entirety. Notification of appointment of the arbitrator shall be made to all those who did not nominate the arbitrator in question.

Challenging and dismissal of arbitrators

Clause 11 Arbitrators must remain independent and impartial throughout. Any arbitrator nominated who believes that there may be a reason for his admissibility to be challenged must notify the parties and the secretariat. In this case, he can only accept appointments with the agreement of the parties. The arbitrator once appointed shall refrain from such acts as shall in the eyes of the parties raise doubts as to his independence or to his impartiality. Should such circumstances arise after the arbitrator has accepted to act he shall immediately notify the arbitration committee.

Any party can require the Arbitration Committee to take steps to challenge an arbitrators appointment. The request shall be sent to the secretariat within one month of notification of the appointment of the arbitrator or within one month of the occurrence of the event or disclosure of the information or fact relied upon as the reason for the challenge. The time limits are strict and must be complied with if a valid request is to be made.

The Arbitration Committee has an inherent power to object to an arbitrator who has been appointed when his independence or his impartiality appear to be in doubt or have been discovered after his appointment. It has a further inherent jurisdiction to cancel the appointment of an arbitrator who is not complying with the terms of his appointment and who fails to ensure that the arbitration is completed within a reasonable time. The Committee shall give its decision after hearing the arbitrator concerned, the parties to the arbitration and, if the need be and is believed that the same may be of relevance, the other arbitrators.

When withdrawal or the cancellation of an appointment of an arbitrator occurs, the Arbitration Committee will take steps to replace him. The Committee will propose the name of a new arbitrator for the agreement of the parties. In the event of failure of the parties to agree within one month, the Committee will appoint an arbitrator from the approved list.

Replacement of arbitrators

Clause 12 Where unforeseen circumstances prevent an arbitrator from fulfilling his role, the Committee may give notice in writing to this effect and seek a solution with the agreement of the parties. Should agreement not be reached within one month of the date of the said circumstances or their becoming known, the Committee shall appoint an arbitrator from the approved list.

Failure to appoint arbitrators within time limits

Clause 13 If the arbitrator(s) has/have not been appointed within the three months of the date on which the request for arbitration was served upon the respondent and, when the arbitration is taking place in France or where the parties thereto have consented to French procedural law applying, either party may apply for such appointment to be made by summons to the President of the Tribunal de Grande Instance (of Lille) (High Court) (in Lille). That same party shall serve a copy of the summons and the Court's decision upon the secretariat.

PART IV

THE HEARING

A. Place of Hearing

Clause 14 Unless the parties decide otherwise, the hearing shall take place in Lille (France). Nevertheless, the Committee may decide on another venue in view of the circumstances of the case.

B.   Language of Arbitration

Clause   15   If the parties have not chosen the applicable language this will be fixed by the Court taking into account the circumstances of the case and the language of the Contract.

C.   Procedure for the Hearing

Statement of facts/mission statement

Clause   16   As soon as the Tribunal has been established and the matters in issue have been set out by the statements of the parties that follow the request for arbitration and the Respondent's reply, the Tribunal will set out a statement of the issues in question which will contain but not exclusively:

Identification of the parties and of the arbitrators.

Whether the arbitration is international or internal.

The address and country of residence chosen by the parties for the purpose of the proceedings.

Identifying the matter in issue.

Setting out such matters as may be relevant to the choice of law and of procedure and, if the case may be, the giving of power to the Tribunal to act as mediator in accordance with clauses 21, 29 and 30 hereof.

Indicating the place where the arbitration shall take place.

The language for the arbitration.

Setting up the time limits for discovery of documents and schedules of evidence.

Setting out the time limits applicable under the two first paragraphs of clause 26 for the making of the award.

Nature of the mission statement

Clause   17   The statement shall be signed by the arbitrators and by the parties to the arbitration. If one party refuses to sign the tribunal shall draw attention to this refusal, the reasons which have brought about such refusal and the reasons given for such refusal.

Once the statement has been signed or, if the case may be, endorsed with the conditions mentioned in the proceeding paragraph, the statement should be dated and sent to the secretariat for the matter to be listed.

Validity of the arbitration agreement

Clause   18   The Tribunal is empowered to give a ruling, either at the request of a party or of its inherent jurisdiction, upon the existence or the validity of the agreement or its own jurisdiction.

Amendments to the subject matter in issue

Clause   19   Amendments are permitted during the course of the arbitration to include related matters that the Tribunal regards as being linked to the original dispute.

When the Tribunal accepts the amendments, it will issue a supplemental statement in order that the matters in issue are clearly set out. The provisions of clause 17 apply to the amended statement.

Joinder of arbitrations

Clause 20 A party may apply to the Arbitration Committee for the case to be joined with other cases, where such a link exists between the cases, that the proper administration of justice requires joinder.

If joinder is ordered on matters which are in the same arbitral jurisdiction, then, by virtue of the order, the Tribunal's jurisdiction is extended to cover all the cases.

If joinder is ordered where more than one jurisdiction is involved, the order for joinder shall establish a Tribunal consisting of three arbitrators. The two arbitrators or the two chairmen of the arbitration bodies involved shall appoint a third arbitrator from the approved list.

In the event that it proves impossible to appoint the third arbitrator within one month of the order, the order shall lapse.

Rules of procedure

Clause 21 Rules of procedure shall be in accordance with the law applicable chosen by the parties and in default of such choice with the Tribunal's own rules.

When arbitration questions a country's commercial interests, the procedure is subject to these rules whenever there is no conflict with the law of that country.

Clause 22 The hearings shall be in private unless the parties agree to the contrary.

Clause 23 The arbitration Tribunal shall with the agreement of the parties, have power to decline to receive oral evidence or oral admissions whether generally or in respect of such matter as he/they may specify and to make their determination on the basis of written submissions only.

Presence of the parties

Clause 24 The Tribunal shall, in all circumstances, follow the principles and ensure that the other parties follow the principle of the right to be heard. No party can be forced to take part in arbitration proceedings without having been heard or properly summoned thereto.

The Tribunal may request that parties provide explanations of facts pleaded in the matter as well as explanations of the law applicable which the Tribunal considers necessary for the dispute to be resolved.

The parties shall notify each other of the evidence upon which they propose to rely to base their claims, and the documents upon which they will rely and intend to produce and the precedents and legal arguments upon which they will rely in order that each one of them can properly prepare their case for the hearing.

From the date upon which the arbitration has been requested, all communications between the parties should be made via the secretariat or directly but with a copy to the secretariat.

From the moment of the commencement of the arbitration, written notices shall be served upon parties at the address given by them in the mission statement.

Means of investigation

Clause 25 The Tribunal may order at a request of a party any admissible investigation and, in particular, it may appoint any person of its choice to clarify a question of fact which requires explanation by an expert.

The Tribunal can also visit sites and take evidence from parties agreeing thereto.

If one party refuses to attend for a joint meeting with the other party the Tribunal may draw from the refusal all necessary conclusions.

No investigation will be ordered under this clause to make up for a failure in preparing its case by the party who makes the request.

The Tribunal will restrict such investigations to those that are sufficient in order to resolve the dispute between the parties, endeavouring to limit the same to those that are the most simple and the least burdensome.

Time limit for the award

Clause 26 The Arbitration clause or agreement will impose upon the Tribunal the time limits within which it must deliver its award.

In default of a time limit being fixed, the arbitration shall not last longer than six months from the date upon which the last of the arbitrators accepts his appointment.

The Tribunal may, with the approval of the Committee, or of its inherent jurisdiction, extend the time limit under the agreement or the rules for a period of three months. Such an extension is only permitted once.

The time limits under the Contract or the rules may nevertheless always be extended for an unlimited time with the agreement of the parties.

A party or the Tribunal may always request the Committee to extend the agreed time limits for a limited period. The Committee may grant such requests upon giving reasons if it is satisfied that, for reasons not attributable to the arbitrators, the termination of the arbitration proceedings has been delayed.

D. Interim and Protective Orders

Clause 27 Any party may request the tribunal to make interim orders that may be found necessary concerning the subject matter of the dispute. The tribunal may require security for the costs incurred by such interlocutory applications.

Clause 28 The terms of the previous clause nevertheless shall not prevent a party applying to the appropriate judicial authorities for interim or protective orders either before the matter has been submitted to the tribunal or in exceptional circumstances when extremely urgent during the course of the hearing. However, an interim payment shall not be the subject of a request to the judicial authorities once the tribunal has been seised of the matter.

PART V

THE AWARD

A decision ex aequo et bono

Clause 29 The Tribunal may give its ruling as *amiable compositeur* if the arbitration agreement or subsequent agreement between the parties entitles it so to act.

Applicable law

Clause 30 Where the subject matter of an arbitration involves business dealings within one jurisdiction the applicable law is that of the said country.

Where the arbitration is international the tribunal will decide the issues in accordance with the law chosen by the parties. In default of such choice the tribunal will decide the applicable law under which to decide the issues.

The tribunal will take note in all cases of the practices usual in any particular trade.

Settlement

Clause 31 Throughout the arbitration proceedings the parties may, either of their own initiative or at that of the tribunal, reach an agreement on all or part of the matters in dispute.

The nature of the agreement even if it relates to part only of the matters in dispute shall be set out in a signed document and transmitted without delay to the tribunal. The arbitrators may sign this formal document. The tribunal may at the request of the parties make an award based on the agreement between the parties. Clauses 34 and 35 hereof shall apply to such an award.

The award

Clause 32 The tribunal can give final awards as well as interim interlocutory awards limited in their scope.

Such awards are made in writing and shall contain reasons even when the tribunal gives a ruling in its capacity as mediator.

The tribunal may order its award to be implemented forthwith. The parties undertake to comply with the award immediately and to act in good faith expressly agreeing not to follow other courses of action.

Clause 33 When an award is made by three arbitrators it is a majority decision. In the event that no majority can be obtained (i.e. a tie) the Chair of the tribunal alone will make the award having advised the committee of the reasons that required him to do so.

Draft award

Clause 34 The draft award must be signed by the arbitrators and then forwarded to the committee for their endorsement.

The committee may recommend alterations of a presentational nature. It may also draw the attention of the arbitrators to matters of content.

When the committee's approval has been endorsed upon an award which has not yet been signed by each of the arbitrators the absence of such signature shall be noted.

Contents of the award

Clause 35 The award shall have endorsed thereon the date and place where it was given, the name of the arbitrators concerned, the name surname and titles of the parties concerned as well as their address or registered office and if appropriate the names of the lawyers or all other persons who represented or assisted the parties.

The award is then signed by the arbitrators.

It shall not disclose whether the decision was unanimous, by a majority or decided on the Chair's casting vote. Any dissenting decision shall not be set out in the award nor annexed thereto.

Confidentiality

Clause 36 The award is secret and shall not be published without the agreement of the parties. CAREN may publish details of decisions made in arbitrations effected under its aegis. Such summaries shall maintain the anonymity of the parties and will only reveal those facts which may be necessary for an understanding of the matter and of the decision which was reached.

Rectification and correction of material errors on appreciation of the facts and for increase or reduction of quantum of the award

Clause 37 The award brings to an end the tribunal's role in the dispute which it was asked to decide.

However the tribunal may upon formal request made by any party be asked to decide matters of interpretation, correction of material error in order that the award may be finalised or to reinforce it if the tribunal has failed to make a decision on every matter put before it or if it has gone beyond the limit of that which it was required to decide. The tribunal will give reasons after having heard the parties.

The remedies set out in the preceding paragraph shall only be admissible within six months of the date of the award. Material errors and omissions can also be corrected by the tribunal of its inherent jurisdiction the parties having been heard or summoned to make representations.

Should it prove impossible to assemble the same tribunal reference must be made to the provisions of clause 12 hereof.

The provisions of Clauses 34 and 35 hereof apply also to the interpretative and corrective decisions. Such decisions shall require endorsement by the committee and be registered with the secretary who shall place them with the original award.

PART VI

COSTS AND FEES

Clause 38 An administration fee for the arbitration and the fees of the arbitrators is chargeable in accordance with the CAREN scale of fees annexed.

When the amount in question has to be evaluated this is done by the committee as soon as possible after the date of filing the mission statement by the secretariat.

When the parties do not wish to reveal the value of the matters at stake the costs and fees are left entirely to the discretion of the committee.

The committee can reduce the amounts which would apply if the scale were used.

The committee can increase the amount of the costs for administration when in the course of the proceedings addditional matters have arisen which justify an increase.

In exceptional cases and for good reasons given, the committee can increase the fees paid to the arbitrator.

Clause 39 The secretariat or in the event of complexity the committee can fix the amount and the date of payment of the deposit on account of costs and fees. The amount payable shall be divided equally between the parties. If one or other of the parties fail to make payment the claimant is responsible for the payment of the amounts unpaid from the date of a request sent by the secretariat.

The tribunal can also request a deposit on account of its fees from the time when the same have been fixed by the committee. In addition the tribunal can request payment of personal expenses incurred by the arbitrators once they have been approved by the committee.

PART VII

CONCLUSION

Date of applicability of these rules

Clause 40 These rules shall come into force on the 1st day of January 1995 and apply to all requests for arbitration registered with the secretariat from that date.

All amendments to these rules approved before registration of a request for arbitration by the secretariat under Clause 2 hereof shall apply to arbitrations registered thereafter.

The arbitrators are responsible for ensuring that their decisions under these rules do not conflict with the substantive law applicable to the arbitration in question.

Supremacy of French version

Clause 41 These rules are intended to be translated into several languages. In the event of differences of interpretation the French text shall be final.

CHARTERED INSTITUTE OF ARBITRATORS

© **The Chartered Institute of Arbitrators**

International Arbitration Centre
24 Angel Gate
City Road
London EC1V 2RS
Tel: 0044–171–837 4483
Fax: 0044–0171–837 4185

ARBITRATION RULES 1988

These Rules are published by the Chartered Institute of Arbitrators, to help parties and arbitrators take maximum advantage of the flexible procedures available in arbitration for the resolution of disputes quickly and economically. The Rules provide that the wishes of the parties regarding procedure will be respected so far as possible, but they also seek to ensure that the Arbitrator will have sufficient powers to direct the proceedings if the parties cannot agree on procedure or will not cooperate. The Rules may be used without reference to the Institute (unless the Institute is required to act as Appointing Authority in accordance with Article 2.1).

The Arbitration Rules of the Chartered Institute of Arbitrators are not intended for use in arbitrations relating to international contracts or disputes (i.e. where the parties come from different countries). In such cases, reference should be made to the Rules of the London Court of International Arbitration.

SUGGESTED CLAUSES

1. Parties to a contract who wish to have any *future* disputes referred to arbitration under the Rules of the Chartered Institute of Arbitrators may insert in the contract an arbitration clause in the following form:

Any dispute arising out of or in connection with this contract shall be referred to and finally resolved by arbitration under the Rules of the Chartered Institute of Arbitrators, which Rules are deemed to be incorporated by reference into this clause.

2. Parties to an *existing* dispute who wish to refer it to arbitration under the Rules of the Chartered Institute of Arbitrators may agree to do so in the following terms:

We, the undersigned, agree to refer to arbitration under the Rules of the Chartered Institute of Arbitrators the following dispute which has arisen between us:
(Brief description of matters to be referred to arbitration)

Signed_____(Claimant)

Signed_____(Respondent)

Date_____

3.   Where the Rules of the Chartered Institute of Arbitrators apply:
   (a)   The parties may if they wish specify an Appointing Authority to appoint the arbitrator (or arbitrators) if the parties fail to do so or cannot agree. If no Appointing Authority is specified, then the Rules provide the ·President or a Vice-President for the time being of the Chartered Institute of Arbitrators will act as Appointing Authority. The following provision may be suitable if some other Appointing Authority is required:

   The Appointing Authority shall be (name of institution or person).

   (b)   The Rules provide a sole arbitrator will be appointed unless the parties agree otherwise. If the parties wish to specify a three-man tribunal, the following provision may be suitable:

   The arbitral tribunal shall consist of three arbitrators one of whom shall be appointed by each party and the third by the Appointing Authority.

CHARTERED INSTITUTE OF ARBITRATORS ARBITRATION RULES

adopted to take effect from 1 January 1988

Where any agreement, submission or reference provides for arbitration under the Rules of the Chartered Institute of Arbitrators, the parties shall be taken to have agreed that the arbitration shall be conducted in accordance with the following Rules, or such amended Rules as the Chartered Institute of Arbitrators may have adopted to take effect, before the commencement of the arbitration.

Article 1   Commencement of Arbitration

1.1   Any party wishing to commence an arbitration under these rules ('the Claimant') shall send to the other party ('the Respondent') a written request for arbitration ('the Request') which shall include, or be accompanied by:
   (a)   the names and addresses of the parties to the arbitration;
   (b)   copies of the contractual documents in which the arbitration clause is contained or under which the arbitration arises;

(c) a brief statement describing the nature and circumstances of the dispute, and specifying the relief claimed;

(d) a statement of any matters (such as the Appointing Authority, the number of arbitrators, or their qualifications or identities) with respect to which the requesting party wishes to make a proposal;

(e) if the arbitration agreement calls for each party to appoint an arbitrator, the name and address (and telephone, telex and fax numbers, if known) of the arbitrator appointed by the Claimant.

The arbitration shall be deemed to commence on the date of receipt by the Respondent of the Request for Arbitration.

1.2   For the purpose of facilitating the choice of arbitrators, within 30 days of receipt of Request for Arbitration, the Respondent may send to the Claimant a Response containing:

(a) confirmation or denial of all or part of the claims;

(b) a brief statement of the nature and circumstances of any envisaged counterclaims;

(c) comment (including confirmation of agreement) in response to any proposals contained in the Request, as called for under Article 1.1(d), on matters relating to the conduct of the arbitration;

(d) if the arbitration agreement calls for each party to appoint an arbitrator, the name and address (and telephone, telex and fax numbers if known) of the arbitrator appointed by the Respondent.

1.3   Failure to send a Response shall not preclude the Respondent from denying the claim nor from setting out a counterclaim in its Statement of Defence. However, if the arbitration agreement calls for each party to appoint an arbitrator, failure to send a Response or to name an appointed arbitrator in it within the time specified in Article 1.2 shall constitute a waiver of the right to appoint an arbitrator.

Article 2   Appointing Authority

2.1   The parties may agree to nominate an Appointing Authority. Failing such nomination the Appointing Authority shall be the President or a Vice-President for the time being of the Chartered Institute of Arbitrators.

2.2   Any application to the Appointing Authority to act in accordance with these Rules shall be accompanied by:

(a) Copies of the Request and Response and any other related correspondence;

(b) Confirmation that a copy of the application has been received by the other party;

(c) Particulars of any method or criteria of selection of arbitrators agreed by the parties.

The Appointing Authority may require payment of a fee for its services.

Article 3   Appointment of Arbitrator

3.1   Provided that the final number is uneven, the parties may agree on the number of arbitrators in the Tribunal. Failing such agreement there shall be a sole arbitrator. In these Rules, the expression 'the Arbitrator' includes a sole arbitrator or all the arbitrators where more than one is appointed.

3.2   The Arbitrator shall be and remain at all times wholly independent and impartial, and shall not act as advocate for any party. Before appointment if so requested by either party or the Appointing Authority any proposed arbitrator shall furnish a resume of his past and present professional activities (which will be communicated to the parties). In any event any arbitrator if so requested by either party or the Appointing Authority shall sign a declaration to the effect that there are no circumstances likely to give rise to any justified doubts as to his impartiality or independence, and that he will forthwith disclose any such circumstances to the parties if they should arise after that time and before the arbitration is concluded.

3.3   The Arbitrator may be appointed by agreement of the parties. Failing such agreement within 30 days of the commencement of the arbitration in accordance with Article 1, the Arbitrator shall upon the application of either party be appointed by the Appointing Authority.

3.4   Where the parties have agreed there shall be three arbitrators, they may also agree that each party shall appoint an arbitrator. If either party fails to make and notify the other party of such appointment within 30 days of the commencement of the arbitration under Article 1, that appointment shall be made by the Appointing Authority.

3.5   Where the parties have agreed that each shall appoint an arbitrator then, unless otherwise agreed by the parties, a third arbitrator shall be appointed by the Appointing Authority.

3.6   Where there are three or more arbitrators, they may agree who shall act as Chairman of the arbitral tribunal. Failing such agreement the Chairman shall be designated by the Appointing Authority.

3.7   If any arbitrator, after appointment, dies, is unable to act, or refuses to act, the Appointing Authority will, upon request by a party or by the remaining arbitrators, appoint another arbitrator.

Article 4   Communications between Parties and the Arbitrator

4.1   Where the Arbitrator sends any communication to one party, he shall send a copy to the other party.

4.2   Where a party sends any communication (including Statements under Article 6) to the Arbitrator, it shall be copied to the other party and be shown to the Arbitrator to have been so copied.

4.3   The addresses of the parties for the purpose of all communications during the proceedings shall be those set out in the Request, or as either party may at any time notify to the Arbitrator and to the other party. Any communication by post shall be deemed to be received in the ordinary course of mail unless the contrary is proved.

4.4   With the agreement of the parties, the Arbitrator may appoint the Registrar of the Chartered Institute of Arbitrators to act as arbitration administrator (whether or not the Chartered Institute of Arbitrators is acting as Appointing Authority). Where the Registrar is so appointed, all communications and notices between a party and the Arbitrator in the course of the arbitration (except at meetings and hearings) will be addressed through the Registrar, and in the case of communications to the Arbitrator will be deemed received by him when received by the Registrar.

Article 5   Conduct of the Proceedings

5.1   In the absence of procedural rules agreed by the parties or contained herein, the Arbitrator shall have the widest discretion allowed by law to ensure the just, expeditious, economical, and final determination of the dispute.

5.2   Any party wishing the Arbitrator to adopt a simplified or expedited procedure should apply to the Arbitrator for this within 15 days of notification of the Arbitrator's acceptance of his appointment.

5.3   In the case of a three-member tribunal the Chairman may, after consulting the other arbitrators, make procedural rulings alone.

Article 6   Submission of Written Statements and Documents

6.1   Subject to any procedural rules agreed by the parties or determined by or requested from the Arbitrator under Article 5, the written stage of the proceedings shall be as set out in this Article (and in accordance with Article 4).

6.2   Within 30 days of receipt by the Claimant of notification of the Arbitrator's acceptance of the appointment, the Claimant shall send to the Arbitrator a Statement of Case setting out in sufficient detail the facts and any contentions of law on which it relies and the relief claimed.

6.3   Within 30 days of receipt of the Statement of Case, the Respondent shall send to the Arbitrator a Statement of Defence stating in sufficient detail which of the facts and contentions of law in the Statement of Case it admits or denies, on what grounds, and on what other facts and contentions of law it relies. Any Counterclaims shall be submitted with the Statement of Defence in the same manner as claims are set out in the Statement of Case.

6.4   Within 30 days of receipt of the Statement of Defence, the Claimant may send to the Arbitrator a Statement of Reply which, where there are Counterclaims, shall include a Defence to Counterclaims.

6.5   If the Statement of Reply contains a Defence to Counterclaims, the Respondent may within a further 30 days send to the Arbitrator a Statement of Reply regarding Counterclaims.

6.6   All Statements referred to in this Article shall be accompanied by copies (or, if they are especially voluminous, lists) of all essential documents on which the party concerned relies and which have not previously been submitted by any party, and (where appropriate) by any relevant samples.

6.7   As soon as practicable following completion of the submission of the Statements specified in this Article, the Arbitrator shall proceed in such manner as has been agreed by the parties, or pursuant to his authority under these Rules.

Article 7   Party Representatives

Any party may be represented by persons of their choice, subject to such proof of authority as the Arbitrator may require. The names and addresses of such representatives must be notified to the other party.

Article 8   Hearings

8.1   Subject to Article 12, each party has the right to be heard before the Arbitrator, unless the parties have agreed to documents-only arbitration.

8.2   The Arbitrator shall fix the date, time and place of any meetings and hearings in the arbitration, and shall give the parties reasonable notice thereof.

8.3   The Arbitrator may in advance of hearings provide the parties with a list of matters or questions to which he wishes them to give special consideration.

8.4   All meetings and hearings shall be in private unless the parties agree otherwise.

Article 9   Witnesses

9.1   The Arbitrator may require each party to give notice of the identity of witnesses it intends to call. The Arbitrator may also require before a hearing the exchange of witnesses statements and of expert reports.

9.2   The Arbitrator has discretion to allow, limit, or (subject to Article 10.2) refuse to allow the appearance of witnesses, whether witnesses of fact or expert witnesses.

9.3   Any witness who gives oral evidence may be questioned by each party or its representative, under the control of the Arbitrator, and may be required by the Arbitrator to testify under oath or affirmation in accordance with the Arbitration Act 1950. The Arbitrator may put questions at any stage of the examination of the witnesses.

9.4   The testimony of witnesses may be presented in written form, either as signed statements or by duly sworn affidavits. Subject to Article 9.2 any party may request that such a witness should attend for oral examination at a hearing. If the witness fails to attend, the Arbitrator may place such weight on the written testimony as he thinks fit, or may exclude it altogether.

Article 10   Experts Appointed by the Arbitrator

10.1   Unless otherwise agreed by the parties, the Arbitrator:

(a)   may appoint one or more experts to report to the Arbitrator on specific issues;

(b)   may require a party to give any such expert any relevant information or to produce, or to provide access to, any relevant documents, goods or property for inspection by the expert.

10.2   Unless otherwise agreed by the parties, if a party so requests or if the Arbitrator considers it necessary, the expert shall, after delivery of his written or oral report, participate in a hearing, at which the parties shall have the opportunity to question him and to present expert witnesses in order to testify on the points at issue.

10.3   The provisions of Article 10.2 shall not apply to an assesor appointed by agreement of the parties, nor to an expert appointed by the Arbitrator to advise him solely in relation to procedural matters.

Article 11   Additional Powers of the Arbitrator

11.1   Unless the parties at any time agree otherwise, the Arbitrator shall have the power to:
(a)   allow any party, upon such terms (as to costs and otherwise) as he shall determine, to amend claims or counterclaims;
(b)   extend or abbreviate any time limits provided by these Rules or by his directions;
(c)   conduct such enquiries as many appear to the Arbitrator to be necessary or expedient;
(d)   order the parties to make any property or thing available for inspection, in their presence, by the Arbitrator or any expert;
(e)   order any party to produce to the Arbitrator, and to the other parties for inspection, and to supply copies of any documents or classes of documents in their possession, custody or power which the Arbitrator determines to be relevant.

11.2   If the parties so agree the Arbitrator shall also have the power to:
(a)   order the rectification in any contract or arbitration agreement of any mistake which he determines to be common to the parties;
(b)   rule on the existence, validity or determination of the contract;
(c)   rule on his own jurisdiction, including any objections with respect to the existence or validity of the arbitration agreement or to his terms of reference.

Article 12   Jurisdiction of the Arbitrator

12.1   In addition to the Jurisdiction to exercise the powers defined elsewhere in these Rules, the Arbitrator shall have jurisdiction to:
(a)   determine any question of law arising in the arbitration;
(b)   receive and take into account such written or oral evidence as he shall determine to be relevant, whether or not strictly admissible in law;
(c)   proceed in the arbitration and make an award notwithstanding the failure or refusal of any party to comply with these Rules or with the Arbitrator's written orders or written directions, or to exercise its right to present its case, but only after giving that party written notice that he intends to do so.

12.2   If the Claimant fails to attend any hearing of which due notice has been given, the Arbitrator may make an award on the substantive issue and an award as to costs, with or without a hearing, but such an award must be an Interim Award with the provision that it shall become a Final Award after 42 days if no application for a hearing is made by the Claimant during that period. If the Respondent fails to submit a Statement of Defence or to attend any hearing after due notice has been given, the Arbitrator may conduct the hearing in the absence of the Respondent and make an Award.

Article 13   Deposits and Security

13.1   The Arbitrator may direct the parties, in such proportions as he deems just, to make one or more deposits to secure the Arbitrator's fees and expenses. Such deposits shall be made to and held by the Arbitrator, or the

Chartered Institute of Arbitrators or some other person or body to the order of the Arbitrator, as the Arbitrator may direct, and may be drawn from as required by the Arbitrator. Interest on sums deposited, if any, shall be accumulated to the deposits.

13.2   The Arbitrator shall have the power to order any party to provide security for the legal or other costs of any other party by way of deposit or bank guarantee or in any other manner the Arbitrator thinks fit.

13.3   The Arbitrator shall also have the power to order any party to provide security for all or part of any amount in dispute in the arbitration.

Article 14   The Award

14.1   The Arbitrator shall make his award in writing and, unless all the parties agree otherwise, shall state the reasons upon which his award is based. The award shall state its date and shall be signed by the Arbitrator.

14.2   Where there is more than one arbitrator and they fail to agree on any issue, they shall decide by a majority. Failing a majority decision on any issue, the Chairman of the tribunal shall make the award alone as if he were sole arbitrator. If an arbitrator refuses or fails to sign the award, the signatures of the majority shall be sufficient, provided that the reason for the omitted signature is stated.

14.3   The Arbitrator shall be responsible for delivering the award or certified copies thereof to the parties, provided that he has been paid his fees and expenses.

14.4   The Arbitrator may make interim awards or separate awards on different issues at different times.

14.5   If, before the award is made, the parties agree on a settlement of the dispute, the Arbitrator shall either issue an order for termination of the reference to arbitration or, if requested by both parties and accepted by the Arbitrator, record the settlement in the form of a consent award. The Arbitrator shall then be discharged and the reference to arbitration concluded, subject to payment by the parties of any outstanding fees and expenses of the Arbitrator.

Article 15   Correction of Awards and Additional Awards

15.1   Within 14 days of receiving an award, unless another period of time has been agreed upon by the parties, a party may by notice to the Arbitrator request the Arbitrator to correct in the award any errors in computation, any clerical or typographical errors or any errors of similar nature. If the Arbitrator considers the request to be justified, he shall make the corrections within 14 days of receiving the request. Any correction shall be notified in writing to the parties and shall become part of the award.

15.2   The Arbitrator may correct any error of the type referred to in Article 15.1 on his own initiative within 14 days of the date of the award.

15.3   Unless otherwise agreed by the parties, a party may request the Arbitrator, within 10 days of the date of the award, and with notice to the other party, to make an additional award as to claims presented in the reference to arbitration but not dealt with in the award. If the Arbitrator considers the request to be justified, he shall notify the parties within 7 days and shall make the additional award within 30 days.

15.4   The provisions of Article 14 shall apply to any correction of the award and to any additional award.

Article 16   Costs

16.1   The Arbitrator shall specify in the award the total amount of his fees and expenses, including the charges of the arbitration administrator (if any). Unless the parties shall agree otherwise after the dispute has arisen, the Arbitrator shall determine the proportions in which the parties shall pay such fees and expenses, provided that the parties will be jointly and severally liable to the Arbitrator for payment of all such fees and expenses until they have been paid in full. If the Arbitrator has determined that all or any of his fees and expenses shall be paid by any party other than a party which has already paid them to the Arbitrator, the latter party shall have the right to recover the appropriate amount from the former.

16.2   The Arbitrator has power to order in his award that all or a part of the legal or other costs of one party shall be paid by the other party. The Arbitrator also has power to tax these costs and may do so if requested by the parties.

16.3   If the Arbitration is abandoned, suspended or concluded, by agreement or otherwise, before the final award is made, the parties shall be jointly and severally liable to pay to the Arbitrator his fees and expenses as determined by him together with the charges of the arbitration administrator (if any).

Article 17   Exclusion of Liability

17.1   The Arbitrator, the Appointing Authority (and the arbitration administrator if any) shall not be liable to any party for any act or omission in connection with any arbitration conducted under these Rules, save for the consequences of conscious and deliberate wrongdoing.

17.2   After the award has been made and the possibilities of correction and additional awards referred to in Article 15 have lapsed or been exhausted, the Arbitrator, the Appointing Authority (and the arbitration administrator if any) shall not be under any obligation to make any statement to any person about any matter concerning the arbitration, and no party shall seek to make any arbitrator or the Appointing Authority or the arbitration administrator a witness in any legal proceedings arising out of the arbitration.

Article 18   Waiver

A party which is aware of non-compliance with these Rules and yet proceeds with the arbitration without promptly stating its objection to such non-compliance, shall be deemed to have waived its right to object.

SHORT FORM ARBITRATION RULES 1991

SUGGESTED CLAUSES

1.   Parties to a contract who wish to have any *future* disputes referred to arbitration under the Short Form Arbitration Rules of the Chartered Institute

of Arbitrators may insert in the contract an arbitration clause in the following form:

> Any dispute arising out of or in connection with this contract shall be referred to and finally resolved by arbitration under the Short Form Arbitration Rules of the Chartered Institute of Arbitrators, which Rules are deemed to be incorporated by reference into this clause.

2. Parties to an *existing* dispute who wish to refer it to arbitration under the Short Form Arbitration Rules of the Chartered Institute of Arbitrators may agree to do so in the following terms:

> We, the undersigned, agree to refer to arbitration under the Rules of the Chartered Institute of Arbitrators the following dispute which has arisen between us:
>
> (Brief description of matters to be referred to arbitration)

Signed_____(Claimant)

Signed_____(Respondent)

Date_____

3. Where the Short Form Arbitration Rules of the Chartered Institute of Arbitrators apply:

(a) The parties may if they wish specify an Appointing Authority to appoint the arbitrator (or arbitrators) if the parties fail to do so or cannot agree. If no Appointing Authority is specified, then the Short Form Arbitration Rules provide the President or a Vice-President for the time being of the Chartered Institute of Arbitrators will act as Appointing Authority. The following provision may be suitable if some other Appointing Authority is required:

> The Appointing Authority shall be (name of institution or person).

(b) The Short Form Arbitration Rules provide a sole arbitrator will be appointed unless the parties agree otherwise. If the parties wish to specify a three-man tribunal, the following provision may be suitable:

> The arbitral tribunal shall consist of three arbitrators one of whom shall be appointed by each party and the third by the Appointing Authority.

REQUEST FOR ARBITRATION UNDER THE SHORT FORM ARBITRATION RULES

The Chartered Institute of Arbitrators
International Arbitration Centre
24 Angel Gate
City Road
London EC1V 2RS

Claimant/First Party

Name:_____

Address:_____

_____

_____

Tel:_____

Respondent/Second Party

Name:_____

Address:_____

_____

_____

Tel:_____

Contract/Agreement: Date_____
(enclose a copy or summarise briefly)

Arbitration Clause or Agreement:

(A copy of this is essential in the case of a Unilateral Application. A Joint Application may itself be considered an arbitration agreement)

Dispute:

(Enclose brief particulars of the nature, circumstances and location, of dispute, issue for arbitration and amount at issue are all that are required at this stage. The parties will be asked to make detailed submissions in due course)

Other Relevant Details:

(e.g. *Unilateral Application*: date on which other party was requested to concur in appointment of arbitrator, names of arbitrators proposed, etc.

Joint Application: matters on which parties have agreed regarding conduct of the arbitration, etc.)

Signature:

Claimant:_____

Respondent:_____

Date:_____

SHORT FORM ARBITRATION RULES 1991

Preliminary

1. These Rules shall apply to arbitrations which the parties intend to be conducted according to shortened forms of procedure, whether on the basis of:
    1.1 written submissions and documentary evidence only, without a hearing; or
    1.2 a hearing for the purpose of receiving oral submissions and evidence.
The parties may vary any of the provisions of these Rules by agreement.

Commencement of Arbitration

2. An application for arbitration shall be made to the Appointing Authority by the parties on the Appointing Authority's form, accompanied by the prescribed registration fee. At such time as the Appointing Authority thinks fit, it shall appoint an Arbitrator.

Jurisdiction and Powers of the Arbitrator

3. Without prejudice to the jurisdictions and powers set out in the Schedule to these Rules, the Arbitrator shall have the widest discretion permitted by law to ensure the just, expeditious, economical and final determination of the dispute.

4. Without prejudice to any powers conferred on the Arbitrator by law or by the contract between the parties, the Arbitrator may exercise the powers set out in the Schedule to these Rules.

Procedure

5. The parties shall, if possible, agree whether the arbitration is to proceed on the basis of written submissions and documentary evidence only, without a hearing, or whether a hearing is required for the purpose of receiving oral submissions and evidence. If the parties fail to agree, the Arbitrator shall decide which procedure is to be followed and may, if he considers it desirable, call a meeting with the parties to consider the matter. The Arbitrator shall in any case confirm which procedure is to be followed by directions issued to the parties in writing.

6. Within 21 days of the Arbitrator's directions under article 5, the party making the claim ('the Claimant') shall submit to the Arbitrator and to the other party ('the Respondent') a brief statement of claim.

7. Within 21 days of receipt of the Claimant's statement of its claim, the Respondent shall submit to the Arbitrator and to the Claimant:
    7.1 a brief statement of its defence to the claim;
    7.2 a brief statement of any counterclaim.

8.   Within 14 days of receipt of the Respondent's statement(s) under Article 7, the Claimant shall submit to the Arbitrator and to the Respondent:
 8.1   a brief statement of any reply to the defence which it wishes to make:
 8.2   a brief statement of its defence to any counterclaim

9.   Where the Claimant submits a defence to the Respondent's counterclaim, the Respondent may, within 14 days of receipt of the defence to the counterclaim, submit to the Arbitrator and to the Claimant a brief statement of its reply to that defence.

10.   All statements submitted under Articles 6 to 9 above shall include a brief statement of:
 10.1   the party's principal arguments of fact and law;
 10.2   in the case of the claim and of any counterclaim, the remedies sought;
and shall be accompanied by copies of all documents on which the party seeks to rely in support of its case and detailed calculations of any sums claimed.

11.   Submissions will normally be closed on completion of the procedure set out in Articles 6–10. However, the Arbitrator may, in his discretion, permit the parties to make further replies to each other's cases, but shall in every case have the power to determine when the submissions are closed.

12.   The Arbitrator may require the parties to submit to him and to each other:
 12.1   on application to the Arbitrator, such documents as are properly discoverable to help the parties in preparing their submissions;
 12.2   in any case, such further submissions, documents or information as he considers to be necessary.

13.   Within 14 days of the close of submissions or at such other time as he thinks fit, the Arbitrator may in appropriate cases conduct an inspection of the subject-matter of the arbitration. Either party or both parties shall be entitled to attend, but only for the purpose of identifying for the Arbitrator the subject-matter of the dispute or any relevant part(s).

14.   Where, under Article 5, the Arbitrator has directed that a hearing be held, he shall, in consultation with the parties, fix a date and venue for the hearing at the earliest opportunity.

15.   Where, under Article 5, the Arbitrator has directed that the arbitration is to proceed on the basis of written submissions and documentary evidence only, the Arbitrator may nevertheless call the parties to an informal hearing solely for the purpose of seeking clarification of any matters arising from the parties' statements and supporting evidence.

16.   If, during the course of the arbitration, the Arbitrator concludes that the dispute is incapable of proper resolution in accordance with these Rules,

or if, having directed otherwise under Article 5, he considers that a full formal hearing is after all required, he shall advise the parties of his alternative proposals for the conduct of the arbitration. The arbitration shall, unless otherwise directed by the Arbitrator, continue from the point already reached.

17. The parties may, by agreement at any time, serve notice on the Arbitrator that the arbitration shall no longer be conducted in accordance with these Rules.

18. The Arbitrator shall have the power to extend or vary any of the time limits stipulated in these Rules.

Costs

19. In making his award under these Rules, the Arbitrator shall, at his discretion, which shall be exercised judicially, order by whom and in what proportion the parties shall pay his fees and expenses. He shall also decide who shall pay the parties' own costs.

20. In determining the parties' liability for their own costs under Article 19, the Arbitrator shall award all costs which have been reasonably incurred, having received representations as to costs from the parties.

Miscellaneous

21. The Appointing Authority reserves the right to appoint a substitute arbitrator if the original appointee dies, is incapacitated or is for any reason unable to deal expeditiously with the dispute following acceptance of the appointment.

22. Awards made under these Rules shall be final and binding on the parties.

23. Neither the Appointing Authority nor the Arbitrator shall be liable to any party for any act or omission in connection with any arbitration conducted under these Rules.

24. The Short Form Arbitration Rules 1990 are hereby revoked.

SCHEDULE

JURISDICTION AND POWERS OF THE ARBITRATOR

Jurisdiction

The Arbitrator shall have jurisdiction to:

1. determine any question as to the existence, validity or termination of any contract between the parties;

2.   order the rectification of any contract or the arbitration agreement, but only to the extent required to rectify any manifest error, mistake or omission which he determines to be common to all the parties;

3.   determine any question of law arising in the arbitration;

4.   determine any question as to his own jurisdiction, including any objections with respect to the existence or validity of the arbitration agreement or to his terms of reference;

5.   determine any question of good faith, dishonesty or fraud arising in the dispute, if specifically pleaded by a party.

Powers

6.   The Arbitrator shall, without prejudice to any powers conferred by these Rules, have power to:

(a)   allow any party, upon such terms (as to costs and otherwise) as he shall determine, to amend any statement of case, counterclaim, defence to counterclaim and reply, or any other submissions;

(b)   order the parties to produce relevant information, documents, goods or property for inspection, in their presence, by the Arbitrator;

(c)   order any party to produce to the Arbitrator and to the other party, a list of relevant documents for inspection, and to supply copies of any documents or classes of documents in their possession, custody or power which the arbitrator determines to be relevant;

(d)   allow, limit or refuse to allow the appearance of witnesses, whether witnesses of fact or expert witnesses;

(e)   require, prior to any hearing, the exchange of witnesses' statements and of experts' reports;

(f)   appoint one or more experts to report to the Arbitrator on specific issues and to order a party to produce relevant information, documents, and (so far as is practicable) goods or property or samples thereof for Inspection by the expert;

(g)   seek legal advice in such form as he thinks fit;

(h)   direct the parties, in such proportions as he deems just and in any manner he thinks fit, to make one or more deposits to secure the Arbitrator's fees and expenses;

(i)   order any party to provide security for the legal or other costs of any other party by way of deposit or bank guarantee or in any other manner the Arbitrator thinks fit;

(j)   order any party to provide security for all or part of any amount in dispute in the arbitration;

(k)   proceed in the arbitration notwithstanding the failure or refusal of any party to comply with these Rules or with his orders or directions, or to attend any meeting or hearing, but only after giving that party written notice that he intends to do so;

(l)   express awards in any currency;

(m)   issue an order for termination of the reference to arbitration if the parties agree to settle the dispute before an award is made or, if required by both parties, record the settlement in the form of a consent award.

7. If the parties agree, following an explanation by the Arbitrator of the consequences, the Arbitrator may exercise the following additional powers:

(a) to conduct such enquiries as may appear to him to be necessary or expedient;

(b) to order the preservation, storage, sale or other disposal of any property or thing under the control of any party;

(c) to receive oral or written evidence from any party which he considers relevant, whether or not strictly admissible in law. In particular the Arbitrator may, at his discretion. receive secondary evidence and/or draw appropriate inferences from a party's conduct where that party fails to comply with an order made by the Arbitrator;

(d) to make an award on the basis of faimess and reasonableness, without necessarily being bound by mandatory rules of law.

RULES OF THE ARBITRATION SCHEME FOR THE PLASTICS WINDOW FEDERATION

1. Introduction

1.1   This Scheme applies to applications for arbitration made to the Chartered Institute of Arbitrators (CIArb) in respect of disputes between the members of the Plastics Window Federation and their customers. A dispute may only be referred to arbitration under the Scheme where both parties have agreed to do so after the dispute has arisen.

1.2   The Scheme does not apply to claims for compensation exceeding £20,000, or to claims concerning physical injury, illness, nervous shock or there consequences.

1.3   The Rules apply to disputes between two parties but, if they and the Arbitrator agree, the Rules may be adapted for disputes involving three or more parties.

1.4   Registration fees are payable by each party when an application for arbitration is submitted. Registration fees are charged at £250 per party. Registration fees are returnable only in accordance with Rules 2.5, 4.7 and 5.3.

2 Commencement of Arbitration Proceedings

2.1   To commence arbitration proceedings, a joint application must be submitted to the CIArb through the Plastics Window Federation, on the schemes application form, accompanied by the appropriate fees.

2.2   The arbitration commences when the CIArb writes to the parties telling them that their application has been accepted. At this stage the person making the claim (the 'claimant') will be sent a statement of claim form. See Rule 3.4.

2.3   The Chairman or a Vice-President of the CIArb will appoint an Arbitrator and will inform the parties.

2.4   The CIArb may appoint a substitute Arbitrator, in the event of the Arbitrator resigning, dying or otherwise becoming incapacitated, or for any reason being unable to attend competently and/or expeditiously to his duties.

2.5   If the Arbitrator believes that the dispute is not capable of proper resolution under these Rules, the parties shall be so advised. In that case the

Arbitrator's appointment shall be cancelled, the parties' application for arbitration treated as withdrawn and their registration fees for arbitration refunded. The parties will then be able to pursue the matter through the courts.

2.6   Once appointed the Arbitrator will communicate with or issue directions to the parties. Correspondence with the Arbitrator must be copied to all parties.

3.   Arbitration Procedure

3.1   The Arbitrator shall have the jurisdiction and power to direct the procedure of the arbitration including the amendment of time limits and other procedural requirements. The Arbitrator shall also have the power to:

(a)   allow submission of further evidence and the amendment of claim or defence;

(b)   order the parties to produce goods, documents or property for inspection;

(c)   conduct such enquiries as may appear to the Arbitrator to be desirable;

(d)   receive and take into account any oral or written evidence as the Arbitrator shall decide to be relevant;

(e)   appoint an expert to report on specific issues or take legal advice;

(f)   award interest whether or not claimed;

(g)   proceed with the arbitration if either party fails to comply with these Rules or with the Arbitrator's directions, or if either party fails to attend any meeting or inspection ordered by the Arbitrator but only after giving that party written notice;

(h)   terminate the arbitration if the Arbitrator considers the case to be incapable of resolution under the Scheme or if the parties settle their dispute prior to an Award. If the case is settled the parties must immediately inform the CIArb in writing of the terms of the settlement and the Arbitrator shall record them in a Consent Award enforceable under the Arbitration Acts.

3.2   In addition to the powers conferred by these Rules, the Arbitrator shall have the widest discretion permitted by law to resolve the dispute in a just, speedy, economical and final manner in accordance with natural justice.

3.3   The arbitration will normally proceed on the basis of written argument and evidence which must be submitted in duplicate and in accordance with the following procedure. However, if either party requests it and/or if the Arbitrator considers it appropriate a meeting or inspection may be held. Any such meeting or inspection shall be made in the presence of both parties who may be questioned by the Arbitrator in order to clarify matters in dispute.

3.4   Within 28 days of receipt of the statement of claim form, the claimant shall send the completed form to the CIArb together with all supporting documents to prove their case. The claimant may not raise issues or claim amounts not covered by the application form without the Arbitrator's consent.

3.5   A copy of the statement of claim and supporting documents will be sent by the CIArb to the other party (the 'respondent'), who then has 28 days in which to submit a written statement of defence. Providing notice was given on the application form, the respondent shall submit details and all necessary supporting documents to prove any counterclaim.

3.6   A copy of the statement of defence and supporting documents, and any counterclaim will be sent by the CIArb to the claimant, who is entitled to submit written comments within a further 14 days. Such comments must be restricted to points arising from the respondent's defence (and counter-claim if any). The claimant may not introduce any new matters or new points of claim.

3.7   The Arbitrator will make an Award with reasons after considering all submissions and evidence.

3.8   The CIArb will send a copy of the Award to each party and to the organisation acting as the sponsoring body for the scheme.

3.9   Unless otherwise directed, any amount awarded shall be paid within 21 days of dispatch of the Award to the parties. Such payments shall be made direct to the party entitled to receive it.

3.10   Any Award made under this Scheme is final and legally binding on all parties.

3.11   The Arbitrator shall not be liable to either of the parties for breach of his duty, save where he has been guilty of misconduct, moral turpitude or fraud.

3.12   Any party may request the return of its original documents but must do so within 42 days of the date of dispatch of the Award.

4.   Content of Submissions for Arbitration

4.1   The Statement of Claim shall include:
(a)   nature and basis of the claim;
(b)   the amount of compensation claimed or other remedy sought;
(c)   all supporting documents relied on as evidence.

4.2   If the claimant is unable to submit a copy of any original contract or order, the respondent shall submit a copy of that document with the defence.

4.3   The statement of defence shall include:
(a)   what matters in the opposing documents are accepted or agreed;
(b)   what matters are disputed, with reasons why;
(c)   any supporting documents relied on as evidence.

4.4   Any counterclaim shall include:
(a)   the nature and basis of the counterclaim;
(b)   the amount of compensation claimed or other remedy sought;
(c)   any supporting documents relied on as evidence.

4.5   The response by the claimant to any defence and/or counterclaim shall include:
(a)   what matters in the opposing documents are accepted or agreed;
(b)   what matters are disputed, with reasons why;
(c)   any supporting documents relied on as evidence.

4.6   The respondent shall have a right to comment on any defence to a counterclaim within 14 days of its submission.

4.7   If any party fails to deliver anything required by these Rules and does not supply it within 14 days of a reminder by the CIArb then:
(a)   where a claim or a counterclaim is not delivered it shall be deemed to be abandoned;

(b)   where a claim is abandoned the arbitration will not proceed and the respondent's registration fee will be refunded;

(c)   where a counterclaim is abandoned the arbitration will proceed with the original claim;

(d)   where the failure concerns information requested by the Arbitrator, the arbitration shall proceed as the Arbitrator considers appropriate;

(e)   where the failure is non-delivery of the defence (or the claimant's response to a counterclaim) the Arbitrator may make the Award on the basis of documents received.

5.   Arbitration Costs

5.1   The Arbitrator's fees and expenses and those of any expert or legal adviser appointed by him shall be paid by the CIArb and shall be recovered, along with its administration costs, from the Plastics Window Federation.

5.2   Subject to rule 5.4 below, each party shall bear its own costs of preparing and submitting its case and of attending any hearing. No legal action may be brought to recover these costs.

5.3   The Arbitrator may award that one party shall reimburse the other's registration fee.

5.4   The Arbitrator may also order one party to pay any part of the other's costs where the former has acted unreasonably and caused the opposing party unnecessary expense.

5.5   These provisions for costs will not apply to any application or appeal to the court.

6.   Miscellaneous

6.1   The national law to be applied shall be determined by the Arbitrator if the parties fail to agree. If Scots law applies, substitute Arbiter for Arbitrator throughout these Rules.

6.2   Neither the CIArb nor the Arbitrator can enter into any correspondence regarding an Award issued under this Scheme.

6.3   Neither the CIArb nor the Arbitrator shall be liable to any party for any act or omission in connection with the arbitration conducted under these Rules.

6.4   Nothing herein shall prevent the parties agreeing to settle the differences or dispute arising out of the agreement without recourse to arbitration.

6.5   Nothing herein shall prevent the any party from appealing the Award to the High Court in terms of the Arbitration Acts 1950–1979, should the need arise. This provision applies equally to the law of Scotland.

BRITISH RAILWAYS BOARD ARBITRATION PROCEDURE

RULES (1985 EDITION)

Scope of the Procedure

1.   (i)   This Procedure ('the Procedure') has been established by the Chartered Institute of Arbitrators ('the Institute') and British Railways Board

('the Board') in consultation with the Central Transport Consultative Committee.

(ii)   The Procedure provides informal and inexpensive arbitration as a method of resolving disputes between customers and the Board which the parties agree should be referred to arbitration in accordance with the Board's Code of Practice (1985). An arbitrator appointed under the Procedure will decide such disputes in accordance with the applicable law as determined in accordance with Rules 13(i) below. He will proceed by reference to submissions and documentary evidence supplied by the parties, with no oral hearing.

(iii)   Arbitrations under the Procedure are administered independently by the Institute, and the appointment of arbitrators under the Procedure is within the Institute's exclusive and unfettered control.

(iv)   A customer is not obliged to take advantage of the Procedure in any dispute to which it may apply, but if he does so he will be bound by the arbitrator's decision, and will not be able subsequently to start again with proceedings in the Courts in respect of the same dispute.

2.   (i)   The Procedure applies to any claim for compensation for failure by the Board to carry out its legal obligations under a contract governed by the Board's:

(a)   Conditions of Carriage of passengers and their luggage;
(b)   Left luggage conditions;
(c)   Platform ticket conditions;
(d)   Conditions relating to seat etc reservations;
(e)   Conditions relating to parking of motor vehicles and bicycles.

(ii)   The Procedure does not apply where the claim is within Rule 2(i) but:

(a)   The claim exceeds £1000;
(b)   The claim is for compensation for personal injury;
(c)   The claim involves a complicated issue of law or is otherwise unsuitable for arbitration on documents only;
(d)   The claim has not previously been notified to the Board;
(e)   The application for arbitration under the Procedure has not been made within three months of the Claimant receiving the last reply on the matter from the Board or other relevant body dealing with the matter (unless there are exceptional circumstances);
(f)   Legal proceedings in Court in respect of the claim have been commenced.

(iii)   The Procedure also does not apply to:

(a)   Carriage of articles under the Board's parcels or freight conditions. It should be noted that luggage sent independently of any carriage of a passenger is governed by the Board's parcel conditions, and that a vehicle conveyed under a Motorail ticket is governed by the Board's freight conditions;
(b)   Golden Rail Holidays where a separate arbitration scheme is available through the Association of British Travel Agents, from whom information can be obtained;
(c)   Journeys under international tickets governed by the Uniform Rules concerning the carriage of passengers and their luggage by rail (CIV)

appended to the convention concerning International Carriage by Rail (COTIF). Those rules provide their own system of arbitration;

(d)   Journeys on the services of administrations other than the Board.

3.   A registration fee is payable by any customer submitting an application for arbitration under the Procedure. This is applied towards the Institute's administrative costs unless it is returnable under Rule 6, 8(ix) or 12.

Commencement of Arbitration

4.   (i)   A customer wishing to refer a disputed claim against the Board to arbitration under the Procedure ('the Claimant') must apply on the prescribed application form, which can be obtained from the Institute. The form must be completed and returned to the Institute, together with the registration fees specified in the application form.

(ii)   On receipt of the duly completed application form and the registration fee the Institute will forward the application form to the Board for signature and return, thus bringing the Board into the case as the other party to the arbitration ('the Respondent').

5.   Where the application is outside the time limit specified in Rule 2 the Board may agree to arbitration but reserves the right not to do so. Where it considers the claim is otherwise outside the scope of the Procedure, the Board will not agree to arbitration and will explain its decision in writing to the Claimant.

6.   Arbitration commences when the Institute has received the application form signed by both parties and despatches notice to both parties that it accepts the application. The Claimant's copy of such notice will be accompanied by a Statement of Claim form. If, for any reason, the claim is not admissible, the Claimant's registration fee shall be returned and he may pursue the matter in the Courts.

Subsequent Proceedings

General

7.   The arbitration will be on documents only. Subject to any directions of the Arbitrator, the procedure will be as follows:

(i)   The Claimant is required, within four weeks of receipt of the statement of claim form, to send the completed form, together with the supporting documents, to the Institute (in duplicate). (The Claimant may not, without the consent of the Institute, claim an amount greater than specified on the application for arbitration).

(ii)   A copy of the claim documents will be sent by the Institute to the Board, which is required, within four weeks of receipt of the documents, to send to the Institute (in duplicate) its written defence to the claim together with any supporting documents.

(iii)   A copy of the defence documents will be sent by the Institute to the Claimant, who is entitled to send to the Institute (in duplicate) any written comments which he wishes to make on the defence documents within two weeks of their receipt. They must be restricted to points arising from the Board's defence, and may not introduce any new matters or points from them.

(iv)   The President or a Vice-President of the Institute, at such stage of the proceedings as the Institute considers appropriate, will appoint a sole arbitrator to decide the dispute and the Institute will notify the parties of his appointment.

(v)   The arbitrator will make his award with reference to documents submitted by the parties and transmit his award to the Institute for publication.

(vi)   Unless the parties otherwise agree the arbitrators reasons will be set out or referred to in his award. His award will not contain any directions as to payment of interest, but in arriving at the sum to be awarded in respect of a wholly or partially successful claim, the arbitrator may, in appropriate circumstances, have regard to any lack of promptness by either party in dealing with the complaint and to any lack of proper effort to settle the matter amicably.

(vii)   The Institute will publish the award by sending copies to each of the parties.

(viii)   Unless directed otherwise in the award, within three weeks of despatch to the parties of the copy award, payment shall be made of any monies directed by the award to be paid. Such payment shall be made by the party liable direct to the party entitled, and not through the Institute.

Supplementary

8.   (i)   The arbitrator may, through the Institute, request the provision of any further documents/information which he considers would assist him in his decision. Each party will be given an opportunity to comment on any documents/information supplied by the other party in response to such a request. If the documents/information are not supplied to the Institute within such time as it prescribes, the arbitrator will proceed with the reference on the basis of the documents already before him.

(ii)   Where in the opinion of the arbitrator it is desirable, he may make an examination of any subject matter of the dispute. The parties shall afford the arbitrator all necessary assistance and facilities for the conduct of this examination.

(iii)   Where appropriate, the arbitrator may sit with one or more independent technical advisers appointed by the Institute when considering the documentary evidence submitted to him.

(iv)   Where, in the opinion of the arbitrator, it is desirable that independent examination of any subject matter of the dispute be made, an independent examiner will be appointed by the Institute to make such examination and a written report thereon. The parties shall afford the examiner all necessary assistance and facilities for the conduct of this examination and copies of his report shall be sent by the Institute to the parties who will then be given 14 days in which to comment thereon.

(v)   If the Claimant does not furnish his statement of claim within the time allowed and does not remedy his default within two weeks after despatch to him by the Institute of notice of that default, he will be treated as having abandoned his claim under the Procedure, and the arbitration will not proceed.

(vi)   If the Board does not furnish its defence within the time allowed and does not remedy its default within two weeks after despatch to it by the Institute of notice of that default, then subject to any directions the arbitrator may give the dispute will be decided by him by reference to the documents submitted by the Claimant.

(vii)   If the Claimant does not furnish any comments on the Boards defence within the time allowed and does not request an extension before such time expires the Institute will assume the Claimant does not wish to make any such comments and the case will proceed accordingly.

(viii)   Either party may request an extension of time within which to furnish its submissions. The other party will be notified of such request and if there is any objection then the arbitrator will be asked to give directions.

(ix)   If in the opinion of the arbitrator the dispute is not capable of proper resolution under the rules of this Procedure, he shall advise the parties through the Institute. The arbitrator's appointment shall be deemed revoked and the parties' application for arbitration withdrawn, and the Claimant's registration fee will be refunded. The Claimant will then be at liberty to pursue the matter through the Courts.

Costs

9.   The arbitrator's fees and expenses shall be paid by the Institute and are part of the administrative costs of the Procedure.

10.   The administrative costs of the Procedure are subject to a separate agreement between the Institute and the Board.

11.   Each party bears its own costs of preparing and submitting its case.

12.   The arbitrator has a discretion to give in his award such directions as he considers appropriate with regard to reimbursement to the Claimant by the Institute of the amount of the Claimant's registration fee.

Miscellaneous

13. (i)   The law to apply (English, Scottish etc) may be determined by the arbitrator if the parties fail to agree.

(ii)   Where Scottish law applies, any reference in these Rules to an arbitrator shall be construed as a reference to an arbiter.

14.   The Institute reserves the right to appoint a substitute arbitrator if the arbitrator originally appointed dies or is incapacitated or is for any reason unable to deal expeditiously with the dispute. The parties shall be notified of any substitution.

15.   Awards made under the Procedure are final and binding on the parties. Subject to the right of a party to request the Institute to draw the

arbitrator's attention to any accidental slip or omission which he has power to correct, neither the Institute nor the abitrator can enter into correspondence regarding awards made under the Procedure.

16.   Rights of application or appeal to the Courts are as under the relevant Arbitration Acts provided that:
　　　(i)   The costs provisions of the Procedure shall not apply to any such application or appeal;
　　　(ii)   Either party making such application or appeal (other than an application for leave to enforce the award) will bear its own and the other party's costs (including the costs of any resumed or fresh arbitration resulting from such proceedings) irrespective of the outcome of such proceedings.

17.   Neither the Institute nor the arbitrator shall be liable to any party for any act or omission in connection with any arbitration conducted under these Rules save that the arbitrator (but not the Institute) shall be liable for any conscious or deliberate wrongdoing on his own part.

ARBITRATION SCHEME FOR THE BONDED COACH HOLIDAY SECTION OF THE BUS AND COACH COUNCIL

RULES (1990 EDITION)

Scope of the Scheme

1.   The Scheme provides an inexpensive and informal method of resolving disputes arising between members of Bonded Coach Holiday Section of the Bus and Coach Council ('BCH') and their customers in connection with bookings for inclusive holidays (eg. holidays for which the price payable is inclusive of travel and accommodation).

2.   Claims may be made under the Scheme by or on behalf of any person named in the document(s) constituting the holiday booking, and in these Rules 'customer' includes all such persons in respect of whom a claim is made.

3.   No claim may be made under the Scheme for compensation:
　　　(i)   in an amount greater than £1,500 per person or in excess of £7,500 per booking form.
　　　(ii)   solely or mainly in respect of physical injury or illness or the consequences of such injury or illness.
Claims may also be excluded by the Arbitrator under Rule 8(iv) on the grounds that the dispute is not capable of proper resolution on documents only.

4.   A registration fee is payable by each party when an application for arbitration is submitted. These fees are charged on the scale set out in the application form. They are applied towards defraying the Institute's administrative costs and are non-returnable except as provided in Rules 8(ii) and

8(iv) although either party may be required to reimburse the other's registration fee under Rule 12.

Institution of Arbitration proceedings

5. A joint application for arbitration must be made to the Institute through BCH on the prescribed application form, accompanied by the appropriate registration fees.

6. The arbitration commences, for the purpose of these Rules, when the Institute dispatches to the parties written notice of acceptance of the application. The notice sent to the customer will be accompanied by a claim form.

Procedure

General

7. Subject to any directions issued by the the arbitrator and to the provisions of 7(i) and 8(ii) below, the arbitration will be on documents only and the procedure will be as follows:

(i) The customer is required, within 28 days of receipt of the claim form, to send the completed form, together with supporting documents in duplicate, to the Institute.

(ii) The customer may not generally claim an amount greater than that specified on the application form. If he does, however, the arbitrator subsequently appointed will have a discretion as to whether to allow this.

(iii) A copy of the claim documents will be sent by the Institute to the BCH member, who is required, within 28 days of receipt of the documents, to send to the Institute its written defence to the claim, together with any supporting documents in duplicate.

(iv) A copy of the defence documents will be sent by the Institute to the customer, who is entitled to send to the Institute any written comments which he wishes to make on the defence documents within 14 days of their receipt. Such comments should be in duplicate. They must be restricted to points arising from the defence, and may not introduce any new matters or points of claim.

(v) At such stage of the proceedings as the Institute in its discretion considers appropriate the President or Vice-President of the Institute will appoint a sole arbitrator to decide the dispute and the Institute will notify the parties of his appointment.

(vi) The arbitrator will make his award with reference to the documents submitted by the parties and transmit his award to the Institute for publication.

(vii) Unless the parties otherwise agree the arbitrator's reasons will be sent out or referred to in his award.

(viii) The Institute will issue the award by sending copies to each of the parties. In normal circumstances the Institute will also send a copy to BCH.

(ix) Unless directed otherwise in the award, within 21 days of despatch to the parties of the copy award, payment shall be made of any monies directed by the award to be paid. Such payment shall be sent by the party liable direct to the party entitled and not through the Institute of the BCH.

Supplementary

8. (i)   The arbitrator may, through the Institute, request the provision of any further documents/information which he considers would assist him in his decision. A copy of any documents/information so provided will be sent by the Institute to the other party who will be allowed a reasonable time to comment. If the documents/information are not supplied to the Institute within such time as it prescribes, the arbitrator will proceed with the reference on the basis of the documents already before him.

(ii)   If the customer does not furnish his claim within the time allowed and does not remedy his default within 14 days after despatch to him by the Institute of notice of that default, he will be treated as having abandoned his claim. The arbitration will not proceed and the BCH member's registration fee will be refunded to him.

(iii)   If the BCH member does not furnish its defence within the time allowed and does not remedy its default within 14 days after despatch to it by the Institute of notice of that default, then (subject to any further directions the arbitrator may issue) the dispute will be decided by the arbitrator by reference to the documents submitted by the customer.

(iv)   If in the opinion of the arbitrator the dispute is not capable of proper resolution on documents only, he shall advise the parties through the Institute, with his proposals for how else the arbitration should proceed. If the parties accept these proposals the arbitration shall proceed accordingly provided that the special costs provisions of the Rules shall no longer apply. Failing such agreement the arbitrator's appointment shall be deemed revoked and the parties' application for arbitration deemed withdrawn, and the parties' registration fees will be refunded. The claimant will then be at liberty to pursue the matter through the courts.

Costs

9.   The arbitrator's fees and expenses shall be paid by the Institute and are part of the administrative costs of the Scheme.

10.   The administrative costs of the Scheme are subject to a separate agreement between the Institute and BCH.

11.   Each party bears its own costs of preparing and submitting its case.

12.   The arbitrator has a discretion to give in his award such directions as he considers appropriate with regard to reimbursement of either party by the other of the amount of its registration fee.

Miscellaneous

13.   The law to apply (English, Scots etc) shall be determined by the arbitrator if the parties fail to agree.

14.   The Institute reserves the right to appoint a substitute arbitrator if the arbitrator originally appointed dies or is incapacitated or is for any reason

unable to deal expeditiously with the dispute. The parties shall be notified of any substitution.

15.   Awards made under the Scheme are final and binding on the parties. Subject to the right of a party to request the Institute to draw the arbitrator's attention to any accidental slip or omission which he has power to correct; neither the Institute nor the arbitrator can enter into correspondence regarding awards made under the Scheme.

16.   Rights of application or appeal (if any) to the courts are as per the relevant Arbitration Acts provided that:

(i)   The special costs provisions of the scheme shall not apply to any such application or appeal;

(ii)   Either party making any such application or appeal (other than an application of leave to enforce the award) will bear its own and the other party's costs (including the costs of any resumed or fresh arbitration resulting from such proceedings) irrespective of the outcome of such proceedings.

17.   Neither the Institute nor the arbitrator shall be liable to any party for any act or omission in connection with any arbitration conducted under these Rules save that the arbitrator (but not the Institute) shall be liable for any conscious wrongdoing on his part.

SURVEYORS AND VALUERS ARBITRATION SCHEME

RULES (1993 EDITION)

Introduction

1.   These Rules apply to applications for arbitration made to the Chartered Institute of Arbitrators ('the Institute') on or after 1 June 1993 in respect of disputes between members of the Royal Institution of Chartered Surveyors ('RICS'), i.e. chartered surveyors, the Incorporated Society of Valuers and Auctioneers ('ISVA'), i.e. incorporated valuers, and their clients. A dispute may only be referred to arbitration under the Scheme where both parties have agreed to do so after the dispute has arisen.

2.   The Scheme applies to disputes involving:

(i)   a chartered surveyor or incorporated valuer practising in England and Wales, Scotland, Northern Ireland, the Channel Islands or the Isle of Man;

(ii)   a client who has instructed the chartered surveyor or incorporated valuer;

(iii)   an allegation that that chartered surveyor or incorporated valuer is liable in contract to that client for breach of professional duty.

For the purposes of this Rule, 'chartered surveyor or incorporated valuer' includes a partnership, a limited company or an unlimited company carrying on practice as surveyors or valuers, of which at least one partner or director is a chartered surveyor or incorporated valuer.

3.   No claim may be made under the Scheme:

(i)   in respect of physical injury, illness or nervous shock or the consequences of any of these;

(ii)   where the property or land to which the dispute relates is situated outside the territories listed in Rule 2(i);

(iii)   if the issues are unusually complicated and their resolution is likely to require a hearing and oral evidence.

4.   The Rules are designed primarily for arbitrations between the two parties only. With the agreement of the Institute and of all parties concerned, the Rules may be adapted for arbitrations between three or more parties.

5.   A registration fee is payable by each party when an application for arbitration is submitted and is specified in the Institute's application form. It is non-returnable except as provided in Rules 9(v) and (vii) although either party may be required to reimburse the other's registration fee under Rule 12.

Commencing Arbitration Proceedings

6.   A joint application for arbitration must be submitted to the Institute on its application form, signed by both parties and accompanied by the registration fee.

7.   The arbitration commences under these Rules when the Institute sends the parties written notice of acceptance of the application. The notice sent to the client ('the Claimant') will be accompanied by a claim form.

Procedure

General

8.   The Institute will appoint a sole arbitrator to decide the dispute and notify the parties of the appointment. Subject to any directions issued by the arbitrator and to the provisions of these Rules, the arbitration will be on documents only and the procedure will be as follows:—

(i)   The Claimant shall, within 28 days of receipt of the claim form, send the completed form together with the supporting documents, in duplicate, to the Institute.

(ii)   The Claimant may not generally claim an amount greater than that specified on the application form. If he/she does, however, the arbitrator will have a discretion as to whether to allow this.

(iii)   A copy of the claim documents will be sent by the Institute to the chartered surveyor or incorporated valuer ('the Respondent') who shall, within 28 days of the receipt of the documents, send to the Institute a written defence to the claim, together with any supporting documents in duplicate. The Respondent may include with its defence a counterclaim in respect of any balance of payment alleged to be due on the contract between the parties. The Respondent may not make any other counterclaim against the Claimant unless:

(a)   notice of it was contained in the parties' application for arbitration; and

(b)   the arbitrator consents to the making of such counterclaim.

(iv)   A copy of the defence documents will be sent by the Institute to the Claimant, who may send to the Institute any written comments which he/she wishes to make on them and a defence to any counterclaim within 14 days of their receipt. Such comments must be in duplicate and the Institute will send a copy to the Respondent. They must refer only to points arising from the defence and any counterclaim and may not introduce any new matters or points of claim.

(v)   The arbitrator will make his/her award by reference to the documents submitted by the parties and his/her reasons will be set out or referred to in the award.

(vi)   Any compensation ordered may include or be limited to any amount of fees owing to the Respondent for which a counterclaim has been made.

(vii)   The Institute will send copies of the award to each party and to the RICS or ISVA (as appropriate).

(viii)   Unless the award states otherwise, payment shall be made of any monies directed by the award to be paid within 21 days of despatch of the award. Such payment shall be made by the party liable direct to the party entitled, and not through the arbitrator, the Institute, the RICS or the ISVA. Enforcement of the award is the responsibility of the parties and the Institute cannot assist.

(ix)   If either party has sent original documents in support of its case to the Institute that party may, within six weeks of despatch of the award, request the return of those documents. Subject to that, case papers will be retained by the Institute and may be disposed of.

Supplementary

9.   (i)   The arbitrator may require the parties to provide any further documents/information which he/she considers would assist him/her in his/her decision. If the documents/information are not supplied to the Institute within such time as it prescribes, the arbitrator may proceed with the reference on the basis of the documents already before him/her.

(ii)   The arbitrator may make an examination of the land or property to which the dispute relates. The parties shall give the arbitrator all necessary assistance for the conduct of this examination.

(iii)   The arbitrator may appoint an independent expert or call for expert evidence from the parties. The parties will be given an opportunity to comment on any evidence obtained.

(iv)   The arbitrator may at his/her discretion appoint a legal or technical assessor to assist him/her in considering the documentary evidence submitted by the parties.

(v)   If the Claimant does not submit his/her claim within the time allowed and fails to do so within 14 days of a reminder by the Institute he/she will be treated as having abandoned his/her claim. The arbitration will not proceed and the Respondent's registration fee will be returned.

(vi)   If the Respondent does not submit its defence within the time allowed and fails to do so within 14 days of a reminder by the Institute the arbitrator may decide the dispute by reference to the documents submitted by the Claimant.

(vii)   If the arbitrator concludes that the dispute is not capable of proper resolution under these Rules, he/she shall so advise the parties. Failing agreement as to how the arbitration should otherwise proceed (including proposals as to costs) the arbitrator's appointment shall be deemed revoked, the parties application for arbitration shall be deemed withdrawn and their registration fees will be refunded. The Claimant will then be able to pursue the matter through the courts.

Costs

10.   The administrative costs of the Scheme, including the fees and expenses of the arbitrator, any independent expert appointed by the arbitrator under Rule 9(iii) and any assessor appointed under Rule 9(iv), shall be paid by the RICS or ISVA (as appropriate). The maximum potential liability of an unsuccessful Claimant for costs, under the Scheme will therefore be limited to his her own and the other party's registration fee in accordance with Rule 12 below.

11.   Each party bears its own legal and other costs of preparing and submitting its case (including legal costs), and may not recover them in court proceedings against the other party.

12.   The arbitrator may, in the award, order one party to reimburse the other's registration fee.

Miscellaneous

13.   (i)   The applicable law (English, Scots, Northern Irish etc) shall be determined by the arbitrator if the parties fail to agree.

(ii)   Where Scots law applies, any reference in these Rules to an 'arbitrator' shall be construed as a reference to an 'arbiter' and Scottish arbitration procedures shall apply.

14.   The Institute may appoint a substitute arbitrator if the original appointee dies, is incapacitated or is for any reason unable to deal quickly with the dispute. The parties shall be notified of any substitution.

15.   The arbitrator's award shall be final and binding on the parties. Subject to a party's right to draw attention to any accidental slip or omission which the arbitrator has power by law to correct, neither the Institute nor the arbitrator can enter into correspondence regarding awards made under the Scheme.

16.   The parties may apply or appeal to the courts under the relevant Arbitration Acts, but:

(i)   the special costs provisions of the Scheme shall not apply to any such application or appeal;

(ii)   the party making an application or appeal (other than an application for leave to enforce the award) will bear its own and the other party's costs (including the costs of any resumed or fresh arbitration) regardless of the outcome of such proceedings, unless the relevant court orders otherwise.

17.   Neither the Institute nor the arbitrator shall be liable to any party for any act or omission in connection with any arbitration conducted under these Rules. However, the arbitrator (but not the Institute) shall be liable for any wrongdoing on his/her own part arising from bad faith.

ARBITRATION SCHEME FOR THE ASSOCIATION OF BRITISH TRAVEL AGENTS

The Chartered Institute of Arbitrators,
International Arbitration Centre,
24 Angel Gate,
City Road,
London EC1V 2RS
Tel: 0171 837 4483
Fax: 0171 837 4185

Explanatory Notes

Arbitration is a dispute resolution process in which a third, but independent, person makes a final and legally enforceable decision. It is the only judicial and binding alternative to going to court.

This Scheme provides for the settling of disputes between members of the Association of British Travel Agents (ABTA) and their customers which they are unable amicably to resolve themselves. It is administered independently of ABTA and has been set up in consultation with the Office of Fair Trading. Your attention is drawn to the scheme rules provided overleaf.

Application for arbitration may be made to the Institute on the attached form and on payment of a registration fee. The registration fee may at the discretion of the arbitrator be refunded to the successful party by the other party and each party is responsible for its own costs (including legal costs). The customer must agree to be bound by the arbitrator's decision and the ABTA member will agree to be bound in all cases.

The procedure is simple, quick, informal and inexpensive. Each party may present a written statement of its arguments in the dispute, together with supporting documents, and comment on the arguments and evidence of the other party. The arbitrator makes his decision without an oral hearing on documents only and it is important to include all evidence upon which you wish to rely.

The Scheme is not designed to deal with complicated disputes which should be dealt with by more formal oral hearing and evidence procedures to ensure their proper resolution. This includes claims exceeding £1,500 per person and £7,500 per booking, whichever is the lower, and claims arising from injury, illness or death.

The arbitrators selected for appointment by the President or a Vice-President of the Institute are Fellows of the Institute and all appointments are within the Institute's exclusive and unfettered control.

Arbitrations conducted under the Scheme are subject to the laws of England and Wales, Scotland or Northern Ireland (as the case may be).

RULES (1994 EDITION)

Introduction and Scope of the Scheme

1. The Scheme applies to disputes arising out of the provision of any services by members of the Association of British Travel Agents (ABTA) to their customers. Claims may be made by or on behalf of any person named in the booking form or other contractual documents and in these Rules 'customer' includes all persons on whose behalf a claim is made.

2. These Rules apply to applications for arbitration received on or after 1 September 1994.

3. No claim may be made under the Scheme:
    (i)   For compensation exceeding £1,500 per person and £7,500 per booking, whichever is the lower;
    (ii)   In respect of injury, illness or death or the consequences of any of these.

4. In considering the parties' cases, the arbitrator shall have regard to ABTA's Tour Operators' Code of Conduct and/or its Travel Agents' Code of Conduct. In the event of a conflict between a rule of law and a provision of either code, the interpretation most favourable to the customer shall prevail.

5. These Rules are designed primarily for arbitrations between two parties, that is to say, between a customer and a travel agent or a tour operator. However, a customer may also apply for arbitration against both a travel agent and a tour operator.

Institution of Arbitration Proceedings

6. The parties must make a joint application for arbitration to the Institute, accompanied by their registration fees.

7. In general, the parties' registration fees are charged on the scale set out in the Institute's application form, but;
    (i)   Where a travel agent and a tour operator are joined in the same application, each shall pay half the registration fee.
    (ii)   Where the only customer claiming is a child under the age of 12, a registration fee shall be payable by the person making a claim on his behalf. Unless Rules 10(iii) or (v) apply, registration fees are non-returnable.

8. Unless there is a good reason for any delay the customer must apply for arbitration within 9 months of completion of the return journey.

Procedure

The Institute will appoint a sole arbitrator to determine the dispute and notify the parties of the appointment. Subject to any directions given by the arbitrator, the arbitration procedure will be on documents only, as follows:

General

9. (i)   The Institute will acknowledge receipt of the application to the parties and will also send the party making the claim (the 'Claimant') a claim form.

(ii)   The Claimant shall return the completed claim form and supporting documents to the Institute within 28 days. Additional copies of these documents shall be submitted to the Institute for each Respondent.

(iii) A claim exceeding the amount specified in the application form will not be permissible.

(iv)   The Institute will send a copy of the claim documents to the other party/parties ('the Respondent(s)'), who shall, within 28 days of receipt, send to the Institute a written defence, together with supporting documents. Additional copies of these documents shall be submitted to the Institute for the Claimant and for any other Respondent.

(v)   The Institute will send a copy of each of the defence documents to the Claimant, who may send to the Institute written comments on the defence(s), in duplicate/triplicate (as appropriate), within 14 days. No new matters or points of claim may be raised by the comments.

(vi)   Where there are two Respondents, the Institute will send a copy of each Respondent's defence to the other for comment. Any such comments must be submitted within 28 days and must be restricted to points arising from the documents.

(vii) The arbitrator will give an award with reasons which the Institute will forward to the parties and forward a copy to ABTA.

(viii) Payment ordered by an award shall be paid within 21 days, unless directed otherwise in the award. Payment must be made directly between the parties and not through the arbitrator, the Institute or ABTA. Enforcement of the award is the parties' responsibility and the Institute is unable to assist. Enforcement should in the first instance be sought through ABTA.

(ix)   Original documents will be returned to the parties after six weeks have elapsed from the date of the award if requested by the parties within this time, and only if the request accompanied by a self addressed envelope of suitable size and appropriate prepaid postage.

Supplementary

10. (i)   The arbitrator may, through the Institute, request the provision of any further documents/information or submission which he considers would assist him in his decision. If the documents/information or submissions are not sent to the Institute within the time prescribed, the arbitrator will proceed with the reference on the basis of the documents already before him.

(ii)   Documents submitted by the parties otherwise than under Rules 9(i)-(iv) and 10(i) will not be admissible as of right but at the arbitrator's sole discretion. Where a party submits such documents, the arbitrator will decide whether or not they are admissible. Where the documents are held to be admissible, the other party will be sent copies and be entitled to comment on them before an award is made.

(iii) If the Claimant does not submit his claim within the time allowed and does not send one within 14 days of a reminder by the Institute he will be treated as having abandoned his claim. The arbitration will not proceed and the Respondent's registration fee will be returned.

(iv) If a Respondent does not submit its defence within the time allowed and does not send one within 14 days of a reminder by the Institute the arbitrator will be appointed and, subject to any directions he may give, the dispute will be decided by him be reference to the documents submitted by the Claimant.

(v) If, in the arbitrator's opinion (which shall be final), the dispute is not capable of proper resolution on documents only, he shall advise the parties, through the Institute. The arbitrator's appointment shall be revoked, the parties' application for arbitration shall be withdrawn and their registration fees will be refunded. The Claimant may then pursue the matter through the courts.

Costs

11. The arbitrator's fees and expenses shall be paid by the Institute and are part of the administrative costs of the Scheme. The said costs are subject to separate agreement between the Institute and ABTA.

12. Each party shall bear its own costs of preparing and submitting its case (including legal costs).

13. The arbitrator may, at his discretion, direct the reimbursement by one party of the other's registration fee.

14. No legal proceedings may be brought by one party against the other for recovery of any of the costs set out in Rules 11 and 12 or any other cost incurred in pursuing the arbitration.

Miscellaneous

15. (i) The law to apply (English, Scots etc) shall be determined by the arbitrator if the parties fail to agree.

(ii) Where Scots law applies, any reference in these Rules to an arbitrator shall be construed as a reference to an arbiter.

16. The Institute reserves the right to appoint a substitute arbitrator if the arbitrator originally appointed dies, is incapacitated or is for any reason unable to deal expeditiously with the dispute. The parties shall be notified of any substitution.

17. Awards made under the Scheme shall be final and binding on the parties.

18. Subject to the right of one party to request the Institute to draw the arbitrator's attention to any accidental slip or omission which he has power to correct by law, neither the Institute nor the arbitrator can enter into correspondence regarding award made under the Scheme.

19.   A party may make an application or appeal to the courts under the relevant Arbitration Acts but:

(i)   The special costs provisions of Rules 11–13 shall not apply to any such application or appeal;

(ii)   Either party making any such application or appeal (other than an application for leave to enforce the award) will bear its own and the other party's costs (including the costs of any resumed or fresh arbitration resulting from such proceedings) regardless of the outcome of those proceedings.

20.   Neither the Institute nor the arbitrator shall be liable to any party for any act or omission in connection with any arbitration conducted under these Rules save that the arbitrator (but not the Institute) shall be liable for any wrongdoing on his own part arising from bad faith.

PERSONAL INSURANCE ARBITRATION SERVICE

RULES (1996 EDITION)

Introduction

1.   The Service provides an informal method of resolving disputes by arbitration (once the normal complaints procedure of the insurance company has been exhausted) where an insured person, or, on the case of a life policy, a person entitled to claim under it ('the Claimant'), claims to have suffered financial loss through alleged failure of the insurance company ('the Insurer') to fulfil its obligation under a contract of insurance.

2.   Provided that the dispute falls within the Scope of the Service as applicable to the particular Insurer, the Service applies to persons resident in the United Kingdom who have taken out or who are (in the case of a life policy) beneficiaries under insurance effected in a private capacity through policies issued in the United Kingdom.

3.   A joint application for arbitration must be made through the Insurer to the Institute on the prescribed application form.

4.   The arbitration commences when the Institute despatches to the parties written notice of acceptance of the application. The Claimant's copy of this notice will be accompanied by a claim form.

General Provisions

5.   The resolution of disputes shall be subject to the provisions in the contract and in accordance with the applicable law and the applicable Statements of Insurance Practice issued by the Association of British Insurers, that is to say:

(i)   The Statement of General Insurance Practice;

(ii)   The Statement of Long-Term Insurance Practice;

(iii)   The Code of Practice for Selling of General Insurance.

In the event of conflict between the applicable law and the relevant Statement, the interpretation more favourable to the Claimant shall prevail.

Procedure

General

6. The Institute will appoint a sole Arbitrator to decide the dispute and will notify the Parties of his appointment. Subject to any directions issued by the Arbitrator and to the provisions of rules 6(iv) and 7(viii) below, the arbitration will be as follows:

(i) The Claimant is required, within 28 days of receipt of the claim form, to send the completed form, together with supporting documents, in duplicate, to the Institute.

(ii) A copy of the claim documents will be sent by the Institute to the Insurer, who is required, within 28 days of receipt of the documents, to send to the Institute a written defence to the claim, together with any supporting documents in duplicate.

(iii) A copy of the defence documents will be sent by the Institute to the Claimant, who is entitled to send to the Institute, in duplicate, any written comments which he wishes to make on the defence documents within 14 days of receipt. Comments must be restricted to points arising from the Insurers defence and may not introduce any new matters or points of claim.

(iv) At the request of either Party or at his own instigation the Arbitrator has a discretion to call the Parties to an informal hearing.

(v) The Arbitrator will make his Award with reasons by reference to the documents submitted by the Parties and to the evidence submitted at any informal hearing. The Institute will publish the Award by sending a copy to each of the Parties.

(vi) Unless the Arbitrator directs otherwise, within 21 days of despatch to the Parties of the copy Award, payment shall be made of any moneys directed by the Award to be paid. Payment shall be made direct to the Party entitled and not through the Institute.

Supplementary

7. (i) If the Claimant does not submit his claim or a reasonable explanation for his failure to do so within the time allowed and does not submit one within 14 days of a reminder being sent by the Institute, he will be treated as having abandoned his claim and the arbitration will not proceed.

(ii) If the Insurer fails to submit its defence within the time allowed and does not send one within 14 days of a reminder being sent by the Institute, then, subject to any directions the Arbitrator may make, the dispute will be decided by him with reference to the documents submitted by the Claimant.

(iii) The Arbitrator may, through the Institute, request the provision of any further documents/information which he considers would assist him in his decision and the documents/information shall be supplied to the Institute within such time as is directed by the Arbitrator.

(iv) Where the Arbitrator is of the opinion that expert evidence or further expert evidence is required, he may call for such evidence as he thinks necessary, whether oral or in writing. The Parties will be given an opportunity to comment on this evidence.

(v)   If, in the opinion of the Arbitrator, it is desirable for him to make an examination of the subject matter of the dispute, the Parties shall afford the Arbitrator all necessary assistance and facilities for the conduct of this examination.

(vi)   The Arbitrator may sit with one or more independent technical advisers appointed by the Institute when considering the documentary evidence submitted to him if he considers this to be necessary.

(vii)   If, in the opinion of the Arbitrator, it is desirable that independent examination of the subject matter of the dispute be made, an independent examiner will be appointed by the Institute to make such an examination and a written report. The Parties shall afford the examiner all necessary assistance and facilities for the conduct of this examination and will be given an opportunity to comment on the report.

(viii)   If, in the Arbitrator's opinion (which shall be final), the dispute is not capable of proper resolution by means of these procedures, he shall advise the Parties, through the Institute, with his proposals, if any, for how else the arbitration should proceed. If the Parties accept these proposals, the arbitration shall proceed accordingly, provided that the special costs provisions of Rules 8–10 shall no longer apply. Failing such an agreement, the Arbitrator's appointment shall be deemed revoked and the Parties' application for arbitration shall be deemed withdrawn. The Claimant will then be at liberty to pursue the matter through the courts.

Costs

8.   The Insurer shall in any event pay the following costs:
(i)   The Arbitrator's fees and expenses;
(ii)   The Institute's administrative charges;
(iii)   The fees of any independent technical advisor appointed under Rule 7 (vi) or independent examiner appointed under Rule 7(vii).

9.   The Parties shall pay their own costs (including any legal costs) of preparing and submitting their cases.

10.   Determination of liability for costs incurred by the Claimant in attending a hearing shall be at the Arbitrator's discretion.

Miscellaneous

11.   The law to apply (of England and Wales, Scotland or Northern Ireland) shall be determined by the Arbitrator if the Parties fail to agree. Where Scots law applies, any reference in these Rules to an Arbitrator shall be construed as a reference to an Arbiter.

12.   The Institute reserves the right to appoint a substitute Arbitrator if the Arbitrator originally appointed dies, is incapacitated or is for any reason unable to deal expeditiously with the dispute. The Parties shall be notified of any substitution.

13.   Awards made under the Scheme are final and binding on the Parties. Subject to the right of a Party to request the Institute to draw the Arbitrator's

attention to any accidental slip or omission which he has power to correct, neither the Institute nor the Arbitrator can enter into correspondence regarding Awards made under the Scheme.

14.   A Party may make an appeal or application to the courts under the relevant Arbitration Acts but:

(i)   The special costs provisions of Rules 8–10 shall not apply to any such application or appeal;

(ii)   The Party making any such application or appeal (other than an application for leave to enforce the Award), will bear its own and the other Party's costs (including the costs of any resumed or fresh arbitration resulting from such proceedings) irrespective of the outcome of such proceedings, unless otherwise directed by the court to which the application or appeal is addressed.

15.   Neither the Institute nor the Arbitrator shall be liable to any Party for any act or omission in connection with any arbitration conducted under these Rules, save that the Arbitrator (but not the Institute) shall be liable for any conscious or deliberate wrongdoing on his own part.

CHARTERED INSTITUTE OF ARBITRATORS
IRISH BRANCH

The Chartered Institute of Arbitrators, Irish Branch
5, Wilton Place, Dublin 2
Tel: (00 + 353-1-8394077)
Fax: (00 + 353-1-8326587)

Standard Arbitration Clause

Parties to a contract who wish to have any dispute referred to arbitration under these Rules are recommended to insert in their contract an arbitration clause in the following form:

'Any dispute or difference of any kind whatsoever which arises or occurs between the parties in relation to any thing or matter arising under out of or in connection with this agreement shall be referred to arbitration under the Arbitration Rules of the Chartered Institute of Arbitrators – Irish Branch.'

Application of Rules

The Arbitration Rules of the Chartered Insitute of Arbitrators – Irish Branch may be used without reference to the Branch.

ARBITRATION RULES

adopted to take effect from 1 April 1990

Rule 1   Applicability

1.1   Where any agreement, submission or reference provides for arbitration under the Arbitration Rules of The Chartered Insitute of Arbitrators –

Irish Branch ('the Branch') the arbitration shall be conducted in accordance with the following Rules or such amended Rules as the Branch may adopt from time to time and which shall have taken effect before the commencement of the arbitration.

1.2   In any other circumstances where a dispute is referred to arbitration these Rules may be used in whole or in part by agreement of the parties.

Rule 2   Singular and Plural

In the following Rules words importing the singular also include the plural and vice versa where the context requires and in particular the expression 'Arbitrator' includes all the Arbitrators where more than one has been appointed.

Rule 3   Request for Nomination of Arbitrator

Where a request for the nomination of an Arbitrator is made to the Branch, the Request for Nomination of Arbitrator form should be completed and sent to the Branch at 5 Wilton Place, Dublin 2.

Rule 4   Selection of Arbitrator

On accepting a Request for Nomination of Arbitrator the Branch (unless all the parties have previously agreed on an Arbitrator) shall select and nominate an Arbitrator to determine the dispute and shall advise the parties who shall formally appoint the Arbitrator.

Rule 5   Number of Arbitrators

5.1   Unless the parties have agreed otherwise the nomination shall be of a single Arbitrator, usually but not necessarily chosen from the Branch's own Panels of Arbitrators. In making a nomination the Branch shall taken into consideration any agreement reached or representation made by the parties.

5.2   If the parties have each nominated an Arbitrator the Branch shall nominate those Arbitrators together with a sufficient number of additional Arbitrators, selected by the Branch, to ensure the total number of Arbitrators is uneven.

Rule 6   Chairman of Tribunal

The Branch shall nominate the Arbitrator or one of the Arbitrators it selects as the Chairman of the arbitral tribunal.

Rule 7   Replacement of Arbitrator

If after appointment any arbitrator dies, refuses, fails or in the opinion of the Branch becomes unable or unfit to act, the Branch shall upon request appoint another arbitrator in his place.

Rule 8   Suitability of Arbitrator

In selecting an Arbitrator the Branch shall so far as possible have regard to the nature of the contract and to the nature and circumstances of the dispute.

Rule 9   Independence and Impartiality of Arbitrators

Any Arbitrator (whether or not nominated by the parties) conducting an arbitration under these Rules shall be and shall remain at all times wholly independent and impartial and shall not act as advocate for any party.

Rule 10   Extension of Proceedings

Nothing in these Rules shall preclude an Arbitrator from acting, where all the parties involved so agree, in Representative Proceedings, Third Party Proceedings or Consolidated Proceedings.

Rule 11   Communications

11.1   Where a party sends any communication (including any notice or Statement made under these Rules) to the Arbitrator, it shall include a copy for the Arbitrator and also send copies to all the other parties at the same time and confirm to the Arbitrator that it has done so.

11.2   The Arbitrator shall likewise copy any communication to a party to all the other parties at the same time.

Rule 12   Address of Party

For the purpose of all communications during the proceedings the address of a party shall be that set out in the Request for Nomination of Arbitrator or such other address as the parties shall later agree or as any party shall notify to the Arbitrator or if there be no such address its last known place of business or its last known address.

Rule 13   Delivery of Communication

13.1   Any notice or communication in any arbitration under these Rules shall be deemed to have been properly delivered if dispatched by post, cable, telex, facsimile transmission or by hand to the address notified to the Arbitrator by the party concerned as the address for service or as provided in Rule 12.

13.2   If any party to whom a notice or communication has to be sent for the purpose of these Rules cannot be found or if for any reason service upon such party cannot readily be effected in accordance with these Rules, the Arbitrator may dispense with such service upon such party or may order substituted service in such form as the Arbitrator thinks fit.

Rule 14   Jurisdiction

The Arbitrator shall have the jurisdiction and the powers to direct the procedure in the arbitration necessary to ensure the just expeditious economical and final determination of the dispute as set out in the schedule of Jurisdiction and Powers of the Arbitrator.

Rule 15   Procedure

In the absence of any other Directions the procedure of the arbitration shall be that set out in the following Rules.

Rule 16   Directions

Directions from the Arbitrator to the parties shall be in writing or, if given orally, shall be confirmed in writing by the Arbitrator within seven days. With or without preliminary meetings, the Arbitrator shall give Directions for the progress of the arbitration.

Rule 17   Orders

If the parties shall themselves agree upon any interlocutory matters, they shall seek the approval of the Arbitrator thereto and the Arbitrator if he so approves shall incorporate any such agreement in an Order.

Rule 18   Objections

Any application to the Arbitrator on any matter relating to the arbitration shall be in writing. On receiving a copy of such application any party may within seven days thereof make an objection in writing to the Arbitrator and shall send a copy to the applicant and shall notify the Arbitrator that such a copy has been sent. Upon receipt of any such application or objection the Arbitrator may give such Directions as appear to him appropriate with or without hearing the parties.

Rule 19   Adjournments

The Arbitrator may adjourn a meeting or hearing for such period as he may deem appropriate if a party appears by a legal or professional representative without proper notice having been given to the other parties or for such other reason as he may deem sufficient.

Rule 20   Joint Statement of Matters in Dispute

Wherever possible, the parties shall prepare a joint statement setting out concisely the matters which are in dispute between them and amounts and other reliefs sought and shall submit that statement to the Arbitrator.

Rule 21   Statement of Claim, Defence & Reply

21.1   Unless the Arbitrator directs otherwise, where a joint statement of the matters in dispute cannot be prepared the following procedure shall apply.

21.2   The party who requested the arbitration ('*the Claimant*') shall send to the Arbitrator a Statement of Claim setting out in sufficient detail the facts and contentions of law on which it relies and the relief it claims.

21.3   The other party ('*the Respondent*') shall send to the Arbitrator a Statement of Defence stating in sufficient detail which of the facts and contentions of law in the Statement of Claim it admits or denies on what grounds and on what other facts and contentions of law it relies. If it has a counterclaim, this shall be set out in the Statement of Defence as a Statement of Claim.

21.4   After receipt of the Statement of Defence, the Claimant may send the Arbitrator a Statement of Reply.

21.5   Where there is a counterclaim, the Claimant shall send the Arbitrator a Statement of Defence to the counterclaim to which the Respondent may make a Statement of Reply.

21.6   All Statements of Claim, Defence and Reply shall be accompanied by copies (or, if they are especially voluminous, lists) of the essential documents on which the party concerned relies and which have not previously been submitted by any party and, where practicable, by relevant samples.

21.7   After the submission of all the Statements, the Arbitrator shall give Directions for the further conduct of the arbitration.

21.8   The Arbitrator shall determine the time limits within which the Statements of Claim, Defence and Reply are to be submitted.

21.9   At the conclusion of pleadings, the Arbitrator may direct the parties to set out concisely the matters which are then in dispute and may direct the parties to draw up a Scott Schedule.

Rule 22   Meetings and Hearings

22.1   The Arbitrator may at any time fix the date, time and place of meetings and hearings in the arbitration and shall give all the parties adequate notice of these. Subject to any adjournment which the Arbitrator may allow, the final hearing shall be continued on successive working days until it is concluded.

22.2   Unless the parties shall agree otherwise the Arbitrator may be accompanied by one pupil grade member of the Institute at meetings or hearings.

22.3   Provided that it gives the Arbitrator and the other parties not less than ten days prior notice, or such shorter notice as may be directed by the Arbitrator, any party may be represented at any meeting or hearing by a legal or other professional practitioner. The appearance of the representative as an advocate shall not prevent his appearance as a witness in the same proceedings provided that the capacity in which he is appearing at any one time is made clear.

22.4   The Arbitrator may in his discretion disallow as costs of the arbitration the fees and expenses of legal representatives of the parties provided that he gives notice of his intention to do so.

Rule 23   The Award

The Arbitrator shall make his Award in writing and as soon as practicable after the conclusion of the final hearing he shall publish his Award and notify the parties that the Award is ready to be taken up.

Rule 24   Majority Decision

Where there is more than one Arbitrator and they disagree on any matter or question they shall decide by a majority; failing a majority, the Chairman alone shall decide.

Rule 25   Settlements

25.1   If before the publication of the Arbitrator's final Award the parties arrive at a settlement of their disputes they shall immediately so notify the Arbitrator in writing.

25.2   The Arbitrator may direct that documents be prepared and signed by all the parties recording the terms of the agreement which unless the parties have otherwise agreed shall be incorporated in an Award.

25.3   If the parties' agreement does not determine all matters in dispute, the outstanding differences shall be settled by the Arbitrator in a further Award or Awards.

Rule 26   Costs of the Arbitrator

26.1   The Arbitrator in his terms of acceptance shall state the basis on which his costs will be charged in accordance with the Schedule of Costs contained herein.

26.2   From the commencement of the arbitration all the parties shall be jointly and severally liable to the Arbitrator for his costs until they are paid.

26.3   The Arbitrator shall specify the total amount of his costs in his Award. Unless all the parties agree otherwise he shall determine (in the exercise of his absolute discretion) which party or parties shall pay his costs.

26.4   After notification by the Arbitrator any party may take up the Award upon payment to the Arbitrator of all his costs then still outstanding whereupon the Arbitrator shall send a copy of the Award to the other party or parties.

26.5   If the Award has not been taken up within ten days of the notification the Arbitrator may by action at law proceed to recover all his outstanding costs from any or all of the parties.

26.6.   If the Arbitrator has determined that all or any part of his costs shall be paid by any party other than the party which has already paid them in taking up the Award that party shall have the right to recover the appropriate amount from the party liable for the payment.

26.7   If the arbitration is abandoned, suspended or concluded by agreement or otherwise before the final Award is made the parties shall pay to the Arbitrator his costs incurred to that time in such proportions as they shall agree or failing agreement as the Arbitrator shall determine.

Rule 27   Simplified Procedure

27.1   Where the value of all matters in dispute between the parties does not exceed such sum as may from time to time be determined by the Branch or in any other arbitration where the parties so agree:

27.2   The Branch will nominate a single Arbitrator;

27.3   The Arbitrator may determine the dispute at an informal hearing attended by all the parties;

27.4   Alternatively, the Arbitrator may determine the dispute on the documents submitted to him by the parties, voluntarily or on his Direction, without any hearing.

Rule 28   Exclusion of Liability

28.1   The Arbitrator and the branch shall not be liable to any party for any act or omission or negligence in connection with any arbitration conducted under these Rules, save for the consequences of conscious and deliberate wrongdoing.

28.2   After the Award has been made and any corrections and additional Awards made, the Arbitrator and the Branch shall not be under any obligation to make any statement to any person about any matter concerning the arbitration and no party shall seek to make any Arbitrator or the Branch a witness in any legal proceedings arising out of the arbitration and the parties agree that the Arbitrator is not compellable as a witness.

SCHEDULE OF COSTS

[Not reproduced here.]

SCHEDULE OF JURISDICTION AND POWERS OF THE ARBITRATOR

A   By submitting to arbitration under the foregoing Rules the parties shall be taken to have conferred on the Arbitrator the following jurisdiction and powers to be exercised by him so far as the law allows and in his discretion as he may judge expedient for the purpose of ensuring the just expeditious economical and final determination of the dispute referred to him.

B   The Arbitrator shall have jurisdiction to:

1   Determine any question as to the validity extent or continuation in force of any contract between the parties.

2   Order the correction or amendment of any such contract and of the arbitration agreement submission or reference but only to the extent required to rectify any manifest error mistake or omission which he determines to be common to all the parties.

3   Determine any question of law arising in the arbitration (including any question as to which system or law governs the dispute).

4   Determine any question as to his own jurisdiction.

5   Determine any question of good faith or dishonesty arising in the dispute.

6   Order any party to furnish him with such further details of its case in fact or in law as he may require.

7   Proceed in the arbitration following the failure or refusal of any party to comply with these rules or with his Orders or Directions or to attend any meeting or hearing but only after giving that party written notice that he intends so to do.

8   Receive and take into account such written or oral evidence as he shall determine to be relevant whether or not strictly admissible in law.

9   Make one or more interim Awards.

10   Order the parties to make interim payments towards the costs of the Arbitrator.

11   Hold meetings and hearings in Ireland and elsewhere.

12   Express his Award in any currency.

13   Award interest on any sum from and to any date and at such rates as he determines to be appropriate provided that:

interest has been claimed or counterclaimed as special damages; or

he finds the sum to have been due but not paid up to the date of the Award; or

he finds the sum to have been paid late but after the commencement of the proceedings.

14   Correct any accidental mistake or omission in his Award.

15   Apportion the parties costs in the arbitration between the parties.

16   Require witnesses to be examined on oath or affirmation and administer oaths to or take affirmations of witnesses.

17   Direct on such terms and conditions as he may determine that evidence by given by affidavit.

C   Unless the parties at any time agree otherwise the Arbitrator shall have power on the application of any party or of his own motion but in either case only after hearing or receiving any representations from the parties to:

1   Allow other parties to be joined in the arbitration with their express consent and make a single final Award determining all disputes between them.

2   Allow any party upon such terms (as to costs and otherwise) as he shall determine to amend its Statement of Claim, Defence or Reply.

3   Extend or abbreviate any time limits provided by these Rules or by his Directions.

4   Rely on his own expert knowledge and experience in any field provided that the parties ha e been informed of his being possessed of such knowledge or experience.

5   Appoint one or more advisors or experts on any matter (including law) to assist him in the arbitration.

6   Direct the parties to submit to him for subsequent exchange written statements (whether or not verified by oath or affirmation) of the proposed evidence of experts and direct which of the makers of such statements are to attend before him for oral examination.

7   Order the parties to make any property or thing available for his inspection and inspect it in the presence of the parties.

8   Order the parties to produce to him and to each other and to supply copies of any documents or classes of documents in their possession or power which he determines to be relevant.

9   Order the preservation or storage of any property or thing under the control of any of the parties and which property or thing is the subject of the reference.

10   Make interim Orders for security for any party's own costs and/or to secure all or part of any amounts in dispute in the arbitration.

D In addition the Arbitrator shall have such further jurisdiction and powers as may be allowed to him by law and by the contract between the parties.

ARBITRATION ARRANGED BY THE CHARTERED INSTITUTE OF ARBITRATORS — IRISH BRANCH ON BEHALF OF TOUR OPERATOR

ADMINISTERED UNDER THE RULES OF THE CHARTERED INSTITUTE OF ARBITRATORS — IRISH BRANCH

ARBITRATION RULES

(For use in Holiday Arbitrations)

Rule 1   Applicability

1.1   Where any agreement, submission or reference provides for arbitration under the Arbitration Rules of the Chartered Institute of Arbitrators (Irish Branch) 'the Branch', the arbitration shall be conducted in accordance with the following Rules.

Rule 2   Request for Nomination of Arbitration

Where a request for the nomination of an Arbitrator is made to the Branch, the Request for Nomination Form should be completed and sent to the Branch at 5 Wilton Place, Dublin 2

Rule 3   Selection of Arbitrator

On Accepting a request for Nomination of Arbitrator, the Chairman or, in his absence, the Vice-Chairman shall nominate an Arbitrator to determine the dispute and shall advise the parties.

Rule 4   Number of Arbitrators

The nomination shall be of a single arbitrator.

Rule 5   Replacement of Arbitrator

If, after appointment, any Arbitrator dies, refuses, fails or, in the opinion of the Branch, becomes unable or unfit to act, the Chairman, shall, upon request, appoint another Arbitrator in his place.

Rule 6   Communications

6.1   Where a party sends out any communication (including any notice or Statement made under these Rules) to the Arbitrator, it shall send copies to all of the other parties at the same time and confirm to the Arbitrator that it has done so.

6.2 The Arbitrator shall likewise copy any communication to a party to all the other parties at the same time.

6.3 For the purpose of all communications during the proceedings, the address of a party shall be that set out in the Request for Nomination of Arbitrator unless otherwise notified to the Arbitrator.

6.4 Any notice or communication shall be deemed to have been properly delivered if dispatched by post, telex, facsimile transmission or by hand to the address of the party concerned.

6.5 The Arbitrator may, where appropriate, upon the application of either party, order substituted service of any communication in such form as the Arbitrator thinks fit.

Rule 7 Jurisdiction

The Arbitrator shall have the jurisdiction and the powers to direct the procedure in the Arbitration necessary to ensure the just, expeditious, economical and final determination of the dispute.

Rule 8 Procedure

In the absence of any other Directions, the Procedure of the Arbitration shall be that set out in the following Rules.

Rule 9 Directions

Directions from the Arbitrator to the parties shall be in writing or, if given orally, shall be confirmed in writing by the Arbitrator.

Rule 10 Orders

If the parties shall themselves agree upon any procedural matters, they shall seek the approval of the Arbitrator to them.

Rule 11 Objections

Any application to the Arbitrator shall be in writing. On receiving a copy of such application, any party may within seven days thereof make an objection in writing to the Arbitrator, with a copy to the other party (See Rule 6.1) On receipt of any such application or objection, the Arbitrator may give such Directions as appear to him appropriate with or without hearing the parties.

Rule 12 Adjournments

The Arbitrator may adjourn a meeting or hearing for such period as he may deem appropriate, if the party appears by a legal or professional representative without proper notice having been given to the other parties, or for such other reason as he may deem sufficient.

Rule 13   Statement of Claim Defence and Reply

13.1   The party who requested the arbitration ('the Claimant' shall send to the Arbitrator a Statement of Claim setting out in sufficient detail the facts, contentions of law on which it relies, and the relief it claims.

13.2   The other party ('the Respondent') shall send to the Arbitrator a Statement of Defence stating in a sufficient detail which of the facts and contentions of law in the Statement of Claim it admits or denies, on what grounds and on what other facts and contentions of law it relies. If it has a counterclaim, this shall be set out in the Statment of Defence, as a Statement of Claim.

13.3   After receipt of the Statement of Defence, the Claimant may send the Arbitrator a Statement of Reply.

13.4   Where there is a counterclaim, the Claimant shall send the Arbitrator a Statement of Defence to the counterclaim, to which the Respondent may make a Statement of Reply.

13.5   All Statements of Claim, Defence and Reply shall be accompanied by copies of the essential documents on which the party concerned relies.

13.6   The Arbitrator shall determine the time limits within which the Statements of Claim, Defence and Reply are to be submitted.

Rule 14   Meetings and Hearings

14.1   The Arbitrator shall fix the date, time and place of any hearing.

14.2   Alternatively, the Arbitrator may determine the dispute on the documents submitted to him by the parties, without any hearing.

Rule 15   The Award

The Arbitrator shall make his Award in writing as soon as practicable after the conclusion of the final hearing.

Rule 16   Settlements

If, before the publication of the Arbitrators final Award the parties arrive at a settlement of their disputes, they shall immediately so notify the Arbitrator in writing, and shall pay to the Arbitrator his costs incurred so that time in such proportions as they shall agree or, failing agreement, as the Arbitrator shall determine.

Rule 17   Costs

17.1   The parties shall be jointly and severally liable to the Arbitrator for his costs until they are paid.

17.2   The Arbitrator shall have full power and discretion to tax and settle costs of the arbitration and, where appropriate, his own costs and to determine which party shall pay such costs.

17.3   If the Arbitrator has determined that all or any costs shall be paid by any party other than the party which has already paid them, that party shall have the right to recover the appropriate amount from the party liable.

Rule 18   Exclusion of Liability

The Arbitrator and the Branch shall not be liable to any party for any act or omission or negligence in connection with any Arbitration conducted under these rules.

DIS
GERMAN INSTITUTION OF ARBITRATION

Deutsche Institution für Schiedsgerichtsbarkeit e.V.
Secretary General, Jens Bredow
Schedestrasse 13
Postfach 1446
53113 Bonn 1
Tel: +49-228/21 00 23-24
Fax: +49-228/21 22 75
Telex: 8 86 805 diht d

ARBITRATION RULES

1 January 1992

Arbitration Agreement

The German Institution of Arbitration recommends all parties wishing to make reference to DIS Arbitration in their contracts to use the following arbitration clause:

'All disputes arising from the contract (. . . description of the contract . . .) including its validity shall be finally settled according to the Arbitration Rules of the German Institution of Arbitration e.V. (DIS) without recourse to the ordinary courts of law. The arbitration tribunal may also decide on the validity of this arbitration agreement.'

It may be advisable to supplement the arbitration agreement, e.g. by an agreement concerning the venue of the arbitration tribunal or a decision by a sole arbitrator. In international relations it is advisable to agree on the substantive law to be applied as well as on the language of the proceedings.

Form of the Agreement

If a dispute is to be settled according to the following arbitration rules an arbitration agreement is necessary which must in principle be in writing. According to the international norm, this requirement is fulfilled if the arbitration agreement is contained in a contract signed by the parties or in letters, telegrams, telexes or telefax exchanged by the parties. The form of an arbitration agreement under German Law is governed by §1027 ZPO (Code of Civil Procedure: CCP):

§ 1027   CCP

I.   The Arbitration agreement must be concluded expressly and in writing; the instrument must not contain any agreements other than those referring to the arbitration procedure. Admission to the arbitral discussions on the substance of the case overrides any faults in form.

II.   The above provision does not apply if the arbitration agreement is a business matter for the two parties and if neither of the two parties belongs to the trading professions set out in Section 4 of the Commercial Code.

III.   In so far as, in accordance with para.2, the arbitration agreement does not have to be laid down in writing, each party may require a written instrument concerning the agreement.

ARBITRATION RULES OF THE
GERMAN INSTITUTION OF ARBITRATION*
(DEUTSCHE INSTITUTION FÜR
SCHIEDSGERICHTSBARKEIT e. V. (DIS))

§ 1   Application

These Arbitration Rules shall be applied to disputes which following an agreement concluded by the parties are to be decided by an arbitration tribual in accordance with the DIS Arbitration Rules without recourse to the ordinary courts of law.

§ 2   Choice of Arbitrators

The parties shall be free in their choice of the arbitrators. Upon request, the German Institution of Arbitration shall make suggestions for the choice of arbitrators.

§ 3   Number of Arbitrators

3.1   The arbitration tribunal shall consist of three arbitrators, unless the parties have agreed to nominate a sole arbitrator.

3.2   In procedures entailing only German parties, the chairman of the arbitration tribunal or the sole arbitrator must be qualified to hold judicial office.

§ 4   Request for Arbitration

4.1   The claimant shall file the statement of claim with the DIS Secretariat. Arbitration proceedings shall commence upon receipt of the statement of claim at the Secretariat.

---

*Translation of the German original. Should this translation in any way differ from the German original, the latter is binding.

4.2   The request must contain:
— identification of the parties,

— specification of the arbitation agreement,
— a definite statement on the subject-matter of the claim and on the reason for the claim,
— the claims requested,
— the appointment of an arbitrator or, where the parties have agreed on a sole arbitrator, a proposal for his joint appointment.

The statement of claim should contain a statement of the sum involved in the dispute.

4.3 The DIS Secretariat shall without delay serve the statement of claim to the respondent.

§ 5 Arbitration Tribunal with Three Arbitrators

5.1 On service of the request for arbitration the DIS Secretary General shall require the respondent to appoint an arbitrator within a period of 30 days. The Secretary General shall be entitled to extend this period after having heard the claimant. Where the respondent has not appointed an arbitrator within this time, the DIS Appointing Committee shall, on application by the claimant, appoint the arbitrator.

5.2 The two arbitrators shall elect the chairman of the arbitration tribunal and notify without delay the DIS Secretariat and the parties of this election. With regard to the election the arbitrators should take into account unanimous wishes of the parties. Where the two arbitrators have not given notification of the election of the chairman of the arbitration tribunal within 30 days after the request of the Secretary General, the DIS Appointing Committee shall, on application by a party, appoint the chairman of the arbitration tribunal.

§ 6 Sole Arbitrator

Where parties have not reached agreement on a sole arbitrator within a period of 30 days after service of the statement of claim to the respondent, the DIS Appointing Committee shall, on application by one of the parties, appoint the sole arbitrator.

§ 7 Acceptance of the Office as Arbitrator

Each arbitrator shall declare without delay to the DIS Secretariat whether he accepts the office as arbitrator. The DIS Secretariat shall notify the parties.

§ 8 Rejection of an Arbitrator

8.1 An arbitrator may be rejected
— in cases where a state judge would be barred from exercising judicial office,
— for fear of bias or
— for undue delay in fulfilling his duties as an arbitrator.

8.2 Within 2 weeks of cognisance of the reason for the rejection, a statement giving reasons for the rejection shall be made to the Secretary General of the Institution, which shall notify the arbitrators and the parties and set the rejected arbitrator and the other party a reasonable time-limit to make a statement. If the rejected arbitrator does not resign and the other party does not declare his agreement to the rejection within the time allowed, the rejecting party shall submit to the competent court within 2 weeks a motion of rejection by giving reasons.

8.3   If the other party declares his agreement to rejection or if the arbitrator resigns after rejection or if the motion of rejection is accepted with final and binding effect, the party that appointed the rejected arbitrator shall appoint another arbitrator, or the two arbitrators shall elect another chairman. §§ 5 and 6 shall apply *mutatis mutandis.*

§ 9   Default of Arbitrator

Where an arbitrator defaults his duties, § 8 shall apply *mutatis mutandis.*

§ 10   Costs of the Arbitration Tribunal

10.1   The arbitrators are entitled to remuneration (fees and expenses, value-added tax), for which the parties to the arbitration agreement are jointly and severally liable.

10.2   The fees shall be determined according to the sum involved in the dispute to be assessed by the arbitration tribunal in accordance with the statutory provisions.

10.3   Each arbitrator is entitled to a fee for his services.

10.4   Where proceedings are terminated in an early stage, the arbitration tribunal may at its equitable discretion reduce the fees in correspondence with the duration of the proceedings.

10.5   The German Institution of Arbitration is entitled to a service fee.

10.6   The amount of the fees shall be calculated according to the schedule of the Arbitration Rules.

§ 11   Venue of the Arbitration Tribunal

Where the parties have not agreed on a venue for the arbitration tribunal, the venue shall be determined by the arbitration tribunal. Meetings of the arbitration tribunal may also be held in other places.

§ 12   Proceedings

12.1   The chairman of the arbitration tribunal shall preside over the proceedings.

12.2   The chairman may make the proceedings dependent upon advance payments on the costs of the arbitration tribunal by requesting payment of half of the advance from each party.

§ 13   Pleadings, Summons, Directions

13.1   The statement of the arbitration claim, pleadings with applications on the merits or a withdrawal of the claim, summons and directions of the arbitration tribunal setting time-limits shall be served to the parties by registered letter with a receipt acknowledging delivery. All other pleadings, notifications and records may be sent by ordinary mail. All documents and information sent by a party to the arbitration tribunal shall at the same time also be transmitted to the other party.

13.2   Where a document subject to service pursuant to § 13.1 is received by other means, service shall be deemed to have been effected at the time of actual receipt.

13.3   A legal representative is to be served in lieu of the party.

§ 14   Hearing

14.1   Before the arbitration award is rendered, a hearing shall be held unless the parties have expressly waived the right to a hearing or unless, at the arbitration tribunal's discretion, a hearing is dispensable.

14.2   The chairman shall request the parties to make full statements on the relevant facts and the appropriate applications.

14.3   The parties shall be given a hearing at every stage of the proceedings.

§ 15   Default of a Party

15.1   When the respondent, without sufficient excuse, fails to submit a reply to the claim within a time-limit set by the chairman, or where a party, without sufficient excuse omits during the further course of proceedings and within a time-limit set by the chairman to fulfil a requirement imposed by the arbitration tribunal, or in spite of a proper summons has not appeared and was not represented at the hearing, the arbitration tribunal shall continue the proceedings.

15.2   The reasons for the excuse have to be substantiated upon request of the arbitration tribunal.

15.3   A default of a party shall not be deemed to be an admission of the factual submissions of the other party. The arbitration tribunal shall freely assess the defaulting conduct of a party.

§ 16   Proceedings of the Arbitration Tribunal

The arbitration tribunal shall handle the proceedings at its own free discretion.

§ 17   Establishment of the Facts

17.1   The arbitration tribunal shall establish the facts. It may order at its own discretion and, in particular, it may examine witnesses and experts and order the production of documents. It shall not be limited by applications of the parties in taking of evidence.

17.2   The arbitration tribunal shall be deemed to be authorised by the parties to refer to the competent state court to have an oath sworn by a witness or by an expert or another act performed which does not lie within its competence.

§ 18   Written Record of Oral Proceedings

A written record shall be made of oral proceedings. Such record shall be signed by the chairman.

The parties will receive a copy of the written record.

§ 19   Arbitration Settlement

19.1   At every stage of the proceedings the arbitration tribunal shall seek to reach an amicable settlement of the dispute or of individual issues in dispute.

19.2   A settlement shall be entered into the written record. On application of a party, the written record shall be signed by the arbitrators and the parties.

19.3   In order to secure enforcement of a settlement, a declaration of submission to immediate execution can be requested from the parties. In such case the written record verifying the settlement must be signed by the parties and the arbitrators and specify the date on which the settlement was reached. The written record shall be deposited at the registry of the competent court.

§ 20   Deliberation of Arbitration Award

20.1   The arbitration tribunal shall encourage an expeditious conduct of the proceedings and render the arbitration award within a reasonable time.

20.2   The arbitration award and all decisions preceding the arbitration award shall be made with a majority of votes of the arbitration tribunal.

20.3   An arbitration award shall be bound by the request of the parties.

§ 21   Applicable Law

21.1   The arbitration tribunal shall decide in accordance with the legal provisions agreed upon by the parties. A reference to a particular national law without further specifications by the parties shall be understood as a direct reference to the substantive law of that state and not to its conflict of laws rules.

21.2   Where the parties have not agreed on the applicable law, the arbitration tribunal shall decide in accordance with the legal provisions of the conflict of laws rules that it holds applicable.

21.3   Only upon express authorisation by the parties may the arbitration tribunal decide in accordance with equity (ex aequo et bono, amiable composition).

21.4   The arbitration tribunal shall in all cases take account of the parties' contractual provisions and current commercial practices and usages.

§ 22   Costs

22.1   The arbitration tribunal shall decide which party is to bear the costs of the arbitration proceedings, including the costs incurred by the parties and those necessary for the appropriate conduct of the matter.

22.2   In principle, the unsuccessful party shall bear the costs of the arbitration proceedings. Where a party is partly successful, the arbitration tribunal may offset the costs or divide them proportionally between the parties.

22.3 § 22.1 and § 22.2 shall apply mutatis mutandis where the proceedings have been terminated without an arbitration award and so far as the parties have not reached an agreement on the costs.

§ 23   Form of Arbitration Award

23.1   The arbitration award must be drawn up in writing and substantiated with reasons. Thus, it shall contain:

a)   an identification of the parties to the arbitration proceedings;
b)   an identification of the arbitrators;
c)   the venue of the arbitration tribunal;
d)   the date of drawing up;
e)   the operative provisions of the arbitration award with the decision as to what is bound to be right between the parties;
f)   the statement of facts;
g)   the reasons;
h)   the signatures of all members of the arbitration tribunal.

23.2   Where signature cannot be procured from one arbitrator, the signature of the other arbitrators shall suffice. The chairman of the arbitration tribunal shall make a note under the arbitration award that signature could not be procured from the arbitrator concerned.

23.3   The chairman of the arbitration tribunal shall ensure production of the required number of originals of the award.

§ 24   Service and Deposit of the Award

24.1   One original of the award shall be served to each party by registered letter with a receipt acknowledging delivery. §13.2 shall apply mutatis mutandis.

24.2   The award shall be deposited together with evidence of service at the registry of the competent court in the absence of any other agreement of the parties — except in the case of declaration of enforceability.

24.3   Each arbitrator shall be deemed to be authorised by the arbitrators and by the parties to furnish the parties with the arbitration award or the settlement and to deposit them at the registry of the competent court. The DIS Secretariat shall also be authorised to deposit the arbitration award or the settlement.

§ 25   Effect of the Award

The award shall be final and between the parties it shall have the effect of a final and binding court judgment.

§ 26   Disclosure of the Award

The chairman shall send an authentic copy of the award to the Secretariat of the Institution with the information whether the parties have consented to disclosure of the award. The Institution may disclose the arbitration award only with the consent of the parties, yet the names of the parties and the arbitrators and other individual data shall not be disclosed.

§ 27 Secrecy

If consent to disclosure of the arbitration award has not been given, the arbitrators shall preserve utmost secrecy of the proceedings and of all the facts which have come to their knowledge as arbitrator. The arbitration tribunal shall oblige to secrecy all persons invited by it to act in the proceedings.

Schedule to § 10.6 of the Arbitration Rules.

[*This schedule is not reproduced here.*]

GERMAN INSTITUTION OF ARBITRATION
DEUTSCHE INSTITUTION FÜR SCHIEDSGERICHTSBARKEIT
e. V.

GUIDE TO THE CONDUCT OF ARBITRATION PROCEEDINGS

This guide appears in Part VII, on Conduct and Ethics later in this book.

FEDERATION OF OILS, SEEDS AND FATS
ASSOCIATIONS LTD

20 St Dunstan's Hill,
London EC3R 8HL
Tel: 0044-171-283-5511/2707
Fax: 0044-171-623-1310
Telex: 8812757

RULES OF ARBITRATION AND APPEAL

revised and effective from 1 January 1995

Any dispute arising out of a contract or contracts subject to these Rules, including any questions of law arising in connection therewith, shall be referred to arbitration in London (or elsewhere if so agreed) in accordance with the Arbitration Acts 1950, 1975 and 1979 or any statutory modification or re-enactment thereof for the time being in force.

Each Party engaging in an arbitration or an appeal pursuant to these Rules, whether or not a Member of the Federation, is deemed therefore to abide by these Rules and to agree with the Federation to be liable to the Federation (jointly and severally with the other parties to the arbitration or appeal) for all fees and expenses incurred in connection with the arbitration or appeal, which said fees and expenses shall, upon notification by the Federation under the provisions of Rules 1(b), 1(f), 6(b) and 9, be and become a debt due to the Federation.

1. Appointment of Arbitrators/Umpire

(a) Each party shall appoint an arbitrator who shall have accepted the appointment. However the two parties may by agreement appoint a sole arbitrator who shall have accepted the appointment. Any reference to arbitrators in these Rules shall also be taken to refer to a sole arbitrator. Each party shall advise the Federation promptly of the name of any arbitrator which that party has appointed.

(b) If two arbitrators have been appointed they shall, if and when they disagree, appoint an umpire. If the arbitrators fail to agree on the appointment of an umpire, they shall notify the Federation which shall appoint an umpire. The Federation shall charge a fee, to be fixed by the Council from time to time, on such appointment.

(c) Only full Members or their nominated representative/s to the Federation shall have the right to act as arbitrators or umpires subject to retirement at age 75, if still active in the trade, or two years after retirement, whichever comes first. No person shall be eligible to act who, or whose company or firm, has any direct or indirect interest in the transaction in dispute. No person shall be eligible to proceed as an arbitrator or umpire who is already proceeding as an arbitrator or umpire in 10 disputes, excluding arbitrations on quality and/or condition and any arbitration stayed by Order of the Court. Any arbitration other than on quality and/or condition that is being held as between the first Seller and the last Buyer in a string shall be counted as a single dispute.

(d) If the party claiming arbitration has notified the other party and the Federation in accordance with Rule 2(a) or (b) and that party fails to appoint an arbitrator within the time specified, or in the event that an arbitrator refuses to act, becomes incapable of acting or ineligible to act, or delays unduly, and the party who made the appointment omits to appoint a substitute, then the other party may apply to the Federation in accordance with Rule 1(f) for the appointment of an arbitrator to act on behalf of the party who failed to appoint an arbitrator or substitute as the case may be.

(e) Any application to the Federation as mentioned under Rule 1(b) and (d) above shall be accompanied by a copy of the notice of claim for arbitration.

(f) The Federation on receiving an application to appoint under Rule 1(d) shall charge the appropriate fee fixed by the Council from time to time. The Federation will notify the party who has failed to make an appointment or a substitution of its arbitrator, as the case may be, that the Federation intends to make such an appointment unless that party makes it own appointment with 14 consecutive days of notice being despatched to it by the Federation. In the absence of an appointment being notified to the Federation within the stipulated period the Federation shall make such an appointment.

2. Procedure for Claiming Arbitration and Time Limits

(a) Claims on quality and/or condition:

(i) If the claim is not to be supported by certificate/s of contractual analysis/ses, the party claiming arbitration shall despatch the notice of claim with the name of his appointed arbitrator to the other party within 21 consecutive days from the date of completion of discharge of the goods and shall at the same time notify the Federation and despatch sealed sample/s to the office of the Federation, where such sample/s shall be held at the disposal of the arbitrators and/or unpire. The other party shall nominate an arbitrator and notify his name to the Federation within 7 consecutive days from receipt of such notice. Notwithstanding the above, if the claimant requires a supporting analysis then a further sample shall have been despatched to the analyst within 21 consecutive days from the date of completion of discharge of the goods.

For FOB, ex tank, ex mill and ex store contracts under 2(a) the word 'delivery' shall be read in place of 'discharge'.

(ii)   If the claim is to be supported by certificate/s of contractual analysis/ses, the notice under (i) shall be despatched and the Federation notified within 14 consecutive days from the date of the final analysis certificate. The other party shall nominate an arbitrator and notify his name to the Federation within 7 consecutive days from the receipt of such notice.

(iii)   If the claim relates to goods sold as fair average quality and the contract provides for a standard average for the month of shipment being made, the notice shall be despatched and the Federation notified within 14 consecutive days of the publication in the trade lists that the standard has been or will not be made. The other party shall nominate an arbitrator and notify his name to the Federation within 7 consecutive days from the receipt of such notice.

If the arbitration is not proceeded with within 14 consecutive days of the appointment of the arbitrator acting for the respondent, then either party may apply to the Federation in accordance with Rule 1(d) for the appointment of a substitute.

(b)   Claims other than on quality and/or condition shall be notified by the claimant with the name of an arbitrator to the other party and to the Federation within the time limits stipulated in this Rule:

(i)   For goods sold

(1)   On CIF terms: not later than 120 consecutive days after the expiry of the contract period of shipment or of the date of completion of final discharge of the goods whichever period shall last expire.

(2)   On FOB terms: not later than 120 consecutive days after the expiry of the contract period of shipment.

(3)   On any other terms: not later than 120 consecutive days after the last day of the contractual delivery period.

(ii)   In respect of any monies due by one party to the other, not later than 60 consecutive days after the dispute has arisen. The other party shall nominate an arbitrator and notify his name to the Federation within 30 consecutive days from receipt of such notice.

(c)   Claims for arbitration shall be made in accordance with the Notices Clause of the contract. The provisions of the Non-Business Days Clause shall also apply.

(d)   In the event of non-compliance with any of the preceding provisions of this Rule, and of such non-compliance being raised by the respondents as a defence, claims shall be deemed to be waived and absolutely barred unless the arbitrators, umpire or Board of Appeal referred to in these Rules, shall, in their absolute discretion, otherwise determine, whereupon the substantive case shall be considered first by the arbitrators and subsequently, if necessary, by an umpire and Board of Appeal in accordance with these Rules.

(e)   Failure to notify the Federation as required by Rule 1(a), 2(a) or 2(b) shall not in itself debar a claim for arbitration nor prevent an arbitration proceeding but shall be taken into account by arbitrators, umpire or Board of Appeal in exercising their discretion under Rule 2(d).

3.   Lapse of Claim

If neither the claimant nor the respondent submits any documentary evidence or submissions to the arbitrator appointed by or for him with the copy to the other party within the period of one year from the date of appointment of the first named arbitrator, then the claim to arbitration shall be deemed to have lapsed on expiry of the said period of one year unless before that date the claim is renewed by a further claim for arbitration to be made by either party notifying the other before the expiry date. Any such renewal shall be for a period of one year from the date of the giving of notice of renewal when it shall lapse again unless renewed in the like manner as the first renewal or unless by then documentary evidence or submissions have been submitted by either the claimant or the respondent. In the event of failure to renew a claim as provided in this Rule such claim shall be deemed to have been withdrawn and abandoned unless the arbitrator/s shall in his/their absolute discretion otherwise determine upon such terms as he/they think fit.

4.   Procedure for Arbitrations

(a)   Claims under Rule 2(a) (quality and/or condition)

(i)   The party claiming arbitration shall despatch in writing his submission together with supporting documents to his appointed arbitrator in triplicate and to the party against whom arbitration is claimed within 10 consecutive days of the claim for arbitration.

(ii)   If the party against whom a claim is made wishes to reply to the claimants submission, such reply together with supporting documents shall be despatched in writing to his arbitrator in triplicate and to the other party within 14 consecutive days of the receipt thereof. Failing receipt of such reply, the arbitrators shall proceed with the arbitration without delay.

(iii)   In arbitration under Rule 2(a)(i) and (iii), the Award of the arbitrator/s or umpire shall be despatched to FOSFA International for typing within 28 consecutive days from the date of the claim or the date of the publication of the standard.

(b)   Claims under 2(b) (other than on quality and/or condition)

(i)   The party claiming arbitration shall despatch in writing his submission together with supporting documents to his appointed arbitrator in triplicate and to the other party against whom arbitration is claimed without delay.

(ii)   If the party against whom a claim is made wishes to reply, such reply together with supporting documents shall be despatched in writing to his appointed arbitrator in triplicate and to the other party without delay. Failing receipt of such reply, the arbitrators shall proceed with the arbitration without delay.

(c)   Upon receiving particulars of the dispute or claim in accordance with Rule 4(a)(i) or 4(b)(i) an arbitrator shall immediately notify the Federation, using the appropriate form. When arbitrators appoint an umpire they shall also notify the Federation, using the appropriate form.

(d)   A sole arbitrator or the arbitrators, by mutual agreement, or the umpire, or the Board of Appeal, as the case may be, shall have discretion to extend the time limits under Rule 4(a).

(e)   If one party has submitted any document to the arbitrator/s which has not been submitted to the other party, then a copy thereof shall be supplied to that party by the arbitrator/s prior to the hearing.

(f)   The arbitrator/s or the umpire, as the case may be, shall have the power to request further information or documents from either of the parties, to hear oral submissions or evidence if they or he so desire and to make such directions relating to the conduct of the arbitration as they or he think fit. The parties shall be entitled to a reasonable period within which to comply with any such request but the arbitrators or the umpire, as the case may be, having given reasonable notice, may made an Award if such requests have not been complied with.

(g)   If either party has expressed a wish to be present, the arbitrators or the umpire shall give reasonable notice to the parites of the date, time and place when any oral evidence or additional submissions may be heard and both parties to the arbitration or their authorised representatives may attend any such hearing but may not have present or be represented by counsel, solicitor or any member of the legal profession wholly or principally engaged in legal practice.

(h)   The arbitrator/s or the umpire at their absolute discretion may require the claimant to lodge a deposit with the Federation on account of the fees, costs and expenses of the arbitration before proceeding. If after the expiration of 14 consecutive days after the notification to the claimant of the deposit is paid. In the event that the deposit is not paid within 28 consecutive days the arbitration shall be deemed to be permanetly stayed unless the arbitrator/s or umpire in the exercise of their absolute discretion decide to continue the arbitration.

(i)   If any party to an arbitration considers that either arbitrator or the umpire is failing to exercise all reasonable despatch in entering on or proceeding with the arbitration then that party may notify the Federation accordingly in writing with full details. Upon receipt of such notice the Federation shall call upon the arbitrator or umpire to explain the reasons for the delay. The arbitrator or umpire must furnish the Federation with such an explanation within seven days of the Federation's request for such an explanation. If the Federation is not satisfied with the arbitrator's or umpire's explanation the Federation shall fix a seven day period in which the arbitrator or umpire is to take the next step required to be done in proceeding with the arbitration. Should the arbitrator or umpire fail to respond to the Federation's request for an explanation or fail to take the next step required to be done in proceeding with the arbitration, within the seven day period then the Federation shall have the right to require the arbitrator or umpire to resign his position as arbitrator or umpire in that particular arbitration. The arbitrator or umpire shall be deemed to have resigned his position fourteen consecutive days after despatch to him of the Federation's written requirement that he resigns his appointment unless otherwise decided by the Federation.

An arbitrator or umpire who is called upon to resign his position as arbitrator or umpire under this provision shall not be entitled to receive any remuneration in respect of his services provided in the particular arbitration in question unless otherwise decided by the Federation. Where an arbitrator resigns his position under this provision then the party who appointed the arbitrator shall appoint another duly qualified arbitrator in his place within fourteen days of the notice being despatched in accordance with the provisions of Rule 1 hereof. If that party does not so appoint then the Federation shall make such an appointment and shall charge the defaulting party the appropriate fee fixed by the Council from time to time being in force.

Where an umpire resigns his position under this provision then the two arbitrators who have appointed him shall appoint another umpire in his place, within seven days of being notified of the resignation of the umpire. If the arbitrators do not so appoint then the Federation shall make such an appointment in accordance with its powers under Rule 1(b) hereof.

In circumstances where an arbitrator or umpire is removed from an arbitration by the Federation as provided for above, the Federation may, by a decision of the Council, also suspend or remove that person's right to act as an arbitrator or umpire and to serve on the appeals panel.

5. Jurisdiction

(a) Prior to proceeding with an arbitration, arbitrators shall satisfy themselves that they have jurisdiction. If arbitrators agree that they have no jurisdiction they shall jointly advise the parties in writing.

(b) If the arbitrators cannot agree that they have jurisdiction they shall appoint an umpire under Rule 1(b) who shall first determine the question of jurisdiction.

(c) If the umpire decides that he has no jurisdiction then he shall advise the arbitrators in writing who shall advise the parties in writing.

(d) If the umpire decides that he does have jurisdiction, he shall proceed with the arbitration without delay.

6. Procedure for Arbitration Awards

(a) Awards, which shall incorporate the reasons therefore, shall be in writing on the official form of the Federation and the arbitrators or the umpire shall have the power to assess and award their fees and award by whom these and other fees and expenses of the arbitration shall be paid. The Federation's fees shall be those in force as prescribed by the Council of the Federation.

(b) When an award has been signed, it shall be the duty of the arbitrators or the umpire to lodge the original and two copies with the Federation who shall date them and give notice to the parties named in the award that the award is at their disposal upon payment of the fees and expenses of the arbitration. Such payment must be received by the Federation within 42 days of the date of the award or the parties shall forfeit their right to appeal against the award under Rule 7 below. On receipt of payment, the Federation shall immediately send the original award to the party who has paid and send a copy to the other party. Until payment has been made, the contents of the award shall under no circumstances be divulged.

(c)   Should the contract form part of a string of contracts which are in all material points identical in terms, except as to date and price, then:

(i)   In any arbitration for quality and/or condition, as mentioned in Rule 2(a)(i), (ii) and (iii) above, the arbitration shall be held as between the first Seller and the last Buyer in the string as though they were contracting parties.

Any Award so made (in these Rules called the String Award) shall, subject to the right of appeal as provided in these Rules, be binding on all the intermediate parties in the string, and may be enforced by any intermediate party against him immediate contracting party as though a separate award had been made under each contract.

(ii)   In other cases arbitration shall only be held as between the first Seller and the last Buyer in a string as though they were contracting parties if all parties in the string agree in writing and provided each intermediate party shall have submitted his contract and all relevant information to the arbitrators.

A separate Award shall be made in respect of each contract.

7.   Procedure for Claiming Appeal and Time Limits

(a)   Any party to an award of arbitration shall have the right to appeal to the Appeals Panel of the Federation provided (i) that payment of the fees and expenses of the arbitration was made to the Federation within 42 days of the date of the award as per Rule 6(b) and (ii) that notice of appeal is received by the Secretary of the Federation not later than 12.00 hours on the 28th consecutive day after the date on which the award is sent to the parties, in accordance with Rule 6(b) above.

(b)   The appellant when giving notice of appeal to the Federation shall arrange to pay to the Federation a deposit as prescribed by the Council of the Federation on account of fees, costs and expenses of the appeal, which is to be received by the Secretary of the Federation not later than 7 consecutive days after receipt of the notice of appeal.

If due to currency regulations payment of the deposit is not possible within the 7 day time limit an extension of 14 consecutive days shall be granted for the payment of the deposit provided that the appellant has produced satisfactory evidence from a bank that the application for the transfer of the deposit has been made.

(c)   The appellant shall, within the 42 day time limit, inform the other principal to the contract that he has lodged an appeal. Every notice given to a party to any string Award shall be passed on with due despatch by that party and such passing on, provided it is done with due despatch, shall be deemed to be in compliance with the procedure for claiming appeal.

(d)   Should it not be possible to perform any of the foregoing acts within the time limits stipulated, application may be made to the Federation for an extension of the time limit, which extension may be granted at the absolute discretion of the Federation.

8. Procedure for Appointment of Boards of Appeal

(a) The appeal shall be determined by a Board of Appeal consisting of five members appropriately appointed by the Federation from the Appeals Panel. No member of the Panel who, or whose company or firm, has any direct or indirect interest in the transaction in dispute or who has acted as arbitrator or umpire in the case, nor any member of the same company or firm to which either of the arbitrators or the umpire belong, shall be entitled to be appointed a member of the Board of Appeal.

(b) In the case of illness or death, or refusal, or incapacity, or inability to act, of any member appointed to serve on a Board of Appeal, the Federation shall appoint a substitute from the Appeals Panel in his place. Nevertheless if only four members of the Board Panel are able to serve on the day of the substantive hearing, they may, subject to the agreement of the parties or of their duly authorised representatives, exercise all the powers of the Board of Appeal.

(c) In the event of appeals lodged by more than one party in relation to the same Award, the Federation shall consolidate such appeals for hearing by the same Board of Appeal.

9. Procedure at Appeals

(a) Each party may state their case orally and/or in writing and may appear either personally or be represented by a person nominated to the Federation by a full member company or firm or a person who is a full member of the Federation and duly appointed in writing, but shall not be represented by or have present at the hearing of such appeal, Counsel or Solicitor, or any member of the legal profession wholly or principally engaged in legal practice, unless, at the sole discretion of the Board of Appeal, the case is of special importance, and in such cases the other party shall have the same rights.

(b) The Board of Appeal shall issue a reasoned Award signed by a minimum of three members of the Board of Appeal and counter-signed by the Secretary to the Board of Appeal and when so signed shall be the Award of the Board of Appeal which shall be final and binding.

(c) In respect of any String Award made by a Board of Appeal such String Award shall be binding on the first Sellers, the last Buyers, and all the intermediate parties in the string and may be enforced by any intermediate party against his immediate contracting party as though a separate award had been made under each contract.

(d) The board of Appeal shall have the power to require from time to time a further deposit/s to be made by either party and shall award the payment of appeal fees, costs and expenses of and incidental to the appeal. If an Award is remitted to a Board of Appeal by order of the Court the Board shall have the power to require a deposit to be made by the party/ies that made application to the Court on account of the fees, costs and expenses of any hearing by the Board of submissions by the parties or of any meeting of the Board occasioned by such remission. No interest shall be payable on any deposit or further deposit made by any party to an appeal under the provisions either of this Rule of Rule 7.

(e)   If the appellant, on receiving from the Board of Appeal notice of the date fixed for the hearing of the appeal, requests a postponement of more than 14 days or at the first or any subsequent hearing of the appeal requests an adjournment, then in such events the Board of Appeal may at their absolute discretion direct that as a condition of granting a postponement or an adjournment all or any part of the money required by the terms of the award of arbitration to be paid by either party to the other shall be deposited in a bank (either in England or abroad) as the Board of Appeal may direct. Such money shall be held by such bank in an account in the name of the Federation and otherwise in such terms as the Board of Appeal directs.

The Board of Appeal shall, where such money has been deposited, in their Award direct how and to which of the parties the amount so held shall be paid out. Provided that, if in the opinion of the Board of Appeal after hearing the parties, the appellant shall have delayed unduly the proceedings of his appeal, he shall after due warning and if the Board of Appeal so decides, be deemed to have withdrawn his appeal in which case the money on deposit (with interest, if any, less tax) shall immediately become due and payable to the party or parties entitled thereto under the terms of the Award of Arbitration.

10.   Withdrawal of Appeals

(a)   An appellant shall have the right at any time before the hearing of the appeal to withdraw his appeal subject to payment of such costs, if any, as the Federation or the Board of Appeal may determine:

(i)   On notice being received from the appellant at least 24 hours before the appointment of the Board of Appeal half of the deposit shall be returned.

(ii)   On notice being received at least 72 hours before the time fixed for the hearing by the Board of Appeal one quarter shall be returned.

(iii)   If such notice of withdrawal is received after that time no part of the deposit shall be returned.

(iv)   When an appeal is withdrawn before any action has been taken by the Federation the deposit shall be refunded.

(b)   In the event of such withdrawal as aforesaid any other party to an Award of Arbitration shall have a right of appeal against that award to the Arbitration and Appeal Panel of the Federation in accordance with the provisions of Rule 7 save that the time limit for giving notice of appeal laid down in Rule 7 shall be 12.00 hours on the 21st consecutive day after the date of the Federation's notice to that party of the aforesaid withdrawal.

11.   General

(a)   (i)   Any objection to the membership of a Board of Appeal on the ground that a member of the Board of Appeal was not eligible to serve must be made in writing and established to the satisfaction of the Council of the Federation before the hearing of the substantive case has commenced.

(ii)   If such objection is made the Federation in its absolute discretion shall have the power to appoint a substitute member or members of a Board of Appeal from the Appeals Panel up to the beginning of the hearing of the substantive case.

(iii)   No award of a Board of Appeal shall be questioned or invalidated on the ground of any irregularity in the appointment of the Board of Appeal or any of its members or on the ground that any member of the Board of Appeal was not eligible to serve.

(b)   Any notice may be delivered personally or left at the place where the party to whom it is to be delivered is carrying on business or (by reason of the provisions of the contract) is to be considered to be carrying on business. A copy shall be delivered to the Federation.

(c)   If an Arbitration or an Appeal Award is not taken up by any of the parties to the dispute within 28 consecutive days after the date of the Award, the Federation shall call upon the claimant or the appellant, as the case may be, to take up the Award. If the claimant or the appellant fail to take up the Award, the Council of the Federation may post on the Federation's notice board and/or circularise to members in any way thought fit a notification to that effect. The parties to any such arbitration or appeal held under these Rules shall be deemed to have consented to the Council taking such action.

(d)   In the event of any party to an arbitration or appeal held under these Rules neglecting or refusing to carry out or abide by an Award of arbitrators or umpire or Board of Appeal made under these Rules, the Council of the Federation may post on the Federation's notice board and/or circularise to members in any way thought fit a notification to that effect. The parties to any such arbitration or appeal shall be deemed to have consented to the Council taking such action.

THE GRAIN AND FEED TRADE ASSOCIATION

The Grain & Feed Trade Association,
Mrs. Pamela Kirby Johnson, Director General
GAFTA House, 6 Chapel Place,
Rivington Street, London EC2A 3DQ
Tel: 0044-171 814 9666
Fax: 0044-171 814 8383
Tx: 886984 GAFTA G
E-Mail Address: post@gafta.demon.co.uk

ARBITRATION RULES

effective 1 March 1994

1. Preliminary

1.1   Any dispute arising out of a contract embodying these Rules shall be referred to arbitration in accordance with the following provisions.

1.2   Arbitration shall take place in London, or elsewhere if mutually agreed by the parties.

1.3   The provisions of the Arbitration Acts 1950, 1975 and 1979, and of any statutory modification or re-enactment thereof for the time being in force, shall apply to every arbitration and appeal held under these Rules save insofar as such provisions are modified by or are inconsistent with these Rules.

1.4   In these Rules:—

(a)   'Council' means the Council of the Association.

(b)   'Officers' means the President, Deputy President, the two Vice Presidents, the Director General and Secretary of the Association.

(c)   The masculine gender shall include the feminine gender.

1.5   Each party engaging in an arbitration or an appeal pursuant to these Rules, whether or not a Member of the Association, is deemed thereby to agree to abide by these Rules and to agree with the Association to be liable to the Association (jointly and severally with the other parties to the arbitration or appeal) for all fees and expenses incurred in connection with the arbitration or appeal or any remissions, which said fees and expenses shall, upon notification by the Association be and become a debt due to the Association. Any costs incurred by the Association in connection with Rule 4, will be debited direct to the respective party by the Association when deemed appropriate.

2. Procedure for Claiming Arbitration and Time Limits

2.1   A party claiming arbitration shall notify the other party that he is claiming arbitration within the time limits stipulated in this Rule, and shall, no later than 7 consecutive days from the last day for claiming arbitration, appoint an arbitrator in accordance with Rule 3.

2.2   Technical

(a)   In respect of Contracts for the Sale of Goods:

(i)   On CIF terms: not later than 90 consecutive days after the expiry of the contract period of shipment including extension if any, or after the date of completion of final discharge of the ship at port of destination whichever period shall last expire;

(ii)   on FOB terms: not later than 90 consecutive days after the date of the last bill of lading or after the expiry of the contract period of delivery, including extension if any, whichever shall first expire;

(iii)   on any other terms: not later than 90 consecutive days after the last day of the contractual delivery period.

(b)   In respect of claims arising out of certificates of analysis for which allowances are not fixed by the terms of the contract, not later than 21 consecutive days from the date of receipt by the claimant of the final certificate of analysis.

(c)   In respect of any monies due by one party to the other, not later than 90 consecutive days of the dispute having arisen.

2.3   Quality and/or Condition (excluding Rye Terms Clause) Grain, Pulses and Cereal By-Products

Contract Numbers: 2, 3, 12, 13, 14, 14a, 16, 23, 24, 25, 27, 28, 30, 31, 32, 35, 36, 41, 43 54a, 59, 60, 61, 62, 64, 75, 77, 78, 79, 79a, 80, 80a, 83, 84, 85, 86, 94, 94a, 110, 111.

(a)   When the sale has been a sale on sample, or by specification, or by Grade No. 1 Marrowfat Peas, not later than 14 consecutive days after the date of completion of final discharge of the ship at port of destination.

(b)   When the sale has been of fair average quality to be assessed upon the basis of and by comparison with the Association's Official FAQ Standard of the month during which the bill of lading is dated, not later than 14 consecutive days after publication by the Association that the Standard has been, or will not be, made.

(c)   When the sale has been of fair average quality against a Standard which is officially adopted by the Association, not later than 14 consecutive days after completion of final discharge of the ship at port of destination, or not later than 14 consecutive days after publication by the Association that the Standard has been, or will not be, adopted, whichever period shall last expire.

(d)   In respect of quality and/or condition of goods sold otherwise than for shipment, not later than 28 consecutive days after the date of delivery, or for goods sold ex store/silo, not later than 35 consecutive days after the date of invoice.

(e)   In respect of containerised goods within 14 consecutive days from the unstuffing of the container, but not later than 28 consecutive days after the date of completion of final discharge of the ship at port of destination.

2.4   Quality and/or Condition (excluding Rye Terms Clause)
Feeding Stuffs
Contract Numbers: 1, 4, 6, 8, 9, 10, 15, 17, 22, 95, 96, 97, 98, 99, 100, 100a, 101, 102, 103, 104, 107, 108, 109, 112, 113, 114, 116, 118, 119.

(a)   In respect of quality and/or condition of goods sold for shipment, not later than 28 consecutive days after the date of completion of final discharge of the ship at port of destination.

(b)   In respect of quality and/or condition of goods sold otherwise than for shipment, not later than 28 consecutive days after the date of delivery, or for goods sold ex store/silo, not later than 35 consecutive days after the date of invoice.

2.5   Rye Terms
In respect of the 'Rye Terms' Clause within 10 consecutive days after the date of completion of final discharge of the ship at port of destination.

2.6   Finality
Every arbitration for quality and/or condition claimed in accordance with Rules 2:3, 2:4 and 2:5 must be proceeded with as follows:

(a)   When the sale has been a sale on sample, or by specification, or by Grade No. 1 Marrowfat Peas within 28 consecutive days after the date of completion of final discharge of the ship at port of destination.

(b)   When the sale has been of fair average quality or by description in respect of Grains, Pulses and Cereal By-Products (Contracts listed in Clause 2.3), within 28 consecutive days of the publication by the Association that the Standard has been, or will not be, adopted or made, or within 28 consecutive days after the date of completion of final discharge of the ship at port of destination, whichever period shall last expire.

(c)   When the sale has been of fair average quality in respect of Feeding Stuffs (Contracts listed in Clause 2.4), within 60 consecutive days of the date of appointment of an arbitrator by or on behalf of the party against whom arbitration has been claimed.

(d)   In respect of goods sold otherwise than for shipment (unless sold on sample, by specification or by Grade No. 1 Marrowfat Peas or of fair average quality), within 28 consecutive days of arbitration having been claimed.

(e) When the goods have been bought or sold on terms known as 'Rye Terms', within 21 consecutive days after the date of completion of final discharge of the ship at port of destination.

(f) For Contract No. 75 — Condition (fly and/or weevil) — within 10 consecutive days of the claim for arbitration.

2.7 In the event of non-compliance with any of the preceding provisions of this Rule and of such non-compliance being raised by the respondents as a defence, claims shall be deemed to be waived and absolutely barred, unless the arbitrator(s) shall in his/their absolute discretion, otherwise determine. If the arbitrator(s) do not exercise his/their discretion to admit a claim then the board of appeal, on appeal, shall have the power in its absolute discretion to determine otherwise, but not so as to over-rule or set aside any determination already made by the arbitrator(s) to admit a claim.

2.8 No award by the arbitrator(s) shall be questioned or invalidated on appeal or otherwise on the ground that the claim was not made within the time limits stipulated in this Rule if the respondents to the claim did not raise the matter in his submissions so as to enable the arbitrator(s) to consider whether or not to exercise the discretion vested in him/them by Rule 2.7.

2.9 Lapse of Claim

If neither the claimants nor the respondents submits any documentary evidence or submissions to the Association with a copy to the other party within the period of 1 year from the date of the appointment of the first named arbitrator, then the claim to arbitration shall be deemed to have lapsed on the expiry of the said period of 1 year unless before that date the claim is renewed by either party notifying the other during the 30 days prior to the expiry date. The claim may be thus renewed for successive periods of 1 year by either party serving on the other notice of renewal of the claim to arbitration, such notice to be served during the 30 days prior to the expiry of the previous notice. If the claim is not so renewed then it shall lapse unless prior to the expiry of the last notice of renewal documentary evidence or submissions have been submitted by either the claimants or the respondents.

In the event of failure to renew a claim as provided in this Rule such claim shall be deemed to have been withdrawn and abandoned unless the arbitrator(s) or board of appeal on appeal shall in his/their absolute discretion otherwise determine upon such terms as he/they may think fit.

3. Appointment of Arbitrators

3.1 A party claiming arbitration shall within the time limits specified in Rule 2 either:—

(a) Appoint an arbitrator and give notice to the other party of the name of the arbitrator so appointed or

(b) apply to the Association for the appointment of an arbitrator as provided in Rule 3.6.

The other party shall within 9 consecutive days of such notice of appointment either appoint a second arbitrator or accept the appointment of the claimants' appointed arbitrator as sole arbitrator in the dispute.

3.2 Where two arbitrators have been appointed, the Association shall on receipt of the first statements and evidence submitted in accordance with the provisions of Rule 4, appoint a third arbitrator. The third arbitrator shall be the chairman of the tribunal so formed and his name shall be notified to the parties by the Association, together with a time table for the steps required under Rule 4. If either party has sent his statements and/or evidence and has not been notified by the Association of the name of the third arbitrator he may apply to the Association for the appointment of a third arbitrator.

3.3   It shall be the duty of the chairman of the tribunal (or of the sole arbitrator if such be appointed) to ensure the prompt progress of the arbitration. Any delay in the proceedings on the part of the tribunal (or of the sole arbitrator) may be notified to the Association.

3.4   An arbitrator appointed under these Rules shall be either a Member of the Association or, with the consent of his principals, an employee of a Member, but in either case shall be a person engaged or who has been engaged in the Trade and shall not be interested in the transaction nor directly interested as a member of a company or firm named as a party to the arbitration, nor financially retained by any such company or firm, nor a member of nor financially retained by any company or firm financially associated with any party to the arbitration.

3.5   (a)   An appointment of an arbitrator shall be valid provided that:—

(i)   the party making the appointment has notified the arbitrator of his appointment, and

(ii)   either that arbitrator has signified his acceptance of the appointment to the party appointing him prior to the hearing or, if the originally appointed arbitrator shall be unwilling or unable to act, the appointing party has appointed a substitute who has signified his acceptance of the appointment prior to the hearing.

(iii)   in the case of a third arbitrator, when his acceptance has been communicated to the first two arbitrators.

(b)   In arbitrations for quality and/or condition when parties claim to be in a string, intermediate parties may pass on the name(s) of the arbitrator(s) without his/their prior acceptance provided that subsequently the provisions of Rule 5.1 are complied with.

3.6   Any party requiring an arbitrator to be appointed on his behalf may apply to the Association for an appointment. The Association shall appoint an arbitrator to act for the party applying provided that such application is addressed in writing to the Association and provided that a copy has been despatched to the other party within the time limit stipulated in Rule 3.1. Such application for an appointment shall for the purpose of any time limit stipulated in these Rules be equivalent to the appointment of an arbitrator by the applicant.

3.7   If one party has appointed an arbitrator, despatched notice of the appointment in writing to the other party, and called upon that party either to concur with the appointment of that arbitrator as sole arbitrator or to appoint an arbitrator, and the other party fails to comply within 9 consecutive days of the notice being served, then the party claiming arbitration may apply to the Association for the appointment of an arbitrator to act on behalf of the party who has failed to appoint. Provided that the application is accompanied by evidence that (a) the parties had, prima facie, entered into a contract subject to these Rules, (b) notice was despatched to the other party that arbitration was claimed and (c) notice was despatched to the other party that application was being made to the Association for the appointment of an arbitrator and the appropriate fee ruling at the date of application had been paid, the Association shall appoint an arbitrator to act on behalf of the party who failed to appoint an arbitrator to act on his behalf.

3.8 If an arbitrator dies, or refuses to act, or becomes incapable of acting, or fails to proceed with the arbitration, or is found to be ineligible, the party appointing such arbitrator shall forthwith appoint a substitute. If a substitute is not appointed by the appointing party within 5 consecutive days after the notice of such death, refusal, incapacity, failure or finding of ineligibility as the case may be, the Association shall have the power to appoint an arbitrator, and in the case of failure to proceed, to set down a date for the arbitration, provided that application is made in accordance with the second sentence of Rule 3.7.

3.9 Any party making an application to the Association for the appointment of an arbitrator in accordance with Rule 3.6, 3.7 or 3.8 may be required by the Association to pay a deposit of such sum as the Association may require on account of any fees and expenses thereafter arising if the arbitrator(s) should decide that under the provisions of Rule 6 he/they have no jurisdiction.

3.10 The arbitrator(s) may call upon either party to deposit with the Association such sum or sums as he/they consider appropriate on account of fees, costs and expenses prior to the commencement of the arbitration hearing.

3.11 If the arbitration is abandoned, suspended or concluded by agreement or otherwise, before the final award is made, the parties shall be jointly and severally liable to pay to the Association, the arbitrator(s)' and Association's costs, fees and expenses.

4. Arbitration Procedure

All statements and evidence provided for below shall in every case be delivered by being sent by each party to the other party, with 3 copies to the Association. Failure to send all 3 copies to the Association will render the party responsible liable to the Association for the costs of copying such documents for forwarding to the arbitrators. In cases where a sole arbitrator is appointed, only one copy need be sent to the Association.

4.1 The claimants shall draw up a clear and concise statement of his case which, together with a copy of the contract and such documentary evidence as he wishes to put it, shall be delivered as required under this Rule.

4.2 The other party shall, on receipt of his copy of the claimants' case and documents, draw up a clear and concise statement of his defence (and counterclaim, if any) which, together with all supporting documents, shall be delivered as required under this Rule.

4.3 The claimants shall then have the right to submit further written comments and/or documents in reply, such to be delivered as required by this Rule.

4.4 Where samples are involved the above procedure shall apply with regard to the exchange of statements and documentary evidence, but having due regard to the finality time limits the arbitrator(s) may examine samples prior to the completion of this exchange.

4.5 Nothing in this Rule shall prevent the other party from delivering his statement and documentary evidence before receiving documents/statements from the claimants.

4.6　Any party or his representative (not being a solicitor or barrister, or other legally qualified advocate, wholly or principally engaged in private practice) shall be entitled to make further submissions orally in addition to those made under this Rule. If any party to the arbitration wishes to attend the arbitration hearing he should notify the Association who shall, after consultation with the arbitrators, on receipt of such notice, inform the parties of the expected date, time and place of the arbitration hearing.

No person (including any solicitor/barrister or other legally qualified advocate or advisor wholly or principally engaged in private practice) other than the parties and witnesses shall be permitted to attend the arbitration hearing, which shall be in private, unless the arbitrator(s) otherwise decide(s).

5.　String Arbitrations (Quality and/or Condition)

5.1　In the event of a contract forming part of a string of contracts which are in all material points identical in terms, except as to price, any arbitration for quality and/or condition may be held between the first seller and the last buyer in the string as though they were contracting parties, provided that every party against whom arbitration is claimed and who claims to be in a string shall have supplied his contract and all relevant information to the arbitrator(s).

Any award so made, hereinafter referred to as a string award, shall, subject to the right of appeal (except an award in respect of condition where the goods have been bought and sold on terms known as 'Rye Terms'), be binding on all intermediate parties in the string and may be enforced by an intermediate party against his immediate contracting party as though a separate award had been made under each contract.

6.　Preliminary Issues

6.1　Where the arbitrator(s) decide(s), at any time after being appointed, and prior to making an award, that the dispute is not one arising out of a contract embodying these Rules, he/they shall forthwith certify in writing that, in consequence, he has/they have no jurisdiction under these Rules to arbitrate on the dispute, and he/they shall forthwith notify the Association in writing that the dispute shall be deemed to be one which is not subject to the Arbitration Rules of the Association and accordingly such Rules shall not apply thereto. The Association will notify the parties of the arbitrator(s)' decision and will invoice the claimants for any costs, fees and expenses incurred. Such decision shall be final and binding upon the parties and upon the Association, subject to the right of appeal to the Committee of Appeal by either party in accordance with the provisions stipulated in Rule 8.

6.2　Upon being notified as aforesaid a board of appeal shall be appointed by the Association to determine the preliminary issue and such other matters relating to the dispute as the parties may, by mutual agreement, submit to the board of appeal.

6.3　The board of appeal may in its absolute discretion lay down the procedure to be adopted at the determination of the preliminary issue and may order the parties to the dispute to lodge with the Association within a specified time such fees as the board of appeal considers reasonable as a condition of the determination of the preliminary issue.

6.4 The board of appeal shall either uphold or reverse the decision of the arbitrator(s) on the preliminary issue.

6.5 In the event of the board of appeal upholding the arbitrator(s) on a preliminary issue the board of appeal shall certify accordingly and the Association shall notify the parties and the arbitrator(s) that the dispute is deemed to be one which is not subject to these Rules and accordingly that these Rules shall not apply thereto, and will invoice the appellants for any costs, fees and expenses incurred.

6.6 In the event of the board of appeal reversing the decision of the arbitrator(s) on a preliminary issue, the board of appeal shall certify accordingly and shall notify the parties, the arbitrator(s) and the Association and shall order that the dispute be referred to arbitration afresh, whereupon:—

(a) The dispute shall be deemed to be one arising out of a contract embodying these Rules.

(b) The arbitrator(s) formerly appointed shall thereupon cease to act.

(c) The board of appeal may in its absolute discretion extend the time limits in Rules 2 and 3. Provided that:

(i) No arbitrator previously appointed under the provisions of Rule 3 to determine such dispute shall be re-appointed when the dispute is referred as aforesaid.

(ii) No objections shall be taken under Rules 2 and 3 that time has expired if the requirements of Rules 2 and 3 were previously validly complied with and if the board of appeal has extended the time limits stipulated in Rules 2 and 3.

6.7 The decision of the board of appeal on the preliminary issue shall be conclusive and binding upon the parties and upon any subsequent arbitrator(s) or board of appeal to whom the dispute may be referred under these Rules.

6.8 The determination of the preliminary issue shall not preclude a subsequent appeal under these Rules as hereinafter provided, save that no member of the board of appeal which determined the preliminary issue shall be eligible to vote for or serve on a board of appeal which subsequently determines the appeal against the award of arbitration in the dispute.

6.9 The board of appeal appointed to determine the preliminary issue shall, on the joint application of the parties, have power to hear the merits of the dispute and to make an award thereon in lieu of ordering the dispute to be remitted to arbitration under Rule 6.6, and such award shall be deemed in all respects to be an award of a board of appeal under these Rules.

6.10 The board of appeal shall have absolute discretion to make such order by way of costs in respect of the preliminary issue as it deems just and equitable.

6.11 For the purposes of Rule 6, the arbitrator(s) and board of appeal shall have the power to rule on their own jurisdiction, including any objections with respect to the existence or validity of the arbitration agreement or of the existence or validity of the contract of which the arbitration clause forms part. For this purpose an arbitration clause which forms part of a contract and which provides for arbitration under these Rules, shall be treated as an agreement independent of the other terms of the contract.

7. Awards of Arbitration

7.1 All awards of arbitration shall be in writing on an official form issued by the Association and shall be signed by the sole arbitrator or by all members of the Tribunal. The arbitrator(s) shall have the power to award the costs of and connected with the reference, and may assess his/their fees. The Association's fees shall be those for the time being in force as prescribed by the Council.

7.2 The award shall state the arbitrators' reasons therefor and whether any sum awarded carries interest thereon.

7.3 The arbitrators shall, on the application of either party, before the arbitration award is made, have the power to extend the time for appealing in any case in which he/they consider(s) it just or necessary so to do. Any such extension must be stated in the award of arbitration.

7.4 Upon the signing of an award it shall be the duty of the arbitrator(s) to lodge it, with not less than two official copies, with the Association. The Association shall then give notice to the parties named in the award, that the award is at their disposal upon payment of the fees and expenses to the Association. If payment is not received by the Association within 14 days from such notice, the Association may call upon any one of the parties named, to take up the award and in such case the party so called upon shall pay the fees and expenses as directed.

Upon receipt of the fees by the Association, the Association shall then date and issue the award to the parties.

7.5 Awards of arbitration (subject to the right of appeal hereinafter mentioned) shall be conclusive and binding on the parties with respect both to the matter in dispute and to all expenses of and incidental to the reference and to the award.

7.6 No award by arbitrator(s) shall be questioned or invalidated on the ground that the arbitrator(s) (or any of them) is/are not qualified or entitled to act as provided in Rule 3 unless objection to his/their acting, is made before the hearing of such arbitration is begun.

8. Right of Appeal

8.1 No appeal shall be allowed on awards for condition where the goods have been sold on terms 'Guaranteed sound on arrival' and/or on 'Rye Terms'.

8.2 If any party, except as provided in Rule 8.1, be dissatisfied with an arbitration award, a right of appeal shall lie to a board of appeal provided that the following conditions are complied with:—

(a) No later than 12 noon on the 30th consecutive day after the date of the award of arbitration the appellants shall:—

(i) give a written notice of appeal to the Association,

(ii) give a notice of his intention to lodge an appeal to the other party with a copy to the Association,

(iii) and (subject to the provisions of Rule 14) make payment to the Association of the appeal fee stated on the award of arbitration on account of the costs fees and expenses of the appeal.

(b)   The total fees and expenses of the arbitration award shall be paid before the appeal is heard.

(c)   The appellants shall pay such further sum or sums on account of fees, costs and expenses as may be called for by the Association at any time after the lodging of the appeal and prior to the publication of the award by the board of appeal. The fees charged by the board of appeal shall be in accordance with the scale of fees laid down by the Council from time to time.

8.3   In cases of appeals lodged by more than one party in relation to the same award any two of the Officers shall have the power to consolidate such appeals for hearing by the same board of appeal.

8.4   If neither the appeal fee required under Rule 8.2(a) nor evidence from a bank as required by Rule 14.1 has been received by the Association within 35 consecutive days of receipt of the notice of appeal, such notice shall be deemed to have been withdrawn and the right of appeal waived unless, prior to the expiry of that period of 35 consecutive days the appellant has applied to the board of appeal for an extension and the board of appeal has, in its absolute discretion on hearing evidence from the appellants as to why further time is required, granted an extension.

9.   Boards of Appeal

9.1   Boards of appeal shall be elected and constituted in accordance with the Rules and Regulations of the Association and each board of appeal shall, when so elected, appoint one of its members to be its chairman.

9.2   In the case of illness or death, or refusal, or incapacity, or inability to act, of any member elected to serve on a board of appeal, the next member of the Committee of Appeal duly appointed for this purpose, shall become a member of the board of appeal in his place. In the event of no substitute being available the remaining four members of the board may, subject to the agreement of the parties, or of their duly authorised representatives exercise all the powers of the board of appeal.

10.   Appeal Procedure

10.1   All submissions, statements and evidence provided for below (which may include new evidence not before the arbitrators) shall in every case be delivered by being sent by each party to the other with six copies to the Association. Failure to send all six copies to the Association will render the party responsible liable to the Association for the costs of copying such documents for forwarding to the board of appeal.

10.2   The parties shall deliver their submissions, statements and evidence on appeal as above provided in accordance with the following:—

(a)   By the appellants within 28 days of the giving of the written notice of appeal provided for in Rule 8.2;

(b)   By the respondents, in response, within 28 days of the giving by the appellants of his documents under (a) above;

(c)   By the appellants in reply (if required) within 14 days of the giving by the respondents of his response under (b) above.

The Association will set down the appeal for hearing taking due regard to the above timetable, or some other time table which the board of appeal may decide.

10.3   Each party to an appeal from an arbitration award may, in addition to the documents lodged in accordance with Rule 10.1, state its case orally at the hearing either personally or by a representative or agent engaged or who has been engaged in the trade and duly appointed in writing but shall not be represented at the hearing of such appeal by (nor have present) a solicitor or barrister or other legally qualified advocate or advisor, wholly or principally engaged in private practice, unless special leave shall previously have been obtained in writing from the board of appeal, which leave the board of appeal may in its absolute discretion grant or refuse.

10.4   An appeal involves a new hearing of the dispute and the board of appeal may confirm, vary, amend or set-aside the award of the arbitrator(s). In particular (but not by way of restriction), the board of appeal may:—

(a)   Vary an award by increasing or reducing, if the board shall see fit, the liability of either party.

(b)   Correct any errors in the award or otherwise alter or amend it.

(c)   Award interest on any sum(s) awarded.

(d)   Award the payment of costs and expenses incidental to the hearing of the arbitration and the appeal; such costs and expenses shall normally follow the event.

10.5   The award of the board of appeal, whether confirming, varying, amending or setting aside the original award of arbitration, shall be signed by the chairman of the board of appeal, and, when so signed, shall be deemed to be the award of the board of appeal, and shall be final, conclusive and binding.

10.6   Where a party gives notice to a board of appeal pursuant to Section 1 (6)(a) of the Arbitration Act 1979 that a reasoned award will be required with a view to a possible judicial review of the award as provided for in the Arbitration Act 1979, then, at the discretion of the board of appeal both parties may be represented at the hearing by solicitor or barrister or other legally qualified advocate.

10.7   An award of arbitration shall be confirmed, unless the board of appeal decide by a majority to vary, amend or set it aside.

10.8   (a)   If the appellants, on receiving from the board of appeal notice of the date fixed for the hearing of the appeal, requests a postponement of more than 14 days, or at the first or any subsequent hearing of the appeal requests an adjournment, then in such event the board of appeal may in their absolute discretion direct that as a condition of granting an adjournment all or any part of the money required by the terms of the award of arbitration to be paid by either party to the other shall be deposited in such bank and in such currency (either in the United Kingdom or abroad) as the board of appeal may direct. Such money shall be held by such bank in an account in the name of the Association and otherwise on such terms as the board of appeal may direct. The board of appeal shall, where such money has been deposited, direct in their award how and to which of the parties the amount so held shall be paid out. Provided that, if in the opinion of the board of appeal after hearing the parties, the appellant shall be guilty of undue delay in proceeding with his appeal, he shall, after due warning and if the board of appeal so decides, be deemed to have withdrawn his appeal (with the consequences as stated in Rule 11) in which event the money on deposit (with interest if any, less any tax deductible) shall immediately become due and payable to the party and/or parties entitled thereto under the terms of the award of arbitration.

(b) If the appellants fail to make such payment as aforesaid in accordance with the directions of the board of appeal, and within such time as the board of appeal stipulates, then (subject to the provisions of Rule 14) the appeal shall be deemed to be withdrawn.

10.9 If the board of appeal shall determine that any of the conditions in Rules 8 to 14 have not been complied with, it may in its absolute discretion extend the time for compliance (notwithstanding that the time may already have expired) or dispense with the necessity for compliance and may proceed to hear and determine the appeal as if each and all of those conditions had been complied with. The determination by the board of appeal of any matter to which this paragraph applies shall be final, conclusive and binding.

10.10 No award of a board of appeal or decision by a board of appeal on a preliminary issue, as defined in Rule 6, shall be questioned or invalidated on the ground of any irregularity in the election of the board of appeal or of any of its members, or on the ground that any member of the board of appeal was not eligible to serve, unless objection is made in writing and established to the satisfaction of the board of appeal before the hearing of the appeal or of the preliminary issue is begun.

11. Withdrawals of Appeals

11.1 An appellant from an arbitration award shall have the right, at any time before an award is made, to withdraw his appeal and the Association shall forthwith notify all parties to the arbitration that the appeal has been withdrawn. On notice being received from the appellant within 10 consecutive days of the date on which the appeal has been duly lodged with the Association in accordance with Rule 8, half of the fees shall be returned, and on notice being received not later than 48 hours before the time fixed for the hearing a quarter of the fees shall be returned, but on any later withdrawal no part of the fees shall be returned.

11.2 In the event of such withdrawal as aforesaid the other party to an award of arbitration shall have the right of appeal against that award to a board of appeal in accordance with the provisions of Rule 8, save that the time limit laid down in Rule 8.2 shall be 12 noon on the 30th consecutive day after the date of the Association's notice to that party of the aforesaid withdrawal.

12. Appeals on String Contracts

12.1 In any case in which a string award shall have been made by arbitrator(s) as aforesaid and the first seller, or the last buyer, or any intermediate party bound thereby shall be dissatisfied therewith (whether the award shall be in his favour or against him), the first seller, the last buyer, and any intermediate party (as the case may be) or any of them shall be entitled to appeal against that award to a board of appeal, provided that each of the following provisions, in addition to the provisions of Rule 8, shall first have been complied with:—

(a) If the appellants is an intermediate party he shall state in such notice of appeal whether he is appealing as a buyer or a seller.

(b) If the appellants is the first seller or the last buyer he shall, when giving notice of appeal, also despatch written notice thereof to the party in immediate contractual relationship with him.

(c) If the appellants is an intermediate party and is appealing as a buyer or a seller he shall when giving notice of appeal also despatch written notice thereof to his own immediate seller or buyer, as the case may be.

(d) Every notice given to an intermediate party by a first seller, a last buyer or by another intermediate party in accordance with the provisions of paragraph 12.1 hereof shall be passed on with due despatch, and such passing on shall, as between the intermediate party passing the same on and the party to whom the same is passed on, be deemed to be in compliance with the said conditions relating to appeals.

12.2 All appeals to which this Rule applies shall be held in the like manner in which the corresponding arbitrations are required by Rule 5 to be held. Any award made by a board of appeal shall in all respects have the like effect and shall be enforceable in the like manner as is provided in that Rule in the case of awards made in the corresponding arbitration, and non-compliance with any provisions of Rule 12.1(d) shall in no way limit or affect the rights and jurisdiction of the board of appeal.

13. Taking Up Appeal Awards

13.1 The Association may call upon either of the disputing parties to take up the award of the board of appeal and in such case the party so called upon shall take up the award and pay the fees, costs and expenses. Upon receipt of the fees, costs and expenses by the Association, the Association shall then date and issue the award to the parties.

14. Currency Regulations

14.1 If an appellant is precluded by currency regulations from paying any money due to be paid by him as required under Rule 8, and notifies the Association in writing (a) in the case of payment of the appeal fee when giving notice of appeal and (b) in the case of any further sum being called for under Rule 8.2(e) or being directed to be paid under Rule 10.8, within 9 consecutive days of the money being demanded, accompanied in every case by evidence from a bank that he has already made application for the transfer of the required sum, he shall be entitled to an extension of up to 35 consecutive days from the date when the said payment became due in which to pay such sum.

15. Defaulters

15.1 In the event of any party to an arbitration or an appeal held under these Rules neglecting or refusing to carry out or abide by a final award of the arbitrator(s) or board of appeal made under these Rules, the Council of the Association may post on the Association's Notice Board and/or circularise Members in any way thought fit notification to that effect. The parties to any such arbitration or appeal shall be deemed to have consented to the Council taking such action as aforesaid.

15.2   In the event that parties do not pay the arbitration or appeal fees and expenses when called upon to do so by the Association in accordance with these Rules, the Council may post on the Asociation's Notice Board and/or circularise Members in any way thought fit notification to that effect. The parties to any such arbitration or appeal shall be deemed to have consented to the Council taking such action as aforesaid.

16. Notices

16.1   All notices to be given under these Rules shall be given by letter, telex, telegram or by other method of rapid written communication (excluding facsimile) and shall be deemed to be properly given if proved to have been despatched within the required time limits.

A notice to the brokers or agents named in the contract shall be deemed a notice under these Rules. So far as concerns such notices, this Rule overrides, in relation to them, any provisions as to notices that may be contained in the contract.

16.2   Except at a hearing, all notices, proceedings and documents to be served on members of a board of appeal shall be given by the means specified in Rule 16.1 to the Secretary of the Association at the Association's Offices and when so given shall be deemed to be properly served. For the purposes of any time limits receipt of such notices by the Association shall be deemed to be the date of receipt by the board of appeal.

16.3   Notwithstanding the provisions of Rules 16.1 and 16.2, notices to the Association may be given by facsimile.

17. Discretion to Extend Time Limits

17.1   Whenever it shall appear to the Council that by reason of a state of war, war-like operation, strike, lockout, riot or civil commotion, parties to contracts which have been or may hereafter be made incorporating these Rules, have been or may be prevented from exercising any of their rights within the time limits prescribed by these Rules, the Council shall have, and shall be deemed always to have had, the power to extend any of such time limits at any time and from time to time and to any extent necessary to enable justice to be done between the parties. Such extension may be made generally or with reference to any particular dispute.

In the event of the Council deciding so to extend any such time limits with reference to any particular dispute, notice thereof shall be given by the Council to such of the parties to the contract as may be available.

18. Samples

18.1   All samples sent to the Association for arbitration, testing and/or other purposes shall become and be the absolute property of the Association.

CHAMBER OF COMMERCE AND INDUSTRY OF GENEVA (CCIG)

©1992 Chamber of Commerce and Industry of Geneva (CCIG)

Chamber of Commerce and Industry of Geneva
(C.C.I.G.)
case postale 5039
Contact: Mrs Janine Uzan-Spira,
General Counsel
Member of the Arbitration Committee
4, bd du Théâtre, 1204 Geneva, Switzerland
Tel: 0041-22 819.91.11
Fax: 0041-22 819.91.00

Model clause

Any disputes arising with respect to or in connection with this agreement shall be finally decided by one or more arbitrators in accordance with the Rules of arbitration of the Chamber of Commerce and Industry of Geneva.

(Clause in German and French are available from CCIG.)

ARBITRATION RULES

Effective as of 1 January 1992

A.   GENERAL PROVISIONS

1.   Scope of the Rules

1.1   These Rules apply whenever the parties have agreed to submit their disputes to CCIG arbitration.

1.2   Arbitration agreements referring to the Arbitration Directives of the CCIG of June 1, 1980 are considered as referring to the present Rules unless one of the parties objects.

2.   Arbitration Committee

2.1   The CCIG shall provide all necessary assisstance to the parties for the organization of the arbitration pursuant to these Rules.

2.2   For this purpose, the CCIG shall appoint an Arbitration Committee which shall perform the functions of the CCIG according to these Rules. The Arbitration Committee shall consist of three to five members, one of which shall be an officer or employee of the CCIG. The members of the Arbitration Committee shall be appointed by the CCIG for three years. Such members may not serve as arbitrators or counsel in CCIG arbitrations.

3.   Place of Arbitration

Unless otherwise agreed, the place of arbitration shall be Geneva.

4. Confidentiality

CCIG arbitration is confidential. The parties, the arbitrators and the CCIG undertake not to disclose to third parties any facts or other information relating to the dispute or the arbitral proceedings. The parties, the arbitrators and CCIG shall refrain from publishing or causing others to publish the award, unless the parties to the arbitration agree to such publication.

5. Notifications

The awards and orders of the arbitral tribunal as well as other decisions of the arbitral tribunal and those of the CCIG shall be notified to the parties at the address shown in the request for arbitration, or at any other address subsequently specified, by any means of communication permitting proof of receipt.

6. Time Limits

The CCIG may extend the time limits provided in the present Rules if the circumstances so justify.

B.   COMMENCING THE ARBITRATION PROCEEDINGS

7. Request for Arbitration

7.1   The party wishing to initiate an arbitration under these Rules shall deliver its request to the CCIG. Such request shall contain:

(a)   the names, capacities and addresses of the parties, including telephone and telefax or telex numbers;

(b)   a copy of the contract containing the arbitration agreement or any other document showing that the arbitration is governed by these Rules;

(c)   a statement of the facts and legal argument on which the claimant's case is based, together with supporting documents;

(d)   the claimant's prayer for relief, *i.e.* a brief and precise description of each claim;

(e)   an estimate of the amount in dispute, if no definite sum of money is claimed;

(f)   relevant information regarding the number and choice of arbitrators within the meaning of Articles 10 and 11.

7.2   The request shall be delivered in as many copies as there are other parties, together with an additional copy for each arbitrator and for the CCIG. The CCIG shall send the request to the respondent.

8. Answer

8.1   The respondent shall communicate its answer to the CCIG within thirty days from the receipt of the request. The answer shall contain:

(a)   a statement of the defenses together with supporting documents, including any objection concerning the arbitration agreement;

(b)   any counterclaim, together with the information provided in Article 7.1(d)–(e);

(c) relevant information regarding the number and choice of the arbitrators within the meaning of Articles 10 and 11.

8.2 The answer shall be delivered in as many copies as there are other parties, together with an additional copy for each arbitrator and for the CCIG. The CCIG shall send the answer to the claimant.

8.3 The provisions of this Article are subject to Article 18 with respect to the participation of a third party.

C. FORMATION OF THE ARBITRAL TRIBUNAL

9. Agreement to Arbitrate

The CCIG shall poceed with the formation of the arbitral tribunal, unless it is apparent from the outset that there is manifestly no agreement to arbitrate referring to the CCIG.

10. Independence and Qualifications of the Arbitrators

10.1 Every arbitrator, whether a sole arbitrator, chairperson or coarbitrator, shall be and remain independent from the parties and has the obligation to disclose immediately any circumstances likely to affect independence with respect to the parties or any one of them.

10.2 Every arbitrator shall have the qualifications agreed by the parties and the availability required to conduct the arbitration to an expeditious completion.

10.3 The sole arbitrator or the chairperson may not have the same nationality as one of the parties unless the parties agree otherwise or have the same nationality.

11. Number of Arbitrators

11.1 The parties are free to agree that the arbitral tribunal shall consist of a sole arbitrator or of three arbitrators.

11.2 In the absence of such an agreement, the tribunal shall consist of a sole arbitrator, unless the CCIG decides to form a tribunal of three arbitrators on account of the amount in dispute, of the nature and of the complexity of the dispute.

12. Appointment of the Arbitrators

Sole Arbitrator

12.1 The parties may select the sole arbitrator by mutual agreement. In the absence of such a selection within a thirty-day time limit set by the CCIG, the CCIG shall appoint the sole arbitrator.

Tribunal of Three Arbitrators

12.2 If the agreement to arbitrate provides for a tribunal of three arbitrators, each party shall select a coarbitrator respectively, in the request for arbitration and in the answer. In the absence of a selection by a party, the CCIG shall appoint the coarbitrator.

If the CCIG decides to form a tribunal of three arbitrators pursuant to Article 11.2, each party shall select a coarbitrator upon the request of the CCIG. Failing such a selection by a party within a thirty-day time limit set by the CCIG, the CCIG shall appoint the coarbitrator.

Within a thirty-day time limit starting from the date when the coarbitrators learned from the CCIG of their appointment, the coarbitrators shall select a chairperson. Failing such selection of a chairperson, the CCIG shall appoint the chairperson.

Confirmation of the Arbitrators

12.3   Every arbitrator selected by the parties, either separately or jointly, or by the coarbitrators, shall be deemed to be appointed only upon confirmation by the CCIG. The CCIG may refuse the confirmation, without indicating any reasons, if it considers that the arbitrator does not fulfill the requirements of Article 10.

13.   Challenge

13.1   An arbitrator may be challenged upon the ground that he or she does not fulfill the requirements of Article 10.1, that he or she does not possess the qualifications agreed by the parties, or that he or she manifestly does not have the availability required to conduct the arbitration to an expeditious completion.

13.2   Challenges are within the exclusive jurisdiction of the CCIG. The challenge petition shall be submitted to the CCIG immediately after the party making such challenge becomes aware of the relevant facts. It shall specify the facts and circumstances upon which the challenge is based.

13.3   The CCIG shall ask the other parties, the challenged arbitrator and the other arbitrators to submit written observations and shall render a decision summarily stating reasons.

13.4   In domestic arbitrations, the mandatory provisions of the Swiss Intercantonal Arbitration Convention of 27 March 1969 are reserved.

14.   Removal

14.1   An arbitrator may be removed by written agreement of the parties.

14.2   An arbitrator can also be removed by the CCIG if he or she refuses to carry out his or her functions or is manifestly unable to do so. The CCIG invites the parties, the contested arbitrator and the other arbitrators to submit written observations and shall render a decision summarily motivated.

14.3   In domestic arbitrations, the mandatory provisions of the Swiss Intercantonal Arbitration Convention of 27 March 1969 are reserved.

15.   Replacement

15.1   In case of death, removal, successful challenge or resignation of an arbitrator, such arbitrator shall be replaced pursuant to the provisions of Article 12.

15.2   Unless otherwise agreed by the parties or otherwise decided by the arbitral tribunal, the proceeding shall continue with the new arbitrator from the point where the previous arbitrator ceased to perform his or her duties.

D.   MULTIPLE REQUESTS FOR ARBITRATION, MULTIPARTY ARBITRATION

16.   Multiple Requests

16.1   If an arbitration is initiated between parties already involved in another arbitration governed by these Rules, the CCIG may assign the second case to the arbitral tribunal appointed to decide the first case, in which case the parties shall be deemed to have waived their right to select an arbitrator in the second case.

16.2   In order to decide upon such assignment, the CCIG shall take into account all the circumstances, including the links between the two cases and the progress already made in the first case.

17.   Multiparty Arbitration in General

17.1   In arbitration proceedings comprising more than two parties, including in case of participation of a third party within the meaning of Article 18, the number of arbitrators shall be determined in accordance with Article 11.

17.2   The parties may agree on a method of selection of the coarbitrators. In the absence of such an agreement, the coarbitrators shall be appointed by the CCIG, which shall take into account any proposals by the parties.

17.3   The chairperson or the sole arbitrator shall be appointed in accordance with Article 12.

18.   Participation of a Third Party

18.1   If a respondent intends to cause a third party to participate in the arbitration, it shall so state in its answer and shall state the reasons for such participation. The respondent shall deliver to the CCIG an additional copy of its answer.

18.2   The CCIG shall send the answer to the third party whose participation is sought, the provisions of Articles 8 and 9 being applicable by analogy.

18.3   Upon receipt of the third party's answer, the CCIG shall decide on the participation of the third party in the already pending proceeding, taking into account all of the circumstances. If the CCIG accepts the participation of the third party, it shall proceed with the formation of the arbitral tribunal in accordance with Article 17; if it does not accept the participation, it shall proceed according to Article 12.

18.4   The decision of the CCIG regarding the participation of third parties shall not prejudice the decision of the arbitrators on the same subject. Regardless of the decision of the arbitrators on such participation, the formation of the arbitral tribunal cannot be challenged.

E. PROCEDURE BEFORE THE ARBITRAL TRIBUNAL

19. Applicable Rules

Unless otherwise agreed by the parties, the procedure before the arbitral tribunal shall be governed by the provisions in this chapter and any additional rules established by the parties or, if none, by the arbitrators.

20. Communications

Subject to Article 5 of these Rules, the arbitral tribunal shall determine the means of communication between itself and the parties.

21. Conciliation

The arbitral tribunal may at any time seek to conciliate the parties. Any settlement may be embodied in an arbitral award rendered by consent of the parties.

22. Assistance

Each party has the right to be assisted by the counsel of its choice, regardless of the nationality or residence of such counsel.

23. Provisional or Conservatory Measures

23.1   Each party may request provisional or conservatory measures from a state authority having jurisdiction or from the arbitral tribunal.

23.2   The arbitral tribunal shall request the respondent party to state its position and shall render an order based on an adversarial proceeding within a short time.

23.3   In case of utmost urgency, the arbitral tribunal may order provisional or conservatory measures upon mere presentation of the request, provided that the other party shall be heard subsequently.

23.4   In domestic arbitrations, the mandatory provisions of the Swiss Intercantonal Arbitration Convention of 27 March 1969 are reserved.

24. Additional Briefs

At the request of a party or upon its own initiative, the arbitral tribunal shall order the exchange of additional briefs if the circumstances so justify.

25. Documents

25.1   Each party shall produce the documents upon which it relies in conjunction with the written pleadings provided in Articles 7, 8 and 24.

25.2   Exceptionally, the arbitral tribunal may permit the production of new documents if the parties so agree, if the party wishing to produce the new document could not do so within the applicable time limit, or if the relevance of the document did not become apparent until after expiry of the time limit.

25.3   Each party may request in due course the production of documents in the custody of the opponent. If the parties disagree, the arbitral tribunal may order production of the documents, on condition that the requesting party demonstrates the likely existence and relevance of such documents.

26. Witnesses

26.1   The party wishing to have a witness heard shall deliver a preliminary statement signed by such witness, unless the witness refuses. Unless otherwise decided by the arbitral tribunal, the preliminary statements shall be delivered at the latest fifteen days before the hearing at which evidence is to be taken.

26.2   At the hearing at which evidence is taken, each party shall examine its witnesses, if it deems necessary in order to complete the preliminary statements. The opponent shall thereafter ask the questions that it deems relevant. The arbitrators may ask their own questions at any time.

27. Experts

27.1   Each party may consult and present one or more experts of its choice to be heard by the arbitral tribunal. The provisions regarding the examination of witnesses shall apply by analogy.

27.2   The arbitral tribunal may, of its own motion or at the request of a party, appoint one or more experts. The arbitral tribunal shall consult the parties with respect to the appointment and terms of reference of such experts.

28. Records

The examination of witnesses, experts and parties shall be recorded by a stenographer. At the request of the parties or if it deems appropriate, the arbitral tribunal may substitute any process permitting the preservation of the entire statements or of their essential elements.

F. AWARD

29. Reasons

Unless othwise agreed by the parties, the award shall state reasons in a concise manner. It shall confirm the undertaking of confidentiality contained in Article 4 of these Rules.

30. Notification

The CCIG shall notify the award to the parties provided that all the costs of arbitration have been paid. The CCIG shall keep a copy of the award for ten years.

G.   EXPEDITED PROCEDURE

31.   Special Provisions

If the parties so agree, the arbitration shall be conducted according to an expedited procedure. Such arbitrations shall be governed by the foregoing provisions, subject to the following changes:

(a)   the CCIG may shorten the time limits for the appointment of arbitrators;

(b)   upon deposit of the request for Arbitration, each party may state its position only once in writing on the claims asserted against it;

(c)   unless the parties authorize the arbitral tribunal to decide on the basis of the documentary evidence only, the arbitral tribunal shall hold a single hearing for the examination of the parties, witnesses and expert witnesses as well as for the oral argument;

(d)   the award shall be rendered within six months from the date when the CCIG hands the file over to the arbitrators;

(e)   the award shall summarily state reasons, unless the parties waive the requirement of reasons.

H.   COSTS OF ARBITRATION

32.   Definition of Costs

The costs of arbitration include the fees and disbursements of the CCIG as well as the fees and expenses of the arbitral tribunal.

33.   Fees and Disbursements of the CCIG

33.1   The fees of the CCIG shall be CHF 4000 for arbitrations where the amount in dispute does not exceed CHF 2000000 and CHF 6000 for arbitrations involving a higher amount. The CCIG may amend these charges should the cost of administering arbitrations so require.

33.2   The fees of the CCIG shall be paid at the time of filing the request for Arbitration, failing which the CCIG shall not proceed with the case.

33.3   The CCIG shall assess an additional charge when an arbitrator is challenged.

33.4   The disbursements of the CCIG include the actual costs incurred by the CCIG, such as telephone, telefax, photocopies and courier services.

34.   Fees and Expenses of the Arbitral Tribunal

34.1   The fees of the arbitrators shall in principles be computed according to the time reasonably spent on the resolution of the dispute at an hourly rate subject to limits established in proportion to the amount in dispute. The CCIG schedule in force at the time of the filing of the request shall apply.

34.2   The expenses of the arbitral tribunal include the actual expenses incurred by the arbitral tribunal, such as the costs of travel, meeting room rental, the remuneration of interpreters, the recording and transcribing of hearings, telephones, telefax, photocopies and courier services.

35. Advance

35.1   When the arbitral tribunal is being formed, the CCIG shall determine the amount of the advance towards the costs of arbitration, subject to possible changes during the arbitration. The filing of a counterclaim or a new claim shall result in the determination of separate advances.

35.2   The advances shall be paid in two instalments of 50% each. The first instalment shall be paid at the beginning of the proceeding or following the filing of a new claim within the time limits set by the CCIG. The CCIG shall hand over the file to the arbitral tribunal as soon as the first instalment is paid. The second instalment shall be paid during the proceeding at a date to be set by the CCIG in agreement with the arbitrators.

35.3   Each instalment shall be payable in equal shares by the claimant and the respondent. If a party does not pay its share, the other party may substitute for it; if the share is not paid, the claim to which such share relates, after notice, shall be deemed to be withdrawn.

35.4   Any supplementary advance fixed by the CCIG in agreement with the arbitrators shall be paid in a single instalment in comformity with Article 35.3.

35.5   The advance shall bear interest at a usual rate. Such interest is included in the final computation of the arbitration costs in favour of the parties having advanced the amounts bearing interest.

35.6   If the arbitral tribunal orders an expert report, the expert shall commence work only after payment by the parties, or by one of them, of an advance determined by the arbitral tribunal and intended to cover the costs of the expertise.

36. Assessment of the Costs of Arbitration in the Award

36.1   At the end of the proceeding, the CCIG shall determine the final amount of the costs of arbitration. Such costs shall be stated in the arbitral award, which shall also determine which party shall bear such costs or in which proportion the parties shall share them.

36.2   In addition, the arbitral tribunal shall in principle adjudge that the losing party contribute towards the attorney's fees of the other party.

INTERNATIONAL CHAMBER OF COMMERCE (ICC)

ICC Rules of Conciliation and Arbitration (1988)
ICC Publication No. 447/3 – ISBN 92.842.1165.4(E)
Published in its official English version by the International Chamber of Commerce.
Copyright © 1993 – International Chamber of Commerce (ICC), Paris
Available from: *ICC Publishing S.A.,* 38 Cours Albert 1er, 75008 Paris, France.

38 cours Albert 1er,
75008 Paris
Tel: 0033-1-49.53.28.28
Fax: 0033-1-49.53.29.33

ICC RULES OF CONCILIATION AND ARBITRATION

in force from 1 January 1988

STANDARD ICC ARBITRATION CLAUSE

The ICC recommends that all parties wishing to make reference to ICC arbitration in their contracts use the following clause:

English

'All disputes arising in connection with the present contract shall be finally settled under the Rules of Conciliation and Arbitration of the International Chamber of Commerce by one or more arbitrators appointed in accordance with the said Rules.'

An arbitration clause is available for/in most commercial languages from the ICC.

Parties are reminded that it may be desirable for them to stipulate in the arbitration clause itself the law governing the contract, the number of arbitrators and the place and language of the arbitration. The parties' free choice of the law governing the contract and of the place and language of the arbitration is not limited by the ICC Rules of Arbitration.

Attention is called to the fact that the laws of certain countries require that parties to contracts expressly accept arbitration clauses, sometimes in a precise and particular manner.

RULES OF OPTIONAL CONCILIATION

Preamble

Settlement is a desirable solution for business disputes of an international character.

The International Chamber of Commerce therefore sets out these Rules of Optional Conciliation in order to facilitate the amicable settlement of such disputes.

Article 1

All business disputes of an international character may be submitted to conciliation by a sole conciliator appointed by the International Chamber of Commerce.

Article 2

The party requesting conciliation shall apply to the Secretary of the International Court of Arbitration of the International Chamber of Commerce setting out succinctly the purpose of the request and accompanying it with the fee required to open the file, as set out in Appendix III hereto.

Article 3

The Secretary of the International Court of Arbitration shall, as soon as possible, inform the other party of the request for conciliation. The party will be given a period of 15 days to inform the Secretariat whether it agrees or declines to participate in the attempt to conciliate.

If the other party agrees to participate in the attempt to conciliate it shall so inform the Secretariat within such period.

In the absence of any reply within such period or in the case of a negative reply the request for conciliation shall be deemed to have been declined. The Secretariat shall, as soon as possible, so inform the party which had requested conciliation.

Article 4

Upon receipt of an agreement to attempt conciliation, the Secretary General of the International Court of Arbitration shall appoint a counciliator as soon as possible. The conciliator shall inform the parties of his appointment and set a time-limit for the parties to present their respective arguments to him.

Article 5

The conciliator shall conduct the conciliation process as he thinks fit, guided by the principles of impartiality, equity and justice.

With the agreement of the parties, the conciliator shall fix the place for conciliation.

The conciliator may at any time during the conciliation process request a party to submit to him such additional information as he deems necessary.

The parties may, if they so wish, be assisted by counsel of their choice.

Article 6

The confidential nature of the conciliation process shall be respected by every person who is involved in it whatever capacity.

Article 7

The conciliation process shall come to an end:

(a)   Upon the parties signing an agreement. The parties shall be bound by such agreement. The agreement shall remain confidential unless and to the extent that its execution or application require disclosure.

(b)   Upon the production by the conciliator of a report recording that the attempt to conciliate has not been successful. Such report shall not contain reasons.

(c)   Upon notification to the conciliator by one or more parties at any time during the conciliation process of an intention no longer to pursue the conciliation process.

Article 8

Upon termination of the conciliation, the conciliator shall provide the Secretariat of the International Court of Arbitration with the settlement agreement signed by the parties or with his report of lack of success or with a notice from one or more parties of the intention no longer to pursue the conciliation process.

Article 9

Upon the file being opened, the Secretariat of the International Court of Arbitration shall fix the sum required to permit the process to proceed, taking into consideration the nature and importance of the dispute. Such sum shall be paid in equal shares by the parties.

This sum shall cover the estimated fees of the conciliator, expenses of the conciliation, and the administrative expenses as set out in Appendix III hereto.

In any case where, in the course of the conciliation process, the Secretariat of the Court shall decide that the sum originally paid is insufficient to cover the likely total costs of the conciliation, the Secretariat shall require the provision of an additional amount which shall be paid in equal shares by the parties.

Upon termination of the conciliation, the Secretariat shall settle the total costs of the process and advise the parties in writing.

All the above costs shall be borne in equal shares by the parties except and insofar as a settlement agreement provides otherwise.

A party's other expenditures shall remain the responsibility of that party.

Article 10

Unless the parties agree otherwise, a conciliator shall not act in any judicial or arbitration proceeding relating to the dispute which has been the subject of the conciliation process whether as an arbitrator, representative or counsel of a party.

The parties mutually undertake not to call the conciliator as a witness in any such proceedings, unless otherwise agreed between them.

Article 11

The parties agree not to introduce in any judicial or arbitration proceeding as evidence or in any manner whatsoever:

(a)   any views expressed or suggestions made by any party with regard to the possible settlement of the dispute

(b)   any proposals put forward by the conciliator;

(c)   the fact that a party had indicated that it was ready to accept some proposal for a settlement put forward by the conciliator.

RULES OF ARBITRATION

Article 1   International Court of Arbitration

1   The International Court of Arbitration of the International Chamber of Commerce is the arbitration body attached to the International Chamber of Commerce. Members of the Court are appointed by the Council of the

International Chamber of Commerce. The function of the Court is to provide for the settlement by arbitration of business disputes of an international character in accordance with these Rules.

2   In principle, the Court meets once a month. It draws up its own internal regulations.

3   The Chairman of the International Court of Arbitration or his deputy shall have power to take urgent decisions on behalf of the court, provided that any such decision shall be reported to the Court at its next session.

4   The Court may, in the manner provided for in its internal regulations, delegate to one or more groups of its members the power to take certain decisions provided that any such decision shall be reported to the Court at its next session.

5   The Secretariat of the International Court of Arbitration shall be at the Headquarters of the International Chamber of Commerce.

Article 2   The Arbitral Tribunal

1   The International Court of Arbitration does not itself settle disputes. Insofar as the parties shall not have provided otherwise, it appoints, or confirms the appointments of, arbitrators in accordance with the provisions of this Article. In making or confirming such appointment, the Court shall have regard to the proposed arbitrator's nationality, residence and other relationships with the countries of which the parties or the other arbitrators are nationals.

2   The disputes may be settled by a sole arbitrator or by three arbitrators. In the following Articles the word 'arbitrator' denotes a single arbitrator or three arbitrators as the case may be.

3   Where the parties have agreed that the disputes shall be settled by a sole arbitrator, they may, by agreement, nominate him for confirmation by the Court. If the parties fail so to nominate a sole arbitrator within 30 days from the date when the Claimant's Request for Arbitration has been communicated to the other party, the sole arbitrator shall be appointed by the Court.

4   Where the dispute is to be referred to three arbitrators, each party shall nominate in the Request for Arbitration and the Answer thereto respectively one arbitrator for confirmation by the Court. Such person shall be independent of the party nominating him. If a party fails to nominate an arbitrator, the appointment shall be made by the Court.

The third arbitrator, who will act as chairman of the arbitral tribunal, shall be appointed by the Court, unless the parties have provided that the arbitrators nominated by them shall agree on the third arbitrator within a fixed time-limit. In such a case the Court shall confirm the appointment of such third arbitrator. Should the two arbitrators fail, within the time-limit fixed by the parties or the Court, to reach agreement on the third arbitrator, he shall be appointed by the Court.

5   Where the parties have not agreed upon the number of arbitrators, the Court shall appoint a sole arbitrator, save where it appears to the Court that the dispute is such as to warrant the appointment of three arbitrators. In such a case the parties shall each have a period of 30 days within which to nominate an arbitrator.

6   Where the Court is to appoint a sole arbitrator or the chairman of an arbitral tribunal, it shall make the appointment after having requested a proposal from a National Committee of the ICC that it considers to be appropriate. If the Court does not accept the proposal made, or if said National Committee fails to make the proposal requested within the time-fixed by the Court, the Court may repeat its request or may request a proposal from another appropriate National Committee.

Where the Court considers that the circumstances so demand, it may choose the sole arbitrator or the chairman of the arbitral tribunal from a country where there is no National Committee, provided that neither of the parties objects within the time-limit fixed by the Court.

The sole arbitrator or the chairman of the arbitral tribunal shall be chosen from a country other than those of which the parties are nationals. However, in suitable circumstances and provided that neither of the parties objects within the time-limit fixed by the Court, the sole arbitrator or the chairman of the arbitral tribunal may be chosen from a country of which any of the parties is a national.

Where the Court is to appoint an arbitrator on behalf of a party which has failed to nominate one, it shall make the appointment after having requested a proposal from the National Committee of the country of which the said party is a national. If the Court does not accept the proposals made, or if said National Committee fails to make the proposal requested within the time-limit fixed by the Court, or if the country of which the said party is a national has no National Committee, the Court shall be at liberty to choose any person whom it regards as suitable, after having informed the National Committee of the country of which such person is a national, if one exists.

7   Every arbitrator appointed or confirmed by the Court must be and remain independent of the parties involved in the arbitration.

Before appointment or confirmation by the Court, a prospective arbitrator shall disclose in writing to the Secretary General of the Court any facts or circumstances which might be of such a nature as to call into question the arbitrator's independence in the eyes of the parties. Upon receipt of such information, the Secretary General of the Court shall provide it to the parties in writing and fix a time-limit for any comments from them.

An arbitrator shall immediately disclose in writing to the Secretary General of the Court and the parties any facts or circumstances of a similar nature which may arise between the arbitrator's appointment or confirmation by the Court and the notification of the final award.

8   A challenge of an arbitrator, whether for an alleged lack of independence or otherwise, is made by the submission to the Secretary General of the Court of a written statement specifying the facts and circumstances on which the challenge is based.

For a challenge to be admissible, it must be sent by a party either within 30 days from reciept by that party of the notification of the appointment or confirmation of the arbitrator by the Court; or within 30 days from the date when the party making the challenge was informed of the facts and circumstances on which the challenge is based, if such date is subsequent to the receipt of the aforementioned notification.

9   The Court shall decide on the admissibility, and at the same time if need be on the merits, of a challenge after the Secretary General of the Court

has accorded an opportunity for the arbitrator concerned, the parties and any other members of the arbitral tribunal to comment in writing within a suitable period of time.

10   An arbitrator shall be replaced upon his death, upon the acceptance by the Court of a challenge, or upon the acceptance by the Court of the arbitrator's resignation.

11   An arbitrator shall also be replaced when the Court decides that he is prevented *de jure* or *de facto* from fulfilling his functions, or that he is not fulfilling his functions in accordance with the Rules or within the prescibed time-limits.

When, on the basis of information that has come to its attention, the Court considers applying the preceding sub-paragraph, it shall decide on the the matter after the Secretary General of the Court has provided such information in writing to the arbitrator concerned, the parties and any other members of the arbitral tribunal, and accorded an opportunity to them to comment in writing within a suitable period of time.

12   In each instance where an arbitrator is to be replaced, the procedure indicated in the preceding paragraphs 3, 4, 5 and 6 shall be followed. Once reconstituted, and after having invited the parties to comment, the arbitral tribunal shall determine if and to what extent prior proceedings shall again take place.

13   Decisions of the Court as to the appointment, confirmation, challenge or replacement of an arbitrator shall be final.

The reasons for decisions by the Court as to the appointment, confirmation, challenge, or replacement of an arbitrator on the grounds that he is not fulfilling his functions in accordance with the Rules or within the prescribed time-limits, shall not be communicated.

Article 3   Request for Arbitration

1   A party wishing to have recourse to arbitration by the International Chamber of Commerce shall submit its Request for Arbitration to the Secretariat of the International Court of Arbitration, through its National Committee or directly. In this latter case the Secretariat shall bring the Request to the notice of the National Committee concerned.

The date when the Request is received by the Secretariat of the Court shall, for all purposes, be deemed to be the date of commencement of the arbitral proceedings.

2   The Request for Arbitration shall *inter alia* contain the following information:

    (a)   names in full, description, and addresses of the parties,

    (b)   a statement of the Claimant's case,

    (c)   the relevant agreements, and in particular the agreement to arbitrate, and such documentation or information as will serve clearly to establish the circumstances of the case,

    (d)   all relevant particulars concerning the number of arbitrators and their choice in accordance with the provisions of Article 2 above.

3   The Secretariat shall send a copy of the Request and the documents annexed thereto the Defendant for his Answer.

Article 4   Answer to the Request

1   The Defendant shall within 30 days from the receipt of the documents referred to in paragraph 3 of Article 3 comment on the proposals made concerning the number of arbitrators and their choice and, where appropriate, nominate an arbitrator. He shall at the same time set out his defence and supply relevant documents. In exceptional circumstances the Defendant may apply to the Secretariat for an extention of time for the filing of his defence and his documents. The application must, however, include the Defendant's comments on the proposals made with regard to the number of arbitrators and their choice and also, where appropriate, the nomination of an arbitrator. If the Defendant fails so to do, the Secretariat shall report to the International Court of arbitration, which shall proceed with the arbitration in accordance with these Rules.

2   A copy of the answer and of the documents annexed thereto, if any, shall be communicated to the Claimant for his information.

Article 5   Counter-claim

1   If the Defendant wishes to make a counter-claim, he shall file the same with the Secretariat, at the same time as his Answer as provided for in Article 4.

2   It shall be open to the Claimant to file a Reply with the Secretariat within 30 days from the date when the counter-claim was communicated to him.

Article 6   Pleadings and written statements, notifications or communications

1   All pleadings and written statements submitted by the parties, as well as all documents annexed thereto, shall be supplied in a number of copies sufficient to provide one copy for each party, plus one for each arbitrator, and one for the Secretariat.

2   All notifications or communications from the Secretariat and the arbitrator shall be validly made if they are delivered against receipt or forwarded by registered post to the address or last known address of the party for whom the same are intended as notified by the party in question or by the other party as appropriate.

3   Notification or communication shall be deemed to have been effected on the day when it was received, or should, if made in accordance with the preceding paragraph, have been received by the party itself or by its representative.

4   Periods of time specified in the present Rules or in the Internal Rules or set by the International Court of Arbitration pursuant to its authority under any of these Rules shall start to run on the day following the date a notification or communication is deemed to have been effected in accordance with the preceding paragraph. When, in the country where the notification or communication is deemed to have been effected, the day next following such date is an official holiday or a non-business day, the period of time shall commence on the first following working day. Official holidays and non-

working days are included in the calculation of the period of time. If the last day of the relevant period of time granted is an official holiday or a non-business day in the country where the notification or communication is deemed to have been effected, the period of time shall expire at the end of the first following working day.

Article 7   Absence of agreement to arbitrate

Where there is no *prima facie* agreement between the parties to arbitrate or where there is an agreement but it does not specify the International Chamber of Commerce, and if the Defendant does not file an Answer within the period of 30 days provided by paragraph 1 of Article 4 or refuses arbitration by the International Chamber of Commerce, the Claimant shall be informed that the arbitration cannot proceed.

Article 8   Effect of the agreement to arbitrate

1   Where the parties have agreed to submit to arbitration by the International Chamber of Commerce, they shall be deemed thereby to have submitted *ipso facto* to the present Rules.

2   If one of the parties refuses or fails to take part in the arbitration, the arbitration shall proceed notwithstanding such refusal or failure.

3   Should one of the parties raise one or more pleas concerning the existence or validity of the agreement to arbitrate, and should the International Court of Arbitration be satisfied of the *prima facie* existence of such an agreement, the Court may, without prejudice to the admissibility or merits of the plea or pleas, decide that the arbitration shall proceed. In such a case any decision as to the arbitrator's jurisdiction shall be taken by the arbitrator himself.

4   Unless otherwise provided, the arbitrator shall not cease to have jurisdiction by reason of any claim that the contract is null and void or allegation that it is inexistent provided that he upholds the validity of the agreement to arbitrate. He shall continue to have jurisdiction, even though the contract itself may be inexistent or null and void, to determine the respective rights of the parties and to adjudicate upon their claims and pleas.

5   Before the file is transmitted to the arbitrator, and in exceptional circumstances even thereafter, the parties shall be at liberty to apply to any competent judicial authority for interim or conservatory measures, and they shall not by so doing be held to infringe the agreement to arbitrate or to affect the relevant powers reserved to the arbitrator.

Any such application and any measures taken by the judicial authority must be notified without delay to the Secretariat of the International Court of Arbitration. The Secretariat shall inform the arbitrator thereof.

Article 9   Advance to cover costs of arbitration

1   The International Court of Arbitration shall fix the amount of the advance on costs in a sum likely to cover the costs of arbitration of the claims which have been referred to it.

Where, apart from the principle claim, one or more counter-claims are submitted, the Court may fix separate advances on costs for the principle claim and the counter-claim or counter-claims.

2   The advance on costs shall be payable in equal shares by the Claimant or Claimants and the Defendant or Defendants. However, any one party shall be free to pay the whole of the advance on costs in respect of the claim or the counter-claim should the other party fail to pay its share.

3   The Secretariat may make the transmission of the file to the arbitrator conditional upon the payment by the parties or one of them of the whole or part of the advance on costs to the International Chamber of Commerce.

4   When the Terms of Reference are communicated to the Court in accordance with the provisions of Article 13, the Court shall verify whether the requests for the advance on costs have been complied with.

The Terms of Reference shall only become operative and the arbitrator shall only proceed in respect of those claims for which the advance on costs has been duly paid to the International Chamber of Commerce.

Article 10   Transmission of the file to the arbitrator

Subject to the provisions of Article 9, the Secretariat shall transmit the file to the arbitrator as soon as it has received the Defendant's Answer to the Request for Arbitration, at the latest upon the expiry of the time-limits fixed in Articles 4 and 5 above for the filing of these documents.

Article 11   Rules governing the proceedings

The rules governing the proceedings before the arbitrator shall be those resulting from these Rules and, where these Rules are silent, any rules which the parties (or, failing them, the arbitrator) may settle, and whether or not reference is thereby made to a municipal procedural law to be applied to the arbitration.

Article 12   Place of arbitration

The place of arbitration shall be fixed by the International Court of Arbitration, unless agreed upon the parties.

Article 13   Terms of Reference

1   Before proceeding with the preparation of the case, the arbitrator shall draw up, on the basis of the documents or in the presence of the parties and in the light of their most recent submissions, a document defining his Terms of Reference. This document shall include the following particulars:
    (a)   the full names and description of the parties,
    (b)   the addresses of the parties to which notifications or communications arising in the course of the arbitration may validly be made,
    (c)   a summary of the parties' respective claims,
    (d)   definition of the issues to be determined,
    (e)   the arbitrator's full name, description and address,
    (f)   the place of arbitration,

(g) particulars of the applicable procedural rules and, if such is the case, reference to the power conferred upon the arbitrator to act as amiable compositeur,

(h) such other particulars as may be required to make the arbitral award enforceable in law, or may be regarded as helpful by the International Court of Arbitration or the arbitrator.

2   The document mentioned in paragraph 1 of this Article shall be signed by the parties and the arbitrator. Within two months of the date when the file has been transmitted to him, the arbitrator shall transmit to the Court the said document signed by himself and by the parties. The Court may, pursuant to a reasoned request from the arbitrator or if need be on its own initiative, extend this time-limit if it decides it is necessary to do so.

Should one of the parties refuse to take part in the drawing up of the said document or to sign the same, the Court, if it is satisfied that the case is one of those mentioned in paragraphs 2 and 3 of Article 8, shall take such action as is necessary for its appoval. Thereafter the Court shall set a time-limit for the signature of the statement by the defaulting party and on expiry of that time-limit the arbitration shall proceed and the award shall be made.

3   The parties shall be free to determine the law to be applied by the arbitrator to the merits of the dispute. In the absence of any indication by the parties as to the applicable law, the arbitrator shall apply the law designated as the proper law by the rule of conflict which he deems appropriate.

4   The arbitrator shall assume the powers of an amiable compositeur if the parties are agreed to give him such powers.

5   In all cases the arbitrator shall take account of the provisions of the contract and the relevant trade usages.

Article 14   The arbitral proceedings

1   The arbitrator shall proceed within as short a time as possible to establish the facts of the case by all appropriate means. After study of the written submissions of the parties and of all documents relied upon, the arbitrator shall hear the parties together in person if one of them so requests; and failing such a request he may of his own motion decide to hear them.

In addition, the arbitrator may decide to hear any other person in the presence of the parties or in their absence provided they have been duly summoned.

2   The arbitrator may appoint one or more experts, define their Terms of Reference, receive their reports and/or hear them in person.

3   The arbitrator may decide the case on the relevant documents alone if the parties so request or agree.

Article 15

1   At the request of one of the parties or if necessary on his own initiative, the arbitrator, giving reasonable notice, shall summon the parties to appear before him on the day and at the place appointed by him and shall so inform the Secretariat of the International Court of Arbitration.

2   If one of the parties, although duly summoned, fails to appear, the arbitrator, if he is satisfied that the summons was duly received and the party

is absent without valid excuse, shall have power to proceed with the arbitration, and such proceedings shall be deemed to have been conducted in the presence of all parties.

3   The arbitrator shall determine the language or languages of the arbitration, due regard being paid to all the relevant circumstances and in particular to the language of the contract.

4   The arbitrator shall be in full charge of the hearings, at which all the parties shall be entitled to be present. Save with the approval of the arbitrator and of the parties, persons not involved in the proceedings shall not be admitted.

5   The parties may appear in person or through duly accredited agents. In addition, they may be assisted by advisers.

Article 16

The parties may make new claims or counter-claims before the arbitrator on condition that these remain within the limits fixed by the Terms of Reference provided for in Article 13 or that they are specified in a rider to that document, signed by the parties and communicated to the International Court of Arbitration.

Article 17   Award by consent

If the parties reach a settlement after the file has been transmitted to the arbitrator in accordance with Article 10, the same shall be recorded in the form of an arbitral award made by consent of the parties.

Article 18   Time-limit for award

1   The time-limit within which the arbitrator must render his award is fixed at six months. Once the terms of Article 9(4) have been satisfied, such time-limit shall start to run from the date of the last signature by the arbitrator or of the parties of the document mentioned in Article 13, or from the expiry of the time-limit granted to a party by virtue of Article 13(2), or from the date that the Secretary General of the International Court of Arbitration notifies the arbitrator that the advance on costs is paid in full, if such notification occurs later.

2   The Court may, pursuant to a reasoned request from the arbitrator or if need be on its own initiative, extend this time-limit if it decides it is necessary to do so.

3   Where no such extension is granted and, if appropriate, after application of the provisions of Article 2(11), the Court shall determine the manner in which the dispute is to be resolved.

Article 19   Award by three arbitrators

When three arbitrators have been appointed, the award is given by a majority decision. If there be no majority, the award shall be made by the Chairman of the arbitral tribunal alone.

Article 20   Decision as to costs of arbitration

1   The arbitrator's award shall, in addition to dealing with the merits of the case, fix the costs of the arbitration and decide which of the parties shall bear the costs or in what proportions the costs shall be borne by the parties.

2   The costs of the arbitration shall include the arbitrator's fees and the administrative costs fixed by the International Court of Arbitration in accordance with the scale annexed to the present Rules, the expenses, if any, of the arbitrator, the fees and expenses of any experts, and the normal legal costs incurred by the parties.

3   The Court may fix the arbitrator's fees at a figure higher or lower than that which would result from the application of the annexed scale if in the exceptional circumstances of the case this appears to be necessary.

Article 21   Scrutiny of award by the Court

Before signing an award, whether partial or definitive, the arbitrator shall submit it in draft form to the International Court of Arbitration. The Court may lay down modifications as to the form of the award and without affecting the arbitrator's liberty of decision, may also draw his attention to points of substance. No award shall be signed until it has been approved by the Court as to its form.

Article 22   Making of award

The arbitral award shall be deemed to be made at the place of the arbitration proceedings and on the date when it is signed by the arbitrator.

Article 23   Notification of award to parties

1   Once an award has been made, the Secretariat shall notify to the parties the text signed by the arbitrator; provided always that the costs of the arbitration have been fully paid to the International Chamber of Commerce by the parties or by one of them.

2   Additional copies certified true by the Secretary General of the International Court of Arbitration shall be made available on request and at any time, to the parties but to no one else.

3   By virtue of the notification made in accordance with paragraph 1 of this article, the parties waive any other form of notification or deposit on the part of the arbitrator.

Article 24   Finality and enforceability of award

1   The arbitral award shall be final.

2   By submitting the dispute to arbitration by the International Chamber of Commerce, the parties shall be deemed to have undertaken to carry out the resulting award without delay and to have waived their right to any form of appeal insofar as such waiver can validly be made.

Article 25   Deposit of award

An original of each award made in accordance with the present Rules shall be deposited with the Secretariat of the International Court of Arbitration.

The arbitrator and the Secretariat of the Court shall assist the parties in complying with whatever further formalities may be necessary.

Article 26   General rule

In all matters not expressly provided for in these Rules, the International Court of Arbitration and the arbitrator shall act in the spirit of these Rules and shall make every effort to make sure that the award is enforceable at law.

APPENDIX I

STATUTES OF THE INTERNATIONAL COURT OF ARBITRATION

Article 1   Appointment of members

The members of the International Court of Arbitration of the International Chamber of Commerce are appointed for a term of three years by the Council of that Chamber pursuant to Article 5.3i of the Constitution, on the proposal of each National Committee.

Article 2   Composition

The International Court of Arbitration shall be composed of a Chairman, of eight Vice-Chairmen, of a Secretary General and of one or several Technical Advisers chosen by the Council of the International Chamber of Commerce either from among the members of the Court or apart from them, and of one member for, and appointed by, each National Committee.

The chairmanship may be exercised by two Co-Chairmen; in this case, they shall have equal rights, and the expression 'the Chairman', used in the Rules of Conciliation and Arbitration, shall apply to either of them equally.

When a member of the Court does not reside in the city where International Headquarters of the International Chamber of Commerce is situated, the Council may appoint an alternate member.

If the Chairman is unable to attend a session of the Court, he shall be replaced by one of the Vice-Chairmen.

Article 3   Function and powers

The function of the International Court of Arbitration is to ensure the application of the Rules of Conciliation and Arbitration of the International Chamber of Commerce, and the Court has all the necessary powers for that purpose. It is further entrusted, if need be, with laying before the Commission on International Arbitration any proposals for modifying the Rules of Conciliation and Arbitration of the International Chamber of Commerce which it considers necessary.

Article 4   Deliberations and quorum

The decisions of the International Court of Arbitration shall be taken by a majority vote, the Chairman having a casting vote in the event of a tie. The deliberations of the Court shall be valid when at least six members are present.

The Secretary General of the International Chamber of Commerce, the Secretary General of the Court and the Technical Adviser or Advisers shall attend in an advisory capacity only.

APPENDIX II

INTERNAL RULES OF THE INTERNATIONAL COURT OF ARBITRATION

Role of the International Court of Arbitration

1   The International Court of Arbitration may accept jurisdiction over business disputes not of an international business nature, if it has jurisdiction by reason of an arbitration agreement.

Confidential character of the work of the International Court of Arbitration

2   The work of the International Court of Arbitration is of a confidential character which must be respected by everyone who participates in that work in whatever capacity.

3   The sessions of the International Court of Arbitration, whether plenary or those of a Committee of the Court, are open to its members and to the Secretariat.

However, in exceptional circumstances and, if need be, after obtaining the opinion of members of the Court, the Chairman of the International Court of Arbitration may invite honorary members of the Court and authorize observers to attend. Such persons must respect the confidential character of the work of the Court.

4   The documents submitted to the Court or drawn up by it in the course of the proceedings it conducts are communicated only to members of the Court and to the Secretariat.

The Chairman or the Secretary General of the Court may nevertheless authorize researchers undertaking work of a scientific nature on international trade law to acquaint themselves with certain documents of general interest, with the exception of memoranda, notes, statements and documents remitted by the parties within the framework of arbitration proceedings.

Such authorization shall not be given unless the beneficiary has undertaken to respect the confidential character of the documents made available and to refrain from any publication in their respect without having previously submitted the text for approval to the Secretary General of the Court.

Participation of members of the International Court of Arbitration in ICC arbitration

5   Owing to the special responsibilities laid upon them by the ICC Rules of Arbitration, the Chairman, the Vice-Chairmen and the Secretariat of the

International Court of Arbitration may not personally act as arbitrators or as counsel in cases submitted to ICC arbitration.

The members of the International Court of Arbitration may not be directly appointed as co-arbitrators, sole arbitrator or Chairman of an arbitral tribunal by the International Court of Arbitration. They may however be proposed for such duties by one or more of the parties, subject to confirmation by the Court.

6   When the Chairman, a Vice-Chairman or a member of the Court is involved, in any capacity whatsoever, in proceedings pending before the Court, he must inform the Secretary General of the Court as soon as he becomes aware of such involvement.

He must refrain from participating in the discussions or in the decisions of the Court concerning the proceedings and he must be absent from the courtroom whenever the matter is considered.

He will not receive documentation or information submitted to the Court during the proceedings.

Relations between the members of the Court and the ICC National Committees

7   By virtue of their capacity, the members of the International Court of Arbitration are independent of the ICC National Committees which proposed them for nomination by the ICC Council.

Furthermore, they must regard as confidential, vis-à-vis the said National Committees, any information concerning individual disputes with which they have become acquainted in their capacity as members of the Court except when they have been requested, by the Chairman of the Court or by its Secretary General, to communicate that information to their respective National Committees.

Committee of the Court

8   In accordance with the provisions of Article 1(4) of the ICC Rules of Arbitration, the International Court of Arbitration hereby establishes a Committee of the Court composed as follows, and with the following powers.

9   The Committee consists of a Chairman and two members. The Chairman of the International Court of Arbitration acts as the Chairman of the Committee. He may nevertheless designate a Vice-Chairman of the Court to replace him during a session of the Committee.

The other two members of the Committee are appointed by the Court from among the Vice-Chairmen or the other members of the Court. At each meeting of the Court it appoints the members who are to attend the meeting of the Committee to be held before the next plenary session of the Court.

10   The Committee meets when convened by its Chairman, in principle twice a month.

11   (a)   The Committee is empowered to take any decision within the jurisdiction of the Court, with the exception of decisions concerning challenges of arbitrators (Arts. 2(8) and 2(9) of the ICC Rules of Arbitration), allegations that an arbitrator is not fulfilling his functions (Art. 2(11) of the ICC Rules of Arbitration) and appoval of draft awards other than awards made with the consent of the parties.

(b)   The decisions of the Committee are taken unanimously.

(c)   When the Committee cannot reach a decision or deems it preferable to abstain, it transfers the case to the next plenary session of the Court, making any suggestions it deems appropriate.

(d)   The Committee's proceedings are brought to the notice of the Court at its next plenary session.

Absence of an arbitration agreement

12   Where there is no *prima facie* arbitration agreement between the parties or where there is an agreement but it does not specify the ICC, the Secretariat draws the attention of the Claimant to the provisions laid down in Article 7 of the Rules of Arbitration. The Claimant is entitled to require the decision to be taken by the International Court of Arbitration.

This decision is of an administrative nature. If the Court decides that the arbitration solicited by the Claimant cannot proceed, the parties retain the right to ask the competent jurisdiction whether or not they are bound by an arbitration agreement in the light of the law applicable.

If the Court considers *prima facie* that the proceedings may take place, the arbitrator appointed has the duty to decide as to his own jurisdiction and, where such jurisdiction exists, as to the merits of the dispute.

Joinder of claims in arbitration proceedings

13   When a party presents a Request for Arbitration in connection with a legal relationship already submitted to arbitration proceedings by the same parties and pending before the International Court of Arbitration, the Court may decide to include that claim in the existing proceedings, subject to the provisions of Article 16 of the ICC Rules of Arbitration.

Advances to cover costs of arbitration

14   When the International Court of Arbitration has set separate advances on costs for a specific case in accordance with Article 9(1) (sub para. 2) of the ICC Rules of Arbitration, the Secretariat requests each of the parties to pay the amount corresponding to its claims, without prejudice to the right of the parties to pay the said advances on costs in equal shares, if they deem it advisable.

15   When a request for an advance on costs has not been complied with, the Secretariat may set a time-limit, which must not be less than 30 days, on the expiry of which the relevant claim, whether principal claim or counter-claim, shall be considered as withdrawn. This does not prevent the party in question from lodging a new claim at a later date.

Should one of the parties wish to object to this measure, he must make a request, within the aforementioned period, for the matter to be decided by the Court.

16   If one of the parties claims a right to a set-off with regard to either a principal claim or counter-claim, such a set-off is taken into account in determining the advance to cover the costs of arbitration, in the same way as a separate claim, insofar as it may require the arbitrators to consider additional matters.

Arbitral awards : form

17   When it scrutinizes draft arbitral awards in accordance with article 21 of the ICC rules of Arbitration, the International Court of Arbitration pays particular attention to the respect of the formal requirements laid down by the law applicable to the procceedings and, where relevant, by the mandatory rules of the place of arbitration, notably with regard to the reasons for awards, their signature and the admissibility of dissenting opinions.

Arbitrators' fees

18   In setting the arbitrators' fees on the basic of the scale attached to the ICC Rules of Arbitration, the International Court of Arbitration takes into consideration the time spent, the rapidity of the proceedings and the complexity of the dispute so as to arrive at a figure within the limits specified or, when circumstances require, higher or lower then those limits (Art. 20(3) of the ICC Rules of Arbitration).

[. . .]

APPENDIX III

SCHEDULE OF CONCILIATION AND ARBITRATION COSTS
[*Not reproduced here.*]

ICC PRE-ARBITRAL REFEREE PROCEDURE

rules in force as of 1 January 1990

ICC RULES FOR A PRE-ARBITRAL REFEREE PROCEDURE (1990)

ICC Publication No. 482 – ISBN 92.842.11.1.8 (E)
Published in its official English version by the International Chamber of Commerce.
Copyright © 1990 — International Chamber of Commerce (ICC), Paris.
Available from: *ICC Publishing S.A.*, 38 Cours Albert 1er, 75008 Paris, France.
Tel: (1) 49.53.28.28
Fax: (1) 49.53.29.33
Telex: 640 003 F

STANDARD CLAUSE FOR AN ICC PRE-ARBITRAL REFEREE PROCEDURE

The ICC recommends that all parties wishing to make reference to the ICC Rules for a Pre-Arbitral Referee Procedure use the following clause in their contracts:

English

'Any party to this contract shall have the right to have recourse to and shall be bound by the Pre-arbitral Referee Procedure of the International Chamber of Commerce in accordance with its Rules.'

Parties are reminded that if they wish to have recourse to ICC Arbitration as well as to the ICC Pre-arbitral Referee Procedure, a specific reference to both procedures should be stipulated. For that purpose the following clause is recommended:

> 'Any party to this contract shall have the right to have recourse to and shall be bound by the Pre-arbitral Referee Procedure of the International Chamber of Commerce in accordance with its Rules.'
>
> 'All disputes arising in connection with the present contract shall be finally settled under the Rules of Conciliation and Arbitration of the International Chamber of Commerce by one or more arbitrators appointed in accordance with the said Rules.'

RULES FOR A PRE-ARBITRAL REFEREE PROCEDURE

Article 1 Definitions

1.1 These Rules concern a procedure called the 'Pre-arbitral Referee Procedure' which provides for the immediate appointment of a person (the 'Referee') who has the power to make certain orders prior to the arbitral tribunal or national court competent to deal with the case (the 'competent jurisdiction') being seized of it.

1.2 The Secretariat of the ICC International Court of Arbitration (the 'Secretariat') shall act as the Secretariat of the Pre-arbitral Referee Procedure.

1.3 (a) In these Rules any reference to a party includes a party's employees or agents. (b) Any reference to the 'Chairman' means the Chairman of the ICC International Court of Arbitration or includes, in his absence, a Vice-Chairman.

Article 2 Powers of the Referee

2.1 The powers of the Referee are:

(a) To order any conservatory measures or any measures of restoration that are urgently necessary to prevent either immediate damage or irreparable loss and so to safeguard any of the rights or property of one of the parties;

(b) To order a party to make to any other party or to another person any payment which ought to be made;

(c) To order a party to take any step which ought to be taken according to the contract between the parties, including the signing or delivery of any document of the procuring by a party of the signature or delivery of a document;

(d) To order any measures necessary to preserve or establish evidence.

2.1.1 These powers may be altered by express written agreement between the parties.

2.2 The Referee shall not have power to make any order other than that requested by any party in accordance with Article 3.

2.3 Unless the parties otherwise agree in writing, a Referee appointed in accordance with these Rules shall not act as arbitrator in any subsequent proceedings between those parties or in any other proceedings in which there is any issue or question which is the same as or connected with any which had been raised in the proceedings before the Referee.

2.4   If the competent jurisdiction becomes seized of the case after the appointment of the Referee, the Referee shall nevertheless retain the power to make an order within the time provided by Article 6.2 unless the parties otherwise agree or the competent jurisdiction orders otherwise.

2.4.1   Except as provided in Article 2.4 above or by the relevant rules of the competent jurisdiction, once the competent jurisdiction becomes seized of the case it alone may order any further provisional or conservatory measures that it considers necessary. For such purpose the competent jurisdiction, if its rules so permit, shall be deemed to have been authorised by the parties to exercise the powers conferred on the Referee by Article 2.1.

Article 3   Request for Referee and Answer

3.1   An agreement to use the Pre-arbitral Referee Procedure must be in writing.

3.2   A party who requires the appointment of a Referee must send two copies of its Request and of any annexed documents to the Secretariat. Such party must at the same time notify the other party or parties of the Request by the quickest method of delivery available, including telefax.

3.2.1   Each such Request must be accompanied by the amount required to open the file, as set out in Article B.1 of the Appendix to these Rules.

3.2.2   The Request must be drawn up in whatever language may have been agreed upon in writing by the parties or, in the absence of any such agreement, in the same language as the agreement to use the Pre-arbitral Referee Procedure. If this language is not English, French or German a translation of the Request into one of these languages must accompany the Request. The annexed documents may be submitted in their original language without translation except where it is necessary in order to understand the Request. The Request shall be in writing and shall contain in particular:

(a)   the names and addressess of the parties to the agreement together with a brief description of the legal relationships between the parties;

(b)   a copy of the agreement on which the Request is based;

(c)   the order or orders requested and an explanation of the grounds relied on so as to show that the Request falls within Article 2.1;

(d)   as the case may be, the name of the Referee chosen by agreement of the parties;

(e)   any information concerning the choice of the Referee required to be appointed including as appropriate technical or professional qualifications, nationality and language requirements;

(f)   confirmation that the request has been sent to every other party, stating the means by which this has been done and enclosing proof of transmission, such as postal registration form, receipt from a private courier or telefax receipt.

3.3   The requesting party shall, if required by the Secretariat, establish when a copy of the Request was received by each party to whom it was sent or when it should be treated as having been received by said party.

3.4   The other party or parties must submit to the Secretariat in writing an Answer to the Request within 8 days from the receipt of the copy of the Request sent in accordance with Article 3.2 above and must send at the same time a copy to the requesting party and to any other party using the quickest method of delivery available including telefax. The Answer must state any order requested by that party or parties.

Article 4   Appointment of the Referee and Transmission of File

4.1   The Referee may be chosen by the parties by agreement before or after a Request is made pursuant to Article 3 in which case the name and address of the Referee shall be sent immediately to the Secretariat. Upon receipt of the Answer or upon the expiry of the time set out in Article 3.4, whichever is sooner, and having verified the *prima facie* existence of the agreement of the parties, the Chairman shall appoint the Referee agreed upon.

4.2   If a Referee is to be appointed under Article 3.2.2(e), the Chairman shall, upon the expiry of the time limit set out in Article 3.4, appoint the Referee in the shortest time possible, taking account of his technical or professional qualifications, his nationality, residence, other relationships with the countries in which the parties are established or with which they are otherwise connected, and any submissions of any party concerning the choice of a Referee.

4.3   Once the Referee has been appointed, the Secretariat shall so notify the parties and shall transmit the file to him. Thereafter all documentation from the parties must be sent directly to the Referee with a copy to the Secretariat. All documentation from the Referee to the parties must be copied to the Secretariat.

4.4   Any party may challenge a Referee appointed under Article 4.2. In such case the Chairman, after giving the other party and the Referee an opportunity to comment, shall take within the shortest time possible a final decision as to the validity of the challenge. His decision shall be within his sole discretion and shall not itself be subject to challenge or appeal by any party.

4.5   Another person shall be appointed (a) where a Referee dies or is prevented or unable to carry out his functions, or (b) it is decided under Article 4.4. that a challenge is valid or (c) if the Chairman decides, after giving the Referee an opportunity to comment, that he is not fulfilling his functions in accordance with the Rules or within any applicable time limit. Such an appointment shall be made in accordance with Article 4.2 (but subject to Article 4.4). In such case the new Referee shall proceed afresh.

4.6   The reasons for any decision about an appointment, challenge or replacement of any Referee shall not be disclosed.

Article 5   The Proceedings

5.1   If any party shall not have presented an Answer by the time the file has been transmitted to the Referee then the requesting party may be required by the Referee to establish to his satisfaction that a copy of the Request was received or should be treated as having been received by that party before he proceeds further. If the Referee is not so satisfied he shall notify the relevant party of his right to submit an Answer and shall set a time limit within which the Answer shall be submitted. Any such action by the arbitral Referee shall not affect the validity of his appointment.

5.2 Any decision as to the Referee's jurisdiction shall be taken by the Referee.

5.3 Within the limits of the powers conferred on him by Article 2.1. and subject to any agreement of the parties the Referee shall conduct the proceedings in the manner which he considers appropriate for the purpose for which he was appointed including:

- considering the written documents submitted by the parties,
- informing the parties of any further investigation or inquiry that he may consider necessary,
- making such further investigation or inquiry, which may include him visiting any place where the contract is being carried out or the establishments of the parties or any other relevant place, obtaining the report of an expert, and hearing any person he chooses in connection with the dispute, either in the presence of the parties or, if they have been duly convened, in their absence. The results of these investigations and inquiries shall be communicated to the parties for comment.

5.4 In acceding to these Rules the parties undertake to provide the Referee with every facility to implement his terms of reference and, in particular, to make avialable to him all documents which he may consider necessary and also grant free access to any place for the purpose of any investigation or inquiry. The information given to the Referee shall remain confidential between the parties and the Referee.

5.5 The Referee may convene the parties to appear before him within the shortest time limit possible on a date and at a place fixed by him.

5.6 If one of the parties does not make a submission, comment or appear as required by the Referee, and the Referee is satisfied that the party concerned has received or should have received the relevant communication he may nonetheless continue with the proceedings and may make his order.

Article 6 The Order

6.1 The decisions taken by the Referee shall be sent by him to the Secretariat in the form of an order giving reasons.

6.2 The Referee shall make and send the order within 30 days from the date on which the file was transmitted to him. This time limit may be extended by the Chairman upon a reasoned request from the Referee or on his own initiative if he thinks it is necessary to do so.

6.3 The Referee's order does not pre-judge the substance of the case nor shall it bind any competent jurisdiction which may hear any question, issue or dispute in respect of which the order has been made. The order of the Referee shall however remain in force unless and until the Referee or the competent jurisdiction has decided otherwise.

6.4 The Referee may make the carrying out of his order subject to such conditions as he thinks fit including (a) that a party shall commence proceedings before the competent jurisdiction on the substance of the case within a specified period, (b) that a party for whose benefit an order is made shall provide adequate security.

6.5 The Secretariat shall notify the parties of the order of the Referee provided that it shall have received the full amount of the advance on costs fixed by the Secretariat. Only orders so notified are binding upon the parties.

6.6   The parties agree to carry out the Referee's order without delay and waive their right to all means of appeal or recourse or opposition to a request to a Court or to any other authority to implement the order insofar as such waiver can validly be made.

6.7   Unless otherwise agreed between the parties and subject to any mandatory order, any submissions, communications or documents (other than the order) established or made solely for the purpose of the Pre-arbitral Referee Procedure shall be confidential and shall not be given to the competent jurisdiction.

6.8   The Referee shall not be obliged to explain or give further additional reasons for any order after it has been notified by the Secretariat under Article 6.5. Neither the ICC nor any of its employees or persons acting as Chairman or Vice-Chairman, nor any person acting as Referee shall be liable to any person for any loss or damage arising out of any act or ommission in connection with the Rules except that the Referee may be liable for the consequences of conscious and deliberate wrongdoing.

6.8.1   The competent jurisdiction may determine whether any party who refuses or fails to carry out an order of the Referee is liable to any other party for loss or damage caused by such refusal or failure.

6.8.2   The competent jurisdiction may determine whether a party who requested the Referee to issue an order the carrying out of which caused damage to another party is liable to such other party.

Article 7   Costs

7.1   The costs of the Pre-arbitral Referee Procedure comprise: (a) an administrative charge as set out in the Appendix to these Rules, (b) the fees and expenses of the Referee to be determined as set out in the Appendix and (c) the costs of any expert. The Referee's order shall state who shall bear the costs of the Pre-arbitral Referee Procedure and in what proportion. A party who made an advance or other payment is respect of costs which it was not liable to have made under the Referee's order shall be entitled to recover the amount paid from the party who ought to have made the payment.

7.2   The costs of and payment for any procedure under these Rules are as set out in the Appendix hereto.

THE ICC INTERNATIONAL CENTRE FOR EXPERTISE

new rules in force as from 1 January 1993

ICC International Centre for Expertise (1993)
ICC Publication No. 520 — ISBN 92.842.1149.2 (E)
Published in its official English version by the International Chamber of Commerce.
Copyright © 1993 — International Chamber of Commerce (ICC), Paris.
Available from: *ICC Publishing S.A.*, 38 Cours Albert 1er, 75008 Paris, France.
Tel: (1) 49.53.28.28
Fax: (1) 49.53.29.33
Telex: 640 003 F

MODEL EXPERTISE CLAUSE

'The parties to this agreement agree to have recourse, if the need arises, to the International Centre for Expertise of the International Chamber of Commerce in accordance with the ICC's Rules for Expertise'.

Note: Since expertise and arbitral proceedings are distinct, the ICC recommends parties to separate technical and legal disputes in contracts by inserting the model clause for expertise, in addition to the arbitration clause.

This does not prevent the possible use by ICC arbitrators of the services of the International Centre for Expertise if they need to appoint technically qualified experts.

Parties wishing to make reference to ICC arbitration are reminded that they should include the following clause in their contracts:

'All disputes arising in connection with the present contract shall be finally settled under the Rules of Conciliation and Arbitration of the International Chamber of Commerce by one or more arbitrators appointed in accordance with the said Rules'.

Request for the Centre's services

Parties wishing to use the Centre's services should contact:
The ICC International Centre for Expertise
38, Cours Albert 1er
75008 Paris
France
Tel: 0033–1–49 53 28 28
Telex: 640 003 ICCARBIF
Telefax: 0033–1–49 53 29 33

ICC RULES FOR EXPERTISE

SECTION I

General provisions

Article 1   The International Centre for Expertise

1   The International Centre for Expertise which was established by the International Chamber of Commerce (ICC) has for its function the appointment or the proposal of experts in connection with international business transactions.

2   The Centre consists of a Standing Committee and a Secretariat. The Standing Committee is composed of five members (a chairman and four members) of different nationalities all of whom are appointed by the ICC for a three-year renewable term. The Secretariat of the Centre is assumed by the ICC.

Article 2   Recourse to the International Centre for Expertise

1   Any request for the appointment or proposal of an expert shall be submitted to the ICC International Centre for Expertise, at the ICC Headquarters in Paris.

2   The Request shall contain inter alia the following information:
— names, description and addresses of the parties involved;
— where applicable, a copy of the parties' agreement to have recourse to the ICC International Centre for Expertise;
— any relevant indications concerning the choice of an expert;
— a descriptive summary of the expert's brief.

Article 3   Manner in Which an Expert is Chosen

Any appointment or proposal of an expert as well as any decision on the replacement of an expert, in accordance with Articles 4, 5, and 7, shall be made as quickly as possible by the Chairman of the Standing Committee after consultation with members of the Standing Committee.

SECTION II

Proposal of an expert

Article 4

At the request of an arbitral tribunal or any person, the Chairman of the Standing Committee may propose the name(s) of one or more experts. The Centre's intervention ends on notification of the proposal.

SECTION III

Appointment of an expert and expertise procedure

Article 5   Appointment of an Expert

1   Where the parties have agreed to have recourse to the ICC International Centre for Expertise, one or more parties may request the Centre to appoint an expert. If the request for appointment is not made jointly by all the parties to the agreement, the Secretariat of the Centre shall send a copy of the request to the other party or parties who may make representations within a time limit fixed by the Secretariat according to the circumstances of the case.

2   Subject to Article 6, the Chairman of the Standing Committee shall confirm the choice of the expert nominated by the parties by mutual consent. Failing such an agreement, the Chairman shall appoint an expert.

Article 6   The Expert's independence

Prior to an appointment, the Centre shall invite the prospective expert to submit a declaration confirming his independence of the parties.

Article 7   Replacement of an Expert

1   The Chairman of the Standing Committee shall decide on the replacement of an expert who has died or resigns or is unable to carry out his functions.

The Chairman may replace the expert, after having considered his observations, if any, where objections are made by one of the parties concerning the person appointed as expert.

2   The Chairman may also replace the expert if he should find, after having considered the expert's observations, if any, that the expert is not fulfilling his functions in accordance with the Rules or within any prescribed time limits.

Article 8   The Expert's Brief

1   (a)   The expert is empowered to make findings within the limits set by the request for expertise, after giving the parties an opportunity to make submissions.

(b)   The expert may also be empowered, by express agreement between the parties, either in a prior agreement or in their request for the appointment of an expert, to:

— recommend, as needed, those measures which he deems most appropriate for the performance of the contract and/or those which would be necessary in order to safeguard the subject matter;

— supervise the carrying out of the contractual operations.

2   In agreeing to the application of these Rules the parties undertake to provide the expert with all facilities in order to implement his Brief and, in particular, to make available all documents he may consider necessary and also to grant him free access to any place where the expertise operations are being carried out. The information given to the expert will be used only for the purpose of the expertise and shall remain confidential.

3   Unless otherwise agreed the findings or recommendations of the expert shall not be binding upon the parties.

Article 9   Notification of the Expert's Report

The expert shall send his report to the Centre in as many copies as there are parties plus one for the Centre. Thereafter, the Centre shall notify the expert's report to the parties.

SECTION IV

Costs of the expertise

[*Not reproduced here.*]

INTERNATIONAL MARITIME ARBITRATION ORGANISATION (1979, 1990)

ICC Publication No. 324 — ISBN 92.842.0116.8 (E)
Published in its official English version by the International Chamber of Commerce.

ICC/CMI RULES

STANDARD CLAUSE

'All disputes arising from this contract/Charter Party shall be finally settled
in accordance with the ICC-CMI International Maritime Arbitration Rules
by one or more arbitrators appointed in accordance with the said Rules'.

It is advisable to indicate the place of arbitration, the law to be applied to
the issues of the dispute, the number of arbitrators and the language of the
arbitration.

RULES

The ICC-CMI arbitral organisation

Article 1

The International Chamber of Commerce (ICC) and the Comité Maritime
International (CMI) have jointly decided, with a view to providing a service
to the maritime world at large, to issue rules for the conduct of arbitration
disputes relating to maritime affairs including *inter alia* contracts of charter-
ing, contracts of carriage by sea or of combined transport, contracts of marine
insurance, salvage, general average, shipbuilding and ship repairing contracts,
contracts of sale of vessels and other contracts creating rights in vessels.

Article 2

1   An institutional body known as the 'Standing Committee on Maritime
Arbitration' (hereinafter referred to as the Standing Committee) will have the
duty of ensuring the application of these Rules.

2   The Standing Committee shall be composed of twelve members: six
appointed by the ICC and six by the CMI.

The members of the Standing Committee shall be appointed for three
years.

3   The Chairman of the Standing Committee, selected from among its
members, shall be appointed jointly by the ICC and the CMI.

Likewise from among the members of the Standing Committee, two
Vice-Chairmen shall be appointed: one by the ICC and one by the CMI.

4   The Secretariat of the Standing Committee shall be provided by the
ICC and its costs shall be met by the parties seeking arbitration under these
Rules.

The seat of the Standing Committee will be 38, Cours Albert 1er, 75008 Paris (France), where the meetings of the Standing Committee will be held unless otherwise agreed.

5   The Standing Committee shall have power to deliberate when at least two of the members appointed by the ICC and two of the members appointed by the CMI are present. Decisions shall be taken within the Committee by a simple majority. If no majority is attained, the Chairman of the meeting shall have a casting vote.

Request for arbitration and defendant's answer

Article 3

1   Where the parties have agreed that disputes between them shall be referred to arbitration under these Rules, such disputes shall be settled in accordance with these Rules subject to such modification as the parties may agree.

2   A party wishing to have recourse to ICC-CMI maritime arbitration shall submit its Request to the Secretariat of the Standing Committee with a copy of it to the Defendant.

The date when the Request is received by the Secretariat shall be deemed, for all purposes, to be the date of commencement of the arbitration proceedings.

3   The Request for arbitration shall contain the following information:

(a)   names in full, description, and addresses of the parties;

(b)   a summary of the claimant's points of claim;

(c)   the document containing the arbitration clause or the arbitration agreement;

(d)   such documents as are deemed relevant to clarify the subject matter of the dispute;

(e)   all relevant particulars concerning the number and appointment of arbitrators.

4   Disputes shall be settled by a sole arbitrator or by three arbitrators if circumstances so require. In the following Articles, the word 'arbitrator' denotes a single arbitrator or three arbitrators as the case may be.

Article 4

1   The Defendant shall within 21 days from the date on which he receives the Claimant's request for arbitration state whether he agrees that the dispute be submitted to arbitration according to these Rules and, if so, comment on the proposals made concerning the number and appointment of arbitrators and, where appropriate, nominate an arbitrator.

2   If the Defendant objects to submitting the dispute to arbitration according to these Rules, the Claimant shall have a period of 15 days from the day such objection is communicated to him to comment on the Defendant's objection. If the Claimant agrees that there is no agreement that the dispute be submitted to arbitration under these Rules, the parties will be informed by the Secretariat that the proceedings are discontinued. If the Claimant maintains that there is a valid arbitration agreement, the matter

shall be referred to the Standing Committee and resolved according to the provisions of Article 5.

3   The Defendant's failure to reply within the time mentioned above to the Claimant's request for arbitration shall be considered as an objection to the request.

4   The Defendant shall have a period of 30 days from the date when he has notified the Secretariat of his agreement to the Claimant's request for arbitration or, failing such agreement, from the date when he has received notice of the Standing Committee's decision that the arbitration shall proceed, to file his defence and supply relevant documents.

5   Within the last-mentioned time limit the Defendant may in his defence make a counter-claim to which the Claimant may file a reply within 21 days from the date it was communicated to him.

6   The time limits stipulated in this Article may, upon the request of either party, be extended by the Secretariat but not for more than an additional period of 30 days unless the parties otherwise agree. If a longer extension is requested, or failing such an agreement if the Secretariat refuses to grant an extension, the request shall be submitted to the Standing Committee.

Validity of the arbitration agreement

Article 5

1   Should one of the parties raise one or more pleas concerning the existence or validity of the agreement to arbitrate, and should the Standing Committee be satisfied of the prima facie existence of such an agreement, the Standing Committee may, without prejudice to the admissibility or merits of the plea or pleas, decide that the arbitration shall proceed. In such a case any decision as to the arbitrator's jurisdiction shall be taken by the arbitrator himself.

2   Unless otherwise provided, the arbitrator shall not cease to have jurisdiction by reason of any claim that the contract containing the arbitration agreement is null and void or allegation that it is non-existent provided that he upholds the validity of the agreement to arbitrate. He shall continue to have jurisdiction, even though the contract itself may be non-existent or null and void, to determine the respective rights of the parties and to adjudicate upon their claims and pleas.

3   If one of the parties refuses or fails to take part in the arbitration, the arbitration shall proceed notwithstanding such refusal or failure.

Constitution of the arbitral tribunal

Article 6

1   Insofar as the parties have not themselves appointed arbitrators, and unless the parties have otherwise agreed, the Standing Committee shall appoint arbitrators in accordance with the provisions of this Article.

2   Where the parties have agreed that the disputes shall be settled by a sole arbitrator and fail so to nominate him within 30 days from the date when the Claimant's Request for Arbitration has been communicated to the other party, the sole arbitrator shall be appointed by the Standing Committee.

3   Where the dispute is to be referred to three arbitrators, each party shall nominate in the Request for Arbitration and in the Answer thereto one arbitrator. Such person shall be independent of the party nominating him. If a party fails to nominate an arbitrator, the appointment shall be made by the Standing Committee. The third arbitrator, who will act as chairman of the arbitral tribunal, shall be appointed by the arbitrators nominated by the parties (unless the parties have nominated such third arbitrator) within a fixed time limit. Should the two arbitrators fail, within the time limit fixed by the parties or the Standing Committee, to reach agreement on the third arbitrator, he shall be appointed by the Standing Committee.

4   Where the parties have not agreed upon the number of arbitrators, the Standing Committee shall appoint a sole arbitrator, save where it appears to the Standing Committee that the dispute is such as to warrant the appointment of three arbitrators. In such a case the parties shall each have a period of 21 days within which to nominate an arbitrator.

5   Where the Standing Committee is to appoint a sole arbitrator or the Chairman of an arbitral tribunal, the sole arbitrator or the chairman of an arbitral tribunal shall be chosen from a country other than those of which the parties are nationals. However, in suitable circumstances and provided that neither of the parties objects, the sole arbitrator or the chairman of the arbitral tribunal may be chosen from a country of which any one of the parties is a national.

6   Should an arbitrator be challenged by one of the parties, the Standing Committee, as sole judge of the grounds of challenge shall make a decision which shall be final.

7   If an arbitrator dies or is prevented from carrying out his functions or has to resign consequent upon a challenge or for any other reason, or if the Standing Committee, after having considered the arbitrator's observations, decides that the arbitrator is not fulfilling his functions in accordance with the Rules or within the prescribed time limits, he shall be replaced. In all such cases the procedure indicated in the preceding paragraphs 2, 3 and 5 shall be followed.

When an arbitrator is replaced, prior hearings may be repeated at the discretion of the new arbitral tribunal.

Deposit of costs

Article 7

1   The Standing Committee shall fix the amount of the deposit in a sum likely to cover the administrative costs of arbitration of the claims which have been referred to it and, after consulting the arbitrator, his fee and costs.

Where, apart from the principle claim, one or more counterclaims are submitted, the Standing Committee may fix separate deposits for the principal claim and the counterclaim or counterclaims.

2   It is for the Claimant or Counterclaimant as the case may be to make the deposit(s) referred to in (1) above.

3   The Secretariat may make the transmission of documents to the arbitrator conditional upon the payment by the parties or one of them of the whole or part of the deposit to the Secretariat of the Standing Committee.

4   Before proceeding to establish the facts of the case, in accordance with the provisions of Article 11, the arbitrator shall inquire of the Secretariat whether the requests for deposit have been complied with.

The arbitrator shall only proceed in respect of those claims for which he has received confirmation from the Secretariat of the payment of the deposit.

Place of arbitration, procedure and applicable law

Article 8

The place of arbitration shall be that agreed by the parties. In the absence of such an agreement, the place of arbitration will be fixed by the Standing Committee.

Article 9

Unless otherwise agreed, the Rules governing the proceedings before the arbitrator shall be those set out in these Rules and, where these Rules are silent, any Rules which the parties (or, failing them, the arbitrator) may settle.

Article 10

1   The parties shall be free to determine the law to be applied by the arbitrator to the merits of the dispute. In the absence of any indication by the parties as to the applicable law, the arbitrator shall apply the law designated as the proper law by the rule of conflict of laws which he deems appropriate.

2   The arbitrator shall assume the powers of an amiable compositeur only if the parties have agreed to give him such powers.

Arbitration proceedings

Article 11

1   All pleadings and written statements submitted by the parties, as well as all documents annexed thereto, shall be sent with one copy of each to the Secretariat, the other party and the arbitrator. When the arbitrator has not yet been appointed the copies intended for him shall be sent to the Secretariat which, subject to the provisions of Article 7(3), shall transmit them to the arbitrator when appointed.

All notifications or communications from the parties, the Secretariat and the arbitrator shall be validly made if they are delivered against receipt or forwarded by registered post to the address or last known address of the party for whom the same are intended.

Notification or communication shall be deemed to have been effected on the day when it was received, or should, if made in accordance with the preceding paragraph, have been received by the party itself or by its representative.

2 The parties shall be at liberty to apply to any competent judicial authority for such measures as are outside the jurisdiction of the arbitrator and they shall not by so doing be held to infringe the agreement to arbitrate or to affect the relevant powers reserved to the arbitrator.

3 The arbitrator shall proceed within as short a time as possible to establish the facts of the case. He may fix time limits. After study of the written submissions of the parties and of all documents relied upon, the arbitrator shall hear the parties if one of the parties so requests; failing such a request he may of his own motion decide to hear them.

In addition, the arbitrator may decide to hear any other person in the presence of the parties or in their absence provided they have been duly summoned.

4 The arbitrator may appoint one or more experts, define their terms of reference, receive their reports and/or hear them in person in the presence of the parties or in their absence provided they have been duly summoned.

5 The arbitrator may decide the case on the relevant documents alone if the parties so request or agree.

6 At the request of one of the parties or if necessary on his own initiative, the arbitrator, giving reasonable notice, shall summon the parties to appear before him on the day and at the place appointed by him and shall so inform the Secretariat.

7 If one of the parties, although duly summoned, fails to appear, the arbitrator, if he is satisfied that the summons was duly received and the party is absent without valid excuse, shall have power to proceed with the arbitration.

Such proceedings shall then be deemed to have been conducted in the presence of all parties.

8 The arbitrator shall determine the language or languages of the arbitration, due regard being paid to all the relevant circumstances and in particular to the language of the contract.

9 The arbitrator shall be in full charge of the hearings, at which all the parties shall be entitled to be present. Save with the approval of the arbitrator and of the parties, persons not involved in the proceedings shall not be admitted.

10 The parties may appear in person or through duly appointed representatives. In addition, they may be assisted by advisers.

The arbitration award

Article 12

1 If the parties reach a settlement the same shall, if the parties so request and the arbitrators agree, be recorded in the form of an arbitral award made by the consent of the parties.

2 The arbitrator shall make his award within six months after the date for the constitution of the arbitral tribunal. The Standing Committee may, if necessary, extend this time.

3 Where no such extension is granted and, if appropriate, after application of the provisions of Article 6(7), the Standing Committee shall determine the manner in which the dispute is to be resolved.

4   When three arbitrators have been appointed, the award is given by a majority decision. If there be no majority, the award shall be made by the chairman of the arbitral tribunal.

5   The arbitrator's award shall, in addition to dealing with the merits of the case, fix the costs of the arbitration and decide which of the parties shall bear the costs or in what proportions the costs shall be borne by the parties.

The costs of the arbitration shall include the arbitrator's costs and fees, the fees and expenses of any experts, the normal legal costs incurred by the parties, and the administrative costs fixed by the Standing Committee.

6   The arbitrator shall, when fixing his fee, take into account the complexity of the subject matter and the time spent.

The arbitrator's decision on his own fees may be appealed to the Standing Committee within 30 days after the notification of the award.

Article 13

The arbitral award shall be deemed to be made at the place of the arbitration proceedings and on the date when it is signed by the arbitrator.

Article 14

1   Once an award has been made, the Secretariat shall notify to the parties the text signed by the arbitrator, provided always that the costs of the arbitration have been fully paid by the parties or by one of them.

2   Additional copies certified as true by the Secretariat shall be made available, on request and at any time, to the parties but to no one else.

3   By virtue of the notification made in accordance with (1) of this article, the parties waive any other form of notification or deposit of the award.

Article 15

1   The arbitral award shall be final.

2   By submitting the dispute to the ICC-CMI International Maritime Arbitration Rules, the parties shall be deemed to have undertaken to carry out the resulting award without delay and to have waived their right to any form of appeal insofar as such waiver can validly be made.

Article 16

An original of each award made in accordance with the present Rules shall be deposited with the Secretariat.

The Secretariat and, when requested by the Secretariat, the arbitrator shall assist the parties in complying with whatever further formalities may be necessary.

Article 17

In all matters not expressly provided for in these Rules, the Standing Committee and the arbitrator shall act in the spirit of these Rules and shall make every effort to make sure that the award is enforceable at law.

INSTITUTION OF CIVIL ENGINEERS'

ARBITRATION PROCEDURE (1983)

ICE ARBITRATION PROCEDURE (February 1983)

Copyright: The Institution of Civil Engineers, the Association of Consulting Engineers and the Federation of Civil Engineering Contractors. Published by: Thomas Telford Services Ltd.,
attn: Publishing Director,
1, Heron Quay,
London E14 4JD
Tel: 0044-171-987-6999
Fax: 0044-171-538-4101

This Procedure (approved February 1983) has been prepared by The Institution of Civil Engineers to be used with the ICE Conditions of Contract (fifth edition) for the settlement of disputes by arbitration under Clause 66 thereof. It replaces The ICE Arbitration Procedure (1973). This Procedure is also suitable for other engineering arbitrations.

PART A

REFERENCE AND APPOINTMENT

Rule 1 Notice to refer

1.1 A dispute of difference shall be deemed to arise when a claim or assertion made by one party is rejected by the other party and that rejection is not accepted. Subject only to Clause 66(1) of *the ICE Conditions of Contract* (if applicable) either party may then invoke arbitration by serving a *Notice to Refer* on the other party.

1.2 The Notice to Refer shall list the matters which the issuing party wishes to be referred to arbitration. Where Clause 66 of the ICE Conditions of Contract applies the Notice to Refer shall also state the date when the matters listed therein were referred to the Engineer for his decision under Clause 66(1) and the date on which the Engineer gave his decision thereon or that he has failed to do so.

Rule 2 Appointment of sole Arbitrator by agreement

2.1 After serving the Notice to Refer either party may serve upon the other a *Notice to Concur* in the appointment of an Arbitrator listing therein the names and addresses of any persons he proposes as Arbitrator.

2.2 Within 14 days thereafter the other party shall

(a) agree in writing to the appointment of one of the persons listed in the Notice to Concur, or

(b) propose a list of alternative persons.

2.3 Once agreement has been reached the issuing party shall write to the person so selected inviting him to accept the appointment enclosing a copy of the Notice to Refer and documentary evidence of the other party's agreement.

2.4   If the person so selected accepts the appointment he shall notify the issuing party in writing and send a copy to the other party. The date of posting or service as the case may be of this notification shall be deemed to be the date on which the Arbitrator's appointment is completed.

Rule 3   Appointment of sole Arbitrator by the President

3.1   If within one calendar month from service of the Notice to Concur the parties fail to appoint an Arbitrator in accordance with Rule 2 either party may then apply to the President to appoint an Arbitrator. The parties may also agree to apply to the President without a Notice to Concur.

3.2   Such application shall be in writing and shall include copies of the Notice to Refer, the Notice to Concur (if any) and any other relevant documents. The application shall be accompanied by the appropriate fee.

3.3   The Institution will send a copy of the application to the other party stating that the President intends to make the appointment on a specified date. Having first contacted an appropriate person and obtained his agreement the President will make the appointment on the specified date or such later date as may be appropriate which shall then be deemed to be the date on which the Arbitrator's appointment is completed. The Institution will notify both parties and the Arbitrator in writing as soon as possible thereafter.

Rule 4   Notice of further disputes or differences

4.1   At any time before the Arbitrator's appointment is completed either party may put forward further disputes or differences to be referred to him. This shall be done by serving upon the other party an additional Notice to Refer in accordance with Rule 1.

4.2   Once his appointment is completed the Arbitrator shall have jurisdiction over any issue connected with and necessary to the determination of any dispute or difference already referred to him whether or not the connected issue has first been referred to the Engineer for his decision under Clause 66(1) of the ICE Conditions of Contract.

PART B

POWERS OF THE ARBITRATOR

Rule 5   Power to control the proceedings

5.1   The Arbitrator may exercise any or all of the powers set out or necessarily to be implied in this Procedure on such terms as he thinks fit. These terms may include orders as to costs, time for compliance and the consequences of non-compliance.

5.2   Powers under this Procedure shall be in addition to any other powers available to the Arbitrator.

Rule 6   Power to order protective measures

6.1   The arbitrator shall have power

(a)   to give directions for the detention storage sale or disposal of the whole or any part of the subject matter of the dispute at the expense of one or both of the parties

(b)   to give directions for the preservation of any document or thing which is or may become evidence in the arbitration

(c)   to order the deposit of money or other security to secure the whole or any part of the amount(s) in dispute

(d)   to make an order for security for costs in favour of one or more of the parties and

(e)   to order his own costs to be secured.

6.2   Money ordered to be paid under this Rule shall be paid without delay into a separate bank account in the name of a stakeholder to be appointed by and subject to the directions of the Arbitrator.

Rule 7   Power to order concurrent hearings

7.1   Where disputes or differences have arisen under two or more contracts each concerned wholly or mainly with the same subject matter and the resulting arbitrations have been referred to the same Arbitrator he may with the agreement of all the parties concerned or upon the application of one of the parties being a party to all contracts involved order that the whole or any part of the matters at issue shall be heard together upon such terms or conditions as the Arbitrator thinks fit.

7.2   Where an order for concurrent Hearings has been made under Rule 7.1 the Arbitrator shall nevertheless make and publish separate Awards unless the parties otherwise agree but the Arbitrator may if he thinks fit prepare one combined set of Reasons to cover all the Awards.

Rule 8   Powers at the hearing

8.1   The Arbitrator may hear the parties their representatives and/or witnesses at any time or place and may adjourn the arbitration for any period on the application of any party or as he thinks fit.

8.2   Any party may be represented by any person including in the case of a company or other legal entity a director officer employee or beneficiary of such company or entity. In particular, a person shall not be prevented from representing a party because he is or may be also a witness in the proceedings. Nothing shall prevent a party from being represented by different persons at different times.

8.3   Nothing in these Rules or in any other rule custom or practice shall prevent the Arbitrator from starting to hear the arbitration once his appointment is completed or at any time thereafter.

8.4   Any meeting with or summons before the Arbitrator at which both parties are represented shall if the Arbitrator so directs be treated as part of the hearing of the arbitration.

Rule 9   Power to appoint assessors or to seek outside advice

9.1   The Arbitrator may appoint a legal technical or other assessor to assist him in the conduct of the arbitration. The Arbitrator shall direct when such assessor is to attend hearings of the arbitration.

9.2   The Arbitrator may seek legal technical or other advice on any matter arising out of or in connection with the proceedings.

9.3   Further and/or alternatively the Arbitrator may rely upon his own knowledge and expertise to such extent as he thinks fit.

PART C

PROCEDURE BEFORE THE HEARING

Rule 10   The preliminary meeting

10.1   As soon as possible after accepting the appointment the Arbitrator shall summon the parties to a preliminary meeting for the purpose of giving such directions about the procedure to be adopted in the arbitration as he considers necessary.

10.2   At the preliminary meeting the parties and the Arbitrator shall consider whether and to what extent

(a)   Part F (Short Procedure) or Part G (Special Procedure for Experts) of these Rules shall apply

(b)   the arbitration may proceed on documents only

(c)   progress may be facilitated and costs saved by determining some of the issues in advance of the main Hearing

(d)   the parties should enter into an exclusion agreement (if they have not already done so) in accordance with s. 3 of the Arbitration Act 1979 (where the Act applies to the arbitration)

and in general shall consider such other steps as may minimise delay and expedite the determination of the real issues between the parties.

10.3   If the parties so wish they may themselves agree directions and submit them to the Arbitrator for his approval. In so doing the parties shall state whether or not they wish Part F or Part G of these Rules to apply. The Arbitrator may then approve the directions as submitted or (having first consulted the parties) may vary them or substitute his own as he thinks fit.

Rule 11   Pleadings and discovery

11.1   The Arbitrator may order the parties to deliver pleadings or statements of their cases in any form he thinks appropriate. The Arbitrator may order any party to answer the other party's case and to give reasons for any disagreement.

11.2   The Arbitrator may order any party to deliver in advance of formal discovery copies of any documents in his possession custody or power which relate either generally or specifically to matters raised in any pleading statement or answer.

11.3   Any pleading statement or answer shall contain sufficient detail for the other party to know the case he has to answer. If sufficient detail is not provided the Arbitrator may of his own motion or at the request of the other party order further and better particulars to be delivered.

11.4   If a party fails to comply with any order made under this Rule the Arbitrator shall have power to debar that party from relying on the matters in respect of which he is in default and the Arbitrator may proceed with the arbitration and make his Award accordingly. Provided that the Arbitrator shall first give notice to the party in default that he intends to proceed under this Rule.

Rule 12   Procedural meetings

12.1   The Arbitrator may at any time call such procedural meetings as he deems necessary to identify or clarify the issues to be decided and the procedures to be adopted. For this purpose the Arbitrator may request particular persons to attend on behalf of the parties.

12.2   Either party may at any time apply to the Arbitrator for leave to appear before him on any interlocutory matter. The Arbitrator may call a procedural meeting for the purpose or deal with the application in correspondence or otherwise as he thinks fit.

12.3   At any procedural meeting or otherwise the Arbitrator may give such directions as he thinks fit for the proper conduct of the arbitration. Whether or not formal pleadings have been ordered under Rule 11 such directions may include an order that either or both parties shall prepare in writing and shall serve upon the other party and the Arbitrator any or all of the following
   (a)   a summary of that party's case
   (b)   a summary of that party's evidence
   (c)   a statement or summary of the issues between the parties
   (d)   a list and/or a summary of the documents relied upon
   (e)   a statement or summary of any other matters likely to assist the resolution of the disputes or differences between the parties.

Rule 13   Preparation for the hearing

13.1   In addition to his powers under Rules 11 and 12 the Arbitrator shall also have power
   (a)   to order that the parties shall agree facts as facts and figures as figures where possible
   (b)   to order the parties to prepare an agreed bundle of all documents relevant to the arbitration. The agreed bundle shall thereby be deemed to have been entered in evidence without further proof and without being read out at the Hearing. Provided always that either party may at the Hearing challenge the admissibility of any document in the agreed bundle.
   (c)   to order that any experts whose reports have been exchanged before the Hearing shall be examined by the Arbitrator in the presence of the parties or their legal representatives and not by the parties or their legal representatives themselves. Where such an order is made either party may put questions whether by way of cross-examination or re-examination to any party's expert after all experts have been examined by the Arbitrator provided that the party so doing shall first give notice of the nature of the questions he wishes to put.

13.2   Before the Hearing the Arbitrator may and shall if so requested by the parties read the documents to be used at the Hearing. For this or any other purpose the Arbitrator may require all such documents to be delivered to him at such time and place as he may specify.

Rule 14 Summary awards

14.1 The Arbitrator may at any time make a *Summary Award* and for this purpose shall have power to award payment by one party to another of a sum representing a reasonable proportion of the final nett amount which in his opinion that party is likely to be ordered to pay after determination of all the issues in the arbitration and after taking into account any defence or counterclaim upon which the other party may be entitled to rely.

14.2 The Arbitrator shall have power to order the party against whom a Summary Award is made to pay part or all of the sum awarded to a stakeholder. In default of compliance with such an order the Arbitrator may order payment of the whole sum in the Summary Award to the other party.

14.3 The Arbitrator shall have power to order payment of costs in relation to a Summary Award including power to order that such costs shall be paid forthwith.

14.4 A Summary Award shall be final and binding upon the parties unless and until it is varied by any subsequent Award made and published by the same Arbitrator or by any other arbitrator having jurisdiction over the matters in dispute. Any such subsequent Award may order repayment of monies paid in accordance with the Summary Award.

PART D
PROCEDURE AT THE HEARING

Rule 15 The hearing

15.1 At or before the Hearing and after hearing representations on behalf of each party the Arbitrator shall determine the order in which the parties shall present their cases and/or the order in which the issues shall be heard and determined.

15.2 The Arbitrator may order any submission or speech by or on behalf of any party to be put into writing and delivered to him and to the other party. A party so ordered shall be entitled if he so wishes to enlarge upon or vary any such submission orally.

15.3 The Arbitrator may on the application of either party or of his own motion hear and determine any issue or issues separately.

15.4 If a party fails to appear at the Hearing and provided that the absent party has had notice of the Hearing or the Arbitrator is satisfied that all reasonable steps have been taken to notify him of the Hearing the Arbitrator may proceed with the Hearing in his absence. The Arbitrator shall nevertheless take all reasonable steps to ensure that the real issues between the parties are determined justly and fairly.

Rule 16 Evidence

16.1 The Arbitrator may order a party to submit in advance of the Hearing a list of the witnesses he intends to call. That party shall not thereby be bound to call any witness so listed and may add to the list so submitted at any time.

16.2　No expert evidence shall be admissible except by leave of the Arbitrator. Leave may be given on such terms and conditions as the Arbitrator thinks fit. Unless the Arbitrator otherwise orders such terms shall be deemed to include a requirement that a report from each expert containing the substance of the evidence to be given shall be served upon the other party within a reasonable time before the Hearing.

16.3　The Arbitrator may order disclosure or exchange of proofs of evidence relating to factual issues. The Arbitrator may also order any party to prepare and disclose in advance a list of points or questions to be put in cross-examination of any witness.

16.4　Where a list of questions is disclosed whether pursuant to an order of the Arbitrator or otherwise the party making disclosure shall not be bound to put any question therein to the witness unless the Arbitrator so orders. Where the party making disclosure puts a question not so listed in cross-examination the Arbitrator may disallow the costs thereby occasioned.

16.5　The Arbitrator may order that any proof of evidence which has been disclosed shall stand as the evidence in chief of the deponent provided that the other party has been or will be given an opportunity to cross-examine the deponent thereon. The Arbitrator may also at any time before such cross-examination order the deponent or some other identified person to deliver written answers to questions arising out of the proof of evidence.

16.6　The Arbitrator may himself put questions to any witness and/or require the parties to conduct enquiries tests or investigations. Subject to his agreement the parties may ask the Arbitrator to conduct or arrange for any enquiry test or investigation.

PART E
AFTER THE HEARING

Rule 17　The award

17.1　Upon the closing of the Hearing (if any) and after having considered all the evidence and submissions the Arbitrator will prepare and publish his Award.

17.2　When the Arbitrator has made and published his Award (including a Summary Award under Rule 14) he will so inform the parties in writing and shall specify how and where it may be taken up upon due payment of his fee.

Rule 18　Reasons

18.1　Whether requested by any party to do so or not the Arbitrator may at his discretion state his Reasons for all or any part of his Award. Such Reasons may form part of the Award itself or may be contained in a separate document.

18.2　A party asking for Reasons shall state the purpose for his request. If the purpose is to use them for an appeal (whether under s. 1 of the Arbitration Act 1979 or otherwise) the requesting party shall also specify the points of law with which he wishes the Reasons to deal. In that event the

Arbitrator shall give the other party an opportunity to specify additional points of law to be dealt with.

18.3   Reasons prepared as a separate document may be delivered with the Award or later as the Arbitrator thinks fit.

18.4   Where the Arbitrator decides not to state his Reasons he shall nevertheless keep such notes as will enable him to prepare Reasons later if so ordered by the High Court.

Rule 19   Appeals

19.1   If any party applies to the High Court for leave to appeal against any Award or decision or for an order staying the arbitration proceedings or for any other purpose that party shall forthwith notify the Arbitrator of the application.

19.2   Once any Award or decision has been made and published the Arbitrator shall be under no obligation to make any statement in connection therewith other than in compliance with an order of the High Court under s. 1(5) of the Arbitration Act 1979.

PART F

SHORT PROCEDURE

Rule 20   Short procedure

20.1   Where the parties so agree (either of their own motion or at the invitation of the Arbitrator) the arbitration shall be conducted in accordance with the following *Short Procedure.*

20.2   Each party shall set out his case in the form of a file containing

(a)   a statement as to the orders or awards he seeks

(b)   a statement of his reasons for being entitled to such orders or awards and

(c)   copies of any documents on which he relies (including statements) identifying the origin and date of each document

and shall deliver copies of the said file to the other party and to the Arbitrator in such manner and within such time as the Arbitrator may direct.

20.3   After reading the parties' cases the Arbitrator may view the site or the Works and may require either or both parties to submit further documents or information in writing.

20.4   Within one calendar month of completing the foregoing steps the Arbitrator shall fix a day when he shall meet the parties for the purpose of

(a)   receiving any oral submissions which either party may wish to make and/or

(b)   the Arbitrator's putting questions to the parties their representatives or witnesses.

For this purpose the Arbitrator shall give notice of any particular person he wishes to question but no person shall be bound to appear before him.

20.5   Within one calendar month following the conclusion of the meeting under Rule 20.4 or such further period as the Arbitrator may reasonably require the Arbitrator shall make and publish his Award.

Rule 21   Other matters

21.1   Unless the parties otherwise agree the Arbitrator shall have no power to award costs to either party and the Arbitrator's own fees and charges shall be paid in equal shares by the parties. Where one party has agreed to the Arbitrator's fees the other party by agreeing to this Short Procedure shall be deemed to have agreed likewise to the Arbitrator's fees.

21.2   Either party may at any time before the Arbitrator has made and published his Award under this Short Procedure require by written notice served on the Arbitrator and the other party that the arbitration shall cease to be conducted in accordance with this Short Procedure. Save only for Rule 21.3 the Short Procedure shall thereupon no longer apply or bind the parties but any evidence already laid before the Arbitrator shall be admissible in further proceedings as if it had been submitted as part of those proceedings and without further proof.

21.3   The party giving written notice under Rule 21.2 shall thereupon in any event become liable to pay

(a)   the whole of the Arbitrator's fees and charges incurred up to the date of such notice and

(b)   a sum to be assessed by the Arbitrator as reasonable compensation for the costs (including any legal costs) incurred by the other party up to the date of such notice.

Payment in full of such charges shall be a condition precedent to that party's proceeding further in the arbitration unless the Arbitrator otherwise directs. Provided that non-payment of the said charges shall not prevent the other party from proceeding in the arbitration.

PART G

SPECIAL PROCEDURE FOR EXPERTS

Rule 22   Special procedure for experts

22.1   Where the parties so agree (either of their own motion or at the invitation of the Arbitrator) the hearing and determination of any issues of fact which depend upon the evidence of experts shall be conducted in accordance with the following *Special Procedure*.

22.2   Each party shall set out his case on such issues in the form of a file containing

(a)   a statement of the factual findings he seeks

(b)   a report or statement from and signed by each expert upon whom that party relies and

(c)   copies of any other documents referred to in each expert's report or statement or on which the party relies on identifying the origin and date of each document

and shall deliver copies of the said file to the other party and to the Arbitrator in such manner and within such time as the Arbitrator may direct.

22.3   After reading the parties' cases the Arbitrator may view the site or the Works and may require either or both parties to submit further documents or information in writing.

22.4   Thereafter the Arbitrator shall fix a day when he shall meet the experts whose reports or statements have been submitted. At the meeting each expert may address the Arbitrator and put questions to any other expert representing the other party. The Arbitrator shall so direct the meeting as to ensure that each expert has an adequate opportunity to explain his opinion and to comment upon any opposing opinion. No other person shall be entitled to address the Arbitrator or question any expert unless the parties and the Arbitrator so agree.

22.5   Thereafter the Arbitrator may make and publish an Award setting out with such details or particulars as may be necessary his decision upon the issues dealt with.

Rule 23   Costs

23.1   The Arbitrator may in his Award make orders as to the payment of any costs relating to the foregoing matters including his own fees and charges in connection therewith.

23.2   Unless the parties otherwise agree and so notify the Arbitrator neither party shall be entitled to any costs in respect of legal representation assistance or other legal work relating to the hearing and determination of factual issues by this Special Procedure.

PART H

INTERIM ARBITRATION

Rule 24   Interim arbitration

24.1   Where the Arbitrator is appointed and the arbitration is to proceed before completion or alleged completion of the Works then save in the case of a dispute arising under Clause 63 of the ICE Conditions of Contract the following provisions shall apply in addition to the foregoing Rules and the arbitration shall be called an Interim Arbitration.

24.2   In conducting an Interim Arbitration the Arbitrator shall apply the powers at his disposal with a view to making his Award or Awards as quickly as possible and thereby allowing or facilitating the timely completion of the Works.

24.3   Should an Interim Arbitration not be completed before the Works or the relevant parts thereof are complete the Arbitrator shall within 14 days of the date of such completion make and publish his Award findings of fact or Interim Decision pursuant to Rule 24.5 hereunder on the basis of evidence given and submissions made up to that date together with such further evidence and submissions as he may in his discretion agree to receive during the said 14 days. Provided that before the expiry of the said 14 days the parties may otherwise agree and so notify the Arbitrator.

24.4   For the purpose only of Rule 24.3 the Arbitrator shall decide finally whether and if so when the Works or the relevant parts thereof are complete.

24.5   In an Interim Arbitration the Arbitrator may make and publish any or all of the following
    (a)   a Final Award or an Interim Award on the matters at issue therein

(b) findings of fact

(c) a Summary Award in accordance with Rule 14

(d) an Interim Decision as defined in Rule 24.6.

An Award under (a) above or a Finding under (b) above shall be final and binding upon the parties in any subsequent proceedings. Anything not expressly identified as falling under either of headings (a) (b) or (c) above shall be deemed to be an Interim Decision under heading (d). Save as aforesaid the Arbitrator shall not make an Interim Decision without first notifying the parties that he intends to do so.

24.6 An *Interim Decision* shall be final and binding upon the parties and upon the Engineer (if any) until such time as the Works have been completed or any Award or decision under Rule 24.3 has been given. Thereafter the Interim Decision may be re-opened by another Arbitrator appointed under these Rules and where such other Arbitrator was also the Arbitrator appointed to conduct the Interim Arbitration he shall not be bound by his earlier Interim Decision.

24.7 The Arbitrator in an Interim Arbitration shall have power to direct that Part F (Short Procedure) and/or Part G (Special Procedure for Experts) shall apply to the Interim Arbitration.

PART J

MISCELLANEOUS

Rule 25 Definitions

25.1 In these Rules the following definitions shall apply.

(a) 'Arbitrator' includes a tribunal of two or more Arbitrators or an Umpire.

(b) 'Institution' means the Institution of Civil Engineers.

(c) 'ICI Conditions of Contract' means the Conditions of Contract for use in connection with Works of Civil Engineering Construction published jointly by the Institution, the Association of Consulting Engineers and the Federation of Civil Engineering Contractors.

(d) 'Other party' includes the plural unless the context otherwise requires.

(e) 'President' means the President for the time being of the Institution or any Vice-President acting on his behalf.

(f) 'Procedure' means the Institution of Civil Engineers' Arbitration Procedure (1983) unless the context otherwise requires.

(g) 'Award', 'Final Award' and 'Interim Award' have the meanings given to those terms in or in connection with the Arbitration Acts 1950 to 1979. 'Summary Award' means an Award made under Rule 14 hereof.

(h) 'Interim Arbitration' means an arbitration in accordance with Part H of these Rules. 'Interim Decision' means a decision as defined in Rule 24.6 hereof.

Rule 26 Application of the ICE procedure

26.1 This Procedure shall apply to the conduct of the arbitration if

(a) the parties at any time so agree

(b) the President when making an appointment so directs, or

(c) the Arbitrator so stipulates at the time of his appointment.

Provided that where this Procedure applies by virtue of the Arbitrator's stipulation under (c) above the parties may within 14 days of that appointment agree otherwise in which event the Arbitrator's appointment shall terminate and the parties shall pay his reasonable charges in equal shares.

26.2 This Procedure shall not apply to arbitrations under the law of Scotland for which a separate *ICE Arbitration Procedure (Scotland)* is available.

26.3 Where an arbitration is governed by the law of a country other than England and Wales this Procedure shall apply to the extent that the applicable law permits.

Rule 27 Exclusion of liability

27.1 Neither the Institution nor its servants or agents nor the President shall be liable to any party for any act omission or misconduct in connection with any appointment made or any arbitration conducted under this Procedure.

INTERNATIONAL CENTRE FOR THE SETTLEMENT OF INVESTMENT DISPUTES

International Centre for Settlement of Investment Disputes,
1818 H Street, NW, Washington DC 20433, USA.
Tel: 001 202 458 1534.
Fax: 001 202 522 2615

A copy of the Convention appears in Part V International Documents.

RULES OF PROCEDURE FOR THE INSTITUTION OF CONCILIATION AND ARBITRATION PROCEEDINGS (INSTITUTION RULES)

26 September 1984

Rule 1 The Request

(1) Any Contracting State or any national of a Contracting State wishing to institute conciliation or arbitration proceedings under the Convention shall address a request to that effect in writing to the Secretary-General at the seat of the Centre. The request shall indicate whether it relates to a conciliation or an arbitration proceeding. It shall be drawn up in an official language of the Centre, shall be dated, and shall be signed by the requesting party.

(2) The request may be made jointly by the parties to the dispute.

Rule 2   Contents of the Request

(1)   The request shall:

(a)   designate precisely each party to the dispute and state the address of each;

(b)   state, if one of the parties is a constituent subdivision or agency of a Contracting State, that it has been designated to the Centre by that State pursuant to Article 25(1) of the Convention;

(c)   indicate the date of consent and the instruments in which it is recorded, including, if one party is a constituent subdivision or agency of a Contracting State, similar data on the approval of such consent by that State unless it had notified the Centre that no such approval is required;

(d)   indicate with respect to the party that is a national of a Contracting State:

(i)   its nationality on the date of consent; and

(ii)   if the party is a natural person:

(A)   his nationality on the date of the request; and

(B)   that he did not have the nationality of the Contracting State party to the dispute either on the date of consent or on the date of the request; or

(iii)   if the party is a juridical person which on the date of consent had the nationality of the Contracting State party to the dispute, the agreement of the parties that it should be treated as a national of another Contracting State for the purposes of the Convention; and

(e)   contain information concerning the issues in dispute indicating that there is, between the parties, a legal dispute arising directly out of an investment.

(2)   The information required by subparagraphs (1)(c) and (1)(d)(iii) shall be supported by documentation.

(3)   'Date of consent' means the date on which the parties to the dispute consented in writing to submit it to the Centre; if both parties did not act on the same day, it means the date on which the second party acted.

Rule 3   Optional Information in the Request

The request may in addition set forth any provisions agreed by the parties regarding the number of conciliators or arbitrators and the method of their appointment, as well as any other provisions agreed concerning the settlement of the dispute.

Rule 4   Copies of the Request

(1)   The request shall be accompanied by five additional signed copies. The Secretary-General may require such further copies as he may deem necessary.

(2)   Any documentation submitted with the request shall conform to the requirements of Administrative and Financial Regulation 30.

Rule 5   Acknowledgement of the Request

(1)   On receiving a request the Secretary-General shall:

(a)   send an acknowledgement to the requesting party;

(b)   take no other action with respect to the request until he has received payment of the prescribed fee.

(2)   As soon as he has received the fee for lodging the request, the Secretary-General shall transmit a copy of the request and of the accompanying documentation to the other party.

Rule 6   Registration of the Request

(1)   The Secretary-General shall, subject to Rule 5(1)(b), as soon as possible, either:

(a)   register the request in the Conciliation or the Arbitration Register and on the same day notify the parties of the registration; or

(b)   if he finds, on the basis of the information contained in the request, that the dispute is manifestly outside the jurisdiction of the Centre, notify the parties of his refusal to register the request and of the reasons therefor.

(2)   A proceeding under the Convention shall be deemed to have been instituted on the date of the registration of the request.

Rule 7   Notice of Registration

The notice of registration of a request shall:

(a)   record that the request is registered and indicate the date of the registration and of the dispatch of that notice;

(b)   notify each party that all communications and notices in connection with the proceeding will be sent to the address stated in the request, unless another address is indicated to the Centre;

(c)   unless such information has already been provided, invite the parties to communicate to the Secretary-General any provisions agreed by them regarding the number and the method of appointment of the conciliators or arbitrators;

(d)   invite the parties to proceed, as soon as possible, to constitute a Conciliation Commission in accordance with Articles 29 to 31 of the Convention, or an Arbitral Tribunal in accordance with Articles 37 to 40; and

(e)   be accompanied by a list of the members of the Panel of Conciliators or of Arbitrators of the Centre.

Rule 8   Withdrawal of the Request

The requesting party may, by written notice to the Secretary-General, withdraw the request before it has been registered. The Secretary-General shall promptly notify the other party, unless, pursuant to Rule 5(1)(b), the request had not been transmitted to it.

Rule 9   Final Provisions

(1)   The texts of these Rules in each official language of the Centre shall be equally authentic.

(2)   These Rules may be cited as the 'Institution Rules' of the Centre.

RULES OF PROCEDURE FOR ARBITRATION PROCEEDINGS (ARBITRATION RULES)

26 September 1984

CHAPTER I

ESTABLISHMENT OF THE TRIBUNAL

Rule 1   General Obligations

(1)   Upon notification of the registration of the request for arbitration, the parties shall, with all possible dispatch, proceed to constitute a Tribunal, with due regard to Section 2 of Chapter IV of the Convention.*

(2)   Unless such information is provided in the request, the parties shall communicate to the Secretary-General as soon as possible any provisions agreed by them regarding the number of arbitrators and the method of their appointment.

(3)   Except if each member of the Tribunal is appointed by agreement of the parties, nationals of the State party to the dispute or of the State whose national is a party to the dispute may be appointed by a party only if appointment by the other party to the dispute of the same number of arbitrators of either of these nationalities would not result in a majority of arbitrators of these nationalities.

(4)   No person who had previously acted as a conciliator or arbitrator in any proceeding for the settlement of the dispute may be appointed as a member of the Tribunal.

* See Section V of this book

Rule 2   Method of Constituting the Tribunal in the Absence of Previous Agreement

(1)   If the parties, at the time of the registration of the request for arbitration, have not agreed upon the number of arbitrators and the method of their appointment, they shall, unless they agree otherwise, follow the following procedure:

(a)   the requesting party shall, within 10 days after the registration of the request, propose to the other party the appointment of a sole arbitrator or of a specified uneven number of arbitrators and specify the method proposed for their appointment;

(b)   within 20 days after receipt of the proposals made by the requesting party, the other party shall:

(i)   accept such proposals; or

(ii)   make other proposals regarding the number of arbitrators and the method of their appointment;

(c)   within 20 days after receipt of the reply containing any such other proposals, the requesting party shall notify the other party whether it accepts or rejects such proposals.

(2)   The communications provided for in paragraph (1) shall be made or promptly confirmed in writing and shall either be transmitted through the

Secretary-General or directly between the parties with a copy to the Secretary-General. The parties shall promptly notify the Secretary-General of the contents of any agreement reached.

(3) At any time 60 days after the registration of the request, if no agreement on another procedure is reached, either party may inform the Secretary-General that it chooses the formula provided for in Article 37(2)(b) of the Convention. The Secretary-General shall thereupon promptly inform the other party that the Tribunal is to be constituted in accordance with that Article.

Rule 3   Appointment of Arbitrators to a Tribunal Constituted in Accordance with Convention Article 37(2)(b)

(1) If the Tribunal is to be constituted in accordance with Article 37(2)(b) of the Convention:
(a)   either party shall in a communication to the other party:
(i)   name two persons, identifying one of them, who shall not have the same nationality as nor be a national of either party, as the arbitrator appointed by it, and the other as the arbitrator proposed to be the President of the Tribunal; and
(ii)   invite the other party to concur in the appointment of the arbitrator proposed to be the President of the Tribunal and to appoint another arbitrator;
(b)   promptly upon receipt of this communication the other party shall, in its reply:
(i)   name a person as the arbitrator appointed by it, who shall not have the same nationality as nor be a national of either party; and
(ii)   concur in the appointment of the arbitrator proposed to be the President of the Tribunal or name another person as the arbitrator proposed to be President;
(c)   promptly upon receipt of the reply containing such a proposal, the initiating party shall notify the other party whether it concurs in the appointment of the arbitrator proposed by that party to be the President of the Tribunal.
(2) The communications provided for in this Rule shall be made or promptly confirmed in writing and shall either be transmitted through the Secretary-General or directly between the parties with a copy to the Secretary-General.

Rule 4   Appointment of Arbitrators by the Chairman of the Administrative Council

(1) If the Tribunal is not constituted within 90 days after the dispatch by the Secretary-General of the notice of registration, or such other period as the parties may agree, either party may, through the Secretary-General, address to the Chairman of the Administrative Council a request in writing to appoint the arbitrator or arbitrators not yet appointed and to designate an arbitrator to be the President of the Tribunal.
(2) The provision of paragraph (1) shall apply *mutatis mutandis* in the event that the parties have agreed that the arbitrators shall elect the President of the Tribunal and they fail to do so.

(3)   The Secretary-General shall forthwith send a copy of the request to the other party.

(4)   The Chairman shall, with due regard to Articles 38 and 40(1) of the Convention, and after consulting both parties as far as possible, comply with that request within 30 days after its receipt.

(5)   The Secretary-General shall promptly notify the parties of any appointment or designation made by the Chairman.

Rule 5   Acceptance of Appointments

(1)   The party or parties concerned shall notify the Secretary-General of the appointment of each arbitrator and indicate the method of his appointment.

(2)   As soon as the Secretary-General has been informed by a party or the Chairman of the Administrative Council of the appointment of an arbitrator, he shall seek an acceptance from the appointee.

(3)   If an arbitrator fails to accept his appointment within 15 days, the Secretary-General shall promptly notify the parties, and if appropriate the Chairman, and invite them to proceed to the appointment of another arbitrator in accordance with the method followed for the previous appointment.

Rule 6   Constitution of the Tribunal

(1)   The Tribunal shall be deemed to be constituted and the proceeding to have begun on the date the Secretary-General notifies the parties that all the arbitrators have accepted their appointment.

(2)   Before or at the first session of the Tribunal, each arbitrator shall sign a declaration in the following form:

'To the best of my knowledge there is no reason why I should not serve on the Arbitral Tribunal constituted by the International Centre for Settlement of Investment Disputes with respect to a dispute between .... and...................

'I shall keep confidential all information coming to my knowledge as a result of my participation in this proceeding, as well as the contents of any award made by the Tribunal.

'I shall judge fairly as between the parties, according to the applicable law, and shall not accept any instruction or compensation with regard to the proceeding from any source except as provided in the Convention on the Settlement of Investment Disputes and in the Regulations and Rules made pursuant thereto.

'A statement of my past and present professional, business and other relationships (if any) with the parties is attached hereto.'

Any arbitrator failing to sign a declaration by the end of the first session of the Tribunal shall be deemed to have resigned.

Rule 7   Replacement of Arbitrators

At any time before the Tribunal is constituted, each party may replace any arbitrator appointed by it and the parties may by common consent agree to replace any arbitrator. The procedure of such replacement shall be in accordance with Rules 1, 5 and 6.

Rule 8   Incapacity or Resignation of Arbitrators

(1)   If an arbitrator becomes incapacitated or unable to perform the duties of his office, the procedure in respect of the disqualification of arbitrators set forth in Rule 9 shall apply.

(2)   An arbitrator may resign by submitting his resignation to the other members of the Tribunal and the Secretary-General. If the arbitrator was appointed by one of the parties, the Tribunal shall promptly consider the reasons for his resignation and decide whether it consents thereto. The Tribunal shall promptly notify the Secretary-General of its decision.

Rule 9   Disqualification of Arbitrators

(1)   A party proposing the disqualification of an arbitrator pursuant to Article 57 of the Convention shall promptly, and in any event before the proceeding is declared closed, file its proposal with the Secretary-General, stating its reasons therefor.

(2)   The Secretary-General shall forthwith:

(a)   transmit the proposal to the members of the Tribunal and, if it relates to a sole arbitrator or to a majority of the members of the Tribunal, to the Chairman of the Administrative Council; and

(b)   notify the other party of the proposal.

(3)   The arbitrator to whom the proposal relates may, without delay, furnish explanations to the Tribunal or the Chairman, as the case may be.

(4)   Unless the proposal relates to a majority of the members of the Tribunal, the other members shall promptly consider and vote on the proposal in the absence of the arbitrator concerned. If those members are equally divided, they shall, through the Secretary-General, promptly notify the Chairman of the proposal, of any explanation furnished by the arbitrator concerned and of their failure to reach a decision.

(5)   Whenever the Chairman has to decide on a proposal to disqualify an arbitrator, he shall take that decision within 30 days after he has received the proposal.

(6)   The proceeding shall be suspended until a decision has been taken on the proposal.

Rule 10   Procedure during a Vacancy on the Tribunal

(1)   The Secretary-General shall forthwith notify the parties and, if necessary, the Chairman of the Administrative Council of the disqualification, death, incapacity or resignation of an arbitrator and of the consent, if any, of the Tribunal to a resignation.

(2)   Upon the notification by the Secretary-General of a vacancy on the Tribunal, the proceeding shall be or remain suspended until the vacancy has been filled.

Rule 11   Filling Vacancies on the Tribunal

(1)   Except as provided in paragraph (2), a vacancy resulting from the disqualification, death, incapacity or resignation of an arbitrator shall be promptly filled by the same method by which his appointment had been made.

(2)   In addition to filling vacancies relating to arbitrators appointed by him, the Chairman of the Administrative Council shall appoint a person from the Panel of Arbitrators:

(a)   to fill a vacancy caused by the resignation, without the consent of the Tribunal, of an arbitrator appointed by a party; or

(b)   at the request of either party, to fill any other vacancy, if no new appointment is made and accepted within 30 days of the notification of the vacancy by the Secretary-General.

(3)   The procedure for filling a vacancy shall be in accordance with Rules 1, 4(4), 4(5), 5 and, *mutatis mutandis*, 6(2).

Rule 12   Resumption of Proceeding after Filling a Vacancy

As soon as a vacancy on the Tribunal has been filled, the proceeding shall continue from the point it had reached at the time the vacancy occurred. The newly appointed arbitrator may, however, require that the oral procedure be recommenced, if this had already been started.

CHAPTER II

WORKING OF THE TRIBUNAL

Rule 13   Sessions of the Tribunal

(1)   The Tribunal shall hold its first session within 60 days after its constitution or such other period as the parties may agree. The dates of that session shall be fixed by the President of the Tribunal after consultation with its members and the Secretary-General. If upon its constitution the Tribunal has no President because the parties have agreed that the President shall be elected by its members, the Secretary-General shall fix the dates of that session. In both cases, the parties shall be consulted as far as possible.

(2)   The dates of subsequent sessions shall be determined by the Tribunal, after consultation with the Secretary-General and with the parties as far as possible.

(3)   The Tribunal shall meet at the seat of the Centre or at such other place as may have been agreed by the parties in accordance with Article 63 of the Convention. If the parties agree that the proceeding shall be held at a place other than the Centre or an institution with which the Centre has made the necessary arrangements, they shall consult with the Secretary-General and request the approval of the Tribunal. Failing such approval, the Tribunal shall meet at the seat of the Centre.

(4)   The Secretary-General shall notify the members of the Tribunal and the parties of the dates and place of the sessions of the Tribunal in good time.

Rule 14   Sittings of the Tribunal

(1)   The President of the Tribunal shall conduct its hearings and preside at its deliberations.

(2)   Except as the parties otherwise agree, the presence of a majority of the members of the Tribunal shall be required at its sittings.

(3)   The President of the Tribunal shall fix the date and hour of its sittings.

Rule 15   Deliberations of the Tribunal

(1)   The deliberations of the Tribunal shall take place in private and remain secret.

(2)   Only members of the Tribunal shall take part in its deliberations. No other person shall be admitted unless the Tribunal decides otherwise.

Rule 16   Decisions of the Tribunal

(1)   Decisions of the Tribunal shall be taken by a majority of the votes of all its members. Abstention shall count as a negative vote.

(2)   Except as otherwise provided by these Rules or decided by the Tribunal, it may take any decision by correspondence among its members, provided that all of them are consulted. Decisions so taken shall be certified by the President of the Tribunal.

Rule 17   Incapacity of the President

If at any time the President of the Tribunal should be unable to act, his functions shall be performed by one of the other members of the Tribunal, acting in the order in which the Secretary-General had received the notice of their acceptance of their appointment to the Tribunal.

Rule 18   Representation of the Parties

(1)   Each party may be represented or assisted by agents, counsel or advocates whose names and authority shall be notified by that party to the Secretary-General, who shall promptly inform the Tribunal and the other party.

(2)   For the purposes of these Rules, the expression 'party' includes, where the context so admits, an agent, counsel or advocate authorised to represent that party.

CHAPTER III

GENERAL PROCEDURAL PROVISIONS

Rule 19   Procedural Orders

The Tribunal shall make the orders required for the conduct of the proceeding.

Rule 20   Preliminary Procedural Consultation

(1)   As early as possible after the constitution of a Tribunal, its President shall endeavor to ascertain the views of the parties regarding questions of procedure. For this purpose he may request the parties to meet him. He shall, in particular, seek their views on the following matters:

(a)   the number of members of the Tribunal required to constitute a quorum at its sittings;

(b)   the language or languages to be used in the proceeding;

(c)   the number and sequence of the pleadings and the time limits within which they are to be filed;

(d)   the number of copies desired by each party of instruments filed by the other;

(e)   dispensing with the written or the oral procedure;

(f)   the manner in which the cost of the proceeding is to be apportioned; and

(g)   the manner in which the record of the hearings shall be kept.

(2)   In the conduct of the proceeding the Tribunal shall apply any agreement between the parties on procedural matters, except as otherwise provided in the Convention or the Administrative and Financial Regulations.

Rule 21   Pre-Hearing Conference

(1)   At the request of the Secretary-General or at the discretion of the President of the Tribunal, a pre-hearing conference between the Tribunal and the parties may be held to arrange for an exchange of information and the stipulation of uncontested facts in order to expedite the proceeding.

(2)   At the request of the parties, a pre-hearing conference between the Tribunal and the parties, duly represented by their authorised representatives, may be held to consider the issues in dispute with a view to reaching an amicable settlement.

Rule 22   Procedural Languages

(1)   The parties may agree on the use of one or two languages to be used in the proceeding, provided that, if they agree on any language that is not an official language of the Centre, the Tribunal, after consultation with the Secretary-General, gives its approval. If the parties do not agree on any such procedural language, each of them may select one of the official languages (i.e. English, French and Spanish) for this purpose.

(2)   If two procedural languages are selected by the parties, any instruments may be filed in either language. Either language may be used at the hearings, subject, if the Tribunal so requires, to translation and interpretation. The orders and the award of the Tribunal shall be rendered and the record kept in both procedural languages, both versions being equally authentic.

Rule 23   Copies of Instruments

Except as otherwise provided by the Tribunal after consultation with the parties and the Secretary-General, every request, pleading, application, written observation, supporting documentation, if any, or other instrument shall be filed in the form of a signed original accompanied by the following number of additional copies:

(a) before the number of members of the Tribunal has been determined: five;

(b) after the number of members of the Tribunal has been determined: two more than the number of its members.

Rule 24   Supporting Documentation

Supporting documentation shall ordinarily be filed together with the instrument to which it relates, and in any case within the time limit fixed for the filing of such instrument.

Rule 25   Correction of Errors

An accidental error in any instrument or supporting document may, with the consent of the other party or by leave of the Tribunal, be corrected at any time before the award is rendered.

Rule 26   Time Limits

(1) Where required, time limits shall be fixed by the Tribunal by assigning dates for the completion of the various steps in the proceeding. The Tribunal may delegate this power to its President.

(2) The Tribunal may extend any time limit that it has fixed. If the Tribunal is not in session, this power shall be exercised by its President.

(3) Any step taken after expiration of the applicable time limit shall be disregarded unless the Tribunal, in special circumstances and after giving the other party an opportunity of stating its views, decides otherwise.

Rule 27   Waiver

A party which knows or should have known that a provision of the Administrative and Financial Regulations, of these Rules, of any other rules or agreement applicable to the proceeding, or of an order of the Tribunal has not been complied with and which fails to state promptly its objections thereto, shall be deemed—subject to Article 45 of the Convention—to have waived its right to object.

Rule 28   Cost of Proceeding

(1) Without prejudice to the final decision on the payment of the cost of the proceeding, the Tribunal may, unless otherwise agreed by the parties, decide:

(a) at any stage of the proceeding, the portion which each party shall pay, pursuant to Administrative and Financial Regulation 14, of the fees and expenses of the Tribunal and the charges for the use of the facilities of the Centre;

(b)   with respect to any part of the proceeding, that the related costs (as determined by the Secretary-General) shall be borne entirely or in a particular share by one of the parties.

(2)   Promptly after the closure of the proceeding, each party shall submit to the Tribunal a statement of costs reasonably incurred or borne by it in the proceeding and the Secretary-General shall submit to the Tribunal an account of all amounts paid by each party to the Centre and of all costs incurred by the Centre for the proceeding. The Tribunal may, before the award has been rendered, request the parties and the Secretary-General to provide additional information concerning the cost of the proceeding.

CHAPTER IV

WRITTEN AND ORAL PROCEDURES

Rule 29   Normal Procedures

Except if the parties otherwise agree, the proceeding shall comprise two distinct phases: a written procedure followed by an oral one.

Rule 30   Transmission of the Request

As soon as the Tribunal is constituted, the Secretary-General shall transmit to each member a copy of the request by which the proceeding was initiated, of the supporting documentation, of the notice of registration and of any communication received from either party in response thereto.

Rule 31   The Written Procedure

(1)   In addition to the request for arbitration, the written procedure shall consist of the following pleadings, filed within time limits set by the Tribunal:
    (a)   a memorial by the requesting party;
    (b)   a counter-memorial by the other party;
and, if the parties so agree or the Tribunal deems it necessary;
    (c)   a reply by the requesting party; and
    (d)   a rejoinder by the other party.

(2)   If the request was made jointly, each party shall, within the same time limit determined by the Tribunal, file its memorial and, if the parties so agree or the Tribunal deems it necessary, its reply; however, the parties may instead agree that one of them shall, for the purposes of paragraph (1), be considered as the requesting party.

(3)   A memorial shall contain: a statement of the relevant facts; a statement of law; and the submissions. A counter-memorial, reply or rejoinder shall contain an admission or denial of the facts stated in the last previous pleading; any additional facts, if necessary; observations concerning the statement of law in the last previous pleading; a statement of law in answer thereto; and the submissions.

Rule 32   The Oral Procedure

(1)   The oral procedure shall consist of the hearing by the Tribunal of the parties, their agents, counsel and advocates, and of witnesses and experts.

(2)   The Tribunal shall decide, with the consent of the parties, which other persons besides the parties, their agents, counsel and advocates, witnesses and experts during their testimony, and officers of the Tribunal may attend the hearings.

(3)   The members of the Tribunal may, during the hearings, put questions to the parties, their agents, counsel and advocates, and ask them for explanations.

Rule 33   Marshalling of Evidence

Without prejudice to the rules concerning the production of documents, each party shall, within time limits fixed by the Tribunal, communicate to the Secretary-General, for transmission to the Tribunal and the other party, precise information regarding the evidence which it intends to produce and that which it intends to request the Tribunal to call for, together with an indication of the points to which such evidence will be directed.

Rule 34   Evidence: General Principles

(1)   The Tribunal shall be the judge of the admissibility of any evidence adduced and of its probative value.

(2)   The Tribunal may, if it deems it necessary at any stage of the proceeding:

    (a)   call upon the parties to produce documents, witnesses and experts; and

    (b)   visit any place connected with the dispute or conduct inquiries there.

(3)   The parties shall cooperate with the Tribunal in the production of the evidence and in the other measures provided for in paragraph (2). The Tribunal shall take formal note of the failure of a party to comply with its obligations under this paragraph and of any reasons given for such failure.

(4)   Expenses incurred in producing evidence and in taking other measures in accordance with paragraph (2) shall be deemed to constitute part of the expenses incurred by the parties within the meaning of Article 61(2) of the Convention.

Rule 35   Examination of Witnesses and Experts

(1)   Witnesses and experts shall be examined before the Tribunal by the parties under the control of its President. Questions may also be put to them by any member of the Tribunal.

(2)   Each witness shall make the following declaration before giving his evidence:

'I solemnly declare upon my honour and conscience that I shall speak the truth, the whole truth and nothing but the truth.'

(3)   Each expert shall make the following declaration before making his statement:

'I solemnly declare upon my honour and conscience that my statement will be in accordance with my sincere belief.'

Rule 36   Witnesses and Experts: Special Rules

Notwithstanding Rule 35 the Tribunal may:

(a)   admit evidence given by a witness or expert in a written deposition; and

(b)   with the consent of both parties, arrange for the examination of a witness or expert otherwise than before the Tribunal itself. The Tribunal shall define the subject of the examination, the time limit, the procedure to be followed and other particulars. The parties may participate in the examination.

Rule 37   Visits and Inquiries

If the Tribunal considers it necessary to visit any place connected with the dispute or to conduct an inquiry there, it shall make an order to this effect. The order shall define the scope of the visit or the subject of the inquiry, the time limit, the procedure to be followed and other particulars. The parties may participate in any visit or inquiry.

Rule 38   Closure of the Proceeding

(1)   When the presentation of the case by the parties is completed, the proceeding shall be declared closed.

(2)   Exceptionally, the Tribunal may, before the award has been rendered, reopen the proceeding on the ground that new evidence is forthcoming of such a nature as to constitute a decisive factor, or that there is a vital need for clarification on certain specific points.

CHAPTER V

PARTICULAR PROCEDURES

Rule 39   Provisional Measures

(1)   At any time during the proceeding a party may request that provisional measures for the preservation of its rights be recommended by the Tribunal. The request shall specify the rights to be preserved, the measures the recommendation of which is requested, and the circumstances that require such measures.

(2)   The Tribunal shall give priority to the consideration of a request made pursuant to paragraph (1).

(3)   The Tribunal may also recommend provisional measures on its own initiative or recommend measures other than those specified in a request. It may at any time modify or revoke its recommendations.

(4)   The Tribunal shall only recommend provisional measures, or modify or revoke its recommendations, after giving each party an opportunity of presenting its observations.

(5)   Nothing in this Rule shall prevent the parties, provided that they have so stipulated in the agreement recording their consent, from requesting any judicial or other authority to order provisional measures, prior to the institution of the proceeding, or during the proceeding, for the preservation of their respective rights and interests.

Rule 40   Ancillary Claims

(1)   Except as the parties otherwise agree, a party may present an incidental or additional claim or counter-claim arising directly out of the subject-matter of the dispute, provided that such ancillary claim is within the scope of the consent of the parties and is otherwise within the jurisdiction of the Centre.

(2)   An incidental or additional claim shall be presented not later than in the reply and a counter-claim no later than in the counter-memorial, unless the Tribunal, upon justification by the party presenting the ancillary claim and upon considering any objection of the other party, authorises the presentation of the claim at a later stage in the proceeding.

(3)   The Tribunal shall fix a time limit within which the party against which an ancillary claim is presented may file its observations thereon.

Rule 41   Objections to Jurisdiction

(1)   Any objection that the dispute or any ancillary claim is not within the jurisdiction of the Centre or, for other reasons, is not within the competence of the Tribunal shall be made as early as possible. A party shall file the objection with the Secretary-General no later than the expiration of the time limit fixed for the filing of the counter-memorial, or, if the objection relates to an ancillary claim, for the filing of the rejoinder—unless the facts on which the objection is based are unknown to the party at that time.

(2)   The Tribunal may on its own initiative consider, at any stage of the proceeding, whether the dispute or any ancillary claim before it is within the jurisdiction of the Centre and within its own competence.

(3)   Upon the formal raising of an objection relating to the dispute, the proceeding on the merits shall be suspended. The President of the Tribunal, after consultation with its other members, shall fix a time limit within which the parties may file observations on the objection.

(4)   The Tribunal shall decide whether or not the further procedures relating to the objection shall be oral. It may deal with the objection as a preliminary question or join it to the merits of the dispute. If the Tribunal overrules the objection or joins it to the merits, it shall once more fix time limits for the further procedures.

(5)   If the Tribunal decides that the dispute is not within the jurisdiction of the Centre or not within its own competence, it shall render an award to that effect.

Rule 42   Default

(1)   If a party (in this Rule called the 'defaulting party') fails to appear or to present its case at any stage of the proceeding, the other party may, at any time prior to the discontinuance of the proceeding, request the Tribunal to deal with the questions submitted to it and to render an award.

(2)   The Tribunal shall promptly notify the defaulting party of such a request. Unless it is satisfied that that party does not intend to appear or to present its case in the proceeding, it shall, at the same time, grant a period of grace and to this end:

(a)   if that party had failed to file a pleading or any other instrument within the time limit fixed therefor, fix a new time limit for its filing; or

(b)   if that party had failed to appear or present its case at a hearing, fix a new date for the hearing.

The period of grace shall not, without the consent of the other party, exceed 60 days.

(3)   After the expiration of the period of grace or when, in accordance with paragraph (2), no such period is granted, the Tribunal shall resume the consideration of the dispute. Failure of the defaulting party to appear or to present its case shall not be deemed an admission of the assertions made by the other party.

(4)   The Tribunal shall examine the jurisdiction of the Centre and its own competence in the dispute and, if it is satisfied, decide whether the submissions made are well-founded in fact and in law. To this end, it may, at any stage of the proceeding, call on the party appearing to file observations, produce evidence or submit oral explanations.

Rule 43   Settlement and Discontinuance

(1)   If, before the award is rendered, the parties agree on a settlement of the dispute or otherwise to discontinue the proceeding, the Tribunal, or the Secretary-General if the Tribunal has not yet been constituted, shall, at their written request, in an order take note of the discontinuance of the proceeding.

(2)   If the parties file with the Secretary-General the full and signed text of their settlement and in writing request the Tribunal to embody such settlement in an award, the Tribunal may record the settlement in the form of its award.

Rule 44   Discontinuance at Request of a Party

If a party requests the discontinuance of the proceeding, the Tribunal, or the Secretary-General if the Tribunal has not yet been constituted, shall in an order fix a time limit within which the other party may state whether it opposes the discontinuance. If no objection is made in writing within the time limit, the other party shall be deemed to have acquiesced in the discontinuance and the Tribunal, or if appropriate the Secretary-General, shall in an order take note of the discontinuance of the proceeding. If objection is made, the proceeding shall continue.

Rule 45   Discontinuance for Failure of Parties to Act

If the parties fail to take any steps in the proceeding during six consecutive months or such period as they may agree with the approval of the Tribunal, or of the Secretary-General if the Tribunal has not yet been constituted, they shall be deemed to have discontinued the proceeding and the Tribunal, or if appropriate the Secretary-General, shall, after notice to the parties, in an order take note of the discontinuance.

CHAPTER VI

THE AWARD

Rule 46   Preparation of the Award

The award (including any individual or dissenting opinion) shall be drawn up and signed within 60 days after the closure of the proceeding. The Tribunal may, however, extend this period by a further 30 days if it would otherwise be unable to draw up the award.

Rule 47   The Award

(1)   The award shall be in writing and shall contain:
    (a)   a precise designation of each party;
    (b)   a statement that the Tribunal was established under the Convention, and a description of the method of its constitution;
    (c)   the name of each member of the Tribunal, and an identification of the appointing authority of each;
    (d)   the names of the agents, counsel and advocates of the parties;
    (e)   the dates and place of the sittings of the Tribunal;
    (f)   a summary of the proceeding;
    (g)   a statement of the facts as found by the Tribunal;
    (h)   the submissions of the parties;
    (i)   the decision of the Tribunal on every question submitted to it, together with the reasons upon which the decision is based; and
    (j)   any decision of the Tribunal regarding the cost of the proceeding.
(2)   The award shall be signed by the members of the Tribunal who voted for it; the date of each signature shall be indicated.
(3)   Any member of the Tribunal may attach his individual opinion to the award, whether he dissents from the majority or not, or a statement of his dissent.

Rule 48   Rendering of the Award

(1)   Upon signature by the last arbitrator to sign, the Secretary-General shall promptly:
    (a)   authenticate the original text of the award and deposit it in the archives of the Centre, together with any individual opinions and statements of dissent; and
    (b)   dispatch a certified copy of the award (including individual opinions and statements of dissent) to each party, indicating the date of dispatch on the original text and on all copies.

(2)   The award shall be deemed to have been rendered on the date on which the certified copies were dispatched.

(3)   The Secretary-General shall, upon request, make available to a party additional certified copies of the award.

(4)   The Centre shall not publish the award without the consent of the parties. The Centre may, however, include in its publications excerpts of the legal rules applied by the Tribunal.

Rule 49   Supplementary Decisions and Rectification

(1)   Within 45 days after the date on which the award was rendered, either party may request, pursuant to Article 49(2) of the Convention, a supplementary decision on, or the rectification of, the award. Such a request shall be addressed in writing to the Secretary-General. The request shall:
    (a)   identify the award to which it relates;
    (b)   indicate the date of the request;
    (c)   state in detail:
        (i)   any question which, in the opinion of the requesting party, the Tribunal omitted to decide in the award; and
        (ii)   any error in the award which the requesting party seeks to have rectified; and
    (d)   be accompanied by a fee for lodging the request.

(2)   Upon receipt of the request and of the lodging fee, the Secretary-General shall forthwith:
    (a)   register the request;
    (b)   notify the parties of the registration;
    (c)   transmit to the other party a copy of the request and of any accompanying documentation; and
    (d)   transmit to each member of the Tribunal a copy of the notice of registration, together with a copy of the request and of any accompanying documentation.

(3)   The President of the Tribunal shall consult the members on whether it is necessary for the Tribunal to meet in order to consider the request. The Tribunal shall fix a time limit for the parties to file their observations on the request and shall determine the procedure for its consideration.

(4)   Rules 46–48 shall apply, *mutatis mutandis,* to any decision of the Tribunal pursuant to this Rule.

(5)   If a request is received by the Secretary-General more than 45 days after the award was rendered, he shall refuse to register the request and so inform forthwith the requesting party.

CHAPTER VII

INTERPRETATION, REVISION AND ANNULMENT OF THE AWARD

Rule 50   The Application

(1)   An application for the interpretation, revision or annulment of an award shall be addressed in writing to the Secretary-General and shall:
    (a)   identify the award to which it relates;

(b)   indicate the date of the application;

(c)   state in detail:

(i)   in an application for interpretation, the precise points in dispute;

(ii)   in an application for revision, pursuant to Article 51(1) of the Convention, the change sought in the award, the discovery of some fact of such a nature as decisively to affect the award, and evidence that when the award was rendered that fact was unknown to the Tribunal and to the applicant, and that the applicant's ignorance of that fact was not due to negligence;

(iii)   in an application for annulment, pursuant to Article 52(1) of the Convention, the grounds on which it is based. These grounds are limited to the following:

- that the Tribunal was not property constituted;
- that the Tribunal has manifestly exceeded its powers;
- that there was corruption on the part of a member of the Tribunal;
- that there has been a serious departure from a fundamental rule of procedure;
- that the award has failed to state the reasons on which it is based;

(d)   be accompanied by the payment of a fee for lodging the application.

(2)   Without prejudice to the provisions of paragraph (3), upon receiving an application and the lodging fee, the Secretary-General shall forthwith:

(a)   register the application;

(b)   notify the parties of the registration; and

(c)   transmit to the other party a copy of the application and of any accompanying documentation.

(3)   The Secretary-General shall refuse to register an application for:

(a)   revision, if, in accordance with Article 51(2) of the Convention, it is not made within 90 days after the discovery of the new fact and in any event within three years after the date on which the award was rendered (or any subsequent decision or correction);

(b)   annulment, if, in accordance with Article 52(2) of the Convention, it is not made:

(i)   within 120 days after the date on which the award was rendered (or any subsequent decision or correction) if the application is based on any of the following grounds:

- the Tribunal was not properly constituted;
- the Tribunal has manifestly exceeded its powers;
- there has been a serious departure from a fundamental rule of procedure;
- the award has failed to state the reasons on which it is based;

(ii)   in the case of corruption on the part of a member of the Tribunal, within 120 days after discovery thereof, and in any event within three years after the date on which the award was rendered (or any subsequent decision or correction).

(4)   If the Secretary-General refuses to register an application for revision, or annulment, he shall forthwith notify the requesting party of his refusal.

Rule 51   Interpretation or Revision: Further Procedures

(1)   Upon registration of an application for the interpretation or revision of an award, the Secretary-General shall forthwith:

(a)   transmit to each member of the original Tribunal a copy of the notice of registration, together with a copy of the application and of any accompanying documentation; and

(b)   request each member of the Tribunal to inform him within a specified time limit whether that member is willing to take part in the consideration of the application.

(2)   If all members of the Tribunal express their willingness to take part in the consideration of the application, the Secretary-General shall so notify the members of the Tribunal and the parties. Upon dispatch of these notices the tribunal shall be deemed to be reconstituted.

(3)   If the Tribunal cannot be reconstituted in accordance with paragraph (2), the Secretary-General shall so notify the parties and invite them to proceed, as soon as possible, to constitute a new Tribunal, including the same number of arbitrators, and appointed by the same method, as the original one.

Rule 52   Annulment: Further Procedures

(1)   Upon registration of an application for the annulment of an award, the Secretary-General shall forthwith request the Chairman of the Administrative Council to appoint an *ad hoc* Committee in accordance with Article 52(3) of the Convention.

(2)   The Committee shall be deemed to be constituted on the date the Secretary-General notifies the parties that all members have accepted their appointment. Before or at the first session of the Committee, each member shall sign a declaration conforming to that set forth in Rule 6(2).

Rule 53   Rules of Procedure

The provisions of these Rules shall apply *mutatis mutandis* to any procedure relating to the interpretation, revision or annulment of an award and to the decision of the Tribunal or Committee.

Rule 54   Stay of Enforcement of the Award

(1)   The party applying for the interpretation, revision or annulment of an award may in its application, and either party may at any time before the final disposition of the application, request a stay in the enforcement of part or all of the award to which the application relates. The Tribunal or Committee shall give priority to the consideration of such a request.

(2)   If an application for the revision or annulment of an award contains a request for a stay of its enforcement, the Secretary-General shall, together with the notice of registration, inform both parties of the provisional stay of the award. As soon as the Tribunal or Committee is constituted it shall, if either party requests, rule within 30 days on whether such stay should be continued; unless it decides to continue the stay, it shall automatically be terminated.

(3)   If a stay of enforcement has been granted pursuant to paragraph (1) or continued pursuant to paragraph (2), the Tribunal or Committee may at any time modify or terminate the stay at the request of either party. All stays shall automatically terminate on the date on which a final decision is rendered

on the application, except that a Committee granting the partial annulment of an award may order the temporary stay of enforcement of the unannulled portion in order to give either party an opportunity to request any new Tribunal constituted pursuant to Article 52(6) of the Convention to grant a stay pursuant to Rule 55(3).

(4)   A request pursuant to paragraph (1), (2) (second sentence) or (3) shall specify the circumstances that require the stay or its modification or termination. A request shall only be granted after the Tribunal or Committee has given each party an opportunity of presenting its observations.

(5)   The Secretary-General shall promptly notify both parties of the stay of enforcement of any award and of the modification or termination of such a stay, which shall become effective on the date on which he dispatches such notification.

Rule 55   Resubmission of Dispute after an Annulment

(1)   If a Committee annuls part or all of an award, either party may request the resubmission of the dispute to a new tribunal. Such a request shall be addressed in writing to the Secretary-General and shall:

(a)   identify the award to which it relates;

(b)   indicate the date of the request;

(c)   explain in detail what aspect of the dispute is to be submitted to the Tribunal; and

(d)   be accompanied by a fee for lodging the request.

(2)   Upon receipt of the request and of the lodging fee, the Secretary-General shall forthwith;

(a)   register it in the Arbitration Register;

(b)   notify both parties of the registration;

(c)   transmit to the other party a copy of the request and of any accompanying documentation; and

(d)   invite the parties to proceed, as soon as possible, to constitute a new Tribunal, including the same number of arbitrators, and appointed by the same method, as the original one.

(3)   If the original award had only been annulled in part, the new Tribunal shall not reconsider any portion of the award not so annulled. It may, however, in accordance with the procedures set forth in Rule 54, stay or continue to stay the enforcement of the unannulled portion of the award until the date its own award is rendered.

(4)   Except as otherwise provided in paragraphs (1)–(3), these Rules shall apply to a proceeding on a resubmitted dispute in the same manner as if such dispute had been submitted pursuant to the Institution Rules.

CHAPTER VIII

GENERAL PROVISION

Rule 56   Final Provisions

(1)   The texts of these Rules in each official language of the Centre shall be equally authentic.

(2)   These Rules may be cited as the 'Arbitration Rules' of the Centre.

JAPAN
COMMERCIAL ARBITRATION ASSOCIATION

TOKYO OFFICE
Taishoseimei Hibiya Bldg. 9-1, Yurakucho 1-chome, Chiyoda-ku, Tokyo 100, Tel.: 0081 -3 (3287) 3061, Fax.: 0081 -3 (3287) 3054

OSAKA OFFICE
The Osaka Chamber of Commerce & Industry Bldg. 2-8, Honmachibashi, Chuo-ku, Osaka, Tel.: 0081 -6 (944) 6164, Fax.: 0081 -6 (946) 8865

KOBE OFFICE
The Kobe Chamber of Commerce & Industry, 1, Minatojima-Nakamachi 6-chome, Chuo-ku, Kobe, Tel.: 0081 -78 (303) 5806, Fax.: 0081 -78 (303) 2312

NAGOYA OFFICE
The Nagoya Chamber of Commerce & Industry, 10-19, Sakae 2-chome, Naka-ku, Nagoya, Tel.: 0081 -52 (221) 7211, Fax.: 0081 -52 (231) 5213

COMMERCIAL ARBITRATION RULES

STANDARD ARBITRATION CLAUSE

All disputes, controversies or differences which may arise between the parties hereto, out of, in relation to or in connection with this Agreement shall be finally settled by arbitration in *(town)*, Japan in accordance with the Commercial Arbitration Rules of the Japan Commercial Arbitration Association.

COMMERCIAL ARBITRATION RULES

CHAPTER I

GENERAL PROVISIONS

Rule 1   Purpose

1   The purpose of these Rules shall be to provide such matters as are necessary for arbitration at the Japan Commercial Arbitration Association (hereinafter the 'Association').

2   Arbitration under the UNCITRAL Arbitration Rules adopted by the United Nations Commission on International Trade Law on 28 April, 1976 and the Administrative and Procedural Rules for Arbitration under the UNCITRAL Arbitration Rules shall be governed otherwise.

Rule 2   Application of these rules

1   These Rules shall apply where the parties have agreed to submit their dispute to arbitration under the Rules of the Association or simply arbitration at the Association (hereinafter the 'arbitration agreement').

2   These Rules shall apply if the parties agree, in writing, during the course of arbitral proceedings provided for in Rule 1, Paragraph 2, to conduct such arbitral proceedings pursuant to these Rules. In the case of such an agreement, the Arbitral proceedings already conducted shall remain valid.

Rule 3   Interpretation of these rules

If any question arises concerning the interpretation of these Rules, the Association's interpretation shall prevail; provided that the interpretation of an arbitral tribunal shall, after such interpretation is made, prevail over that of the Association in the arbitration case before such tribunal.

Rule 4   Arbitration agreement

1   Arbitration agreements shall be made in writing.
2   When the parties have entered into an arbitration agreement, these Rules shall be deemed incorporated in such agreement; provided that the parties may agree otherwise to the extent that such agreement does not violate the spirit of these Rules.

Rule 5   Arbitral tribunal

1   Arbitration under these Rules shall be conducted by an arbitral tribunal composed of one or more arbitrators who have been appointed pursuant to the provisions of Rules 20 through 26 (including the application mutatis mutandis of Rule 26 under the provisions of Rule 41, Paragraph 2) and Rule 29.
2   If the arbitral tribunal is composed of more than one arbitrator, the arbitrators may, after all of them have been appointed, agree upon and appoint a presiding arbitrator from among themselves.

Rule 6   Decision of arbitral tribunal

1   If the number of arbitrators is more than one, decisions of the arbitral tribunal, including the arbitral award, shall be made by a majority of votes of the arbitrators.
2   If the voting of the arbitral tribunal results in a tie, the presiding arbitrator, if one has been appointed, shall cast the deciding vote.

Rule 7   Secretariat and tribunal clerk

1   Clerical work with respect to arbitration under these Rules shall be conducted by the Secretariat of the Association (hereinafter the 'secretariat').
2   Clerical work of the arbitral tribunal shall be conducted by a staff member of the Association who has been appointed by the Association as the clerk in charge of such clerical work (hereinafter the 'clerk in charge').

Rule 8   Panel of arbitrators

The Association shall prepare and maintain a panel of arbitrators to facilitate the appointment of arbitrators.

Rule 9   Representation and assistance

A party may be represented or assisted by any person of its choice in the proceedings under these Rules. Subsequent to such selection, the arbitral tribunal may, for good cause, reject a party's selection of such representative or assistant.

Rule 10   Definition

1   'Basic Date' under these Rules shall be the date after the lapse of three (3) weeks from the date on which the Association sends a notice of acceptance of the request for arbitration provided for in Rule 13, Paragraph 1; provided that, if the respondent proves that it received such notice of acceptance after such date, the date on which the respondent received such notice shall be the Basic Date.

2   'Party or parties' under these Rules shall be either a claimant or respondent or both. Multiple claimants or respondents shall be deemed to be one party for purposes of the appointment of arbitrators.

3   'Document or documents' under these Rules shall include any document in which the contents of a communication have been recorded mechanically by way of telex, facsimile or other means.

4   'Agreement in writing' under these Rules shall mean the meeting of minds acknowledged in writing and the document need not be a single instrument.

Rule 11   Means of communication

Communication during arbitration under these Rules shall be by way of a document or other means of communication followed by a document.

CHAPTER II

REQUEST FOR ARBITRATION

Rule 12   Request for arbitration

1   To request the initiation of arbitral proceedings, the claimant shall submit to the Association a written request for arbitration setting forth the following:

    (1)   a demand that the dispute be referred to arbitration under these Rules;

    (2)   a reference to the arbitration agreement that is invoked;

    (3)   the full personal or corporate names of the parties and their addresses;

    (4)   if the claimant is represented by an agent, the name and address of such agent;

    (5)   the relief or remedy claimed;

    (6)   a summary of the dispute; and

    (7)   the basis for the claim and the manner or method of proof.

2   The claimant shall submit to the Association, together with the written request for arbitration, a copy of the arbitration clause or the separate arbitration agreement containing the arbitration agreement provided for in (2) of the preceding Paragraph.

3   If the claimant is represented by an agent in the arbitral proceedings, such agent shall submit a power of attorney to the Association together with the written request for arbitration.

4   The claimant shall, when it requests the initiation of arbitral proceedings, pay the request fee and the administrative fee provided for in the Arbitration Fee Regulations of the Association. If the claimant fails to pay such request fee and/or administrative fee, the Association may treat the request for arbitration as if it had not been made and return the written request for arbitration to the claimant with notification to such effect.

5   Arbitral proceedings shall be deemed to be initiated on the date on which the Association receives the written request for arbitration.

Rule 13   Acceptance and notification of request for arbitration

1   The Association, upon confirmation that the request for arbitration has been made in conformity with the provisions of Paragraphs 1 through 3 of the preceding Rule, shall notify, without delay, the claimant and the respondent of the acceptance of the request for arbitration. Copies of the written request for arbitration and the arbitration agreement shall be attached to the notice sent to the respondent.

2   The Association shall designate one of its offices as the secretariat in charge of administrative services and give notice thereof to each party when the Association notifies the parties of the acceptance of the request for arbitration provided for in the preceding Paragraph.

Rule 14   Request for separation of arbitral proceedings

1   If a request for arbitration against multiple respondents is submitted and any respondent submits a written request for separation of arbitral proceedings within three (3) weeks from the Basic Date and prior to the establishment of the arbitral tribunal, the claimant shall submit a new request for arbitration against each of such respondent and the other respondent(s).

2   All newly submitted requests for arbitration under the preceding Paragraph shall be deemed to have been submitted on the date on which the Association received the initial request for arbitration; provided that the Basic Date shall be determined based on the newly submitted requests for arbitration.

3   The provisions of Paragraph 1 shall not preclude the application of Rule 41.

Rule 15   Answer

1   The respondent shall, within four (4) weeks from the Basic Date, submit to the Association a written answer setting forth the following:

(1)   the full personal or corporate names of the parties and their addresses;

(2) if the respondent is represented by an agent, the name and address of such agent;

(3) confirmation or denial of the claims;

(4) a summary of the dispute; and

(5) the basis for the answer and the manner or method of proof.

2   If the respondent is represented by an agent in the arbitral proceedings, such agent shall submit a power of attorney to the Association together with the written answer.

3   Subsequent to submission of the written answer, the Association shall send, without delay, a copy thereof to the other party or parties and, if an arbitrator has or arbitrators have been appointed, to such arbitrator or arbitrators.

4   If the written answer contains a counterclaim, the provisions of the following Rule shall apply to such counterclaim.

Rule 16   Counterclaim

1   The respondent may, only within six (6) weeks from the Basic Date, submit a counterclaim that is related to the claimant's claim(s) and covered by the same arbitration agreement. The arbitral tribunal shall examine any such counterclaim together with the claimant's claim(s).

2   The provisions of Rules 12, 13 and 15 shall apply mutatis mutandis to any counterclaim provided for in the preceding Paragraph.

Rule 17   Amendments to claims or counterclaims

1   Either the claimant or the counterclaimant may, to the extent that the claim and counterclaim are covered by the same arbitration agreement, amend or supplement its claim (which shall hereinafter include a counterclaim for purposes of this Rule) by submitting a written request for amendment to the Association; provided that, after the establishment of the arbitral tribunal, such claimant or counterclaimant shall submit a written application for approval of such amendment to the arbitral tribunal and obtain its approval thereof.

2   The arbitral tribunal shall hear the other party's opinion before giving the approval provided for in the preceding Paragraph.

3   The arbitral tribunal shall not give any approval provided for in Paragraph 1 if it considers it inappropriate to approve such amendment in view of the substantial delay in conducting the arbitral proceedings or prejudice to the other party that such amendment will cause or any other circumstances.

4   The provisions of Rules 15 or 16 shall apply mutatis mutandis to an answer to or counterclaim with respect to an amended claim; provided that such answer or counterclaim shall be submitted within three (3) weeks from the date on which the secretariat or the clerk in charge sends written notice of such amendment to such other party.

Rule 18   Number of copies of documents to be submitted

The number of copies of documents to be submitted pursuant to the provisions of Rule 12, Paragraph 1 and Rule 15, Paragraph 1 (including the application mutatis mutandis of such provisions under Rule 16, Paragraph 2 and Paragraph 4 of the preceding Rule) and the provisions of Paragraph 1 of the preceding Rule shall be equal to the number of arbitrators (three (3) if not yet determined) and the other party or parties plus one (1); provided that one copy of a power of attorney shall suffice.

Rule 19   Withdrawal of request for arbitration

1   The claimant may, within thirty (30) days after the initiation of arbitral proceedings and before the appointment of any arbitrator, withdraw its request for arbitration upon written notice.

2   Except as provided in the preceding Paragraph, the claimant may withdraw its request for arbitration only with the written consent of the respondent.

3   Withdrawal of the request for arbitration shall become effective when the written notice of withdrawal and, in the case provided for in the preceding Paragraph, the respondent's written consent thereto reach the Association.

CHAPTER III

APPOINTMENT OF ARBITRATORS

Rule 20   Qualification of arbitrators

No person having a beneficial interest in the case under arbitration shall be an arbitrator.

Rule 21   Agreement of parties

1   The parties may, by written agreement, appoint one or more arbitrators or determine the number, the method or the period of time (or all of the above) of appointment of the arbitrators.

2   The parties shall notify the Association, within, at the latest, three (3) weeks from the Basic Date, of the contents of an agreement provided for in the preceding Paragraph.

Rule 22   Appointment of arbitrators where the parties have determined the method of appointment

1   If the parties have entered into an agreement provided for in the latter part of Paragraph 1 of the preceding Rule, an arbitrator shall be appointed pursuant to such agreement.

2   If one or both of the parties fails or fail to notify the Association of the appointment of an arbitrator, as provided for in the preceding Paragraph, within the period of time for appointment agreed upon by the parties or, if the parties have not agreed upon such period of time, within four (4) weeks from the earlier of the date on which the notice provided for in Paragraph 2 of the preceding Rule reaches the Association or the date provided for in the same Paragraph, the Association shall appoint such arbitrator. If the Association is to make such an appointment, it shall respect, to the extent possible,

the contents of the agreement provided for in Paragraph 1 of the preceding Rule.

3 If the Association appoints an arbitrator under the provisions of the preceding Paragraph, the provisions of Rule 24, Paragraph 3 shall apply mutatis mutandis.

4 If the parties have not entered into an agreement provided for in the latter part of Paragraph 1 of the preceding Rule with respect to the number of arbitrators, such number shall be determined pursuant to the provisions of the following Rule.

Rule 23   Number of arbitrators

If the parties fail to notify the Association, within three (3) weeks from the Basic Date, of their agreement with respect to the number of arbitrators, such number shall be one (1); provided that if either party requests in writing, within four (4) weeks from the Basic Date, that such number be three (3) and the Association determines that such request is appropriate, such number shall be three (3).

Rule 24   Appointment of arbitrator—single arbitrator

1 If the number of arbitrators is one (1) under the agreement provided for in Rule 21 or the provisions of the preceding Rule, the parties shall agree upon and appoint an arbitrator.

2 If the parties fail to notify the Association of the appointment of an arbitrator provided for in the preceding Paragraph within four (4) weeks from the date when the notice provided for in Rule 21, Paragraph 2 reaches the Association if the number of arbitrators fixed under an agreement provided for in Rule 21 is one (1) or the last day of the third week immediately following the Basic Date if the number of arbitrators fixed under the provisions of the preceding Rule is one (1), the Association shall appoint such arbitrator. If the Association is to make such an appointment, it shall respect, to the extent possible, the contents of an agreement, if one exists, provided for in Rule 21, Paragraph 1.

3 If the Association is to appoint an arbitrator pursuant to the provisions of the preceding Paragraph, the Association shall give due consideration to a written request, submitted by either party within one (1) week from the date on which it is determined that the Association shall make such appointment, that a person of a different nationality from those of the parties be appointed as such arbitrator.

Rule 25   Appointment of arbitrators—more than one arbitrator

1 If the parties agree under the provisions of Rule 21 that there shall be more than one arbitrator but not on the method of appointment or if the number of arbitrators is fixed at three (3) pursuant to the proviso of Rule 23, each party shall appoint the same number of arbitrators, the sum of which shall not exceed the number of arbitrators thus fixed, and if the number thus fixed is an odd number, the arbitrators appointed thereby shall appoint one (1) more arbitrator.

2   The parties shall appoint, within four (4) weeks from the date on which they have given notice under the provisions of Rule 21, Paragraph 2 or from the date on which the number of arbitrators is fixed at three (3) pursuant to the proviso of Rule 23, the same number of arbitrators which each party should appoint pursuant to the provisions of the preceding Paragraph.

3   If either party fails to appoint an arbitrator or arbitrators within the period of time provided for in the preceding Paragraph, the Association shall appoint such arbitrator or arbitrators.

4   If the number of arbitrators is odd and the arbitrators appointed by the parties or the arbitrators appointed pursuant to the provisions of the preceding Paragraph fail to appoint one (1) more arbitrator within three (3) weeks from the date on which the last of such arbitrators was appointed, the Association shall appoint such arbitrator.

5   If the Association is to make the appointment under the provisions of the preceding Paragraph, the provisions of Paragraph 3 of the preceding Rule shall apply mutatis mutandis.

Rule 26   Appointment of arbitrators where third party participates in proceedings

1   If, prior to the establishment of an arbitral tribunal, a third party participates or is allowed to participate in arbitral proceedings under the provisions of Rule 40, one or more arbitrators shall be appointed by agreement of the claimant, the respondent and such third party.

2   If the appointment of the number of arbitrators fixed by the agreement provided for in the preceding Paragraph has not been completed within three (3) weeks from the date on which such third party has participated in arbitral proceedings, the Association shall appoint the arbitrator(s) yet to be appointed.

3   If the number of arbitrators has not been agreed upon by the date fixed under the provisions of the preceding Paragraph, the Association shall appoint the number of arbitrator(s) determined by the Association.

Rule 27   Notice of appointment of arbitrator

1   Upon appointment of an arbitrator by a party or the arbitrators, such party or arbitrators shall, without delay, submit to the Association a written notice of appointment of arbitrator setting forth such arbitrator's name, address and occupation, together with such arbitrator's written acceptance of appointment. The Association shall, without delay, send a copy of such notice to the other party and the arbitrator(s) already appointed.

2   Upon appointment of an arbitrator by the Association, it shall, without delay, notify the parties and the arbitrator(s) already appointed of such arbitrator's name, address and occupation.

Rule 28   Allocation of expenses of non-resident arbitrator

1   If a party has appointed an arbitrator who is not resident in Japan, such party shall bear the expenses required due to such arbitrator's non-residence; provided that the arbitral tribunal may allocate such expenses in a manner different therefrom.

2   If the Association has, or the arbitrators have, appointed an arbitrator who is not resident in Japan, the arbitral tribunal shall allocate such expenses in its arbitral award.

Rule 29   Replacement of arbitrator

1   If an arbitrator resigns or dies, the Association shall, without delay, notify the parties and the remaining arbitrator(s) thereof.

2   If the arbitrator who resigns or dies is one appointed by a party or parties or the remaining arbitrators, the party or parties or the remaining arbitrators shall appoint a substitute arbitrator within three (3) weeks from the date on which such party or parties or such arbitrators receive the notice provided for in the preceding Paragraph. If the arbitrator who resigns or dies is one appointed by the Association, the Association shall appoint a substitute arbitrator within three (3) weeks from the date on which it learns of such resignation or death.

3   If such party or parties or arbitrators fails or fail to appoint a substitute arbitrator within the period of time provided for in the preceding Paragraph, the Association shall appoint such substitute arbitrator.

Rule 30   Removal of arbitrator

1   The Association may remove any arbitrator who fails to perform its duties or unduly delays in the performance of its duties, or is legally or actually unable to perform its duties.

2   The provisions of Paragraph 2 of the preceding Rule shall apply mutatis mutandis to the appointment of a substitute arbitrator.

CHAPTER IV

ARBITRAL PROCEEDINGS

Section 1   Examination Proceedings

Rule 31   Supervision of examination proceedings

1   The examination proceedings, including hearings, shall be conducted under the supervision of the arbitral tribunal.

2   The arbital tribunal shall treat the parties equally and give each party sufficient opportunity to state and prove its case and present a defense against the other party's case.

Rule 32   Hearings

1   The date and place of hearings shall be decided by the arbitral tribunal upon consultation with the parties. If a hearing lasts more than one (1) day, it shall be held on consecutive days, to the extent possible.

2   After the date and place of hearing have been decided, the clerk in charge shall, without delay, notify the parties thereof. One notice shall suffice even if hearings are held on consecutive days.

3   Oral argumentations on the law and the facts and applications to present evidence and examination thereof shall occur at hearings.

4   The date of a hearing shall be changed at the request of both parties. In the event that one of the parties requests that the date of a hearing be changed, the arbitral tribunal may change such date only if it determines that there are unavoidable circumstances.

5   The request provided for in the preceding Paragraph shall be made in writing, unless made at a hearing.

Rule 33   Submission of written statements

1   Each party may submit to the arbitral tribunal, at hearings or otherwise, written statements setting forth such party's case on the law and the facts (hereinafter the 'written statements'). The arbitral tribunal may urge the submission of written statements.

2   Any party submitting written statements shall submit to the Association a number of copies thereof equal to the number of arbitrators and parties. The clerk in charge shall keep one copy for the record and, without delay, deliver personally or send one copy each to the arbitrators and parties (except the party submitting such written statements).

3   The arbitral tribunal shall confirm at hearings the receipt of the written statements submitted otherwise than at a hearing.

Rule 34   Clarification of the case

The arbitral tribunal may, to assist it in understanding the case, require a party to explain such party's case or conduct an on-site inspection or investigation in the presence of the parties.

Rule 35   Examination of evidence

1   Each party shall have the burden of proving the facts relied on to support such party's claim or defense.

2   The arbitral tribunal may, when it deems it necessary, examine evidence that a party has not applied to present.

3   Such examination of evidence may be made other than at a hearing. If the arbitral tribunal decides to examine evidence other than at a hearing, the parties shall be given the opportunity to be present.

4   The arbitral tribunal is not authorized to administer an oath to any witness or expert.

5   The arbitral tribunal may, when it deems it necessary or when there has been a petition from a party, refer inquiries to, and request responses from, public or private bodies. The arbitral tribunal shall disclose responses thus obtained to the parties.

Rule 36   Application to present evidence

1   A party may apply to present evidence by submitting any of the following documents to arbitral tribunal:

(1)   application for documentary evidence (a document explaining the documentary evidence attached thereto);

(2)   application to examine a witness (a written application, specifying the witness and the matters with respect to which such witness is to be examined, to examine a witness); or

(3)   application for an expert opinion or verification (a written application for an expert opinion or verification setting forth the matters for which an expert opinion is required or the items to be verification and the method thereof).

2   An application to present evidence may be made other than at a hearing.

3   Any party submitting any of the documents provided for in Paragraph 1 shall submit to the Association a number of copies thereof equal to the number of arbitrators and parties. The clerk in charge shall keep one of the copies for the record and promptly deliver personally or send one copy each to the arbitrators and the parties (except the party submitting such document).

4   A party, except the party who has applied to present evidence, may submit to the arbitral tribunal a document setting forth its views with respect to the application to present evidence. If a party does submit such a document, the provisions of the preceding two (2) Paragraphs shall apply mutatis mutandis.

5   The arbitral tribunal may, any time after the lapse of a reasonable period of time necessary for the document provided for in Paragraph 4 to be submitted, determine whether to adopt or reject the application to present evidence. After the arbitral tribunal makes such determination, the clerk in charge shall, without delay, notify the parties of the result thereof.

6   The arbitral tribunal shall, a hearing, confirm its receipt of documents provided for in Paragraphs 1 and 4 that are submitted other than at a hearing and determine whether to adopt or reject any applications to present evidence (or, if already determined pursuant to the provisions of the preceding Paragraph, confirm such determination).

Rule 37   Principle of appearance by the parties

1   Hearings shall in principle be held in the presence of both parties.

2   If one or both parties fails or fail to appear without good cause, a hearing may be held in its or their absence; provided that, if both of the parties fail to appear, the examination proceedings may not be terminated on the date when such hearing is held.

3   If one of the parties fails to appear, the examination proceedings may be conducted based on the allegations and proof of the party who has appeared.

Rule 38   Allocation of the cost of examining evidence and other expenses

The necessary costs incurred to examine evidence, make inquiries and conduct inspections or investigations under the provisions of Rule 34 shall, if such expense was the result of an order by the arbitral tribunal, be equally borne by the parties and, if such expense was the result of a petition by a party, be borne by such party; provided that, notwithstanding the foregoing, the arbitral tribunal may reallocate expenses in view of the circumstances.

Rule 39   Assignment of arbitrator's authority

The arbitral tribunal may, when it deems it necessary and upon obtaining the consent of the parties, cause one or more of the arbitrators constituting the arbitral tribunal to examine witnesses, make verifications, conduct inspections or investigations under the provisions of Rule 34 or mediate a settlement.

Rule 40   Participation in proceedings

1   Any person who is not a party to a particular arbitration may, upon the consent of such person and all the parties to such arbitration, participate in such arbitration as a claimant or be allowed to participate therein as a respondent.

2   If the participation in the arbitration provided for in the preceding Paragraph occurs before the establishment of the arbitral tribunal, the arbitrators shall be appointed subject to the provisions of Rule 26 and, if such participation occurs after the establishment of the arbitral tribunal, the composition thereof shall not be affected.

3   Notwithstanding that the consent provided for in Paragraph 1 has been given, the arbitral tribunal may deny participation in the arbitration if the arbitral tribunal determines that such participation will delay the arbitral proceedings or for any other proper reason.

4   The provisions of Rule 12 shall apply mutatis mutandis to an application for participation in the arbitration; provided that the administrative fee mentioned in Rule 12, Paragraph 4 shall be repaid if such participation is denied.

Rule 41   Examination of multiple requests for arbitration in the same proceedings

1   If the Association or the arbitral tribunal determines that it is necessary to consolidate multiple requests for arbitration that contain claims that are essentially mutually related, the arbitral tribunal, after obtaining the written consent of all the relevant parties, may examine such cases together in the same proceedings; provided that, if multiple requests for arbitration arise out of the same arbitration agreement, no consent of the parties is necessary.

2   If it is determined, pursuant to the provisions of the preceding Paragraph, that multiple requests for arbitration are to be disposed of in the same proceedings, the provisions of Paragraph 2 of the preceding Rule shall apply mutatis mutandis to the appointment of arbitrators.

Rule 42   Closed proceedings, obligation of confidentiality

1   Arbitral proceedings and records thereof shall be closed to the public.

2   The arbitrators, the staff of the Association, the parties and their representatives or assistants shall not disclose facts related to arbitration cases

or facts learned through arbitration cases; provided that disclosure may be made subject to the conditions provided in a consent of the arbitral tribunal.

Rule 43 Minutes of hearings and other matters

1 The clerk in charge shall, for each hearing, take minutes stating the date, time and place of the hearing, the names of those attending the hearing and a summary record of the hearing, obtain, without delay, confirmation of the contents thereof from the arbitrators and the parties and file or otherwise preserve the minutes at the Association.

The clerk in charge may, subject to the consent of the arbitral tribunal, make tape-recordings or video-recordings of hearings.

2 The clerk in charge shall, when the arbitral tribunal has so ordered or a party has so requested, arrange for the making of a stenographic transcript. Such order or request shall, in principle, be made not less than three (3) weeks before the date of the hearing at which stenography is required.

3 The cost of making a stenographic transcript shall, if ordered by the arbitral tribunal, be borne equally by each party or, if ordered at a party's request, be borne by the requesting party; provided that the arbitral tribunal may, in view of the circumstances, allocate such cost among the parties.

Rule 44 Interpretation and translation

1 The clerk in charge shall, when the arbitral tribunal has so ordered or a party has so requested, arrange for interpreting. Such order or request shall, in principle, be made not less than three (3) weeks before the date when interpreting is required.

2 The provisions of Paragraph 3 of the preceding Rule shall apply mutatis mutandis to the cost of interpreting.

3 The provisions of the preceding two (2) paragraphs shall apply mutatis mutandis to the translation of documents.

Rule 45 Conclusion and reopening of examination proceedings

1 The arbitral tribunal may decide to conclude the examination upon determining that the proceedings have matured enough for the arbitral tribunal to render an arbitral award or that the proceedings should be terminated because it is impossible to continue. If such decision is made other than at a hearing, an appropriate period of time for advance notice shall be provided.

2 The arbitral tribunal shall declare the proceedings closed upon determining that the proceedings should be terminated and concluding the examination. The provisions applied to arbitral awards shall apply mutatis mutandis to such declaration.

3 The arbitral tribunal may, if it deems it necessary, reopen the examination. The arbitral tribunal shall, if it decides to reopen the examination, promptly notify the parties in writing of such decision and the reasons therefor.

4 An examination shall, in principle, not be reopened after the lapse of three (3) weeks from the date of the decision to conclude the examination.

Rule 46   Right to object

A party who knows or ought to know that the arbitral proceedings have not been conducted properly and who fails to object without delay, shall be deemed to have waived its right to object; provided that no party shall be deemed to have waived any right that it cannot waive.

Rule 47   Examination proceedings only on documents

1   The parties may, at any time, by written agreement, request examination based only on documents. If the parties make such a request, the proceedings already conducted shall remain valid.

2   If it is a violation of the spirit of the provisions of these Rules to apply them to examination proceedings based only on documents, the arbitral tribunal's determination shall prevail.

Section 2   Arbitral Award

Rule 48   Time of arbitral award

1   Once the arbitral tribunal has determined that the proceedings have matured enough for it to render an arbitral award and concluded the examination, the arbitral tribunal shall make an arbitral award within five (5) weeks from the date of such conclusion; provided that the arbitral tribunal may, if if deems it necessary in view of the complexities of the case or for any other reason, extend such period of time to an appropriate period of not more than eight (8) weeks.

2   The arbitral tribunal shall, upon conclusion of the examination pursuant to the preceding Paragraph, notify the parties of the period of time during which it shall make an arbitral award.

Rule 49   Arbitral award

1   The arbitral award shall state the following and bear the signature and seal of each arbitrator; provided that the statement of Item (4) below shall be omitted if the parties have agreed that no statement is necessary and in the case provided for in the following Paragraph and the reason for such omission shall be set forth in the arbitral award:

(1)   the full personal or corporate names of the parties and their addresses;

(2)   if a party is represented by an agent, the name and address of such agent;

(3)   the text of the award;

(4)   the reason for the award; and

(5)   the date of the award.

2   If the arbitral tribunal deems it appropriate, it may, at the request of the parties reaching a settlement during the course of the arbitral proceedings, set forth the contents of any such settlement in its arbitral award.

3   The arbitral tribunal shall set forth in the text of its arbitral award the total amount and the allocation of the administrative fee, the hearing fee, the

necessary expenses incurred during the proceedings and the arbitrators' remuneration and shall, if there is a party who has deposited an amount of money less than the amount allocated in the text of the arbitral award, set forth an order to the effect that the balance shall be paid to the other party.

4   If there are more than one arbitrators and an arbitrator fails to sign and affix its seal to the arbitral award, the arbitral tribunal shall set forth the reasons for such failure in the arbitral award.

Rule 50   Service and deposit of arbitral award

1   The clerk in charge shall serve an authenticated copy of the arbitral award on each party by hand delivery, by delivery-certified registered mail or any other method proving receipt.

2   Service under the preceding Paragraph shall occur after the fees, the necessary expenses incurred during the proceedings and the arbitrators' remuneration have been fully paid to the Association.

3   After serving authenticated copies of the arbitral award, the clerk in charge shall, without delay, deposit the original text of the arbitral award with a court of appropriate jurisdiction together with certificates of service.

Rule 51   Interim award

The arbitral tribunal may, when it deems it appropriate, make an interim award to decide a dispute arising during the course of the arbitral proceedings. The provisions of Rule 49, Paragraph 1 and Rule 50, Paragraph 1 shall apply mutatis mutandis to such interim award; provided that the statement of a reason for the interim award may be dispensed with.

CHAPTER V

SUPPLEMENTARY RULES

Rule 52   Language

1   The language or languages to be used in arbitral proceedings shall be Japanese or English or both. The arbitral tribunal shall, except where the parties have agreed on one or both of such languages, determine, without delay, the language or languages to be used. The arbitral tribunal shall, in so determining, take into consideration whether interpreting or translating will be required and how the cost thereof should be allocated.

2   Arbitral proceedings conducted, prior to the determination of language or languages pursuant to the preceding Paragraph, in a language other than the language or languages so determined shall remain valid. The Association may, if such language is one other than Japanese or English, require the submission of Japanese or English translations.

3   If it is determined that both Japanese and English are to be the languages used during arbitral proceedings, either Japanese or English may be, at a party's option, used during all arbitral proceedings, including hearings, provided that the arbitral award shall be written in Japanese and English, both versions of which shall be official, and if a discrepancy in

interpretation arises between the two (2) versions, the interpretation of the Japanese version shall prevail.

Rule 53   Extension of period of time

1   The parties may, by written agreement, extend any period of time provided for in these Rules, except for the period of time provided for in Rule 10, Paragraph 1, Rule 15, Paragraph 1, Rule 16, Paragraph 1, Rule 19, Paragraph 1 and Rule 24, Paragraph 3 (including the application mutatis mutandis of the provisions or such Paragraph under the provisions of Rule 25, Paragraph 5). In the event of such an extension, the parties shall, without delay, notify the arbitral tribunal (or, hereinafter, for purposes of this Rule, the Association if the arbitral tribunal has not been established) thereof.

2   The arbitral tribunal may, if it deems it necessary, extend a period of time provided for in these Rules (including a period of time determined by the arbitral tribunal). In the event of such an extension, the arbitral tribunal shall, without delay, notify the parties thereof.

Rule 54   Obligation to pay fees, etc.

1   The parties shall be jointly and severally liable for payment to the Association of the fees provided for in the Arbitration Fee Regulations, necessary expenses incurred during the proceedings and the arbitrators' remuneration.

2   Any dispute arising between the Association and the parties with respect to the payments provided for in the preceding Paragraph shall be determined by the arbitral tribunal established to determine the dispute between the parties.

Rule 55   Allocation of fees and expenses

In addition to the expenses provided for in Rule 28, Paragraphs 1 and 2, Rule 38 and Rule 43, Paragraph 3 (including the application mutatis mutandis of the provisions of such Paragraph under the provisions of Rule 44, Paragraphs 2 and 3), the parties shall bear, in the manner provided below, the fees provided for in the Arbitration Fee Regulations and the necessary expenses incurred during the proceedings:

(1)   the request fee shall be borne by the party requesting the initiation of arbitral proceedings;

(2)   the administrative fee, hearing fee and necessary expenses incurred during the proceedings shall be borne subject to the allocation determined by the arbitral tribunal and set forth in the arbitral award; and

(3)   the hearing schedule alteration fee shall be borne, if the alteration is requested by one of the parties, by such party, and, in any other case, equally by both parties.

Rule 56   Allocation of remuneration for arbitrators

The parties shall bear equally the cost of the remuneration fixed by the Association for the arbitrators; provided that the arbitral tribunal may, in view of the circumstances, allocate such cost in any other manner.

Rule 57 Payment to the association

1 The parties shall pay to the Association, in the manner and within the period of time determined by the arbitral tribunal, a sum of money fixed by it to cover the hearing fee, the hearing schedule alteration fee, the arbitrators' remuneration and necessary expenses incurred during the proceedings.

2 If a party fails to make payment as provided for in the preceding Paragraph, the arbitral tribunal may suspend or terminate the arbitral proceedings unless the other party makes such payment on behalf of the first party.

3 If, subsequent to termination of the arbitral proceedings, the total sum of money paid under the provisions of Paragraph 1 exceeds the total sum of the administrative fees and other fees and expenses determined by the arbitral tribunal under the provisions of Rule 49, Paragraph 3 and the hearing schedule alteration fee, the Association shall refund the difference to either or both of the parties.

Rule 58 Official version of these rules

These Rules have been prepared in Japanese and in English and both versions are official; provided that, in the event that a discrepancy in interpretation arises between the two versions, the interpretation of the Japanese version shall prevail.

Supplementary Provisions

1 These Rules shall come into effect on October 1, 1992.

2 The Commercial Arbitration Rules, as amended on June 1, 1991 (hereinafter the 'Former Rules'), are hereby repealed.

3 Any arbitral proceedings initiated before these Rules come into effect shall be governed by the Former Rules; provided that subsequent proceedings may, upon agreement of the parties, be conducted pursuant to these Rules. In the event of such an agreement between the parties, the proceedings that already have been conducted pursuant to the Former Rules shall remain valid.

ARBITRATION FEE REGULATIONS

[Not reproduced here.]

ADMINISTRATIVE AND PROCEDURAL RULES FOR ARBITRATION UNDER THE UNCITRAL ARBITRATION RULES

effective 1 June, 1991

MODEL CLAUSE

Any dispute, controversy or claim arising out of or relating to this contract, or the breach, termination or invalidity thereof, shall be settled by arbitration in accordance with the UNCITRAL Arbitration Rules as at present in force.

Any such arbitration shall be administered by the Japan Commercial Arbitration Association in accordance with the Administrative and Procedural Rules for Arbitration under the UNCITRAL Arbitration Rules.

The appointing authority shall be the Japan Commercial Arbitration Association.

(1)   The number of arbitrators shall be_____(one or three).

(2)   The place of arbitration shall be_____.

(3)   The language(s) to be used in the arbitral proceedings shall be Japanese or/and English.

Article 1   Application of these rules

1   The Japan Commercial Arbitration Association (hereinafter the 'Association') shall, in either of the following cases, provide administrative services for arbitration under the UNCITRAL Arbitration Rules adopted at the United Nations Commission on International Trade Law on 28 April 1976 (hereinafter 'the UNCITRAL Arbitration Rules') in accordance with the provisions of articles 2 through 12 below:

(a)   Where the parties have agreed in advance to have the Association provide administrative services for arbitration under the UNCITRAL Arbitration Rules, or

(b)   Where the parties have agreed, with respect to a matter in which a request for arbitration has been submitted to the Association under its Commercial Arbitration Rules, to conduct the arbitral proceedings under the UNCITRAL Arbitration Rules.

2   The proceedings of an arbitration administered under the preceding paragraph shall, as to matters not provided for in these Rules, be conducted in accordance with the provisions of the UNCITRAL Arbitration Rules.

Article 2   Appointing authority

When a request for arbitration has been submitted under these Rules and the Association has been designated by the agreement of the parties as the appointing authority, the Association shall perform the functions of the appointing authority as set forth in the UNCITRAL Arbitration Rules.

Article 3   Request for arbitration and acceptance thereof

1   The party requesting the initiation of arbitral proceedings in a case described in article 1, paragraph 1, subparagraph (a) (hereinafter the 'claimant') shall submit to the Association a written request for arbitration setting forth the matters referred to in article 3, paragraph 3 and article 18, paragraph 2 of the UNCITRAL Arbitration Rules.

2   Arbitral proceedings shall be deemed to be initiated on the date on which the written request for arbitration referred to in the preceding paragraph is received by the Association.

3   The Association shall, where the written request for arbitration referred to in paragraph 1 is in conformity with the provisions of article 3, paragraph 3 and article 18, paragraph 2 of the UNCITRAL Arbitration Rules and when the request fee and the administrative fee have been paid, give notice to the

claimant and the other party (hereinafter the 'respondent') of its acceptance of the request for arbitration. The Association shall attach a copy of the written request for arbitration to the notice of acceptance given to the respondent.

4   The provisions of the preceding three paragraphs shall apply *mutatis mutandis* to a counterclaim made by the respondent.

5   The parties shall, when they have reached agreement as provided in article 1, paragraph 1, subparagraph (b), give written notice to the Association of such agreement. In such a case, the arbitral proceedings conducted theretofore shall remain valid.

Article 4   Withdrawal of request for arbitration

1   The claimant may, within 30 days after the initiation of the arbitral proceedings and when no arbitrator has been appointed, withdraw the request for arbitration by giving written notice.

2   Except as provided in the preceding paragraph, the claimant may withdraw the request for arbitration only with the written consent of the respondent.

3   Withdrawal of the request for arbitration shall become effective when the written notice of withdrawal and, in the case mentioned in the preceding paragraph, the respondent's written consent thereto reach the Association.

Article 5   Secretariat and clerk in charge of administrative services

1   The Association shall, promptly after accepting a request for arbitration, designate one of its offices as the secretariat in charge of administrative services and give each party, together with the notice of acceptance under article 3, paragraph 3, notice thereof.

2   The Association shall, when the arbitral tribunal has been constituted, designate one of the personnel of the Association as the clerk in charge of the clerical affairs of the arbitral tribunal (hereinafter the 'clerk in charge') and give each party and the arbitral tribunal notice thereof.

Article 6   Communications

1   Except at hearings, communications between the arbitral tribunal and a party and communications between the parties shall be done in writing through the Association.

2   The communications referred to in the preceding paragraph shall, notwithstanding the provisions of article 2 of the UNCITRAL Arbitration Rules, be deemed to have been received by the addressee when received by the Association.

Article 7   Cooperation concerning hearings and other meetings

1   The Association shall, upon request of the arbitral tribunal, cooperate with the arbitral tribunal in the coordination of scheduling for determining the time, place, etc. of hearings and other meetings, in the preparation of the hearing room, and in other matters necessary for the conduct of the arbitral proceedings.

2   If facilities other than those provided by the Association are used for a hearing, the parties shall bear the expense thereof.

Article 8   Taking of minutes of hearing

1   The clerk in charge shall, for each hearing date, take minutes setting forth the date, time, place, and names of those attending the hearing as well as a summary of the hearing and shall keep such minutes at the Association. The clerk in charge may, subject to the permission of the arbitral tribunal, make tape-recordings or video-recordings of hearings.

2   The clerk in charge shall, when the arbitral tribunal has so ordered or a party has so requested, arrange for the making of a stenographic transcript. Such order or request shall, in principle, be made not less than 21 days before the date of the hearing at which stenography is required.

3   The expense of making a stenographic transcript shall, where it is by order of the arbitral tribunal, be borne one half each by the claimant and the respondent or, where it is at a party's request, be borne by the requesting party. The arbitral tribunal may, however, in view of the circumstances, revise such shares of burden.

4   The expense of making a stenographic transcript shall not be included in the administrative fee.

Article 9   Language and interpretation/translation

1   The language or languages to be used in the arbitral proceedings shall be Japanese or English or both of them. The arbitral tribunal shall, except where the parties have agreed on one or both of these languages, promptly determine the language or languages to be used. The arbitral tribunal shall, when so determining, take into consideration whether interpretation or translation would be required and how the burden of the expense thereof would be allocated.

2   Arbitral proceedings conducted, prior to the determination of language or languages under the preceding paragraph, in a language other than the language or languages so determined shall remain valid notwithstanding the 2nd sentence of article 17, paragraph 1 of the UNCITRAL Arbitration Rules.

3   The clerk in charge shall, when the arbitral tribunal has so ordered or a party has so requested, arrange for interpretation. Such order or request shall, in principle, be made not less than 21 days before the day when interpretation is required.

4   The expense of interpretation shall, where it is by order of the arbitral tribunal, be borne one half each by the claimant and the respondent or, where it is at a party's request, be borne by the requesting party. The arbitral tribunal may, however, in view of the circumstances, revise such shares of burden.

5   The expense of interpretation shall not be included in the administrative fee.

6   The provisions of the preceding two paragraphs shall apply *mutatis mutandis* to the translation of documents.

Article 10   Service and deposit of award

1   The Association shall serve authenticated copies of the award upon the parties by hand delivery, by delivery-certified registered mail, or by any other method recognised by law.

2   Service under the preceding paragraph shall take place after the fees, costs, etc. stipulated in article 11 have been paid.

3   The Association shall, promptly after serving authenticated copies of the award, deposit the original text thereof with the competent court together with certificates of service.

Article 11   Fees and costs

1   The claimant shall, at the time of requesting the initiation of arbitral proceedings, pay a request fee and an administrative fee to the Association in accordance with its Arbitration Fee Regulations. This shall also apply where the respondent makes a counterclaim.

2   The parties shall, in accordance with the Arbitration Fee Regulations, pay the hearing fee for each hearing date on such hearing date. A party applying for alteration of the date, time, or place of a scheduled hearing shall, in accordance with the Arbitration Fee Regulations, pay the hearing schedule alteration fee for each alteration at the time of such alteration.

3   Notwithstanding the provisions of article 41, paragraphs 1 and 2 of the UNCITRAL Arbitration Rules, the Association may, as necessary, request either or both of the parties to pay all or part of the fees and costs in advance.

4   If a party fails to pay the fees or costs stipulated ih the preceding three paragraphs, the arbitral tribunal may suspend or terminate the arbitral proceedings. However, this shall not apply if the fees and costs that should have been paid by the party are paid by the other party.

5   When terminating the arbitral proceedings, the arbitral tribunal shall, in addition to fixing the amounts of the various costs referred to in article 38 of the UNCITRAL Arbitration Rules, fix the amounts of the administrative fee, the hearing fees, and the costs stipulated in these Rules as well as determining the party to bear such amounts or the manner in which the burden of such amounts should be allocated. Notwithstanding the provisions of article 41, paragraph 5 of the UNCITRAL Arbitration Rules, the Association shall make an accounting of fees and costs paid in advance and, if there is an unexpended balance, refund same to either or both of the parties.

Article 12   Other services

The Association may, upon request of the arbitral tribunal or the parties, provide such services, other than those referred to in the preceding articles, as may be deemed appropriate by the Association.

THE JCT ARBITRATION RULES (18 JULY 1988)

Rule 1   Arbitration Agreements

1   These rules are the 'JCT Arbitration' Rules' referred to in the Arbitration Agreements in:

    1   The Standard Form of Building   Article 5 and clause 41
Contract 1980 Edition, as amended

2 The Standard Forms of Employer/	Clause 10 (NSC/2)
Nominated Sub-Contractor Agreement (NSC/2	Clause 8 (NSC/2a)

and NSC/2a)1980 Edition as amended

3 The JCT Standard Forms of Nominated	Article 3 and clause 38

Sub-Contract NSC/4 and NSC/4a, 1980 Edition,
as amended

4 The JCT Warranty by a Nominated	Clause 4

Supplier (TNS/2: Schedule 3 of the JCT
Standard Form of Tender by Nominated
Supplier), as amended

5 The Standard Form of Building Contract	Article 5 and clause 39

with Contractor's Design 1981 Edition, as
amended

6 The Intermediate Form of Building	Article 5 and section 9

Contract for Works of simple content 1984
Edition, as amended

7 The Standard Form of Sub-Contract	Article 4 and clause 35

Conditions for Sub-Contractors named under the
Intermediate Form of Building Contract
(NAM/SC) 1984 Edition, as amended

8 The Standard Form of Management	Article 8 and section 9

Contract 1987 Edition, as amended

9 The Standard Form of Works	Works Contract/1,
Contract/1, and Works Contract/2) 1987 Edition	Section 3
for use with Standard Form of Management	Article 3 and Works
Contract, as amended	Contract/2 section 9

10 The Standard Form of Employer/Works	Clause 7

Contractor Agreement (Works Contract/1) 1987
Edition, as amended

11 The Agreement for Minor Building	Article 4 and clause 9

Works 1980 Edition, as amended

Rule 2   Interpretation and provisions as to time

2.1   The party who has required a dispute to be referred to arbitration is referred to as 'the Claimant'; the other party is referred to as 'the Respondent'. Where the Arbitrator has been appointed on a joint application the Arbitrator shall decide who will be the Claimant and who will be the Respondent.

2.2   The Claimant and Respondent are referred to as 'the parties' and this expression where the context so admits includes the Claimant and Respondent in any arbitration who have been joined in the proceedings under the relevant joinder provisions in the contract or sub-contract or other agreement referred to in Rule 1.

2.3   'Days' means calendar days but in computing any period of days referred to in these Rules all public holidays, the four days following Easter Monday, December 24, 27, 28, 29, 30 and 31 shall be excluded.

2.4   'Arbitration Agreement' means the relevant provisions of a contract, sub-contract or agreement under one of the contracts, sub-contracts or agreements referred to in Rule 1.

2.5   'Notification Date' means the date of notification by the Arbitrator to the parties of his acceptance of the appointment to proceed with the reference in accordance with the Arbitration Agreement and these Rules.

2.6   Where the context so admits 'award' includes as interim award.

2.7   No time required by these Rules, or by any direction of the Arbitrator, may be extended by agreement of the parties without the express written concurrence of the Arbitrator.

Rule 3   Service of statements, documents and notices—content of statements

3.1   Each party shall notify the other party and the Arbitrator of the address for service upon him of statements, documents or notices referred to in the Rules.

3.2   The service of any statements, documents or notices referred to in these Rules shall be
   by actual delivery to the other party or
   by first class post or
   where a FAX number has previously been given to the sending party, by FAX (facsimile transmission) to that number.
Where service is by FAX, for record purposes the statement, document or notice served by FAX must forthwith be sent by first class post or actually delivered.

3.3   Subject to proof to the contrary service shall be deemed to have been effected for the purpose of these Rules upon actual delivery or two days, excluding Saturdays and Sundays, after the date of posting or upon the facsimile transmission having been effected.

3.4   Any statement referred to in these Rules shall:
   be in writing
   set out the factual and legal basis relied upon and
   be served upon the other party and a copy sent to the Arbitrator.

3.5   Without prejudice to any award in respect of general damages any statement of case or of counterclaim shall so far as practicable specify the remedy which the party seeks and where a monetary sum is being sought the amount sought in respect of each and every head of claim.

Rule 4   Conduct of the arbitration—application of Rule 5, Rule 6 or Rule 7—preliminary meeting

4.1   Not later than 21 days from the Notification Date the Arbitrator shall, unless he and the parties otherwise agree, hold a preliminary meeting with the parties at such place and on such day and at such time as the Arbitrator directs.

4.2   (1)   At the preliminary meeting, or if the Arbitrator and the parties have agreed that no preliminary meeting be held then not later than 21 days from the Notification Date, the parties shall jointly decide whether Rule 5 (procedure without hearing), Rule 6 (full procedure with hearing) or, subject to Rule 4.2.2, Rule 7 (short procedure with hearing) shall apply to the conduct of the arbitration.

(2)   If the Claimant wishes Rule 7 to apply to the conduct of the arbitration he shall, within a reasonable time after the commencement of the

arbitration and at least 7 days before a decision under Rule 4.2.1 is required, formulate his case in writing in sufficient detail to identify the matters in dispute and submit that written case to the Respondent with a copy to the Arbitrator and state that at the preliminary meeting he will request the Respondent to agree that Rule 7 shall apply to the conduct of the arbitration. A preliminary meeting shall be held and if at that meeting the parties so agree the provisions of Rule 7 shall thereafter apply and the Arbitrator shall issue any necessary directions thereunder; if at that meeting the parties do not so agree the Arbitrator shall issue a direction under Rule 4.3.1 as to whether Rule 5 or Rule 6 shall apply to the conduct of the arbitration.

4.3   (1)   If the parties have not jointly decided under Rule 4.2 which Rule shall apply to the arbitration the Arbitrator shall direct that Rule 5 shall apply unless the Arbitrator having regard to any information supplied by, and/or any representations made by, the parties directs that Rule 6 shall apply.

(2)   A direction under Rule 4.3.1 shall be issued within 28 days of the Notification Date or, if a preliminary meeting has been held, not later than 7 days after the date of the preliminary meeting.

4.4   Whichever of the Rules 5, 6 or 7 applies to the conduct of the arbitration all the other Rules so far as relevant and applicable shall apply.

Rule 5   Procedure without hearing

5.1   Rule 5 applies to the conduct of the arbitration where:

(1)   the parties have so decided under Rule 4.2.1; or

(2)   the provisions of Rule 4.3.1 have come into effect and the Arbitrator has not directed that Rule 6 shall apply.

5.2   The times for service required by Rule 5.3 shall apply unless, at a preliminary meeting, or, if no preliminary meeting has been held, then within 28 days of the Notification Date, the Arbitrator, after considering any representations made by the parties, has directed any times for service different from those required by Rule 5.3 in which case the times stated in such direction shall be substituted for the times required by Rule 5.3.

5.3   (1)   The Claimant shall, within 14 days after the date when Rule 5 becomes applicable, serve a statement of case.

(2)   If the Claimant serves a statement of case within the time or times allowed by these Rules the Respondent shall, within 14 days after service of the Claimant's statement of case, serve

a statement of defence to the Claimant's statement of case; and

a statement of any counterclaim.

(3)   If the Respondent serves a statement of defence within the time or times allowed by these Rules the Claimant may, within 14 days after such service, serve a statement of reply to the defence.

(4)   If the Respondent serves a statement of counterclaim within the time or times allowed by these Rules the claimant shall, within 14 days after such service, serve a statement of defence to the Respondent's counterclaim.

(5)   If the Claimant serves a statement of defence to the Respondent's statement of counterclaim within the time or times allowed by these Rules the Respondent may, within 14 days after such service, serve a statement of reply to the defence.

(6)   The Claimant with

his statement of case and

any statement setting out a reply to the Respondent's statement of defence and

his statement of defence to any statement of counterclaim by the Respondent

and the Respondent with

his statement of defence and

any statement of counterclaim and

any statement setting out a reply to the Claimant's statement of defence to any counterclaim

shall include a list of any documents the Claimant or Respondent as the case may be considers necessary to support any part of the relevant statement and a copy of those documents identifying clearly in each document that part or parts on which reliance is or is being placed.

5.4   If a party does not serve a statement of

case, defence, reply to the defence, counterclaim, defence to the counterclaim or reply to the defence to the counterclaim

within the relevant time required by Rule 5.3 or directed under Rule 5.2 the Arbitrator shall notify the parties that he proposes to proceed on the basis that the party will not be serving the same unless within 7 days of the date of service of that notification the relevant statement is served. If within 7 days of the date of service of that notification the relevant statement is not received the Arbitrator shall proceed on the basis that that party will not be serving the same. If the relevant statement is subsequently served it shall be of no effect unless the Arbitrator is satisfied that there was a good and proper reason both why an application was not made within the time required by Rule 5.7.1 and why a statement was not served within 7 days of the service of his notice given under Rule 5.4.

5.5   If the Claimant either does not serve his statement of case within the time or times allowed by these Rules or if served it is of no effect by reason of Rule 5.4 the Arbitrator shall make an award dismissing the claim and ordering the Claimant to pay the Arbitrator's fees and expenses and any costs hitherto incurred by the Respondent.

5.6   Provided that where either party has, or the parties have, previously delivered to the Arbitrator a statement or statements setting out the matter or matters in dispute including the factual and legal basis relied upon together with the information where relevant required by Rule 3.5 and a list of any documents and a copy of those documents as required by Rule 5.3.6, the Arbitrator may direct that such statement or statements shall stand in place of all or any of the statements or documents to be delivered in compliance with the requirements of Rule 5.3.

5.7   (1)   Subject to a written application by the Claimant or Respondent for an extension of the times for service required by Rule 5.3 or directed under Rule 5.2 being served upon the Arbitrator before the expiry of the relevant time for service, the Arbitrator may in his discretion extend by direction in writing to the Claimant and the Respondent the times for service required by Rule 5.3 or directed under Rule 5.2 provided he is satisfied that the reason for the application was in respect of matters which could reasonably be considered to be outside the control of the applicant.

(2)   A copy of any written application under Rule 5.7.1 shall be served upon the other party who may, within 5 days of such service, serve written comments thereon upon the Arbitrator and serve a copy thereof upon the applicant. In exercising his discretion under rule 5.7.1 the Arbitrator shall take such written comments into account.

5.8   Where the Arbitrator considers that any document listed in any of the statements referred to in Rule 5.3 or in any statement to which Rule 5.6 refers requires further clarification by an interview with the parties or otherwise, or that some further document is essential for him properly to decide on the matters in dispute the Arbitrator may require such clarification or further document by notice in writing to the Claimant or the Respondent as appropriate and shall serve a copy of that notice upon the party not required to provide such clarification or further document. Such clarification by an interview with the parties or otherwise shall be obtained in accordance with the directions of the Arbitrator and such further document shall be supplied to the Arbitrator with a copy to the other party by the Claimant or Respondent forthwith upon receipt of the notice in writing from the Arbitrator.

5.9   (1)   The Arbitrator shall publish his award within 28 days
after receipt of the last of the statements and documents referred to in Rule 5.3 or
after the expiry of the last of the times allowed by these Rules for their service
whichever is the earlier.

(2)   The Arbitrator may decide to publish his award later than the expiry of the aforementioned 28 days period and if so he shall, prior to the expiry thereof, immediately notify the parties in writing when his award will be published.

Rule 6   Full procedure with hearing

6.1   Rule 6 applies to the conduct of the arbitration where:
(1)   the parties have so decided under Rule 4.2.1; or
(2)   the provisions of Rule 4.3.1 have come into effect and the Arbitrator has directed that Rule 6 shall apply.

6.2   Rule 6.3 shall apply except to the extent that the Arbitrator otherwise directs or, subject to Rule 2.7, the parties otherwise agree.

6.3   (1)   The Claimant shall, within 28 days after the date when Rule 6 becomes applicable, serve a statement of case.

(2)   If the Claimant serves a statement of case within the time or times allowed by these Rules the Respondent shall, within 28 days after service of the Claimant's statement of case, serve
a statement of defence to the Claimant's statement of case; and
a statement of any counterclaim.

(3)   If the Respondent serves a statement of defence within the time or times allowed by these Rules the Claimant may, within 14 days after such service, serve a statement of reply to the defence.

(4)   If the Respondent serves a statement of counterclaim within the time or times allowed by these Rules the Claimant shall, within 28 days after such service, serve a statement of defence to the Respondent's counterclaim.

(5)   If the Claimant serves a statement of defence to the Respondent's statement of counterclaim within the time or times allowed by these Rules the Respondent may, within 14 days after such service, serve a statement of reply to the defence.

(6)   The Claimant with

his statement of case and

any statement setting out a reply to the Respondent's statement of defence and

his statement of defence to any statement of counterclaim by the Respondent

and the Respondent with

his statement of defence and

any statement of counterclaim and

any statement setting out a reply to the claimant's statement of defence to any counterclaim

shall include a list of any documents the Claimant or Respondent as the case may be considers necessary to support any part of the relevant statement and a copy of the principal documents on which reliance will be placed identifying clearly in each document the relevant part or parts on which reliance will be placed.

6.4   If a party does not serve a statement of case, defence, reply to the defence, counterclaim, defence to the counterclaim or reply to the defence to the counterclaim within the relevant time required by Rule 6.3 or directed or agreed under Rule 6.2 the Arbitrator shall notify the parties that he proposes to proceed on the basis that the party will not be serving the same unless within 7 days of the date of service of that notification the relevant statement is served. If within 7 days of the date of service of that notification the relevant statement is not received the Arbitrator shall proceed on the basis that the party will not be serving the same. If the relevant statement is subsequently served it shall be of no effect unless the Arbitrator is satisfied that there was a good and proper reason both why an application was not made within the time required by Rule 6.7.1 and why a statement was not served within 7 days of his notice given under Rule 6.4.

6.5   If the Claimant either does not serve his statement of case within the time or times allowed by these Rules or if served it is of no effect by reason of Rule 6.4 the Arbitrator shall make an award dismissing the claim and ordering the Claimant to pay the Arbitrator's fees and expenses and any costs hitherto incurred by the Respondent.

6.6   Provided that where either party has, or the parties have, previously delivered to the Arbitration a statement or statements setting out the matter or matters in dispute including the factual and legal basis relied upon together with the information where relevant required by Rule 3.5 and a list of any documents and a copy of the principal documents as required by Rule 6.3.6, the Arbitrator may direct that such statement or statements shall stand in place of all or any of the statements or documents to be delivered in compliance with Rule 6.3.

6.7   (1)   Subject to a written application by the Claimant or Respondent for an extension of the times for service required by Rule 6.3 or directed or agreed under Rule 6.2 being served upon the Arbitrator before the expiry of the relevant time for service, the Arbitrator may in his discretion extend by direction in writing to the Claimant and the Respondent the times for service required by Rule 6.3 or directed or agreed under Rule 6.2.

(2) A copy of any written application under Rule 6.7.1 shall be served upon the other party who may, within 5 days of such service, serve written comments thereon upon the Arbitrator and serve a copy thereof upon the applicant. In exercising his discretion under Rule 6.7.1 the Arbitrator shall take such written comments into account.

6.8 The Arbitrator shall, after receipt of the last of the statements and documents referred to in Rule 6.3 or after the expiry of the last of the times allowed by these Rules for their service, whichever is the earlier, after consultation with the parties, notify the parties in writing of the date(s) when and the place where the oral hearing will be held. The Arbitrator shall immediately notify the parties in writing of any change in such date(s) or place.

6.9 (1) The Arbitrator shall publish his award within 28 days of the close of the hearing.

(2) The Arbitrator may decide to publish his award later than the expiry of the aforementioned 28 day period and if so he shall, prior to the expiry thereof, immediately notify the parties in writing when his award will be published.

Rule 7   Short procedure with hearing

7.1 (1) Rule 7 applies to the conduct of the arbitration where the parties have so decided under Rule 4.2.2.

(2) Each party shall bear his own costs unless for special reasons the Arbitrator at his discretion otherwise directs.

7.2 Within 21 days of the date when Rule 7 has become applicable the hearing shall be held at such place and on such day and at such time as the Arbitrator shall direct. No evidence except the documents referred to in Rule 7.3 may be adduced at the hearing except as the Arbitrator may otherwise direct or allow.

7.3 (1) Not later than 7 days before the hearing documents necessary to support the oral submissions and the relevant part or parts thereof shall be identified to the other party and a copy of any such document not in the possession of the other party shall be served upon that party.

(2) A copy of the documents referred to in Rule 7.3.1 shall be served upon the Arbitrator 7 days before the hearing and shall be available at the hearing.

7.4 The Arbitrator may direct that such procedures shall be followed at the hearing and such documents made available as he considers necessary for the just and expeditious determination of the dispute.

7.5 At the end of the hearing the Arbitrator shall

either   thereupon make his award and if made orally shall forth-
                with confirm his award in writing

or   publish his award within 7 days of the hearing.

The Arbitrator may decide to publish his award later than the expiry of the aforementioned 7 day period and if so, he shall, prior to the expiry thereof, immediately notify the parties in writing when his award will be published.

Rule 8 Inspection by Arbitrator

8.1 The Arbitrator may inspect any relevant work, goods or materials whether on the site or elsewhere. Such inspection shall not be treated as a hearing of the dispute.

8.2 Where under Rule 8.1 the Arbitrator has decided that he will inspect:

where Rule 5 applies, as soon as the parties have served all their written statements or the last of the times for such service allowed by these Rules has expired the Arbitrator shall fix a date not more than 10 days in advance for his inspection and inform the parties of the date and time selected;

where Rule 6 or Rule 7 applies, the Arbitrator shall fix a date for his inspection and shall inform the parties of the date and time selected.

8.3 (1) The Arbitrator may require the Claimant or the Respondent, or a person appointed on behalf of either of them, to attend the inspection solely for the purpose of identifying relevant work, goods or materials.

(2) No other person may attend the Arbitrator's inspection unless the Arbitrator shall otherwise direct.

Rule 9 Arbitrator's fees and expenses—costs

9.1 From the Notification Date the parties shall be jointly and severally liable to the Arbitrator for the payment of his fees and expenses.

9.2 In an arbitration which continues for more than 3 months after the Notification Date the Arbitrator shall be entitled to render fee notes at no less than 3-monthly intervals and the same shall be payable 14 days after delivery.

9.3 The Arbitrator shall, unless the parties inform him that they have otherwise agreed, include in his award his decision on the liability of the parties as between themselves for the payment of his fees and expenses and, subject to Rule 7.1.2, on the payment by one party of any costs of the other party.

9.4 The Claimant shall, unless the Respondent has previously done so, take up an award of the Arbitrator and pay his fees and expenses (or any balance thereof if Rule 9.2 has applied) within 10 days of the notification given by the Arbitrator to the parties of publication of the award as provided in Rule 11.3.

Rule 10 Payment to trustee-stakeholder

10.1 If the Arbitrator publishes an award in favour of the Claimant before he has published his award on all matters in a counterclaim by the Respondent, the Arbitrator upon application by the Claimant or the Respondent and after considering any representations by the parties may direct that the whole or a part of the amount so awarded shall be deposited by the Respondent with a deposit-taking bank to hold as a trustee-stakeholder (as described in Rule 10.3) pending a direction of the Arbitrator under Rule 10.2.1 or of the parties under Rule 10.2.2 or of the court under Rule 10.2.3.

10.2 The trustee-stakeholder shall hold any amount deposited as a result of a direction of the Arbitrator under Rule 10.1 in trust for the parties until such time as either

(1)   the Arbitrator shall direct the trustee-stakeholder (whether as a result of his award or as a result of an agreement between the parties reported to the Arbitrator or otherwise) to whom the amount deposited, including any interest accrued thereon, should be paid by the trustee-stakeholder; or

(2)   if the Arbitrator is deceased or otherwise unable to issue any direction to the trustee-stakeholder under Rule 10.2.1 and the Arbitrator has not been replaced, the parties in a joint letter signed by or on behalf of each of them direct the trustee-stakeholder to whom the amount deposited, including any interest accrued thereon, should be paid by the trustee-stakeholder; or

(3)   a court of competent jurisdiction gives directions.

10.3   An amount so deposited may, notwithstanding the trust imposed, be held by the trustee-stakeholder as an ordinary bank deposit to the credit of the bank as a trustee-stakeholder in respect of the party making the deposit pursuant to a direction of the Arbitrator under Rule 10.1 and in respect of such deposit the trustee-stakeholder shall pay such usual interest which shall accrue to and form part of the deposit subject to the right of the trustee-stakeholder to deduct its reasonable and proper charges and, if deductible, any tax in respect of such interest from the amount deposited.

Rule 11   The award

11.1   The Arbitrator shall only give reasons for his award where and to the extent required by either party by notice in writing to the Arbitrator with a copy to the other party.

11.2   (1)   The Arbitrator may from time to time publish an interim award.

(2)   If in any interim award the parties are directed to seek agreement on an amount or amounts due but such agreement is not reached by the parties within 28 days of receipt of that award (or within such other lesser or greater period as the Arbitrator may direct) the Arbitrator shall, on the basis of such further appropriate evidence or submissions as he may require, publish a further award on the amount due in respect of any liability or liabilities set out in the interim award.

11.3   On publishing an award the Arbitrator shall simultaneously send to the parties by first class post, a notification that his award is published and of the amount of his fees and expenses (or any balance thereof if Rule 9.2 has applied).

11.4   An Arbitrator's award can be taken up by either party on payment to the Arbitrator of his fees and expenses. The Arbitrator shall forthwith deliver the original award to the party who paid his fees and expenses and shall simultaneously send a certified copy of the award to the other party.

11.5   If, before an award is published, the parties agree on a settlement of the dispute the parties shall so notify the Arbitrator. The Arbitrator shall issue an order for the termination of the arbitration or, if requested by both parties and accepted by the Arbitrator, record the settlement in the form of a consent award. The Arbitrator's fees and expenses shall be paid upon notification that such order or consent award is ready for taking up and on payment thereof the Arbitrator shall be discharged and the reference to arbitration concluded.

Rule 12   Powers of Arbitrator

12.1   In addition to any powers conferred by law, the Arbitrator shall have the following powers:

(1)   after consultation with the parties to take legal or technical advice on any matter arising out of or in connection with the arbitration;

(2)   to give directions for protecting, storing, securing or disposing of property the subject of the dispute, at the expense of the parties or of either of them;

(3)   to order that the Claimant or Counter-Claimant give security for the costs of the arbitration or any part thereof, and/or for the fees and expenses of the Arbitrator, in such form and of such amount as the Arbitrator may determine;

(4)   to proceed in the absence of a party or his representative provided that reasonable notice of the Arbitrator's intention to proceed has been given to that party in accordance with the provisions of these Rules, including if there is to be a hearing, notice of the date and place thereof;

(5)   at his discretion to direct that the costs, if not agreed, shall be taxed by the Arbitrator;

(6)   to direct the giving of evidence by affidavit;

(7)   to order any party to produce to the Arbitrator, and to the other party for inspection, and to supply copies of, any documents or classes of documents in the possession power or custody of the party which the Arbitrator determines to be relevant.

12.2   Subject to the Arbitration Acts 1950 to 1979 any non-compliance by the Arbitrator with these Rules, including those relating to time, shall not of itself affect the validity of an award.

12.3   If during the arbitration it appears to the Arbitrator to be necessary for the just and expeditious determination of the dispute that a Rule for the conduct of the arbitration other than that previously applicable shall apply, the Arbitrator, after considering any representations made by the parties, may so direct and shall give such further directions as he may deem appropriate.

LONDON COURT OF INTERNATIONAL ARBITRATION

London Court of International Arbitration
12 Carthusian St.,
London EC1M 6EB
Tel: +44 71 417 8228
+44 71 417 8404
(Correspondence should be addressed to the Registrar.)

RECOMMENDED CLAUSES FOR CONTRACTS

Alternative clauses are set out for:
— arbitration under the LCIA Rules
— arbitration under the UNCITRAL Rules
— conciliation under the UNCITRAL Rules
— combined conciliation and arbitration

Future Disputes

Parties to an international contract who wish to have any future disputes referred to LCIA administered arbitration, conciliation or a combination of both, are recommended to insert one of the following clauses in the contract:

A   LCIA Arbitration Rules

'Any dispute arising out of or in connection with this contract, including any question regarding its existence, validity or termination, shall be referred to and finally resolved by arbitration under the Rules of the London Court of International Arbitration, which Rules are deemed to be incorporated by reference into this clause.

  (i)   The number of arbitrators shall be ... (one or three)
  (ii)   The place of arbitration shall be ... (City or Country)
  (iii)   The language to be used in the arbitral proceedings shall be . . .
  (iv)   The governing law of the contract shall be the substantive law
of . . .'

B   UNCITRAL Arbitration Rules

'Any dispute, controversy or claim arising out of or relating to the contract, or the breach, termination or invalidity thereof, shall be settled by arbitration in accordance with the UNCITRAL Arbitration Rules as at present in force.

  (i)   Any such arbitration shall be administered by the London Court of International Arbitration (LCIA)
  (ii)   The standard LCIA administrative procedures and Schedule of Costs in force at the time of the arbitration shall apply
  (iii)   The appointing authority shall be the LCIA
  (iv)   The number of arbitrators shall be ... (one or three)
  (v)   The place of arbitration shall be ... (City or Country)
  (vi)   The language to be used in the arbitral proceedings shall be . . .
  (vii)   The governing law of the contract shall be the substantive law
of . . .'

C   UNCITRAL Conciliation Rules

'Where, in the event of a dispute arising out of or relating to this contract, the parties wish to seek amicable settlement of that dispute by conciliation, the conciliation shall take place in accordance with the UNCITRAL Conciliation Rules at present in force.

  (i)   Any such conciliation shall be administered by the London Court of International Arbitration (LCIA)
  (ii)   The standard LCIA administrative procedures and Schedule of Costs in force at the time of the conciliation shall apply
  (iii)   The appointing authority shall be the LCIA
  (iv)   The number of conciliators shall be . . . (one, two or three).'

D   Combined Clause

'If a dispute arises out of or in connection with this contract, including any question as to its existence, validity or termination, the parties agree to first seek amicable settlement by conciliation under the UNCITRAL Conciliation Rules administered by the London Court of International Arbitration.

In the event of the dispute not being settled within . . . days, or such further period as the parties shall agree in writing, after the appointment of the conciliator, the dispute shall be referred to and finally resolved by arbitration under the Rules of the London Court of International Arbitration

(alternatively under the UNCITRAL Arbitration Rules administered by the LCIA)
which Rules are deemed to be incorporated by reference into this clause.
   (i)   The appointing authority shall be the LCIA
   (ii)   The number of arbitrators shall be . . . (one or three)
   (iii)   The place of arbitration shall be . . . (City or Country)
   (iv)   The language to be used in the arbitral proceedings shall be . . .
   (v)   The governing law of the contract shall be the substantive law
of . . .'

Existing Disputes

If a dispute has arisen when the contract or agreement does not contain an arbitration or conciliation clause, or when the parties wish to change a clause to provide for LCIA administered arbitration or conciliation, the following forms of agreement are recommended, to be selected as appropriate:

E   Arbitration

'A dispute having arisen between the parties concerning . . . the parties hereby agree that the matter shall be referred to and finally resolved by arbitration under the Rules of the London Court of International Arbitration

(alternatively under the UNCITRAL Arbitration Rules administered by the LCIA)
   (i)   The appointing authority shall be the LCIA
   (ii)   The number of arbitrators shall be . . . (one or three)
   (iii)   The place of arbitration shall be . . . (City or Country)
   (iv)   The language to be used in the arbitral proceedings shall be . . .
   (v)   The governing law of the agreement/contract shall be the substantive law of . . . '

F   Conciliation

'A dispute having arisen between the parties concerning . . . the parties hereby agree to seek an amicable settlement by conciliation under the UNCITRAL Conciliation Rules administered by the London Court of International Arbitration.

(i)   The standard LCIA administered procedures and Schedule of Costs shall apply

(ii)   The appointing authority shall be the LCIA

(iii)   The number of conciliators shall be . . . (one, two or three).'

G   Combined Clause

'A dispute having arisen between the parties concerning . . . the parties hereby agree to first seek an amicable settlement by conciliation under the UNCITRAL Conciliation Rules administered by the London Court of International Arbitration.

In the event of the dispute not being settled within . . . days after the appointment of the conciliator, the dispute shall be referred to and finally resolved by arbitration under the Rules of the London Court of International Arbitration

(alternatively under the UNCITRAL Arbitration Rules administered by the LCIA)

(i)   The appointing authority shall be the LCIA

(ii)   The number of arbitrators shall be . . . (one or three)

(iii)   The place of arbitration shall be . . . (City or Country)

(iv)   The language to be used in the arbitral proceedings shall be . . .

(v)   The governing law of the agreement/contract shall be the substantive law of . . .'

LCIA RULES

effective from 1 January 1985

Where any agreement, submission or reference provides for arbitration under the Rules of the London Court of International Arbitration (the LCIA), the parties shall be taken to have agreed that the arbitration shall be conducted in accordance with the following Rules, or such amended Rules as the Court may have adopted to take effect before the commencement of the arbitration.

The Arbitration Court of the LCIA, in these Rules called 'The Court', has the function of ensuring the application of the Rules.

Article 1   Request for arbitration

Any party wishing to commence an arbitration under these Rules ('the Claimant') shall send to the Registrar of the Court ('the Registrar') a written request for arbitration ('the Request') which shall include, or be accompanied by:

(a)   the names and addresses of the parties to the arbitration;

(b)   copies of the contractual documents in which the arbitration clause is contained or under which the arbitration arises;

(c)   a brief statement describing the nature and circumstances of the dispute, and specifying the relief claimed;

(d)   a statement of any matters (such as the place or language of the arbitration, or the number of arbitrators, or their qualifications or identities) on which the parties have already agreed in relation to the conduct of the arbitration, or with respect to which the requesting party wishes to make a proposal;

(e)   if the arbitration agreement calls for party nomination of arbitrators, the name and address (and telephone and telex numbers, if known) of the Claimant's nominee;

(f)   the fee prescribed in the Schedule of Costs;

and shall confirm to the Registrar that copies have been served on the other parties. The date of receipt by the Registrar of the Request for Arbitration shall be deemed to be the date on which the arbitration has commenced.

Article 2   Response by respondent

2.1   For the purpose of facilitating the choice of arbitrators, within 30 days of receipt of its copy of the Request for Arbitration the Respondent may send to the Registrar a Response containing:

(a)   confirmation or denial of all or part of the claims;

(b)   a brief statement of the nature and circumstances of any envisaged counterclaims;

(c)   comment in response to any statements contained in the Request, as called for under Article 1(d), on matters relating to the conduct of the arbitration;

(d)   if the arbitration agreement calls for party nomination of arbitrators, the name and address (and telephone and telex numbers if known) of the Respondent's nominee;

and shall confirm to the Registrar that copies have been served on the other parties.

2.2   Failure to send a Response shall not preclude the Respondent from denying the claim nor from setting out a counterclaim in its Statement of Defence. However, if the arbitration agreement calls for party nomination of arbitrators, failure to send a Response or to nominate an arbitrator in it shall constitute a waiver of the opportunity to nominate an arbitrator.

Article 3   The arbitral tribunal

3.1   In these Rules, the expression 'the Tribunal' includes a sole arbitrator or all the arbitrators where more than one is appointed. All arbitrators (whether or not nominated by the parties) conducting an arbitration under these Rules shall be and remain at all times wholly independent and impartial, and shall not act as advocates for any party. Before appointment by the Court, if the Registrar so requests, any arbitrator shall furnish a resumé of his past and present professional positions (which will be communicated to the parties). In any event every arbitrator shall sign a declaration to the effect that there are no circumstances likely to give rise to any justified doubts as to his impartiality or independence, and that he will forthwith disclose any such circumstances to the Court and to all the parties if they should arise after that time and before the arbitration is concluded.

3.2   The Court will appoint the Tribunal to determine the dispute as soon as practicable after receipt by the Registrar of the Response, or after the expiry of 30 days following receipt by the Respondent of the Request if no Response is received, provided that the Registrar is satisfied that the Request has been properly served. A sole arbitrator will be appointed unless the parties have agreed otherwise, or unless the Court determines that in view of all the circumstances of the case a three-member tribunal is appropriate.

3.3   The Court alone is empowered to appoint arbitrators and such appointment will be made in the name of the Court by the President or any Vice President of the Court. The Court will appoint arbitrators with due regard for any particular method or criteria of selection agreed by the parties. In selecting arbitrators consideration will be given, so far as possible, to the nature of the contract, the nature and circumstances of the dispute, and the nationality, location and languages of the parties. Where the parties are of different nationalities, then unless they have agreed otherwise, sole arbitrators or chairmen are not to be appointed if they have the same nationality as any party (the nationality of parties being understood to include that of controlling shareholders or interests). If the parties have agreed that they are to nominate arbitrators themselves, or to allow two arbitrators, or a third party, to nominate an arbitrator, the Court may refuse to appoint such nominees if it determines that they are not suitable or independent or impartial. In the case of a three-member Tribunal the Court will designate the Chairman, who will not be a party-nominated abitrator.

3.4   If the arbitration agreement calls for party nominations, and the Respondent fails to make such a nomination within the time limit established by Article 2, the Court will forthwith appoint an arbitrator in place of the arbitrator to be nominated by the Respondent. If the Request does not contain a nomination by the Claimant, and the Claimant fails to make such a nomination with the same time limit, the Court will likewise make that appointment.

3.5   In the event that the Court determines that a nominee is not suitable or independent or impartial, or if an appointed arbitrator is to be replaced, the Court shall have discretion to decide whether or not to follow the original nominating process. If it so decides any opportunity for renomination shall be waived if not exercised within 30 days, after which the Court shall appoint the replacement as soon as practicable.

3.6   If any arbitrator, after appointment, dies, refuses, or in the opinion of the Court becomes unable or unfit to act, the Court will, upon request by a party or by the remaining arbitrators, appoint another arbitrator in accordance with the provisions of Article 3.5. If in the opinion of the Court an arbitrator acts in manifest violation of these Rules, or does not conduct the proceedings with reasonable diligence, he will be considered unfit.

3.7   An arbitrator may be challenged if circumstances exist that give rise to justifiable doubts as to his impartiality or independence. A party may challenge an arbitrator it has nominated, or in whose appointment it has participated, only for reasons of which it becomes aware after the appointment has been made.

3.8   A party who intends to challenge an arbitrator shall, within fifteen days of the constitution of the Tribunal or after becoming aware of any circumstances referred to in Article 3.6 or 3.7, whichever is the later, send a written statement of the reasons for the challenge to the Court. Unless the challenged arbitrator withdraws or the other party agrees to the challenge within 15 days of receipt of the written statement of challenge, the Court shall decide on the challenge.

3.9 The decision of the Court with respect to all matters referred to in this Article shall be final. Such decisions are deemed to be administrative in nature, and the Court shall not be required to give reasons for them. To the extent permitted by the law of the place of arbitration the parties shall be taken to have waived any right of appeal in respect of any such decisions to a court of law or other judicial authority. If such appeals remain possible due to mandatory provisions of the law of the place of arbitration, the Court shall, subject to the provisions of the applicable law, decide whether the arbitral proceedings are to continue notwithstanding an appeal.

Article 4   Communications between parties and the Tribunal

4.1 Until the Tribunal is finally constituted and the Court determines that it would be appropriate for the parties and the Tribunal to communicate directly, all communications between parties and arbitrators shall be made through the Registrar. If and when the Court directs that communication shall take place directly between the Tribunal and the parties (with simultaneous copies to the Registrar) all further reference in these Rules to the Registrar shall thereafter be read as references to the Tribunal.

4.2 Where the Registrar, on behalf of the Tribunal, sends any communication to one party, he shall send a copy to each of the other parties.

4.3 Where any party sends any communication (including Statements under Article 6) to the Registrar, it shall include a copy for each arbitrator, and it shall also send copies to all the other parties and confirm to the Registrar in writing that it has done so.

4.4 The addresses of the parties for the purpose of all communications during the proceedings shall be those set out in the Request, or as any party may at any time notify to the Registrar and to the other parties.

Article 5   Conduct of the proceedings

5.1 The parties may agree on the arbitral procedure, and are encouraged to do so.

5.2 In the absence of procedural rules agreed by the parties or contained herein, the Tribunal shall have the widest discretion allowed under such law as may be applicable to ensure the just, expeditious, economical, and final determination of the dispute.

5.3 In the case of a three-member tribunal the Chairman may, after consulting the other arbitrators, make procedural rulings alone.

Article 6   Submission of written statements and documents

6.1 Subject to any procedural rules agreed by the parties or determined by the Tribunal under Article 5, the written stage of the proceedings shall be as set out in this Article.

6.2 Within 30 days of receipt of notification from the Court of the appointment of the Tribunal, the Claimant shall send to the Registrar a Statement of Case setting out in sufficient detail the facts and any contentions of law on which it relies, and the relief claimed.

6.3   Within 40 days of receipt of the Statement of Case, the Respondent shall send to the Registrar a Statement of Defence stating in sufficient detail which of the facts and contentions of law in the Statement of Case it admits or denies, on what grounds, and on what other facts and contentions of law it relies. Any counterclaims shall be submitted with the Statement of Defence in the same manner as claims are set out in the Statement of Case.

6.4   Within 40 days of receipt of the Statement of Defence, the Claimant may send to the Registrar a Statement of Reply which, where there are counterclaims, shall include a Defence to Counterclaims.

6.5   If the Statement of Reply contains a Defence to Counterclaims, the Respondent has a further 40 days to send to the Registrar a Statement of Reply regarding Counterclaims.

6.6   All Statements referred to in this Article shall be accompanied by copies (or, if they are especially voluminous, lists) of all essential documents on which the party concerned relies and which have not previously been submitted by any party, and (where appropriate) by any relevant samples.

6.7   As soon as practicable following completion of the submission of the Statements specified in this Article, the Tribunal shall proceed in such manner as has been agreed by the parties, or pursuant to its authority under these Rules. If the Respondent fails to submit a Statement of Defence, or if at any point any party fails to avail itself of the opportunity to present its case in the manner directed by the Tribunal, the Tribunal may nevertheless proceed with the arbitration and make the award.

Article 7   Place of arbitration

7.1   The parties may choose the place of arbitration. Failing such a choice, the place of arbitration shall be London, unless the Tribunal determines in view of all the circumstances of the case that another place is more appropriate.

7.2   The Tribunal may hold hearings and meetings anywhere convenient, subject to the provisions of Article 10.2, and provided that the award shall be made at the place of arbitration.

Article 8   Language of arbitration

8.1   The language(s) of the arbitration shall be that of the document(s) containing the arbitration agreement, unless the parties have agreed otherwise.

8.2   If a document is drawn up in a language other than the language(s) of the arbitration, and no translation of such document is submitted by the party producing the document, The Tribunal, or if the Tribunal has not been appointed the Court, may order that party to submit a translation in a form to be determined by the Tribunal or the Court.

Article 9   Party representatives

Any party may be represented by legal practitioners or any other representatives, subject to such proof of authority as the Tribunal may require.

Article 10   Hearings

10.1   Any party has the right to be heard before the Tribunal, unless the parties have agreed on documents-only arbitration.

10.2   The Tribunal shall fix the date, time and place of any meetings and hearings in the arbitration, and the Registrar shall give the parties reasonable notice thereof.

10.3   The Tribunal may in advance of hearings submit to the parties a list of questions which it wishes them to treat with special attention.

10.4   All meetings and hearings shall be in private unless the parties agree otherwise.

Article 11   Witnesses

11.1   Before any hearing, the Tribunal may require any party to give notice of the identity of witnesses it wishes to call, as well as the subject matter of their testimony and its relevance to the issues.

11.2   The Tribunal has discretion to allow, refuse, or limit the appearance of witnesses, whether witnesses of fact or expert witnesses.

11.3   Any witness who gives oral evidence may be questioned by each of the parties or their legal practitioners, under the control of the Tribunal. The Tribunal may put questions at any stage of the examination of the witnesses.

11.4   The testimony of witnesses may be presented in written form, either as signed statements or by duly sworn affidavits. Subject to Article 11.2 any party may request that such a witness should attend for oral examination at a hearing. If he fails to attend, the Tribunal may place such weight on the written testimony as it thinks fit, or exclude it altogether.

11.5   Subject to the mandatory provisions of any applicable law it shall be proper for any party or its legal practitioners to interview any witness or potential witness prior to his appearance at any hearing.

Article 12   Experts appointed by the Tribunal

12.1   Unless otherwise agreed by the parties, the Tribunal:

(a)   may appoint one or more experts to report to the Tribunal on specific issues;

(b)   may require a party to give any such expert any relevant information or to produce, or to provide access to, any relevant documents, goods or property for inspection by the expert.

12.2   Unless otherwise agreed by the parties, if a party so requests or if the Tribunal considers it necessary, the expert shall, after delivery of his written or oral report, participate in a hearing at which the parties shall have the opportunity to question him, and to present expert witnesses in order to testify on the points at issue.

Article 13   Additional powers of the Tribunal

13.1   Unless the parties at any time agree otherwise, and subject to any mandatory limitations of any applicable law, the Tribunal shall have the power, on the application of any party or of its own motion, but in either case only after giving the parties a proper opportunity to state their views, to:

(a)   determine what are the rules of law governing or applicable to any contract, or arbitration agreement or issue between the parties;

(b)   order the correction of any such contract or arbitration agreement, but only to the extent required to rectify any mistake which it determines to be common to all the parties and then only if and to the extent to which the rules of law governing or applicable to the contract permit such correction;

(c)   allow other parties to be joined in the arbitration with their express consent, and make a single final award determining all disputes between them;

(d)   allow any party, upon such terms (as to costs and otherwise) as it shall determine, to amend claims or counterclaims;

(e)   extend or abbreviate any time limits provided by these Rules or by its directions;

(f)   conduct such enquiries as may appear to the Tribunal to be necessary or expedient;

(g)   order the parties to make any property or thing available for inspection, in their presence, by the Tribunal or any expert;

(h)   order the preservation, storage, sale or other disposal of any property or thing under the control of any party;

(i)   order any party to produce to the Tribunal, and to the other parties for inspection, and to supply copies of, any documents or classes of documents in their possession or power which the Tribunal determines to be relevant.

13.2   By agreeing to arbitration under these Rules the parties shall be taken to have agreed to apply only to the Tribunal, and not to any court of law or other judicial authority, for an order under paragraphs (g), (h) or (i) of Article 13.1.

Article 14   Jurisdiction of the tribunal

14.1   The Tribunal shall have the power to rule on its own jurisdiction, including any objections with respect to the existence or validity of the arbitration agreement. For that purpose, an arbitration clause which forms part of a contract shall be treated as an agreement independent of the other terms of the contract. A decision by the Tribunal that the contract is null and void shall not entail ipso jure the invalidity of the arbitration clause.

14.2   A plea that the Tribunal does not have jurisdiction shall be raised not later than in the Statement of Defence. A plea that the Tribunal is exceeding the scope of its authority shall be raised promptly after the Tribunal has indicated its intention to decide on the matter alleged to be beyond the scope of its authority. In either case the Tribunal may nevertheless admit a late plea under this paragraph if it considers the delay justified.

14.3   In addition to the jurisdiction to exercise the powers defined elsewhere in these Rules, the Tribunal shall have jurisdiction to determine any question of law arising in the arbitration; proceed in the arbitration notwithstanding the failure or refusal of any party to comply with these Rules or with the Tribunal's orders or directions, or to attend any meeting or hearing, but only after giving that party written notice that it intends to do so; and to receive and take into account such written or oral evidence as it shall determine to be relevant, whether or not strictly admissible in law.

Article 15   Deposits and security

15.1   The Tribunal may direct the parties, in such proportions as it deems just, and subject to the confirmation of the Court that the amounts are in conformity with the Schedule of Costs, to make one or several interim or final payments on account of the costs of the arbitration. Such deposits shall be made to and held by the Court to the order of the Chairman of the Tribunal or sole arbitrator, and may be drawn from as required by the Tribunal. Interest on sums deposited, if any, shall be accumulated to the deposits.

15.2   The Tribunal shall have the power to order any party to provide security for the legal or other costs of any other party by way of deposit or bank guarantee or in any other manner the Tribunal thinks fit.

15.3   By agreeing to arbitration under these Rules the parties shall be taken to have agreed to apply only to the Tribunal, and not to any court of law or other judicial authority, for an order under Article 15.1, or for an order for security for costs under Article 15.2.

15.4   Without prejudice to the right of any party to apply to a competent court for pre-award conservatory measures (except those referred to in Articles 15.1 and 15.2), the Tribunal shall also have the power to order any party to provide security for all or part of any amount in dispute in the arbitration.

15.5   In the event that orders under paragraphs 1, 2 and 4 of this Article are not complied with, the Tribunal may disregard claims or counterclaims by the non-complying party, although it may proceed to determine claims or counterclaims by complying parties.

Article 16   The award

16.1   The Tribunal shall make its award in writing and, unless all the parties agree otherwise, shall state the reasons upon which its award is based. The award shall state its date and shall be signed by the arbitrator or arbitrators.

16.2   If any arbitrator refuses or fails to comply with the mandatory provisions of any applicable law relating to the making of the award, having been given a reasonable opportunity to do so, the remaining arbitrators shall proceed in his absence.

16.3   Where there is more than one arbitrator and they fail to agree on any issue, they shall decide by a majority. Failing a majority decision on any issue, the Chairman of the Tribunal shall make the award alone as if he were sole arbitrator. If an arbitrator refuses or fails to sign the award, the signatures of the majority shall be sufficient, provided that the reason for the omitted signature is stated.

16.4   The sole arbitrator or chairman shall be responsible for delivering the award to the Court, which shall transmit certified copies to the parties provided that the costs of the arbitration have been paid to the Court in accordance with Article 18.

16.5   Awards may be expressed in any currency, and the Tribunal may award that simple or compound interest shall be paid by any party on any sum which is the subject of the reference at such rates as the Tribunal determines to be appropriate, without being bound by legal rates of interest, in respect of any period which the Tribunal determines to be appropriate ending not later than the date upon which the award is complied with.

16.6   The Tribunal may make separate final awards on different issues at different times, which shall be subject to correction under the procedure specified in Article 17. Such awards shall be enforceable.

16.7   In the event of a settlement, the Tribunal may render an award recording the settlement if any party so requests. If the parties do not require a consent award, then on confirmation in writing by the parties to the Court that a settlement has been reached the Tribunal shall be discharged and the reference to arbitration concluded, subject to payment by the parties of any outstanding costs of the arbitration in accordance with Article 18.

16.8   By agreeing to arbitration under these Rules, the parties undertake to carry out the award without delay, and waive their right to any form of appeal or recourse to a court of law or other judicial authority, insofar as such waiver may be validly made. Awards shall be final and binding on the parties as from the date they are made.

Article 17   Correction of awards and additional awards

17.1   Within thirty days of receipt of the award, unless another period of time has been agreed upon by the parties, a party may by notice to the Registrar request the Tribunal to correct in the award any errors in computation, any clerical or typographical errors or any errors of a similar nature. If the Tribunal considers the request to be justified, it shall make the corrections within thirty days of receipt of the request. Any correction, which shall take the form of a separate memorandum, shall become part of the award.

17.2   The Tribunal may correct any error of the type referred to in Article 17.1 on its own initiative within thirty days of the date of the award.

17.3   Unless otherwise agreed by the parties, a party may, within thirty days of receipt of the award, and with notice to the other party or parties, request the Tribunal to make an additional award as to claims presented in the arbitral proceedings but not dealt with in the award. If the Tribunal considers the request to be justified, it shall make the additional award within sixty days.

17.4   The provisions of Article 16 shall apply mutatis mutandis to a correction of the award and to any additional award.

Article 18   Costs

18.1   The costs of the arbitration (other than the legal or other costs incurred by the parties themselves) shall be in accordance with the Schedule of Costs applicable to these Rules as of the date of the Request for Arbitration.

18.2   The Tribunal shall specify in the award the total amount of the costs of the arbitration, subject to the confirmation of the Court that the amount is in conformity with the Schedule of Costs. Unless the parties shall agree otherwise, the Tribunal shall determine the proportions in which the parties shall pay all or part of them to the Court. If the Tribunal has determined that all or any part of the costs of the arbitration shall be paid by any party other than a party which has already paid them to the Court, the latter shall have the right to recover the appropriate amount from the former.

18.3   The Tribunal shall have the authority to order in its award that all or a part of the legal or other costs of a party (apart from the costs of the arbitration) be paid by another party.

18.4   If the arbitration is abandoned, suspended or concluded, by agreement or otherwise, before the final award is made, the parties shall be jointly and severally liable to pay to the Court the costs of the arbitration as determined by the Tribunal, subject to the confirmation by the Court that the amount is in conformity with the Schedule of Costs. In the event that the costs so determined are less than the deposits made, there shall be a refund in such proportions as the parties may agree, or, failing agreement, in the same proportions as the deposits were made.

Article 19   Exclusion of liability

19.1   Neither the court nor any arbitrator shall be liable to any party for any act or omission in connection with any arbitration conducted under these Rules, save that arbitrators (but not the Court) may be liable for the consequences of conscious and deliberate wrongdoing.

19.2   After the award has been made and the possibilities of correction and additional awards referred to in Article 17 have lapsed or been exhausted, neither the Court nor any arbitrator shall be under any obligation to make any statement to any person about any matter concerning the arbitration, nor shall any party seek to make any arbitrator or any officer of the Court a witness in any legal proceedings arising out of the arbitration.

Article 20   General rules

20.1   A party who knows that any provision of, or requirement under, these Rules has not been complied with and yet proceeds with the arbitration without promptly stating its objection to such non-compliance, shall be deemed to have waived its right to object.

20.2   In all matters not expressly provided for in these Rules, the Court and the Tribunal shall act in the spirit of these Rules and shall make every reasonable effort to ensure that the award is legally enforceable.

LONDON MARITIME ARBITRATORS' ASSOCIATION

London Maritime Arbitrators' Association,
G. T. Hardee Esq.,
Honorary Secretary,
46/48 Rivington Street,
London EC2A 3QP
Tel: 00 + 44-171 613 5401
Fax: 00 + 44-171 613 5394

THE LMAA TERMS (1994)

effective for appointments on and after 1 January 1994

Preliminary

1.   These Terms may be referred to as 'the LMAA Terms (1994)'.

2.   (a)   In these Terms, unless the context otherwise requires,
     (i)   'The Association' means the London Maritime Arbitrators'
Association;
            'Member of the Association' includes both full and supporting
            members;
            'President' means the President for the time being of the Association
     (ii)   'Tribunal' includes a sole arbitrator, a tribunal of two or more
arbitrators, and an umpire
     (iii)   'Original arbitrator' means an arbitrator appointed (whether
initially or by substitution) by or at the request of a party as its nominee and
any arbitrator duly appointed so to act following failure of a party to make its
own nomination.
     (b)   Save where original arbitrators, having disagreed, are thereafter
requested and agree to act as advocates for presentation of the dispute to an
umpire, an original arbitrator will at all times act with judicial impartiality and
with exactly equal duties towards both parties and is in no sense to be
considered as the representative of his appointer.

3.   (a)   The Terms apply to all arbitration proceedings commenced on
and after 1st January 1994 whenever the dispute (unless it arises under an
agreement providing for application to the arbitration of other specified rules
or terms) is referred to members of the Association by their appointment as
sole or original arbitrators and the dispute arises out of a transaction of a kind
which, if it were to have been litigated in the High Court, would have been
tried in the Admiralty or Commercial Courts. The Terms likewise apply
whenever a sole or original arbitrator, not being a member, expressly accepts
appointment on these Terms.
     (b)   For the foregoing purpose arbitration proceedings shall be treated
as having commenced upon acceptance of appointment (i) by a sole arbitrator
or (ii) whichever original arbitrator is first appointed.

Jurisdiction and powers

4.   (a)   Subject to sub-paragraph (b) below, by submitting to arbitration
under these Terms the parties confer upon the tribunal the jurisdiction and
powers set out in the First Schedule.
     (b)   A party shall be entitled to make application to the High Court,
instead of to the tribunal, in relation to any interlocutory matters over which
the High Court has jurisdiction; save that applications for security for costs
shall be made to the High Court only with the concurrence of the other party
or with leave of the tribunal.

Tribunal's fees

5.   Provisions regulating fees payable to the tribunal and other related matters are set out in the Second Schedule. Save as therein or herein otherwise provided, payment of the tribunal's fees and expenses is the joint and several responsibility of the parties.

Arbitration on documents

6.   If it is agreed that an arbitration is to be on documents (i.e. without an oral hearing) it is the responsibility of the parties to agree the procedure to be followed and to inform the tribunal of the agreement reached. The procedure set out in the Third Schedule should normally be adopted, with any such modifications as may be appropriate: and in default of agreement the tribunal will give appropriate directions.

7.   Applications for directions should not be necessary but, if required, they should be made in accordance with paragraph 10.

Oral hearings

8.   A time-table for preparation of the case for hearing should, whenever possible, be agreed between the parties and the tribunal should then be informed by the claimant of the agreement reached. In default of agreement, application for directions should be made in accordance with paragraph 10.

9.   (a)   A hearing date will not be fixed, save in exceptional circumstances, until the preparation of a case is sufficiently advanced to enable the duration of the hearing to be properly estimated; this will normally be after discovery has been completed.
   (b)   Unless the case calls for a preliminary meeting with the tribunal (see paragraph 11), it is the duty of the parties or their advisers, prior to application for a hearing date, to consult together (i) to assess the expected readiness and the likely duration of the hearing, (ii) to plan the preparatory work still to be done, and (iii) to consider whether any other directions are required from the tribunal when the hearing date is requested.
   (c)   Following such consultation, application for a hearing date must be made in writing, indicating the expected date of readiness and likely duration of the hearing.
   (d)   Following fixture of the hearing date a booking fee will be payable in accordance with the provisions of the Second Schedule.

Interlocutory applications

10.   (a)   Application to the tribunal for directions should, save in special circumstances, be made only after the other party has been afforded a reasonable opportunity to agree the terms of the directions proposed.
   (b)   If agreement is not reached, the applicant should apply to the tribunal, setting out the terms of the directions proposed. The application must be copied to the other party, who must respond to the tribunal (copy

to the applicant) stating the grounds of objection. The response must be made within three working days, or such further time as the tribunal may allow on the application of the respondent party.

(c)   Unless either party has requested an oral hearing, the tribunal will make its order following receipt of the response or, in default of response within the time allowed, upon expiry of that time.

(d)   Prior to appointment of a third arbitrator, original arbitrators shall, if in agreement, be entitled to give directions without the need to appoint a third arbitrator for that purpose.

(e)   Communications regarding interlocutory matters should be made expeditiously.

Preliminary meetings

11.   (a)   In cases where there are circumstances which merit preliminary informal discussion with the tribunal (including most cases involving a hearing of more than five days' duration) any application for a hearing should be preceded by a discussion between the parties' representatives to review the progress of the case; to reach agreement, so far as possible, upon further preparation for, and the conduct of, the hearing; to identify matters for discussion with the tribunal; and to prepare for submission to the tribunal an agenda of matters for approval or determination by it.

(b)   Following the discussion between the parties' representatives, the parties should request a preliminary meeting with the tribunal, submitting their agenda together with an updated pleadings bundle and giving their estimates of readiness for hearing and the likely duration of the hearing.

(c)   The preliminary meeting with the tribunal will be informal. Its object is to secure agreement so far as possible on the conduct of the arbitration generally, and to give any such directions as the tribunal considers fit.

(d)   There is set out in the Fourth Schedule a guidance document indicating topics which may be appropriate for consideration prior to and, if still outstanding, at the preliminary meeting.

Settlement

12.   It is the duty of the claimant (a) to notify the tribunal immediately if the arbitration is settled or otherwise terminated and (b) to inform the tribunal of the parties' agreement as to the manner in which payment will be made of any outstanding fees and expenses of the tribunal, e.g. for interlocutory work not covered by any booking fee paid.

13.   Any booking fee paid will be dealt with in accordance with the provisions of paragraph (B) (1) (c) of the Second Schedule. Any other fees and expenses of the tribunal shall be settled, promptly and at latest within 28 days of presentation of the relevant account(s), in accordance with the agreement of the parties or, in default of agreement, the parties shall be jointly and severally responsible for such fees and expenses.

Adjournment

14.   If a case is for any reason adjourned part-heard, the tribunal will be entitled to an interim payment, payable in equal shares or otherwise as the tribunal may direct, in respect of fees and expenses already incurred, appropriate credit being given for the booking fee.

15.   The provisions of paragraph (B)(1)(d) of the Second Schedule shall apply in relation to adjournments ordered prior to the start of the hearing.

Umpires

16.   An umpire who attends the principal hearing or any interlocutory application shall be entitled to remuneration accordingly for his services, irrespective of whether or not he is thereafter required to enter upon the reference, and as from the date of his appointment he shall, for the purposes of paragraphs 5 and 11–15 above, be treated as if he were a member of the tribunal.

Availability of arbitrators

17.   (a)   In cases where it is known at the outset that an early hearing is essential, the parties should consult and ensure the availability of the arbitrator(s) to be appointed by them.

   (b)   If, in cases when the tribunal has already been constituted, the fixture of an acceptable hearing date is precluded by the commitments of the original appointee(s) the provisions of the Fifth Schedule shall apply.

The award

18.   The time required for preparation of an award must vary with the circumstances of the case. The award should normally be available within not more than six weeks from the close of the proceedings. In many cases, and in particular where the matter is one of urgency, the interval should be substantially shorter.

19.   The members of a tribunal need not meet together for the purpose of signing their award or of effecting any corrections thereto.

20.   Where the reference is to a tribunal of three arbitrators, the majority view shall prevail in relation to any head of claim or counterclaim upon which unanimity is lacking. In the event of there being no majority the view of the third arbitrator shall prevail.

21.   Unless a reasoned award is requested under Section 1 of the Arbitration Act 1979, the tribunal will normally supply the parties, on a confidential basis, with a document outlining the reasons for its decision. The document will not form part of the award, nor (unless the Court should otherwise direct) may it be relied upon or referred to by the parties in any proceedings relating to the award.

22.   If any award has not been paid for and collected within one month of the date of publication, the tribunal may give written notice to either party requiring payment of the costs of the award whereupon such party shall be obliged to pay for and collect the award within fourteen days.

23.   If, following the making of an interim award, outstanding matters are amicably resolved the tribunal should be promptly advised so that the file can be closed and documents disposed of.

24.   If the tribunal considers that an arbitration decision merits publication then, provided such publication is not objected to by either or both of the parties, it may be published under such arrangements as the Association may effect from time to time. The publication will be so drafted as to preserve anonymity as regards the identity of the parties and of the tribunal.

General

25.   Three months after publication of any final award the tribunal will notify the parties of its intention to dispose of the documents and to close the file, and it will act accordingly unless otherwise requested within 14 days of such notice being given.

26.   In relation to any matters not expressly provided for herein the tribunal shall act in accordance with the tenor of these Terms.

THE FIRST SCHEDULE

(A) Jurisdiction

The tribunal shall have jurisdiction in relation to the following matters:—

(1)   To determine all disputes arising under or in connection with the transaction the subject of the reference, including (so far as the tribunal considers that course to be both practicable and desirable) any application for rectification of the contract and any further disputes arising subsequent to the commencement of the arbitration proceedings. Provided however that, unless the parties otherwise agree, this jurisdiction shall not extend to determination of a dispute as to whether the transaction was the subject of an agreement binding in law upon the parties.

(2)   To proceed to an award on any claim or counterclaim on the application of the claimant party and without the need for an oral hearing if the respondent party (a) has failed to furnish defence submissions to such claim or counterclaim within such time as the tribunal has directed by final and peremptory order, and (b) (except where an arbitration on documents only has been agreed) has declined or failed to take advantage of an opportunity to apply to the tribunal for an oral hearing.

(3)   To impose, in relation to any final and peremptory order, such terms as the tribunal considers appropriate in the event of non-compliance with the order.

(4)   To make interim orders, upon the application of a respondent party to a claim or counterclaim, for the provision of security for that party's costs

of the reference, with power to order a stay (either temporary or permanent) of the arbitration or to make such other direction as may in the circumstances be appropriate or if appropriate make an award dismissing the claim.

(5)   At the request of the parties or either of them or of its own volition, to correct any accidental mistake, omission, or error of calculation in its award, any such request to be made within 28 days of the collection of the award. Any correction may be effected in writing on the original award or in a separate memorandum which shall become part of the award.

(B)   Powers

Without derogation from all powers with which it is otherwise invested or with which it may be invested pursuant to application made to the High Court under Section 5(2) of the Arbitration Act 1979, the tribunal shall have the following specific powers, to be exercised as the circumstances may require for the most efficient and expeditious conduct of the reference:

(1)   To receive and act upon such oral or written evidence as it determines to be relevant, whether or not the evidence is strictly admissible in law.

(2)   To limit the number of expert witnesses, to direct that experts' reports be exchanged in advance of the hearing and, if the tribunal thinks fit, to direct that there be a 'without prejudice' meeting of such experts within such period before or after the disclosure of the reports as the tribunal may direct, for the purpose of identifying those parts of their evidence which are at issue.

(3)   To direct, in appropriate circumstances, that statements of witnesses of fact be exchanged in advance of the hearing and be received as their evidence-in-chief.

(4)   To appoint, upon the application of any party, an expert assessor or assessors to sit with and advise the tribunal upon any matters which are outside its own expertise; the fees of any assessor(s) so appointed to form part of the cost of the award.

(5)   To direct, upon the application of any party or of its own volition, that anything the subject of the reference be made available for inspection by or on behalf of the tribunal or any party.

(6)   To require the parties to attend a preliminary meeting to deal with matters referred to in the fourth schedule or otherwise in the tribunal's discretion.

(C)   Multi-party disputes

A tribunal or tribunals shall have the following powers in relation to multi-party disputes:

(1)   To direct in appropriate cases that the references shall be heard concurrently and to give all such directions as to procedure as the interests of fairness, economy and expedition may require.

(2)   Upon the application of any party to an existing reference, the tribunal shall have power to direct that there be joined in that reference any other party or parties who, by written consent, have indicated readiness to be so joined; and the arbitration shall then proceed as though the tribunal had been appointed to deal with all associated disputes between the respective interests on a consolidated basis.

THE SECOND SCHEDULE

TRIBUNAL'S FEES

(A) Appointment fee

An appointment fee is payable on appointment by the appointing party or by the party at whose request the appointment is made. The appointment fee shall be a standard fee fixed by the Committee of the Association from time to time. Unless otherwise agreed, the appointment fee of an umpire or third arbitrator shall in the first instance be paid by the claimant.

(B) Booking fee

(1) (a) For a hearing of up to ten days' duration there shall be payable to the tribunal a booking fee of £250 per person or such sum as the Committee of the Association may from time to time decide, for each day reserved. The booking fee will be invoiced to the party asking for the hearing date to be fixed or to the parties in equal shares if both parties ask for the hearing date to be fixed as the case may be and shall be paid within 14 days of confirmation of the reservation or six months in advance of the first day reserved ('the start date'), whichever date be the later. If the fee is not paid in full by the due date the tribunal will be entitled to cancel the reservation but either party may secure reinstatement of the reservation by payment within seven days of any balance outstanding.

(b) For hearings over ten days duration the booking fee in sub-paragraph (1)(a) above shall for each day reserved be increased by 30% in the case of a hearing of up to 15 days and 60% in the case of a hearing up to 20 days and may, at the discretion of the tribunal, be subscribed in non-returnable stage payments. For hearings in excess of 20 days the booking fee to be at the rate for a hearing of 20 days plus such additional sum as may be agreed between the parties in the light of the length of the proposed hearing.

(c) Where the case proceeds to an award, or is settled subsequent to the start of the hearing, appropriate credit will be given for the booking fee in calculating the cost of the award or, as the case may be, the amount payable to the tribunal upon settlement of the case.

(d) Where a hearing date is vacated prior to the start date the booking fee will be retained by the tribunal (i) in full if the date is vacated less than three months before the start date (ii) as to 50% if the date is vacated three months or more before the start date. Any interlocutory fees and expenses incurred will also be payable or, as the case may be, deductible from the refund under (ii).

(2) An arbitrator or umpire who, following receipt of his booking fee or any part thereof, is for any reason replaced is, upon settlement of his fees for any interlocutory work, responsible for transfer of his booking fee to the person appointed to act in his place. In the event of death the personal representatives shall have a corresponding responsibility.

ACCOMMODATION

(1)   If accommodation and/or catering is arranged by the tribunal, the cost will normally be recovered as part of the cost of the award, but where a case is adjourned part-heard or in other special circumstances, the tribunal reserves the right to direct that the cost shall be provisionally paid by the parties in equal shares (or as the tribunal may direct) promptly upon issue of the relevant account. Prior to booking accommodation and/or catering the tribunal may, if they think fit, request that they be provided with security sufficient to cover their prospective liabilities in respect thereof.

(2)   If accommodation is reserved and paid for by the parties and it is desired that the cost incurred be the subject of directions in the award, the information necessary for that purpose must be furnished promptly to the tribunal.

THE THIRD SCHEDULE

ARBITRATION ON DOCUMENTS

RECOMMENDED PROCEDURE

If parties wish a dispute to be decided without an oral hearing the procedure set out in paragraphs 1–5 below is recommended for adoption by agreement.

When this procedure (or any modification) has been agreed, the tribunal should be so informed. The tribunal must be promptly advised if, at a later stage, the parties or either of them consider that an oral hearing is going to be necessary.

The exchange of submissions, etc., will take place directly between the parties unless the case is being handled by others (e.g. by lawyers or a Club) on their behalf.

Copies of all submissions, comments and documents must be supplied simultaneously to the tribunal, and all communications with the tribunal must be copied to the other party.

All documents relied on must be legibly copied and translations supplied as necessary.

(1)   Claimants' written submissions, together with copies of supporting documents, to be furnished by them within 28 days after the agreement by the parties to adopt the procedure.

(2)   Respondents' written submissions (including those relating to any counterclaim), together with copies of any documents relied on additional to those already provided by the claimants, to be furnished by them within 28 days after receipt of the claimants' submissions and documents.

(3)   If there is no counterclaim, claimants' final comments (if any) on the claim to be furnished within 21 days after receipt of the respondents' submissions and documents.

(4)   If there is a counterclaim:

(a)   claimants to furnish comments and any additional documents relative to the counterclaim within 28 days after receipt of the respondents' submissions and documents;

(b)   respondents' final comments (if any) on the counterclaim to be furnished within 21 days after receipt of the claimants' comments and additional documents (if any).

(5)   The tribunal will then give notice to the parties of its intention to proceed to its award and will so proceed unless either party within seven days requests, and is thereafter granted, leave to provide further submissions and/or documents.

THE FOURTH SCHEDULE

PRELIMINARY MEETINGS

Paragraph 11 of the Terms envisages that where the hearing of a case is expected to last more than five days, or if there are other special circumstances, the representatives should first review the progress of the matter and consider preparations for the hearing, and thereafter a preliminary meeting should take place with the tribunal to consider those matters (see paragraph 11 of the Terms for fuller details).

This Schedule sets out, in check-list form, topics which may be appropriate for consideration. The representatives' discussion should lead to a measure of procedural agreement, and any remaining areas for discussion with the tribunal can be identified and the scope for specific directions from the tribunal thus reduced.

In complex cases, more than one preliminary meeting may be required in order to deal with developments since, or any matters stood over at, a prior meeting.

Because cases vary so much, the procedure and matters for consideration must be flexible. Inevitably, certain matters must be left to the discretion of the parties' advisers (e.g. what facts can be agreed, how evidence is to be dealt with, what level of representation is required, etc.); those mentioned in the check-list are not, in all instances, matters on which the tribunal can or will rule. This makes it all the more important that the representatives first consider in a comprehensive, realistic and co-operative way all the relevant points listed, always bearing in mind the underlying object of the anticipated meetings: to achieve the speediest, cheapest and most efficient resolution of the parties' disputes.

1. **Pleadings**
     (i)   closed (including particulars)?
     (ii)   amendments required?
     (iii)   are all issues still alive?

2. **Discovery**
     (i)   completed?
     (ii)   disputes re outstanding discovery.

3. **The Hearing**
A.   General
     (i)   preliminary issues appropriate for determination? (e.g. interpretation of contract, liability only, etc.)

    (ii)   any issues suitable for determination on written submissions alone?

B. Evidence (Fact)
    (i)   can some facts/figures be agreed?
    (ii)   exchange lists of witnesses of fact (indicating broadly areas each will deal with)?
    (iii)   presentation of some evidence-in-chief by proofs or affidavits appropriate? If so, what arrangements should be made re exchange prior to hearing?
    (iv)   admission of some evidence (perhaps formal or of marginal importance) in proof or affidavit form only?

C. Evidence (Expert)
    (i)   expert(s) needed? If so, should numbers be limited, generally or by reference to specific aspects of dispute?
    (ii)   when should reports be exchanged (leaving enough time for reply reports to be supplied well before hearing)?
    (iii)   should a 'without prejudice meeting' of experts be held?
    (iv)   could tribunal deal with technical aspects on basis of reports, without need to call experts?
    (v)   could an independent assessor usefully assist tribunal?

D. Inspection
Would tribunal be assisted by attending trials or experiments, or inspecting any object featuring in the dispute?

E. Documents
    (i)   if possible provide agreed chronology, dramatis personae, list of telex answerbacks, agreed statement of accounts.
    (ii)   arrangements of documents (e.g. different bundles for different topics, or as appropriate) and dates by which bundles to be produced.
    (iii)   unnecessary inclusion of documents to be avoided.
    (iv)   when documents voluminous, consider copying only key bundles, holding other material available for reference and copying if required.

F. Advance Reading
    (i)   provision of pleadings and other suitable material (e.g. experts' reports) to tribunal as far in advance of hearing as possible.
    (ii)   should time be set aside during hearing, after appropriate opening, for private reading of any documents by tribunal (to reduce time otherwise involved in reading documents out)?

G. Multi-Party Disputes
    (i)   procedure generally.
    (ii)   consolidated, concurrent or consecutive hearings?

H. Representation
  Level of representation at hearing appropriate to case.

4. Hearing Dates

(The fixing of dates will, in the majority of cases, be most usefully considered after the matters covered in paragraph 3 have been reviewed, for they are bound to have a considerable bearing on how long the hearing is likely to take, and when the parties can be ready.)

(i)   estimated duration of hearing.

(ii)   when can parties realistically be expected to be ready?

(iii)   any problems re availability of witnesses? (If so, can these be mitigated by taking evidence in advance, or using proofs/affidavits?)

(iv)   availability of tribunal (see LMAA Terms, paragraph 17 and Fifth Schedule).

(v)   accommodation required and numbers attending.

(vi)   any special facilities required (e.g. transcripts, interpreters, etc.).

(vii)   arrangements for accommodation, etc.: who to book/pay for?

THE FIFTH SCHEDULE

RECONSTITUTION OF THE TRIBUNAL

The following provisions are directed to avoiding delay which the parties or either of them consider unacceptable, but if both parties prefer to retain a tribunal as already constituted they remain free so to agree.

(1)   The governing factor will be the ability of the tribunal to fix a hearing date within a reasonable time of the expected readiness date as notified by the parties on application for a date (see paragraph 9(c) of the Terms), or, if they are not agreed as to the expected readiness date, within a reasonable time of whichever forecast date the tribunal considers more realistic.

(2)   For hearings of up to 10 days estimated duration, what constitutes a reasonable time will (unless the parties apply for a date further ahead) be determined by reference to the estimated length of hearing as follows:-

ESTIMATED DURATION		REASONABLE TIME
(i)	Up to 2 days	3 months
(ii)	3–5 days	6 months
(iii)	6–10 days	10 months

'Relevant time-scale' is used below to mean whichever of the foregoing periods is applicable and, in cases of more than 10 days duration, such corresponding time-scale as the tribunal may consider appropriate.

(3)   A sole arbitrator who is unable to offer a date within the relevant time-scale will offer to retire and, if so requested by the parties or either of them, will retire upon being satisfied that an appropriate substitute appointment has been effected by the parties; in event of their disagreement, either party may request the President to make the necessary substitute appointment.

(4)   In all other cases, unless all members of the tribunal are able to offer a matching date within the relevant time-scale:

(A)   the tribunal will have regard to any agreed preference of the parties, but if there is no agreed preference the tribunal will fix:

(i)   the earliest hearing date that can be given by any member(s) able to offer a guaranteed date within the relevant time-scale; or

(ii)   if a guaranteed date within the relevant time-scale cannot be offered by any member of the tribunal, the earliest date thereafter which can be guaranteed by any member(s) of the tribunal;

on the basis, in either case, that any member then unable (by reason of a prior commitment) to guarantee the date so fixed will (unless that prior commitment has meanwhile cleared) retire by notice given six clear weeks prior to the start date.

(B)   Upon notification of any such retirement an appropriate substitution will be effected as follows:—

(i)   If an original arbitrator retires the substitute shall be promptly appointed by his appointer; or failing such appointment at least 21 days prior to the start date the substitute will then be appointed by the umpire or third arbitrator or, if an umpire or third arbitrator has not yet been appointed, the substitute will be appointed by the President;

(ii)   If an umpire or third arbitrator retires the substitute will be appointed by the original arbitrators.

(5)   For the purpose of paragraph (4):

(A)   'Appropriate substitution' means appointment of a substitute able to match the hearing date established in accordance with sub-paragraph (A);

(B)   'Start date' means the first date reserved for the hearing;

(C)   An umpire or third arbitrator will retain power to make any necessary substitution under sub-paragraph (B)(i) notwithstanding that he may himself have given notice of retirement under sub-paragraph (A) and an original arbitrator will retain the like power under sub-paragraph (B)(ii).

(6)   Applications to vacate dates fixed by implementation of this Schedule will be granted only in exceptional circumstances. The convenience of counsel and/or expert witnesses will not normally be treated as justifying vacation of the date.

THE LMAA SMALL CLAIMS PROCEDURE and COMMENTARY

revised 1 January 1994

THE LMAA SMALL CLAIMS PROCEDURE

1. Introduction

These provisions shall be known as the LMAA Small Claims Procedure ('the Small Claims Procedure').

2. Appointment of Arbitrator

(a)   If a dispute has arisen and the parties have agreed that it should be referred to arbitration under the Small Claims Procedure, then, unless a sole arbitrator has already been agreed on, either party may start the arbitration by giving notice to the other requiring him to join in appointing a sole arbitrator. If within fourteen days the parties have agreed on a sole arbitrator and the intended arbitrator has accepted the appointment, the Claimant shall within a further fourteen days send to the Respondent (with copies to the arbitrator) a letter of claim accompanied by copies of all relevant documents and shall further send to the arbitrator a remittance in his favour for the small claims fee as defined in para 3(b).

(b)   If the parties have not within fourteen days agreed on a sole arbitrator, either party may apply in writing to the Honorary Secretary, London Maritime Arbitrators Association for the appointment of a sole arbitrator by the President. Such application shall be copied to the other party and shall be accompanied by a copy of the letter of claim together with copies of all relevant documents and a remittance for the said small claims fee plus £100 plus VAT where applicable in favour of the LMAA. The President, having considered the nature of the dispute, shall appoint an appropriate arbitrator and shall give notice to the parties. The LMAA shall send to the arbitrator the letter of claim and the documents together with the said small claims fee, and shall retain the balance in respect of administrative expenses.

3.   The Arbitrator's Fee

(a)   The fixed fee includes the appointment fee, interlocutories, a hearing not exceeding one day (if required by the arbitrator pursuant to para 5(g)), the writing of the Award and the assessment of costs (if any). It does not include expenses, such as the hire of an arbitration room, which shall in the first instance be paid by the Claimant on demand.

(b)   The small claims fee shall be £750 (plus VAT where applicable) or such standard fee as shall be fixed from time to time by the Committee of the LMAA.

(c)   If the case is settled amicably before an award has been written, the arbitrator may retain out of the small claims fee a sum sufficient to compensate him for services thus far rendered and any balance shall be repaid.

4.   Right of Appeal Excluded

The right of appeal to the Courts is excluded, and, immediately following the appointment of the arbitrator, each party shall send to the arbitrator a letter confirming that such right of appeal is excluded.

5.   Procedure

(a)   A letter of defence and details of counterclaim (if any) accompanied in each case by copies of all relevant documents including any experts' reports shall be delivered to the Claimant within twenty-eight days from the receipt of the letter of claim or from the date of the appointment of the arbitrator, whichever shall be the later.

(b)   Letter of reply and defence to counterclaim (if any) within a further twenty-one days.

(c)   Where there is a counterclaim, letter of reply to defence to counterclaim within a further fourteen days.

(d)   No extension to the above time limits will be granted unless application is made before expiry of the existing time limit. Any extensions granted shall not in total exceed twenty eight days.

(e)   If a party fails to communicate to the arbitrator its letter of defence, letter of reply and defence to counterclaim, or letter of reply to defence to counterclaim within the time limits set out above or set by an extension of time granted by the arbitrator, the arbitrator shall on application by the other party notify the defaulting party that unless the outstanding communication is received within fourteen days he will proceed to the award on the basis of the submissions and documents before him to the exclusion of all others. Any pleading submitted by a defaulting party subsequent to expiry of such extended time limit shall not be admissible.

(f)   Copies of all the above letters and documents shall be sent to the arbitrator and to the other party, or if the other party is acting through a solicitor or representative, to that solicitor or representative.

(g)   There shall be no hearing unless, in exceptional circumstances, the arbitrator requires this.

(h)   In the case of an oral hearing the arbitrator shall have power to allocate the time available (which shall be limited to one working day) between the parties in such manner that each party has an equal opportunity in which to present his case.

(i)   All communications or notifications under this procedure may be by letter, telex or telefax.

6.   Disclosure of Documents

(a)   There shall be no Discovery, but, if in the opinion of the arbitrator a party has failed to produce any relevant document(s), he may order the production of such document(s) and may indicate to the party to whom the order is directed that, if without adequate explanation he fails to produce the document(s), the arbitrator may proceed on the assumption that the contents of that document(s) do not favour that party's case.

(b)   The expression 'relevant documents' includes all documents relevant to the dispute, whether or not favourable to the party holding them. It includes witness statements, expert's reports and the like on which he intends to rely, but does not include documents which are not legally disclosable.

7.   The Award

The Award will be made within one month, in a documents only case, from the date when the arbitrator has received all relevant documents and submissions, or, where there is an oral hearing, from the close of the hearing.

8.   Costs

The arbitrator may give directions with regard to the ultimate responsibility for his fee and expenses and with regard to legal costs and may assess such costs. Such assessment shall be on a commercial basis and unless the parties otherwise agree the amount which one party may be ordered to pay to the other in respect of legal costs shall not exceed £1,250, but in small cases the arbitrator may in his discretion limit such amount to £625, or such other standard maximum/minimum figures as shall be fixed from time to time by the committee of the LMAA.

9. General

The arbitrator may in exceptional cases depart from or vary the above provisions at his entire discretion.

COMMENTARY ON
THE LMAA SMALL CLAIMS PROCEDURE

The Small Claims Procedure has been introduced to provide a simplified, quick and inexpensive procedure for the resolution of small claims. It is supplementary to the Documents Only procedure contained in the Third Schedule to the LMAA Terms 1994.

It is suggested that it should be used where neither the claim nor any counterclaim exceeds the sum of $50,000. It is not suitable for use where there are complex issues or where there is likely to be examination of witnesses. On the other hand, the Procedure may be suitable for handling larger claims where there is a single issue at stake.

Attention is drawn to the following features:

1. Reference to a Sole Arbitrator

This will provide a saving both in time and expense. It is expected and hoped that in most cases the parties will be able to agree on the sole arbitrator. Where they cannot agree, application may be made to the LMAA, and the President will then make the appointment. There will be a charge of £100 to cover the administrative expenses.

2. Arbitrator to Receive a Fixed Fee

So that the parties know where they stand at an early stage, it is provided that the arbitrator will receive a fixed fee of £750. Members of the LMAA have agreed to do this as a service to the industry, though it will be appreciated that, having regard to current rates of remuneration, it may in many cases involve some financial sacrifice. Any expenses must be paid in addition.

3. Informal Procedure

There will be no formal pleadings and no discovery as such. Each party will be informed of the case against him by a simple exchange of letters accompanied by copies of all relevant documents, including witness statements. A strict but reasonable timetable is imposed, and, if a party fails to comply with a final time limit set by the arbitrator, the arbitrator will proceed to his award on the basis of the documents already received.

There is substituted for discovery (a procedure frequently used to gain time) an obligation on the parties to disclose all relevant documents with their letters of claim or defence. Should a party fail in this obligation, the arbitrator is given power to order production of any missing documents and to give warning to that party that, if he fails to produce them without adequate explanation, the arbitrator may proceed on the basis that those documents do not favour that party's case.

4. Legal Representation

The use of lawyers is not excluded, but it is thought that in many cases they will not be necessary. But it should be borne in mind that advice from a lawyer can often indicate to a party the strength or weakness of his case and can assist in reaching an amicable settlement; also, if settlement cannot be reached, the case may be presented by a lawyer in a more orderly and concise manner.

5. The Costs

The power of an arbitrator to award costs has been retained as an important feature of London arbitration. It operates to deter spurious claims or defences and may assist in promoting an amicable settlement. The arbitrator is given power to tax or assess legal costs, but on a commercial and strict basis. The amount recoverable will be limited to £1,250, or in small cases £625, or such other sums as may be fixed by the Committee of the LMAA.

6. The Award

The arbitrator will normally make his Award within one month from the date on which he has received all the papers.

7. Exclusion of Appeal

To ensure that the dispute is brought to a conclusion without delay or additional costs the right of appeal to the Courts is excluded. By way of confirmation, each party is required, immediately after the appointment of the arbitrator, to write to him confirming that the right of appeal is excluded.

8. Discretion

It is expected that in the great majority of cases the strict timetable and provisions of the Procedure will be observed and enforced, but in exceptional cases there is discretion for the arbitrator to vary or depart from them.

THE LMAA CONCILIATION TERMS 1991

THE LMAA CONCILIATION CLAUSE

In the event of a dispute arising out of or in connexion with this Agreement and the parties desire to seek an amicable solution to that dispute by conciliation, the conciliation shall be conducted in accordance with the LMAA Conciliation Terms currently in force.

Article 1 Preliminary

1.1 These terms may be referred to as 'The LMAA Conciliation Terms 1991'.

1.2   In these Terms, unless the context otherwise requires,

   (a)   'Association' means the London Maritime Arbitrators Association;
   (b)   'President' means the President for the time being of the Association;
   (c)   'Conciliation' means and includes conciliation, mediation, and any other form of dispute resolution other than litigation and arbitration;
   (d)   'Conciliator' means and includes one or more persons appointed or nominated for the purpose of conciliation.

Article 2   Application and purpose of the terms

2.1   These Terms apply to conciliation of disputes arising out of or relating to a contractual or other legal relationship, whether commercial or maritime, where the parties seeking an amicable settlement of their disputes have agreed that the Terms shall apply.
2.2   The parties may agree to exclude or vary any of these Terms at any time.

Article 3   Number of conciliators

Unless the parties otherwise agree, there shall be one conciliator. Where the parties agree that there shall be more than one conciliator, each party shall appoint or be represented by a conciliator. The conciliator or conciliators shall be appointed within 30 days from the commencement of the conciliation procedure as mentioned in Article 4 below.

Article 4   Commencement of the conciliation procedure

4.1   The party initiating conciliation shall send to the other party or parties a written invitation to conciliate under these Terms, briefly setting out the matters in dispute.
4.2   The conciliation procedure shall be deemed to have commenced when the other party or parties accept the invitation to conciliation in writing.
4.3   If the other party, or if one of the other parties, rejects the invitation, or if the other party or parties fail to respond to the invitation within 30 days, or any other period (being not less than 15 nor more than 45 days) that may be stated in the invitation, there will also be no conciliation procedure. Provided that, if there are more than two parties and one accepts but the other or others do not, then conciliation in accordance with these Terms between the party making the invitation and the party accepting shall take place if they so agree.

Article 5   Appointment of conciliator

5.1   If the parties are unable to agree on the appointment of a conciliator, they may make application in writing to the President for the appointment of a conciliator. Such application shall be accompanied by a brief summary of the matters in dispute. Each party shall send a copy of its application and the summary to the other parties. The President may call for such further information as he may require. He shall then appoint the conciliator and shall notify the parties of his name and address.

5.2   Where the parties have agreed that each party should appoint a conciliator and one or more of the parties has failed to make the appointment, the party or parties who have made the appointment may apply in writing to the President for the appointment of a conciliator on behalf of the defaulting party or parties, and the procedure indicated in the preceding paragraph shall be followed.

Article 6   Duties and powers of the conciliator

6.1   The conciliator shall assist the parties in an independent and impartial manner in their attempt to reach an amicable settlement of their dispute. He shall be guided by the principles of objectivity, fairness and justice, giving consideration to, among other things, the rights and obligations of the parties, the usages of the trade in question and the circumstances surrounding the dispute, including any previous business practices between the parties or some of them.

6.2   The conciliator may conduct the conciliation in such manner as he considers appropriate, taking into account the circumstances of the case, any wishes the parties may express, including any request that the conciliator hear oral statements, and the need for a speedy settlement of the dispute.

6.3   The conciliator may at any time make proposals for the settlement of the dispute. Such proposal may be oral or in writing and need not be accompanied by any reasons therefor.

6.4   The conciliator may invite the parties to meet with him or may communicate with them orally or in writing. He may meet or communicate with the parties together or with each of any or them separately.

6.5   Where the conciliator receives factual information concerning the dispute from a party, he shall disclose the substance of that information to the other party or parties so that that other party or those other parties may have the opportunity to present any explanation which it or they consider appropriate. However, when a party gives information to the conciliator subject to a specific condition that it be kept confidential, the conciliator shall not disclose that information to any other party.

6.6   The conciliator may, with the consent of the parties, call any witness whom he thinks may be able to assist in the conciliation.

Article 7   Co-operation of parties with conciliator

The parties will in good faith co-operate with conciliator and in particular will endeavour to comply with requests by him to submit written materials, provide evidence and attend meetings.

Article 8   Settlement agreement

8.1   Where it appears to the conciliator that there exist elements of a settlement which would be acceptable to the parties, he may formulate the terms of a possible settlement and submit them to the parties for their observations. He may reformulate the terms in the light of such observations.

8.2   If the parties reach agreement on the settlement of the dispute, they shall draw up and sign a written agreement. The conciliator may draw up, or assist the parties in drawing up, the settlement agreement.

8.3   The parties, by signing the settlement agreement, put an end to the dispute and are bound by the agreement.

8.4   The conciliator may, if so requested by the parties, draw up the settlement agreement in the form of an arbitration award.

Article 9   Confidentiality

The conciliator and the parties must keep confidential all matters relating to the conciliation proceedings. Confidentiality extends also to the settlement agreement (or arbitration award, if that be the case), except where its disclosure is necessary for purposes of implementation and enforcement.

Article 10   Termination of conciliation procedure

10.1   The conciliation procedure is terminated—

(a)   by the signing of the settlement agreement by the parties or by the signing of an arbitration award, on the date of such agreement or award;

(b)   by a written declaration of the parties to the effect that further efforts at conciliation are no longer justified, on the date of the declaration;

(c)   by a written declaration of a party to the other party or parties to the effect that the conciliation procedure is terminated, on the date of the declaration;

(d)   by a written declaration of the conciliator to the effect that further efforts at conciliation are no longer justified, on the date of the declaration.

Article 11   Resort of arbitration or judicial proceedings

The parties undertake not to initiate or pursue, during the conciliation procedure, any arbitration or judicial proceedings in respect of a dispute that is the subject of the conciliation procedure, except that a party may initiate arbitration or judicial proceedings, where in his opinion such proceedings are necessary for preserving his rights.

Article 12   Costs

12.A   The Conciliator's Costs

12.A.1   Upon termination of the conciliation procedure, the conciliator shall fix the costs of the conciliation and shall give written notice thereof to the parties, who shall, unless otherwise ordered by the conciliator, be liable to pay the same in equal proportions. Such costs shall include the conciliator's fees, which, unless agreed beforehand, shall be reasonable in amount having regard to the time involved, the amount in dispute and the complexity of the case, any out of pocket expenses and the expenses of any witnesses called by the conciliator with the consent of the parties.

12.A.2   If any party fails to pay the conciliator's costs or his proportion thereof within 90 days from the termination of the conciliation procedure, the other party or parties shall be jointly and severally liable to indemnify the conciliator in respect of such failure.

12.A.3   The conciliator may, on his appointment or at any time or times thereafter, order the parties to pay to him a deposit on account of his costs.

12.B   The Parties' Costs

12.B.1   Normally each party shall bear its own costs.

12.B.2   However, if the conciliator should be of the opinion that any party has not genuinely tried to co-operate in the conciliation or has been obstructive, so that the conciliation procedure has been thwarted or has been made more expensive, he may order that that party should pay all or part of the costs of any other party; and, if such costs cannot be amicably agreed, the conciliator may assess and decide the amount to be paid and a certificate signed by the conciliator shall be conclusive and binding on the parties.

Article 13   Role of the conciliator in other proceedings

The parties and the conciliator undertake that the conciliator will not act as arbitrator, witness, lawyer, adviser or representative of any party in arbitration or judicial proceedings in respect of a dispute that is the subject of the conciliation procedure.

Article 14   Admissibility of evidence in other proceedings

14.1   Unless all parties to the present conciliation procedure otherwise agree, the parties undertake not to reveal, introduce or rely on the following as evidence in any arbitration or judicial proceedings, whether or not those proceedings relate to the dispute that is the subject of the conciliation procedure:

(a)   views expressed or proposals made by any party with a view to a possible settlement of the dispute;

(b)   admissions made by any party in the course of the conciliation procedure;

(c)   proposals made by the conciliator;

(d)   the fact that a party had indicated its willingness to accept a proposal for settlement made by the conciliator.

14.2   The parties further undertake, unless all parties otherwise agree, not to refer to or rely on any documents which might have been disclosed during the conciliation procedure, whether voluntarily or at the request of the conciliator or other party, but which would otherwise have been privileged and to return all such documents and all copies thereof to the party disclosing them.

LONDON METAL EXCHANGE (LME)

The London Metal Exchange Limited,
56 Leadenhall Street,
London EC3A 2BJ
Telephone: + 44 (0)171 264 5555
Telefax: 8951367
Fax: +44 (0)171 680 0505

ARBITRATION REGULATIONS

June 1995

1. Definitions and Interpretations

1.1   In these Arbitration Regulations, the following words and expressions shall, unless the context otherwise requires, bear the meanings set opposite them:—

'Administrative Procedure' a notice posted in the Exchange containing a procedure for implementing the Rules or any part thereof;

'Arbitration Regulations' the regulations set out in Part 8 of the Rules;

'Chief Executive' includes the Deputy Chief Executive and any other person for the time being appointed to perform the duties of Chief Executive of the Company;

'Claimant' the person commencing an arbitration by serving a Notice to Arbitrate;

'Close of Pleadings' the end of a period of 28 days after the time for submission of the points of reply, unless otherwise ordered by the Tribunal;

'the Company' The London Metal Exchange Limited;

'Counter Notice' a notice served by the Respondent pursuant to Regulation 2.4 of Part 8 of the Rules;

'Deposit' such sum as may be specified by Administrative Procedure from time to time;

'the Directors' the Board of Directors of the Company;

'Member' a member of the Company;

'Notice to Arbitrate' a Notice served by the Claimant pursuant to Regulation 2.1 of Part 8 of the Rules;

'Panel' the Arbitration Panel of the Company;

'Panel Committee' a committee appointed by the Directors to oversee the conduct of arbitrations pursuant to the Arbitration Regulations, and in particular to perform the functions and powers referred to in the Arbitration Regulations;

'Registration Fee' such sum as may be specified by Administrative Procedure from time to time;

'Respondent' the person receiving a Notice to Arbitrate served by the Claimant;

'Rules' means these rules and regulations as the same may be amended in accordance with Article 58 of the Articles;

'Secretary' any person appointed to perform the duties of Secretary of the Company, and for the purpose only of Part 8 of the Rules, any person to whom the functions and powers of the Secretary referred to therein may be delegated from time to time;

'Tribunal' the tribunal of one, two or three arbitrators appointed in accordance with Regulation 3 of Part 8 of the Rules;

'Working Day' any weekday, Monday to Friday inclusive, which is not a public holiday in England and Wales.

1.2   Reference to a period of days shall mean consecutive days, calculated with reference to London Time, whether or not they are Working Days.

Where an act is required to be done within a specified period of days after a specified event, the first day of the period shall be the day after the specified event occurs. The period shall end at 5.00pm (London Time) on the last day of the period.

1.3 (a) Words importing the singular shall, where the context permits, include the plural and *vice versa*. Words importing gender shall include each gender. Words importing persons shall, where the context permits or requires, include partnerships and corporations.

(b) Where reference is made to a Regulation in any Part of the Rules it shall be deemed to be a reference to a Regulation in that Part unless the context otherwise requires.

1.4 The headings in these Arbitration Rules are inserted for convenience only and are to be ignored for the purposes of construction.

2. Commencement

2.1 A Claimant shall commence an arbitration pursuant to these Arbitration Regulations by serving a Notice to Arbitrate on the Respondent, and by sending a copy of the Notice to Arbitrate to the Secretary accompanied by the Registration Fee and Deposit. The Deposit shall be paid by cash or cheque drawn on a London clearing bank made payable to The London Metal Exchange Limited.

2.2 Subject to Regulation 6.3, the Notice to Arbitrate shall contain at least the following information:—

(a) the address for service of the Claimant;

(b) a brief statement of the nature and circumstances of the dispute including a brief description of any contract, sufficient to enable the Respondent to identify it, to which the dispute relates;

(c) a brief statement of the relief claimed;

(d) the Claimant's proposal with regard to the number of arbitrators to form the Tribunal;

(e) the Claimant's nomination of one arbitrator from the Panel; and

(f) the person and address of the Respondent to which the Notice to Arbitrate has been sent.

2.3 The Secretary shall acknowledge receipt of the Deposit and Registration Fee, indicating the date on which payment was made, and shall copy such acknowledgement to the Respondent. The Notice to Arbitrate shall not be valid, and time shall not start to run for the purpose of any other provisions of these Arbitration Regulations until the Deposit and Registration Fee have been paid and all the above information has been supplied to the Respondent and to the Secretary.

2.4 Within 21 days of receipt of the Notice to Arbitrate, the Respondent shall send to the Claimant, with a copy to the Secretary, a Counter Notice which shall contain:—

(a) the address for service of the Respondent;

(b) confirmation that the Respondent agrees to the number of arbitrators proposed by the Claimant, or the Respondent's counter proposal;

(c) if relevant, the Respondent's nomination of one arbitrator from the Panel.

2.5   If the Respondent fails to serve the Counter Notice then, on application by the Claimant in writing to the Secretary, the Secretary shall proceed with the appointment of the Tribunal as set out in Regulation 3.

3.   Appointment of Tribunal

3.1   Subject to Regulation 3.5, two arbitrators shall form the Tribunal unless the parties to the dispute agree that either one or three arbitrators should form the Tribunal.

3.2   Within 7 days of receipt of the Counter Notice, or of the Claimant's application referred to in Regulation 2.5, the Secretary shall:—

(a)   if the Tribunal is to consist of a single arbitrator

(1)   appoint the arbitrator agreed by the parties; or

(2)   if the parties do not agree on the identity of the arbitrator, appoint an arbitrator who may, but need not, be an arbitrator nominated by one of the parties;

(b)   unless the Tribunal is to consist of a single arbitrator, appoint

(1)   the arbitrator nominated by the Claimant; and

(2)   the arbitrator nominated by the Respondent or, in default, an arbitrator;

(c)   send to each arbitrator a copy of the Notice to Arbitrate and the Counter Notice, if any, and any accompanying documents;

(d)   notify the parties of steps taken pursuant to Regulations 3.2(a), 3.2(b) and 3.2(c).

3.3   If the Tribunal is to consist of three arbitrators, the two arbitrators appointed pursuant to Regulation 3.2(b) shall, within 7 days of their appointment, nominate the third and notify the Secretary of their choice or inform the Secretary that they are unable to agree. The Secretary shall within 7 days thereafter:—

(a)   appoint the third arbitrator if necessary having made the choice of third arbitrator himself;

(b)   send the third arbitrator a copy of the documents referred to in Regulation 3.2(c);

(c)   notify the parties and other arbitrators of steps taken pursuant to Regulations 3.3(a) and 3.3(b).

3.4   For the purpose of these Arbitration Regulations, the Tribunal shall be taken to have been appointed on the date the Secretary sends notification to the parties pursuant to Regulation 3.2(d) or 3.3(c) as the case may be.

3.5   If the Tribunal consists of two arbitrators then, upon request to the Secretary by

(a)   either party at any time prior to 14 days after Close of Pleadings, or

(b)   either of the arbitrators at any time before an award is made,

the Secretary shall, in consultation with the existing arbitrators and providing, in the event the request is made by a party, at least one arbitrator is of the view that a third arbitrator should be appointed, appoint a third arbitrator.

3.6   The third arbitrator shall be the chairman of the Tribunal.

3.7   Any arbitrator chosen and appointed by the Secretary shall be chosen from the Panel.

3.8   In every case in which the Secretary appoints an arbitrator he shall, before doing so, ascertain the arbitrator's ability and willingness to act. If any arbitrator is unable or unwilling to act, the Secretary shall, subject to Regulation 3.13, appoint a replacement.

3.9   The arbitrators may only nominate arbitrators who are members of the Panel.

3.10   All arbitrators, whether or not nominated by the parties, shall be and remain at all times wholly independent and impartial and shall not act as advocates for either party.

3.11   If at any time after his appointment any arbitrator is unable or unwilling to act for any reason, then within 7 days of receipt of a written request from the arbitrator himself, any of the other members of the Tribunal, or either party, the Secretary shall, subject to Regulation 3.13, appoint a replacement.

3.12   Either party may challenge the appointment of an arbitrator within 28 days of the appointment of that arbitrator or, if later, within 28 days of becoming aware of the facts and circumstances on which the challenge is based, on grounds of non-independence, partiality, unfitness or inability to act by sending a written statement of its reasons for the challenge to the Secretary. Unless the other party agrees to the challenge or the arbitrator withdraws within 7 days, the Secretary shall refer the matter to the Panel Committee who shall determine whether the challenge should be sustained and, if so and subject to Regulation 3.13, the Secretary shall appoint a replacement within a further 7 days.

3.13   If the arbitrator to be replaced pursuant to Regulations 3.7, 3.11 or 3.12 is one who either party was originally entitled to nominate, that party shall be entitled to nominate the replacement. If the arbitrator to be replaced was the third arbitrator, the other two shall be entitled to nominate the replacement. The Secretary, before appointing the replacement, shall consult with the parties or arbitrators accordingly. The Secretary shall appoint the arbitrator so nominated or, in default of any such nomination within a time specified by the Secretary, choose and appoint the replacement arbitrator.

3.14   The Secretary shall have power, on the application of either party or on his own motion, and on notice to both parties, to extend or abridge any of the time limits specified in this Regulation 3 or in Regulation 2.

4. Procedure

4.1   In the absence of any express provision in these Arbitration Regulations the Tribunal shall have the widest discretion permitted by law to determine the procedure to be adopted, and to ensure the just, expeditious, economical and final determination of the dispute.

4.2   A party who knows that any provision of, or requirement under, these Arbitration Regulations has not been complied with and yet proceeds with the arbitration without promptly stating its objection to such non-compliance, shall be deemed to have waived its right to object.

5. Notices and Communications

5.1   Unless otherwise ordered by the Tribunal, all notices required by these Arbitration Regulations shall be in writing. Notices and all other documents shall be sent by first class post where available, or airmail, fax or telex or delivered by hand.

5.2   Documents sent between the parties shall be sent to the other party's address for service or, if none has yet been specified, to the address of the other party specified in the contract containing the agreement to refer the dispute to arbitration, failing which to the principal place of business of the other party.

5.3   In every case in which either party sends any document to the Secretary or the Tribunal that party shall where relevant provide sufficient copies for each member of the Tribunal, and shall also at the same time send a copy to the other party.

5.4   Subject to satisfactory evidence being produced by the sender and unless the intended recipient proves otherwise:—

(a)   documents sent by post shall be deemed to have been received;

(1)   if posted within the United Kingdom to an address in the United Kingdom, 2 Working Days after posting;

(2)   subject to 5.4(a)(1), if posted within the European Community to an address in the European Community, 5 Working Days after posting;

(3)   in all other cases, 10 Working Days after posting;

(b)   faxes or telexes shall be deemed to have been received at the time transmission ceases;

(c)   by hand deliveries shall be deemed to have been received at the time of delivery to the address stated on their face.

In the event that the sender utilises more than one of the methods above then documents shall be deemed to have been received by the faster method used.

References in these Arbitration Regulations to receipt of documents shall be construed accordingly. In the event of a dispute prior to the appointment of the Tribunal the Secretary shall in his absolute discretion determine if and/or when receipt is deemed to have occurred.

5.5   Unless these Arbitration Regulations otherwise state, or unless otherwise directed by the Secretary (if no Tribunal has been appointed) or by the Tribunal, all notices and other documents received on a day which is not a Working Day, or after 5.00 pm on any Working Day, shall be deemed to have been received on the next following Working Day. Time of receipt shall be determined with reference to local time in the place where the notice or other document is received.

6.   Submission and Documents

6.1   Unless otherwise ordered by the Tribunal, the procedure following appointment of the Tribunal shall be as set out in the rest of this Regulation.

6.2   Within 21 days after the appointment of the Tribunal, the Claimant shall send to the Tribunal and to the Respondent written points of claim which set out any facts or contentions of law on which it relies, and the relief claimed.

6.3   The Claimant may serve the points of claim on the Respondent at the same time as the Notice to Arbitrate. If so, the information required by Regulations 2.2(b) and 2.2(c) need not be contained in the Notice to Arbitrate, and no further copies of the points of claim need be served pursuant to Regulation 6.2.

6.4   Within 21 days of receipt of the points of claim, or of the appointment of the Tribunal if later, the Respondent shall send to the Tribunal and to the

Claimant written points of defence stating in sufficient detail which of the facts and contentions of law in the points of claim it admits or not, or denies, on what grounds, and on what other facts and contentions of law it relies. Any counterclaims shall be submitted with the points of defence in the same manner as claims are set out in the points of claim.

6.5 Within 21 days of receipt of the points of defence, the Claimant may send to the Tribunal and to the Respondent written points of reply which, where there are counterclaims, shall include points of defence to counter-claims.

6.6 If the points of reply contain points of defence to counterclaims, the Respondent may, within 21 days of receipt, send to the Tribunal and to the Claimant written points of reply regarding counterclaims.

6.7 No further submissions shall be served without an order from the Tribunal.

6.8 All submissions referred to in this Regulation shall be accompanied by legible copies, or if they are especially voluminous, lists of all essential documents on which the party concerned relies, and where appropriate, by any relevant samples.

6.9 Any document not in English shall be accompanied by a translation into English and a note explaining who prepared the translation and his qualifications, if any, to do so. Translations may but do not need to be notarised. The authority to be accorded to any translation is a matter for the Tribunal.

6.10 Within 7 days after Close of Pleadings the Tribunal shall give directions for the subsequent procedure of the arbitration and may convene a hearing for this purpose.

6.11 All submissions, information and documents produced or sent to the Secretary, Panel Committee, either party, any arbitrator or expert during the course of an arbitration, whether voluntarily or pursuant to any order, and every interim and final award made by any Tribunal, shall be treated as confidential, and shall not be used by the Secretary, Panel Committee, either party, arbitrator or expert for any purpose other than the arbitration.

6.12 For the avoidance of doubt, Regulation 6.11 shall not preclude the use of any award, together with any necessary supporting documents or information:—

(a) for the purpose of enforcing such award in any competent court; nor

(b) in any subsequent arbitration or court proceedings in connection with a plea of *res judicata* or issue estoppel or otherwise that a party to such subsequent proceedings is estopped, by virtue of the award, from bringing a claim against the party relying upon the award.

7. Hearings

7.1 Either party has the right to be heard before the Tribunal, unless the parties have agreed on documents-only arbitration.

7.2.1 The Tribunal shall fix the date, time and place of any meetings and hearings in the arbitration, and shall give the parties reasonable notice thereof.

7.2.2 Subject to Regulation 7.2.3, all hearings shall take place at the offices of the Company or such other venue in England and Wales, but not elsewhere, as may be mutually agreed between the Tribunal and parties.

7.2.3 Provided the Tribunal itself remains in England or Wales, the Tribunal may in its discretion direct hearings to be conducted without the physical presence of every participant in the same room but such that every participant is linked, for the duration of his participation, through a telecommunication system or systems permitting each participant clearly to hear and speak to every other participant and, if the Tribunal so directs, to see every other participant.

7.3 The Tribunal may in advance of hearings submit to the parties a list of questions which it wishes them to treat with special attention.

8. Party Representatives

8.1 Neither party shall be represented at any hearing by a legal practitioner without the consent of the Tribunal, such consent to be requested not later than Close of Pleadings. If such consent be granted by the Tribunal to one party the other party shall automatically have an equivalent right.

8.2 Nothing in Regulation 8.1 shall preclude either party from otherwise seeking legal advice.

8.3 Subject to Regulation 8.1, either party may be represented at any hearing by any representative, subject to such proof of authority as the Tribunal may require.

9. Witnesses

9.1 Before any hearing, the Tribunal may require either party to give notice of the identity and qualification of witnesses it wishes to call and may require the parties to exchange statements of evidence to be given by the witnesses a specified time in advance of the hearing.

9.2 The Tribunal may allow, refuse, or limit the appearance of witnesses, whether witnesses of fact or expert witnesses.

9.3 Any witness who gives oral evidence may be questioned by each of the parties or their representative, under the control of the Tribunal. The Tribunal may put questions at any stage of the examination of the witnesses.

9.4 The Tribunal may allow the evidence of a witness to be presented in written form either as a signed statement or by a duly sworn affidavit. Subject to Regulation 9.2 either party may request that such a witness should attend for oral examination at a hearing. If he fails to attend, the Tribunal may place such weight on the written evidence as it thinks fit, or exclude it altogether.

10. Powers of Tribunal

10.1 Without prejudice to any powers which may be given to the Tribunal elsewhere in these Arbitration Regulations, the Tribunal shall have power either on its own motion or on the application of either party:—

(a) to order either party to take specified steps within a specified time;

(b) to extend or abridge any time limits specified in these Arbitration Regulations, or in any order;

(c) to continue with the reference in default of appearance or of any other act by either party in like manner as a judge of the High Court might continue with proceedings in that court where a party fails to comply with an order of that court or a requirement of rules of the court, including, for the avoidance of doubt and without limitation, power to strike out all or any part of any submission and to make any award consequent upon any such striking out, in the event a party fails

    (1)   within the time specified in these Arbitration Regulations or in any order or

    (2)   if no time is specified, within a reasonable time

to do any act required by these Arbitration Regulations or to comply with any order;

    (d)   at any time to permit either party to amend any submissions;

    (e)   to stay arbitration proceedings in favour of proceedings in the High Court or other forum and, in an appropriate case, to make it a condition of the stay that one of the parties commence proceedings in the High Court or such other forum forthwith;

    (f)   to order either party to produce and to supply copies of, any documents in that party's possession, custody or power, which, in the event of dispute, the Tribunal determines to be relevant;

    (g)   to order either party to answer interrogatories;

    (h)   to require the parties to provide a written statement of their respective cases in relation to particular issues, to provide a written answer and to give reasons for any disagreement;

    (i)   to order the inspection, preservation, storage, interim custody, sale or other disposal of any property or thing relevant to the arbitration under the control of either party;

    (j)   to make orders authorising any samples to be taken, or any observation to be made, or experiment to be tried which may, in the Tribunal's discretion, be necessary or expedient for the purposes of obtaining full information or evidence:

    (k)   to appoint one or more investigators or experts to report to the Tribunal on specified issues;

    (l)   to order either party, 'the payer', to make an interim payment to the other party, 'the payee', of such amount as the Tribunal shall in its discretion think just, not exceeding a reasonable proportion of the monetary award which in the opinion of the Tribunal is likely to be recovered by the payee after taking into account any set-off or counterclaim on which the payer may be entitled to rely;

    (m)   to order either party to provide security for all or part of any amount of dispute in the arbitration;

    (n)   to make an interim order that either party shall pay to the other party or to the Tribunal or to the Company a proportion of any costs of an administrative nature necessarily incurred by that party or by the Tribunal or by the Company or by an investigator or expert in respect of the progress or conduct of the arbitration, with the intent that such costs should, so far as reasonably possible, be borne equally by the parties pending the final award of the Tribunal;

    (o)   to order either party to provide security for the legal or other costs of the other party in any manner the Tribunal thinks fit;

    (p)   to order specific performance of any contract;

    (q)   to open up, revise and review any certificate, opinion or decision of any person whose certificate, opinion or decision is subject to reference to arbitration;

(r)   to order the rectification of any agreement subject to any rule of law which would restrict this power;

(s)   to delegate the power to make procedural rulings to the chairman of the Tribunal, including the power to determine in the event of dispute, whether a ruling is procedural.

10.2   The Tribunal shall have the power to rule on its own jurisdiction, including any objections with respect to the existence or validity of the arbitration agreement, or of the existence of validity of the contract of which the arbitration clause forms part. For this purpose, an arbitration clause which forms part of a contract and which provides for arbitration under these Arbitration Regulations shall be treated as an agreement independent of the other terms of the contract. A decision by the Tribunal that the contract is null and void shall not entail *ipso jure* the invalidity of the arbitration clause.

10.3   A plea that the Tribunal does not have jurisdiction shall be raised not later than in the points of defence. A plea that the Tribunal is exceeding the scope of its authority shall be raised promptly after the Tribunal has indicated its intention to decide on the matter alleged to be beyond the scope of its authority. In either case the Tribunal may nevertheless admit a late plea under this Regulation 10.3 if it considers the delay justified.

11.   Consolidation

11.1   On the appointment of a Tribunal, and whenever requested to do so by either party, the Panel Committee shall review pending arbitrations and, if it appears to the Panel Committee that

(a)   some common question of law or fact arises in two or more of them, or

(b)   the rights to relief claimed therein are in respect of or arise out of the same transaction or series of transactions, or

(c)   for some other reason it is desirable to make a direction under this Regulation,

the Panel Committee shall so inform the parties to all relevant arbitrations and may, upon the application of one or more of the parties to any of the arbitrations, and after consultation with the Tribunals and the parties, direct those arbitrations to be consolidated on such terms as it considers just or may direct them to be heard at the same time or one immediately after another or may order any of them to be stayed until after the determination of any of them.

11.2   For the purposes of Regulation 11.1, the Panel Committee may require any party to any relevant arbitration to provide it with copies of all that party's submissions and other documents connected with the arbitration which appear to the Panel Committee to be relevant.

11.3   If two or more arbitrations are to be consolidated pursuant to Regulation 11.1 above, and all parties to the consolidated arbitration are in agreement as to the choice of arbitrators the same shall be appointed by the Secretary but if all parties cannot agree within 21 days after the date of the direction under Regulation 11.1 the Panel Committee shall have power to choose and appoint three arbitrators as the Tribunal for the consolidated arbitration and to choose and appoint any replacement arbitrators which may thereafter be necessary.

11.4   The Tribunal in any consolidated arbitration shall have power at any time, on the application of any party to the consolidated arbitration or on its own motion, and on such terms as it considers just to order that the arbitration as between any two or more parties proceed separately, but under the same Tribunal, from the arbitration as between any other two or more parties, and to make any directions consequent thereon as the Tribunal considers expedient for the future conduct of all such proceedings.

12.   Interim and Summary Measures

12.1   Notwithstanding the agreement to arbitrate either party shall be entitled to make an application to the High Court for relief under RSC Order 14 or Order 29 rules 1–4, 6 or 7A, and such application shall not be deemed incompatible with the agreement to arbitrate or as a waiver of that agreement.

12.2   A party applying to a court for relief under RSC Order 29 shall within 7 days commence an arbitration (if one has not already been commenced) against the party against whom such relief is sought.

13.   Awards

13.1   The Tribunal shall make its award in writing and shall give reasons for the award. The award shall be dated and shall be signed in England or Wales by the members of the Tribunal.

13.2.1   If the Tribunal consists of two arbitrators and they fail to agree on any issue they shall request the Secretary to appoint a third arbitrator pursuant to Regulation 3.5.

13.2.2   If the Tribunal consists of three arbitrators and they fail to agree on any issue, they shall decide by a majority. If an arbitrator refuses or fails to sign the award, the signatures of the majority shall be sufficient, provided that the reason for the omitted signature is stated.

13.3   Where a decision on any issue is by a majority, the award may contain reasons by the dissenting arbitrator for his dissent, in the discretion of that arbitrator.

13.4   Awards may be expressed in any currency claimed in the arbitration.

13.5   In addition to the statutory power to award interest, the Tribunal shall have the power to award interest at such rate and for such period as it considers fit on any sum after its due date but before commencement of the arbitration.

13.6   The Tribunal may make separate final awards on different issues at different times.

13.7   In the event of a settlement, the Tribunal may make an award recording the settlement if either party so requests.

13.8   Awards shall be final and binding on the parties as from the date they are made.

13.9   If all members of the Tribunal consider that the award contains any points which are of significant importance or interest to Members, they shall communicate such points to the Directors. The Directors, in consultation with the Tribunal, shall determine whether and how such points should be brought to the attention of Members while keeping the names of the parties confidential.

13.10   The award of the arbitrators shall be deposited by them with the Secretary who shall notify each party of such receipt. Either party may thereupon take up the award upon payment by that party of the costs and expenses of the arbitration as specified in the award (including the remuneration of the arbitrators) notwithstanding any direction in the award as to the ultimate responsibility therefor. Until the award is taken up by one of the parties it shall confer no rights upon either party. Upon the award being taken up by either party, a copy thereof shall forthwith be sent by the Secretary to the other party. In the event of the award not being taken up by either party within a period of 28 days from the notification by the Secretary of its receipt to the parties, the Deposit referred to in Regulation 1 above shall be forfeited, and the Secretary may in his absolute discretion call upon the parties or either of them (a) to take up the award and (b) to pay forthwith the costs and expenses of the award (including the remuneration of the arbitrators) or any part or proportion thereof whereupon the party or parties so called upon shall forthwith pay the costs and expenses as aforesaid and take up the award.

14.   Costs and Deposit

14.1   The Tribunal shall have power to specify in the award the amount of the costs of the arbitration (which expression shall, for the purpose of this Regulation 14, include the Tribunal's own remuneration, and any costs relating to the progress or conduct of the arbitration incurred by the Tribunal or by the Company including the costs of and fees payable to any person who has reported to or advised the Tribunal or the Company on any matter), and shall determine the proportions in which they shall be borne by the parties.

14.2   The Tribunal shall have power:—

(a)   to order in its award that all or part of the legal or other costs of one party be paid by the other party; and

(b)   to determine or assess the amount of those costs, if agreed by the parties, and for this purpose shall not be *functus officio*.

14.3   If the arbitration is abandoned, suspended, stayed or concluded, by agreement or otherwise, before the final award is made, the parties shall be jointly and severally liable to pay the costs of the arbitration, as determined by the Tribunal, and for this purpose the Tribunal shall not be *functus officio*.

14.4   In any determination or award made by the Tribunal pursuant to Regulations 14.1, 14.2 and 14.3 the Tribunal shall, or at any time on the application of either party the Tribunal may provide for the return or other disposal of the deposit or any part thereof to such persons as it shall in its absolute discretion consider fit.

15.   The Secretary and the Panel Committee

15.1   Subject only to Regulations 15.2 and 15.3, the Secretary and the Panel Committee shall have sole and exclusive jurisdiction over all matters referred for decision to each of them respectively by any provision of these Arbitration Regulations, and their decisions upon such matters shall be final and binding.

15.2   The Panel Committee may exercise any of the functions and powers of the Secretary referred to in these Arbitration Regulations. It may delegate to the Secretary any of its own functions and powers, either generally or in relation to specific matters.

15.3   In the event of conflict between a decision of the Secretary and a decision of the Panel Committee, the latter shall prevail.

16.   Exclusion of Liability

None of the Secretary, the Panel Committee, any arbitrator, or the Company shall be liable to any party for any act or omission in connection with any arbitration, save that the Secretary, the Panel Committee and the arbitrators may be liable for the consequences of conscious and deliberate wrongdoing.

17.   Governing Law

These Arbitration Regulations shall be governed by and construed in accordance with English Law.

MILAN CHAMBER OF NATIONAL AND INTERNATIONAL ARBITRATION

20123 Milan (Italy)
Palazzo Mezzanotte - Piazza degli Affari 6
Tel. 00-39-2- 8515.4536 - 8515.4444 - 8515.4515 - 8645.3607
Telefax 00-39-2- 8515.4384

INTERNATIONAL ARBITRATION RULES 1996

Standard Arbitration Clauses

Clause for sole arbitrator

All disputes arising out of the present contract (1), including those concerning its validity, interpretation, performance and termination, shall be referred to a sole arbitrator according to the International Arbitration Rules of the Chamber of National and International Arbitration of Milan, which the parties declare that they know and accept in their entirety.
The sole arbitrator shall decide according to the norms . . . (2) .
   The language of the arbitration shall be . . .

Clause for arbitral tribunal

All disputes arising out of the present contract (1), including those concerning its validity, interpretation, performance and termination, shall be referred to an arbitral tribunal consisting of three arbitrators, one being the President, according to the International Arbitration Rules of the Chamber of National and International Arbitration of Milan, which the parties declare that they know and accept in their entirety.
   The arbitrators shall decide according to the norms . . . (2).
   The language of the arbitration shall be . . .

Clause for multi-party arbitration

All disputes arising out of the present contract (1), including those concerning its validity, interpretation, performance and termination, shall be settled, independent of the number of the parties, by an arbitral tribunal consisting of three arbitrators, one being the President, directly appointed by the Chamber of National and International Arbitration of Milan, the International Arbitration Rules of which the parties declare that they know and accept in their entirety.

The arbitrators shall decide according to the norms . . . (2).

The language of the arbitration shall be . . .

Submission Agreement (3)

The undersigned (4) .... and ...., considering that a dispute has arisen between them concerning (5) ....

agree

to refer this dispute to the decision of (6) ...., according to the International Arbitration Rules of the Chamber of National and International Arbitration of Milan, which the parties declare that they know and accept in their entirety.

The arbitrator(s) shall decide according to the norms . . . (2).

The language of the arbitration shall be . . .

(Date)...

(Signature)...

(1)   Where the arbitration clause is contained in a document other than the contract to which it pertains, the contract referred to shall be indicated.

(2)   The parties may indicate the norms applicable to the merits of the dispute; alternatively, they may provide that the arbitrator decide *ex aequo et bono*.

(3)   The submission agreement is an agreement concluded where the dispute has already arisen between the parties and no arbitration clause has been previously concluded.

(4)   Indicate the name and domicile (seat, if a company) of the parties.

(5)   Indicate (in a general manner) the subject matter of the dispute, referring if necessary to the contract out of which the dispute arises.

(6)   Indicate the number of the arbitrators (one or three).

The Chamber of Arbitration

1.   The Chamber of National and International Arbitration of Milan, an entity of the Chamber of Commerce of Milan, does not adjudicate disputes: it administers arbitral proceedings under these Rules through its bodies.

The Chamber of Arbitration also provides technical and contractual expertise and conciliation services on national and international contracts.

Upon request, the Chamber of Arbitration appoints arbitrators and experts in arbitral proceedings not administered according to these Rules.

2.   The Chamber of Arbitration applies these Rules through its Arbitral Council and Secretariat.

3.   The Chamber of Arbitration is an Appointing Authority under the Arbitration Rules of the United Nations Commission for International Trade Law (UNCITRAL).

At the request of the parties, the Chamber of Arbitration administers arbitral proceedings according to the UNCITRAL Rules.

The Arbitral Council

1.   The Arbitral Council is composed of a Honorary President, an Executive President and five members appointed for three years by the Board of the Chamber of Commerce of Milan.

A maximum of two foreign members may be co-opted and appointed by the Board of the Chamber of Commerce of Milan.

The members of the Arbitral Council may not be appointed as arbitrators in proceedings administered by the Chamber of Arbitration.

2.   The Arbitral Council administers the arbitral proceedings held under these Rules.

In particular, it may:

— exercise a preliminary control on the existence and validity of the arbitration agreement and take measures on jurisdiction and connected proceedings where the arbitral body has not yet been formed;

— appoint, replace and decide on the challenge of arbitrators;

— extend the time limit for filing the arbitral award;

— determine the costs of the proceedings.

3.   The meetings of the Arbitral Council are valid where half of its members plus one are present; the Council deliberates by majority of the members present. In case of deadlock, the vote of the Honorary President or his deputy shall prevail.

The Secretariat

The Secretariat assists the Arbitral Council and performs the administrative tasks indicated in these Rules.

In particular;

— it receives the Request for Arbitration and ascertains whether it meets all requirements;

— it receives all procedural acts, ascertains their regularity and forwards them, in full compliance with the principle of adversarial proceedings;

— it gives logistical support in the proceedings to the arbitrator;

— it may request deposits on the costs of the proceedings, which are finally determined by the Arbitral Council.

Article 1   Arbitration agreement

1.   The arbitral procedure laid down in these Rules shall apply where the parties have concluded an arbitration agreement referring to the Chamber of Commerce of Milan or the Chamber of Arbitration of Milan or its Rules.

2.   Where a party raises an objection as to the existence or validity of the arbitration agreement before the arbitral body has been formed, the Arbitral Council shall decide on the matter and declare whether the arbitration may proceed.

If the arbitration proceeds, the arbitrator shall decide on his jurisdiction at the first hearing.

3.   Where there is no arbitration agreement or the arbitration agreement does not contain at least one of the indications under para. 1 of this Article, the party wishing nonetheless to commence arbitration according to the Rules of the Chamber of Arbitration of Milan may request to do so by filing a Request for Arbitration with the Chamber of Arbitration according to Article 2 of these Rules.

If the other party does not agree with this request within thirty days of receiving the Request for Arbitration, the Secretariat informs the requesting party that the arbitration cannot take place.

Article 2   Request for arbitration

1.   The party wishing to commence proceedings shall file a signed Request for Arbitration with the Chamber of Arbitration, containing:

(a)   the name and address of the parties and their domicile for the proceedings, if any;

(b)   the document containing the clause or submission or, in the case indicated under Article 1.3 of these Rules, the request to the other party to accept arbitration before the Chamber of Arbitration of Milan;

(c)   all indications, if any, as to the language of the arbitration, the norms applicable to the merits of the dispute or the *ex aequo et bono* decision;

(d)   a description of the facts and claims and a (summary) indication of the economic value of the dispute, if possible;

(e)   the evidence, if any, in support of its claim and any document which the party deems appropriate to enclose;

(f)   the designation of the arbitrator or all indications necessary for selecting him;

(g)   the original power of attorney to counsel, if any.

2.   The Request for Arbitration shall be filed with the Chamber of Arbitration as follows: one original for the Chamber of Arbitration and one for each defendant, plus as many copies as are the arbitrators.

When filing the Request, claimant shall pay the registration fee indicated in the annexed Schedule.

3.   Where the document under (b) is lacking or the other party does not accept arbitration in the case under Article 1.3 of these Rules, the Secretariat shall declare that the arbitration cannot take place.

4.   The Secretariat shall forward the Request for Arbitration to the other party through a bailiff, by registered mail with advice of receipt or by any other means allowing for a proof that the notice has been received.

Article 3   Statement of defence and counterclaim by defendant

1.   Within thirty days of receiving the Request, defendant shall file its signed Statement of Defence with the Chamber of Arbitration, containing:

(a)   the name and address of defendant and its domicile for the proceedings, any;

(b)   all indications, if any, as to the language of the arbitration, the norms applicable to the merits of the dispute or the *ex aequo et bono* decision;

(c)   its defence and all counterclaims, if any, with a (summary) indication of their economic value;

(d)   the evidence, if any, in support of its defence and counterclaim and any document which the party deems appropriate to enclose;

(e)   the designation of the arbitrator or all necessary indications for selecting him;

(f)   the original power of attorney to counsel, if any.

2.   The Statement of Defence by defendant shall be filed with the Chamber of Arbitration as follows: one original for the Chamber of Arbitration and one for each opposing party, plus as many copies as are the arbitrators.

When filing its Statement, defendant shall pay the registration fee indicated in the annexed Schedule.

3.   In case of counterclaim by defendant, claimant may file a Reply within thirty days of receiving notice of the counterclaim.

4.   The Secretariat shall forward the Statement of Defence by defendant to the other party through a bailiff, by registered mail with advice of receipt or by any other means allowing for a proof that the notice has been received.

Article 4   Deposit on the costs of the proceedings

1.   The Secretariat shall give a provisional estimate of the economic value of the dispute on the basis of the documents mentioned in Articles 2 and 3, and request the parties to pay an equal part of the deposit on the costs of the proceedings as indicated in Article 22 of the Rules.

The economic value of the dispute shall be estimated on the basis of all the claims presented by all the parties and their economic value.

2.   Where one or more counterclaims have been filed, the Secretariat may request the parties to pay separate deposits for the main claim and the counterclaim.

3.   Where the value of the dispute is initially undetermined, the deposit on the costs of the proceedings to be paid by the parties shall be determined by the Secretariat.

Article 5   Appointment of the arbitrator

1.   Disputes under these Rules shall be settled by a sole arbitrator or by a Tribunal of three arbitrators or more, provided their number is uneven. In the absence of a specific provision by the parties as to the number of arbitrators, the dispute shall be settled by a sole arbitrator appointed by the Arbitral Council, unless the Arbitral Council deems that the dispute, because of its characteristics, is to be referred to a Tribunal of three arbitrators.

2.   *Sole arbitrator*

Unless otherwise agreed, the sole arbitrator shall be appointed by the Arbitral Council.

Where the parties have provided for the common designation of the sole arbitrator, such designation shall be made within fifteen days of the filing of the Statement of Defence by defendant.

If the parties cannot reach an agreement, the arbitrator shall be appointed by the Council.

3. *Arbitral tribunal*

Unless otherwise agreed, the Tribunal shall be formed in the following manner:

(a)   each party shall designate an arbitrator in the Request for Arbitration and the Statement of Defence, respectively; if a party fails to do so, the arbitrator shall be appointed by the Arbitral Council;

(b)   the third arbitrator, being the President of the Tribunal, shall be appointed by the Arbitral Council. The parties may, however, provide that the third arbitrator be designated by common agreement of the two arbitrators designated by the parties. In this case, if the two arbitrators fail to reach an agreement within the time limit indicated by the parties, or set by the Chamber of Arbitration where the parties have not indicated it, the third arbitrator shall be appointed by the Arbitral Council;

(c)   all the arbitrators who have not been directly appointed by the Arbitral Council (i.e. those designated by the parties and the third arbitrator designated by common agreement by the two arbitrators) shall be confirmed by the Arbitral Council; if the arbitrator is not confirmed, the new arbitrator shall again be designated by the party or by the two arbitrators.

4.   Where it appoints the sole arbitrator or the President of the Tribunal, the Arbitral Council shall appoint a person of a nationality other than that of the parties, where they do not have the same nationality.

5. *Plurality of parties*

Where there are more than two parties to the arbitration and their interests contrast and cannot be reduced to two opposing interests, in the absence of a specific provision in the arbitration clause as to the number or manner of appointment of the arbitrators, the Arbitral Council shall directly appoint a Tribunal of three arbitrators, one being the President of the Tribunal.

In the presence of a specific provision in the arbitration clause or a factual situation leading to a Tribunal of more than three arbitrators, the Arbitral Council shall appoint as many arbitrators as are needed to obtain in any case an uneven number of arbitrators.

Article 6   Acceptance and statement of independence by the arbitrator

1.   Within ten days of receiving notice of his appointment from the Chamber of Arbitration, the arbitrator shall give notice of his acceptance to the Chamber.

2.   When giving notice of his acceptance, the arbitrator shall state in writing:

— any relationship with the parties or their counsel which may affect his independence and impartiality;

— any personal or economic interest, either direct or indirect, in the subject matter of the dispute;

— any prejudice or reservation as to the subect matter of the dispute which may affect his impartiality.

Where necessary, due to supervening facts, this Statement shall be repeated in the course of the arbitral proceedings until the award is filed.

3.   A new arbitrator, replacing the party-designated arbitrator who has not accepted the mandate shall again be designated by the party, within ten days of the notification of non-acceptance.

Article 7   Replacement of the arbitrator in case of challenge, resignation, impossibility or obstructive behaviour

1.   Within ten days of receiving notice of the Statement of the Arbitrator provided for in Article 6, or of becoming aware of a new ground, each party may, under pain of expiry, file a reasoned challenge against the arbitrator with the Secretariat.

The Arbitral Council shall render a final decision on the challenge, after having heard the arbitrator, which may also be only in writing.

The Arbitral Council may remove the arbitrator on its own initiative.

2.   The arbitrator may resign in the course of the proceedings for serious reasons, by giving written notice thereof to the Arbitral Council.

3.   The arbitrator shall be replaced in case of death or supervening impossibility.

4.   In case of obstructive behaviour by the arbitrator, such as inactivity, unjustified delay or negligence in performing his tasks, the Arbitral Council shall issue a first warning in writing. If the arbitrator still does not fulfil his duties, the Council shall remove him and appoint another arbitrator in his place.

5.   In all cases of replacement provided for in this Article, the Arbitral Council shall decide on the manner of appointment of the new arbitrator and determine the fees due to the arbitrator who has been replaced, taking into account the work done.

6.   In all cases of replacement of the arbitrator provided for in the present Article, the new sole arbitrator or the new Arbitral Tribunal shall decide whether to repeat all or some of the acts in the proceedings. Where all acts are to be repeated, the time limit for rendering the award starts running *ex novo* from the moment in which the renewal order has been issued.

Article 8   Transmission of the file to the arbitrator

The Secretariat shall forward the Request for Arbitration and the Statement of Defence by defendant to the arbitrator, together with all annexed documents, only after the parties have paid the initial deposit provided for in Article 4.

Article 9   Arbitral jurisdiction

Arbitral jurisdiction is deemed accepted if defendant does not expressly object to it within the time limit provided for in Article 3.1.

Article 10   Connected disputes

Where more than one proceedings are commenced before the Chamber of Arbitration on connected disputes, the Arbitral Council may, before the first hearing before the arbitral body, suggest to the parties that the proceedings be consolidated and referred to an arbitral body appointed by the Council.

Article 11　Seat of the arbitration

In the absence of an agreement by the parties, the seat of the arbitration is at the seat of the Chamber of Arbitration of Milan, unless the Arbitral Council, taking into account special requests by the parties or the characteristics of the arbitration, determines a different seat before the first hearing before the arbitral body.

The arbitrators may further decide that hearings or single procedural acts take place in a place other than the seat.

Article 12　Language of the arbitration

1.　Where the parties have not agreed on a language within the time limit provided for filing the Statement of Defence by defendant, the language in which the arbitration is to be held shall be determined by the arbitrator, taking into account the circumstances of the arbitration, among others, the language of the contract under which the dispute arises and the language of the correspondence between the parties, in such a manner as to guarantee that the interests of all parties are fully protected.

2.　The acts in the arbitral proceedings precedent to the determination by the arbitrators shall be drawn up in or translated into the language of the contract.

3.　The arbitrator may authorise or request translations or interpretations of single acts of the parties.

Article 13　Norms applicable to the merits

The parties may, also after commencement of the proceedings, agree on the norms applicable to the merits of the dispute or provide that the arbitrator decide *ex aequo et bono*.

If the parties are silent, the arbitrator shall apply the law with which the contract has its closest connection.

In any case the arbitrator shall take into account the provisions of the contract and trade usages.

Article 14　Urgent measures

1.　If this is allowed under the applicable law, the parties may request the arbitrator to issue urgent measures, also in the form of a partial award, in order to prevent events related to the object of the dispute which otherwise could not be avoided.

2.　The arbitrator may make the measure conditional upon a bond, guarantee or other security to be given by the requesting party.

3.　The parties shall comply with the measure forthwith, or in any case within the time limit set therein.

4.　A request by a party to the Judicial Authority to issue an urgent measure is not to be deemed incompatible with the arbitration agreement.

Article 15   Rules governing the proceedings and the taking of evidence

1.   The rules applicable to the procedure shall be those established by the parties before the arbitral body is formed, by these Rules or, in the silence of the Rules, by the arbitrator.

2.   Where the nature of the dispute allows, the arbitrator shall attempt a conciliation between the parties at the first hearing. This conciliation attempt may be renewed at any moment in the evidence taking phase.

3.   The arbitrator may gather evidence both on his own initiative and at the request of a party, in full compliance with the principle of adversarial proceedings.

4.   The arbitrator may hear the parties directly and admit witness evidence, also in writing.

Where witness evidence is admitted, the interested parties shall arrange that the witnesses are present on the day and place of the hearing.

The arbitrator may authorise or request interpreters or translators for the hearing of witnesses.

If a witness is absent without just reason, he may not be subsequently heard unless the interested party requests so and the arbitrator agrees.

5.   The arbitrator may appoint one or more expert witnesses for the arbitral body, define their mission, receive their reports and hear them in adversarial proceedings with any party-appointed expert witness.

At the request of the arbitrator, the expert witness for the arbitral body may also be appointed by the Arbitral Council.

The provisions of Articles 6 and 7 on the acceptance by and the replacement of the arbitrator apply, in so far as they are compatible, to the expert witness for the arbitral body.

The Chamber of Arbitration shall ascertain that the fees of the expert witness for the arbitral body are determined according to the schedule of his professional association.

6.   When the evidence taking phase is concluded, the arbitrator may set a time limit for filing final statements and a last hearing for oral discussion.

7.   Where an arbitral tribunal has been appointed, the tribunal may delegate the evidence taking to its President or one of its members.

8.   If the parties so request, the arbitrator may decide on the basis of documents only, in full compliance with the principle of adversarial proceedings.

Article 16   Hearings and minutes

1.   The date of the hearings shall be determined by the arbitrator and communicated to the parties with adequate notice.

2.   The parties may appear at the hearings either in person or through duly empowered representatives, or be assisted by counsel with power of attorney.

If a party does not appear at the hearing without just reason, the arbitrator shall ascertain whether it was duly summoned and may then proceed with the hearing.

Otherwise, he shall arrange that the party is summoned again.

3.   The arbitrator shall make minutes of all hearings and evidence taking activity; the Secretariat shall forward a copy of the minutes to the parties.

Article 17   Settlement in the course of the proceedings

1.   If the parties reach a settlement before the arbitral body is formed, they shall give notice thereof to the Secretariat, which terminates the proceedings.

2.   If the parties reach a settlement after the arbitral body has been formed, the arbitrator shall make a report, signed by the parties, which relieves him from the obligation to render an award.

If the settlement only concerns part of the dispute, the proceedings continue on the issues not covered by the settlement.

3.   The parties may jointly request the arbitrator, who may refuse, to record their settlement in an award.

Article 18   Deliberation and signing of the award

1.   Where an arbitral tribunal has been appointed, the award shall be deliberated by the arbitrators meeting in personal conference or videoconference, also at a place other than the seat of the arbitration, and shall be set down in writing.

The decision shall be taken unanimously or by majority vote or, where no majority is possible, by the President of the arbitral tribunal.

2.   The award may be signed by the members of the arbitral tribunal at different times and places, also abroad.

Each signature shall indicate its place, day, month and year.

3.   The signatures of the members of the arbitral tribunal may result from different copies of the award, as long as the Secretariat declares them to be true copies of the original.

4.   Where the award is signed only by the majority of the members or by the President of the arbitral tribunal, it shall be expressly declared that the deliberation has taken place in personal conference of all members and that the members who did not sign could not or did not wish to.

Article 19   Contents of the award

1.   The award shall settle all the issues of the dispute, and give reasons therefor.

2.   The award shall indicate or refer to the costs of the proceedings provided for in Article 22 of the Rules and determined by the Arbitral Council of the Chamber.

3.   The arbitrator shall apportion the costs of the proceedings and the legal costs between the parties in the award.

Article 20   Partial award

If, for reasons to be stated in the partial award, he deems that he can decide separately on some of the issues of the dispute, the arbitrator shall render a partial award.

A partial award does not affect the time limit for rendering the final award provided for in Article 21.1, requests for extension excepted.

Article 21   Time limit for filing the award: suspensions and extensions

1.   The arbitrator shall file the award with the Secretariat of the Chamber of Arbitration within six months of the first hearing.

The award shall be filed in as many originals as are the parties plus one.

The Chamber of Arbitration shall forward the award to each party by sending the original award by registered mail with advice of receipt or by any other means allowing for a proof that the notice has been received.

2.   The time limit for filing the award shall be suspended in the case provided for in Article 22.4 of these Rules.

The Arbitral Council may, on its own initiative or at the request of a party or the arbitrator, suspend the proceedings on any other just ground.

3.   The time limit shall be extended only by the Arbitral Council on just grounds.

Article 22   Costs of the proceedings and payments

1.   The costs of the proceedings shall be determined by the Arbitral Council. They shall include:

(a)   the registration fees paid by claimant when filing the Request and by defendant together with its Statement of Defence;

(b)   the administrative fees due to the Secretariat of the Chamber of Arbitration for its activities;

(c)   the fees (and reimbursement of expenses) of the arbitrator, determined on the basis of the economic value of the dispute and the annexed Schedule, taking into account the complexity of the dispute, the rapidity of the proceedings and the work done by the arbitrator. In case of a tribunal, the Arbitral Council may establish different fees for the members of the arbitral tribunal, in particular for the President with respect to the other members;

(d)   the fees (and reimbursement of expenses) of the expert witness for the arbitral body.

2.   The Secretariat may request to the parties, apart from the initial deposit under Article 4, further advance payments on the costs to be finally determined by the Arbitral Council.

3.   The parties shall make equal payments until the end of the proceedings, with the exception of the case where separate deposits are requested as provided for in Article 4.2 of these Rules.

Where a party does not make a requested payment within the time limit given therefor, the payment may be made by the other party. In such case, this sum shall be credited in the award to the party which has paid.

4.   If any of the payments requested during the proceedings is not made, the Chamber of Arbitration shall suspend the proceedings. The time limit shall start running again when the payment is made.

Where a payment is not made within six months of having been requested, the Arbitral Council may declare that the request to which the payment refers has been withdrawn.

5.   Where the proceedings end before the award is rendered, the Arbitral Council shall determine the costs of the proceedings, taking into account the moment when the proceedings have ended and the work done.

6. If the dispute or the proceedings are extraordinarily complex, the Arbitral Council may determine the costs of the proceedings in excess of the Schedule.

Article 23   Scope and application of the rules

These Rules shall apply to all proceedings commenced after 1st May 1996. Where the parties have not indicated which Rules (National or International) apply to the proceedings, the arbitrator shall decide on the matter, on the basis of the national or international nature of the arbitration.

Article 24   Notices and time limits

1.   Notices shall be sent by all means commonly used in business relationships for the sake of rapidity, as long as they allow for a proof of receipt.
2.   Notice of an act shall be deemed sent at the place and on the day of delivery to the addressee by the means provided for in the preceding paragraph.
3.   The time limits indicated in these Rules shall run from the date on which notice thereof is received by the addressee.
The initial day shall be excluded from the calculation of time limits.
Where the date of expiry falls on a Saturday or a holiday, it shall be prorogated to the first following working day.

Article 25   Filing of acts and documents by the parties

1.   The parties shall file with the Chamber of Arbitration: one original of each act for the Chamber of Arbitration and one original for the other party, plus as many copies as there are arbitrators.
2.   Photostatic copies of documents may be filed. Where it is disputed that the copies are true copies of the original, the interested party may request the Secretariat to certify them, by showing the original.
3.   The Secretariat may send copies of acts and documents, stating that they are true copies of the original.
4.   If the parties do not file the requested number of copies, the Secretariat shall make copies at the expense of the failing party.

Article 26   Restitution and keeping of acts

Each party may, within three months of the conclusion of the proceedings, request the restitution of the acts it has filed. The Secretariat keeps the case file for three years after conclusion of the proceedings.

Article 27   Obligation to preserve confidentiality

1.   The Chamber of Arbitration, the arbitrator, the expert and the parties shall keep all information on the development and outcome of the arbitral proceedings confidential.
2.   The parties may expressly authorise the Chamber of Arbitration to publish the award, either in its entirety or in a totally anonymous form as far as the parties and other persons in the proceedings are concerned.

Article 28   General rule

In all cases not expressly provided for in these Rules, the Arbitral Council and the arbitrators shall act according to the general principles underlying these Rules, in such a manner as to guarantee to the parties correct, transparent and rapid proceedings.

CHAMBER OF NATIONAL AND INTERNATIONAL ARBITRATION OF MILAN CODE OF ETHICS FOR ARBITRATORS

[*See Part VII of this book.*]

SCHEDULE OF FEES FOR INTERNATIONAL ARBITRATION SERVICES

[*Not included here.*]

INTERNATIONAL BUREAU OF THE PERMANENT COURT OF ARBITRATION

The Secretary-General and the International Bureau of the Permanent Court of Arbitration may be addressed at:

Peace Palace, Carnegieplaan 2, NL-2517 KJ The Hague.
Tel: +31-70-302.42.42
Fax: +31-70-302.41.67
e-mail: pca@euronet.nl euronet

(The Court also publishes the *Permanent Court of Arbitration Optional Rules for Arbitrating Disputes between Two States,* October 20th, 1992.)

Peace Palace, Carnegieplein 2, 2517 KJ The Hague, The Netherlands, Telephone: (0)70-302.4242, Facsimile: (0)70-302.4167

OPTIONAL RULES

MODEL ARBITRATION CLAUSES FOR USE IN CONNECTION WITH THE PERMANENT COURT OF ARBITRATION OPTIONAL RULES FOR ARBITRATING DISPUTES BETWEEN TWO PARTIES OF WHICH ONLY ONE IS A STATE

Future Disputes

Where a State and a private entity are parties to a contract and wish to have any dispute referred to arbitration under these Rules, they may insert in the contract an arbitration clause in the following form:

1. If any dispute arises between the parties as to the interpretation, application or performance of this contract, including its existence, validity or

termination, either party may submit the dispute to final and binding arbitration in accordance with the Permanent Court of Arbitration Optional Rules for Arbitrating Disputes Between Two Parties of which only one is a State, as in effect on the date of this contract.[1]

Parties may wish to consider adding:

2. *The number of arbitrators shall be* . . . [insert 'one' or 'three'][2].
3. *The language(s) to be used in the arbitral proceedings shall be* . . . [insert choice of one or more languages][3].
4. *The appointing authority shall be* . . . [insert choice][4].
5. This agreement to arbitrate constitutes a waiver of any right to sovereign immunity from execution to which a party might otherwise be entitled with respect to the enforcement of any award rendered by an arbitral tribunal constituted pursuant to this agreement[5].

Notes

1. Parties may agree to vary this model clause. If they consider doing so, they may consult with the Secretary-General of the Permanent Court of Arbitration to ensure that the clause to which they agree will be appropriate in the context of the Rules, and that the functions of the Secretary-General and the International Bureau can be carried out effectively.
2. If the parties do not agree on the number of arbitrators, the number shall be three, in accordance with article 5 of the Rules.
3. If the parties do not agree on the language, or languages, to be used in the arbitral proceedings, this shall be determined by the arbitral tribunal in accordance with article 17 of the Rules.
4. Parties are free to agree upon any appointing authority, e.g., the President of the International Court of Justice, or the head of a specialised body expert in the relevant subject-matter, or an *ad hoc* panel chosen by the parties, or any other officer, institution or individual. The Secretary-General of the Permanent Court of Arbitration will consider accepting designation as appointing authority in appropriate cases. Before inserting the name of an appointing authority in an arbitration clause, it is advisable for the parties to inquire whether the proposed authority is willing to act.
   If the parties do not agree on the appointing authority, the Secretary-General of the Permanent Court of Arbitration at The Hague will designate the appointing authority in accordance with article 6 or 7 of the Rules, as the case may be.
5. Waiver of sovereign immunity from jurisdiction is provided in article 1, paragraph 2 of the Rules.

Existing Disputes

If the parties have not already entered into an arbitration agreement, or if they mutually agree to change a previous agreement in order to provide for arbitration under these Rules, they may enter into an agreement in the following form:

The parties agree to submit the following dispute to final and binding arbitration in accordance with the Permanent Court of Arbitration Optional Rules for Arbitrating Bilateral Disputes Two Parties of which only one is a State, as in effect on the date of this agreement: . . . [insert brief description of dispute].

Parties may wish to consider adding paragraphs 2–5 of the arbitration clause for future disputes as set forth above.

GUIDELINES FOR ADAPTING THESE RULES FOR USE IN ARBITRATING DISPUTES ARISING UNDER MULTIPARTY CONTRACTS

The Permanent Court of Arbitration Optional Rules for Arbitrating Disputes Between Two Parties of which only one is a State can be adapted for use in resolving disputes arising under multiparty contracts. All of the provisions in these Rules are appropriate, except that modifications are needed in the mechanisms for naming arbitrators and sharing costs.

Particular care should be taken in drafting the provisions for appointing arbitrators where there may be so many parties in the arbitration that the tribunal would be of impractical size or structure if each party appointed an arbitrator. One solution sometimes considered in multiparty arbitrations is for the parties to agree that the appointing authority will designate all of the arbitrators if the parties do not do so within a specified period.

Modifications may also be needed in the provisions for sharing the costs of the arbitration.

It is recommended that parties that contemplate including an arbitration provision in a multiparty contract consult in advance with the Secretary-General of the Permanent Court of Arbitration concerning the drafting of that provision in order to ensure that the functions of the Secretary-General and the International Bureau of the Permanent Court of Arbitration can be carried out effectively.

PERMANENT COURT OF ARBITRATION OPTIONAL RULES FOR ARBITRATING DISPUTES BETWEEN TWO PARTIES OF WHICH ONLY ONE IS A STATE

effective 6 July 1993

SECTION I

INTRODUCTORY RULES

Scope of Application

Article 1

1.   Where the parties to a contract have agreed in writing that disputes in relation to that contract shall be referred to arbitration under the Permanent

Court of Arbitration Optional Rules for Arbitrating Disputes Between two parties of which only one is a State, then such disputes shall be referred to arbitration in accordance with these Rules subject to such modification as the parties may agree in writing.

2.   Agreement by a party to arbitration under these Rules constitutes a waiver of any right of sovereign immunity from jurisdiction, in respect of the dispute in question, to which such party might otherwise be entitled. A waiver of immunity relating to the execution of an arbitral award must be explicitly expressed.

3.   These Rules shall govern the arbitration except that where any of these Rules is in conflict with a provision of the law applicable to the arbitration from which the parties cannot derogate, that provision shall prevail.

4.   The International Bureau of the Permanent Court of Arbitration at The Hague (the 'International Bureau') shall have charge of the archives of the arbitration proceeding. In addition, the International Bureau shall, upon written request of all the parties or of the arbitral tribunal, act as a channel of communications between the parties and the arbitral tribunal, and provide secretariat services including, *inter alia,* arranging for hearing rooms, interpretation, and stenographic or electronic records of hearings.

Notice, Calculation of Periods of Time

Article 2

1.   For the purposes of these Rules, any notice, including a notification, communication or proposal, is deemed to have been received if it is physically delivered to the addressee or if it is delivered at the addressee's habitual residence, place of business or mailing address, or, if none of these can be found after making reasonable inquiry, then at the addressee's last-known residence or place of business or mailing address. Notice shall be deemed to have been received on the day it is so delivered.

2.   For the purposes of calculating a period of time under these Rules, such period shall begin to run on the day following the day when a notice, notification, communication or proposal is received. If the last day of such period is an official holiday or a non-business day at the residence or place of usiness of the addressee, the period is extended until the first business day which follows. Official holidays or non-business days occurring during the running of the period of time are included in calculating the period.

Notice of Arbitration

Article 3

1.   The party initiating recourse to arbitration (hereinafter called the 'claimant') shall give to the other party (hereinafter called the 'respondent') a notice of arbitration.

2.   Arbitral proceedings shall be deemed to commence on the date on which the notice of arbitration is received by the respondent.

3.   The notice of arbitration shall include the following:

(a)   A demand that the dispute be referred to arbitration;

(b)   The names and addresses of the parties;

(c)   A reference to the arbitration clause or the separate arbitration agreement that is invoked;

(d)   A reference to the contract out of or in relation to which the dispute arises;

(e)   The general nature of the claim and an indication of the amount involved, if any;

(f)   The relief or remedy sought;

(g)   A proposal as to the number of arbitrators (i.e. one or three), if the parties have not previously agreed thereon.

4.   The notice of arbitration may also include:

(a)   The proposals for the appointments of a sole arbitrator and an appointing authority referred to in article 6, paragraph 1;

(b)   The notification of the appointment of an arbitrator referred to in article 7;

(c)   The statement of claim referred to in article 18.

Representation and Assistance

Article 4

The parties may be represented or assisted by persons of their choice. The names and addresses of such persons must be communicated in writing to the other party, to the International Bureau, and to the arbitral tribunal after it has been appointed; such communication must specify whether the appointment is being made for purposes of representation or assistance.

SECTION II

COMPOSITION OF THE ARBITRAL TRIBUNAL

Number of Arbitrators

Article 5

1.   If the parties have not previously agreed on the number of arbitrators (i.e. one or three), and if within thirty days after the receipt by the respondent of the notice of arbitration the parties have not agreed that there shall be only one arbitrator, three arbitrators shall be appointed.

Appointment of Arbitrators (Articles 6 to 8)

Article 6

1.   If a sole arbitrator is to be appointed, either party may propose to the other:

(a)   The names of one or more persons, one of whom would serve as the sole arbitrator; and

(b)   If no appointing authority has been agreed upon by the parties, the name or names of one or more institutions or persons, one of whom would serve as appointing authority.

2. If within thirty days after receipt by a party of a proposal made in accordance with paragraph 1 the parties have not reached agreement on the choice of a sole arbitrator, the sole arbitrator shall be appointed by the appointing authority agreed upon by the parties. If no appointing authority has been agreed upon by the parties, or if the appointing authority agreed upon refuses to act or fails to appoint the arbitrator within sixty days of the receipt of a party's request therefor, either party may request the Secretary-General of the Permanent Court of Arbitration at The Hague ('the Secretary-General') to designate an appointing authority.

3. The appointing authority shall, at the request of one of the parties, appoint the sole arbitrator as promptly as possible. In making the appointment the appointing authority shall use the following list-procedure, unless both parties agree that the list-procedure should not be used or unless the appointing authority determines in its discretion that the use of the list-procedure is not appropriate for the case:

(a) At the request of one of the parties the appointing authority shall communicate to both parties an identical list containing at least three names;

(b) Within thirty days after the receipt of this list, each party may return the list to the appointing authority after having deleted the name or names to which he objects and numbered the remaining names on the list in the order of its preference;

(c) After the expiration of the above period of time the appointing authority shall appoint the sole arbitrator from among the names approved on the lists returned to it and in accordance with the order of preference indicated by the parties;

(d) If for any reason the appointment cannot be made according to this procedure, the appointing authority may exercise its discretion in appointing the sole arbitrator.

4. In making the appointment, the appointing authority shall have regard to such considerations as are likely to secure the appointment of an independent and impartial arbitrator and shall take into account as well the advisability of appointing an arbitrator of a nationality other than the nationalities of the parties.

Article 7

1. If three arbitrators are to be appointed, each party shall appoint one arbitrator. The two arbitrators thus appointed shall choose the third arbitrator who will act as the presiding arbitrator of the tribunal.

2. If within thirty days after the receipt of a party's notification of the appointment of an arbitrator the other party has not notified the first party of the arbitrator it has appointed:

(a) The first party may request the appointing authority previously designated by the parties to appoint the second arbitrator; or

(b) If no such authority has been previously designated by the parties, or if the appointing authority previously designated refuses to act or fails to appoint the arbitrator within thirty days after receipt of a party's request therefor, the first party may request the Secretary-General to designate the appointing authority. The first party may then request the appointing authority so designated to appoint the second arbitrator. In either case, the appointing authority may exercise its discretion in appointing the arbitrator.

3.   If within thirty days after the appointment of the second arbitrator the two arbitrators have not agreed on the choice of the presiding arbitrator, the presiding arbitrator shall be appointed by an appointing authority in the same way as a sole arbitrator would be appointed under article 6.

Article 8

1.   When an appointing authority is requested to appoint an arbitrator pursuant to article 6 or article 7, the party which makes the request shall send to the appointing authority a copy of the notice of arbitration, a copy of the contract out of or in relation to which the dispute has arisen and a copy of the arbitration agreement if it is not contained in the contract. The appointing authority may require from either party such information as it deems necessary to fulfil its function.

2.   Where the names of one or more persons are proposed for appointment as arbitrators, their full names, addresses and nationalities shall be indicated, together with a description of their qualifications.

3.   In appointing arbitrators pursuant to these Rules, the parties and the appointing authority are free to designate persons who are not members of the Permanent Court of Arbitration at The Hague.

Challenge of Arbitrators (Articles 9 to 12)

Article 9

A prospective arbitrator shall disclose to those who approach him/her in connection with his/her possible appointment any circumstances likely to give rise to justifiable doubts as to his/her impartiality or independence. An arbitrator, once appointed or chosen, shall disclose such circumstances to the parties unless they have already been informed by him/her of these circumstances.

Article 10

1.   Any arbitrator may be challenged if circumstances exist that give rise to justifiable doubts as to the arbitrator's impartiality or independence.

2.   A party may challenge the arbitrator appointed by it only for reasons of which it becomes aware after the appointment has been made.

Article 11

1.   A party which intends to challenge an arbitrator shall send notice of its challenge within thirty days after the appointment of the challenged arbitrator has been notified to the challenging party or within thirty days after the circumstances mentioned in articles 9 and 10 became known to that party.

2.   The challenge shall be notified to the other party, to the arbitrator who is challenged and to the other members of the arbitral tribunal. The notification shall be in writing and shall state the reasons for the challenge.

3.   When an arbitrator has been challenged by one party, the other party may agree to the challenge. The arbitrator may also, after the challenge,

withdraw from his/her office. In neither case does this imply acceptance of the validity of the grounds for the challenge. In both cases the procedure provided in article 6 or 7 shall be used in full for the appointment of the substitute arbitrator, even if during the process of appointing the challenged arbitrator a party had failed to exercise its right to appoint or to participate in the appointment.

Article 12

1. If the other party does not agree to the challenge and the challenged arbitrator does not withdraw, the decision on the challenge will be made:

(a) When the initial appointment was made by an appointing authority, by that authority;

(b) When the initial appointment was not made by an appointing authority, but an appointing authority has been previously designated, by that authority;

(c) In all other cases, by the appointing authority to be designated in accordance with the procedure for designating an appointing authority as provided for in article 6.

2. If the appointing authority sustains the challenge, a substitute arbitrator shall be appointed or chosen pursuant to the procedure applicable to the appointment or choice of an arbitrator as provided in articles 6 to 9 except that, when this procedure would call for the designation of an appointing authority, the appointment of the arbitrator shall be made by the appointing authority which decided on the challenge.

Replacement of an Arbitrator

Article 13

1. In the event of the death or resignation of an arbitrator during the course of the arbitral proceedings, a substitute arbitrator shall be appointed or chosen pursuant to the procedure provided for in articles 6 to 9 that was applicable to the appointment or choice of the arbitrator being replaced. Any resignation by an arbitrator shall be addressed to the arbitral tribunal and shall not be effective unless the arbitral tribunal determines that there are sufficient reasons to accept the resignation, and if the arbitral tribunal so determines the resignation shall become effective on the date designated by the arbitral tribunal. In the event that an arbitrator whose resignation is not accepted by the tribunal nevertheless fails to participate in the arbitration, the provisions of paragraph 3 of this article shall apply.

2. In the event that an arbitrator fails to act or in the event of the *de jure* or *de facto* impossibility of his/her performing his/her functions, the procedure in respect of the challenge and replacement of an arbitrator as provided in the preceding articles shall apply, subject to the provisions of paragraph 3 of this article.

3. If an arbitrator on a three-person tribunal fails to participate in the arbitration, the other arbitrators shall, unless the parties agree otherwise, have the power in their sole discretion to continue the arbitration and to make any decision, ruling or award, notwithstanding the failure of one arbitrator to participate. In determining whether to continue the arbitration or to render

any decision, ruling, or award without the participation of an arbitrator, the other arbitrators shall take into account the stage of the arbitration, the reason, if any, expressed by the arbitrator for such nonparticipation, and such other matters as they consider appropriate in the circumstances of the case. In the event that the other arbitrators determine not to continue the arbitration without the nonparticipating arbitrator, the arbitral tribunal shall declare the office vacant, and a substitute arbitrator shall be appointed pursuant to the provisions of articles 6 to 9, unless the parties otherwise agree on a different method of appointment.

Repetition of Hearings in the Event of the Replacement of an Arbitrator

Article 14

If under articles 11 to 13 the sole or presiding arbitrator is replaced, any hearings held previously shall be repeated; if any other arbitrator is replaced, such prior hearings may be repeated at the discretion of the arbitral tribunal.

SECTION III

ARBITRAL PROCEEDINGS

General Provisions

Article 15

1. Subject to these Rules, the arbitral tribunal may conduct the arbitration in such manner as it considers appropriate, provided that the parties are treated with equality and that at any stage of the proceedings each party is given a full opportunity of presenting its case.

2. If either party so requests at any appropriate stage of the proceedings, the arbitral tribunal shall hold hearings for the presentation of evidence by witnesses, including expert witnesses, or for oral argument. In the absence of such a request, the arbitral tribunal shall decide whether to hold such hearings or whether the proceedings shall be conducted on the basis of documents and other materials.

3. All documents or information supplied to the arbitral tribunal by one party shall at the same time be communicated by that party to the other party and a copy shall be filed with the International Bureau.

Place of Arbitration

Article 16

1. Unless the parties have agreed upon the place where the arbitration is to be held, such place shall be The Hague, The Netherlands. If the parties agree that the arbitration shall be held at a place other than The Hague, the International Bureau shall inform the parties and the arbitral tribunal whether it is willing to provide the secretariat and registrar services referred to in article 1, paragraph 4, and the services referred to in article 25, paragraph 3.

2. The arbitral tribunal may determine the locale of the arbitration within the country agreed upon by the parties. It may hear witnesses and hold meetings for consultation among its members at any place it deems appropriate, having regard to the circumstances of the arbitration.

3. After inviting the views of the parties, the arbitral tribunal may meet at any place it deems appropriate for the inspection of goods, other property or documents. The parties shall be given sufficient notice to enable them to be present at such inspection.

4. The award shall be made at the place of arbitration.

Language

Article 17

1. Subject to an agreement by the parties, the arbitral tribunal shall, promptly after its appointment, determine the language or languages to be used in the proceedings. This determination shall apply to the statement of claim, the statement of defence, and any further written statements and, if oral hearings take place, to the language or languages to be used in such hearings.

2. The arbitral tribunal may order that any documents annexed to the statement of claim or statement of defence, and any supplementary documents or exhibits submitted in the course of the proceedings, delivered in their original language, shall be accompanied by a translation into the language or languages agreed upon by the parties or determined by the arbitral tribunal.

Statement of Claim

Article 18

1. Unless the statement of claim was contained in the notice of arbitration, within a period of time to be determined by the arbitral tribunal, the claimant shall communicate its statement of claim in writing to the respondent and to each of the arbitrators. A copy of the contract, and of the arbitration agreement if not contained in the contract, shall be annexed thereto.

2. The statement of claim shall include the following particulars:
   (a) The names and addresses of the parties;
   (b) A statement of the facts supporting the claim;
   (c) The points at issue;
   (d) The relief or remedy sought.

The claimant may annex to its statement of claim all documents it deems relevant or may add a reference to the documents or other evidence it will submit.

Statement of Defence

Article 19

1. Within a period of time to be determined by the arbitral tribunal, the respondent shall communicate its statement of defence in writing to the claimant and to each of the arbitrators.

2.   The statement of defence shall reply to the particulars (b), (c) and (d) of the statement of claim (article 18, paragraph 2). The respondent may annex to its statement the documents on which it relies for its defence or may add a reference to the documents or other evidence it will submit.

3.   In its statement of defence, or at a later stage in the arbitral proceedings if the arbitral tribunal decides that the delay was justified under the circumstances, the respondent may make a counter-claim arising out of the same contract or rely on a claim arising out of the same contract for the purpose of a set-off.

4.   The provisions of article 18, paragraph 2, shall apply to a counter-claim and a claim relied on for the purpose of a set-off.

Amendments to the Claim or Defence

Article 20

During the course of the arbitral proceedings either party may amend or supplement its claim or defence unless the arbitral tribunal considers it inappropriate to allow such amendment having regard to the delay in making it or prejudice to the other party or any other circumstances. However, a claim may not be amended in such a manner that the amended claim falls outside the scope of the arbitration clause or separate arbitration agreement.

Pleas as to the Jurisdiction of the Arbitral Tribunal

Article 21

1.   The arbitral tribunal shall have the power to rule on objections that it has no jurisdiction, including any objections with respect to the existence or validity of the arbitration clause or of the separate arbitration agreement.

2.   The arbitral tribunal shall have the power to determine the existence or the validity of the contract of which an arbitration clause forms a part. For the purposes of this article, an arbitration clause which forms part of a contract and which provides for arbitration under these Rules shall be treated as an agreement independent of the other terms of the contract. A decision by the arbitral tribunal that the contract is null and void shall not entail *ipso jure* the invalidity of the arbitration clause.

3.   A plea that the arbitral tribunal does not have jurisdiction shall be raised not later than in the statement of defence or, with respect to a counter-claim, in the reply to the counter-claim.

4.   In general, the arbitral tribunal should rule on a plea concerning its jurisdiction as a preliminary question. However, the arbitral tribunal may proceed with the arbitration and rule on such a plea in their final award.

Further Written Statements

Article 22

The arbitral tribunal shall decide which further written statements, in addition to the statement of claim and the statement of defence, shall be required from the parties or may be presented by them and shall fix the periods of time for communicating such statements.

Periods of Time

Article 23

The periods of time fixed by the arbitral tribunal for the communication of written statements (including the statement of claim and statement of defence) should not exceed forty-five days. However, the arbitral tribunal may set longer time limits, or extend the time limits, if it concludes that either is justified.

Evidence and Hearings (Articles 24 and 25)

Article 24

1.   Each party shall have the burden of proving the facts relied on to support its claim or defence.

2.   The arbitral tribunal may, if it considers it appropriate, require a party to deliver to the tribunal and to the other party, within such a period of time as the arbitral tribunal shall decide, a summary of the documents and other evidence which that party intends to present in support of the facts in issue set out in its statement of claim or statement of defence.

3.   At any time during the arbitral proceedings the arbitral tribunal may call upon the parties to produce documents, exhibits or other evidence within such a period of time as the tribunal shall determine. The Tribunal shall take formal note of any refusal to do so, as well as any reasons given for such refusal.

Article 25

1.   In the event of an oral hearing, the arbitral tribunal shall give the parties adequate advance notice of the date, time and place thereof.

2.   If witnesses are to be heard, at least thirty days before the hearing each party shall communicate to the arbitral tribunal and to the other party the names and addresses of the witnesses it intends to present, the subject upon and the languages in which such witnesses will give their testimony.

3.   The International Bureau shall make arrangements for the translation of oral statements made at a hearing and for a record of the hearing if either is deemed necessary by the tribunal under the circumstances of the case, or if the parties have agreed thereto and have communicated such agreement to the tribunal and the International Bureau at least thirty days before the hearing, or such longer period before the hearing as the arbitral tribunal may determine.

4.   Hearings shall be held *in camera* unless the parties agree otherwise. The arbitral tribunal may require the retirement of any witness or witnesses during the testimony of other witnesses. The arbitral tribunal is free to determine the manner in which witnesses are examined.

5.   Evidence of witnesses may also be presented in the form of written statements signed by them.

6.   The arbitral tribunal shall determine the admissibility, relevance, materiality and weight of the evidence offered.

Interim Measures of Protection

Article 26

1.   Unless the parties agree otherwise, the arbitral tribunal may, at the request of either party, take any interim measures it deems necessary to preserve the respective rights of either party or in respect of the subject-matter of the dispute, including measures for conservation of the goods forming the subject-matter in dispute, such as ordering their deposit with a third person or the sale of perishable goods.

2.   Such interim measures may be established in the form of an interim award. The arbitral tribunal shall be entitled to require security for the costs of such measures.

3.   A request for interim measures addressed by any party to a judicial authority shall not be deemed incompatible with the agreement to arbitrate, or as a waiver of that agreement.

Experts

Article 27

1.   The arbitral tribunal may appoint one or more experts to report to it, in writing, on specific issues to be determined by the tribunal. A copy of the expert's terms of reference, established by the arbitral tribunal, shall be communicated to the parties.

2.   The parties shall give the expert any relevant information or produce for his/her inspection any relevant documents or goods that he/she may require of them. Any dispute between a party and such expert as to the relevance of the required information or production shall be referred to the arbitral tribunal for decision.

3.   Upon receipt of the expert's report, the arbitral tribunal shall communicate a copy of the report to the parties which shall be given the opportunity to express, in writing, their opinion on the report. A party shall be entitled to examine any document on which the expert has relied in his/her report.

4.   At the request of either party the expert, after delivery of the report, may be heard at a hearing where the parties shall have the opportunity to be present and to interrogate the expert. At this hearing either party may present expert witnesses in order to testify on the points at issue. The provisions of article 25 shall be applicable to such proceedings.

Failure to Appear or to Make Submissions

Article 28

1.   If, within the period of time fixed by the arbitral tribunal, the claimant has failed to communicate its claim without showing sufficient cause for such

failure, the arbitral tribunal shall issue an order for the termination of the arbitral proceedings. If, within the period of time fixed by the arbitral tribunal, the respondent has failed to communicate its statement of defence without showing sufficient cause for such failure, the arbitral tribunal shall order that the proceedings continue.

2.   If one of the parties, duly notified under these Rules, fails to appear at a hearing, without showing sufficient cause for such failure, the arbitral tribunal may proceed with the arbitration.

3.   If one of the parties, duly invited to produce documentary evidence, fails to do so within the established period of time, without showing sufficient cause for such failure, the arbitral tribunal may make the award on the evidence before it.

Closure of Hearings

Article 29

1.   The arbitral tribunal may inquire of the parties if they have any further proof to offer or witnesses to be heard or submissions to make and, if there are none, it may declare the hearings closed.

2.   The arbitral tribunal may, if it considers it necessary owing to exceptional circumstances, decide, on its own motion or upon application of a party, to reopen the hearings at any time before the award is made.

Waiver of Rules

Article 30

A party which knows that any provision of, or requirement under, these Rules has not been complied with and yet proceeds with the arbitration without promptly stating its objection to such non-compliance, shall be deemed to have waived its right to object.

SECTION IV

THE AWARD

Decisions

Article 31

1.   When there are three arbitrators, any award or other decision of the arbitral tribunal shall be made by a majority of the arbitrators.

2.   In the case of questions of procedure, when there is no majority or when the arbitral tribunal so authorises, the presiding arbitrator may decide on his/her own, subject to revision, if any, by the arbitral tribunal.

Form and Effect of the Award

Article 32

1.   In addition to making a final award, the arbitral tribunal shall be entitled to make interim, interlocutory, or partial awards.

2.   The award shall be made in writing and shall be final and binding on the parties. The parties undertake to carry out the award without delay.

3.   The arbitral tribunal shall state the reasons upon which the award is based, unless the parties have agreed that no reasons are to be given.

4.   An award shall be signed by the arbitrators and it shall contain the date on which and the place where the award was made. Where there are three arbitrators and one of them fails to sign, the award shall state the reason for the absence of the signature.

5.   The award may be made public only with the consent of both parties.

6.   Copies of the award signed by the arbitrators shall be communicated to the parties by the International Bureau. The International Bureau may withhold communicating the award to the parties until all costs of the arbitration have been paid.

7.   If the arbitration law of the country where the award is made requires that the award be filed or registered by the arbitral tribunal, the tribunal shall comply with this requirement within the period of time required by law.

Applicable Law, Amiable Compositeur

Article 33

1.   The arbitral tribunal shall apply the law designated by the parties as applicable to the substance of the dispute. Failing such designation by the parties, the arbitral tribunal shall apply the law determined by the conflict of laws rules which it considers applicable.

2.   The arbitral tribunal shall decide as *amiable compositeur* or *ex aequo et bono* only if the parties have expressly authorised the arbitral tribunal to do so and if the law applicable to the arbitral procedure permits such arbitration.

3.   In all cases, the arbitral tribunal shall decide in accordance with the terms of the contract and shall take into account the usages of the trade applicable to the transaction.

Settlement or other Grounds for Termination

Article 34

1.   If, before the award is made, the parties agree on a settlement of the dispute, the arbitral tribunal shall either issue an order for the termination of the arbitral proceedings or, if requested by both parties and accepted by the tribunal, record the settlement in the form of an arbitral award on agreed terms. The arbitral tribunal is not obliged to give reasons for such an award.

2.   If, before the award is made, the continuation of the arbitral proceedings becomes unnecessary or impossible for any reason not mentioned in paragraph 1, the arbitral tribunal shall inform the parties of its intention to issue an order for the termination of the proceedings. The arbitral tribunal shall have the power to issue such an order unless a party raises justifiable grounds for objection.

3.   Copies of the order for termination of the arbitral proceedings or of the arbitral award on agreed terms, signed by the arbitrators, shall be communicated to the parties by the International Bureau. Where an arbitral

award on agreed terms is made, the provisions of article 32, paragraphs 2 and 4 to 7, shall apply.

Interpretation of the Award

Article 35

1. Within thirty days after the receipt of the award, either party, with notice to the other party, may request that the arbitral tribunal give an interpretation of the award.

2. The interpretation shall be given in writing within forty-five days after the receipt of the request. The interpretation shall form part of the award and the provisions of article 32, paragraphs 2 to 7, shall apply.

Correction of the Award

Article 36

1. Within thirty days after the receipt of the award, either party, with notice to the other party, may request the arbitral tribunal to correct in the award any errors in computation, any clerical or typographical errors, or any errors of similar nature. The arbitral tribunal may within thirty days after the communication of the award make such corrections on its own initiative.

2. Such corrections shall be in writing, and the provisions of article 32, paragraphs 2 to 7, shall apply.

Additional Award

Article 37

1. Within sixty days after the receipt of the award, either party, with notice to the other party, may request the arbitral tribunal to make an additional award as to claims presented in the arbitral proceedings but omitted from the award.

2. If the arbitral tribunal considers the request for an additional award to be justified and considers that the omission can be rectified without any further hearings or evidence, it shall complete its award within sixty days after the receipt of the request.

3. When an additional award is made, the provisions of article 32, paragraphs 2 to 7, shall apply.

Costs (Articles 38 to 40)

Article 38

The arbitral tribunal shall fix the costs of arbitration in its award. The term 'costs' includes only:

    (a) The fees of the arbitral tribunal to be stated separately as to each arbitrator and to be fixed by the tribunal itself in accordance with article 39;

    (b) The travel and other expenses incurred by the arbitrators;

    (c) The costs of expert advice and of other assistance required by the arbitral tribunal;

(d)   The travel and other expenses of witnesses to the extent such expenses are approved by the arbitral tribunal;

(e)   The costs for legal representation and assistance of the successful party if such costs were claimed during the arbitral proceedings, and only to the extent that the arbitral tribunal determines that the amount of such costs is reasonable;

(f)   Any fees and expenses of the appointing authority as well as the expenses of the Secretary-General and the International Bureau.

Article 39

1.   The fees of the arbitral tribunal shall be reasonable in amount, taking into account the amount in dispute, the complexity of the subject-matter, the time spent by the arbitrators and any other relevant circumstances of the case.

2.   If an appointing authority has been agreed upon by the parties or designated by the Secretary-General of the Permanent Court of Arbitration at The Hague, and if that authority has issued a schedule of fees for arbitrators in international cases which it administers, the arbitral tribunal in fixing its fees shall take that schedule of fees into account to the extent that it considers appropriate in the circumstances of the case.

3.   If such appointing authority has not issued a schedule of fees for arbitrators in international cases, any party may at any time request the appointing authority to furnish a statement setting forth the basis for establishing fees which is customarily followed in international cases in which the authority appoints arbitrators. If the appointing authority consents to provide such a statement, the arbitral tribunal in fixing its fees shall take such information into account to the extent that it considers appropriate in the circumstances of the case.

4.   In cases referred to in paragraphs 2 and 3, when a party so requests and the appointing authority consents to perform the function, the arbitral tribunal shall fix its fees only after consultation with the appointing authority which may make any comment it deems appropriate to the arbitral tribunal concerning the fees.

Article 40

1.   Except as provided in paragraph 2, the costs of arbitration shall in principle be borne by the unsuccessful party. However, the arbitral tribunal may apportion each of such costs between the parties if it determines that apportionment is reasonable, taking into account the circumstances of the case.

2.   With respect to the costs of legal representation and assistance referred to in article 38, paragraph (e), the arbitral tribunal, taking into account the circumstances of the case, shall be free to determine which party shall bear such costs or may apportion such costs between the parties if it determines that apportionment is reasonable.

3.   When the arbitral tribunal issues an order for the termination of the arbitral proceedings or makes an award on agreed terms, it shall fix the costs of arbitration referred to in article 38 and 39, paragraph 1, in the text of that order or award.

4. No additional fees may be charged by an arbitral tribunal for interpretation or correction or completion of its award under articles 35 to 37.

Deposit of Costs

Article 41

1. The arbitral tribunal, on its establishment, may request each party to deposit an equal amount as an advance for the costs referred to in article 38, paragraphs (a), (b), (c) and (f). All amounts deposited by the parties pursuant to this paragraph and paragraph 2 of this article shall be paid to the International Bureau, and shall be disbursed by it for such costs, including, *inter alia*, fees to the arbitrators, the Secretary-General and the International Bureau.

2. During the course of the arbitral proceedings the arbitral tribunal may request supplementary deposits from the parties.

3. If an appointing authority has been agreed upon by the parties or designated by the Secretary-General of the Permanent Court of Arbitration at the Hague, and when a party so requests and the appointing authority consents to perform the function, the arbitral tribunal shall fix the amounts of any deposits or supplementary deposits only after consultation with the appointing authority which may make any comments to the arbitral tribunal which it deems appropriate concerning the amount of such deposits and supplementary deposits.

4. If the required deposits are not paid in full within thirty days after the receipt of the request, the arbitral tribunal shall so inform the parties in order that one or another of them may make the required payment. If such payment is not made, the arbitral tribunal may order the suspension or termination of the arbitral proceedings.

5. After the award has been made, the International Bureau shall render an accounting to the parties of the deposits received and return any unexpended balance to the parties.

REFINED SUGAR ASSOCIATION

D. G. Moon, Esq. — Secretary
Forum House,
15–18 Lime Street,
London EC3M 7AQ
Tel: 0044-171-626-1745
Fax: 0044-171-283-3831

RULES RELATING TO ARBITRATION

as amended 17 October 1994

RECOMMENDED ARBITRATION CLAUSE

Parties to a White Sugar Contract who wish to have any disputes referred to arbitration under the following Rules are recommended to insert in the Contract an arbitration clause in the following form:

'All disputes arising out of or in connection with this Contract shall be referred to The Refined Sugar Association for settlement in accordance with the Rules Relating to Arbitration. This Contract shall be governed by and construed in accordance with English Law.'

RULES

1. Any dispute arising out of or in connection with a Contract which the Parties have agreed (either in the Contract or otherwise) to refer to arbitration by The Refined Sugar Association shall be determined in accordance with the following Rules.

2. Any party wishing to commence an arbitration concerning a dispute failing within Rule 1 shall give to the other party seven clear days notice of his intention to claim arbitration.

After the expiry of the seven clear days notice period a written request for arbitration shall be sent to the Secretary.

The Claimant shall then forward to the Secretary the following:

(a) a clear and concise statement of his case, in duplicate;

(b) copies of the contractual documents, in duplicate, in which the arbitration clause is contained or under which the arbitration arises;

(c) any supporting documentary evidence, in duplicate, it thinks proper;

(d) the names, addresses, telexes and facsimile numbers (if appropriate) of the parties to the arbitration;

(e) a non-returnable registration fee (see Rule 3);

(f) if required a deposit on account of the Association's fees, costs and expenses (see Rule 3).

The Council shall thereupon have power to determine, as hereinafter provided, any such matter in dispute. Where both parties to a dispute are members the Council shall have jurisdiction to determine whether a Contract has been made.

The other party shall, not later than thirty days after dispatch to his last known address by the Secretary of a copy of the first party's statement of case and supporting documents, or such extended time as the Council shall in its absolute discretion allow, submit in duplicate to the Secretary a clear and concise statement of his defence together with a copy of such other documentary evidence in duplicate as he thinks proper. A copy of this statement of defence and supporting documents shall be forwarded by the Secretary to the first party.

Each party will in turn be permitted a period of twenty-one days, or such extended time as the Council shall in its absolute discretion allow, within which to submit further written comments and/or documents in reply to the other party's last submission, until the Council shall in its absolute discretion decide to proceed to make its award.

All statements, contracts and documentary evidence must be submitted in the English language. Whenever documentary evidence is submitted in a foreign language this must be accompanied by an officially certified English translation.

3. A non-returnable registration fee of such amount as shall be decided by the Council from time to time shall be paid to the Secretary upon any reference to arbitration. The Council may if it thinks fit at any time require either party to the arbitration to deposit with the Secretary such sum as the Council may think fit on account of the fees, costs and expenses in connection with or arising out of the arbitration.

4. Any notice, document or other correspondence to be served on any party in connection with an arbitration under these Rules may be effected either by (a) courier, (b) first class post, (c) post in a registered letter, (d) telex, (e) cable or (f) facsimile in each case to the usual or last known address or place of business of any party. In the case of a facsimile such notice, document or correspondence shall also be served in accordance with either provision under (a) to (e) above.

5. Should a party in dispute with another party refuse to concur in the reference to arbitration as herein provided, the party referring the matter to arbitration may forthwith obtain an award of the Council on the question in dispute. The Council may at its discretion refuse to arbitrate on any reference made by a Member who has been suspended from the Association or whose Membership has been revoked.

6. Unless the Council shall as hereinbefore provided have refused to arbitrate, neither the Buyer, Seller, Trustee in Bankruptcy, liquidator nor any other person claiming under any of them, shall bring any action against any party to the contract in respect of any dispute arising out of such contract, until such dispute shall have been adjudicated upon in arbitration under these Rules; and the obtaining of an award under these Rules shall be a condition precedent to the right of either contracting party to sue the other in respect of any claim arising out of the contract.

7. When the subject matter and terms of contract are identical, except as to date and price, arbitration may in the Council's absolute discretion and subject to the written agreement of all parties be held as between first Seller and last Buyer as though they were contracting parties and the award made in pursuance thereof shall be binding on all intermediate parties, provided that this Rule shall not apply where a question or dispute shall arise between intermediate parties, not affecting both first Seller and last Buyer, and in such case the arbitration may be held as between the two parties affected by the dispute or, subject as aforesaid in the event of there being more than two such parties, as between the first and last of such parties as though they were contracting parties, and the award made in pursuance thereof shall be binding on all parties affected by the dispute.

8. For the purpose of all proceedings in arbitration, the contract shall be deemed to have been made in England, any correspondence in reference to the offer, the acceptance, the place of payment or otherwise, notwithstanding, and England shall be regarded as the place of performance. Disputes shall be settled according to the law of England wherever the domicile, residence or place of business of the parties to the contract may be or become. Unless the

contract contains any statement expressly to the contrary, the provisions of neither the Convention relating to a Uniform Law on the International Sale of Goods, of 1964, nor the United Nations Convention on Contracts for the International Sale of Goods, of 1980, shall apply thereto.

9.   For determination of a dispute the Council shall appoint not less than three and no more than five persons from the Panel of Arbitrators to act on its behalf. The number of persons appointed to determine a dispute shall be in the absolute discretion of the Council. No such person shall act in an arbitration where he is, or becomes, directly or indirectly interested in the subject matter in dispute. In the event of a person becoming so interested, dying or becoming in any other way in view of the Council incapacitated from acting prior to the first meeting, the Council may appoint another person from the Panel of Arbitrators to take his place, and the arbitration shall thereupon proceed as if that other person had been originally appointed in lieu of the first person. If subsequently an Arbitrator discovers that he is directly involved in the subject matter in dispute, dies or becomes in any other way in the view of the Council incapacitated from acting, then the hearing shall, unless the Council in its absolute discretion decides otherwise, proceed without the necessity of appointing another person from the Panel of Arbitrators. The decision of the persons so appointed to act on behalf of the Council shall be by a majority and, in the event of an equality of votes, the Chairman, who shall have been previously elected by such persons, shall have a second or casting vote. The award of such persons shall be signed by the said Chairman and when so signed shall be deemed to be the award of the Council and shall be final and binding in all cases.

10.   The Council may in its discretion decide the case on the written statements and documents submitted to it without an oral hearing. The Council may, however, call the parties before it, and request the attendance of witnesses, or the provision of further documents, or information in written form, and may also consult the legal advisers of the Association.

Should either or both parties require an oral hearing they shall make their request, in writing, to the Secretary. The Council may grant or refuse such request in their absolute discretion and without assigning any reason.

In the event of an oral hearing, with or without witnesses, each party shall appear either personally or by any agent duly appointed in writing and may be represented at the hearing by counsel or solicitor. One party shall not, however, make any oral statement in the absence of the other, excepting in the case of his opponent failing to appear after notice has been given to him by the Secretary.

The Council shall not be bound by the strict rules of evidence and shall be at liberty to admit and consider any material whatsoever notwithstanding that it may not be admissible under the law of evidence.

Any party requiring a Reasoned Award shall, before the hearing commences, make its request, in writing, to the Secretary.

11.   If a party wishes to withdraw a claim or counterclaim, he shall give notice to that effect to the Secretary. On receipt of such a notice, the Secretary shall inform the other party and shall cancel any arrangements for

the hearing of that claim or counterclaim (unless any other claim or counter-claim remains to be dealt with at the same hearing). The other party shall be entitled to an award dismissing the withdrawn claim or counterclaim with costs, provided that a written request for such an award is received by the Secretary within 28 days after such other party has been informed by the Secretary of the withdrawal. If no such request is received by the Secretary within the said period of 28 days the arbitration shall be deemed to have been terminated by consent so far as it relates to such claim or counterclaim. Such award or termination shall not affect any other claim or counterclaim which is the subject of the same arbitration proceedings, or the Council's right to recover their fees and expenses from either party.

12.   Subject to any agreement to the contrary, the Council shall have the power if it thinks fit:
(a)   to award interest on any sum which becomes due in respect of a contract whether by way of debt or damages and which is paid before the commencement of arbitration proceedings at such rate as it thinks fit and for such period as it thinks fit ending not later than the date of payment;
(b)   where a sum is due in respect of a contract whether by way of debt or damages, to award general damages in respect of the late payment of such sum.

13.   The Arbitration fees shall be in the discretion of the Council in every case, and shall be paid by whom the Council shall determine.
Any expenses incurred by the Association or by the Council, including the expenses incurred in obtaining legal assistance, copies of documents or evidence, shorthand notes, etc., may be added to such fees.
The Council may also make an award or order as to payment of the costs of the parties to the arbitration.

14.   A book shall be kept in which all cases shall be noted, together with the award and fees and expenses charged. The Secretary shall notify the parties as soon as the award is signed and it shall be held by the Secretary at the disposal of either party against payment of fees and expenses incurred by the Association or by the Council. A copy of the award shall be given to the party who does not take up the original. If the award is not taken up within ten days, the Council may order either of the parties to take up the award, and in such case the party so ordered shall take up the award and pay the fees and expenses as directed. The Council shall have the right to invoke arbitration Rule 16, if any party neglects or refuses to abide by any such order.

15.   The award must be honoured within twenty-eight days from the date on which it is taken up.

16.   In the event of a party to an arbitration neglecting or refusing to carry out or abide by any award or order made under arbitration Rule 14, the Council may circularise to Members of the Association in any way thought fit a notification to that effect. The parties to any such arbitration shall be deemed to have consented to the Council taking such action as aforesaid.

17.   In the event of both Parties consenting in writing to the publication to Members of the Association of an Award or any part thereof or summary of its contents, the Council may make available the same to its Members in a form approved by the Parties. The Council shall be entitled to charge a fee to Members for the provision of such information.

ARBITRATION INSTITUTE OF THE STOCKHOLM CHAMBER OF COMMERCE

Arbitration Institute of the Stockholm Chamber of Commerce
PO. Box 160 50, S-103 21 Stockholm, Sweden.
Tel: 00 + 46 - 8 6131800
Telex: 15638 Chamber S
Fax: 00 + 46 - 8 7230176

RULES OF THE ARBITRATION INSTITUTE OF THE STOCKHOLM CHAMBER OF COMMERCE

adopted by the Stockholm Chamber of Commerce and in
force from 1 January 1988

RECOMMENDED ARBITRATION CLAUSE

Any dispute, controversy or claim arising out of or in connection with this contract, or the breach, termination or invalidity thereof, shall be settled by arbitration in accordance with the Rules of the Arbitration Institute of the Stockholm Chamber of Commerce.

The parties are advised to make the following additions to the clause, as required.

The arbitral tribunal shall be composed of .... arbitrators (a sole arbitrator).

The place of arbitration shall be ....

The language(s) to be used in the arbitral proceedings shall be
....

RECOMMENDED GOVERNING LAW CLAUSE

This contract shall be governed by the law of ....
(insert jurisdiction).

I.   ORGANISATION OF THE INSTITUTE

§ **1**   The Arbitration Institute of the Stockholm Chamber of Commerce ('the Institute') is an organ within the Stockholm Chamber of Commerce ('the Chamber') for dealing with matters of arbitration. Its objects are to assist in the settlement of domestic and international disputes in accordance with the Rules of the Institute set forth in §§ 5–34 hereof,

to assist in the settlement of disputes in accordance with other rules adopted by the Institute*

to assist, pursuant to its own decision in each case, in proceedings which take place in a manner that differs wholly or partly from that contemplated by the rules referred to above,

and to provide information concerning arbitration matters.

§ 2   The Institute shall have a Board composed of three members who shall be appointed for a period of three years by the Executive Committee of the Chamber. One of the members, who shall act as Chairman, shall be a judge having experience of business disputes, while one of the others shall be a practising lawyer, and one a person who enjoys the confidence of the business community.

Each member shall have a personal deputy appointed by the Executive Committee for the same three-year period as the member. The deputy shall have the same qualifications as the member for whom he is a deputy.

For special reasons, the Executive Committee may remove a member or a deputy.

If a member or a deputy resigns or is removed during his term of office, the Executive Committee will nominate another person to serve as member or deputy during the balance of the term.

References below to 'the Chairman' or 'members' apply equally to a deputy serving in the place of the Chairman or a member.

§ 3   Two members of the Board shall form a quorum. If no majority is attained, the Chairman shall have a casting vote. Decisions of the Board are final and cannot be reviewed by the Chamber.

§ 4   The Institute shall have a secretariat composed of one or several persons employed by the Chamber. The secretariat shall be under the direction of a Secretary-General who shall be a lawyer.

---

*The Arbitration Institute of the Stockholm Chamber of Commerce has adopted Conciliation Rules and Rules for Procedures under the UNCITRAL Arbitration Rules.

II.   ARBITRATION RULES OF THE INSTITUTE

A.   Composition of Arbitral Tribunals

Number of arbitrators and manner of their appointment

§ 5   If the parties have not agreed on the number of arbitrators, they shall be three in number.

If the parties have agreed that the dispute is to be decided by a sole arbitrator, then the appointment shall be made by the Institute. In other cases each party shall appoint an equal number of arbitrators and the Institute one arbitrator, who shall be chairman of the tribunal.

If the parties have so agreed, the Institute shall appoint all members of the tribunal.

If an arbitrator appointed by a party dies, such party shall appoint another arbitrator in his place. If the arbitrator had been appointed by the Institute, the Institute shall appoint another arbitrator in his place.

If an arbitrator resigns or is discharged, the Institute shall appoint another arbitrator. If the arbitrator had been appointed by a party, such party shall be consulted by the Institute.

If a party fails to appoint an arbitrator within the time prescribed by the Institute, then the Institute shall make the appointment.

Duty of an arbitrator to disclose grounds for his disqualification

§ 6   A person who is asked whether he wishes to accept appointment as an arbitrator shall disclose to the person approaching him any circumstances which might be deemed to diminish trust in his impartiality or independence (disqualification). If he is nevertheless appointed, he shall at once make the same disclosure to the parties and the other arbitrators.

An arbitrator who becomes aware in the course of the arbitral proceedings of any circumstances which may disqualify him must immediately inform the parties and the other arbitrators thereof.

Challenge of arbitrators

§ 7   If a party wishes to challenge an arbitrator he shall do so in writing. Such a challenge shall state the reasons therefor and shall be notified to the Institute, the arbitrators and each other party.

Any challenge by a party of an arbitrator must be made immediately but in any event within thirty days of the date on which the allegedly disqualifying circumstance becomes known to the party. A party who fails to notify a challenge within the prescribed time is deemed to have waived his right to make such challenge.

Decisions of challenges will be made by the Institute.

Discharge of arbitrators

§ 8   If the Institute finds that an arbitrator is disqualified it shall discharge him.

The Institute may also decide to discharge an arbitrator on the ground of any lawful excuse or failure to perform his duties in an adequate manner.

Before a decision on discharge is made the Institute shall solicit the views of the parties and the arbitrators.

B.   Initiation of Proceedings Procedures of the Institute

Request for arbitration

§ 9   Arbitration is initiated by the filing by a party with the Institute of a request for arbitration which shall include:

    (a)   A statement of the names and addresses of the parties;

    (b)   An account of the dispute;

    (c)   A preliminary statement of the relief claimed by the claimant;

    (d)   A copy of the agreement on which the claim is based and of the arbitration agreement if the latter is not included in the former; and, where applicable,

(e)   A statement identifying the arbitrator or arbitrators appointed by the claimant.

Dismissal

§   **10**   If it is obvious that the Institute lacks competence over the dispute, the claimant's request for arbitration shall be dismissed.

The respondent's reply, etc.

§   **11**   If it is not obvious that jurisdiction is lacking, the request shall be communicated by the Institute to the respondent. The respondent shall be asked to submit a reply to the Institute which shall include:

(a)   A statement commenting on the request made by the claimant; and, where applicable,

(b)   A statement identifying the arbitrator or arbitrators appointed by the respondent.

If the respondent desires to raise any objection concerning the validity or applicability of the arbitration agreement, such objection shall be made in the reply together with a statement of the grounds therefor.

If the respondent desires to make a counterclaim or plead a set-off, a statement to that effect shall be made in the reply, including an account of the dispute and a preliminary statement of the relief claimed. A counterclaim or a plea by way of set-off must be comprised by the arbitration agreement.

The respondent's reply shall be communicated to the claimant. The claimant shall be given an opportunity to comment on any objections and pleas advanced by the respondent.

Failure by the respondent to submit a reply shall not prevent the proceedings in the case from continuing.

Amplification. Time limits

§   **12**   The Institute may request a party to amplify any submission to the Institute. If the claimant fails to comply with such a request, the Institute may decide to dismiss the case. If the respondent fails to do so, such failure shall not prevent the proceedings in the case from continuing.

If the respondent should fail to amplify his counterclaim or plea for a set-off, such claim or plea may be dismissed by the Institute.

If the Institute has requested a party to perform any act within a specified time, such time limit may be extended by the Institute.

Security for costs

§   **13**   The Institute shall fix a sum which shall be paid to the Institute and which, together with accrued interest, shall constitute security for the costs of the proceedings. The amount thereof is fixed in accordance with regulations issued by the Institute. The Institute may fix separate sums for a counterclaim and a plea by way of set-off. After notification by the arbitral tribunal the Institute may in the course of the proceedings decide to increase the sums to be paid.

Each party shall as a rule contribute half of such sums of money as are referred to in the preceding paragraph. One party may, however, pay the entire sum.

If a party fails to make a required payment the Institute shall afford the other party an opportunity to do so. If, this notwithstanding, the required payment is not made, the case shall be wholly or partly dismissed or stayed.

The Institute may, both in the course of the proceedings and thereafter, draw on the security to pay fees to the arbitrators and other costs of the proceedings.

The Institute may decide that the security may partly consist of a bank guarantee or other security.

Decisions of the institute

§ **14**   When the exchange of written submissions pursuant to §§ 9–12 has been concluded, then, unless it is obvious that jurisdiction is lacking, the Institute shall:

(a)   Appoint a chairman of the arbitral tribunal and, if necessary, another arbitrator pursuant to § 5;

(b)   Determine the place of arbitration unless the parties have done so; and

(c)   Fix the amount of the security and the time within which each party shall pay his share thereof.

Referral of a case to the arbitral tribunal

§ **15**   As soon as the arbitral tribunal has been appointed and the security been provided, the Institute shall refer the case to the arbitral tribunal.

C.   The Proceedings Before the Arbitral Tribunal

The procedure before the arbitral tribunal

§ **16**   The arbitral tribunal shall determine the manner in which the proceedings will be conducted. In so doing, the arbitral tribunal shall comply with the stipulations of the parties in the arbitration agreement and these Rules and shall have regard to the wishes of the parties.

The arbitral tribunal shall deal with the case in an impartial, practical and speedy fashion. Each party shall be given a sufficient opportunity to present his case.

If the arbitral tribunal is composed of three or more members, the chairman may, if the other arbitrators have so authorised him, decide questions of procedure on his own.

Language

§ **17**   Unless the parties have agreed on the language or languages to be used in the proceedings, the arbitral tribunal shall make a determination in such respect.

Statement of claim and defence

§ **18** 1. The claimant shall submit a statement of claim which, unless such information has already been provided in the case, shall include:

(a) The specific relief claimed.

(b) The circumstances which constitute the material facts on which the claimant relies in support of his claim.

The statement of claim in addition ought to include a preliminary statement of the evidence which the claimant desires to adduce.

2. The respondent shall submit a defence, which, unless such information has previously been provided in the case, shall include:

(a) A statement as to whether and to what extent the respondent accepts or opposes the relief claimed by the claimant;

(b) If the claim is denied in whole or in part, the circumstances which constitute the material facts on which such denial is based and specifying whether the respondent admits or denies the material facts relied upon by the claimant; and, if the respondent so pleads,

(c) A specific plea by way of set-off or counterclaim and the grounds on which it is based.

The defence further ought to include a preliminary statement of the evidence which the respondent desires to adduce.

3. The arbitral tribunal may decide on the submission by the parties of additional written statements.

Amendment to claim or defence

§ **19** A party may amend his claim or defence in the course of the proceedings if his case, as amended, is still comprised by the arbitration agreement and unless the arbitral tribunal considers it inappropriate having regard to the point of time at which the request is made, the prejudice that may be caused to the other party or other circumstances.

The provisions of the preceding paragraph shall apply equally to the right of a party to introduce a plea for a set-off or a counterclaim.

Oral hearing

§ **20** An oral hearing shall, as a rule, be arranged. Guided by the wishes of the parties, the arbitral tribunal shall determine the time at which such a hearing shall take place, its duration and how it shall be organised, including the manner in which evidence is to be presented.

If an arbitrator is replaced in the course of the proceedings, the newly composed tribunal shall decide whether and to what extent a prior oral hearing shall be repeated.

Evidence

§ **21** At the request of the arbitral tribunal, the parties shall state the evidence on which they wish to rely, specifying what they wish to prove with each piece of evidence, and shall produce the documentary evidence on which they rely.

The arbitral tribunal determines whether written affidavits may be submitted.

The arbitral tribunal may refuse to accept evidence offered to it if it considers that such evidence is not required or is irrelevant or that proof can be established by other means in a considerably simpler fashion or at considerably lesser expense.

After having conscientiously scrutinised and evaluated everything that has occurred in the proceedings, the arbitral tribunal shall determine what has been proved in the case.

Expert

§ **22** Unless the parties provide otherwise, the arbitral tribunal may appoint an expert to give his opinion on a particular matter.

Failure of a party to appear, etc.

§ **23** If one of the parties, without showing valid cause, fails to appear at a hearing or otherwise to comply with an order of the arbitral tribunal, such failure will not prevent the arbitral tribunal from proceeding with the case and rendering an award.

Waiver of procedural irregularities

§ **24** A party who fails during the proceedings to object within a reasonable time to any deviation from provisions of the arbitration agreement or other rules applicable to the proceedings shall be deemed to have waived his right to invoke such irregularity.

Voting

§ **25** When a vote is taken, that opinion shall prevail which has received more votes than any other opinion. If such a majority is not attained the opinion of the chairman shall prevail.

D. The Award

Time for making an award

§ **26** An award shall be made not later than one year after the case has been referred to the arbitral tribunal. At the request of the arbitral tribunal, the Institute may, however, if appropriate extend this period.

Separate award

§ **27** A separate issue or part of the matter in dispute between the parties may, at the request of a party, be decided by a separate award. If any party objects, such an award may be rendered only if there are special reasons therefor.

Where a party has partially admitted a claim, the arbitral tribunal may give a separate award on the part that has been admitted.

Award

§ **28** The award shall be rendered at the place of arbitration. The award shall contain an order or declaration and the reasons therefor and shall be signed by all the arbitrators. An award may be rendered even in the absence of the signature of an arbitrator provided that the award has been signed by a majority of the arbitrators and contains a verification by them that the arbitrator whose signature is missing took part in deciding the dispute.

An arbitrator may attach a dissenting opinion to the award.

If a settlement is made the arbitral tribunal may at the request of the parties confirm such settlement in an award.

Costs

§ **29** The arbitral tribunal shall decide in the award which amounts of compensation are due to the Institute and the arbitrators, respectively. The parties are jointly and severally liable for the payment of such sums.

The losing party shall be ordered to pay such compensation and costs as well as the costs of the other party unless the circumstances call for a different result.

If a case is terminated before an award has been rendered, the arbitral tribunal may decide that the parties shall pay compensation to the Institute and the arbitrators. If a case is terminated before it has been referred to the arbitral tribunal, the Institute will determine the amount of compensation due to it.

An award may be rendered even if it deals only with costs.

Fees of arbitrators

§ **30** The fees of arbitrators shall be reasonable in amount and shall be determined taking into account the time spent by the arbitrators, the complexity of the case, the amount in dispute and other circumstances.

Correction of an award, etc.

§ **31** Any obvious miscalculation or clerical error in an award shall be corrected by the arbitral tribunal.

If a party so requests within 30 days of receiving the award the tribunal may decide a question which should have been decided in the award but which was not decided therein.

If a party so requests within 30 days of receiving the award the arbitral tribunal may provide an interpretation thereof in writing.

Before the arbitral tribunal takes any action, the parties shall be afforded an opportunity to express their views.

E. Miscellaneous Provisions

Compensation due to the Institute

§ **32** The amount of compensation due to the Institute will be determined in accordance with regulations issued by the Institute.

Filing of awards, etc.

§ **33** An arbitral tribunal must after the close of the proceedings submit to the Institute one copy of each award and written order issued in the case as well as of all recorded minutes therein.

Effectiveness

§ **34** These Rules shall enter into force on 1 January 1988 and will replace the former Rules of the Institute.

If an arbitration agreement has been concluded prior to 1 January 1988, the former Statutes or former Rules of the Institute shall apply unless the parties agree otherwise.

TRIBUNAL ARBITRAL DU SPORT
COURT OF ARBITRATION FOR SPORT

Avenue de l'Elysée 28, CH-1006 Lausanne
Tel. (00 + 41.21) 617 57 24
Fax (00 + 41.21) 617 26 06.

Examples of Arbitration Agreements:
Agreement for insertion in a contract:

Any dispute arising from the present contract which the parties are unable to settle amicably, shall be settled exclusively and definitely by a tribunal — of one or three members — constituted in accordance with the Statute and Regulations of arbitration of the Court of Arbitration for Sport (CAS). The parties undertake to abide by the provisions of the said Statute and Regulations and execute in good faith the award to be rendered. They agree to establish the seat of the tribunal in . . . and to apply . . . law.

Agreement to be made between parties on the occasion of a dispute (arbitration agreement):

The parties agree that the dispute which has arisen between them in the . . . case shall be settled exclusively and definitely by a tribunal — of one or three members — constituted in accordance with the Statute and Regulations of the Court of Arbitration for Sport (CAS). The procedure shall be conducted in accordance with the said Statute and Regulations. The parties undertake to comply with these and to enforce in good faith the award rendered. The arbitration shall take place at . . . and . . . law shall be applicable.

Arbitration agreement to be inserted into the provisions of statutes (recourse to the TAS in the event of dispute or appeal against an internal decision)

—Any dispute arising from the present Statutes and Regulations of the . . . Federation which cannot be settled amicably, shall be settled finally by a tribunal

*composed in accordance with the Statute and Regulations of the Court of Arbitration
for Sport to the exclusion of any recourse to ordinary courts. The parties undertake
to comply with the said Statute and Regulations, and to accept in good faith the
award rendered and in no way hinder its execution.*

—*Disputes between the . . . Federation and one or several of its members which are
not settled finally by a decision by a body of the . . . Federation, may be submitted
for arbitration by one or other of the parties to the Court of Arbitration for Sport
(CAS) in Lausanne. Any decision taken by the said Court shall be without appeal
and binding on the parties concerned.*

CODE OF SPORTS-RELATED ARBITRATION

in force as from 22 November 1994
(and revised to 6 April 1995)

STATUTES OF THE BODIES WORKING
FOR THE SETTLEMENT OF SPORTS-RELATED DISPUTES

A   Joint Dispositions

Article

S1   In order to settle, through arbitration, sports-related disputes, two
bodies are hereby created:
  • the International Council of Arbitration for Sport (ICAS) and
  • the Court of Arbitration for Sport (CAS).
The disputes referred to in the preceding paragraph include, in particular,
those connected with doping. The disputes to which a federation, association
or other sports body is party are a matter for arbitration in the sense of this
Code, only insofar as the statutes or regulations of the said sports bodies or
a specific agreement so provide.
   The seat of the ICAS and the CAS is established in Lausanne, Switzerland.

S2   The task of the ICAS is to facilitate the settlement of sports-related
disputes through arbitration and to safeguard the independence of the CAS
and the rights of the parties. To this end, it looks after the administration and
financing of the CAS.

S3   The CAS, which has a list of arbitrators, procures the arbitral resolution
of disputes arising within the field of sport through the intermediary of
arbitration provided by Panels composed of one or three arbitrators.
   It comprises an Ordinary Arbitration Division and an Appeals Arbitration
Division.

B   The International Council of Arbitration for Sport (ICAS)

1   Composition

S4   The ICAS is composed of twenty members, namely high-level jurists
appointed in the following manner:

    a. four members are appointed by the International Sports Federations (IFs), viz. three by the Summer Olympic IFs (ASOIF), one by the Winter Olympic IFs (AIWF), chosen from within or from outside their membership;

    b. four members are appointed by the Association of the National Olympic Committees (ANOC), chosen from within or from outside its membership;

    c. four members are appointed by the International Olympic Committee (IOC), chosen from within or from outside its membership;

    d. four members are appointed by the twelve members of the ICAS listed above, after appropriate consultation with a view to safeguarding the interests of the athletes;

    e. four members are appointed by the sixteen members of the ICAS listed above and chosen from among personalities independent of the bodies designating the other members of the ICAS.

S5 The members of the ICAS are appointed for a renewable period of four years.

Upon their appointment, the members of the ICAS sign a declaration undertaking to exercise their function in a personal capacity, with total objectivity and independence, in conformity with this Code.

They are, in particular, bound by the confidentiality obligation which is provided in Article R43.

The members of the ICAS may not appear on the list of arbitrators of the CAS nor act as counsel to one of the parties in proceedings before the CAS.

If a member of the ICAS resigns, dies or is prevented from carrying out his functions for any other reason, he is replaced, for the remaining period of his mandate, in conformity with the terms applicable to his appointment.

2 Attributions

S6 The ICAS exercises the following functions:
1. It adopts and amends this Code.
2. It elects from among its members for a renewable period of four years:
   - the President proposed by the IOC,
   - two Vice-Presidents (one proposed by the IFs and one by the NOCs), responsible for deputising for the President if necessary, by order of seniority in age,
   - the President of the Ordinary Arbitration Division and the President of the Appeals Arbitration Division of the CAS,
   - the deputies of the two Division Presidents.
3. It appoints the personalities who are to constitute the list of arbitrators of the CAS (Article S3).
4. It exercises those functions concerning the challenge and removal of arbitrators, and any other functions which the Procedural Rules confer upon it.
5. It looks after the financing of the CAS. To this end, inter alia:
5.1 it receives and manages, in conformity with the financial regulations of the CAS, the funds allocated to its operations;
5.2 it approves the CAS budget prepared by the Court Office of the CAS;

5.3   it approves the annual accounts of the CAS established by the Court Office of the CAS.

6.   It appoints the Secretary General of the CAS.

7.   It supervises the activities of the Court Office of the CAS.

8.   If it deems such action appropriate, it sets up regional or local, permanent or ad hoc arbitration structures.

9.   If it deems such action appropriate, it creates a legal aid fund to facilitate access to CAS arbitration and determines the terms of implementation.

10.   It may take any other action which it deems likely to protect the rights of the parties and, in particular, to best guarantee the total independence of the arbitrators and to promote the settlement of sports-related disputes through arbitration.

S7   The ICAS exercises its functions either itself, or through the intermediary of its Board, made up of the President and two Vice-Presidents of the ICAS, the President of the Ordinary Arbitration Division and the President of the Appeals Arbitration Division of the CAS.

The ICAS may not delegate to the Board the functions listed under Article S6, paragraphs 1, 2, 3, 5.2 and 5.3.

3   Operation

S8   The ICAS meets whenever the activity of the CAS so requires, but at least once a year.

The ICAS constitutes a quorum when at least half of its members participate in taking a decision. Decisions are taken during meetings or by correspondence by a simple majority of the voting members, the President having the casting vote in the event of a tie. However, any modification of this Code requires a majority of two-thirds of the members of ICAS. ICAS members may not act by proxy.

The Secretary General of the CAS takes part in the decision-making with a consultative voice, and acts as Secretary to the ICAS.

S9   The President of the ICAS is also President of the CAS. He is also responsible for the ordinary administrative tasks within the remit of the ICAS.

S10   The Board of the ICAS meets at the invitation of the ICAS President.

The CAS Secretary General participates in the decision-making with a consultative voice, and acts as Secretary to the Board.

The Board constitutes a quorum if three of its members participate in taking a decision. Decisions are taken during meetings or by correspondence with a simple majority of those voting; the President has the casting vote in the event of a tie.

S11   A member of the ICAS or the Board may be challenged when circumstances allow legitimate doubt to be cast on his independence vis-à-vis one of the parties to an arbitration which must be the subject of a decision by the ICAS or the Board pursuant to Article S6, paragraph 4. He shall spontaneously disqualify himself when the subject of a decision is an arbitration procedure in which appears, as a party, a sports body to which he belongs or in which a member of the law firm to which he belongs is an arbitrator or counsel.

The member disqualified shall not take part in the deliberations concerning the arbitration in question and shall not receive any information on the activities of the ICAS and the Board concerning such arbitration.

C   The Court of Arbitration for Sport (CAS)

1   Mission

S12   The CAS sets in operation Panels which have the task of providing for the resolution by arbitration of disputes arising within the field of sport in conformity with the Procedural Rules (Articles R27 et seq.).

To this end, the CAS attends to the constitution of Panels and the smooth running of the proceedings. It places at the disposal of the parties the necessary infrastructure.

The responsibility of such Panels is, inter alia:

   a.   to resolve the disputes that are referred to them through ordinary arbitration;

   b.   to resolve through the appeals arbitration procedure disputes (including doping-related disputes) concerning the decisions of disciplinary tribunals or similar bodics of federations, associations or other sports bodies, insofar as the statutes or regulations of the said sports bodies or a specific agreement so provide;

   c.   to give non-binding advisory opinions at the request of the IOC, the IFs, the NOCs, the associations recognised by the IOC and the Olympic Games Organising Committees (OCOGs).

2   Arbitrators

S13   The personalities designated by the ICAS, in conformity with Article S6, paragraph 3, appear on the list of arbitrators for a renewable period of four years.

There are one hundred and fifty of these arbitrators.

S14   In establishing the list of CAS arbitrators, the ICAS shall call upon personalities with a legal training and who possess recognised competence with regard to sport and respect, in principle, the following distribution:

- thirty arbitrators from among the persons proposed by the IOC, chosen from within its membership or from outside;
- thirty arbitrators from among the persons proposed by the IFs, chosen from within their membership or outside;
- thirty arbitrators from among the persons proposed by the NOCs, chosen from within their membership or outside;
- thirty arbitrators chosen after appropriate consultations with a view to safeguarding the interests of the athletes;
- thirty arbitrators chosen from among persons independent of the bodies responsible for proposing arbitrators in conformity with the present article.

If necessary, the ICAS shall complete the list.

S15   The proposals for designating such arbitrators that shall constitute the list referred to in Article S14, shall be notified to the ICAS within the time limit which the latter shall establish.

The list of CAS arbitrators and all modifications to such list are published.

S16   In appointing the personalities who appear on the list of arbitrators, the ICAS shall, wherever possible, ensure fair representation of the different continents.

S17   Subject to the provisions of the Procedural Rules (Articles R27 et seq.), if a CAS arbitrator resigns, dies or is prevented from carrying out his functions for any other reason, he may be replaced, for the remaining period of his mandate, in conformity with the terms applicable to his appointment.

S18   The personalities who appear on the list of arbitrators may be called upon to serve on Panels constituted by either one of the CAS Divisions.

Upon their appointment, the CAS arbitrators sign a declaration undertaking to exercise their functions personally with total objectivity and independence, and in conformity with the provisions of this Code.

S19   CAS arbitrators are bound by the duty of confidentiality, which is provided in Article R43.

3   Organisation of the CAS

S20   The CAS is composed of two divisions, the Ordinary Arbitration Division and the Appeals Arbitration Division.

a.   The Ordinary Arbitration Division constitutes Panels, the mission of which is to resolve disputes submitted to the ordinary procedure, and performs, through the intermediary of its President, all other functions in relation to the smooth running of the proceedings conferred upon it by the Procedural Rules (Articles R27 et seq.).

b.   The Appeals Arbitration Division constitutes Panels, the mission of which is to resolve disputes (including doping-related disputes) concerning the decisions of disciplinary tribunals or similar bodies of federations, associations or other sports bodies insofar as the statutes or regulations of the said sports bodies or a specific agreement so provide. It performs, through the intermediary of its President, all other functions in relation to the smooth running of the proceedings conferred upon it by the Procedural Rules (Articles R27 et seq.).

Arbitration proceedings submitted to the CAS are assigned by the Court Office to one of these two Divisions according to their nature. Such assignment may not be contested by the parties or raised by them as a cause of irregularity.

S21   The President of one or other of the two Divisions of the CAS may be challenged if circumstances exist that give rise to legitimate doubts with regard to his independence vis-à-vis one of the parties to an arbitration assigned to his Division. He shall spontaneously disqualify himself when, in arbitration proceedings assigned to his Division, one of the parties is a sports body to which he belongs, or when a member of the law firm to which he belongs is acting as arbitrator or counsel.

When the President of one of the two Divisions is challenged, the functions relating to the smooth running of the proceedings conferred upon him by the Procedural Rules (Articles R27 et seq.), are performed by the President of the CAS and the President of the Division may not receive any information concerning the activities of the CAS regarding the arbitration proceedings which led to the disqualification.

S22 The CAS includes a Court Office composed of a Secretary General and secretaries, who replace the Secretary General when required.

The Court Office performs the functions which are assigned to it by this Code.

D Miscellaneous Provisions

S23 The present Statutes are supplemented by the Procedural Rules adopted by the ICAS.

S24 The English text and the French text are authentic. In the event of any divergence, the French text shall prevail.

S25 The present Statutes may be amended by the decision of the ICAS, in conformity with Article S8.

S26 The present Statutes and Procedural Rules come into force through the decision of the twelve members of the ICAS, nominated for the first time by the IOC, the IFs and the NOCs taken by a two-thirds majority.

PROCEDURAL RULES

A General Provisions

R27 Application of the Rules

These Procedural Rules apply whenever the parties have agreed to refer a sports-related dispute to the CAS. Such disputes may arise out of a contract containing an arbitration clause or be the subject of a later arbitration agreement (ordinary arbitration proceedings) or involve an appeal against a decision given by the disciplinary tribunals or similar bodies of a federation, association or sports body where the statutes or regulations of such bodies, or a specific agreement provides for an appeal to the CAS (appeal arbitration proceedings).

Such disputes may involve matters of principle relating to sport or matters of pecuniary or other interests brought into play in the practice or the development of sport and, generally speaking, any activity related or connected to sport.

These Procedural Rules also apply where the CAS is called upon to give an advisory opinion (consultation proceedings).

R28 Seat

The seat of the CAS and of each Arbitration Panel ('Panel') is in Lausanne, Switzerland. However, should circumstances so warrant, and after consultation with all parties, the President of the Panel or, failing him, the President of the relevant Division may decide to hold a hearing in another place.

R29 Language

The CAS working languages are French and English. In the absence of agreement between the parties, and taking into account all pertinent circumstances, the President of the Panel shall select one of these two languages as the language of the arbitration at the start of the proceedings before the Panel.

The parties may choose another language provided that the Arbitration Panel agrees. The parties shall advise the CAS of such a choice. In the event of such a choice, the Panel may order that the parties bear all or part of the translation and interpreting costs.

R30 Representation and Assistance

The parties may be represented or assisted by persons of their choice. The names, addresses, telephone and facsimile numbers of the persons representing the parties shall be communicated to the Court Office, the other party and the Panel after its formation.

R31 Notifications and Communications

All notifications and communications that the CAS or the Panel intend for the parties shall be made through the Court Office. The notifications and communications shall be written in French or in English and sent to the address shown in the arbitration request, statement of appeal or application for an opinion, or to any other address specified at a later date.

All arbitration awards, orders, and other decisions made by the CAS and the Panel shall be notified by any means permitting proof of receipt.

All communications from the parties intended for the CAS or the Panel, including the arbitration request, statement of appeal, application for an opinion and request for participation of a third party, as well as the reply shall be sent to the CAS in as many copies as there are parties, counsel and arbitrators, together with one additional copy for the CAS itself.

R32 Time Limit

Upon application on justified grounds, either the President of the Panel or, failing him, the President of the relevant Division, may extend the time-limits provided in these Procedural Rules, if the circumstances so warrant.

R33   Independence and Qualifications of Arbitrators

Every arbitrator shall be and remain independent of the parties and shall immediately disclose any circumstances likely to affect independence with respect to any of the parties.

Every arbitrator shall appear on the list drawn up by the ICAS in accordance with the Statutes which are part of this Code and shall have the availability required to expeditiously complete the arbitration.

R34   Challenge

An arbitrator may be challenged if the circumstances give rise to legitimate doubts over his independence. The challenge shall be brought immediately after the ground for the challenge has become known.

Challenges are in the exclusive power of the ICAS which may exercise such power through its Board in accordance with the Statutes which are part of this Code. The challenge shall be brought by way of a petition setting forth the facts giving rise to the challenge. The ICAS or its Board shall rule on the challenge after the other parties, the challenged arbitrator and the other arbitrators have been invited to submit written comments. It shall give brief reasons for its decision.

R35   Removal

An arbitrator may be removed by the ICAS if he refuses to or is prevented from carrying out his duties. The ICAS may delegate this function to its Board. The Board shall invite the parties, the arbitrator in question and the other arbitrators to submit written comments and shall render a brief reasoned decision.

R36   Replacement

In the event of resignation, death, challenge or removal of an arbitrator, such arbitrator shall be replaced in accordance with the provisions applicable to his appointment. Unless otherwise agreed by the parties or otherwise decided by the Panel, the proceedings shall continue without repetition of the procedure which took place prior to the replacement.

R37   Provisional and Conservatory Measures

No party may apply for provisional or conservatory measures under these Procedural Rules before the request for arbitration or the statement of appeal, which implies the exhaustion of internal remedies, has been filed with the CAS.

The President of the relevant Division, prior to the transfer of the file to the Panel, or thereafter the Panel may, upon application by one of the parties, make an order for provisional or conservatory measures. In agreeing to submit to these Procedural Rules any dispute subject to appeal arbitration proceedings, the parties expressly waive their rights to request such measures from state authorities. This waiver does not apply to provisional or conservatory measures in connection with disputes subject to ordinary arbitration proceedings.

If an application for provisional measures is filed, the President of the relevant Division or the Panel invites the opponent to express his position within fifteen days or within a shorter time-limit if circumstances so require. The President of the relevant Division or the Panel shall issue an order within a short time. In case of utmost urgency, the President of the relevant Division, prior to the transfer of the file to the Panel, or thereafter the President of the Panel may issue an order upon mere presentation of the application, provided that the opponent shall be heard subsequently.

Temporary and conservatory measures may be made conditional upon the provision of security.

B   Special Provisions Applicable to the Ordinary Arbitration Proceedings

R38   Request for Arbitration

The party intending to submit a reference to arbitration under these Procedural Rules shall file a request with the CAS containing:
- a brief statement of the facts and legal argument, including a statement of the issue to be submitted to the CAS for determination;
- the claimant's request for relief;
- a copy of the contract containing the arbitration agreement or of any document providing for arbitration in accordance with these Procedural Rules;
- any relevant information about the number and choice of the arbitrator(s), in particular if the arbitration agreement provides for three arbitrators, the name and address of the arbitrator chosen by the claimant from the CAS list of names.

Upon filing its request, the claimant shall pay the fee provided in Article R64.1.

R39   Initiation of the Arbitration by the CAS and Answer

Unless it is apparent from the outset that there is manifestly no agreement to arbitrate referring to the CAS, the Court Office shall take all appropriate actions to set the arbitration in motion. To this effect, it in particular communicates the request to the respondent, calls upon the parties to express themselves on the law applicable to the merits of the dispute and sets time-limits for the respondent to submit any relevant information about the number and choice of the arbitrator(s), in particular to appoint an arbitrator from the CAS list, as well as to file an answer to the request for arbitration. The answer shall contain:

- a brief statement of the defence;
- any defence of lack of jurisdiction;
- any counterclaim.

R40   Formation of the Panel

R40.1   Number of Arbitrators

The Panel is composed of one or three arbitrators. If the arbitration agreement does not specify the number of arbitrators, the President of the Division shall determine the number taking into acount the amount in litigation and the complexity of the dispute.

R40.2   Appointment of the Arbitrators

The parties may agree on the method of appointment of the arbitrators. In the absence of an agreement, the arbitrators shall be appointed in accordance with the following paragraphs.

If, by virtue of the arbitration agreement or of a decision of the President of the Division, a sole arbitrator is to be appointed, the parties may select him by mutual agreement within a time-limit of twenty days set by the Court Office upon receipt of the request. In the absence of an agreement within such time-limit, the President of the Division shall proceed with the appointment.

If, by virtue of the arbitration agreement or of a decision of the President of the Division, three arbitrators are to be appointed, the claimant shall appoint its arbitrator in the request or within the time-limit set in the decision on the number of arbitrators and the respondent shall appoint its arbitrator within the time-limit set by the Court Office upon receipt of the request. In the absence of such appointment, the President of the Division shall proceed with the appointment in lieu of the parties. The two arbitrators so appointed shall select the President of the Panel by mutual agreement within a time-limit set by the Court Office. In the absence of an agreement within such time-limit, the President of the Division shall appoint the President of the Panel in lieu of the two arbitrators.

R40.3   Confirmation of the Arbitrators and Transfer of the File

Any arbitrator selected by the parties or by other arbitrators shall only be deemed appointed after confirmation by the President of the Division. Before proceeding with such confirmation, the latter shall ascertain that the arbitrator fulfils the requirements of Article R33.

Once the Panel is formed, the Court Office takes notice of the formation and transfers the file to the arbitrators.

R41   Multiparty Arbitration

R41.1   Plurality of Claimants/Respondents

If the request for arbitration names several claimants and/or respondents, the CAS shall proceed with the formation of the Panel in accordance with the number of arbitrators and the method of appointment agreed by all parties. In the absence of such an agreement, the President of the Division shall decide on the number of arbitrators in accordance with Article R40.1.

If a sole arbitrator is to be appointed, Article R40.2 shall apply. If three arbitrators are to be appointed and there are several claimants, the claimants shall jointly appoint an arbitrator. If three arbitrators are to be appointed and there are several respondents, the respondents shall jointly appoint an arbitrator. In the absence of such a joint appointment, the President of the Division shall proceed with the appointment in lieu of the claimants/respondents. If (i) three arbitrators are to be appointed, (ii) there are several claimants and several respondents, and (iii) either the claimants or the respondents fail to jointly appoint an arbitrator, then both coarbitrators shall be appointed by the President of the Division in accordance with Article R40.2. In all cases, the coarbitrators shall select the President of the Panel in accordance with Article R40.2.

R41.2   Joinder

If a respondent intends to cause a third party to participate in the arbitration, it shall so state in its answer, together with the reasons therefore, and file an additional copy of its answer. The Court Office shall communicate this copy to the person the participation of which is requested and set such person a time-limit to state its position on its participation and to submit a response pursuant to Article R39. It shall also set a time-limit for the claimant to express its position on the participation of the third party.

R41.3   **Intervention**

If a third party intends to participate as a party in the arbitration, it shall file with the CAS an application to this effect, together with the reasons therefore within the time-limit set for the respondent's answer to the request for arbitration. To the extent applicable, such application shall have the same contents as a request for arbitration. The Court Office shall communicate a copy of this application to the parties and set a time-limit for them to express their position on the participation of the third party and to file, to the extent applicable, an answer pursuant to Article R39.

R41.4   **Joint Provisions on Joinder and Intervention**

A third party may only participate in the arbitration if it is bound by the arbitration agreement or if itself and the other parties agree in writing.

Upon expiration of the time-limit set in Articles R41.2 and R41.3, the President of the Division shall decide on the participation of the third party, taking into account, in particular, the prima facie existence of an arbitration agreement as referred to in Article R39 above. Such decision shall be without prejudice to the decision of the Panel on the same matter.

If the President of the Division accepts the participation of the third party, the CAS shall proceed with the formation of the Panel in accordance with the number of arbitrators and the method of appointment agreed by all parties. In the absence of such an agreement, the President of the Division shall decide on the number of arbitrators in accordance with Article R40.1. If a sole arbitrator is to be appointed, Article R40.2 shall apply. If three arbitrators are to be appointed, the coarbitrators shall be appointed by the

President of the Division and shall choose the President of the Panel in accordance with Article R40.2.

Regardless of the decision of the Panel on the participation of the third party, the formation of the Panel cannot be challenged. In the event that the Panel accepts the participation, it shall, if required, issue related procedural directions.

R42 Conciliation

The President of the Division, before the transfer of the file to the Panel, and thereafter the Panel may at any time seek to resolve the dispute by conciliation. Any settlement may be embodied in an arbitral award rendered by consent of the parties.

R43 Confidentiality

Proceedings under these Procedural Rules are confidential. The parties, the arbitrators and the CAS undertake not to disclose to any third party any facts or other information relating to the dispute or the proceedings. Awards shall not be made public unless the award itself so provides or all parties agree.

R44 Procedure before the Panel

R44.1 Written Submissions

The procedure before the Panel comprises written submissions, if the Panel deems it appropriate, and an oral hearing. Upon the receipt of the file, the President of the Panel, if appropriate, shall issue directions in connection with the written submissions. As a general rule, there shall be one statement of claim, one response and, if the circumstances so require, one reply and one second response. The parties may, in the statement of claim and in the response, raise claims not contained in the request for arbitration and in the answer to the request. Thereafter, no party may raise any new claim without the consent of the other party.

Together with their written submissions, the parties shall produce all written evidence upon which they intend to rely. After the exchange of the written submissions, the parties shall not be authorised to produce further written evidence, except by mutual agreement or if the Panel so permits on the basis of exceptional circumstances.

In their written submissions, the parties shall specify any witnesses and experts which they intend to call and state any other evidentiary measure which they request.

R44.2 Hearing

Once the exchange of pleadings is closed, the President of the Panel shall issue directions with respect to the hearing and in particular set the hearing date. As a general rule, there shall be one hearing during which the Panel hears the parties, the witnesses and the expert as well as the parties' final oral arguments, for which the respondent has the floor last.

The President of the Panel shall conduct the hearing and ascertain that the statements made are concise and limited to the subject of the written presentations, to the extent that these presentations are relevant. Except if the parties agree otherwise, the hearings are not public. There shall be minutes of the hearing. Any person heard by the Panel may be assisted by an interpreter at the cost of the party which called such upon.

The parties may call to be heard by the Panel such witnesses and experts which they have specified in their written submissions.

Before hearing any witness, expert or interpreter, the Panel shall solemnly invite such persons to tell the truth, subject to the sanctions of perjury.

Once the hearing is closed, the parties shall not be authorised to produce further written pleadings, except if the Panel so orders.

R44.3   Evidentiary Proceedings Ordered by the Panel

A party may request the Panel to issue an order that the other party produces documents in its custody or under its control. The party seeking such production shall demonstrate that the documents are likely to exist and to be relevant.

If it deems it appropriate to supplement the presentations of the parties, the Panel may at any time order the production of additional documents or the examination of witnesses, appoint and hear experts, and proceed with any other procedural act.

The Panel shall consult the parties with respect to the appointment and terms of reference of such expert. The expert appointed by the Panel shall be and remain independent of the parties and shall immediately disclose any circumstances likely to affect independence with respect to any of the parties.

R44.4   Expedited Procedure

With the consent of the parties, the Panel may proceed in an expedited manner for which it shall issue appropriate directions.

R45   Law Applicable to the Merits

The Panel shall decide the dispute according to the rules of law chosen by the parties or, in the absence of such a choice, according to Swiss law. The parties may authorise the Panel to decide *ex aequo et bono*.

R46   Award

The award shall be made by a majority decision, or, in the absence of a majority, by the President alone. The award shall be written, dated and signed. Unless the parties agree otherwise, it shall briefly state reasons. The signature of the President of the Panel shall suffice.

The award shall be final and binding upon the parties. It may not be challenged by way of an action for setting aside to the extent that the parties have no domicile, habitual residence, or business establishment in Switzerland and that they have expressly excluded all setting aside proceedings in the arbitration agreement or in an agreement entered into subsequently, in particular at the outset of the arbitration.

C Special Provisions Applicable to the Appeal Arbitration Proceedings

R47 Appeal

A party may appeal from the decision of a disciplinary tribunal or similar body of a federation, association or sports body, insofar as the statutes or regulations of the said body so provide or as the parties have concluded a specific arbitration agreement and insofar as the appellant has exhausted the legal remedies available to him prior to the appeal, in accordance with the statutes or regulations of the said sports body.

R48 Statement of Appeal

The appellant shall submit to the CAS a statement of appeal containing:

- a copy of the decision appealed from;
- the appellant's request for relief;
- the appointment of the arbitrator chosen by the appellant from the CAS list, unless the parties have agreed to a Panel composed of a sole arbitrator;
- if applicable, an application to stay the execution of the decision appealed from, together with reasons;
- a copy of the provisions of the statutes or regulations or the specific agreement providing for appeal to the CAS.

Upon filing the statement, the appellant shall pay the fee provided for under Article R65.2.

R49 Time-limit for Appeal

In the absence of a time-limit set in the statutes or regulations of the federation, association, sports body concerned, or of a previous agreement, the time-limit for appeal shall be twenty-one days from the communication of the decision which is appealed from.

R50 Number of Arbitrators

The appeal shall be submitted to a Panel of three arbitrators, except if the appellant establishes at the time of the statement of appeal that the parties have agreed to a Panel composed of a sole arbitrator or if the President of the Division considers that the matter is an emergency and the appeal should be submitted to a sole arbitrator.

R51 Appeal Brief

Within ten days following the expiration of the time-limit for the appeal, the appellant shall file with the CAS a brief stating the facts and legal arguments giving rise to the appeal, together with all exhibits and specification of other evidence upon which he intends to rely, failing which the appeal shall be deemed withdrawn.

R52   Initiation of the Arbitration by the CAS

Unless it is apparent from the outset that there is manifestly no agreement to arbitrate referring to the CAS, the CAS shall take all appropriate actions to set the arbitration in motion. To this effect, the Court Office shall, in particular, communicate the statement of appeal to the respondent, and the President of the Division shall proceed with the formation of the Panel in accordance with Articles R53 and R54. If applicable, he shall also decide promptly on an application for a stay.

R53   Appointment of Arbitrator by Respondent

Unless the parties have agreed to a Panel composed of a sole arbitrator or the President of the Division considers that the appeal is an emergency and must be submitted to a sole arbitrator, the respondent shall appoint an arbitrator within ten days after the receipt of the statement of appeal. In the absence of an appointment within such time-limit, the President of the Division shall proceed with the appointment in lieu of the respondent.

R54   Appointment of the Sole Arbitrator or of the President and Confirmation of the Arbitrators by the CAS

If, by virtue of the parties' agreement or of a decision of the President of a Division, a sole arbitrator is to be appointed, the President of the Division shall appoint the sole arbitrator upon receipt of the motion for appeal.

If three arbitrators are to be appointed, the President of the Division shall appoint the President of the panel upon appointment of the arbitrator by the respondent. The arbitrators selected by the parties shall only be deemed appointed after confirmation by the President of the Division. Before proceeding with such confirmation, the President of the Division shall ascertain that the arbitrators fulfil the requirement of Article R33.

Once the Panel is formed, the Court Office takes notice of the formation of the Panel and transfers the file to the arbitrators.

R55   Answer of Respondent

Within twenty days from the receipt of the grounds for the appeal, the respondent shall submit to the CAS an answer containing:
- a statement of defence;
- any defence of lack of jurisdiction;
- any exhibits or specification of other evidence upon which the respondent intends to rely.

R56   Statement of Appeal and Answer Complete

Unless the parties agree otherwise or the President of the Panel orders otherwise on the basis of exceptional circumstances, the parties shall not be authorised to supplement their argumentation, nor to produce new exhibits, nor to specify further evidence on which they intend to rely after the submission of the grounds for the appeal and of the answer.

R57   Scope of Panel's Review, Hearing

The Panel shall have full power to review the facts and the law. Upon transfer of the file, the President of the Panel shall issue directions in connection with the hearing for the examination of the parties, the witnesses and the experts, as well as for the oral arguments. He may also request communication of the file of the disciplinary tribunal or similar body, the decision of which is subject to appeal. Articles R44.2 and R44.3 shall apply.

R58   Law Applicable

The Panel shall decide the dispute according to the applicable regulations and the rules of law chosen by the parties or, in the absence of such a choice, according to the law of the country in which the federation, association or sports body is domiciled.

R59   Award

The award shall be rendered by a majority decision, or in the absence of a majority, by the President alone. It shall be written, dated and signed. The award shall state brief reasons. The signature of the President shall suffice.

The Panel may decide to communicate the holding of the award to the parties, prior to the reasons. The award shall be final from such written communication.

The award shall be final and binding upon the parties. It may not be challenged by way of an action for setting aside to the extent that the parties have no domicile, habitual residence, or business establishment in Switzerland and that they have expressly excluded all setting aside proceedings in the arbitration agreement or in an agreement entered into subsequently, in particular at the outset of the arbitration.

The holding of the award shall be communicated to the parties within four months after the filing of the statement of appeal. Such time-limit may be extended by the President of the Appeals Arbitration Division upon a motivated request from the President of the Panel.

The award or a summary setting forth the results of the proceedings shall be made public by the CAS, unless both parties agree that they should remain confidential.

D   Special Provisions Applicable to the Consultation Proceedings

R60   Request for Opinion

The IOC, the IFs, the NOCs, the associations recognised by the IOC, the OCOGs, may request an advisory opinion from the CAS about any legal issue with respect to the practice or development of sports or any activity related to sports. The request for an opinion shall be addressed to the CAS and accompanied by any document likely to assist the Panel entrusted with giving the opinion.

R61   Initiation by the CAS

When a request is filed, the CAS President shall review whether it may be the subject of an opinion. In the affirmative, he shall proceed with the formation of a Panel of one or three arbitrators from the CAS list and designate the President. He shall formulate, in his own discretion, the questions submitted to the Panel and forward these questions to the Panel.

R62   Opinion

Before rendering its opinion, the Panel may request additional information. The opinion may be published with the consent of the party which requested it. It does not constitute a binding arbitral award.

E   Interpretation

R63   A party may apply to the CAS for the interpretation of an award issued in an ordinary or appeals arbitration, whenever the holding of the award is unclear, incomplete, ambiguous or whenever its components are contradictory among themselves or contrary to the reasons, or whenever it contains clerical mistakes or a miscalculation of figures.

When an application for interpretation is filed, the President of the relevant Division shall review whether there is ground for interpretation. If there is ground, he shall submit the request to the Panel which has rendered the award for interpretation. The arbitrators of the Panel who are unable to act shall be replaced in accordance with Article R36. The Panel shall rule on the request within one month following the submission of the request to the Panel.

F   Costs of the Proceedings

R64   Ordinary Arbitration

R64.1   Upon filing of the request, the claimant shall pay a minimum fee of Swiss francs 500.—, without which the CAS shall not proceed. The CAS shall in any event keep this fee. The panel shall take it into account when assessing the final amount of the fees.

R64.2   Upon formation of the Panel, the Court Office shall fix, subject to later changes, the amount and the method of payment of the advance of costs. The filing of a counterclaim or a new claim shall result in the determination of separate advances.

To determine the amount of the advance, the Court Office shall fix an estimate of the costs of arbitration, which shall be borne by the parties in accordance with Article R64.4. The advance shall be paid in equal shares by the claimant and the respondent. If a party fails to pay its share, the other may substitute for it; in the absence of substitution, the claim to which the unpaid share relates shall be deemed withdrawn.

R64.3 Each party shall advance the cost of its own witnesses, experts and interpreters.

If the Panel appoints an expert, retains an interpreter or orders the examination of a witness, it shall issue directions with respect to an advance of costs, if appropriate.

R64.4 At the end of the proceedings, the Court Office shall determine the final amount of the cost of arbitration, which shall include the fee of the CAS, the costs and fees of the arbitrators computed in accordance with the CAS fee scale, the contribution towards the costs and expenses of the CAS, and the costs of witnesses, experts and interpreters.

R64.5 The foregoing costs shall be stated in the arbitral award, which shall also determine which party shall bear such costs or in which portion the parties shall share them. As a general rule, the award shall grant the prevailing party a contribution toward its legal fees and other expenses incurred in connection with the proceedings and, in particular, the costs of witnesses and interpreters. When granting such contribution, the Panel shall take into account the outcome of the proceedings, as well as the conduct and the financial resources of the parties.

R65 Appeals Arbitration

R65.1 Subject to Articles R65.2 and R65.4, the proceedings shall be free.

The fees and costs of the arbitrators, calculated in accordance with the CAS fee scale, together with the costs of the CAS are borne by the CAS.

R65.2 Upon submission of the statement of appeal, the appellant shall pay a minimum fee of Swiss francs 500.— without which the CAS shall not proceed and the appeal shall be deemed withdrawn. The CAS shall in any event keep this fee.

R65.3 The costs of the parties, witnesses, experts and interpreters shall be advanced by the parties. In the award, the Panel shall decide which party shall bear them or in what proportion the parties shall share them, taking into account the outcome of the proceedings, as well as the conduct and financial resources of the parties.

R65.4 If all circumstances so warrant, the President of the Appeals Arbitration Division may decide to apply Articles R64.4 and R64.5 to an appeals arbitration.

R66 Consultation Proceedings

The Court Office shall determine, after consultation with the person requesting the opinion, to what extent and upon what terms such person shall contribute towards the costs of the consultation procedure.

G   Miscellaneous Provisions

R67   The arbitration agreements entered into prior to November 22, 1994 shall be deemed to refer to the present Rules, unless both parties request the application of the Rules in force prior to November 22, 1994.

R68   The French text and the English text are authentic. In the event of any discrepancy, the French text shall prevail.

R69   The Procedural Rules may be amended by the decision of the Council, in conformity with Article S8.

RULES FOR THE RESOLUTION OF DISPUTES ARISING DURING THE OLYMPIC GAMES

THE INTERNATIONAL COUNCIL OF ARBITRATION FOR SPORT
(ICAS)
In view of Rule 74 of the Olympic Charter;
In view of articles S6, paragraphs 1, 8 and 10; S8, S23 and R69 of the Code of Sports-related Arbitration;
After having deliberated,

ADOPTS

the present rules which form an integral part of the Code of Sports-related Arbitration;

Article 1   Application of the Present Rules and Jurisdiction of the Court of Arbitration for Sport (CAS)

The purpose of the present rules is to provide, in the interests of the athletes and of sport, for the resolution by arbitration of any disputes which may arise during the Olympic Games (hereinafter the OG) and which result from or affect the holding of the OG. They apply to any dispute falling within the jurisdiction of the CAS.

Article 2   Ad hoc Division

For the period of the OG, the ICAS shall establish an ad hoc Division of the CAS (hereinafter the ad hoc Division), the function of which is to provide for the resolution by arbitration of the disputes covered by article 1 by means of Panels set up in accordance with the present rules. The ad hoc Division consists of arbitrators appearing on a special list, a President and his or her deputy, and an ad hoc Court Office.

Article 3   Special List of Arbitrators

The ICAS, acting through its Board, shall draw up the special list of arbitrators referred to in article 2.
This special list consists only of arbitrators who appear on the CAS general list of arbitrators and who are present at the OG. The ICAS Board shall indicate for each arbitrator the place where his or her presence is principally required.

The special list of arbitrators shall be published before the opening of the OG. However, it may be subsequently modified by the ICAS Board where necessary.

Article 4   President of the ad hoc Division

The ICAS Board shall elect a person to assume the duties of President of the ad hoc Division and a deputy. The President and his or her deputy shall be chosen from among the members of the ICAS. They must be independent of the parties and, where necessary, disqualify themselves in one another's favour.

Article 5   Ad hoc Court Office

The CAS shall establish an ad hoc Court Office placed under the authority of the CAS Secretary General.

Article 6   Language of Arbitration

The proceedings shall be conducted in English or French.

Article 7   Seat of Arbitration

The seat of the ad hoc Division and of the Panel is determined by the President of the ad hoc Division.

Article 8   Representation and Assistance

The parties may be represented or assisted by persons of their choice in so far as circumstances permit, particularly with regard to the time limit set for the award. The names, addresses, telephone and facsimile numbers of the persons representing the parties and details of any other written forms of electronic communication by which they may be reached shall appear in the application referred to in article 10 or be submitted at the start of the hearing.

Article 9   Notifications and Communications

(a)   All notifications and communications from the ad hoc Division (Panel, President or Court Office) shall be given as follows:

— *to the claimant*: by delivery to the address at the OG site appearing in the request or by facsimile or any other written forms of electronic communication specified in the request or, in the absence of all of the above, by deposit at the Court Office.

— *to the respondent*: by delivery, facsimile or other written forms of electronic communication to his or her office or place of residence at the site of the OG.

The ad hoc Division may also give notifications and communications by telephone and confirm them subsequently in writing. In the absence of written confirmation, the communication is nevertheless valid if the addressee had actual knowledge of it.

(b)   Notifications and communications from the parties shall be delivered or faxed to the Court Office with the exception of the application referred to in article 10 which must be delivered to the Court Office in return for a receipt.

Article 10   Application

Any individual and legal entity wishing to bring before the ad hoc Division of the CAS a dispute within the meaning of article 1 of the present rules shall file a written application with the ad hoc Court Office.

The application shall include:
— a copy of the decision being challenged, where applicable;
— a brief statement of the facts and legal arguments on which the application is based;
— the claimant's request for relief;
— where applicable, an application for a stay of the effects of the decision being challenged or for any other preliminary relief of an extremely urgent nature;
— any appropriate comments on the basis for CAS jurisdiction, in particular confirmation that the claimant has signed the entry form for the OG;
— the claimant's address at the site of the OG and, where applicable, the facsimile numbers and details of any other written forms of electronic communication by which the claimant can be reached for the purposes of the proceedings and, where applicable, the same information for the person representing the claimant.

The application shall be written in English or French.

Article 11   Formation of the Panel

Upon receipt of the application, the President of the ad hoc Division constitutes a Panel composed of three arbitrators appearing on the special list within the meaning of article 2 of the rules (the 'Panel'). The Court Office shall convey the application to the Panel.

Article 12   Independence of the Arbitrators

All arbitrators must sign a declaration of independence before the OG and disclose any circumstance likely to compromise their independence.

The President of the ad hoc Division and his or her deputy are subject to the same obligation.

Article 13   Challenge, Disqualification and Removal of Arbitrators

An arbitrator must disqualify him- or herself spontaneously or, failing that, may be challenged by a party if circumstances give rise to legitimate doubts as to his or her independence. A party may bring a challenge before the President of the ad hoc Division, who shall decide it immediately after giving the parties and the arbitrator concerned the opportunity to be heard, in so far as circumstances permit. The challenge must be brought as soon as the reason for the challenge becomes known.

Any arbitrator may be removed by the President of the ad hoc Division if he or she is prevented from carrying out the assignment or fails to perform his or her duties in accordance with the present rules.

If an arbitrator disqualifies him- or herself spontaneously or if the President of the ad hoc Division accepts a challenge by a party or removes an arbitrator, the President of the ad hoc Division shall immediately appoint an arbitrator to fill the vacancy.

Article 14 Stay of Decision Challenged and Preliminary Relief of Extreme Urgency

In case of extreme urgency, the President of the ad hoc Division or the Panel, where already formed, may rule on an application for a stay of the effects of the challenged decision or for any other preliminary relief without hearing the respondent first. The decision granting such relief ceases to be effective when the Panel gives a decision within the meaning of article 20 of the present rules.

When deciding whether to award any preliminary relief, the Panel shall consider whether the relief is necessary to protect the applicant from irreparable harm, the likelihood of success on the merits of the claim, and whether the interests of the applicant outweigh those of the opponent or of other members of the Olympic Community.

Article 15 Procedure before the Panel

(a) *Defense of lack of jurisdiction*
Any defense of lack of jurisdiction of the Panel must be raised at the start of the proceedings or, at the latest, at the start of the hearing.

(b) *Procedure*
The Panel organises the procedure as it considers appropriate while taking into account the specific needs and circumstances of the case, the interests of the parties, in particular their right to be heard, and the particular constraints of speed and efficiency specific to the present ad hoc procedure.

(c) *Hearing*
Except where it considers another form of procedure more appropriate, the Panel shall summon the parties to a hearing on very short notice immediately upon receipt of the application. It shall append a copy of the application to the summons to appear addressed to the respondent.

At the hearing, the Panel shall hear the parties on the subject matter of the dispute and take all appropriate action with respect to evidence. In particular, the parties shall introduce at the hearing all the evidence they intend to adduce and produce the witnesses, who shall be heard immediately. They may be assisted by an interpreter, whom they shall bring with them, at their own expense.

(d) *Other evidentiary measures*
If a party requests an opportunity to introduce additional evidence which, for legitimate reasons, it was not able to produce at the hearing, the Panel may permit it to the extent necessary to the resolution of the dispute.

The Panel may at any time take any appropriate action with respect to evidence including the appointment of an expert. It shall inform the parties accordingly.

(e) *Failure to appear*

If one party or both parties fail to appear at the hearing or to comply with injunctions, summonses or other communications issued by the Panel, the Panel may nevertheless proceed.

Article 16   The Panel's Power to Review

The Panel shall have full power to review the facts on which the application is based.

Article 17   Law Applicable

The Panel shall rule on the dispute pursuant to the Olympic Charter, the applicable regulations, general principles of law and the rules of law, the application of which it deems appropriate.

Article 18   Time limit

The Panel shall give a decision within 24 hours of the lodging of the application. This time limit may be extended by the President of the ad hoc Division if circumstances so require.

Article 19   Decision-making, Form and Communication of the Decision

The decision is taken by a majority or, in the absence of a majority, by the President of the Panel.

It shall be written, dated and signed by a member of the Panel and, in principle, brief reasons will be stated. It shall be communicated to the parties immediately.

Article 20   Enforceability and Scope of the Decision

(a) *Choice of final award or referral*

Taking into account all the circumstances of the case, including the claimant's request for relief, the nature and complexity of the dispute, the urgency of its resolution, the extent of the evidence required and of the legal issues to be resolved, the parties' right to be heard and the state of the record at the end of the ad hoc arbitration proceedings, the Panel may either make a final award or refer the dispute to arbitration by the CAS in accordance with the Code of Sports-related Arbitration. The Panel may also make an award on part of the dispute and refer the unresolved part of the dispute to regular CAS procedure.

(b) *Preliminary relief in case of referral*

If it referes the dispute to regular CAS procedure, the Panel may, even where the parties have made no application to that effect, grant preliminary relief which will remain in effect until the arbitrators decide otherwise in the regular CAS procedure.

(c) *Referral*

If the Panel refers the dispute to regular CAS procedure, the following provisions shall apply:

(i)   The Panel may set a time limit for the claimant to bring the case before the CAS according to Articles R38 and R48 of the Code of Sports-related Arbitration or provide for ex officio referral. In either case, the time limits laid down by the statutes or regulations of the bodies the decision of which is being challenged or by Article R49 of the Code of Sports-related arbitration do not apply.

(ii)   Depending on the nature of the case, the CAS Court Office shall assign the arbitration to the Ordinary Arbitration Division or to the Appeals Arbitration Division.

(iii)   The Panel formed during the OG remains assigned to the resolution of the dispute for purposes of regular CAS procedure and, by submitting to the present rules, the parties waive any provision to the contrary in the Code of Sports-related Arbitration or in their agreement concerning the number of arbitrators and the way in which the Panel is formed.

(iv)   In the event of ex officio referral, the CAS Court Office shall take any appropriate action which may facilitate the initiation of the regular CAS procedure, having special regard to the present provision.

Article 21   Enforceability; no Remedies

The decision is enforceable immediately and may not be appealed against or otherwise challenged.

Article 22   Cost-free Nature of the Proceedings

The proceedings set out in the present rules are free of charge.

Article 23   Miscellaneous Provisions

The English and French texts are authentic. In the event of any discrepancy, the English text shall prevail.

The present rules may be amended by the ICAS pursuant to Article S8 of the Code of Sports-related Arbitration.

Article 24   Application of the Present Rules to Session of OG

The ICAS will decide for each session of the OG whether the present rules shall apply.

UNCITRAL

UNCITRAL Secretariat
United Nations Commission on International Trade Law,
Vienna International Centre,
POB 500
A-1400 WIEN
Tel: 00 + 43-1-21 345-4060
Fax: 00 + 43-1-21 345-5813

MODEL ARBITRATION CLAUSE

'Any dispute, controversy or claim arising out of or relating to this contract, or the breach, termination or invalidity thereof, shall be settled by arbitration in accordance with the UNCITRAL Arbitration Rules as at present in force.'

Note — Parties may wish to consider adding:
    (a)   The appointing authority shall be . . . (name of institution or person);
    (b)   The number of arbitrators shall be . . . (one or three);
    (c)   The place of arbitration shall be . . . (town or country);
    (d)   The language(s) to be used in the arbitral proceedings shall be . . .

[Whilst various bodies are willing to act as the Appointing Authority under these Rules, the reader might note that the JCAA (q.v.) has published its own Model Clause and supplemental Rules and the L.C.I.A. (q.v.) has published Model Clauses. These are all reproduced in this book.]

UNCITRAL ARBITRATION RULES

Resolution 31/98 adopted by the General Assembly on 15 December 1976

31/98.   Arbitration Rules of the United Nations Commission on International Trade Law

(*Official Records of the General Assembly, Thirty-first Session, Supplement No 17* (A/31/17), chap. V, sect. C.)

The General Assembly,
    Recognising the value of arbitration as a method of settling disputes arising in the context of international commercial relations,
    Being convinced that the establishment of rules for *ad hoc* arbitration that are acceptable in countries with different legal, social and economic systems would significantly contribute to the development of harmonious international economic relations,
    Bearing in mind that the Arbitration Rules of the United Nations Commission on International Trade Law have been prepared after extensive consultation with arbitral institutions and centres of international commercial arbitration,
    Noting that the Arbitration Rules were adopted by the United Nations Commission on International Trade Law at its ninth session after due deliberation,
    1   *Recommends* the use of the Arbitration Rules of the United Nations Commission on International Trade Law in the settlement of disputes arising in the context of international commercial relations, particularly by reference to the Arbitration Rules in commercial contracts,
    2   *Requests* the Secretary-General to arrange for the widest possible distribution of the Arbitration Rules.

SECTION I

INTRODUCTORY RULES

Scope of application

Article 1

1 Where the parties to a contract have agreed in writing that disputes in relation to that contract shall be referred to arbitration under the UNCITRAL Arbitration Rules, then such disputes shall be settled in accordance with these Rules subject to such modification as the parties may agree in writing.

2 These Rules shall govern the arbitration except that where any of these Rules is in conflict with a provision of the law applicable to the arbitration from which parties cannot derogate, that provision shall prevail.

Notice, calculation of periods of time

Article 2

1 For the purposes of these Rules, any notice, including a notification, communication or proposal, is deemed to have been received if it is physically delivered to the addressee or if it is delivered at his habitual residence, place of business or mailing address, or, if none of these can be found after making reasonable enquiry, then at the addressee's last-known residence or place of business. Notice shall be deemed to have been received on the day it is so delivered.

2 For the purposes of calculating a period of time under these Rules, such period shall begin to run on the day following the day when a notice, notification, communication or proposal is received. If the last day of such period is an official holiday or a non-business day at the residence or place of business of the addressee, the period is extended until the first business day which follows. Official holidays or non-business days occurring during the running of the period of time are included in calculating the period.

Notice of arbitration

Article 3

1 The party initiating recourse to arbitration (hereinafter called the 'claimant') shall give to the other party (hereinafter called the 'respondent') a notice of arbitration.

2 Arbitral proceedings shall be deemed to commence on the date on which the notice of arbitration is received by the respondent.

3 The notice of arbitration shall include the following:

    (a) A demand that the dispute be referred to arbitration;

    (b) The names and addresses of the parties;

    (c) A reference to the arbitration clause or the separate arbitration agreement that is invoked;

(d)   A reference to the contract out of or in relation to which the dispute arises;

(e)   The general nature of the claim and an indication of the amount involved, if any;

(f)   The relief or remedy sought;

(g)   A proposal as to the number of arbitrators (i.e. one or three), if the parties have not previously agreed thereon.

4   The notice of arbitration may also include:

(a)   The proposals for the appointments of a sole arbitrator and an appointing authority referred to in article 6, paragraph 1;

(b)   The notification of the appointment of an arbitrator referred to in article 7;

(c)   The statement of claim referred to in article 18.

Representation and assistance

Article 4

The parties may be represented or assisted by persons of their choice. The names and addresses of such persons must be communicated in writing to the other party; such communication must specify whether the appointment is being made for purposes of representation or assistance.

SECTION II

COMPOSITION OF THE ARBITRAL TRIBUNAL

Number of arbitrators

Article 5

If the parties have not previously agreed on the number of arbitrators (ie one or three), and if within fifteen days after the receipt by the respondent of the notice of arbitration the parties have not agreed that there shall be only one arbitrator, three arbitrators shall be appointed.

Appointment of arbitrators (articles 6 to 8)

Article 6

1   If a sole arbitrator is to be appointed, either party may propose to the other:

(a)   The names of one or more persons, one of whom would serve as the sole arbitrator; and

(b)   If no appointing authority has been agreed upon by the parties, the name or names of one or more institutions or persons, one of whom would serve as appointing authority.

2   If within thirty days after receipt by a party of a proposal made in accordance with paragraph 1 the parties have not reached agreement on the choice of a sole arbitrator, the sole arbitrator shall be appointed by the

appointing authority agreed upon by the parties. If no appointing authority has been agreed upon by the parties, or if the appointing authority agreed upon refuses to act or fails to appoint the arbitrator within sixty days of the receipt of a party's request therefor, either party may request the Secretary-General of the Permanent Court of Arbitration at The Hague to designate an appointing authority.

3   The appointing authority shall, at the request of one of the parties, appoint the sole arbitrator as promptly as possible. In making the appointment the appointing authority shall use the following list-procedure, unless both parties agree that the list-procedure should not be used or unless the appointing authority determines in its discretion that the use of the list-procedure is not appropriate for the case:

(a)   At the request of one of the parties the appointing authority shall communicate to both parties an identical list containing at least three names;

(b)   Within fifteen days after the receipt of this list, each party may return the list to the appointing authority after having deleted the name or names to which he objects and numbered the remaining names on the list in the order of his preference;

(c)   After the expiration of the above period of time the appointing authority shall appoint the sole arbitrator from among the names approved on the lists returned to it and in accordance with the order of preference indicated by the parties;

(d)   If for any reason the appointment cannot be made according to this procedure, the appointing authority may exercise its discretion in appointing the sole arbitrator.

4   In making the appointment, the appointing authority shall have regard to such considerations as are likely to secure the appointment of an independent and impartial arbitrator and shall take into account as well the advisability of appointing an arbitrator of a nationality other than the nationalities of the parties.

Article 7

1   If three arbitrators are to be appointed, each party shall appoint one arbitrator. The two arbitrators thus appointed shall choose the third arbitrator who will act as the presiding arbitrator of the tribunal.

2   If within thirty days after the receipt of a party's notification of the appointment of an arbitrator the other party has not notified the first party of the arbitrator he has appointed:

(a)   The first party may request the appointing authority previously designated by the parties to appoint the second arbitrator; or

(b)   If no such authority has been previously designated by the parties, or if the appointing authority previously designated refuses to act or fails to appoint the arbitrator within thirty days after receipt of a party's request therefor, the first party may request the Secretary-General of the Permanent Court of Arbitration at The Hague to designate the appointing authority. The first party may then request the appointing authority so designated to appoint the second arbitrator. In either case, the appointing authority may exercise its discretion in appointing the arbitrator.

3   If within thirty days after the appointment of the second arbitrator the two arbitrators have not agreed on the choice of the presiding arbitrator, the presiding arbitrator shall be appointed by an appointing authority in the same way as a sole arbitrator would be appointed under article 6.

Article 8

1   When an appointing authority is requested to appoint an arbitrator pursuant to article 6 or article 7, the party which makes the request shall send to the appointing authority a copy of the notice of arbitration, a copy of the contract out of or in relation to which the dispute has arisen and a copy of the arbitration agreement if it is not contained in the contract. The appointing authority may require from either party such information as it deems necessary to fulfil its function.

2   Where the names of one or more persons are proposed for appointment as arbitrators, their full names, addresses and nationalities shall be indicated, together with a description of their qualifications.

Challenge of arbitrators (articles 9 to 12)

Article 9

A prospective arbitrator shall disclose to those who approach him in connexion with his possible appointment any circumstances likely to give rise to justifiable doubts as to his impartiality or independence. An arbitrator, once appointed or chosen, shall disclose such circumstances to the parties unless they have already been informed by him of these circumstances.

Article 10

1   Any arbitrator may be challenged if circumstances exist that give rise to justifiable doubts as to the arbitrator's impartiality or independence.

2   A party may challenge the arbitrator appointed by him only for reasons of which he becomes aware after the appointment has been made.

Article 11

1   A party who intends to challenge an arbitrator shall send notice of his challenge within fifteen days after the appointment of the challenged arbitrator has been notified to the challenging party or within fifteen days after the circumstances mentioned in articles 9 and 10 became known to that party.

2   The challenge shall be notified to the other party, to the arbitrator who is challenged and to the other members of the arbitral tribunal. The notification shall be in writing and shall state the reasons for the challenge.

3   When an arbitrator has been challenged by one party, the other party may agree to the challenge. The arbitrator may also, after the challenge, withdraw from his office. In neither case does this imply acceptance of the validity of the grounds for the challenge. In both cases the procedure provided in article 6 or 7 shall be used in full for the appointment of the substitute arbitrator, even if during the process of appointing the challenged arbitrator a party had failed to exercise his right to appoint or to participate in the appointment.

Article 12

1 If the other party does not agree to the challenge and the challenged arbitrator does not withdraw, the decision on the challenge will be made:

(a) When the initial appointment was made by an appointing authority, by that authority;

(b) When the initial appointment was not made by an appointing authority, but an appointing authority has been previously designated, by that authority;

(c) In all other cases, by the appointing authority to be designated in accordance with the procedure for designating an appointing authority as provided for in article 6.

2 If the appointing authority sustains the challenge, a substitute arbitrator shall be appointed or chosen pursuant to the procedure applicable to the appointment or choice of an arbitrator as provided in articles 6 to 9 except that, when this procedure would call for the designation of an appointing authority, the appointment of the arbitrator shall be made by the appointing authority which decided on the challenge.

Replacement of an arbitrator

Article 13

1 In the event of the death or resignation of an arbitrator during the course of the arbitral proceedings, a substitute arbitrator shall be appointed or chosen pursuant to the procedure provided for in articles 6 to 9 that was applicable to the appointment or choice of the arbitrator being replaced.

2 In the event that an arbitrator fails to act or in the event of the *de jure* or *de facto* impossibility of his performing his functions, the procedure in respect of the challenge and replacement of an arbitrator as provided in the preceding articles shall apply.

Repetition of hearings in the event of the replacement of an arbitrator

Article 14

If under articles 11 to 13 the sole or presiding arbitrator is replaced, any hearings held previously shall be repeated; if any other arbitrator is replaced, such prior hearings may be repeated at the discretion of the arbitral tribunal.

SECTION III

ARBITRAL PROCEEDINGS

General provisions

Article 15

1 Subject to these Rules, the arbitral tribunal may conduct the arbitration in such manner as it considers appropriate, provided that the parties are

treated with equality and that at any stage of the proceedings each party is given a full opportunity of presenting his case.

2 If either party so requests at any stage of the proceedings, the arbitral tribunal shall hold hearings for the presentation of evidence by witnesses, including expert witnesses, or for oral argument. In the absence of such a request, the arbitral tribunal shall decide whether to hold such hearings or whether the proceedings shall be conducted on the basis of documents and other materials.

3 All documents or information supplied to the arbitral tribunal by one party shall at the same time be communicated by that party to the other party.

Place of arbitration

Article 16

1 Unless the parties have agreed upon the place where the arbitration is to be held, such place shall be determined by the arbitral tribunal, having regard to the circumstances of the arbitration.

2 The arbitral tribunal may determine the locale of the arbitration within the country agreed upon by the parties. It may hear witnesses and hold meetings for consultation among its members at any place it deems appropriate, having regard to the circumstances of the arbitration.

3 The arbitral tribunal may meet at any place it deems appropriate for the inspection of goods, other property or documents. The parties shall be given sufficient notice to enable them to be present at such inspection.

4 The award shall be made at the place of arbitration.

Language

Article 17

1 Subject to an agreement by the parties, the arbitral tribunal shall, promptly after its appointment, determine the language or languages to be used in the proceedings. This determination shall apply to the statement of claim, the statement of defence, and any further written statements and, if oral hearings take place, to the language or languages to be used in such hearings.

2 The arbitral tribunal may order that any documents annexed to the statement of claim or statement of defence, and any supplementary documents or exhibits submitted in the course of the proceedings, delivered in their original language, shall be accompanied by a translation into the language or languages agreed upon by the parties or determined by the arbitral tribunal.

Statement of claim

Article 18

1 Unless the statement of claim was contained in the notice of arbitration, within a period of time to be determined by the arbitral tribunal, the claimant

shall communicate his statement of claim in writing to the respondent and to each of the arbitrators. A copy of the contract, and of the arbitration agreement if not contained in the contract, shall be annexed thereto.

2   The statement of claim shall include the following particulars:
   (a)   The names and addresses of the parties;
   (b)   A statement of the facts supporting the claim;
   (c)   The points at issue;
   (d)   The relief or remedy sought.

The claimant may annex to his statement of claim all documents he deems relevant or may add a reference to the documents or other evidence he will submit.

Statement of defence

Article 19

1   Within a period of time to be determined by the arbitral tribunal, the respondent shall communicate his statement of defence in writing to the claimant and to each of the arbitrators.

2   The statement of defence shall reply to the particulars (b), (c) and (d) of the statement of claim (article 18, para. 2). The respondent may annex to his statement the documents on which he relies for his defence or may add a reference to the documents or other evidence he will submit.

3   In his statement of defence, or at a later stage in the arbitral proceedings if the arbitral tribunal decides that the delay was justified under the circumstances, the respondent may make a counter-claim arising out of the same contract or rely on a claim arising out of the same contract for the purpose of a set-off.

4   The provisions of article 18, paragraph 2, shall apply to a counter-claim and a claim relied on for the purpose of a set-off.

Amendments to the claim or defence

Article 20

During the course of the arbitral proceedings either party may amend or supplement his claim or defence unless the arbitral tribunal considers it inappropriate to allow such amendment having regard to the delay in making it or prejudice to the other party or any other circumstances. However, a claim may not be amended in such a manner that the amended claim falls outside the scope of the arbitration clause or separate arbitration agreement.

Pleas as to the jurisdiction of the arbitral tribunal

Article 21

1   The arbitral tribunal shall have the power to rule on objections that it has no jurisdiction, including any objections with respect to the existence or validity of the arbitration clause or of the separate arbitration agreement.

2   The arbitral tribunal shall have the power to determine the existence or the validity of the contract of which an arbitration clause forms a part. For

the purposes of article 21, an arbitration clause which forms part of a contract and which provides for arbitration under these Rules shall be treated as an agreement independent of the other terms of the contract. A decision by the arbitral tribunal that the contract is null and void shall not entail *ipso jure* the invalidity of the arbitration clause.

3   A plea that the arbitral tribunal does not have jurisdiction shall be raised not later than in the statement of defence or, with respect to a counter-claim, in the reply to the counter-claim.

4   In general, the arbitral tribunal should rule on a plea concerning its jurisdiction as a preliminary question. However, the arbitral tribunal may proceed with the arbitration and rule on such a plea in their final award.

Further written statements

Article 22

The arbitral tribunal shall decide which further written statements, in addition to the statement of claim and the statement of defence, shall be required from the parties or may be presented by them and shall fix the periods of time for communicating such statements.

Periods of time

Article 23

The periods of time fixed by the arbitral tribunal for the communication of written statements (including the statement of claim and statement of defence) should not exceed forty-five days. However, the arbitral tribunal may extend the time-limits if it concludes that an extension is justified.

Evidence and hearings (articles 24 and 25)

Article 24

1   Each party shall have the burden of proving the facts relied on to support his claim or defence.

2   The arbitral tribunal may, if it considers it appropriate, require a party to deliver to the tribunal and to the other party, within such a period of time as the arbitral tribunal shall decide, a summary of the documents and other evidence which that party intends to present in support of the facts in issue set out in his statement of claim or statement of defence.

3   At any time during the arbitral proceedings the arbitral tribunal may require the parties to produce documents, exhibits or other evidence within such a period of time as the tribunal shall determine.

Article 25

1   In the event of an oral hearing, the arbitral tribunal shall give the parties adequate advance notice of the date, time and place thereof.

2   If witnesses are to be heard, at least fifteen days before the hearing each party shall communicate to the arbitral tribunal and to the other party the

names and addresses of the witnesses he intends to present, the subject upon and the languages in which such witnesses will give their testimony.

3   The arbitral tribunal shall make arrangements for the translation of oral statements made at a hearing and for a record of the hearing if either is deemed necessary by the tribunal under the circumstances of the case, or if the parties have agreed thereto and have communicated such agreement to the tribunal at least fifteen days before the hearing.

4   Hearings shall be held *in camera* unless the parties agree otherwise. The arbitral tribunal may require the retirement of any witness or witnesses during the testimony of other witnesses. The arbitral tribunal is free to determine the manner in which witnesses are examined.

5   Evidence of witnesses may also be presented in the form of written statements signed by them.

6   The arbitral tribunal shall determine the admissibility, relevance, materiality and weight of the evidence offered.

Interim measures of protection

Article 26

1   At the request of either party, the arbitral tribunal may take any interim measures it deems necessary in respect of the subject-matter of the dispute, including measures for the conservation of the goods forming the subject-matter in dispute, such as ordering their deposit with a third person or the sale of perishable goods.

2   Such interim measures may be established in the form of an interim award. The arbitral tribunal shall be entitled to require security for the costs of such measures.

3   A request for interim measures addressed by any party to a judicial authority shall not be deemed incompatible with the agreement to arbitrate, or as a waiver of that agreement.

Experts

Article 27

1   The arbitral tribunal may appoint one or more experts to report to it, in writing, on specific issues to be determined by the tribunal. A copy of the expert's terms of reference, established by the arbitral tribunal, shall be communicated to the parties.

2   The parties shall give the expert any relevant information or produce for his inspection any relevant documents or goods that he may require of them. Any dispute between a party and such expert as to the relevance of the required information or production shall be referred to the arbitral tribunal for decision.

3   Upon receipt of the expert's report, the arbitral tribunal shall communicate a copy of the report to the parties who shall be given the opportunity to express, in writing, their opinion on the report. A party shall be entitled to examine any document on which the expert has relied in his report.

4   At the request of either party the expert, after delivery of the report, may be heard at a hearing where the parties shall have the opportunity to be

present and to interrogate the expert. At this hearing either party may present expert witnesses in order to testify on the points at issue. The provisions of article 25 shall be applicable to such proceedings.

Default

Article 28

1   If, within the period of time fixed by the arbitral tribunal, the claimant has failed to communicate his claim without showing sufficient cause for such failure, the arbitral tribunal shall issue an order for the termination of the arbitral proceedings. If, within the period of time fixed by the arbitral tribunal, the respondent has failed to communicate his statement of defence without showing sufficient cause for such failure, the arbitral tribunal shall order that the proceedings continue.

2   If one of the parties, duly notified under these Rules, fails to appear at a hearing, without showing sufficient cause for such failure, the arbitral tribunal may proceed with the arbitration.

3   If one of the parties, duly invited to produce documentary evidence, fails to do so within the established period of time, without showing sufficient cause for such failure, the arbitral tribunal may make the award on the evidence before it.

Closure of hearings

Article 29

1   The arbitral tribunal may inquire of the parties if they have any further proof to offer or witnesses to be heard or submissions to make and, if there are none, it may declare the hearings closed.

2   The arbitral tribunal may, if it considers it necessary owing to exceptional circumstances, decide, on its own motion or upon application of a party, to reopen the hearings at any time before the award is made.

Waiver of rules

Article 30

A party who knows that any provision of, or requirement under, these Rules has not been complied with and yet proceeds with the arbitration without promptly stating his objection to such non-compliance, shall be deemed to have waived his right to object.

SECTION IV

THE AWARD

Decisions

Article 31

1   When there are three arbitrators, any award or other decision of the arbitral tribunal shall be made by a majority of the arbitrators.

2   In the case of questions of procedure, when there is no majority or when the arbitral tribunal so authorises, the presiding arbitrator may decide on his own, subject to revision, if any, by the arbitral tribunal.

Form and effect of the award

Article 32

1   In addition to making a final award, the arbitral tribunal shall be entitled to make interim, interlocutory, or partial awards.
2   The award shall be made in writing and shall be final and binding on the parties. The parties undertake to carry out the award without delay.
3   The arbitral tribunal shall state the reasons upon which the award is based, unless the parties have agreed that no reasons are to be given.
4   An award shall be signed by the arbitrators and it shall contain the date on which and the place where the award was made. Where there are three arbitrators and one of them fails to sign, the award shall state the reason for the absence of the signature.
5   The award may be made public only with the consent of both parties.
6   Copies of the award signed by the arbitrators shall be communicated to the parties by the arbitral tribunal.
7   If the arbitration law of the country where the award is made requires that the award be filed or registered by the arbitral tribunal, the tribunal shall comply with this requirement within the period of time required by law.

Applicable law, amiable compositeur

Article 33

1   The arbitral tribunal shall apply the law designated by the parties as applicable to the substance of the dispute. Failing such designation by the parties, the arbitral tribunal shall apply the law determined by the conflict of laws rules which it considers applicable.
2   The arbitral tribunal shall decide as *amiable compositeur* or *ex aequo et bono* only if the parties have expressly authorised the arbitral tribunal to do so and if the law applicable to the arbitral procedure permits such arbitration.
3   In all cases, the arbitral tribunal shall decide in accordance with the terms of the contract and shall take into account the usages of the trade applicable to the transaction.

Settlement or other grounds for termination

Article 34

1   If, before the award is made, the parties agree on a settlement of the dispute, the arbitral tribunal shall either issue an order for the termination of the arbitral proceedings or, if requested by both parties and accepted by the tribunal, record the settlement in the form of an arbitral award on agreed terms. The arbitral tribunal is not obliged to give reasons for such an award.
2   If, before the award is made, the continuation of the arbitral proceedings becomes unnecessary or impossible for any reason not mentioned in

paragraph 1, the arbitral tribunal shall inform the parties of its intention to issue an order for the termination of the proceedings. The arbitral tribunal shall have the power to issue such an order unless a party raises justifiable grounds for objection.

3   Copies of the order for termination of the arbitral proceedings or of the arbitral award on agreed terms, signed by the arbitrators, shall be communicated by the arbitral tribunal to the parties. Where an arbitral award on agreed terms is made, the provisions of article 32, paragraphs 2 and 4 to 7, shall apply.

Interpretation of the award

Article 35

1   Within thirty days after the receipt of the award, either party, with notice to the other party, may request that the arbitral tribunal give an interpretation of the award.

2   The interpretation shall be given in writing within forty-five days after the receipt of the request. The interpretation shall form part of the award and the provisions of article 32, paragraphs 2 to 7, shall apply.

Correction of the award

Article 36

1   Within thirty days after the receipt of the award, either party, with notice to the other party, may request the arbitral tribunal to correct in the award any errors in computation, any clerical or typographical errors, or any errors of similar nature. The arbitral tribunal may within thirty days after the communication of the award make such corrections on its own initiative.

2   Such corrections shall be in writing, and the provisions of article 32, paragraphs 2 to 7, shall apply.

Additional award

Article 37

1   Within thirty days after the receipt of the award, either party, with notice to the other party, may request the arbitral tribunal to make an additional award as to claims presented in the arbitral proceedings but omitted from the award.

2   If the arbitral tribunal considers the request for an additional award to be justified and considers that the omission can be rectified without any further hearings or evidence, it shall complete its award within sixty days after the receipt of the request.

3   When an additional award is made, the provisions of article 32, paragraphs 2 to 7, shall apply.

Costs (Articles 38 to 40)

Article 38

The arbitral tribunal shall fix the costs of arbitration in its award. The term 'costs' includes only:

(a) The fees of the arbitral tribunal to be stated separately as to each arbitrator and to be fixed by the tribunal itself in accordance with article 39;

(b) The travel and other expenses incurred by the arbitrators;

(c) The costs of expert advice and of other assistance required by the arbitral tribunal;

(d) The travel and other expenses of witnesses to the extent such expenses are approved by the arbitral tribunal;

(e) The costs for legal representation and assistance of the successful party if such costs were claimed during the arbitral proceedings, and only to the extent that the arbitral tribunal determines that the amount of such costs is reasonable;

(f) Any fees and expenses of the appointing authority as well as the expenses of the Secretary-General of the Permanent Court of Arbitration at The Hague.

Article 39

1   The fees of the arbitral tribunal shall be reasonable in amount, taking into account the amount in dispute, the complexity of the subject-matter, the time spent by the arbitrators and any other relevant circumstances of the case.

2   If an appointing authority has been agreed upon by the parties or designated by the Secretary-General of the Permanent Court of Arbitration at The Hague, and if that authority has issued a schedule of fees for arbitrators in international cases which it administers, the arbitral tribunal in fixing its fees shall take that schedule of fees into account to the extent that it considers appropriate in the circumstances of the case.

3   If such appointing authority has not issued a schedule of fees for arbitrators in international cases, any party may at any time request the appointing authority to furnish a statement setting forth the basis for establishing fees which is customarily followed in international cases in which the authority appoints arbitrators. If the appointing authority consents to provide such a statement, the arbitral tribunal in fixing its fees shall take such information into account to the extent that it considers appropriate in the circumstances of the case.

4   In cases referred to in paragraphs 2 and 3, when a party so requests and the appointing authority consents to perform the function, the arbitral tribunal shall fix its fees only after consultation with the appointing authority which may make any comment it deems appropriate to the arbitral tribunal concerning the fees.

Article 40

1   Except as provided in paragraph 2, the costs of arbitration shall in principle be borne by the unsuccessful party. However, the arbitral tribunal may apportion each of such costs between the parties if it determines that apportionment is reasonable, taking into account the circumstances of the case.

2   With respect to the costs of legal representation and assistance referred to in article 38, paragraph (e), the arbitral tribunal, taking into account the circumstances of the case, shall be free to determine which party shall bear

such costs or may apportion such costs between the parties if it determines that apportionment is reasonable.

3   When the arbitral tribunal issues an order for the termination of the arbitral proceedings or makes an award on agreed terms, it shall fix the costs of arbitration referred to in article 38 and article 39, paragraph 1, in the text of that order or award.

4   No additional fees may be charged by an arbitral tribunal for interpretation or correction or completion of its award under articles 35 to 37.

Deposit of costs

Article 41

1   The arbitral tribunal, on its establishment, may request each party to deposit an equal amount as an advance for the costs referred to in article 38, paragraphs (a), (b) and (c).

2   During the course of the arbitral proceedings the arbitral tribunal may request supplementary deposits from the parties.

3   If an appointing authority has been agreed upon by the parties or designated by the Secretary-General of the Permanent Court of Arbitration at The Hague, and when a party so requests and the appointing authority consents to perform the function, the arbitral tribunal shall fix the amounts of any deposits or supplementary deposits only after consultation with the appointing authority which may make any comments to the arbitral tribunal which it deems appropriate concerning the amount of such deposits and supplementary deposits.

4   If the required deposits are not paid in full within thirty days after the receipt of the request, the arbitral tribunal shall so inform the parties in order that one or another of them may make the required payment. If such payment is not made, the arbitral tribunal may order the suspension or termination of the arbitral proceedings.

5   After the award has been made, the arbitral tribunal shall render an accounting to the parties of the deposits received and return any unexpended balance to the parties.

UNCITRAL CONCILIATION RULES

MODEL CONCILIATION CLAUSE

Where, in the event of a dispute arising out of or relating to this contract, the parties wish to seek an amicable settlement of that dispute by conciliation, the conciliation shall take place in accordance with the UNCITRAL Conciliation Rules as at present in force.

(The parties may agree on other conciliation clauses.)

35/52.   Conciliation Rules of the United Nations
Commission on International Trade Law

(*Official Records of General Assembly, Thirty-fifth Session, Supplement No. 77 (A/35/17), paras 105 and 106.*)

The General Assembly,

Recognising the value of conciliation as a method of amicably settling disputes arising in the context of international commercial relations,

Convinced that the establishment of conciliation rules that are acceptable in countries with different legal, social and economic systems would significantly contribute to the development of harmonious international economic relations,

Noting that the Conciliation Rules of the United Nations Commission on International Trade Law were adopted by the Commission at its thirteenth session after consideration of the observations of Governments and interested organisations,

1. *Recommends* the use of the Conciliation Rules of the United Nations Commission on International Trade Law in cases where a dispute arises in the context of international commercial relations and the parties seek an amicable settlement of that dispute by recourse to conciliation;

2. *Requests* the Secretary-General to arrange for the widest possible distribution of the Conciliation Rules.

Article 1 Application of the Rules

(1) These Rules apply to conciliation of disputes arising out of or relating to a contractual or other legal relationship where the parties seeking an amicable settlement of their dispute have agreed that the UNCITRAL Conciliation Rules apply.

(2) The parties may agree to exclude or vary any of these Rules at any time.

(3) Where any of these Rules is in conflict with a provision of law from which the parties cannot derogate, that provision prevails.

Article 2 Commencement of Conciliation Proceedings

(1) The party initiating conciliation sends to the other party a written invitation to conciliate under these Rules, briefly identifying the subject of the dispute.

(2) Conciliation proceedings commence when the other party accepts the invitation to conciliate. If the acceptance is made orally, it is advisable that it be confirmed in writing.

(3) If the other party rejects the invitation, there will be no conciliation proceedings.

(4) If the party initiating conciliation does not receive a reply within thirty days from the date on which he sends the invitation, or within such other period of time as specified in the invitation, he may elect to treat this as a rejection of the invitation to conciliate. If he so elects, he informs the other party accordingly.

Article 3 Number of Conciliators

There shall be one conciliator unless the parties agree that there shall be two or three conciliators. When there is more than one conciliator, they ought, as a general rule, to act jointly.

Article 4   Appointment of Conciliators

(1)   (a)   In conciliation proceedings with one conciliator, the parties shall endeavour to reach agreement on the name of a sole conciliator;

(b)   In conciliation proceedings with two conciliators, each party appoints one conciliator;

(c)   In conciliation proceedings with three conciliators, each party appoints one conciliator. The parties shall endeavour to reach agreement on the name of the third conciliator.

(2)   Parties may enlist the assistance of an appropriate institution or person in connexion with the appointment of conciliators. In particular,

(a)   a party may request such an institution or person to recommend the names of suitable individuals to act as conciliator; or

(b)   the parties may agree that the appointment of one or more conciliators be made directly by such an institution or person.

In recommending or appointing individuals to act as conciliator, the institution or person shall have regard to such considerations as are likely to secure the appointment of an independent and impartial conciliator and, with respect to a sole or third conciliator, shall take into account the advisability of appointing a conciliator of a nationality other than the nationalities of the parties.

Article 3   Submission of Statements to Conciliator

(1)   The conciliator,* upon his appointment, requests each party to submit to him a brief written statement describing the general nature of the dispute and the points at issue. Each party sends a copy of his statement to the other party.

(2)   The conciliator may request each party to submit to him a further written statement of his position and the facts and grounds in support thereof, supplemented by any documents and other evidence that such party deems appropriate. The party sends a copy of his statement to the other party.

(3)   At any stage of the conciliation proceedings the conciliator may request a party to submit to him such additional information as he deems appropriate.

*In this and all following articles, the term 'conciliator' applies to a sole conciliator, two or three conciliators, as the case may be.

Article 6   Representation and Assistance

The parties may be represented or assisted by persons of their choice. The names and addresses of such persons are to be communicated in writing to the other party and to the conciliator; such communication is to specify whether the appointment is made for purposes of representation or of assistance.

Article 7   Role of Conciliator

(1)   The conciliator assists the parties in an independent and impartial manner in their attempt to reach an amicable settlement of their dispute.

(2)   The conciliator will be guided by principles of objectivity, fairness and justice, giving consideration to, among other things, the rights and obligations of the parties, the usages of the trade concerned and the circumstances surrounding the dispute, including any previous business practices between the parties.

(3)   The conciliator may conduct the conciliation proceedings in such a manner as he considers appropriate, taking into account the circumstances of the case, the wishes the parties may express, including any request by a party that the conciliator hear oral statements, and the need for a speedy settlement of the dispute.

(4)   The conciliator may, at any stage of the conciliation proceedings, make proposals for a settlement of the dispute. Such proposals need not be in writing and need not be accompanied by a statement of the reasons therefor.

Article 8   Administrative Assistance

In order to facilitate the conduct of the conciliation proceedings, the parties, or the conciliator with the consent of the parties, may arrange for administrative assistance by a suitable institution or person.

Article 9   Communication between Conciliator and Parties

(1)   The conciliator may invite the parties to meet with him or may communicate with them orally or in writing. He may meet or communicate with the parties together or with each of them separately.

(2)   Unless the parties have agreed upon the place where meetings with the conciliator are to be held, such place will be determined by the conciliator, after consultation with the parties, having regard to the circumstances of the conciliation proceedings.

Article 10   Disclosure of Information

When the conciliator receives factual information concerning the dispute from a party, he discloses the substance of that information to the other party in order that the other party may have the opportunity to present any explanation which he considers appropriate. However, when a party gives any information to the conciliator subject to a specific condition that it be kept confidential, the conciliator does not disclose that information to the other party.

Article 11   Co-operation of Parties with Conciliator

The parties will in good faith co-operate with the conciliator and, in particular, will endeavour to comply with requests by the conciliator to submit written materials, provide evidence and attend meetings.

Article 12   Suggestions by Parties for Settlement of Dispute

Each party may, on his own initiative or at the invitation of the conciliator, submit to the conciliator suggestions for the settlement of the dispute.

Article 13   Settlement Agreement

(1) When it appears to the conciliator that there exist elements of a settlement which would be acceptable to the parties, he formulates the terms of a possible settlement and submits them to the parties for their observations. After receiving the observations of the parties, the conciliator may reformulate the terms of a possible settlement in the light of such observations.

(2) If the parties reach agreement on a settlement of the dispute, they draw up and sign a written settlement agreement.** If requested by the parties, the conciliator draws up, or assists the parties in drawing up, the settlement agreement.

(3) The parties by signing the settlement agreement put an end to the dispute and are bound by the agreement.

**The parties may wish to consider including in the settlement agreement a clause that any dispute arising out of or relating to the settlement agreement shall be submitted to arbitration.

Article 14   Confidentiality

The conciliator and the parties must keep confidential all matters relating to the conciliation proceedings. Confidentiality extends also to the settlement agreement, except where its disclosure is necessary for purposes of implementation and enforcement.

Article 15   Termination of Conciliation Proceedings

The conciliation proceedings are terminated:

(a)   By the signing of the settlement agreement by the parties, on the date of the agreement; or

(b)   By a written declaration of the conciliator, after consultation with the parties, to the effect that further efforts at conciliation are no longer justified, on the date of the declaration; or

(c)   By a written declaration of the parties addressed to the conciliator to the effect that the conciliation proceedings are terminated, on the date of the declaration; or

(d)   By a written declaration of a party to the other party and the conciliator, if appointed, to the effect that the conciliation proceedings are terminated, on the date of the declaration.

Article 16   Resort to Arbitral or Judicial Proceedings

The parties undertake not to initiate, during the conciliation proceedings, any arbitral or judicial proceedings in respect of a dispute that is the subject of the conciliation proceedings, except that a party may initiate arbitral or judicial proceedings where, in his opinion, such proceedings are necessary for preserving his rights.

Article 17   Costs

(1)   Upon termination of the conciliation proceedings, the conciliator fixes the costs of the conciliation and gives written notice thereof to the parties. The term 'costs' includes only:

    (a)   The fee of the conciliator which shall be reasonable in amount;

    (b)   The travel and other expenses of the conciliator;

    (c)   The travel and other expenses of witnesses requested by the conciliator with the consent of the parties;

    (d)   The cost of any expert advice requested by the conciliator with the consent of the parties;

    (e)   The cost of any assistance provided pursuant to articles 4, paragraph (2) (b), and 8 of these Rules.

(2)   The costs, as defined above, are borne equally by the parties unless the settlement agreement provides for a different apportionment. All other expenses incurred by a party are borne by that party.

Article 8   Deposits

(1)   The conciliator, upon his appointment, may request each party to deposit an equal amount as an advance for the costs referred to in article 17, paragraph (1) which he expects will be incurred.

(2)   During the course of the conciliation proceedings the conciliator may request supplementary deposits in an equal amount from each party.

(3)   If the required deposits under paragraphs (1) and (2) of this article are not paid in full by both parties within thirty days, the conciliator may suspend the proceedings or may make a written declaration or termination to the parties, effective on the date of that declaration.

(4)   Upon termination of the conciliation proceedings, the conciliator renders an accounting to the parties of the deposits received and returns any unexpended balance to the parties.

Article 19   Role of Conciliator in Other Proceedings

The parties and the conciliator undertake that the conciliator will not act as an arbitrator or as a representative or counsel of a party in any arbitral or judicial proceedings in respect of a dispute that is the subject of the conciliation proceedings. The parties also undertake that they will not present the conciliator as a witness in any such proceedings.

Article 20   Admissibility of Evidence in Other Proceedings

The parties undertake not to rely on or introduce as evidence in arbitral or judicial proceedings, whether or not such proceedings relate to the dispute that is the subject of the conciliation proceedings:

    (a)   Views expressed or suggestions made by the other party in respect of a possible settlement of the dispute;

    (b)   Admissions made by the other party in the course of the conciliation proceedings;

    (c)   Proposals made by the conciliator;

(d)   The fact that the other party had indicated his willingness to accept a proposal for settlement made by the conciliator.

INTERNATIONAL ARBITRAL CENTRE
OF THE
FEDERAL ECONOMIC CHAMBER
VIENNA

International Arbitral Centre
of the Federal Economic Chamber,
A-1045 Vienna, Wiedner Hauptstrasse 63, POB 190;
Tel: 00 + 431-501 05/43 98;
Fax: 00 + 431 502 06/270;
Telex: 11 18 71 (buka a);
Cable address: ARBITRAGEBUWIKA WIEN

RULES OF ARBITRATION AND CONCILLIATION

**adopted by the Board of the Federal Economic Chamber
on 3 July 1991 with effect from 1 September 1991**

RECOMMENDED ARBITRATION CLAUSE

'All disputes arising out of this contract or related to its violation, termination or nullity shall be finally settled under the Rules of Arbitration and Conciliation of the International Arbitral Centre of the Federal Economic Chamber in Vienna (Vienna Rules) by one or more arbitrators appointed in accordance with these rules.'

Appropriate supplementary provisions:
  (a)   the number of arbitrators shall be ....(one or three);
  (b)   the substantive law of ....shall be applicable;*
  (c)   the language to be used in the arbitral procedings shall be ....

Parties having concluded the arbitration agreement as businessmen may waive their right to have recourse against an award in Austria on those grounds on which recourse may be had against a court judgment by way of an application for reopening the case. If this is desired, it is recommended that the following be added:

'Pursuant to para. 598 (2) of the Austrian Code of Civil Procedure (ZPO), the parties expressly waive the application of para. 595 (1) figure 7 of the said Code.'

*In this context, consideration should be given to the possible application of the United Nations Convention on Contracts for International Sale of Goods, 1980.

RULES OF ARBITRATION

[Translation from the authentic German text.]

GENERAL PROVISIONS

Jurisdiction

Article 1

1   The International Arbitral Centre of the Federal Economic Chamber in Vienna ('the Centre') has jurisdiction to settle disputes of a commercial nature if a valid arbitration agreement exists and if at least one party has its place of business outside the territory of the Republic of Austria.

2   If parties all of which have their place of business in Austria agree to the jurisdiction of the Centre, the Permanent Arbitral Tribunal of the Vienna Chamber of Commerce or, if another venue in Austria has been agreed, the Permanent Arbitral Tribunal of the Chamber of Commerce within whose territorial jurisdiction the agreed arbitration venue is situated, shall have jurisdiction. The latter tribunal shall conduct the proceedings in accordance with the rules of arbitration for the Permanent Arbitral Tribunals of the Chambers of Commerce.

3   Arbitration proceedings shall be conducted at the seat of the Centre in Vienna. Nevertheless, the parties can agree that the proceedings be conducted at a different place.*

*If an arbitration venue outside Austria is agreed upon, it should be noted that the award will as a rule not be an Austrian award and consequently that any challenge thereto may be governed by a foreign law.

Organisation

Article 2

1   The organs of the Centre are the Board, consisting of the Chairman and at least four other members, and the Secretary.

2   The arbitrators to whom arbitration proceedings are entrusted are also members of the Centre for the duration of their mandate.

Article 3

1   The Chairman and the other members of the Board of the Centre are appointed for a period of office of five years by the Board of the Federal Economic Chamber; they can be reappointed.

2   The meetings of the Board are presided over by the Chairman, or in his absence by the most senior member present. The Board can validly take decisions if an absolute majority of its members is present. The Board shall take decisions by a simple majority. In the event of a tie in voting, the Chairman shall have a casting vote.

3   Members of the Board who are parties to particular arbitration proceedings in any capacity whatsoever shall be excluded from decisions pertaining to those proceedings.

4   The members of the Board must perform their duties to the best of their ability and are not subject to any directives in that respect. They are bound to secrecy on all matters coming to their notice in the course of their duties.

Article 4

1   The Secretary shall be appointed by the Board of the Federal Economic Chamber for a period of office of five years; he can be reappointed.

2   The Secretary shall direct the activities of the Secretariat; the latter shall perform the administrative tasks of the Centre.

3   The Secretary must perform his duties to the best of his ability and is not subject to any directives in that respect. He is bound to secrecy on all matters coming to his notice in the course of his duties.

4   The Secretary shall attend the meetings of the Board in an advisory capacity.

Arbitrators

Article 5

1   Arbitrators should have specific knowledge and experience in legal, commercial or other pertinent matters. They need not be Austrian citizens.

2   The names of persons qualified to act as arbitrators can be placed upon a list of arbitrators to be kept by the Secretary. The Board shall decide upon any addition to or deletion from that list and shall prepare a new list of arbitrators every three years.

3   Inclusion in the list of arbitrators is not a prerequisite for acting as an arbitrator. Insofar as the present rules authorise them to nominate or appoint arbitrators, the parties, the arbitrators nominated by the parties and the Board can nominate or appoint any qualified person as arbitrator.

4   A member of the Board may act only as Chairman of an arbitral tribunal or sole arbitrator.

5   The arbitrators must perform their duties in complete independence and impartiality, to the best of their ability, and are not subject to any directives in that respect. They are bound to observe secrecy in respect of all matters that come to their notice in the course of their duties.

Arbitral Proceedings

Commencement of the Proceedings

Article 6

1   The arbitral proceedings are commenced when a statement of claims drawn up in German or in one of the languages of the arbitration agreement is filed with the Secretariat. The proceedings become pending on receipt of the statement of claims by the Secretariat.

2   One copy of the statement of claims together with enclosures must be submitted for each Defendant, each arbitrator and the Secretariat.

3   The statement of claims must include:
— the designation of the parties and their addresses;
— the document or documents giving evidence of the jurisdiction of the Centre;
— a specific statement of claims and the particulars and supporting documents on which the claims are based;

— the amount in dispute at the time of submission of the statement of claims, unless the claims are not related exclusively to a specific sum of money;

— particulars regarding the number of arbitrators in accordance with Article 9; if a decision by three arbitrators is requested, the nomination of an arbitrator and the address of that person.

4 If the statement of claims is defective or incomplete or if copies of documents or enclosures are missing, the Secretary shall call upon the Claimant to remedy the defect or to submit the necessary copies of documents or enclosures, setting a time-limit; the provisions of the second sentence of paragraph 1 of the present Article shall not be affected thereby.

Article 7

The Secretary shall make service to the Defendant of the statement of claims and one copy each of the rules of arbitration and the list of arbitrators and shall invite the Defendant to submit a memorandum in reply within a period of thirty days, including where appropriate a counter-claim accompanied by the number of copies required in accordance with Article 6 paragraph 2, and to state his wishes with regard to the number of arbitrators in accordance with Article 9. If a decision by three arbitrators is requested, an arbitrator shall also be nominated in the memorandum in reply and the address of that person shall be stated.

Time-Limits, Service and Communications

Article 8

1 Time-limits provided for in the rules of arbitration or set by the Secretary can be prolonged by the latter on request or on his own initiative — possibly also after their expiry — if he considers that the reasons that are presented or that come to his notice in other ways are worthy of consideration.

2 Communications shall be considered as having been validly served if they are forwarded by registered letter, telex or telefax to the addresses indicated by the parties or if the document to be served has been demonstrably delivered.

Nomination and Appointment of Arbitrators

Article 9

1 The parties can agree that their dispute is to be decided either by a sole arbitrator or by a tribunal composed of three arbitrators.

2 When no such agreement has been made and the parties do not agree on the number of arbitrators, the Board shall determine whether the dispute is to be decided by one or three arbitrators.

3 The parties shall be notified of the decision of the Board pursuant to paragraph 2 of the present Article; in the event that proceedings before a sole arbitrator are decided upon, the parties shall be requested to agree on a sole

arbitrator and to indicate that person's name and address within thirty days after service of the request. If no such indication is made within that period, the sole arbitrator shall be appointed by the Board.

4 If the dispute is to be decided by three arbitrators, the party that has not yet nominated an arbitrator shall be requested to indicate the name and address of an arbitrator within thirty days after service of the request. If no such indication is made within that period, the arbitrator for the defaulting party shall be appointed by the Board.

5 If the dispute is to be decided by three arbitrators, the arbitrators nominated by the parties or appointed by the Board shall be requested to agree on a Chairman and to indicate his name and address within thirty days after service of the request. If no such indication is made within that period, the Chairman shall be appointed by the Board.

Article 10

1 Two or more Claimants or two or more Defendants shall mutually agree whether they wish the dispute to be decided by a sole arbitrator or by three arbitrators and, if a decision by three arbitrators is wished, they shall jointly nominate an arbitrator.

2 If there is no agreement among the Claimants or among the Defendants concerning the number of arbitrators, the said Claimants or Defendants shall be requested by the Secretary to agree on the number of arbitrators within thirty days after delivery of the statement of claims.

3 If no agreement as to the number of arbitrators is reached within the period indicated in paragraph 2 of the present Article, the Board shall determine whether the dispute is to be decided by one or three arbitrators.

4 If the Claimants or the Defendants have agreed that the dispute is to be decided by three arbitrators, without having nominated an arbitrator, they shall be requested by the Secretary to indicate the name and address of an arbitrator within thirty days after delivery of the request.

5 If no arbitrator is nominated within the period indicated in paragraph 4 of the present Article, and if the dispute is to be decided by three arbitrators, the arbitrator for the defaulting Claimants or Defendants shall be appointed by the Board.

Challenge of Arbitrators

Article 11

1 An Arbitrator may be challenged if there are sufficient grounds for doubting his independence or impartiality.

2 If a party challenges an arbitrator, it must inform the Secretary thereof stating the grounds for challenge after the latter have come to its notice.

3 A challenge is inadmissible if the party making the challenge has taken part in the proceedings notwithstanding the knowledge which it already had or ought to have had of the grounds of challenge relied upon. A challenge is also inadmissible if the grounds of challenge relied upon come to the knowledge of the party making the challenge in the course of the proceedings but that party made them known with undue delay.

4 The Board shall decide upon the challenge.

Termination of the Mandate of Arbitrators

Article 12

1   Any party may request the termination of the mandate of an arbitrator who does not perform his duties or unduly delays the proceedings. The request must be submitted to the Secretariat. The Board shall decide upon the request.

2   If the inability of an arbitrator to perform the duties of his mandate is not merely temporary, the Board shall terminate his mandate at the request of a party. If an arbitrator is obviously unable to perform his duties, the Board may terminate his mandate even without a request from a party.

Article 13

1   If the challenge of an arbitrator is allowed, if his mandate is terminated, if he has resigned his mandate or has died, then,

(a)   if that arbitrator is a sole arbitrator, the parties shall be requested to agree within thirty days on the nomination of a replacement and to indicate his name and address;

(b)   if that arbitrator is the Chairman of an arbitral tribunal, the remaining arbitrators shall be requested to agree within thirty days on the nomination of a replacement and to indicate his name and address; and

(c)   if that arbitrator has been nominated by a party or has been appointed for a party, the party that nominated him or for which he was appointed shall be requested to nominate a replacement within thirty days and to indicate his name and address.

If no such nomination is received within that period, the new arbitrator shall be appointed by the Board.

2   The new arbitrator shall take over the arbitration proceedings at the point which they had reached on the termination of the previous arbitrator's mandate. If necessary, the arbitral tribunal can order the repetition of individual steps of the proceedings.

Conduct of the Proceedings

Article 14

1   The proceedings may be oral or only in writing. Hearings shall take place at the request of one party or if the sole arbitrator or arbitral tribunal to which the case has been referred considers it necessary.

2   The date of hearings shall be fixed by the sole arbitrator or the Chairman of the arbitral tribunal. Hearings shall not be public. A record of the results of the hearings shall be made.

3   If the arbitrators consider it necessary, they may on their own initiative collect evidence, and in particular may question parties or witnesses, may request the parties to submit documents and may call in experts.

Article 15

The parties shall have the right to be represented by authorised agents of their choice in the proceedings before the arbitrators.

Article 16

1   The arbitrators shall apply the substantive law designated by the parties. Failing such a designation by the parties, the arbitrators shall apply the law that is designated in the choice of law rules that they consider to be authoritative. In any case, the arbitrators shall observe the contract and the usages of trade applicable to the transaction.

2   The arbitrators may not base their decisions on equity unless they have been expressly empowered by the parties.

Article 17

The parties must pursue the proceedings with due expedition. Interruptions of the proceedings for indefinite or unduly long periods shall not be permitted, even at the joint request of the parties. The Board may strike off the list of case proceedings that are not pursued by the parties with due expedition, there being no adequate grounds; the pendency of the proceedings and the mandate of the arbitrators shall thereby be terminated.

The Award

Article 18

1   Awards shall be drawn up in writing and all the necessary copies shall be signed by the arbitrators. The signatures of the majority of the arbitrators shall suffice if the award contains a statement that an arbitrator refuses to sign or that his signature cannot be obtained because of an obstacle which cannot be overcome within a reasonable period of time. If an arbitral tribunal makes an award by a majority decision, mention thereof shall be made in the award at the request of the arbitrator who is in a minority.

2   Awards are confirmed on all the necessary copies by the signature of the Secretary and the stamp of the Centre and served on to the parties.

3   The Chairman or if he is prevented another arbitrator shall confirm on a copy at the request of a party the finality and enforceability of the award.

4   By their agreement to the Vienna Rules, the parties undertake to implement the award.

5   A copy of the award shall be deposited with the Secretariat of the Centre.

Article 19

The cost of the arbitration fixed by the Secretary in accordance with Article 23 paragraph 1 shall be stated in the award that terminates the proceedings. The arbitrators shall decide on the proportions in which these costs as well as the costs duly incurred by the parties in respect of legal representation and any further expenses for due prosecution of legal claims shall be borne by the parties.

Article 20

The parties can require that an award be issued concerning the content of any settlement reached between them.

Article 21

If an award or a settlement is to be enforced, the Secretary may provide the prosecuting party with the information that is known to him regarding the law on enforcement and the enforcement practice of the State in which the award or the settlement are to be enforced free of charge, but without guaranteeing the correctness or completeness of such information.

Costs of the Proceedings

Costs and Deposits

Article 22

1   The Claimant (Counter-claimant) shall pay the registration fee; that fee is intended to cover the costs up to the submission of the files to the arbitrators. If higher outlay is incurred, an additional sum may be prescribed.

2   If there are more than two parties to the proceedings, the registration fee shall be increased by 10% for each additional party.

3   The registration fee shall not be repayable. The registration fee, as well as any additional amount required in accordance with paragraph 1 of the present Article shall be deducted from the Claimant's (Counter-claimant's) share of the deposit against costs of arbitration.

4   Service of the statement of claims (counter-claims) will not be made unless the prescribed registration fee has been paid.

Article 23

1   The costs of arbitration (administrative costs, arbitrators' fees, cash outlay on such as experts' fees, travelling and subsistence expenses of arbitrators and experts, rental amounts, costs of minuting, interpretation and translation) shall be fixed by the Secretary.

2   As soon as it is known whether the dispute is to be decided by a sole arbitrator or by an arbitral tribunal, the Secretary shall fix the amount of the deposit against the expected costs of arbitration. That deposit shall be paid in equal shares by the parties before transmission of the files to the arbitrators and within thirty days after service of the payment request.

3   If the Claimant (Counter-claimant) fails to pay its share within the period fixed, the Secretary may delete the claim or counter-claim from the list of cases of the Centre. He shall inform the parties thereof. The claim (counter-claim) can be resubmitted in accordance with Article 6.

4   If the share of the Defendant (Counter-defendant) is not received within the period fixed, the Secretary shall inform the Claimant (Counter-claimant) thereof and shall request the Claimant or Counter-claimant to pay the failing share of the deposit within thirty days after service of the request. If this amount is not received within the period fixed, the Secretary can delete the claim (counter-claim) from the list of cases of the Centre. He shall inform the parties thereof. The claim (counter-claim) can be resubmitted in accordance with Article 6.

5   If it should be necessary to increase the deposit against costs in the course of the proceedings because of an increase in the amount in dispute, a

procedure analogous to that provided for in paragraphs 2 to 4 of the present Article shall be adopted. Until payment of the additional deposit, the increase of the amount in dispute shall not be taken into account in the arbitral proceedings.

6   If it should be necessary to increase the deposit against costs in the course of the proceedings because the amount fixed for cash outlay is not sufficient, a procedure analogous to that provided for in paragraphs 2 to 4 of the present Article shall be adopted.

7   Reductions in the amount in dispute shall be taken into account in the calculation of arbitrators' fees and administrative costs only if they occurred before transmission of the files to the arbitrators.

8   If the proceedings should be terminated otherwise than by an award or a settlement, the Secretary shall fix the arbitrators' fees and administrative costs at an appropriate level and shall determine the cash outlay.

9   If the arbitrators consider it to be necessary to appoint experts, they shall inform the Secretary thereof, indicating the expected costs. The Secretary will proceed by analogy with the provisions of paragraphs 2 to 4 of the present Article. The arbitrators may appoint an expert only after the deposit against the expected fees and expenses of the expert has been paid to the Secretariat or the payment of the fees and expenses has been ensured by means of a service contract between the experts and the parties. The preceding provisions shall also apply to the appointment of interpreters and translators.

Article 24

1   The administrative costs of the Centre and the arbitrators' fees shall be fixed on the basis of the amount in dispute according to the schedules of costs attached to these Rules. Cash outlays (such as experts' fees, travelling and subsistence expenses of arbitrators and experts, rental amounts, costs of minuting, interpretation and translation) shall be determined according to the actual expenditure.

2   For the purpose of calculating the administrative costs and the arbitrators' fees, the amounts in dispute in respect of the claim and counter-claim shall be added if the parties each pay half of the deposit against costs fixed by the Secretary. If that is not the case, the deposits against costs in respect of the claim and counter-claim shall be calculated separately.

3   A separate calculation shall also be made if the claims presented in the counter-claim bear no relation to the claims presented in the statement of claims.

4   If there are more than two parties to proceedings, the rates for the administrative costs of the Centre and the arbitrators' fees contained in the schedules attached to these Rules shall be increased by 10% for each additional party.

5   In the case of proceedings conducted concerning a number of individual claims or counter-claims, the Secretary may make a separate calculation of the arbitrators' fees according to the amounts in dispute in respect of the individual claims.

6   The rates quoted in the schedule for arbitrators' fees are the fees for sole arbitrators. In any case they shall be raised to two-and-a-half times the

amounts quoted if an arbitral tribunal is appointed and up to three times those amounts in the event of the particular difficulty of a case.

CONCILIATION RULES*

*[Translation from the authentic German text.]

Article 1

At the request of a party, conciliation proceedings can be conducted where the Centre may have jurisdiction as to the subject matter. They are not subject to the existence of a valid arbitration agreement.

Article 2

The request for the opening of conciliation proceedings shall be filed with the Secretariat of the Centre. The latter shall invite the opposing party or parties to reply within thirty days after service of the request. If a party refuses to participate in the conciliation proceedings or does not reply within that period, the attempted conciliation shall be considered as having failed.

Article 3

When the opposing party or parties accepts/accept recourse to conciliation, the Board shall nominate one of its members or another qualified person to act as conciliator. The latter shall study the documents submitted by the parties, shall convene them to a hearing and shall then submit proposals for the amicable settlement of the dispute.

Article 4

If agreement is reached, that shall be the subject of a record signed by the parties and the conciliator. If a valid arbitration agreement exists, the Board shall appoint the conciliator as sole arbitrator, provided that all parties so request. The sole arbitrator must authenticate the agreement in the form of a settlement or, if the parties so wish, make an award on the basis of the agreement.

Article 5

If no agreement is reached, the conciliation shall be considered as having failed. Declarations made by the parties in the course of conciliation proceedings shall not bind them in later arbitration proceedings. Except under the conditions set forth in Article 4 of these Rules, the conciliator may not be appointed as an arbitrator in subsequent arbitration proceedings.

Article 6

The costs of the conciliation proceedings and those of any activity of the conciliator under the conditions set forth in Article 4 shall be fixed by the Secretary at an appropriate share of the costs applicable for arbitration proceedings on the basis of the corresponding amount in dispute (Article 24 paragraph 1 of the Rules of Arbitration). The same shall apply to the deposits against costs to be fixed by the Secretary.

WIPO ARBITRATION CENTER

World Intellectual Property Organization
34, chemin des Colombettes, P.O. Box 18, 1211 Geneva 20, Switzerland;
Tel: (41-22) 730 91 11,
Fax: (41-22) 733 54 28 (WIPO), (41-22) 740 37 00 (Direct to Center)

RECOMMENDED CONTRACT
CLAUSES AND
SUBMISSION AGREEMENTS

The following pages contain alternative contract clauses (for the submission of future disputes under a particular contract) and submission agreements (for the reference of an existing dispute) for the following procedures administered by the WIPO Arbitration Center:

— mediation under the WIPO Mediation Rules,
— arbitration under the WIPO Arbitration Rules,
— expedited arbitration under the WIPO Expedited Arbitration Rules,
— mediation under the WIPO Mediation Rules followed, in the absence of a settlement, by arbitration under the WIPO Arbitration Rules.

Future Disputes

Recommended WIPO mediation clause

'Any dispute, controversy or claim arising under, out of or relating to this contract and any subsequent amendments of this contract, including, without limitation, its formation, validity, binding effect, interpretation, performance, breach or termination, as well as non-contractual claims, shall be submitted to mediation in accordance with the WIPO Mediation Rules. The place of mediation shall be . . . The language to be used in the mediation shall be . . .'

Recommended WIPO arbitration clause

'Any dispute, controversy or claim arising under, out of or relating to this contract and any subsequent amendments of this contract, including, without limitation, its formation, validity, binding effect, interpretation, performance, breach or termination, as well as non-contractual claims, shall be referred to and finally determined by arbitration in accordance with the WIPO Arbitration Rules. The arbitral tribunal shall consist of [three arbitrators][a sole arbitrator]. The place of arbitration shall be . . . The language to be used in the arbitral proceedings shall be . . . The dispute, controversy or claim shall be decided in accordance with the law of . . .'

Recommended WIPO expedited arbitration clause

'Any dispute, controversy or claim arising under, out of or relating to this contract and any subsequent amendments of this contract, including, without limitation, its formation, validity, binding effect, interpretation, performance, breach or termination, as well as non-contractual claims, shall be referred to and finally determined by arbitration in accordance with the WIPO Expedited Arbitration Rules. The place of arbitration shall be . . . The language to be used in the arbitral proceedings shall be . . . The dispute, controversy or claim shall be decided in accordance with the law of . . .'

Recommended clause for WIPO mediation followed, in the absence of a settlement, by arbitration

'Any dispute, controversy or claim arising under, out of or relating to this contract and any subsequent amendments of this contract, including, without limitation, its formation, validity, binding effect, interpretation, performance, breach or termination, as well as non-contractual claims, shall be submitted to mediation in accordance with the WIPO Mediation Rules. The place of mediation shall be . . . The language to be used in the mediation shall be . . .

'If, and to the extent that, any such dispute, controversy or claim has not been settled pursuant to the mediation within [60][90] days of the commencement of the mediation, it shall, upon the filing of a Request for Arbitration by either party, be referred to and finally determined by arbitration in accordance with the WIPO Arbitration Rules. Alternatively, if, before the expiration of the said period of [60][90] days, either party fails to participate or to continue to participate in the mediation, the dispute, controversy or claim shall, upon the filing of a Request for Arbitration by the other party, be referred to and finally determined by arbitration in accordance with the WIPO Arbitration Rules. The arbitral tribunal shall consist of [three arbitiators][a sole arbitrator]. The place of arbitration shall be . . . The language to be used in the arbitral proceedings shall be . . . The dispute, controversy or claim referred to arbitration shall be decided in accordance with the law of . . .'

Existing Disputes

Recommended submission agreement for WIPO mediation

'We, the undersigned parties, hereby agree to submit to mediation in accordance with the WIPO Mediation Rules the following dispute:
[Brief description of the dispute]
'The place of mediation shall be . . . The language to be used in the mediation shall be . . .'

Recommended submission agreement for WIPO expedited arbitration

'We, the undersigned parties, hereby agree that the following dispute shall be referred to and finally determined by arbitration in accordance with the WIPO Arbitration Rules:
[Brief description of the dispute]
'The place of arbitration shall be . . . The language to be used in the arbitral proceedings shall be . . . The dispute shall be decided in accordance with the law of . . .'

Recommended submission agreement for WIPO mediation followed, in the absence of a settlement, by arbitration

'We, the undersigned parties, hereby agree to submit to mediation in accordance with the WIPO Mediation Rules the following dispute:
[Brief description of the dispute]
'The place of mediation shall be . . . The language to be used in the mediation shall be . . .
'We further agree that, if, and to the extent that, the dispute has not been settled pursuant to the mediation within [60][90] days of the commencement of the mediation, it shall, upon the filing of a Request for Arbitration by either party, be referred to and finally determined by arbitration in accordance with the WIPO Arbitration Rules. Alternatively, if, before the expiration of the said period of [60][90] days, either party fails to participate or to continue to participate in the mediation, the dispute shall, upon the filing of a Request for Arbitration by the other party, be referred to and finally determined by arbitration in accordance with the WIPO Arbitration Rules. The arbitral tribunal shall consist of [three arbitrators][a sole arbitrator]. The place of arbitration shall be . . . The language to be used in the arbitral proceedings shall be . . . The dispute referred to arbitration shall be decided in accordance with the law of . . .'

WIPO ARBITRATION RULES

effective from 1 October 1994

I GENERAL PROVISIONS

Abbreviated Expressions

Article 1

In these Rules:
'Arbitration Agreement' means an agreement by the parties to submit to arbitration all or certain disputes which have arisen or which may arise between them; an Arbitration Agreement may be in the form of an arbitration clause in a contract or in the form of a separate contract;
'Claimant' means the party initiating an arbitration;
'Respondent' means the party against which the arbitration is initiated, as named in the Request for Arbitration;

'Tribunal' includes a sole arbitrator or all the arbitrators where more than one is appointed;

'WIPO' means the World Intellectual Property Organization;

'Center' means the WIPO Arbitration Center, a unit of the International Bureau of WIPO.

Words used in the singular include the plural and vice versa, as the context may require.

Scope of Application of Rules

Article 2

Where an Arbitration Agreement provides for arbitration under the WIPO Arbitration Rules, these Rules shall be deemed to form part of that Arbitration Agreement and the dispute shall be settled in accordance with these Rules, as in effect on the date of the commencement of the arbitration, unless the parties have agreed otherwise.

Article 3

(a) These Rules shall govern the arbitration, except that, where any of these Rules is in conflict with a provision of the law applicable to the arbitration from which the parties cannot derogate, that provision shall prevail.

(b) The law applicable to the arbitration shall be determined in accordance with Article 59(b).

Notices, Periods of Time

Article 4

(a) Any notice or other communication that may or is required to be given under these Rules shall be in writing and shall be delivered by expedited postal or courier service, or transmitted by telex, telefax or other means of telecommunication that provide a record thereof.

(b) A party's last-known residence or place of business shall be a valid address for the purpose of any notice or other communication in the absence of any notification of a change by that party. Communications may in any event be addressed to a party in the manner stipulated or, failing such a stipulation, according to the practice followed in the course of the dealings between the parties.

(c) For the purpose of determining the date of commencement of a time-limit, a notice or other communication shall be deemed to have been received on the day it is delivered or, in the case of telecommunications, transmitted in accordance with paragraphs (a) and (b) of this Article.

(d) For the purpose of determining compliance with a time-limit, a notice or other communication shall be deemed to have been sent, made or transmitted if it is despatched, in accordance with paragraphs (a) and (b) of this Article, prior to or on the day of the expiration of the time-limit.

(e) For the purpose of calculating a period of time under these Rules, such period shall begin to run on the day following the day when a notice or other communication is received. If the last day of such period is an official holiday or a non-business day at the residence or place of business of the addressee, the period is extended until the first business day which follows. Official holidays or non-business days occurring during the running of the period of time are included in calculating the period.

(f) The parties may agree to reduce or extend the periods of time referred to in Articles 11, 15(b), 16(b), 17(b), 17(c), 18(b), 19(b)(iii), 41(a) and 42(a).

(g) The Center may, at the request of a party or on its own motion, extend the periods of time referred to in Articles 11, 15(b), 16(b), 17(b), 17(c), 18(b), 19(b)(iii), 67(d), 68(e) and 70(e).

Documents Required to be Submitted to the Center

Article 5

(a) Until the notification by the Center of the establishment of the Tribunal, any written statement, notice or other communication required or allowed under Articles 6 to 36 shall be submitted by a party to the Center and a copy thereof shall at the same time be transmitted by that party to the other party.

(b) Any written statement, notice or other communication so sent to the Center shall be sent in a number of copies equal to the number required to provide one copy for each envisaged arbitrator and one for the Center.

(c) After the notification by the Center of the establishment of the Tribunal, any written statements, notices or other communications shall be submitted by a party directly to the Tribunal and a copy thereof shall at the same time be supplied by that party to the other party.

(d) The Tribunal shall send to the Center a copy of each order or other decision that it makes.

II COMMENCEMENT OF THE ARBITRATION

Request for Arbitration

Article 6

The Claimant shall transmit the Request for Arbitration to the Center and to the Respondent.

Article 7

The date of commencement of the arbitration shall be the date on which the Request for Arbitration is received by the Center.

Article 8

The Center shall inform the Claimant and the Respondent of the receipt by it of the Request for Arbitration and of the date of the commencement of the arbitration.

Article 9

The Request for Arbitration shall contain:

(i) a demand that the dispute be referred to arbitration under the WIPO Arbitration Rules;

(ii) the names, addresses and telephone, telex, telefax or other communication references of the parties and of the representative of the Claimant;

(iii) a copy of the Arbitration Agreement and, if applicable, any separate choice-of-law clause;

(iv) a brief description of the nature and circumstances of the dispute, including an indication of the rights and property involved and the nature of any technology involved;

(v) a statement of the relief sought and an indication, to the extent possible, of any amount claimed;

(vi) any appointment that is required by, or observations that the Claimant considers useful in connection with, Articles 14 to 20.

Article 10

The Request for Arbitration may also be accompanied by the Statement of Claim referred to in Article 41.

Answer to the Request

Article 11

Within 30 days from the date on which the Respondent receives the Request for Arbitration from the Claimant, the Respondent shall address to the Center and to the Claimant an Answer to the Request which shall contain comments on any of the elements in the Request for Arbitration and may include indications of any counter-claim or set-off.

Article 12

If the Claimant has filed a Statement of Claim with the Request for Arbitration pursuant to Article 10, the Answer to the Request may also be accompanied by the Statement of Defense referred to in Article 42.

Representation

Article 13

(a) The parties may be represented by persons of their choice, irrespective of, in particular, nationality or professional qualification. The names, addresses and telephone, telex, telefax or other communication references of representatives shall be communicated to the Center, the other party and, after its establishment, the Tribunal.

(b) Each party shall ensure that its representatives have sufficient time available to enable the arbitration to proceed expeditiously.

(c) The parties may also be assisted by persons of their choice.

III COMPOSITION
AND ESTABLISHMENT OF THE TRIBUNAL

Number of Arbitrators

Article 14

(a) The Tribunal shall consist of such number of arbitrators as has been agreed by the parties.

(b) Where the parties have not agreed on the number of arbitrators, the Tribunal shall consist of a sole arbitrator, except where the Center in its discretion determines that, in view of all the circumstances of the case, a Tribunal composed of three members is appropriate.

Appointment Pursuant to Procedure Agreed Upon by the Parties

Article 15

(a) If the parties have agreed on a procedure of appointing the arbitrator or arbitrators other than as envisaged in Articles 16 to 20, that procedure shall be followed.

(b) If the Tribunal has not been established pursuant to such procedure within the period of time agreed upon by the parties or, in the absence of such an agreed period of time, within 45 days after the commencement of the arbitration, the Tribunal shall be established or completed, as the case may be, in accordance with Article 19.

Appointment of a Sole Arbitrator

Article 16

(a) Where a sole arbitrator is to be appointed and the parties have not agreed on a procedure of appointment, the sole arbitrator shall be appointed jointly by the parties.

(b) If the appointment of the sole arbitrator is not made within the period of time agreed upon by the parties or, in the absence of such an agreed period of time, within 30 days after the commencement of the arbitration, the sole arbitrator shall be appointed in accordance with Article 19.

Appointment of Three Arbitrators

Article 17

(a) Where three arbitrators are to be appointed and the parties have not agreed upon a procedure of appointment, the arbitrators shall be appointed in accordance with this Article.

(b) The Claimant shall appoint an arbitrator in its Request for Arbitration. The Respondent shall appoint an arbitrator within 30 days from the date on which it receives the Request for Arbitration. The two arbitrators thus appointed shall, within 20 days after the appointment of the second arbitrator, appoint a third arbitrator, who shall be the presiding arbitrator.

(c) Notwithstanding paragraph (b), where three arbitrators are to be appointed as a result of the exercise of the discretion of the Center under Article 14(b), the Claimant shall, by notice to the Center and to the Respondent, appoint an arbitrator within 15 days after the receipt by it of notification by the Center that the Tribunal is to be composed of three arbitrators. The Respondent shall appoint an arbitrator within 30 days after the receipt by it of the said notification. The two arbitrators thus appointed shall, within 20 days after the appointment of the second arbitrator, appoint a third arbitrator, who shall be the presiding arbitrator.

(d) If the appointment of any arbitrator is not made within the applicable period of time referred to in the preceding paragraphs, that arbitrator shall be appointed in accordance with Article 19.

Appointment of Three Arbitrators in Case of Multiple Claimants or Respondents

Article 18

(a) Where
(i)   three arbitrators are to be appointed,
(ii)   the parties have not agreed on a procedure of appointment, and
(iii) the Request for Arbitration names more than one Claimant,
the Claimants shall make a joint appointment of an arbitrator in their Request for Arbitration. The appointment of the second arbitrator and the presiding arbitrator shall, subject to paragraph (b) of this Article, take place in accordance with Article 17(b), (c) or (d), as the case may be.

(b) Where
(i)   three arbitrators are to be appointed,
(ii)   the parties have not agreed on a procedure of appointment, and
(iii) the Request for Arbitration names more than one Respondent,
the Respondents shall jointly appoint an arbitrator. If, for whatever reason, the Respondents do not make a joint appointment of an arbitrator within 30 days after receiving the Request for Arbitration, any appointment of the arbitrator previously made by the Claimant or Claimants shall be considered void and two arbitrators shall be appointed by the Center. The two arbitrators thus appointed shall, within 30 days after the appointment of the second arbitrator, appoint a third arbitrator, who shall be the presiding arbitrator.

(c) Where
(i)   three arbitrators are to be appointed,
(ii)   the parties have agreed upon a procedure of appointment, and
(iii) the Request for Arbitration names more than one Claimant or more than one Respondent,
paragraphs (a) and (b) of this Article shall, notwithstanding Article 15(a), apply irrespective of any contractual provisions in the Arbitration Agreement with respect to the procedure of appointment, unless those provisions have expressly excluded the application of this Article.

Default Appointment

Article 19

(a) If a party has failed to appoint an arbitrator as required under Articles 15, 17 or 18, the Center shall, in lieu of that party, forthwith make the appointment.

(b) If the sole or presiding arbitrator has not been appointed as required under Articles 15, 16, 17 or 18, the appointment shall take place in accordance with the following procedure:

(i) The Center shall send to each party an identical list of candidates. The list shall comprise the names of at least three candidates in alphabetical order. The list shall include or be accompanied by a brief statement of each candidate's qualifications. If the parties have agreed on any particular qualifications, the list shall contain only the names of candidates that satisfy those qualifications.

(ii) Each party shall have the right to delete the name of any candidate or candidates to whose appointment it objects and shall number any remaining candidates in order of preference.

(iii) Each party shall return the marked list to the Center within 20 days after the date on which the list is received by it. Any party failing to return a marked list within that period of time shall be deemed to have assented to all candidates appearing on the list.

(iv) As soon as possible after receipt by it of the lists from the parties, or failing this, after the expiration of the period of time specified in the previous sub-paragraph, the Center shall, taking into account the preferences and objections expressed by the parties, invite a person from the list to be the sole or presiding arbitrator.

(v) If the lists which have been returned do not show a person who is acceptable as arbitrator to both parties, the Center shall be authorized to appoint the sole or presiding arbitrator. The Center shall similarly be authorized to do so if a person is not able or does not wish to accept the Center's invitation to be the sole or presiding arbitrator, or if there appear to be other reasons precluding that person from being the sole or presiding arbitrator, and there does not remain on the lists a person who is acceptable as arbitrator to both parties.

(c) Notwithstanding the provisions of paragraph (b), the Center shall be authorized to appoint the sole or presiding arbitrator if it determines in its discretion that the procedure described in that paragraph is not appropriate for the case.

Nationality of Arbitrators

Article 20

(a) An agreement of the parties concerning the nationality of arbitrators shall be respected.

(b) If the parties have not agreed on the nationality of the sole or presiding arbitrator, such arbitrator shall, in the absence of special circumstances such as the need to appoint a person having particular qualifications, be a national of a country other than the countries of the parties.

Communication Between Parties and
Candidates for Appointment as Arbitrator

Article 21

No party or anyone acting on its behalf shall have any *ex parte* communication with any candidate for appointment as arbitrator except to discuss the candidate's qualifications, availability or independence in relation to the parties.

Impartiality and Independence

Article 22

(a)   Each arbitrator shall be impartial and independent.

(b)   Each prospective arbitrator shall, before accepting appointment, disclose to the parties, the Center and any other arbitrator who has already been appointed any circumstances that might give rise to justifiable doubt as to the arbitrator's impartiality or independence, or confirm in writing that no such circumstances exist.

(c)   If, at any stage during the arbitration, new circumstances arise that might give rise to justifiable doubt as to any arbitrator's impartiality or independence, the arbitrator shall promptly disclose such circumstances to the parties, the Center and the other arbitrators.

Availability, Acceptance and Notification

Article 23

(a)   Each arbitrator shall, by accepting appointment, be deemed to have undertaken to make available sufficient time to enable the arbitration to be conducted and completed expeditiously.

(b)   Each prospective arbitrator shall accept appointment in writing and shall communicate such acceptance to the Center.

(c)   The Center shall notify the parties of the establishment of the Tribunal.

Challenge of Arbitrators

Article 24

(a)   Any arbitrator may be challenged by a party if circumstances exist that give rise to justifiable doubt as to the arbitrator's impartiality or independence.

(b)   A party may challenge an arbitrator whom it has appointed or in whose appointment it concurred only for reasons of which it becomes aware after the appointment has been made.

Article 25

A party challenging an arbitrator shall send notice to the Center, the Tribunal and the other party, stating the reasons for the challenge, within 15 days after being notified of that arbitrator's appointment or after becoming aware of the circumstances that it considers give rise to justifiable doubt as to that arbitrator's impartiality or independence.

Article 26

When an arbitrator has been challenged by a party, the other party shall have the right to respond to the challenge and shall, if it exercises this right, send, within 15 days after receipt of the notice referred to in Article 25, a copy of its response to the Center, the party making the challenge and the arbitrators.

Article 27

The Tribunal may, in its discretion, suspend or continue the arbitral proceedings during the pendency of the challenge.

Article 28

The other party may agree to the challenge or the arbitrator may voluntarily withdraw. In either case, the arbitrator shall be replaced without any implication that the grounds for the challenge are valid.

Article 29

If the other party does not agree to the challenge and the challenged arbitrator does not withdraw, the decision on the challenge shall be made by the Center in accordance with its internal procedures. Such a decision is of an administrative nature and shall be final. The Center shall not be required to state reasons for its decision.

Release From Appointment

Article 30

At the arbitrator's own request, an arbitrator may be released from appointment as arbitrator either with the consent of the parties or by the Center.

Article 31

Irrespective of any request by the arbitrator, the parties may jointly release the arbitrator from appointment as arbitrator. The parties shall promptly notify the Center of such release.

Article 32

At the request of a party or on its own motion, the Center may release an arbitrator from appointment as arbitrator if the arbitrator has become *de jure* or *de facto* unable to fulfill, or fails to fulfill, the duties of an arbitrator. In such a case, the parties shall be offered the opportunity to express their views thereon and the provisions of Articles 26 to 29 shall apply *mutatis mutandis*.

Replacement of an Arbitrator

Article 33

(a)   Whenever necessary, a substitute arbitrator shall be appointed pursuant to the procedure provided for in Articles 15 to 19 that was applicable to the appointment of the arbitrator being replaced.

(b)   In the event that an arbitrator appointed by a party has either been successfully challenged on grounds which were known or should have been known to that party at the time of appointment, or has been released from appointment as arbitrator in accordance with Article 32, the Center shall have the discretion not to permit that party to make a new appointment. If it chooses to exercise this discretion, the Center shall make the substitute appointment.

(c)   Pending the replacement, the arbitral proceedings shall be suspended, unless otherwise agreed by the parties.

Article 34

Whenever a substitute arbitrator is appointed, the Tribunal shall, having regard to any observations of the parties, determine in its sole discretion whether all or part of any prior hearings are to be repeated.

Truncated Tribunal

Article 35

(a)   If an arbitrator on a three-person Tribunal, though duly notified and without good cause, fails to participate in the work of the Tribunal, the two other arbitrators shall, unless a party has made an application under Article 32, have the power in their sole discretion to continue the arbitration and to make any award, order or other decision, notwithstanding the failure of the third arbitrator to participate. In determining whether to continue the arbitration or to render any award, order or other decision without the participation of an arbitrator, the two other arbitrators shall take into account the stage of the arbitration, the reason, if any, expressed by the third arbitrator for such non-participation, and such other matters as they consider appropriate in the circumstances of the case.

(b)   In the event that the two other arbitrators determine not to continue the arbitration without the participation of a third arbitrator, the Center shall, on proof satisfactory to it of the failure of the arbitrator to participate in the work of the Tribunal, declare the office vacant, and a substitute arbitrator shall be appointed by the Center in the exercise of the discretion defined in Article 33, unless the parties agree otherwise.

Pleas as to the Jurisdiction of the Tribunal

Article 36

(a)   The Tribunal shall have the power to hear and determine objections to its own jurisdiction, including any objections with respect to form,

existence, validity or scope of the Arbitration Agreement examined pursuant
to Article 59(b).

(b)   The Tribunal shall have the power to determine the existence or
validity of any contract of which the Arbitration Agreement forms part or to
which it relates.

(c)   A plea that the Tribunal does not have jurisdiction shall be raised
not later than in the Statement of Defense or, with respect to a counterclaim
or a set-off, the Statement of Defense thereto, failing which any such plea
shall be barred in the subsequent arbitral proceedings or before any court. A
plea that the Tribunal is exceeding the scope of its authority shall be raised
as soon as the matter alleged to be beyond the scope of its authority is raised
during the arbitral proceedings. The Tribunal may, in either case, admit a
later plea if it considers the delay justified.

(d)   The Tribunal may rule on a plea referred to in paragraph (c) as a
preliminary question or, in its sole discretion, decide on such a plea in the
final award.

(e)   A plea that the Tribunal lacks jurisdiction shall not preclude the
Center from administering the arbitration.

IV   CONDUCT OF THE ARBITRATION

Transmission of the File to the Tribunal

Article 37

The Center shall transmit the file to each arbitrator as soon as the arbitrator
is appointed.

General Powers of the Tribunal

Article 38

(a)   Subject to Article 3, the Tribunal may conduct the arbitration in
such manner as it considers appropriate.

(b)   In all cases, the Tribunal shall ensure that the parties are treated
with equality and that each party is given a fair opportunity to present its case.

(c)   The Tribunal shall ensure that the arbitral procedure takes place
with due expedition. It may, at the request of a party or on its own motion,
extend in exceptional cases a period of time fixed by these Rules, by itself or
agreed to by the parties. In urgent cases, such an extension may be granted
by the presiding arbitrator alone.

Place of Arbitration

Article 39

(a)   Unless otherwise agreed by the parties, the place of arbitration shall
be decided by the Center, taking into consideration any observations of the
parties and the circumstances of the arbitration.

(b)   The Tribunal may, after consultation with the parties, conduct hearings at any place that it considers appropriate. It may deliberate wherever it deems appropriate.

(c)   The award shall be deemed to have been made at the place of arbitration.

Language of Arbitration

Article 40

(a)   Unless otherwise agreed by the parties, the language of the arbitration shall be the language of the Arbitration Agreement, subject to the power of the Tribunal to determine otherwise, having regard to any observations of the parties and the circumstances of the arbitration.

(b)   The Tribunal may order that any documents submitted in languages other than the language of arbitration be accompanied by a translation in whole or in part into the language of arbitration.

Statement of Claim

Article 41

(a)   Unless the Statement of Claim accompanied the Request for Arbitration, the Claimant shall, within 30 days after receipt of notification from the Center of the establishment of the Tribunal, communicate its Statement of Claim to the Respondent and to the Tribunal.

(b)   The Statement of Claim shall contain a comprehensive statement of the facts and legal arguments supporting the claim, including a statement of the relief sought.

(c)   The Statement of Claim shall, to as large an extent as possible, be accompanied by the documentary evidence upon which the Claimant relies, together with a schedule of such documents. Where the documentary evidence is especially voluminous, the Claimant may add a reference to further documents it is prepared to submit.

Statement of Defense

Article 42

(a)   The Respondent shall, within 30 days after receipt of the Statement of Claim or within 30 days after receipt of notification from the Center of the establishment of the Tribunal, whichever occurs later, communicate its Statement of Defense to the Claimant and to the Tribunal.

(b)   The Statement of Defense shall reply to the particulars of the Statement of Claim required pursuant to Article 41(b). The Statement of Defense shall be accompanied by the corresponding documentary evidence described in Article 41(c).

(c)   Any counter-claim or set-off by the Respondent shall be made or asserted in the Statement of Defense or, in exceptional circumstances, at a later stage in the arbitral proceedings if so determined by the Tribunal. Any such counter-claim or set-off shall contain the same particulars as those specified in Article 41(b) and (c).

Further Written Statements

Article 43

(a) In the event that a counter-claim or set-off has been made or asserted, the Claimant shall reply to the particulars thereof. Article 42(a) and (b) shall apply *mutatis mutandis* to such reply.

(b) The Tribunal may, in its discretion, allow or require further written statements.

Amendments to Claims or Defense

Article 44

Subject to any contrary agreement by the parties, a party may amend or supplement its claim, counter-claim, defense or set-off during the course of the arbitral proceedings, unless the Tribunal considers it inappropriate to allow such amendment having regard to its nature or the delay in making it and to the provisions of Article 38(b) and (c).

Communication Between Parties and Tribunal

Article 45

Except as otherwise provided in these Rules or permitted by the Tribunal, no party or anyone acting on its behalf may have any *ex parte* communication with any arbitrator with respect to any matter of substance relating to the arbitration, it being understood that nothing in this paragraph shall prohibit *ex parte* communications which concern matters of a purely organizational nature, such as the physical facilities, place, date or time of the hearings.

Interim Measures of Protection; Security for Claims and Costs

Article 46

(a) At the request of a party, the Tribunal may issue any provisional orders or take other interim measures it deems necessary, including injunctions and measures for the conservation of goods which form part of the subject-matter in dispute, such as an order for their deposit with a third person or for the sale of perishable goods. The Tribunal may make the granting of such measures subject to appropriate security being furnished by the requesting party.

(b) At the request of a party, the Tribunal may, if it considers it to be required by exceptional circumstances, order the other party to provide security, in a form to be determined by the Tribunal, for the claim or counter-claim, as well as for costs referred to in Article 72.

(c) Measures and orders contemplated under this Article may take the form of an interim award.

(d)   A request addressed by a party to a judicial authority for interim measures or for security for the claim or counter-claim, or for the implementation of any such measures or orders granted by the Tribunal, shall not be deemed incompatible with the Arbitration Agreement, or deemed to be a waiver of that Agreement.

Preparatory Conference

Article 47

The Tribunal may, in general following the submission of the Statement of Defense, conduct a preparatory conference with the parties for the purpose of organizing and scheduling the subsequent proceedings.

Evidence

Article 48

(a)   The Tribunal shall determine the admissibility, relevance, materiality and weight of evidence.

(b)   At any time during the arbitration, the Tribunal may, at the request of a party or on its own motion, order a party to produce such documents or other evidence as it considers necessary or appropriate and may order a party to make available to the Tribunal or to an expert appointed by it or to the other party any property in its possession or control for inspection or testing.

Experiments

Article 49

(a)   A party may give notice to the Tribunal and to the other party at any reasonable time before a hearing that specified experiments have been conducted on which it intends to rely. The notice shall specify the purpose of the experiment, a summary of the experiment, the method employed, the results and the conclusion. The other party may by notice to the Tribunal request that any or all such experiments be repeated in its presence. If the Tribunal considers such request justified, it shall determine the timetable for the repetition of the experiments.

(b)   For the purposes of this Article, 'experiments' shall include tests or other processes of verification.

Site Visits

Article 50

The Tribunal may, at the request of a party or on its own motion, inspect or require the inspection of any site, property, machinery, facility, production line, model, film, material, product or process as it deems appropriate. A party may request such an inspection at any reasonable time prior to any hearing, and the Tribunal, if it grants such a request, shall determine the timing and arrangements for the inspection.

Agreed Primers and Models

Article 51

The Tribunal may, where the parties so agree, determine that they shall jointly provide:

(i)   a technical primer setting out the background of the scientific, technical or other specialized information necessary to fully understand the matters in issue; and

(ii)   models, drawings or other materials that the Tribunal or the parties require for reference purposes at any hearing.

Disclosure of Trade Secrets and other Confidential Information

Article 52

(a)   For the purposes of this Article, confidential information shall mean any information, regardless of the medium in which it is expressed, which is

(i)   in the possession of a party,

(ii)   not accessible to the public,

(iii)   of commercial, financial or industrial significance, and

(iv)   treated as confidential by the party possessing it.

(b)   A party invoking the confidentiality of any information it wishes or is required to submit in the arbitration, including to an expert appointed by the Tribunal, shall make an application to have the information classified as confidential by notice to the Tribunal, with a copy to the other party. Without disclosing the substance of the information, the party shall give in the notice the reasons for which it considers the information confidential.

(c)   The Tribunal shall determine whether the information is to be classified as confidential and of such a nature that the absence of special measures of protection in the proceedings would be likely to cause serious harm to the party invoking its confidentiality. If the Tribunal so determines, it shall decide under which conditions and to whom the confidential information may in part or in whole be disclosed and shall require any person to whom the confidential information is to be disclosed to sign an appropriate confidentiality undertaking.

(d)   In exceptional circumstances, in lieu of itself determining whether the information is to be classified as confidential and of such nature that the absence of special measures of protection in the proceedings would be likely to cause serious harm to the party invoking its confidentiality, the Tribunal may, at the request of a party or on its own motion and after consultation with the parties, designate a confidentiality advisor who will determine whether the information is to be so classified, and, if so, decide under which conditions and to whom it may in part or in whole be disclosed. Any such confidentiality advisor shall be required to sign an appropriate confidentiality undertaking.

(e)   The Tribunal may also, at the request of a party or on its own motion, appoint the confidentiality advisor as an expert in accordance with Article 55 in order to report to it, on the basis of the confidential information, on specific issues designated by the Tribunal without disclosing the confidential information either to the party from whom the confidential information does not originate or to the Tribunal.

Hearings

Article 53

(a)   If either party so requests, the Tribunal shall hold a hearing for the presentation of evidence by witnesses, including expert witnesses, or for oral argument or for both. In the absence of a request, the Tribunal shall decide whether to hold such a hearing or hearings. If no hearings are held, the proceedings shall be conducted on the basis of documents and other materials alone.

(b)   In the event of a hearing, the Tribunal shall give the parties adequate advance notice of the date, time and place thereof.

(c)   Unless the parties agree otherwise, all hearings shall be in private.

(d)   The Tribunal shall determine whether and, if so, in what form a record shall be made of any hearing.

Witnesses

Article 54

(a)   Before any hearing, the Tribunal may require either party to give notice of the identity of witnesses it wishes to call, as well as of the subject-matter of their testimony and its relevance to the issues.

(b)   The Tribunal has discretion, on the grounds of redundance and irrelevance, to limit or refuse the appearance of any witness, whether witness of fact or expert witness.

(c)   Any witness who gives oral evidence may be questioned, under the control of the Tribunal, by each of the parties. The Tribunal may put questions at any stage of the examination of the witnesses.

(d)   The testimony of witnesses may, either at the choice of a party or as directed by the Tribunal, be submitted in written form, whether by way of signed statements, sworn affidavits or otherwise, in which case the Tribunal may make the admissibility of the testimony conditional upon the witnesses being made available for oral testimony.

(e)   A party shall be responsible for the practical arrangements, cost and availability of any witness it calls.

(f)   The Tribunal shall determine whether any witness shall retire during any part of the proceedings, particularly during the testimony of other witnesses.

Experts Appointed by the Tribunal

Article 55

(a)   The Tribunal may, after consultation with the parties, appoint one or more independent experts to report to it on specific issues designated by the Tribunal. A copy of the expert's terms of reference, established by the Tribunal, having regard to any observations of the parties, shall be communicated to the parties. Any such expert shall be required to sign an appropriate confidentiality undertaking.

(b) Subject to Article 52, upon receipt of the expert's report, the Tribunal shall communicate a copy of the report to the parties, which shall be given the opportunity to express, in writing, their opinion on the report. A party may, subject to Article 52, examine any document on which the expert has relied in such a report.

(c) At the request of a party, the parties shall be given the opportunity to question the expert at a hearing. At this hearing, the parties may present expert witnesses to testify on the points at issue.

(d) The opinion of any expert on the issue or issues submitted to the expert shall be subject to the Tribunal's power of assessment of those issues in the context of all the circumstances of the case, unless the parties have agreed that the expert's determination shall be conclusive in respect of any specific issue.

Default

Article 56

(a) If the Claimant, without showing good cause, fails to submit its Statement of Claim in accordance with Article 41, the Tribunal shall terminate the proceedings.

(b) If the Respondent, without showing good cause, fails to submit its Statement of Defense in accordance with Article 42, the Tribunal may nevertheless proceed with the arbitration and make the award.

(c) The Tribunal may also proceed with the arbitration and make the award if a party, without showing good cause, fails to avail itself of the opportunity to present its case within the period of time determined by the Tribunal.

(d) If a party, without showing good cause, fails to comply with any provision of, or requirement under, these Rules or any direction given by the Tribunal, the Tribunal may draw the inferences therefrom that it considers appropriate.

Closure of Proceedings

Article 57

(a) The Tribunal shall declare the proceedings closed when it is satisfied that the parties have had adequate opportunity to present submissions and evidence.

(b) The Tribunal may, if it considers it necessary owing to exceptional circumstances, decide, on its own motion or upon application of a party, to reopen the proceedings it declared to be closed at any time before the award is made.

Waiver

Article 58

A party which knows that any provision of, or requirement under, these Rules, or any direction given by the Tribunal, has not been complied with, and yet proceeds with the arbitration without promptly recording an objection to such non-compliance, shall be deemed to have waived its right to object.

V   AWARDS AND OTHER DECISIONS

Laws Applicable to the Substance of the Dispute, the Arbitration and the Arbitration Agreement

Article 59

(a)   The Tribunal shall decide the substance of the dispute in accordance with the law or rules of law chosen by the parties. Any designation of the law of a given State shall be construed, unless otherwise expressed, as directly referring to the substantive law of that State and not to its conflict of laws rules. Failing a choice by the parties, the Tribunal shall apply the law or rules of law that it determines to be appropriate. In all cases, the Tribunal shall decide having due regard to the terms of any relevant contract and taking into account applicable trade usages. The Tribunal may decide as *amiable compositeur* or *ex aequo et bono* only if the parties have expressly authorized it to do so.

(b)   The law applicable to the arbitration shall be the arbitration law of the place of arbitration, unless the parties have expressly agreed on the application of another arbitration law and such agreement is permitted by the law of the place of arbitration.

(c)   An Arbitration Agreement shall be regarded as effective if it conforms to the requirements concerning form, existence, validity and scope of either the law or rules of law applicable in accordance with paragraph (a), or the law applicable in accordance with paragraph (b).

Currency and Interest

Article 60

(a)   Monetary amounts in the award may be expressed in any currency.

(b)   The Tribunal may award simple or compound interest to be paid by a party on any sum awarded against that party. It shall be free to determine the interest at such rates as it considers to be appropriate, without being bound by legal rates of interest, and shall be free to determine the period for which the interest shall be paid.

Decision-Making

Article 61

Unless the parties have agreed otherwise, where there is more than one arbitrator, any award, order or other decision of the Tribunal shall be made by a majority. In the absence of a majority, the presiding arbitrator shall make the award, order or other decision as if acting as sole arbitrator.

Form and Notification of Awards

Article 62

(a)   The Tribunal may make preliminary, interim, interlocutory, partial or final awards.

(b)   The award shall be in writing and shall state the date on which it was made, as well as the place of arbitration in accordance with Article 39(a).

(c)   The award shall state the reasons on which it is based, unless the parties have agreed that no reasons should be stated and the law applicable to the arbitration does not require the statement of such reasons.

(d)   The award shall be signed by the arbitrator or arbitrators. The signature of the award by a majority of the arbitrators, or, in the case of Article 61, second sentence, by the presiding arbitrator, shall be sufficient. Where an arbitrator fails to sign, the award shall state the reason for the absence of the signature.

(e)   The Tribunal may consult the Center with regard to matters of form, particularly to ensure the enforceability of the award.

(f)   The award shall be communicated by the Tribunal to the Center in a number of originals sufficient to provide one for each party, the arbitrator or arbitrators and the Center. The Center shall formally communicate an original of the award to each party and the arbitrator or arbitrators.

(g)   At the request of a party, the Center shall provide it, at cost, with a copy of the award certified by the Center. A copy so certified shall be deemed to comply with the requirements of Article IV(1)(a) of the Convention on the Recognition and Enforcement of Foreign Arbitral Awards, New York, June 10, 1958.

Time Period for Delivery of the Final Award

Article 63

(a)   The arbitration should, wherever reasonably possible, be heard and the proceedings declared closed within not more than nine months after either the delivery of the Statement of Defense or the establishment of the Tribunal, whichever event occurs later. The final award should, wherever reasonably possible, be made within three months thereafter.

(b)   If the proceedings are not declared closed within the period of time specified in paragraph (a), the Tribunal shall send the Center a status report on the arbitration, with a copy to each party. It shall send a further status report to the Center, and a copy to each party, at the end of each ensuing period of three months during which the proceedings have not been declared closed.

(c)   If the final award is not made within three months after the closure of the proceedings, the Tribunal shall send the Center a written explanation for the delay, with a copy to each party. It shall send a further explanation, and a copy to each party, at the end of each ensuing period of one month until the final award is made.

Effect of Award

Article 64

(a)   By agreeing to arbitration under these Rules, the parties undertake to carry out the award without delay, and waive their right to any form of appeal or recourse to a court of law or other judicial authority, insofar as such waiver may validly be made under the applicable law.

(b)   The award shall be effective and binding on the parties as from the date it is communicated by the Center pursuant to Article 62(f), second sentence.

Settlement or Other Grounds for Termination

Article 65

(a)   The Tribunal may suggest that the parties explore settlement at such times as the Tribunal may deem appropriate.

(b)   If, before the award is made, the parties agree on a settlement of the dispute, the Tribunal shall terminate the arbitration and, if requested jointly by the parties, record the settlement in the form of a consent award. The Tribunal shall not be obliged to give reasons for such an award.

(c)   If, before the award is made, the continuation of the arbitration becomes unnecessary or impossible for any reason not mentioned in paragraph (b), the Tribunal shall inform the parties of its intention to terminate the arbitration. The Tribunal shall have the power to issue such an order terminating the arbitration, unless a party raises justifiable grounds for objection within a period of time to be determined by the Tribunal.

(d)   The consent award or the order for termination of the arbitration shall be signed by the arbitrator or arbitrators in accordance with Article 62(d) and shall be communicated by the Tribunal to the Center in a number of originals sufficient to provide one for each party, the arbitrator or arbitrators and the Center. The Center shall formally communicate an original of the consent award or the order for termination to each party and the arbitrator or arbitrators.

Correction of the Award and Additional Award

Article 66

(a)   Within 30 days after receipt of the award, a party may, by notice to the Tribunal, with a copy to the Center and the other party, request the Tribunal to correct in the award any clerical, typographical or computational errors. If the Tribunal considers the request to be justified, it shall make the correction within 30 days after receipt of the request. Any correction, which shall take the form of a separate memorandum, signed by the Tribunal in accordance with Article 62(d), shall become part of the award.

(b)   The Tribunal may correct any error of the type referred to in paragraph (a) on its own initiative within 30 days after the date of the award.

(c)   A party may, within 30 days after receipt of the award, by notice to the Tribunal, with a copy to the Center and the other party, request the

Tribunal to make an additional award as to claims presented in the arbitral proceedings but not dealt with in the award. Before deciding on the request, the Tribunal shall give the parties an opportunity to be heard. If the Tribunal considers the request to be justified, it shall, wherever reasonably possible, make the additional award within 60 days of receipt of the request.

VI   FEES AND COSTS

Fees of the Center

Article 67

(a)   The Request for Arbitration shall be subject to the payment to the Center of a registration fee, which shall belong to the International Bureau of WIPO. The amount of the registration fee shall be fixed in the Schedule of Fees applicable on the date on which the Request for Arbitration is received by the Center.

(b)   The registration fee shall not be refundable.

(c)   No action shall be taken by the Center on a Request for Arbitration until the registration fee has been paid.

(d)   If a Claimant fails, within 15 days after a second reminder in writing from the Center, to pay the registration fee, it shall be deemed to have withdrawn its Request for Arbitration.

Article 68

(a)   An administration fee, which shall belong to the International Bureau of WIPO, shall be payable by the Claimant to the Center within 30 days after the commencement of the arbitration. The Center shall notify the Claimant of the amount of the administration fee as soon as possible after receipt of the Request for Arbitration.

(b)   In the case of a counter-claim, an administration fee shall also be payable by the Respondent to the Center within 30 days after the date on which the counter-claim referred to in Article 42(c) is made. The Center shall notify the Respondent of the amount of the administration fee as soon as possible after receipt of notification of the counter-claim.

(c)   The amount of the administration fee shall be calculated in accordance with the Schedule of Fees applicable on the date of commencement of the arbitration.

(d)   Where a claim or counter-claim is increased, the amount of the administration fee may be increased in accordance with the Schedule of Fees applicable under paragraph (c), and the increased amount shall be payable by the Claimant or the Respondent, as the case may be.

(e)   If a party fails, within 15 days after a second reminder in writing from the Center, to pay any administration fee due, it shall be deemed to have withdrawn its claim or counter-claim, or its increase in claim or counter-claim, as the case may be.

(f)   The Tribunal shall, in a timely manner, inform the Center of the amount of the claim and any counter-claim, as well as any increase thereof.

Fees of the Arbitrators

Article 69

(a)   The amount and currency of the fees of the arbitrators and the modalities and timing of their payment shall be fixed, in accordance with the provisions of this Article, by the Center, after consultation with the arbitrators and the parties.

(b)   The amount of the fees of the arbitrators shall, unless the parties and arbitrators agree otherwise, be determined within the range of minimum and maximum fees set out in the Schedule of Fees applicable on the date of the commencement of the arbitration, taking into account the estimated time needed by the arbitrators for conducting the arbitration, the amount in dispute, the complexity of the subject-matter of the dispute, the urgency of the case and any other relevant circumstances of the case.

Deposits

Article 70

(a)   Upon receipt of notification from the Center of the establishment of the Tribunal, the Claimant and the Respondent shall each deposit an equal amount as an advance for the costs of arbitration referred to in Article 71. The amount of the deposit shall be determined by the Center.

(b)   In the course of the arbitration, the Center may require that the parties make supplementary deposits.

(c)   If the required deposits are not paid in full within 30 days after receipt of the corresponding notification, the Center shall so inform the parties in order that one or other of them may make the required payment.

(d)   Where the amount of the counter-claim greatly exceeds the amount of the claim or involves the examination of significantly different matters, or where it otherwise appears appropriate in the circumstances, the Center in its discretion may establish two separate deposits on account of claim and counter-claim. If separate deposits are established, the totality of the deposit on account of claim shall be paid by the Claimant and the totality of the deposit on account of counter-claim shall be paid by the Respondent.

(e)   If a party fails, within 15 days after a second reminder in writing from the Center, to pay the required deposit, it shall be deemed to have withdrawn the relevant claim or counter-claim.

(f)   After the award has been made, the Center shall, in accordance with the award, render an accounting to the parties of the deposits received and return any unexpended balance to the parties or require the payment of any amount owing from the parties.

Award of Costs of Arbitration

Article 71

(a)   In its award, the Tribunal shall fix the costs of arbitration, which shall consist of:

(i)   the arbitrators' fees,

(ii)   the properly incurred travel, communication and other expenses of the arbitrators,

(iii)   the costs of expert advice and such other assistance required by the Tribunal pursuant to these Rules, and

(iv)   such other expenses as are necessary for the conduct of the arbitration proceedings, such as the cost of meeting and hearing facilities.

(b)   The aforementioned costs shall, as far as possible, be debited from the deposits required under Article 70.

(c)   The Tribunal shall, subject to any agreement of the parties, apportion the costs of arbitration and the registration and administration fees of the Center between the parties in the light of all the circumstances and the outcome of the arbitration.

Award of Costs Incurred by a Party

Article 72

In its award, the Tribunal may, subject to any contrary agreement by the parties and in the light of all the circumstances and the outcome of the arbitration, order a party to pay the whole or part of reasonable expenses incurred by the other party in presenting its case, including those incurred for legal representatives and witnesses.

VII   CONFIDENTIALITY

Confidentiality of the Existence of the Arbitration

Article 73

(a)   Except to the extent necessary in connection with a court challenge to the arbitration or an action for enforcement of an award, no information concerning the existence of an arbitration may be unilaterally disclosed by a party to any third party unless it is required to do so by law or by a competent regulatory body, and then only

(i)   by disclosing no more than what is legally required, and

(ii)   by furnishing to the Tribunal and to the other party, if the disclosure takes place during the arbitration, or to the other party alone, if the disclosure takes place after the termination of the arbitration, details of the disclosure and an explanation of the reason for it.

(b)   Notwithstanding paragraph (a), a party may disclose to a third party the names of the parties to the arbitration and the relief requested for the purpose of satisfying any obligation of good faith or candor owed to that third party.

Confidentiality of Disclosures Made During the Arbitration

Article 74

(a)   In addition to any specific measures that may be available under Article 52, any documentary or other evidence given by a party or a witness in the arbitration shall be treated as confidential and, to the extent that such evidence describes information that is not in the public domain, shall not be used or disclosed to any third party by a party whose access to that information arises exclusively as a result of its participation in the arbitration for any purpose without the consent of the parties or order of a court having jurisdiction.

(b)   For the purposes of this Article, a witness called by a party shall not be considered to be a third party. To the extent that a witness is given access to evidence or other information obtained in the arbitration in order to prepare the witness's testimony, the party calling such witness shall be responsible for the maintenance by the witness of the same degree of confidentiality as that required of the party.

Confidentiality of the Award

Article 75

The award shall be treated as confidential by the parties and may only be disclosed to a third party if and to the extent that

(i)   the parties consent, or

(ii)   it falls into the public domain as a result of an action before a national court or other competent authority, or

(iii)   it must be disclosed in order to comply with a legal requirement imposed on a party or in order to establish or protect a party's legal rights against a third party.

Maintenance of Confidentiality by the Center and Arbitrator

Article 76

(a)   Unless the parties agree otherwise, the Center and the arbitrator shall maintain the confidentiality of the arbitration, the award and, to the extent that they describe information that is not in the public domain, any documentary or other evidence disclosed during the arbitration, except to the extent necessary in connection with a court action relating to the award, or as otherwise required by law.

(b)   Notwithstanding paragraph (a), the Center may include information concerning the arbitration in any aggregate statistical data that it publishes concerning its activities, provided that such information does not enable the parties or the particular circumstances of the dispute to be identified.

VIII   MISCELLANEOUS

Exclusion of Liability

Article 77

Except in respect of deliberate wrongdoing, the arbitrator or arbitrators, WIPO and the Center shall not be liable to a party for any act or omission in connection with the arbitration.

Waiver of Defamation

Article 78

The parties and, by acceptance of appointment, the arbitrator agree that any statements or comments, whether written or oral, made or used by them or their representatives in preparation for or in the course of the arbitration shall not be relied upon to found or maintain any action for defamation, libel, slander or any related complaint, and this Article may be pleaded as a bar to any such action.

SCHEDULE OF FEES

[*Not reproduced here.*]

WIPO EXPEDITED ARBITRATION RULES

effective from 1 October 1994

Summary

The WIPO Expedited Arbitration Rules consist of the WIPO Arbitration Rules modified in certain respects in order to ensure that the arbitration can be conducted in a shortened time frame and at reduced cost. To achieve these objectives, four main modifications have been introduced into the WIPO Arbitration Rules:

(i)   The Statement of Claim must accompany (and not be filed later and separately from) the Request for Arbitration. Similarly, the Statement of Defense must accompany the Answer to the Request.

(ii)   There is always a sole arbitrator.

(iii)   Any hearings before the sole arbitrator are condensed and may not, save in exceptional circumstances, exceed three days.

(iv)   The time limits applying to the various stages of the arbitral proceedings have been shortened. In particular, the proceedings should, whenever reasonably possible, be declared closed within three months (as opposed to nine months under the WIPO Arbitration Rules) of either the delivery of the Statement of Defense or the establishment of the Tribunal, whichever event occurs later, and the final award should, whenever reasonably possible, be made within one month (as opposed to three months under the WIPO Arbitration Rules) thereafter.

List of Modifications

The following is the list of the modifications to the WIPO Arbitration Rules that are made in the WIPO Expedited Arbitration Rules:

1.   The following paragraph is added to Article 4 of the WIPO Arbitration Rules:

'(h)   The Center may, in consultation with the parties, reduce the period of time referred to in Article 11.'

2.   Items (iv) and (v) of Article 9 of the WIPO Arbitration Rules are deleted.
3.   Item (vi) of Article 9 is replaced by the following:

'(vi)   any observations that the Claimant considers useful in connection with Articles 14 and 20.'

4.   Article 10 of the WIPO Arbitration Rules is replaced by the following:

'The Request for Arbitration shall be accompanied by the Statement of Claim in conformity with Article 41(b) and (c).'

5.   Article 11 of the WIPO Arbitration Rules is replaced by the following:

'Within 20 days from the date on which the Respondent receives the Request for Arbitration from the Claimant or within 10 days from the date of the appointment of the Tribunal, whichever event occurs later, the Respondent shall address to the Center and to the Claimant an Answer to the Request which shall contain comments on any of the items in the Request for Arbitration.'

6.   Article 12 of the WIPO Arbitration Rules is replaced by the following:

'The Answer to the Request shall be accompanied by the Statement of Defense in conformity with Article 42(b) and (c).'

7.   Articles 14 to 19 of the WIPO Arbitration Rules are replaced by the following Article:

'Sole Arbitrator
Article 14

(a)   The Tribunal shall consist of a sole arbitrator, who shall be appointed jointly by the parties.
(b)   If the appointment of the sole arbitrator is not made within 15 days after the commencement of the arbitration, the sole arbitrator shall be appointed by the Center.'

8.   In Article 25 of the WIPO Arbitration Rules, the words 'within 15 days' are replaced by the words 'within 7 days.'
9.   Articles 41(a) and 42(a) of the WIPO Arbitration Rules are deleted.
10.   Article 53(b) of the WIPO Arbitration Rules is replaced by the following:

'(b)   If a hearing is held, it shall be convened within 30 days after the receipt by the Claimant of the Answer to the Request and the Statement of Defense. The Tribunal shall give the parties adequate advance notice of the date, time and place of the hearing. Except in exceptional circumstances, hearings may not exceed three days. Each party shall be expected to bring to the hearing such persons as necessary to adequately inform the Tribunal of the dispute.'

11.   The following paragraph is added to Article 53 of the WIPO Arbitration Rules:

'(e)   Within such short period of time after the hearing as is agreed by the parties or, in the absence of such agreement, determined by the Tribunal, each party may communicate to the Tribunal and to the other party a post-hearing brief.'

12.   The following sentence is added to Article 55(a) of the WIPO Arbitration Rules:

'The terms of reference shall include a requirement that the expert report to the Tribunal within 30 days of receipt of the terms of reference.'

13.   In Article 63(a) of the WIPO Arbitration Rules, the words 'nine months' are replaced by the words 'three months' and the words 'three months' are replaced by the words 'one month.'

Consolidated Text

A consolidated text of the WIPO Expedited Arbitration Rules may be obtained from the WIPO Arbitration Center. In that text, two conventions have been followed:

(i)   Provisions that represent modifications of the WIPO Arbitration Rules are printed in bold italics.

(ii)   Where the modifications to the WIPO Arbitration Rules have resulted in the deletion of Articles or paragraphs, the number or letter of the deleted Article or paragraph has been retained accompanied by the annotation [Article [paragraph] not used]. This has been done in order to retain the correspondence between the numbers of Articles in the WIPO Arbitration Rules and in the WIPO Expedited Arbitration Rules.

Schedule of Fees

The Fees of the Center are the same as for an arbitration under the WIPO Arbitration Rules.

The arbitrator's fees are determined in the same way as the fees of an arbitrator in an arbitration under the WIPO Arbitration Rules.

WIPO MEDIATION RULES

effective from 1 October 1994

Abbreviated Expressions

Article 1

In these Rules:

'Mediation Agreement' means an agreement by the parties to submit to mediation all or certain disputes which have arisen or which may arise between them; a Mediation Agreement may be in the form of a mediation clause in a contract or in the form of a separate contract;

'Mediator' includes a sole mediator or all the mediators where more than one is appointed;

'WIPO' means the World Intellectual Property Organization;

'Center' means the WIPO Arbitration Center, a unit of the International Bureau of WIPO.

Words used in the singular include the plural and vice versa, as the context may require.

Scope of Application of Rules

Article 2

Where a Mediation Agreement provides for mediation under the WIPO Mediation Rules, these Rules shall be deemed to form part of that Mediation Agreement. Unless the parties have agreed otherwise, these Rules as in effect on the date of the commencement of the mediation shall apply.

Commencement of the Mediation

Article 3

(a)   A party to a Mediation Agreement that wishes to commence a mediation shall submit a Request for Mediation in writing to the Center. It shall at the same time send a copy of the Request for Mediation to the other party.

(b)   The Request for Mediation shall contain or be accompanied by

(i)   the names, addresses and telephone, telex, telefax or other communication references of the parties to the dispute and of the representative of the party filing the Request for Mediation;

(ii)   a copy of the Mediation Agreement; and

(iii)   a brief statement of the nature of the dispute.

Article 4

The date of the commencement of the mediation shall be the date on which the Request for Mediation is received by the Center.

Article 5

The Center shall forthwith inform the parties in writing of the receipt by it of the Request for Mediation and of the date of the commencement of the mediation.

Appointment of the Mediator

Article 6

(a) Unless the parties have agreed themselves on the person of the mediator or on another procedure for appointing the mediator, the mediator shall be appointed by the Center after consultation with the parties.

(b) The prospective mediator shall, by accepting appointment, be deemed to have undertaken to make available sufficient time to enable the mediation to be conducted expeditiously.

Article 7

The mediator shall be neutral, impartial and independent.

Representation of Parties and Participation in Meetings

Article 8

(a) The parties may be represented or assisted in their meetings with the mediator.

(b) Immediately after the appointment of the mediator, the names and addresses of persons authorized to represent a party, and the names and position of the persons who will be attending the meetings of the parties with the mediator on behalf of that party, shall be communicated by that party to the other party, the mediator and the Center.

Conduct of the Mediation

Article 9

The mediation shall be conducted in the manner agreed by the parties. If, and to the extent that, the parties have not made such agreement, the mediator shall, in accordance with these Rules, determine the manner in which the mediation shall be conducted.

Article 10

Each party shall cooperate in good faith with the mediator to advance the mediation as expeditiously as possible.

Article 11

The mediator shall be free to meet and to communicate separately with a party on the clear understanding that information given at such meetings and in such communications shall not be disclosed to the other party without the express authorization of the party giving the information.

Article 12

(a) As soon as possible after being appointed, the mediator shall, in consultation with the parties, establish a timetable for the submission by each party to the mediator and to the other party of a statement summarizing the background of the dispute, the party's interests and contentions in relation to the dispute and the present status of the dispute, together with such other information and materials as the party considers necessary for the purposes of the mediation and, in particular, to enable the issues in dispute to be identified.

(b)   The mediator may, at any time during the mediation, suggest that a party provide such additional information or materials as the mediator deems useful.

(c)   Any party may at any time submit to the mediator, for consideration by the mediator only, written information or materials which it considers to be confidential. The mediator shall not, without the written authorization of that party, disclose such information or materials to the other party.

Role of the Mediator

Article 13

(a)   The mediator shall promote the settlement of the issues in dispute between the parties in any manner that the mediator believes to be appropriate, but shall have no authority to impose a settlement on the parties.

(b)   Where the mediator believes that any issues in dispute between the parties are not susceptible to resolution through mediation, the mediator may propose, for the consideration of the parties, procedures or means for resolving those issues which the mediator considers are most likely, having regard to the circumstances of the dispute and any business relationship between the parties, to lead to the most efficient, least costly and most productive settlement of those issues. In particular, the mediator may so propose.

    (i)   an expert determination of one or more particular issues;

    (ii)   arbitration;

    (iii)   the submission of last offers of settlement by each party and, in the absence of a settlement through mediation, arbitration conducted on the basis of those last offers pursuant to an arbitral procedure in which the mission of the arbitral tribunal is confined to determining which of the last offers shall prevail;

or

    (iv)   arbitration in which the mediator will, with the express consent of the parties, act as sole arbitrator, it being understood that the mediator may, in the arbitral proceedings, take into account information received during the mediation.

Confidentiality

Article 14

No recording of any kind shall be made of any meetings of the parties with the mediator.

Article 15

Each person involved in the mediation, including, in particular, the mediator, the parties and their representatives and advisors, any independent experts and any other persons present during the meetings of the parties with the mediator, shall respect the confidentiality of the mediation and may not, unless otherwise agreed by the parties and the mediator, use or disclose to any outside party any information concerning, or obtained in the course of, the mediation. Each such person shall sign an appropriate confidentiality undertaking prior to taking part in the mediation.

Article 16

Unless otherwise agreed by the parties, each person involved in the mediation shall, on the termination of the mediation, return, to the party providing it, any brief, document or other materials supplied by a party, without retaining any copy thereof. Any notes taken by a person concerning the meetings of the parties with the mediator shall be destroyed on the termination of the mediation.

Article 17

Unless otherwise agreed by the parties, the mediator and the parties shall not introduce as evidence or in any manner whatsoever in any judicial or arbitration proceeding:

(i)   any views expressed or suggestions made by a party with respect to a possible settlement of the dispute;

(ii)   any admissions made by a party in the course of the mediation;

(iii)   any proposals made or views expressed by the mediator;

(iv)   the fact that a party had or had not indicated willingness to accept any proposal for settlement made by the mediator or by the other party.

Termination of the Mediation

Article 18

The mediation shall be terminated

(i)   by the signing of a settlement agreement by the parties covering any or all of the issues in dispute between the parties;

(ii)   by the decision of the mediator if, in the mediator's judgment, further efforts at mediation are unlikely to lead to a resolution of the dispute;

(iii)   by a written declaration of a party at any time after attending the first meeting of the parties with the mediator and before the signing of any settlement agreement.

Article 19

(a)   Upon the termination of the mediation, the mediator shall promptly send to the Center a notice in writing that the mediation is terminated and shall indicate the date on which it terminated, whether or not the mediation resulted in a settlement of the dispute and, if so, whether the settlement was full or partial. The mediator shall send to the parties a copy of the notice so addressed to the Center.

(b)   The Center shall keep the said notice of the mediator confidential and shall not, without the written authorization of the parties, disclose either the existence or the result of the mediation to any person.

(c)   The Center may, however, include information concerning the mediation in any aggregate statistical data that it publishes concerning its activities, provided that such information does not reveal the identity of the parties or enable the particular circumstances of the dispute to be identified.

Article 20

Unless required by a court of law or authorized in writing by the parties, the mediator shall not act in any capacity whatsoever, otherwise than as a mediator, in any pending or future proceedings, whether judicial, arbitral or otherwise, relating to the subject matter of the dispute.

Registration Fee of the Center

Article 21

(a)   The Request for Mediation shall be subject to the payment to the Center of a registration fee, which shall belong to the International Bureau of WIPO. The amount of the registration fee shall be fixed in accordance with the Schedule of Fees applicable on the date of the Request for Mediation.

(b)   The registration fee shall not be refundable.

(c)   No action shall be taken by the Center on a Request for Mediation until the registration fee has been paid.

(d)   If a party who has filed a Request for Mediation fails, within 15 days after a second reminder in writing from the Center, to pay the registration fee, it shall be deemed to have withdrawn its Request for Mediation.

Fees of the Mediator

Article 22

(a)   The amount and currency of the fees of the mediator and the modalities and timing of their payment shall be fixed, in accordance with the provisions of this Article, by the Center, after consultation with the mediator and the parties.

(b)   The amount of the fees shall, unless the parties and the mediator agree otherwise, be calculated on the basis of the hourly or, if applicable, daily indicative rates set out in the Schedule of Fees applicable on the date of the Request for Mediation, taking into account the amount in dispute, the complexity of the subject-matter of the dispute and any other relevant circumstances of the case.

Deposits

Article 23

(a)   The Center may, at the time of the appointment of the mediator, require each party to deposit an equal amount as an advance for the costs of the mediation, including, in particular, the estimated fees of the mediator and the other expenses of the mediation. The amount of the deposit shall be determined by the Center.

(b)   The Center may require the parties to make supplementary deposits.

(c)   If a party fails, within 15 days after a second reminder in writing from the Center, to pay the required deposit, the mediation shall be deemed to be terminated. The Center shall, by notice in writing, inform the parties and the mediator accordingly and indicate the date of termination.

(d)   After the termination of the mediation, the Center shall render an accounting to the parties of any deposits made and return any unexpended balance to the parties or require the payment of any amount owing from the parties.

Costs

Article 24

Unless the parties agree otherwise, the registration fee, the fees of the mediator and all other expenses of the mediation, including, in particular, the required travel expenses of the mediator and any expenses associated with obtaining expert advice, shall be borne in equal shares by the parties.

Exclusion of Liability

Article 25

Except in respect of deliberate wrongdoing, the mediator, WIPO and the Center shall not be liable to any party for any act or omission in connection with any mediation conducted under these Rules.

Waiver of Defamation

Article 26

The parties and, by accepting appointment, the mediator agree that any statements or comments, whether written or oral, made or used by them or their representatives in preparation for or in the course of the mediation shall not be relied upon to found or maintain any action for defamation, libel, slander or any related complaint, and this Article may be pleaded in bar to any such action.

Suspension of Running of Limitation Period Under the Statute of Limitations

Article 27

The parties agree that, to the extent permitted by the applicable law, the running of the limitation period under the Statute of Limitations or an equivalent law shall be suspended in relation to the dispute that is the subject of the mediation from the date of the commencement of the mediation until the date of the termination of the mediation.

ZÜRCHER HANDELSKAMMER
CHAMBRE DE COMMERCE DE ZURICH
ZURICH CHAMBER OF COMMERCE

Bleicherweg 5 (Börse), Postfach 4031, CH-8022 Zürich
Tel: 0041-1-2210742
Fax: 0041-1-2117615

INTERNATIONAL ARBITRATION RULES
OF ZURICH CHAMBER
OF COMMERCE

(1989 EDITION)

RECOMMENDED ARBITRATION CLAUSES

A. Clause providing for appointment of all three arbitrators by the Zurich Chamber of Commerce.

All disputes arising out of or in connection with the present agreement, including disputes on its conclusion, binding effect, amendment and termination, shall be resolved, to the exclusion of the ordinary courts by an Arbitral Tribunal (or: by a three-person Arbitral Tribunal/a sole arbitrator) in accordance with the International Arbitration Rules of the Zurich Chamber of Commerce. (Optional: The decision of the Arbitral Tribunal shall be final, and the parties waive all challenge of the award in accordance with Article 192 Private International Law Statute.)

B. Clause providing for the appointment of one arbitrator each by the parties.

All disputes arising out of or in connection with the present agreement, including disputes on its conclusion, binding effect, amendment and termination shall be resolved, to the exclusion of the ordinary courts by a three-person Arbitral Tribunal in accordance with the International Arbitration Rules of the Zurich Chamber of Commerce. If there are not more than two parties involved in the procedure, each party nominates an arbitrator. (Optional: The decision of the Arbitral Tribunal shall be final, and the parties waive all challenge of the award in accordance with Article 192 Private International Law Statute.)

C. For contracts between Swiss and Japanese parties the Chamber of Commerce recommends the following clause pursuant to the Swiss-Japanese Trade Arbitration Agreement of June 9, 1983:

All disputes, controversies or differences which may arise between the parties out of or in relation to or in connection with this contract, or the breach thereof, shall be finally settled by arbitration, pursuant to the Swiss-Japanese Trade Arbitration Agreement of June 9, 1983 by which each party hereto is bound.

Should this clause be included, it should be stated whether proceedings are to be conducted in Switzerland or in Japan; in the former case, the International Arbitration Rules of the Zurich Chamber of Commerce apply and in the latter case the Arbitration Rules of the Japan Commercial Arbitration Association.

If there is no clause stating the seat of arbitration this is to be settled by a committee consisting of representatives of both organizations.

A. General Provisions

Article 1 Applicability of the International Arbitration Rules

The present International Arbitration Rules of the Zurich Chamber of Commerce of January 1, 1989 are applicable if, at the time when the arbitration agreement was concluded, at least one party had its registered or actual seat, its domicile or its habitual residence outside Switzerland.

Arbitration between parties having their seat, domicile or habitual residence in Switzerland follows the 'Rules of Conciliation and Arbitration of the Zurich Chamber of Commerce'.

Article 2 Jurisdiction of the Arbitral Tribunal

The Arbitral Tribunal has jurisdiction over arbitrable disputes between the parties.

The management of the Zurich Chamber of Commerce investigates summarily whether there is a valid arbitration agreement between all parties that provides for Zurich Chamber of Commerce arbitration; when such an agreement is lacking it notifies the claimant that the arbitration cannot be conducted.

In all other respects the Arbitral Tribunal decides on its own jurisdiction.

Article 3 Applicable Procedural Law

The procedure follows:

(a) The 12th chapter on international arbitration of the Swiss federal Private International Law Statute of December 18, 1987 (PIL Statute);

(b) These International Arbitration Rules of the Zurich Chamber of Commerce;

(c) The arbitration agreement and other agreements between the parties which are not contrary to the Statute and the International Arbitration Rules;

(d) The orders and decisions of the chairman and the Arbitral Tribunal applying the International Arbitration Rules.

Article 4 Applicable Substantive Law

The Arbitral Tribunal decides according to the substantive law declared applicable by the parties.

If the parties have not chosen an applicable law, the Arbitral Tribunal decides the case according to the law applicable according to the rules of the Private International Law Statute.

If, however, the application of the PIL at the seat, domicile or habitual residence of all parties leads similarly to a different result, the case must be decided accordingly on motion of one of the parties.

Article 5   Award ex aequo et bono

The parties may empower the Arbitral Tribunal to make its award ex aequo et bono.

Article 6   Seat of the Arbitral Tribunal

The seat of the Arbitral Tribunal is at the seat of the Zurich Chamber of Commerce in Zurich.

On motion of a party, the President of the Chamber of Commerce may designate another place as the seat if this is required, or deemed desirable, to enforce the award at the seat, domicile or habitual residence of one of the parties.

Meetings and hearings of the Tribunal may be conducted in places other than the seat.

Article 7   Notifications

Orders, decisions and awards of the Chamber of Commerce and the Arbitral Tribunal are, as a rule, notified by registered letter against receipt, or if necessary by private courier or through diplomatic channels.

Simple notifications and extensions of deadlines may also be notified by ordinary letter, telefax or telex.

B.   Commencement of the Arbitration and Formation of the Arbitral Tribunal

Article 8   Lis Pendens

The arbitration is pending if the prerequisites of Article 181 of the Private International Law Statute are fulfilled.

Article 9   Commencement of Arbitration

The claimant must submit the following, in four copies, to the Zurich Chamber of Commerce:

(a)   A request for arbitration in writing, specifying the names of the parties, their legal nature and their address;

(b)   Either a complaint in the sense of Article 29 subs. 2 or a short written summary of the facts, and the prayers for relief;

(c)   The agreements between the parties relevant to the dispute; in particular the arbitration agreement in the original or in copy;

(d)   In two-party arbitration, if the arbitration agreement provides that the parties shall nominate one member of a three-men arbitral tribunal each: Name and address of the arbitrator nominated by claimant;

(e)   Documents evidencing payment of the registration fee provided in the schedule of fees through transfer to the bank or postal checking account of the Zurich Chamber of Commerce; or, a check payable at a Swiss bank. If these prerequisites are not fulfilled on the Chamber of Commerce's first written request to supply the missing items, the management of the Chamber of Commerce notifies the claimant that the arbitration cannot be conducted.

If only the nomination of an arbitrator is missing, the President of the Chamber of Commerce makes the nomination.

Article 10   Number of Arbitrators

If the parties have not expressly agreed on the number of arbitrators, the President of the Zurich Chamber of Commerce decides, independently from a possible nomination of an arbitrator by claimant, whether a sole arbitrator or a three-person arbitral tribunal shall be appointed.

If the value in litigation exceeds SFr. 1 000 000.-and the parties have not expressly provided for a sole arbitrator, a three-person arbitral tribunal shall be appointed.

For multi-party arbitration a three-person arbitral tribunal is appointed.

Article 11   Appointment of the Chairman or Sole Arbitrator

The board of the Zurich Chamber of Commerce appoints eight or more experienced lawyers as permanent chairmen of the Arbitral Tribunal, amongst them practising lawyers and judges.

For each arbitration, the President of the Chamber of Commerce appoints the chairman or sole arbitrator from amongst the permanent chairmen.

In special cases the President may also appoint another suitable person as chairman of the Arbitral Tribunal or sole arbitrator.

Article 12   Appointment of the Co-arbitrators

If the parties have so agreed in writing, for two-party arbitration they appoint one member of the three-person arbitral tribunal each. For the claimant, Article 9 subs. 1 letter d. applies; the chairman of the Arbitral Tribunal sets a deadline for the respondent to appoint its arbitrator.

If the claimant has appointed an arbitrator and the respondent fails to appoint an arbitrator, the chairman of the Arbitral Tribunal asks the President of the Zurich Chamber of Commerce to appoint an arbitrator instead.

If the parties did not provide that they would appoint arbitrators, or, in multi-party arbitration, the chairman of the Arbitral Tribunal appoints his co-arbitrators from a list of four or more names submitted to him by the President of the Chamber of Commerce.

Article 13   Multi-Party Arbitration

If there are several claimants or several respondents, or if the respondent, within the deadline for the answer, files a claim with the Zurich Chamber of Commerce, against a third party based on an arbitration clause valid according to Article 2 subs. 2 an identical three-men Arbitral Tribunal is appointed according to Article 12 subs. 3 for the first and all other arbitrations.

The Arbitral Tribunal may conduct the arbitrations separately, or consolidate them, partly or altogether.

Article 14   Assignment of further Arbitrations

A new dispute between parties which already have an arbitration pending under the International Arbitration Rules may be assigned by the President of the Zurich Chamber of Commerce to the existing Arbitral Tribunal.

The Arbitral Tribunal may conduct the arbitrations separately, or consolidate them, partly or altogether.

Article 15   Assistance

The Arbitral Tribunal appoints, when required, court reporters and other assistants.

A clerk for the entire arbitration, with or without consultatory voice, may be appointed only with the previous assent of the parties.

Article 16   Challenge of an Arbitrator

An arbitrator may be challenged if circumstances exist that give rise to legitimate doubts concerning his independence.

If the arbitrator contests the challenge, a five-person arbitral supervisory commission appointed by the Board of the Zurich Chamber of Commerce decides by majority decision.

The decision of the arbitral supervisory commission is final.

Article 17   Removal of an Arbitrator

If an arbitrator does not fulfill his duties despite having been called to them by the other arbitrators or the Zurich Chamber of Commerce, the arbitral supervisory commission may remove him by majority decision (Article 16 subs. 2).

The arbitrator must be heard. The decision of the arbitral supervisory commission is final.

Article 18   Replacement of an Arbitrator

If an arbitrator dies or if, through no fault of his, he is no longer able to fulfil his duties, and if the arbitrator had been nominated by a party, the president of the Zurich Chamber of Commerce sets that party a deadline to nominate a new arbitrator.

If the party fails to nominate a new arbitrator, and in all other cases, in particular if an arbitrator was successfully challenged or removed, the President of the Chamber of Commerce appoints the new arbitrator.

The arbitration continues with the new arbitrator where his predecessor left it.

C. Procedure Before the Arbitral Tribunal

Article 19   Good Faith

All participants in the arbitration must act in good faith.

Article 20   Constitution

As a rule after having heard the parties, they are notified by an order of the sole arbitrator or, by a decision of the Arbitral Tribunal, the names, addresses, telephone, telex and telefax numbers of the arbitrators, the parties and their representatives. Further, the decree for directions provides the following:

(a)   Form and number of the briefs and documents to be submitted by the parties;

(b)   One or more languages for the procedure as provided in Article 22;

(c)   If there is, as yet, no detailed complaint: a deadline for the claimant to submit one including attachments;

If there is already a detailed complaint: a deadline for the respondent to submit a written answer including attachments;

(d)   Further provisions for the procedure as deemed necessary by the sole arbitrator or the Arbitral Tribunal, such as provisions for the submission of an extract from the Register of Commerce, or of proxies, or provisions on testimony of witnesses and expert evidence;

(e)   The advances to be paid by the parties, the deadline for payment, and the consequences of non-compliance.

Article 21   Chairman

The chairman leads the arbitration.

He may call in deposits, call meetings and set and extend deadlines.

He represents the Arbitral Tribunal vis-à-vis the courts, the authorities and the Zurich Chamber of Commerce.

Article 22   Language

The Arbitral Tribunal determines the language or languages that must be used in written communications and in hearings. It provides for the necessary translations and, where required, interpreters and decides on the distribution of the costs and the risk of erroneous translation.

As a rule, the procedure with the parties is conducted in the language of the arbitration agreement, and the parties may arrange at their own expense and at their own risk for their own translators and interpreters.

Article 23   Transcript

The Arbitral Tribunal determines to what extent the hearings shall be recorded in a written transcript, or audio-taped.

Article 24   Representation of the Parties

The parties may be represented or counselled before the Arbitral Tribunal by practising lawyers and other natural persons.

If the notification is particularly difficult or time-consuming, the Arbitral Tribunal may order a party to appoint an authorized representative for notifications at a suitable place. If the party fails to comply, the notification is omitted.

Article 25   Plea of Lack of Jurisdiction

A plea of lack of jurisdiction of the Arbitral Tribunal must be raised, at the latest, with the answer on the merits by the respondent.

The Arbitral Tribunal decides on its own jurisdiction after having heard the other party, as a rule by an interim award.

Article 26   Counterclaim

A counterclaim must be raised with the answer. With the agreement of the claimant it may also be raised at a later date.

Article 27   Set-off

The Arbitral Tribunal also has jurisdiction over a set-off defense if the claim that is set off does not fall under the arbitration clause, and even if there exists another arbitration clause or jurisdiction clause for that claim.

Article 28   Provisional and Conservatory Measures

If the parties have not expressly excluded this, the Arbitral Tribunal may order, on motion of a party, provisional or conservatory measures in accordance with Article 183 of the Private International Law Statute.

Article 29   Beginning of Main Proceedings

For the complaint and the answer, and for the counterclaim and the answer to the counterclaim, if any, the procedure is in writing.

In the complaint, the prayers for relief and the value in litigation should be specified, and the factual and legal grounds should be given in detail; in the answer, the respondent must respond in detail to the claims made by the claimant. In these briefs, the proofs must be indicated with precision; witnesses must be identified by name; and the available documents must be submitted in the required number of copies, together with a schedule of documents.

After the above briefs have been submitted, as a rule a hearing is held with the parties in which the Arbitral Tribunal discusses the further proceedings with the parties.

Article 30   Deadlines

The Arbitral Tribunal sets deadlines by indicating the date of expiry.

A deadline is deemed to have been complied with if the submission has been posted before the deadline with the official mails in Switzerland or abroad, or was transmitted by telex or telefax. An advance is deemed to have been made timely if the instructions were given to the bank within the deadline, provided that the payment is credited within one month.

Article 31   Extension of Deadlines

Requests for extensions of deadlines must be submitted before the deadline has expired. The extension requested should be specified.

Article 32   Consequences of Failure to Submit a Brief or to Appear at a Hearing

If a party fails to submit a brief within the deadline or fails to appear at a hearing without adequate excuse, the Arbitral Tribunal may restore the deadline, set a new deadline or call a new hearing and specify the consequences of failure to comply.

If the party fails to comply once more, the Arbitral Tribunal may deem the factual allegations of the other party to be undisputed or may investigate the matter on its own.

Article 33   Continuation and Conclusion of the Main Proceedings

To continue the main proceedings, the chairman sets a deadline for reply and rejoinder briefs, and for reply and rejoinder on the counterclaim, if any; or calls a hearing with the parties. For special reasons, further exchanges of briefs or hearings may be ordered.

With the receipt of the last brief, or with the last oral pleading the main procedure is concluded.

Article 34   New Motions and Allegations

After the pleadings are closed, new or modified motions, allegations of fact, defenses and denials are no longer admissible.

At a later date the Arbitral Tribunal may, by exception, admit new or amended claims if the legal position of the other party is not appreciably worsened and the procedure is not unnecessarily lengthened.

The following new motions, allegations of fact, defenses and denials are exempted:

(a)   Motions that have been prompted by the further proceedings.

(b)   Allegations of fact, defenses and denials that can be proved forthwith by documents already on record or newly submitted.

(c)   Facts that could not reasonably have been presented within the deadline.

(d)   Facts and legal arguments that the Arbitral Tribunal must take into account ex officio.

(e)   Allegations of fact and denial in response to questions by the arbitrators.

Article 35   Proof Procedure

The Arbitral Tribunal makes its findings of fact in adversarial proceedings.

As a rule, it administers proof after the main proceedings are concluded; it may, however, start administering proof earlier.

Article 36   Witnesses

The Arbitral Tribunal sets the rules for the testimony of witnesses. The Arbitral Tribunal may order the oral testimony of a witness. The witness is invited by the party that nominated it, at its own expense.

Article 37   Capacity to Testify

Everybody, including parties and their officers, may be a witness. For the assessment of testimony, Article 44 applies.

Article 38   Right to Refuse Testimony

Testimony may be refused by a party's spouse, and the party's grand-parents, parents, children, grandchildren, brothers and sisters, uncles, aunts and cousins and the spouses of these relatives.

Moreover, a witness may refuse to testify against himself and refuse testimony which would infringe official or professional secrecy protected by criminal law, unless the witness has been freed of its secrecy obligation.

Article 39   Hearing Testimony

Before the witness is heard it must be admonished to tell the truth and notified of the consequences of knowingly false testimony which may consist, under the Swiss Federal Penal Code, in a sentence in penitentiary up to five years, or imprisonment.

The Arbitral Tribunal grants the parties an opportunity to question witnesses.

Article 40   Local Inspection

The Arbitral Tribunal may make a local inspection to ascertain relevant facts.

The parties must tolerate such an inspection.

Article 41   Expertise

Each party may submit written experts' reports.

The Arbitral Tribunal may, ex officio, or on motion of the party, question one or more experts in writing or orally. The parties must be given an opportunity to raise objections against the persons proposed as experts and may proffer questions to be asked of an expert.

The parties and persons who have been appointed as experts by the tribunal, or who have been proposed as such, may not communicate directly with each other.

Article 42   Documents

Each party may call upon the other to supply the Arbitral Tribunal with specified documents relevant to the dispute between the parties.

The Arbitral Tribunal may, in case of refusal, or on its own motion, order the presentation of documents.

Article 43   Comment upon the Evidence

The parties must be given an opportunity to comment upon the evidence.

Article 44   Assessment of the Evidence

The Arbitral Tribunal is free in assessing the evidence. It takes into consideration the conduct of the parties during the procedure, in particular a refusal to cooperate in the administration of proof.

D.   Award

Article 45   Amicable Settlement

With the agreement of the parties the Arbitral Tribunal may, at any stage of the proceedings, seek an amicable settlement.

If the parties have reached an amicable settlement, the Arbitral Tribunal, on motion of a party, issues an award embodying the settlement. If there is no such motion, the sole arbitrator orders or the Arbitral Tribunal issues a decision declaring the procedure closed through amicable settlement.

Article 46   Deliberation and Vote

The three-person Arbitral Tribunal deliberates in closed chambers and decides by simple majority.

If there is no majority, the chairman decides alone; he may not award more than the highest motion of the other arbitrators, nor less than the lowest.

Article 47   Form and Content of the Award

The award must be made in writing and signed by all arbitrators, but the signature of the chairman is sufficient.

It contains:
- (a)   the name of the arbitrators;
- (b)   the seat of the Arbitral Tribunal;
- (c)   the designation of the Parties;
- (d)   the relief prayed for by the parties;
- (e)   the findings of fact and the reasons of law for the decision, and, as the case may be, the considerations ex aequo et bono, unless the parties have expressly waived this requirement;
- (f)   the decision on the merits;
- (g)   the decision as to the amount and allocation of arbitration costs;
- (h)   the decision as to the amount of, and obligation to pay costs;
- (i)   date of the award.

If the procedure is ended without a decision on the merits, the sole arbitrator or the Arbitral Tribunal declares this through a closing order, or decision.

Article 48   Issuance of the Award

The arbitral award is issued by notification to the parties.

Article 49   Finality

The award is final with its issuance.

The arbitral award may not be challenged if none of the parties has its seat, habitual residence or a place of business in Switzerland and they have, by an express declaration in the arbitration agreement, or in a later written agreement excluded all challenge of the arbitral awards (Article 192 PIL).

Otherwise, the award may be challenged only on the grounds enumerated in Article 190 subs. 2 and 3 of the Private International Law Statute.

Article 50   Storage and Deposit

A copy of the award and the file, unless given to the parties, shall be kept for at least ten years by the Zurich Chamber of Commerce.

If a party wishes a deposit of the decision with the 'Obergericht des Kantons Zürich' it must provide for this itself at its own costs. The Arbitral Tribunal provides for this purpose, on request, an additional copy of the award, or a certified copy.

Article 51   Confidentiality

All participants in the proceedings must keep the proceedings and the award confidential towards third parties not concerned, and towards the public in general.

Publications on individual arbitral proceedings by participants are possible only in neutralized form and with previous permission by the President of the Zurich Chamber of Commerce.

E.   Costs and Fees

Article 52   Fees of the Zurich Chamber of Commerce

For its administrative expenses in connection with the appointment of an Arbitral Tribunal the Zurich Chamber of Commerce charges a fee at the initial stage of the arbitral proceedings in accordance with the applicable fee schedule.

Article 53   Costs of the Arbitral Tribunal

The members of the Arbitral Tribunal receive their fee and expenses out of the arbitration fee set in the award in accordance with the applicable fee schedule of the Zurich Chamber of Commerce. If a secretary was appointed with the consent of the parties, half of the fee for an arbitrator is charged.

The expenses and the costs of assistants must be paid separately unless they were borne directly by the parties.

Article 54   Advance for Costs

The sole arbitrator, the Arbitral Tribunal or the chairman may order the payment of one or several deposits by the parties to secure the costs of the procedure.

If the advance carries interest, it is added to the principal.

Article 55   Failure to Pay the Advance

If a party fails to pay the advance ordered, the other party may choose to advance the arbitration costs or renounce the arbitration. If it renounces, the parties are no longer bound to the arbitration agreement with respect to the particular dispute.

Article 56   Allocation of Costs

The costs of the proceedings are, as a rule, borne by the losing party. If no party wins totally, the costs are allocated proportionately.

The Arbitral Tribunal may, for special reasons, depart from this rule, especially if the proceeding became without object or if a party caused unnecessary costs.

Article 57   Compensation of Attorneys' and Parties' Costs and Expenses

As a rule, each party must compensate the other for costs and expenses, in proportion to arbitration costs it has, itself, been charged with.

Before it renders its award, the Arbitral Tribunal sets a deadline to the parties to submit a statement of their costs. It also takes into consideration as costs, the registration fee paid to the Zurich Chamber of Commerce.

Article 58   Use of the Deposits

Out of all deposits including the accumulated interests, the arbitration costs are paid first. A surplus is paid to the representatives of the parties for their clients, or directly to the parties if they are not represented.

If the costs were paid in full, or in part, from an advance that was made by a party against whom they were not awarded, the Arbitral Tribunal must award a corresponding claim for reimbursement to the party against whom the costs were awarded.

F.   Final and Transitory Provisions

Article 59   Entry into Force

These International Arbitration Rules were passed by the board of the Zurich Chamber of Commerce on October 5, 1988. They enter into force on

January 1, 1989 and are applied independently from the time of the making of the arbitral agreement to all arbitrations which were commenced after that date, even if the arbitral agreement mentioned expressly earlier arbitration rules of the Zurich Chamber of Commerce.

Article 60   Transitory provision

Arbitrations which were pending at the coming into force of these international arbitration rules before the Arbitral Tribunal of the Zurich Chamber of Commerce are conducted according to the provisions of the Conciliation and Arbitration Rules of the Zurich Chamber of Commerce of July 1, 1985, unless the parties agree that the new International Arbitration Rules apply.

International Treaties of Switzerland Relating to Arbitration

— Protocol on Arbitration Clauses (signed at Geneva, September 24, 1923)
— Convention on the Execution of Foreign Arbitral Awards (signed at Geneva, September 26, 1927)
— *Convention on the Recognition and Enforcement of Foreign Arbitral Awards* (done at New York on June 10, 1958)
— Enforcement Convention between Switzerland and Belgium of 1959
— Enforcement Convention between the Swiss Confederation and the German Reich of 1929
— Jurisdiction and Enforcement Convention between Switzerland and France of 1869
— Enforcement Convention between Switzerland and Italy of 1933
— Commercial Treaty between the Swiss Confederation and the Federative People's Republic of Yugoslavia of 1948
— *Enforcement Convention between the Swiss Confederation and the Principality of Liechtenstein of 1968*
— Enforcement Convention between the Swiss Confederation and the Republic of Austria of 1960
— Enforcement Convention between Switzerland and Sweden of 1936
— Commercial Treaty between the Swiss Confederation and the Union of Soviet Socialist Republics of 1948
— Enforcement Convention between Switzerland and Spain of 1896
— Enforcement Convention between Switzerland and the Czechoslovak Republic of 1926

PART VII
DOCUMENTS RELATING TO
CONDUCT AND ETHICS

CHARTERED INSTITUTE OF ARBITRATORS

GUIDELINES OF GOOD PRACTICE FOR ARBITRATORS

"Celeriter ac Diligenter"

INTRODUCTION

An arbitrator should be impartial, independent, competent, diligent and discreet. These guidelines seek to indicate the manner in which these abstract qualities may be assessed. For the purpose of these Guidelines the reference to 'he' refers to both male and female arbitrators.

1. Professional Standard

An arbitrator shall proceed diligently and efficiently to provide the parties with a just and effective resolution of their disputes, and shall be and shall remain free from bias.

2. Acceptance of Appointment

A prospective arbitrator shall not solicit appointment and shall accept appointment if offered only if he is fully satisfied that he is able to discharge his duties without bias or the appearance of bias; that he is competent to determine the issues in dispute and has an adequate knowledge of the language of the arbitration; that he is able to give to the arbitration the time and attention which the parties are reasonably entitled to expect.

3. Elements of Bias

3.1   The criteria for assessing questions relating to bias are impartiality and independence. Partiality arises when an arbitrator favours one of the parties, or where he is prejudiced in relation to the subject matter of the dispute.

Dependence arises from relationships between an arbitrator and one of the parties, or with someone closely connected with one of the parties.

3.2   Facts which might lead a reasonable person, not knowing the arbitrator's true state of mind, to consider that the arbitrator is dependent on or connected with a party will create an appearance of bias. The same is true if an arbitrator has a material interest in the outcome of the dispute, or if he has already taken a position in relation to it. The appearance of bias is best overcome by full disclosure as described in Guideline 4 below.

3.3   Any current direct or indirect business relationship between an arbitrator and a party, or with a person who is known to be a potentially important witness, will give rise to justifiable doubts as to a prospective arbitrator's impartiality or independence. He should decline to accept an appointment in such circumstances unless all the parties agree in writing that he may proceed. Examples of indirect relationships are where a member of the prospective arbitrator's family, his firm, or any business partner has a business relationship with one of the parties.

3.4   Past business relationships will not operate as an absolute bar to acceptance of appointment, unless they are of such magnitude or nature as to be, or appear to be, likely to affect a prospective arbitrator's judgment.

3.5   Continuous and substantial social or professional relationships between a prospective arbitrator and a party, or with a person who is known to be a potentially important witness in the arbitration, will give rise to justifiable doubts as to the impartiality or independence of a prospective arbitrator.

4.   Duty of Disclosure

4.1   A prospective arbitrator should disclose all facts or circumstances that may give rise to justifiable doubts as to his impartiality or independence. Failure to make such disclosure creates an appearance of bias, and may of itself be a ground for disqualification even though the non-disclosed facts or circumstances would not of themselves justify disqualification.

4.2   A prospective arbitrator should disclose:

(a)   any past or present business relationship, whether direct or indirect as illustrated in Article 3.3, with any party to the dispute, or any representative of a party, or any person known to be a potentially important witness in the arbitration. With regard to present relationships, the duty of disclosure applies irrespective of their magnitude, but with regard to past relationships only if they were of more than a trivial nature in relation to the arbitrator's professional or business affairs. Non-disclosure of an indirect relationship unknown to a prospective arbitrator will not be a ground for disqualification unless it could have been ascertained by making reasonable enquiries;

(b)   the nature and duration of any substantial social relationships with any party or any person known to be likely to be an important witness in the arbitration;

(c)   the extent of any prior knowledge he may have of the dispute;

(d)   the extent of any commitments which may affect his availability to perform his duties as arbitrator as may be reasonably anticipated.

4.3   The duty of disclosure continues throughout the arbitral proceedings as regards new facts or circumstances.

4.4   Disclosure should be made in writing and communicated to all parties.

5.   Communications with Parties

5.1   When approached with a view to appointment, a prospective arbitrator should make sufficient enquiries in order to inform himself whether there may be any justifiable doubts regarding his impartiality or independence; whether he is competent to determine the issues in dispute; and whether he is able to give the arbitration the time and attention required. He may also respond to enquiries from those approaching him, provided that such enquiries are designed to determine his suitability and availability for the appointment and provided that the merits of the case are not discussed.

5.2   Throughout the arbitral proceedings, an arbitrator should avoid any unilateral communications regarding the case with any party, or its representatives. If such communication should occur, the arbitrator should inform the other party or parties of its substance.

5.3 An arbitrator should not accept any gift or hospitality, directly or indirectly, from any party to the arbitration. An arbitrator should be particularly meticulous in avoiding significant social or professional contacts with any party to the arbitration other than in the presence of the other parties.

6. Duty of Diligence

An arbitrator should devote such time and attention as the parties may reasonably require having regard to all the circumstances of the case, and shall do his best to conduct the arbitration in such a manner that costs do not rise to an unreasonable proportion of the interests at stake.

7. Confidentiality of the Deliberations

The deliberations of the arbitrator, and the contents of the award itself, remain confidential in perpetuity unless the parties release the arbitrator from his obligation.

8. Costs

An arbitrator should be prepared to determine on a commercial basis the costs of the reference if such costs cannot be agreed between the parties and provided that such determination is within his competence.

9. Award

The award should be drafted:

1. using plain English;
2. in a logical format;
3. setting down the reasons leading to the decisions;
4. so that the decisions are certain (e.g. specify totals of money not percentages where possible); and
5. so that the outcome is legally enforceable.

10. Procedure

An arbitrator should adopt a procedure in which to run the arbitration which is in accordance with the wishes of the parties. If the parties are unable to agree a procedure, the arbitrator should set the procedure. The procedure should be such as to resolve the dispute quickly, efficiently and economically.

11. Cancellation Fees

11.1 Cancellation charges are intended to compensate the arbitrator for any loss likely to be suffered as a result of time set aside for a hearing not being required and for the inconvenience caused by cancellations. In fixing the amount of such charges the arbitrator should make full allowance for the possibility of mitigating his loss.

11.2 Provision as to cancellation charges should, if possible, be agreed with the parties no later than the acceptance of the appointment.

12. Retention of Documents

An arbitrator should adopt the following policy:
1. original documents — offer to return them to the relevant party or solicitor at the end of the period for appeal against the award plus one month;
2. photocopied documents — as for original documents;
3. correspondence relating to the appointment, the pleadings, directions, proofs of evidence and documents relating to the calculation of fees — these should be retained for six months for a straightforward case and for up to seven years for a complex case;
4. notes of the arbitration and the report of any assessor — these should be retained for up to seven years;
5. the award — this should be retained indefinitely.

GERMAN INSTITUTION OF ARBITRATION

GUIDE TO THE CONDUCT OF ARBITRATION PROCEEDINGS

German Institution of Arbitration
Deutsche Institution für Schiedsgerichtsbarkeit e. V.,
Schedestrasse 13, Postfach 1446, 5300 Bonn 1,
Tel: 0049-228/21 00 23-24,
Fax: 0049-228/21 22 75,
Telex: 8 86 805 diht d

GUIDE TO THE CONDUCT OF ARBITRATION PROCEEDINGS*

This guide is addressed to arbitrators. It is intended to facilitate the conduct of arbitration proceedings and the observance of the necessary formalities.

1. Impartiality

It is a condition for accepting the function of an arbitrator that members of the arbitration tribunal must be impartial and independent of the parties.

2. Arbitrators' contract

On receipt by the parties of the acceptance by the arbitrator, the arbitrator is committed by contract to the parties and vice versa, based on the law and the Arbitration Rules. Additions need the agreement of all persons concerned. It is advisable to agree in writing or on record (cf. no.8).

3. Rejection

In cases where a state judge is barred from exercising judicial office, an arbitrator is likewise prohibited from taking office and can be rejected. If an arbitrator functions in spite of this, he jeopardises the proceedings.

4. Venue of the arbitration tribunal

The circumstances of the case and the suitability of the place for the parties involved will guide the arbitrators when they have to determine the venue of the arbitration tribunal.

5. Advance payments

An advance payment on the costs of the proceedings is usually paid. Advances are requested and collected by the chairman for the members of the arbitration tribunal. Where the respondent refuses to pay the advance payment, such advance may be requested from the claimant. Advances should be deposited in a fiduciary account. Advances on the remuneration to which the arbitrators are entitled are to be settled with the arbitrators by the chairman of the arbitration tribunal as soon as the proceedings have ended. Advances on expenses can be settled after they have been incurred.

On conclusion of the proceedings the chairman of the arbitration tribunal settles the advance payments with the parties or collects fees and expenses that are still outstanding.

The arbitration tribunal must, at every stage of the proceedings, be aware of the need for a cost-saving mode of the proceedings.

* Translation of the German original

6. Handling of pleadings and files

The chairman of the arbitration tribunal keeps a file of the proceedings, in which the originals of all documents relating to the proceedings (pleadings by the parties, written records, directions etc.) are placed so far as they do not have to be deposited at the competent court. The parties receive one copy each. At least 4 originals of an award are to be signed.

The chairman of the arbitration tribunal keeps the files for a minimum of 5 years, calculated from the time when the award is deposited or from the date of the signing of the award or the settlement.

7. Time-limits

The arbitration tribunal is bound to conduct the proceedings without delays. The chairman of the arbitration tribunal sets the parties reasonable time-limits for submission of pleadings.

The minimum time-limit for summons to appear at a hearing is at least one week from receipt of the summons. The arbitration tribunal should grant well-founded applications by the parties for extension of time-limits or postponement of dates. Suspicion of delaying tactics entitles the arbitration tribunal to request a substantiation of the reasons.

8. Hearing

In agreement with the arbitrators and following the time schedule the chairman of the arbitration tribunal summons the parties for a hearing. In the summons the parties can be requested to produce witnesses at the hearing. Witnesses can also be summoned by the arbitration tribunal. However, they have no obligation to appear before an arbitration tribunal.

The chairman of the arbitration tribunal presides over the hearing. A recording clerk may be appointed.

A written record must be made of the hearing for which the following contents are recommended.

— the place and date of the hearing;
— the names of the arbitrators and the recording clerk;
— a description of the legal dispute;
— the names of the parties, legal and authorised representatives, witnesses, experts and other persons;
— a declaration by the parties that they have no objections to the jurisdiction of the arbitration tribunal;
— a stipulation of the value in dispute;
— a declaration by the parties that they agree on the calculation and payment of the arbitrators' fees;
— a declaration by the parties that the recording clerk is to receive for the account of the parties a remuneration from the chairman of the arbitration tribunal at equitable discretion;
— a declaration by the parties as to the competent court;
— the requests made by the parties;
— a finding that the parties had the opportunity of submitting their points of view and were heard;
— indications given by the arbitration tribunal on the issues;
— the time schedule for further dates of the proceedings with the indication of foreseeable incidents as well as the time schedule for the procedure;
— the description of evidence or a declaration by the parties that they waived the right to have evidence recorded;
— the record of admissions, acknowledgements and waivers;
— an arbitration settlement;
— an agreement by the parties as to the applicable law;
— an agreement by the parties as to whether and under what conditions an award is to be deposited;
— an assessment of the costs incurred by the parties;
— a statement of the receipt of pleadings, of the signature by the members of the arbitration tribunal and by the parties or their representatives and possibly by the recording clerk;
— the signature by the chairman of the arbitration tribunal (cf. §§17 and 18 of the Arbitration Rules).

9. Deliberations of the arbitration tribunal

Only the members of the arbitration tribunal are present during deliberations, which are secret and are to be kept secret.

10. The award

The chairman of the arbitration tribunal serves and, if necessary, deposits the award. Where the chairman of the arbitration tribunal does not fulfil this obligation, the arbitrators may do so. The Secretariat of the Institution is not authorised to effect service of the award but only, as an act of assistance, to deposit the award.

The DIS Secretariat shall be provided with a copy of the award and in cases where it shall make the deposit also with an original. The chairman of the arbitration tribunal shall inform the Secretariat of the Institution whether the parties have agreed to disclosure of the arbitration award.

11.   Obligations of the arbitrators

The arbitrators are bound by the Arbitration Rules, unless the parties have agreed otherwise.

THE GRAIN AND FEED TRADE ASSOCIATION

CODES OF PRACTICE

These Codes are so intimately linked with the GAFTA Rules, they are reproduced with those Rules earlier in this book.

INTERNATIONAL BAR ASSOCIATION

271 Regent Street, London W1R 7PA, England,
Tel: (+44) 0171-629 1206,
Fax: (+44) 0171-409 0456

RULES OF ETHICS
FOR INTERNATIONAL ARBITRATORS

Introductory Note

International arbitrators should be impartial, independent, competent, diligent and discreet. These rules seek to establish the manner in which these abstract qualities may be assessed in practice. Rather than rigid rules, they reflect internationally acceptable guidelines developed by practising lawyers from all continents. They will attain their objectives only if they are applied in good faith.

The rules cannot be directly binding either on arbitrators, or on the parties themselves, unless they are adopted by agreement. Whilst the International Bar Association hopes that they will be taken into account in the context of challenges to arbitrators, it is emphasised that these guidelines are not intended to create grounds for the setting aside of awards by national courts.

If parties wish to adopt the rules they may add the following to their arbitration clause or arbitration agreement.

'The parties agree that the Rules of Ethics for International Arbitrators established by the International Bar Association, in force at the date of the commencement of any arbitration under this clause, shall be applicable to the arbitrators appointed in respect of such arbitration.'

The International Bar Association takes the position that (whatever may be the case in domestic arbitration) international arbitrators should in principle be granted immunity from suit under national laws, except in extreme cases of wilful or reckless disregard of their legal obligations. Accordingly, the International Bar Association wishes to make it clear that it is not the intention of these rules to create opportunities for aggrieved parties to sue international arbitrators in national courts. The normal sanction for breach of an ethical duty is removal from office, with consequent loss of entitlement to remuneration. The International Bar Association also emphasises that these rules do not affect, and are intended to be consistent with, the International Code of Ethics for lawyers, adopted at Oslo on 25 July 1956, and amended by the General Meeting of the International Bar Association at Mexico City on 24 July 1964.

1. Fundamental rule

Arbitrators shall proceed diligently and efficiently to provide the parties with a just and effective resolution of their disputes, and shall be and shall remain free from bias.

2. Acceptance of appointment

2.1   A prospective arbitrator shall accept an appointment only if he is fully satisfied that he is able to discharge his duties without bias.

2.2   A prospective arbitrator shall accept an appointment only if he is fully satisfied that he is competent to determine the issues in dispute, and has an adequate knowledge of the language of the arbitration.

2.3   A prospective arbitrator should accept an appointment only if he is able to give to the arbitration the time and attention which the parties are reasonably entitled to expect.

2.4   It is inappropriate to contact parties in order to solicit appointment as arbitrator.

3. Elements of bias

3.1   The criteria for assessing questions relating to bias are impartiality and independence. Partiality arises when an arbitrator favours one of the parties, or where he is prejudiced in relation to the subject-matter of the dispute.

Dependence arises from relationships between an arbitrator and one of the parties, or with someone closely connected with one of the parties.

3.2   Facts which might lead a reasonable person, not knowing the arbitrator's true state of mind, to consider that he is dependent on a party create an appearance of bias. The same is true if an arbitrator has a material interest in the outcome of the dispute, or if he has already taken a position in relation to it. The appearance of bias is best overcome by full disclosure as described in Article 4 below.

3.3   Any current direct or indirect business relationship between an arbitrator and a party, or with a person who is known to be a potentially important witness, will normally give rise to justifiable doubts as to a prospective arbitrator's impartiality or independence. He should decline to accept an appointment in such circumstances unless the parties agree in writing that he may proceed. Examples of indirect relationships are where a member of the prospective arbitrator's family, his firm, or any business partner has a business relationship with one of the parties.

3.4   Past business relationships will not operate as an absolute bar to acceptance of appointment, unless they are of such magnitude or nature as to be likely to affect a prospective arbitrator's judgment.

3.5   Continuous and substantial social or professional relationships between a prospective arbitrator and a party, or with a person who is known to be a potentially important witness in the arbitration, will normally give rise to justifiable doubts as to the impartiality or independence of a prospective arbitrator.

4.   Duty of disclosure

4.1   A prospective arbitrator should disclose all facts or circumstances that may give rise to justifiable doubts as to his impartiality or independence.

Failure to make such disclosure creates an appearance of bias, and may of itself be a ground for disqualification even though the non-disclosed facts or circumstances would not of themselves justify disqualification.

4.2   A prospective arbitrator should disclose:

(a)   any past or present business relationship, whether direct or indirect as illustrated in Article 3.3, including prior appointment as arbitrator, with any party to the dispute, or any representative of a party, or any person known to be a potentially important witness in the arbitration. With regard to present relationships, the duty of disclosure applies irrespective of their magnitude, but with regard to past relationships only if they were of more than a trivial nature in relation to the arbitrator's professional or business affairs. Non-disclosure of an indirect relationship unknown to a prospective arbitrator will not be a ground for disqualification unless it could have been ascertained by making reasonable enquiries;

(b)   the nature and duration of any substantial social relationships with any party or any person known to be likely to be an important witness in the arbitration;

(c)   the nature of any previous relationship with any fellow arbitrator (including prior joint service as an arbitrator);

(d)   the extent of any prior knowledge he may have of the dispute;

(e)   the extent of any commitments which may affect his availability to perform his duties as arbitrator as may be reasonably anticipated.

4.3   The duty of disclosure continues throughout the arbitral proceedings as regards new facts or circumstances.

4.4   Disclosure should be made in writing and communicated to all parties and arbitrators. When an arbitrator has been appointed, any previous disclosure made to the parties should be communicated to the other arbitrators.

5.   Communications with parties

5.1   When approached with a view to appointment, a prospective arbitrator should make sufficient enquiries in order to inform himself whether there may be any justifiable doubts regarding his impartiality or independence; whether he is competent to determine the issues in dispute; and whether he is able to give the arbitration the time and attention required. He may also respond to enquiries from those approaching him, provided that such enquiries are designed to determine his suitability and availability for the appointment and provided that the merits of the case are not discussed. In the event that a prospective sole arbitrator or presiding arbitrator is approached by one party alone, or by one arbitrator chosen unilaterally by a party (a 'party-nominated' arbitrator), he should ascertain that the other party or parties, or the other arbitrator, has consented to the manner in which he has been approached. In such circumstances he should, in writing or orally, inform the other party or parties, or the other arbitrator, of the substance of the initial conversation.

5.2 If a party-nominated arbitrator is required to participate in the selection of a third or presiding arbitrator, it is acceptable for him (although he is not so required) to obtain the views of the party who nominated him as to the acceptability of candidates being considered.

5.3 Throughout the arbitral proceedings, an arbitrator should avoid any unilateral communications regarding the case with any party, or its representatives. If such communication should occur, the arbitrator should inform the other party or parties and arbitrators of its substance.

5.4 If an arbitrator becomes aware that a fellow arbitrator has been in improper communication with a party, he may inform the remaining arbitrators and they should together determine what action should be taken. Normally, the appropriate initial course of action is for the offending arbitrator to be requested to refrain from making any further improper communications with the party. Where the offending arbitrator fails or refuses to refrain from improper communications, the remaining arbitrators may inform the innocent party in order that he may consider what action he should take. An arbitrator may act unilaterally to inform a party of the conduct of another arbitrator in order to allow the said party to consider a challenge of the offending arbitrator only in extreme circumstances, and after communicating his intention to his fellow arbitrators in writing.

5.5 No arbitrator should accept any gift or substantial hospitality, directly or indirectly, from any party to the arbitration. Sole arbitrators and presiding arbitrators should be particularly meticulous in avoiding significant social or professional contacts with any party to the arbitration other than in the presence of the other parties.

6. Fees

Unless the parties agree otherwise or a party defaults, an arbitrator shall make no unilateral arrangements for fees or expenses.

7. Duty of diligence

All arbitrators should devote such time and attention as the parties may reasonably require having regard to all the circumstances of the case, and shall do their best to conduct the arbitration in such a manner that costs do not rise to an unreasonable proportion of the interests at stake.

8. Involvement in settlement proposals

Where the parties have so requested, or consented to a suggestion to this effect by the arbitral tribunal, the tribunal as a whole (or the presiding arbitrator where appropriate), may make proposals for settlement to both parties simultaneously, and preferably in the presence of each other. Although any procedure is possible with the agreement of the parties, the arbitral tribunal should point out to the parties that it is undesirable that any arbitrator should discuss settlement terms with a party in the absence of the other parties since this will normally have the result that any arbitrator involved in such discussions will become disqualified from any future participation in the arbitration.

9. Confidentiality of the deliberations

The deliberations of the arbitral tribunal, and the contents of the award itself, remain confidential in perpetuity unless the parties release the arbitrators from this obligation. An arbitrator should not participate in, or give any information for the purpose of assistance in, any proceedings to consider the award unless, exceptionally, he considers it his duty to disclose any material misconduct or fraud on the part of his fellow arbitrators.

Chamber of National and International Arbitration of Milan

CODE OF ETHICS FOR ARBITRATORS

1. An arbitrator accepting a mandate in an arbitration administered by the Chamber of National and International Arbitration of Milan shall act according to the Chamber's National and International Rules and this Code of Ethics.

2. When accepting his mandate, the arbitrator shall, to his certain knowledge, be able to perform his task with the necessary competence according to his professional qualifications.

3. When accepting his mandate, the arbitrator shall, to his certain knowledge, be able to perform his task with the necessary impartiality characterising the adjudicating function he undertakes in the interest of all parties.

4. The arbitrator shall guarantee his impartiality by being and remaining independent of any external influence, either direct or indirect, during the entire arbitral proceedings.

5. When giving notice of his acceptance, the arbitrator shall disclose in writing:
   — any relationship with the parties or their counsel which may affect his independence and impartiality;
   — any personal or economic interest, either direct or indirect, in the subject matter of the dispute;

— any prejudice or reservation as to the subject matter of the dispute which may affect his impartiality.

Where necessary due to supervening facts, this Statement shall be repeated in the course of the entire arbitral proceedings until the award is filed.

6.   Where facts that should have been disclosed are subsequently discovered, the arbitrator may be challenged or the Chamber of Arbitration may refuse to confirm him in other arbitral proceedings on this ground.

7.   The party-designated arbitrator who participates in the choice of the third arbitrator because the parties so wish, may contact the party who designated him or its representative in the proceedings in order to ascertain whether the suggested names are acceptable.

8.   The arbitrator may at all stages suggest the possibility of a settlement to the parties but may not influence their decision by indicating that he has already reached a decision on the dispute.

9.   In the course of the arbitral proceedings, the arbitrator shall refrain from all unilateral contact with the parties or their counsel which is not notified to the Chamber of Arbitration so that the Chamber can inform the other parties and arbitrators.

10.   The arbitrator shall refrain from giving the parties, either directly or through their counsel, notice of decisions in the evidence taking phase or on the merits; notice of these decisions may be given exclusively by the Chamber of Arbitration.

11.   The arbitrator shall neither request nor accept any direct arrangement on costs or fees with the party which has designated him. The arbitrator is entitled to reimbursement of expenses and a fee as exclusively determined by the Chamber of Arbitration according to its Schedule of Fees, which is deemed to be approved by the arbitrator when accepting his mandate.

12.   The arbitrator shall encourage a serene and positive development of the arbitral proceedings. In particular, he shall decide on the date and manner of the hearings in such a way as to allow both parties to fully participate therein, in compliance with the principle of equal treatment and adversarial proceedings.

13.   The arbitrator shall give the arbitration all the time and attention which are necessary under the circumstances, acting in the most rapid and economic manner. In particular, he shall avoid superfluous expenses which can increase the costs of the proceedings in a manner not proportionate to the value of the dispute.

14.   The arbitrator who performs his task within an arbitral tribunal shall participate actively in the work of the tribunal so that to give the parties all attention and consideration at the time of decision.

In particular, he shall refrain from any obstructive or intimidatory behaviour with respect to his colleagues, aimed at hindering the proper development of the arbitration towards its conclusion.

15.   The arbitrator who does not comply with the provisions of this Code may be replaced by the Chamber of Arbitration.

Where it is not appropriate to replace the arbitrator in order not to cause useless delay in the arbitral proceedings, the Arbitral Council may sanction the behaviour of the arbitrator, also after the conclusion of the arbitral proceedings, by refusing to confirm him in subsequent arbitral proceedings.

PART VIII
DOCUMENTS RELATING
TO EVIDENCE

INTERNATIONAL BAR ASSOCIATION
SECTION OF BUSINESS LAW

271 Regent Street, London W1R 7PA, England,
Tel: (+0044) 0171-629 1206,
Fax: (+0044) 0171-409 0456

THE IBA RULES OF EVIDENCE

These Supplementary Rules are the product of a working party of Committee D (Procedures for Settling Disputes) of the Section on Business Law of the International Bar Association.

They are solely concerned with the presentation and reception of evidence in arbitrations and are recommended by the International Bar Association for incorporation in, or adoption together with, institutional and other general rules or procedures governing international commercial arbitrations.

Even if not specifically adopted by agreement between the parties, they can serve as a guide to arbitrators conducting such arbitrations when the parties in contention come from law areas having rules of procedures derived from different systems.

They may be referred to as The IBA Rules of Evidence.

It is recommended that when the parties desire to adopt the IBA Rules of Evidence as supplementary to the general rules applicable to a particular arbitration, the following additional clause be adopted:

The IBA Rules of Evidence shall apply together with the General Rules governing any submission to arbitration incorporated in this Contract. Where they are inconsistent with the aforesaid General Rules, these IBA Rules of Evidence shall prevail but solely as regards the presentation and reception of evidence.

Adopted by resolution of the Council on 28 May 1983.

Supplementary rules governing
the presentation and reception
of evidence in international
commercial arbitration

Article 1   Scope of application

1   These are procedural rules governing the presentation of evidence ('the Rules of Evidence') intended to supplement any other rules applicable to the arbitration ('the General Rules'). If the parties have so agreed in writing the Rules of Evidence shall govern the arbitration if and so far as they are not in conflict with mandatory applicable provisions of law. The parties may at any time agree in writing to amend, add to or delete any provision contained in the Rules of Evidence.

2   In so far as the Rules of Evidence and the General Rules applicable to the arbitration are silent, the Arbitrator may in his discretion conduct the taking of evidence as he thinks fit.

3   In case of conflict between any provisions of the Rules of Evidence and the General Rules, the Rules of Evidence shall prevail unless the parties shall otherwise agree in writing.

Article 2   Definitions

'*Arbitrator*' means a single arbitrator, or the panel of arbitrators or a majority of them as the case may be and shall include an umpire;

'*Claimant*' means the party or parties who commenced the arbitration or made the first claim therein;

'*Defendant*' means the party or parties against whom the Claimant made his claim and includes a party making a counter-claim;

'*General Rules*' means the specific rules of arbitration agreed upon by the parties except in so far as evidence is concerned;

'*Introductory Submissions*' means any Request for Arbitration or Statement of Claim or similar document produced by the Claimant, any Answer or Statement of Defence or similar document produced by the Defendant and any other or further documents in the nature of pleadings or submissions, however they may be denominated, produced by the parties in accordance with the General Rules, as well as any further submissions which the General Rules may require to be made before the hearings;

'*Production of Documents*' means the listing of documents relevant to the subject matter of the claims and defences in issue in the possession, custody, or control of a party and the delivery of the List and of copies of such documents to the other parties to the arbitration and to the Arbitrator in accordance with the provisions of these Rules;

'*Witness Statement*' means a written statement complying with the provisions of Article 5(2) below.

Article 3   Introductory submissions

The Introductory Submissions made by any party shall contain (*inter alia*) the means by which the facts relevant to the dispute are intended to be proved by that party, including, for each of such facts, the names of witnesses and reference to documents.

Article 4   Production of documents

1   Each party shall make Production of Documents in respect of all documentation on which such party desires to rely.

2   No later than sixty days after delivery of the last Introductory Submission made by the Defendant or by the date agreed between the parties or determined by the Arbitrator, each party shall exchange his List with every other party and deliver his List to the Arbitrator. Unless a document has been so listed it shall not be produced at the hearing without the consent of the Arbitrator. All documents in the List shall be numbered consecutively, and shall be produced in their entirety unless otherwise agreed or ordered. Each party shall provide the Arbitrator with a copy of each document in his List.

3   A party shall at any time be entitled to a copy of any document listed by another party upon offer of payment of the reasonable copying charge. Such document shall be supplied within fifteen days of the request.

4   A party may by Notice to Produce a Document request any other party to provide him with any document relevant to the dispute between the parties and not listed, provided such document is identified with reasonable particularity and provided further that it passed to or from such other party from or to a third party who is not a party to the arbitration. If a party refuses to comply with a Notice to Produce a Document he may be ordered to do so by the Arbitrator.

5   The Arbitrator shall have the power, upon application by one of the parties or of his own volition, to order a party to produce any relevant document within such party's possession, custody or control.

6   If a party fails to comply with the Arbitrator's order to produce any relevant document within such party's possession, custody or control, the Arbitrator shall draw his conclusions from such failure.

Article 5   Witnesses

1   Within sixty days of the delivery of the last Introductory Submission made by the Defendant or by the date agreed between the parties or determined by the Arbitrator, all parties shall deliver their Witness Statements to the Arbitrator only.

2   Each Witness Statement shall:
(a)   contain the full names and address of the Witness, his relationship to or connection with any of the parties, and a description of his background, qualifications, training and experience if these are relevant to the dispute or to the contents of his Statement;
(b)   contain a full statement of the evidence it is desired by that party to present through the testimony of that witness;
(c)   reflect whether the witness is a witness of fact or an expert, and whether the witness is testifying from his own knowledge, observation or experience, or from information and belief, and if the latter, the source of his knowledge; and
(d)   be signed by the witness, and give the date and place of signature.

3   When the Arbitrator has received the Witness Statement(s) of each party he shall simultaneously deliver copies of all the Witness Statement(s) to all the other parties to the arbitration.

4   Within forty days of the receipt of any Witness Statement from another party a party may submit further or supplementary Witness Statements or Oral Evidence Notices in response to evidence submitted by such other party.

5   Within twenty days of the receipt of any Witness Statement any party may by notice to the Arbitrator and all other parties (an 'Oral Evidence Notice') request the right himself to give oral evidence at the hearing, or for any of his own witnesses or the witnesses of any other party to give oral evidence at the hearing. An Oral Evidence Notice shall stipulate the issues to which that evidence is to relate.

6   Within twenty days of the receipt of any Oral Evidence Notice all parties shall reply thereto. If a party fails to reply he shall be deemed to have agreed to the request contained in that Oral Evidence Notice. If all parties agree, or are deemed to have agreed, to a particular Oral Evidence Notice, the witness named therein shall give oral evidence at the hearing in accordance with the Oral Evidence Notice. The Arbitrator may himself order that any witness gives oral evidence.

7   If a party objects to an Oral Evidence Notice he shall state his reasons, and the question whether the witness shall give oral evidence and, if so, the issues upon which the evidence shall be given, shall be determined by the Arbitrator in his discretion. The Arbitrator may give his decision on this question on the basis of the documents submitted or after hearing the parties, as he may decide.

8   A party may be heard in support of his own case. It shall be proper for a party or his legal advisers to interview witnesses or potential witnesses.

9   Any witness who gives oral evidence shall in the first place be questioned by the Arbitrator, and thereafter submit to examination by the party calling him, cross-examination by all other parties and re-examination by the party calling him.

10   The Arbitrator shall at all times have complete control over the procedure in relation to a witness giving oral evidence, including the right to limit or deny the right of a party to examine, cross-examine or re-examine a witness when it appears to the Arbitrator that such evidence or examination is unlikely to serve any further relevant purpose.

11   The testimony of any witness not giving oral evidence or of a witness in respect of any portion of his evidence not subject to oral testimony, shall be taken by means of his Witness Statement only.

12   A party shall be entitled to stipulate the name of a witness in his Oral Evidence Notice even if no Witness Statement has been produced for that witness, provided that the party states in writing that he has requested the witness to give a Witness Statement but that the witness has refused to do so and that the party has no power to compel him to provide such Statement. If the witness has given the party an informal or partial statement or other document (whether signed or not) the party shall deliver a copy thereof to the Arbitrator and to the other parties at the time he delivers the Oral Evidence Notice relating to that witness.

13   The Arbitrator shall decide what weight to attach to the evidence or Statements of any witness or party.

14   Nothing herein shall preclude the Arbitrator in his discretion from permitting any witness to give oral or written evidence.

Article 6   Scope of proceedings

1   Whenever Terms of Reference or the like are provided for in the General Rules or the parties so agree or the Arbitrator so directs, a list of those witnesses shall be included who will be called to give oral evidence at the hearing and the issues upon which each witness will testify.

2   The Arbitrator may provide for such other matters concerning evidence as he considers advisable with a view to facilitating the conduct of the arbitration.

Article 7   Arbitrator's powers

In addition to the powers available to him under the applicable procedural law and the General Rules under which the arbitration is conducted, the Arbitrator shall have the following powers:

(a) to vary, extend or limit any time-periods provided in the Rules of Evidence, or previously ordered by him;

(b) to order that a witness whose Witness Statement has been delivered be available to be called by any party;

(c) to call witnesses to testify orally or in writing, whether the parties agree thereto or not;

(d) to rule that a witness' evidence be ignored if the witness fails to appear without good cause;

(e) to rely on his own expert knowledge;

(f) to appoint experts to assist him or to give expert evidence or reports in the arbitration;

(g) to regulate the right of the parties to call expert witnesses and to make provisions with regard to their activities and the presentation of their evidence; and

(h) to exercise all the powers he deems necessary to make the arbitration effective and its conduct efficient as regards the taking of evidence.

28 May 1983

THE MEDITERRANEAN AND MIDDLE EAST INSTITUTE OF ARBITRATION

© 1984 Mediterranean and Middle East Institute of Arbitration

MMEIA Secretariat
c/o Av. Mauro Rubino-Sammartano
1, Viale Cassiodoro
20145 Milano
Tel: 00392 4819041/4984729 4980554
Fax: 00392 48008277
Telex 324257 DEFEND 1

STANDARD RULES OF EVIDENCE

16 May 1987

Article 1 Scope of the Rules of Evidence

1.1 The present rules (the Standard Rules of Evidence) supplement upon the agreement of the parties any other rules which may apply to arbitration (The Arbitration Rules).

1.2 Single rules of evidence, which may be found to be in conflict with a mandatory rule of the applicable procedural law, will be replaced by that mandatory rule.

1.3 In case of conflict between the Standard Rules of Evidence and the Rules of Arbitration, the former shall prevail.

1.4 The parties are free jointly to amend, or to cancel, any part of the Standard Rules of Evidence.

1.5 The Arbitrator (which expression shall apply also to a panel of arbitrators, if appointed) shall use his best efforts to achieve two different but not necessarily conflicting objectives:

(i)   to avoid that a party be prevented from presenting its case, because of deadlines (since deadlines are not aimed at preventing a party from presenting its case);

(ii)   to avoid that a party be taken by surprise.

Article 2   Witnesses

2.1   Each party shall be entitled to call its witnesses.

2.2   As a rule, the party wishing to call one or more witnesses will do so by submitting its List of Witnesses to the Arbitrator and to the other parties.

2.3   The List of Witnesses shall contain:

— the full name and address of each witness, his address, position, qualification, his present and past position vis-a-vis the parties and the dispute;

— the area, or areas, on which each witness shall be examined.

2.4   The other party shall be entitled to exchange its own List of Witnesses with the other parties and to deliver it to the Arbitrator within 25 days after receipt of the List of Witnesses.

2.5   If a party objects to a witness, it shall do so during the witness's examination. Only in the event of a party considering that the witness or the area mentioned for his examination is totally irrelevant, it will notify the other parties and the Arbitrator within the above 25 days period.

2.6   Supplementary Lists of Witnesses may be submitted.

2.7   Only in exceptional cases the arbitrator will order that a witness be not called, and if so he shall first invite the parties to argue this point in writing, or to be heard if they so wish; his order shall be fully reasoned.

2.8   The Arbitrator will send the List of Witnesses to each witness, inviting him to appear at the hearing in order to be heard.

2.9   Neither counsel for the parties nor the parties, nor any agent of them shall interview witnesses and no proof of evidence will be submitted to the witness, by counsel or by the parties or their agents.

2.10   Each witness shall be first examined in chief by counsel for the party calling him; then he shall be cross-examined by counsel for the other parties.

Reexamination is allowed.

The Arbitrator is entitled to put questions at the end.

2.11   The Arbitrator will bear in mind that it is up to the parties to prove their case and that they must be entitled to some latitude in examining their witnesses and in testing the other parties' witnesses. The credibility of the witness may also be tested by counsel.

On the other hand, the Arbitrator shall have the duty to prevent totally irrelevant questions or questions clearly aiming at delaying the proceedings, and to prevent that the witness be insulted, or subjected to questions contrary to decency. The Arbitrator will have to intervene in this area only with great care and wisdom.

2.12   Unless it is forbidden by mandatory rules of the applicable procedural law, the witness may be asked to swear an oath, or, if his religion prohibits this, to make a solemn affirmation. The Arbitrator shall have no authority to oblige the witness to swear an oath, but if he refuses to do so, the Arbitrator shall be under a duty to enquire as to the reasons of the witness's refusal and to put them on record.

2.13 Only in the event the Arbitrator is satisfied that the witness could not attend the meeting, the party calling the witness may ask the Arbitrator to request the witness to issue a sworn Affidavit. Nevertheless the witness must at the start of his affidavit state to accept to be examined in the country where he resides or works, if the other party so requests. A sworn Affidavit not containing that statement will not be accepted.

The Arbitrator shall request the affidavit from the witness. The witness will not be approached by counsel for the parties, by the parties or by their agents in order to obtain such affidavit from him or in respect thereto.

2.14 The Arbitrator may not call witnesses of his own motion.

2.15 The purpose of arbitration not being to create restrictions to the parties' right to prove their case, each party is entitled to submit Supplementary Lists of Witnesses even after all other witnesses have been heard and until the date of the final hearing is fixed.

2.16 However, in order to avoid that the other parties be taken by surprise by such new List, they shall be entitled to apply for a postponement, whenever this is reasonable, as well as to submit a Supplementary List or to recall previous witnesses.

2.17 The Arbitrator shall be entitled to order that the fees and costs of the other parties and of the Arbitrator arising from the late application be borne by the applicant whenever this late application is not justified by special reasons.

2.18 The Arbitrator will not refuse to hear a late witness, unless there are very serious reasons to do so, which will have to be stated in detail in the relative order. That order will not be issued without having given to the parties the opportunity to be heard, or to file their written argument within a limited but reasonable time.

2.19 Witnesses shall not be allowed to stay in the hearing room, neither before or after giving their evidence.

2.20 Witnesses may be put in front of each other, on a party's request and be examined and be invited to criticise each other's statements and to discuss them together in front of the Arbitrator.

2.21 The Arbitrator shall be entitled to fix a specific hearing in a place different from the venue of the arbitration, whenever a party applies for this and satisfies him that this is the only way to hear a reluctant or not otherwise available witness; provided that specific venue does not create a major problem to the other parties and the applicant advances the legal fees and costs of the other party and of the Arbitrator.

Article 3 Examination of the Parties

3.1 Counsel for a party shall be entitled to call his Client, or another party to the proceedings, as a witness.

3.2 That party shall be treated as any other witness, and consequently all the hereabove provisions related to witnesses shall apply.

3.3 The Arbitrator shall establish with much care the weight to attach to the testimony given by parties.

Article 4 Arbitrator's Expert

4.1 The Arbitrator shall be entitled to appoint an expert (the Arbitrator's Expert) to advise him on technical or other matters even if the parties call their own expert.

4.2   The Arbitrator's Expert shall be given the opportunity to study the file and to collect information.

4.3   The Arbitrator's Expert may file a written report.

4.4   The Arbitrator shall request clarifications from the Arbitrator's Expert during the hearing and each party is entitled to cross-examine him as any other witness.

4.5   If the Arbitrator intends to rely on his own knowledge on technical or other matters different from the issues of the applicable substantive and procedural laws, he shall mention such intention and disclose such knowledge, in order that the parties be given the opportunity to be heard on that issue, or to call evidence on it.

Article 5   Written Evidence

5.1   Each party shall deliver to the Arbitrator, and exchange with the other parties, a List of all the classes of its documents related to the dispute (the List of Classes of Documents).

5.2   The other parties shall be entitled to request, within 30 days after receipt of such list, a full list of the documents of one or more of such classes (List of Documents), and to inspect one or more of such documents, inspection to take place in such a way as to minimise the inconveniences to the other parties; the applicant shall advance the costs related to discovery, as fixed by the Arbitrator.

5.3   In case of refusal to provide the List of Documents or to allow inspection within 30 days after receipt of a notice to this effect, the other party shall be entitled to apply to the Arbitrator for an Order of Discovery. The parties are entitled to be heard on such application.

5.4   Before issuing such an order, the Arbitrator shall satisfy himself that such documents are not irrelevant to the dispute, and that the application does not aim totally or partly to confuse the matter through the production of a quantity of unnecessary documents.

Any application for discovery will have to be examined by the Arbitrator by proceeding to test the relevance of a portion of such documents. On a party's application, before or after his order, the Arbitrator shall conduct a hearing at which the application or his order will be discussed.

5.5   Whenever the Arbitrator, after such an examination, has the impression that a large number of the documents, production of which is sought, is irrelevant, he shall be entitled to appoint a lawyer as his expert to divide the documents in three classes: those which he considers relevant, the irrelevant ones and those which might be relevant.

The party which seeks production of documents, the relevance of which has been challenged, will have to advance the costs of the expert and to deposit an amount to cover the costs caused to the other party by its inspection (such as the time spent by staff to attend inspection by the other side of the documents which are found to be irrelevant). All the costs caused by the inspection of the irrelevant documents are to be borne by the party which has applied for their production, even if its claim is eventually successful.

Likewise the Arbitrator may, on application, appoint an expert to divide already produced documents into said three categories and to report on them and place the expert and the Arbitrator's costs and the other parties' costs to the charge of the party which has produced irrelevant document even if the claim of that party succeeds.

5.6 Apart from general discovery, the production of specific documents may be ordered by the Arbitrator on a party's application at any stage of the proceedings until the hearing for the final addresses of the parties to the Arbitrator.

5.7 Before deciding on the application, the Arbitrator shall invite the parties to file their written arguments or to be heard if they so wish.

5.8 The unjustified refusal by a party to discover documents as well as the refusal of a party to testify may be used by the Arbitrator as one of the elements of his decision.

Article 6 Hearing of Evidence

6.1 The Arbitrator, while entitled to fix deadlines for the production of documents, for calling witnesses, for amendments of pleadings, will not treat them as a final bar to later activities, whenever that late activity is due to late receipt of information, to late discovery of documents by counsel or by the parties, because of the size of files, of turnover of staff, of pressure of other commitments and similar reasons. Only late applications which are clearly for the purpose of delaying or confusing the proceedings are therefore to be rejected.

6.2 The Arbitrator shall use his best efforts to avoid long delays between the various hearings at which evidence is heard.

6.3 The Arbitrator shall, whenever possible, concentrate the hearing of evidence in several subsequent days and in any event in no more than one or two months time.

He shall fix the relative dates much in advance, for the parties guidance, and shall also fix in advance the hearing for the final addresses, choosing a date shortly subsequent to the last hearing of the evidence.

PART IX
MISCELLANEOUS
DOCUMENTS

THE STANDARD CONSUMER
ARBITRATION SCHEME
GUIDANCE NOTES FOR THE PARTIES

Please read these Guidance Notes and the Rules of the applicable Arbitration Scheme carefully before starting an arbitration. You must remember that the arbitrator will make an award based on the documents and evidence submitted by the parties to the dispute. It is therefore in your interest to state your case clearly and produce all relevant supporting documents. Please note that arbitration under the Scheme is an alternative to a claimant's rights to pursue the matter through the courts. **For the avoidance of doubt, these notes are for guidance only and do not form part of the Rules of the Scheme.**

An Introduction to Arbitration

Arbitration is a private process by which an independent person, called an arbitrator or, in Scotland, an arbiter, resolves a dispute. This person is selected by the parties or on their behalf by an appointing body on the basis of expertise, reputation, training and experience as an arbitrator. An arbitrator will:
— consider the parties' arguments and evidence;
— act fairly and impartially;
— act according to the law.
The law gives an arbitrator power to give directions for the conduct of an arbitration where this is not provided for in the Rules of the Arbitration Scheme.
Arbitration is a long established and effective method of resolving disputes. It is the only real alternative to court action because the arbitrator's decision (the 'award') is final, binding and enforceable in the courts.

A. Guidance Notes for Both Parties

1. Please note that the application form is the parties' agreement to arbitrate. Once signed, you are committed to proceeding in accordance with the Rules of the Arbitration Scheme.
2. Make sure that all information required by the application form is completed. Failure to do so will delay arbitration getting under way.
3. You must not delete the section of the application form which states that you agree to be bound by the arbitrator's award. This will invalidate the application.
4. The arbitrator will normally only be able to deal with the matters referred to and/or the amounts claimed in the application form. It is therefore essential that you are certain that all claims and counterclaims have been included in the application form.
5. You must remember that the arbitrator decides the case purely on the arguments and evidence presented to him by the parties. The claimant must prove the case to the satisfaction of the arbitrator.
6. The Rules of the Scheme are intended to allow the parties to present their cases without the need for legal representation.

7. So far as presentation is concerned, please ensure:

(a) That all documents are produced in a simple and presentable form. It is not essential that case documents are typed but, if they are handwritten, they should be written clearly (or printed if necessary). All photocopied documents must be legible.

(b) That case statements are supported by copies of all relevant documents, eg booking forms, brochures, orders, invoices, contracts, quotations, conditions of engagement, photographs, correspondence, witness statements, certificates, drawings, specifications and calculations. For the purpose of this Arbitration Scheme, videos are only admissible with the consent of the Arbitrator.

(c) That all case statements and supporting evidence are submitted in duplicate and, where applicable, arranged in a chronological sequence with all pages numbered.

(d) That jargon or abbreviations used in case statements are explained in plain English.

8. All correspondence and case statements must quote the Chartered Institute's case reference and the name of the case.

9. All case statements must be submitted together and not piecemeal.

10. You should keep a copy of all documents submitted for possible future reference. You may need to refer to them if the arbitrator asks questions.

11. The arbitrator will not receive information about the case from any other source (eg. a trade association's conciliation service). You must therefore make every point and submit all supporting evidence that you consider relevant. You must also retrieve and submit any documents sent previously to any other body and upon which you intend to rely.

12. The arbitrator is not an investigator, nor is the Chartered Institute. Thus, if you have witnesses to support your case, you must obtain the necessary statements and submit them. It will not be acceptable for you to send a list of witnesses and tell the arbitrator to contact them. It is not sufficient for you merely to say that you have evidence. You must produce it.

13. All communications to the arbitrator must be addressed through the Chartered Institute, unless the arbitrator directs otherwise.

14. The Rules of the Arbitration Scheme give each party one extension of time as of right to submit its case and the Chartered Institute has no power to grant further extensions. If you need further time, over and above what is given by the Rules, you must seek the other party's consent or request a further extension from the arbitrator.

15. Settlements must be notified to the Chartered Institute in writing by both parties, otherwise the arbitration will continue to an award. You should correspond directly with the other party for settlement purposes and not through the Chartered Institute. The parties may wish to ask the arbitrator to incorporate the terms of their settlement into a consent award because this makes enforcement easier should the need arise. Please note that registration fees are *not* refundable in the event of settlement.

16. Where applicable, the arbitrator may undertake a site visit. This is not a hearing or an opportunity to submit further arguments or evidence since its purpose is to allow the parties to show the arbitrator the physical evidence and for the arbitrator to assess whether that evidence supports the arguments and documentary evidence submitted.

17.   It is essential that you deal fully with each and every allegation made in the other party's statement of case. If you do not challenge valid evidence put forward by the other party, the arbitrator will usually treat the allegation supported by that evidence as proved.

18.   Neither the arbitrator not the Chartered Institute may advise a party as to the merits of its case or assist a party in presenting its case. If necessary, advice should be sought from a solicitor, a Citizens Advice Bureau, a law centre or a neighbourhood advice centre.

19.   By agreeing to arbitration, the parties are committing themselves to proceeding and to accepting the final and binding effect of the award. Thus, a party ignores the existence of arbitration proceedings at its peril, especially if the party concerned is the respondent, for in this situation the arbitrator has a discretion to make an award solely on the basis of the documents submitted by the claimant.

20.   The mere fact that you may not like an award made against you (or even in your favour but not for the total amount claimed) does not mean that the award is wrong in law. The Chartered Institute has no power to alter an award or to order an arbitrator to do so.

21.   Some Arbitration Schemes require the parties to pay a registration fee. Although you are responsible for your own costs, the arbitrator may order one party to reimburse the other party's registration fee and will generally order an unsuccessful party to do so. However, a successful party may be ordered to pay the other party's fee if, for example, the successful party has conducted the case in such a way as to put the other party to unnecessary costs or has failed to accept an offer of settlement which equals or exceeds the arbitrator's award.

B.   Guidance Notes for Claimants

1.   Your statement of claim should set out in chronological order the events which have led to the claim and refer to each supporting document in respect of each allegation. The information included in the statement should include references to:

(a)   The relevant parts of any contract;

(b)   Special requirements given to the other party (the 'respondent');

(c)   What was promised and what was received;

(d)   Relevant dates;

(e)   The names of persons concerned (eg. respondent's employees or agents);

(f)   The amount(s) claimed, clearly and precisely quantified;

(g)   The remedies sought, whether compensation, specific performance (ie. performance or completion of contract) or corrective works.

2.   Claimants must prove their case. Where appropriate each allegation or element of the claim should be set out in the form of a table. This will help the arbitrator to appreciate what the differences between the parties really are.

3.   You should avoid merely sending a bundle of all documents in your possession and calling this bundle 'the claim'. The 'claim' is the written statement of claim and the bundle of documents is the supporting evidence.

4.   You should avoid 'dressing up' or exaggerating claims to make weight. Allegations which are not supported by evidence will not assist your case and may in fact damage it.

5. It is not enough for you to show, for example in a holiday case, that your dealings with the respondent led to disappointment. You must show that there was a breach of some term of the contract, express or implied, and that, where appropriate, you took steps to reduce your loss. Allegations must therefore be set out precisely.

6. When making comments on the respondent's defence, you should restrict them to the matters dealt with in the defence and not raise any new points. You must also deal with any counter-allegations made in the defence.

7. If you are represented by a lawyer or other professional adviser, you should communicate with the Chartered Institute only through your adviser. Direct communication may cause unnecessary work and thus delay.

C. Guidance Notes for Respondents

1. The defence should answer each and every point raised by the other party (the 'claimant') clearly and precisely, giving details of any action taken to remedy defects or reduce losses. Remember, any points on the claim which remain unanswered will normally be treated by the arbitrator as having been admitted.

2. Any counterclaim must be supported by all relevant evidence and must be clearly and precisely quantified.

3. If you believe that the claimant has exceeded the financial limits of this Arbitration Scheme, you must say so in your defence so that the matter may be dealt with by the arbitrator. It is no use objecting after the award has been made because your silence will have been treated as acceptance.

4. You do not have an automatic right of reply to the claimant's comments on your defence. If the claimant raises new points or makes allegedly scandalous comments, you may submit a reply to those comments. The arbitrator will decide whether they should be admitted as evidence. If you wish to reply to the claimant's comments, you must telephone the Chartered Institute and follow this up in writing immediately.

D. Checklist

Ask yourself the following questions before submitting the application for arbitration:

1. Should the application be submitted direct to the Chartered Institute or through another body?

2. Have you filled in all the information required by the form (name, address, telephone number, matters to be referred to arbitration and amounts or other remedy claimed)?

3. Have you completed the form legibly? (Please type or write in black ink)

4. Have you signed and dated the form?

5. Have you included the registration fee with the application?

Failure to observe any of the above will cause delay in processing the application.

You should ask yourself the following questions before submitting your statement of claim, defence or counterclaim:

6. Exactly what am I claiming for or defending against?

7.   Why do I believe that something is due to me or nothing is due to the other party?

8.   Have I clearly answered all points in the other party's arguments with which I disagree?

9.   Am I submitting all the documents that the arbitrator will need to consider (if in doubt include them) and have I complied with the time limits?

It is essential that you follow the Rules of the Arbitration Scheme and these Guidance Notes. Failure to do so may lead to delay and unnecessary costs.

ACRONYMS AND ABBREVIATIONS

AAA	American Arbitration Association
ABTA	Association of British Travel Agents
BCH	Bonded Coach Holiday Section of the Bus and Coach Council
c.	chapter
CAREN	Cour d'Arbitrage (Lille, France)
CAS	Court of Arbitration for Sport (=TAS)
CCI	Chambre de Commerce Internationale (=ICC)
CCIG	Chamber of Commerce and Industry of Geneva
CCP	code of civil procedure (see ZPO)
CHF	Swiss Francs
CIArb	Chartered Institute of Arbitrators
CIAS	Conseil International de l'Arbitrage en matière de Sport (=ICAS)
CIF	cost, insurance and freight
CIO	Comité International Olympique (=IOC)
CIRDI	Centre international pour le règlement des différends relatifs aux investments (=ICSID)
CLOUT	Case Law on UNCITRAL Texts (published by UNCITRAL Secretariat, Vienna)
CMI	Comité Maritime International
CNUDDCI	Commission des Nations Unies pour le Droit Commercial International (=UNCITRAL)
DIP	Loi fédérale sur le droit international privé (=PIL)
DIS	Deutsche Institution für Schiedsgerichtsbarkeit, German Institution of Arbitration.
EEA	European Economic Area
EEC	European Economic Community
FAQ	fair average quality
FOB	free on board
FOSFA	Federation of Oils, Seeds and Fats Associations.
GAFTA	Grain and Feed Trade Association
GB	Great Britain
IBA	International Bar Association
ICA	International Court of Arbitration (of the ICC)
ICAS	International Council of Arbitration for Sport (see TAS)
ICC	International Chamber of Commerce
ICE	Institution of Civil Engineers
IOC	International Olympic Committee
ICSID	International Centre for Settlement of Investment Disputes
ISVA	Incorporated Society of Valuers and Auctioneers
IHK	Internationale Handelskammer (=ICC)
JCAA	Japan Commercial Arbitration Association
JCIArb	*Arbitration* the journal of the Chartered Institute of Arbitrators
JCT	Joint Contracts Tribunal
LCIA	London Court of International Arbitration
LMAA	London Maritime Arbitrators' Association
LME	London Metal Exchange

MAL	UNCITRAL Model Law on International Commercial Arbitration (1985)
MMEIA	Mediterranean and Middle East Institute of Arbitration
NI	Northern Ireland
No.	Number
NSC	nominated sub-contractor
OG	Olympic Games
OMPI	Organisation Mondiale de la Propriété Intelectuelle (=WIPO)
Ord.	order
para.	paragrah
PCA	Permanent Court of Arbitration (The Hague)
PIAS	Personal Insurance Arbitration Service (of the CIArb)
PIL	Private International Law (the Swiss PIL Statute of 1987, chapter 12 (articles 176–194) regulates arbitration)
r.	rule
RIBA	Royal Institute of British Architects
RICS	Royal Institution of Chartered Surveyors
RSA	Refined Sugar Association
RSC	Rules of the Supreme Court (England)
s.	section
sch.	schedule
SFr	Swiss Francs
SI	Statutory Instrument (United Kingdom secondary legislation)
TAS	Tribunal Arbitral du Sport (=CAS)
UAR	UNCITRAL Arbitration Rules (1976)
UCR	UNCITRAL Conciliation Rules (1980)
UK	The United Kingdom (of Great Britain and Northern Ireland)
UNCITRAL	United Nations Commission on International Trade Law
WIPO	World Intellectual Property Organization
ZHK	Zürcher Handelskammer (Zurich Chamber of Commerce)
ZPO	Zivilprozessordnung, Code of Civil Procedure (Austria or Germany)

INDEX

Unless otherwise stated, statutes and orders are for the UK or England and Wales. Acronyms used throughout are from the List of Acronyms.